UNTOLD STORIES

Alan Bennett first appeared on the stage in 1960 as one of the authors and performers of the revue *Beyond the Fringe*. His stage plays include *Forty Years On*, *Getting On*, *Habeas Corpus*, *The Old Country*, *Enjoy* and *Kafka's Dick*, and he has written many television plays, notably *A Day Out*, *Sunset Across the Bay*, *A Woman of No Importance* and the series of monologues *Talking Heads*. An adaptation of his television play *An Englishman Abroad* was paired with *A Question of Attribution* in the double bill *Single Spies*, first produced at the National Theatre in 1988. This was followed in 1990 by his adaptation of *The Wind in the Willows* and in 1991 by *The Madness of George III*, both produced at the National Theatre. His stage version of *The Lady in the Van* was first seen in the West End in 1999. His most recent play, *The History Boys*, premiered at the National Theatre in 2004 and won the *Evening Standard* and Critics' Circle awards for Best Play, the Laurence Olivier Award for Best New Play and the South Bank Award.

Untold Stories

ALAN BENNETT

faber and faber

P
PROFILE BOOKS

First published in 2005 by

Faber and Faber Limited
3 Queen Square London WC1N 3AU

and

Profile Books Ltd
3A Exmouth Market
Pine Street Exmouth Market
London EC1R 0JH

This paperback edition published in 2006

Typeset by Faber and Faber Limited
Printed in England by Clays Ltd, St Ives plc

A CIP record for this book
is available from the British Library

ISBN 978-0-571-22831-7
ISBN 0-571-22831-3

2 4 6 8 10 9 7 5 3 1

Contents

Illustrations

———

Introduction

At Christmas when I was a boy and hung my pillowcase at the end of the bed one of the presents I could generally count on was an annual. The comics that I read weekly throughout the year all produced a Christmas annual. There were *Dandy* and *Beano* for me, who was the youngest, *Knockout*, *Wizard* or *Hotspur* for my brother, three years older. Annuals, which were also albums, had a long tradition, stretching back to the Edwardian *Chatterbox,* and even in the wartime 1940s the books were still quite substantial and in gaily decorated hard covers with a medley of strip cartoons, stories and games that kept us absorbed well into the new year, when they could be swapped for other children's annuals.

The appeal of such compendium books was not confined to the young; there were adult annuals, the most notable (and still a staple of second-hand bookshops) *The Saturday Book* with poems, short stories, paintings and autobiography, a revue in book form. The fashion for such adult versions seems to have gone out but I imagine there are children's annuals still, or a version of them. I hope so, as for me they were the beginning of childhood reading, and memories of the feel and smell and the excitement of those Christmas volumes come back to me as I write.

So if I have a model book it is not Jane Austen or Dickens or Evelyn Waugh; it is one of those long-forgotten annuals which lured you on from story to story through pictures and puzzles, a real box of delights. And it is my memories of such volumes that reconcile me to the seemingly scrappy nature of this one. There are no cartoons and few pictures, and it is a mixture of autobiography, diaries, lectures and occasional writings that could at a pinch have been sorted out into two less variegated volumes, autobiography, say, and the rest. But on the model of those childhood annuals long ago I'm happier to see them jumbled together. I've a feeling there was indeed a comic called *Jumble*. Or was that just William's dog?

That's part of it, but there is other stuff in the book which, while I was writing it anyway, I did not expect or want to see published in my lifetime. I had no objection to it being read; I just didn't want to be in the room at the time.

What changed my mind on this was being diagnosed with cancer in June 1997, and having what I was told then was only a fifty/fifty chance of recovery. Though I made no particular secret of it, I didn't go public on my illness as these days tends to be the mode, thinking that if there was time I would write about it. This in due course I did, the account included in this book under the title 'An Average Rock Bun'.

I had regarded some of these writings as tidying up, topics I'd been wanting to write about but had never got round to. A death sentence, like moving house, meant that the tidying up had to be done and done quickly: there was a deadline. My earlier misgivings about what I was prepared to see published in my lifetime now seemed almost laughably irrelevant: none of it was likely to be published in my lifetime, so where was the problem?

To be told you only have a short time to live makes any notion of self-preservation of scant importance, death mocking dignity and reputation, the important thing just to get as much as you can down on paper. (And it was paper in my case, not a screen.) The threat of death, provided it's unaccompanied by diminished energy, can be a laxative and so it was with me. Now I could write what I wanted and leave the question of publication to my executors.

I had not felt particularly cooped up in hospital. There was a good view over to some trees on a hill and playing fields which I took to be part of Harrow School, and sometimes I saw a hawk swooping low over the flat roofs of the hospital. As soon as I could I started going downstairs to sit on a seat near where the cars were parked, a bleak-seeming picture such as might figure in a poem by Larkin, though it did not seem especially bleak to me.

I found, though, that in the months that followed I was spending every moment that I could out of doors, very often sitting in a long chair outside my front door in Camden Town. It was a place I had not had much say in previously, occupied as it was from 1974 to 1989 by Miss Shepherd and her van. Even after she died I could not bring myself to sit there, not out of piety but because there was no shelter from the street, and anybody coming past the house was able to see me as they had been able to see her. In my newly straitened circumstances this was another consideration that ceased to matter.

After I began a course of chemotherapy which entailed two days in hospital every fortnight this urge to be in the open air became a compulsion, and every day I took my place outside my door like a passenger on an ocean liner. I skipped the bouillon but everything else was to hand: books, writing materials and a large straw hat, the chair itself a present from my agent, Rosalind Chatto. Fortunately it was a warm and tranquil autumn, though even on the greyest of days I still lay out in the chair, only rain driving me indoors; I would even sit out on the step in the evening.

Before I had been taken ill (though I never felt ill) I had begun work on some autobiographical sketches, the connecting thread the suicide of my grandfather which went unmentioned in the family for more than forty years. These were to be entitled *Untold Stories*, an extract from which was published in the *London Review of Books* in September 1999.

Even had I been able to, I felt it was inadvisable for the moment anyway to try and write a play. The process invariably ties me in knots and, who knows, maybe that was what had brought on the trouble in the first place. Besides *Untold Stories*, though, I wanted something I could fairly effortlessly scribble down as I sat outside convalescing so I began a series of slightly chattier reminiscences. These came easily, and not having expected to see the enterprise brought to a conclusion it was a surprise when I found I had assembled a batch of a dozen or so memoirs, which were then recorded for BBC TV and published as *Telling Tales*.

Unfortunately the programmes passed almost unnoticed and the book similarly. Had I said more about being ill and the impending curtailment that caused the memoirs to be written there would, I'm sure, have been more attention paid and sympathy extended. But cancer is not a career move, and I kept quiet, which, since I'm still here, turned out to be the right thing to have done. Had I done otherwise I might have died of embarrassment.

My continuing presence in the world meant, though, that the decision about the supposedly posthumous chapters which I had thought to shuffle off onto my executors remained my own. However, in the meantime there had been another development.

In 2001 I had been the subject of a somewhat speculative biography, written without my co-operation and with little help from my friends and acquaintances. Knowing there is not much to be done to prevent such an enterprise, I had given the author no help but not made much of a fuss about it. When the book came out it was thought to be kind but dull, not unlike its subject, with the author complaining rather forlornly about how little help he'd received in his self-imposed task. Still, it was the publication of this book that made me press on with my own autobiographical efforts and start thinking of them as pre-posthumous.

Lastly, my continuing remission from cancer coincided with a long period in which I found myself unable to write . . . or certainly to write plays. It's true I finished *The Lady in the Van* in 1999, but that was really something I'd prepared earlier. After that, though, nothing much seemed to occur, and it may be that the so-called battle against cancer, which in 'An Average Rock Bun' I tend to disclaim, took more out of me than I was aware and that the suppression of the growth which that may have involved was a shutdown all round. Autobiography, though, was different, and with no plot needed and the story given it seemed almost therapy.

Most of the other stuff reflects my interests and occupations. Diaries and autobiography apart, there are a couple of lectures on art, given when I was a Trustee of the National Gallery; the last monologue I wrote for Thora Hird, and an account of recording it; and some writings on visiting churches, a hobby I had as a boy and have taken up again now that I'm getting on and have someone to visit them with.

But there is little here that doesn't have something to do with one or another aspect of my life. I might have preferred to tell it differently – in the form of plays, say, or fiction – but this album is a quicker if less face-saving way of doing it.

'Pass it on,' says Hector in *The History Boys*. 'Just pass it on.'

Untold Stories

There is a wood, the canal, the river, and above the river the railway and the road. It's the first proper country that you get to as you come north out of Leeds, and going home on the train I pass the place quite often. Only these days I look. I've been passing the place for years without looking because I didn't know it was a place; that anything had happened there to make it a place, let alone a place that had something to do with me. Below the wood the water is deep and dark and sometimes there's a boy fishing or a couple walking a dog. I suppose it's a beauty spot now. It probably was then.

'Has there been any other mental illness in your family?' Mr Parr's pen hovers over the Yes/No box on the form and my father, who is letting me answer the questions, looks down at his trilby and says nothing.

'No,' I say confidently, and Dad turns the trilby in his hands.

'Anyway,' says Mr Parr kindly but with what the three of us know is more tact than truth, 'depression isn't really mental illness. I see it all the time.'

Mr Parr sees it all the time because he is the Mental Health Welfare Officer for the Craven district, and late this September evening in 1966 Dad and I are sitting in his bare linoleum-floored office above Settle police station while he takes a history of my mother.

'So there's never been anything like this before?'

'No,' I say, and without doubt or hesitation. After all, I'm the educated one in the family. I've been to Oxford. If there had been 'anything like this' I should have known about it. 'No, there's never been anything like this.'

'Well,' Dad says, and the information is meant for me as much as for Mr Parr, 'she did have something once. Just before we were married.' And he looks at me apologetically. 'Only it was nerves more. It wasn't like this.'

The 'this' that it wasn't like was a change in my mother's personality that had come about with startling suddenness. Over a matter of weeks she had lost all her fun and vitality, turning fretful and apprehensive and inaccessible to reason or reassurance. As the days passed the mood deepened, bringing with it fantasy and delusion; the house was watched, my father made to speak in a whisper because there was someone on the landing, and the lavatory (always central to Mam's scheme of things) was being monitored every time it was flushed. She started to sleep with her handbag under her pillow as if she were in a strange and dangerous hotel, and finally one night she fled the house in her nightgown, and Dad found her wandering in the street, whence she could only be fetched back into the house after some resistance.

Occurring in Leeds, where they had always lived, conduct like this might just have got by unnoticed, but the onset of the depression coincided with my parents' retirement to a village in the Dales, a place so small and close-knit that such bizarre behaviour could not be hidden. Indeed it was partly the knowledge that they were about to leave the relative anonymity of the city for a small community where 'folks knew all your business' and that she would henceforth be socially much more visible than she was used to ('I'm the centrepiece here') that might have brought on the depression in the first place. Or so Mr Parr is saying.

My parents had always wanted to be in the country and have a garden. Living in Leeds all his life Dad looked back on the childhood holidays he had spent on a farm at Bielby in the East Riding as a lost paradise. The village they were moving to was very pretty, too pretty for Mam in her depressed mood: 'You'll see,' she said, 'we'll be inundated with folk visiting.'

4

The cottage faced onto the village street but had a long garden at the back, and it seemed like the place they had always dreamed of. This was in 1966. A few years later I wrote a television play, *Sunset Across the Bay*, in which a retired couple not unlike my parents leave Leeds to go and live in Morecambe. As the coach hits the M62, bearing them away to a new life, the wife calls out, 'Bye bye, mucky Leeds!' And so it had seemed. Now Dad was being told that it was this longed-for escape that had brought down this crushing visitation on his wife. Not surprisingly he would not believe it.

In their last weeks in Leeds Dad had put Mam's low spirits down to the stress of the impending upheaval. Once the move had been accomplished, though, the depression persisted so now he fell back on the state of the house, blaming its bare unfurnished rooms, still with all the decorating to be done.

'Your Mam'll be better when we've got the place straight,' he said. 'She can't do with it being all upset.' So, while she sat fearfully on a hard chair in the passage, he got down to the decorating.

My brother, who had come up from Bristol to help with the move, also thought the state of the house was to blame, fastening particularly on an item that seemed to be top of her list of complaints, the absence of stair-carpet. I think I knew then that stair-carpet was only the beginning of it, and indeed when my brother galvanised a local firm into supplying and fitting the carpet in a couple of days Mam seemed scarcely to notice, the clouds did not lift, and in due course my brother went back to Bristol and I to London.

Over the next ten years this came to be the pattern. The onset of a bout of depression would fetch us home for a while, but when no immediate recovery was forthcoming we would take ourselves off again while Dad was left to cope. Or to care, as the phrase is nowadays. Dad was the carer. We cared, of course, but we still had lives to lead: Dad was retired – he had all the time in the world to care.

'The doctor has put her on tablets,' Dad said over the phone, 'only they don't seem to be doing the trick.' Tablets seldom did, even when one saw what was coming and caught it early. The onset of depression would find her sitting on unaccustomed chairs – the cork stool in the bathroom, the hard chair in the hall that was just there for ornament and where no one ever sat, its only occupant the occasional umbrella. She would perch in the passage, dumb with misery and apprehension, motioning me not to go into the empty living room because there was someone there.

'You won't tell anybody?' she whispered.

'Tell anybody what?'

'Tell them what I've done.'

'You haven't done anything.'

'But you won't tell them?'

'Mam!' I said, exasperated, but she put her hand to my mouth, pointed at the living-room door and then wrote TALKING in wavering letters on a pad, mutely shaking her head.

As time went on these futile discussions would become less intimate (less caring even), the topography quite spread out, with the parties not even in adjoining rooms. Dad would be sitting by the living-room fire while Mam hovered tearfully in the doorway of the pantry, the kitchen in between empty.

'Come in the pantry, Dad,' she'd call.

'What for? What do I want in the pantry?'

'They can see you.'

'How can they see me? There's nobody here.'

'There is, only you don't know. Come in here.'

It didn't take much of this before Dad lapsed into a weary silence.

'Oh, whish't,' he'd say, 'be quiet.'

A play could begin like this, I used to think – with a man on stage, sporadically angry with a woman off stage, his bursts of baffled invective gradually subsiding into an obstinate silence. Resistant to the off-stage entreaties, he continues to ignore her until his persistent refusal to respond gradually tempts the woman into view.

Or set in the kitchen, the empty room between them, no one on stage at all, just the voices off. And what happens when they do come on stage? Violence, probably.

It was all so banal. Missionary for her sunless world, my mother was concerned to convince us in the face of all vehement denial that sooner or later she would be taken away. And of course she was right.

Her other fears . . . of being spied on, listened to, shamed and detected . . . were ordinary stuff too. This was not the territory of grand delusion, her fears not decked out in the showy accoutrements of fashionable neurosis. None of Freud's patients hovered at pantry doors; Freud's *selected* patients, I always felt, the ordinary not getting past, or even to, the first consultation because too dull, the final disillusion to have fled across the border into unreason only to find you are as mundane mad as you ever were sane.

Certainly in all her excursions into unreality Mam remained the shy, unassuming woman she had always been, none of her fantasies extravagant, her claims, however irrational they might be, always modest. She might be ill, disturbed, mad even, but she still knew her place.

It may be objected that madness did not come into it; that, as Mr Parr had said, this was depression and a very different thing. But though we clung to this assurance, it was hard not to think these delusions mad and the tenacity with which she held to them, defended them, insisted on them the very essence of unreason. While it was perhaps naïve of us to expect her to recognise she was ill, or that standing stock still on the landing by the hour together was not normal behaviour, it was this determination to convert you to her way of thinking that made her behaviour hardest to bear.

'I wouldn't care,' Dad said, 'but she tries to get me on the same game.' Not perceiving her irrationalities as symptoms, my father had no other remedy than common sense.

'You're imagining stuff,' he would say, flinging wide the wardrobe door. 'Where is he? Show me!'

The non-revelation of the phantom intruder ought, it seemed to Dad, to dent Mam's conviction, persuade her that she was mistaken. But not a bit of it. Putting her finger to her lips (the man in the wardrobe now having mysteriously migrated to the bathroom), she drew him to the window to point at the fishman's van, looking at him in fearful certainty, even triumph; he must surely see that the fate she feared, whatever it was, must soon engulf them both.

But few nights passed uninterrupted, and Dad would wake to find the place beside him empty, Mam scrabbling at the lock of the outside door or standing by the bedroom window looking out at a car in the car park that she said was watching the house.

How he put up with it all I never asked, but it was always this mission- ary side to her depression, the aggressiveness of her despair and her con- viction that hers was the true view of the world that was the breaking point with me and which, if I were alone with her, would fetch me to the brink of violence. I once nearly dragged her out of the house to confront an elderly hiker who was sitting on the wall opposite, eating his sand- wiches. He would have been startled to have been required to confirm to a distraught middle-aged man and his weeping mother that his shorts and sandals were not some subtle disguise, that he was not in reality an agent of . . . what? Mam never specified. But I would have seemed the mad one and the brute. Once I took her by the shoulders and shook her so hard it must have hurt her, but she scarcely seemed to mind. It just confirmed to her how insane the world had become.

'We used to be such pals,' she'd say to me, shaking her head and refus- ing to say more because the radio was listening, instead creeping upstairs to the cold bedroom to perch on one of the flimsy bedroom chairs, beck- oning me to stay silent and do the same as if this were a satisfactory way to spend the morning.

And yet, as the doctor and everybody else kept saying, depression was not madness. It would lift. Light would return. But when? The young, sympathetic doctor from the local practice could not say. The senior part- ner whom we had at first consulted was a distinguished-looking figure, silver-haired, loud-talking, a Rotarian and pillar of the community. Unsurprisingly he was also a pull your socks up merchant and did not hold with depression. At his happiest going down potholes to assist stricken cavers, he was less adept at getting patients out of their more inaccessible holes.

How long such depressions lasted no doctor was prepared to say, nor anyone else that I talked to. There seemed to be no timetable, this want of a timetable almost a definition of the disease. It might be months (the optimistic view), but one of the books I looked into talked about years, though what all the authorities did seem agreed on was that, treated or not, depression cleared up in time. One school of thought held that time was of the essence, and that the depression should be allowed to run its course unalleviated and unaccelerated by drugs. But on my mother drugs seemed to have no effect anyway, and if the depression were to run its course and it did take years, many months even, what would happen to my father?

Alone in the house, knowing no one in the village well enough to call on them for help, he was both nurse and gaoler. Coaxing his weeping parody of a wife to eat, with every mouthful a struggle, then smuggling himself out of the house to do some hasty shopping, hoping that she would not come running down the street after him, he spent every day and every fitful night besieged by Mam's persistent assaults on reality, foiling her attempts to switch off the television, turn off the lights or pull the curtains against her imaginary enemies, knowing that if he once let her out of his sight she would be scrabbling at the lock of the front door trying to flee this house which was both her prison and her refuge.

Thus it was that after six weeks of what Dad called 'this flaming carry-on' it was as much for his sake as for hers that the doctor arranged that she should be voluntarily admitted to the mental hospital in Lancaster.

Lancaster Moor Hospital is not a welcoming institution. It was built at the beginning of the nineteenth century as the County Asylum and Workhouse, and seen from the M6 it has always looked to me like a gaunt grey penitentiary. Like Dickens's Coketown, the gaol might have been the infirmary and the infirmary the gaol. It was a relief, therefore, to find the psychiatric wing where Mam was to be admitted not part of the main complex but a villa, Ridge Lee, set in its own grounds, and as we left Mam with a nurse in the entrance hall that September morning it seemed almost cheerful. Dad was not uncheerful too, relieved that now at any rate something was going to be done and that 'she's in professional hands'. Even Mam seemed resigned to it, and though she had never been in hospital in her life she let us kiss her goodbye and leave without protest.

It was actually only to be goodbye for a few hours, as visiting times were from seven to eight and though it was a fifty mile round trip from home Dad was insistent that we would return that same evening, his conscientiousness in this first instance setting the pattern for the hundreds of hospital visits he was to make over the next eight years, with never a single one missed and agitated if he was likely to be even five minutes late.

I had reached early middle age with next to no experience of mental illness. At Oxford there had been undergraduates who had had nervous breakdowns, though I never quite believed in them and had never visited the Warnford Hospital on the outskirts of the city where they were usually consigned. Later, teaching at Magdalen, I had had a pupil, an irritating, distracted boy who would arrive two hours late for tutorials or ignore them altogether, and when he did turn up with an essay it would be sixty or seventy pages long. When I complained about him in pretty unfeeling terms one of the Fellows took me on one side and explained kindly that he was 'unbalanced', something that had never occurred to me though it was hard to miss. Part of me probably still thought of neurosis as somehow 'put on', a way of making oneself interesting – the reason why when I was younger I thought of myself as slightly neurotic.

When I was seventeen I had had a friend a few years older than me who, I realise when I look back, must have been schizophrenic. He had several times gone through the dreadful ordeal of insulin-induced comas that were the fashionable treatment then, but I never asked him about it, partly out of embarrassment but also because I was culpably incurious. Going into the army and then to university, I lost touch with him, and it was only in 1966, on the verge of leaving Leeds, that I learned that he had committed suicide.

I went to the funeral at St Michael's, Headingley, the church where in our teens we had both been enthusiastic worshippers. Every Friday night a group of us gathered in the chancel to say the office of Compline with, at the heart of it, Psalm 91: 'Thou shalt not be afraid for any terror by night: nor for the arrow that flieth by day. A thousand shall fall beside thee,' we sang, 'and ten thousand at thy right hand: but it shall not come nigh thee.' Now it had, and as the remnants of our group stood awkwardly outside the church, I reflected that he was the first person of our generation to have died. Oddly it was my mother who was most upset, far more so than her acquaintance with him warranted, the fact that he had not died a natural death but had committed suicide seeming particularly to grieve her in a way I might have thought strange were not her own shadows by that time already beginning to gather.

Driving over the moors to the hospital that evening, I thought how precarious our previous well-being had been, how unwittingly blessed in our collective balance of mind, and how much I'd taken it for granted. I said so to Dad, who just stared out of the window saying nothing. Sanity and its vagaries were much discussed at this time, the fashionable theorists R. D. Laing and Thomas Szasz. Their ideas had never impinged on my father nor were they likely to; balance of mind was something you were entitled to take for granted so far as he was concerned, 'Item no. 1 on the agenda, to get your Mam back to normal.'

Except affliction was normal too, and this one seemingly more common than I'd thought. Arriving at the lighted villa in its own little park, we found we were far from alone, the car park full, the nurse busy at Reception, and hanging about the entrance hall, as in all institutions (hospitals, law courts, passport offices), characters who joked with the staff, were clued up on the routine and, whether visitors or patients, seemed utterly at home. It was one of these knowing individuals, a young man familiar rather than affable, who took us along to what the nurse said was Mam's ward.

He flung open the door on Bedlam, a scene of unimagined wretchedness. What hit you first was the noise. The hospitals I had been in previously were calm and unhurried; voices were hushed; sickness, during visiting hours at least, went hand in hand with decorum. Not here. Crammed with wild and distracted women, lying or lurching about in all the wanton disarray of a Hogarth print, it was a place of terrible tumult. Some of the grey-gowned wild-eyed creatures were weeping, others shouting, while one demented wretch shrieked at short and regular intervals like some tropical bird. Almost worse was a big dull-eyed woman who sat bolt upright on her bed, oblivious to the surrounding tumult, as silent and unmoving as a stone deity.

Obviously, I thought, we have strayed into the wrong ward, much as Elizabeth Taylor did in the film of *Suddenly Last Summer*. Mam was not ill like this. She had nothing to do with the distracted creature who sat by the nearest bed, her gown hitched high above her knees, banging her spoon on a tray. But as I turned to go I saw that Dad was walking on down the ward.

We had left Mam at the hospital that morning looking, even after weeks of illness, not much different from her usual self: weeping and distraught, it's true, but still plump and pretty, clutching her everlasting handbag and still somehow managing to face the world. As I followed my father down the ward I wondered why we were bothering: there was no such person here.

He stopped at the bed of a sad, shrunken woman with wild hair, who cringed back against the pillows.

'Here's your Mam,' he said.

And of course it was only that, by one of the casual cruelties that routine inflicts, she had on admission been bathed, her hair washed and left uncombed and uncurled, so that now it stood out round her head in a mad halo, this straight away drafting her into the ranks of the demented. Yet the change was so dramatic, the obliteration of her usual self so utter and complete, that to restore her even to an appearance of normality now seemed beyond hope. She was mad because she looked mad.

Dad sat down by the bed and took her hand.

'What have you done to me, Walt?' she said.

'Nay, Lil,' he said, and kissed her hand. 'Nay, love.'

And in the kissing and the naming my parents were revealed stripped of all defence. Because they seldom kissed, and though they were the tenderest and most self-sufficient couple, I had never seen my father do anything so intimate as to kiss my mother's hand and seldom since childhood heard them call each other by name. 'Mam' and 'Dad' was what my brother and I called them and what they called each other, their names kept for best. Or worst.

They had been Lil and Walt in their courting days, living on opposite sides of Tong Road in the twenties. Marriage and children had changed them to Mam and Dad, and it took a catastrophe for them to christen themselves again. So when in 1946 he collapsed in the street and was taken to St James's with a perforated ulcer, Dad became Walt once more. And when Mam was crying with pain having had all her teeth out, she was not Mam but Lil. And to him she was Lil now.

There was only one chair by Mam's bed and no room for another; besides, Mam was crying, and Dad too, so I walked round the ward. Though many of the patients were unvisited, their disturbance and distress unalleviated by company, other beds hosted families as stunned and bewildered as we were. They sat huddled round a stricken mother, or a weeping daughter, careful to avoid the eye of other visitors and with none of the convivialities and camaraderie a usual hospital visit engenders.

Yet there were others who seemed entirely at ease in these surroundings, elderly sons of vacant mothers, jovial husbands of demented wives, and some whose faces were more coarse and void than those of whom they were visiting. They sat round the bed in bovine indifference, chatting across the demented creature in their midst, as if the lunacy of a loved one was no more than was to be expected.

It was from this time I conceived a dislike of Lancaster I've never since lost. Having seen madness on that ward, I saw it echoed in face after face in the town. Though it's a pleasant enough place I find the people there less amiable and appealing than elsewhere in Lancashire, with the possible exception of Liverpool. There's an openness and generosity in Blackburn, Preston and Rochdale, maybe because these were virtues fostered in the mills; Lancaster, commercial, agricultural and (like Liverpool) once a port, seems sullen, tight-fisted and at night raw and violent.

Sometime in the course of this terrible hour a neat middle-aged woman stopped at the foot of Mam's bed.

'It's Mary, love. I'm off now. They've just rung me a taxi.' She turned to me. 'Could you just go and see if it's come?'

I went out into the entrance hall, cheered that one of these desperate women could, by a stay even in such unpromising surroundings, be recovered for normality and turned back into a sane and sensible creature. There must after all be hope. But if there was hope there was certainly no taxi, so I went back to the ward. Mary had by now passed on, making her farewells at another bed. I went over to tell her the taxi hadn't come only to find she was now telling her tale to an empty pillow.

In her ensuing bouts of depression Mam was in three hospitals and in each one there was a Mary, a Goodbye Girl who hung about the door, often with her bag packed, accosting everyone who came in, claiming she was about to leave, with the taxi ordered.

'Are you my taxi?' she would say to anyone who came near, though this persistent expectation of departure did not necessarily mean she was dissatisfied with her circumstances, and there are after all worse ways to live than in a constant readiness to depart. The irony was that it would only be when she stopped thinking that she was on the point of departing that she would be pronounced cured and allowed to do so.

The next night I got into conversation with a pleasant young man who was sitting in the entrance hall and whom I took to be a student, possibly at Lancaster University. He was telling me in great detail about a forthcoming visit to Russia and I asked him how he was planning to go.

'By Ribble Motors. They run a coach service to Moscow starting every night from Morecambe Pier.'

If these were lighter moments they hardly seemed so then. A nurse told us that this was the Admissions Ward where, until diagnosis could sort them out, the confused and the senile, the deranged and the merely depressed were lumped together for observation, the implication being that the next ward would be better. It could hardly be worse, and to leave Mam in such a situation a moment longer than we had to seemed unthinkable. I longed to bundle her up then and there and, as in some Dickensian deliverance, convey her far away from this yelling hell-hole to a place that was light and calm and clean.

After two days' obstruction by the ward sister we eventually managed to see the doctor in charge, who was kindly and understanding but as weary and defeated as someone out of Chekhov. He would be happy, he said, to have her transferred to another hospital if we could arrange it. I cannot think nowadays it would be so easy, and there would be the rig-marole of quotas to be considered and competing budgets, but in those days it just meant a visit to the Mental Health Welfare Officer, and it is this errand that has brought us straight from Lancaster to Settle this September night, to Mr Parr's bleak office above the police station.

'Nearly done,' says Mr Parr. 'What did Mrs Bennett's parents die of?'

'Her mother died of cancer,' I say, 'and her father had a heart attack.' Dad shakes his head, meaning that these questions seem to him to have little to do with Mam's current illness. At least that's what I take him to mean and I reckon not to see, because while I tend to agree I don't think now is the time to make an issue of it.

As Mr Parr is noting this down Dad gently touches my knee. This is a man who never touches, seldom kisses, but Oxford-educated as I am and regularly to be seen on television I fail to appreciate the magnitude of the gesture, and blunder on.

'Well, perhaps not a heart attack,' I say. 'It may have been a coronary thrombosis. He dropped dead anyway.'

It was in 1925, in the kitchen at Gilpin Place, the spot pointed out: there by the dresser your Grandad died, plain in the sight of everybody. That they were not living at Gilpin Place at the time never, of course, occurred to me.

The form completed, Mr Parr locks up his office, walks us back along the street to where we have parked the car; he promises to make the arrangements for Mam's transfer the next day, and we say goodnight.

'Did those questions matter?' asks Dad. 'Would they affect the treatment?' I tell him that I don't think so and that what Mr Parr was after, presumably, was whether there had been anything similar in the family before. I start the car. 'Only it was your Grandad Peel. He didn't have a heart attack. He killed himself.'

I turn the engine off, sit there and digest this, Dad volunteering no more information. Eventually, though it doesn't seem to me to affect Mam's situation one way or another, I go and knock on Mr Parr's door and explain that I'd just this minute found out that Mam's father didn't die of a heart attack; he had drowned himself in the canal.

Mr Parr doesn't think it's relevant either, but standing on his doorstep as we drive away he may well be thinking that this is an odd family that censors its own history, and it's that that's relevant.

━━━━━━

As we drove home Dad told me that as soon as the interview started he realised the true facts of Mam's father's death were likely to come out, and it was this that had made him want to put his hand on my knee, lest the suicide be a shock. It had been a shock, but the shocking thing was not the act itself so much as the way it had been concealed and misrepresented for more than forty years.

Truth to tell I found the suicide intriguing too (and felt ashamed a little that I did so). Like a child who longs to be an orphan, or at least not the offspring of his humdrum parents, I was excited by this man who had drowned and had his drowning buried; it made my family more interesting. In 1966 I had just begun to write but had already given up on my own background because the material seemed so thin. This perked things up a bit.

In fairness to myself I had never known my grandfather, nor understandably in the circumstances had he been much talked about. 'He was a lovely feller' was Mam's description of him, her stock phrase for men she liked; his only son, her brother Clarence, was a 'lovely feller' too, killed at Ypres in 1917, and when his time came my father would also be a 'lovely feller'. 'Your Grandad Peel', as he was known to distinguish him from 'Your Grandad Bennett', occurred in some of the family photographs I used to find in the dresser drawer at Grandma's where I went rooting as a child. He was a stocky man with thick dark hair and a moustache, not fierce-looking as some of the men in old photographs were but with no clue as to what he was like. Mam had said he was keen on 'nature study' and knew about trees and flowers; he went on walks.

The drowning, though, straight away shed light on an incident early in her depression which at the time I'd thought almost a joke. Dad had gone out and Mam and I were alone in the house. Motioning me into the passage where we would not be overheard, she whispered that she had done something terrible. I was having none of it, but she got hold of my arm and pulled me up the stairs and pointed to the bathroom but would not go in. There were six inches of water in the bath.

My mother's family, the Peels, had once been well-to-do, owning mills in Halifax, and were descendants, so Mam's sister Myra claimed, of Sir Robert Peel. The youngest of the three sisters, Aunty Myra was the keeper of the family flame, determined that if her present did not amount to much, a sales assistant in White's Ladies' Mantles Shop in Briggate, now living in a back-to-back in Wortley, then the past could be called in to compensate. When my brother was christened, Aunty Myra wanted him given Peel as a middle name, and there was a muttered row at the font when Dad, who thought one name sufficient and two pretentious, would have none of it. He didn't have much time for the Sir Robert Peel business either, or for any attempt to put it on or talk posh, which Aunty Kathleen and Aunty Myra both went in for. But even my mother, who took his line, thought that the family had come down in the world, saying that there had been two branches of the Peels in Halifax, both with mills, and that at the time of the Boer War the run on cloth for uniforms had tempted their branch of the family, her grandfather possibly, to invest in new machinery. With the end of the war came a slump and with it bankruptcy, the other less enterprising branch of the family going on to further prosperity. Certainly every Christmas on the mantelpiece of the back-to-back in Gilpin Place there would be a grand card from some country Peels, whom I took to be the gentry they had become and we might have been. But it may all have been romance; in private life Beatrice Lillie was Lady Peel and my aunties even adduced her as a distant connection.

The mill gone, my grandparents then bought a hardware shop in West Vale outside Halifax but that too went bankrupt, through sheer kind-heartedness my mother said, and letting too much stuff out on credit. There is a picture of the shop in the sheaf of crumpled photographs and newspaper clippings that passes for our family album, the shop assistants lined up on the steps flanked by those Karnak columns of linoleum that enfiladed every hardware store even in my own childhood, and peeping through the door my mother's blurred ten-year-old face.

The shame of this second bankruptcy drove the family to Leeds, where they lived in Wortley, Grandad Peel now managing a gents' outfitters in Wellington Road. The three sisters, Kathleen, Lilian and Lemira, and their elder brother Clarence all went to Green Lane School, its gaunt hulk one of the few buildings undemolished among the new houses dinky as houses in Monopoly that nowadays cover the slopes below Armley Gaol; the school, the gaol and St Bartholomew's Church all that is left of a thriving neighbourhood, the pillars of a sometime community.

All this I sort of knew in 1966 but without ever enquiring into the details, our family history a series of vivid scenes of uncertain chronology and mostly connected with Mam's side of the family. There was Uncle Clarence's death at Ypres and the telegraph boy riding his bike along Bruce Street in 1917, with women stood fearfully on their doorsteps to see which door he would knock at. There was Mam, working upstairs at Stylo Shoes in Briggate in 1926, watching mounted police charge the strikers. There was the outbreak of war, the actual declaration catching us on a tram going down to Vicar Lane bus station to get a bus to safety and

Pateley Bridge; VE night outside Guildford Town Hall, sitting on my Uncle George's shoulders, marvelling at floodlights, which I'd never seen before. And Grandma Peel sitting in her chair at Gilpin Place in 1949, beginning to bleed from the womb, and as Aunty Kathleen cleans her up joking grimly, 'Nay, lass, I'm seventy-nine but I think I must be starting again.'

Still, if I knew little of my mother's family I knew even less about my father's, not that there seemed much to know. My father was not a typical butcher – thin, anxious, dogged all his life by stomach ulcers and a temperament ill-suited to the job. The youngest of four brothers, he had lost his mother at the age of five, when his father, faced with bringing up four sons, had hurriedly remarried. This second wife was a narrow, vicious woman, a stepmother out of a fairy story; she was pious, chapel-going and a hypocrite who beat the youngest boys, Walter and George, and then told lies about them to her new husband so that when he came home from work he gave them the strap again. Whereas the elder boys were old enough to escape the house and too big to beat, Dad and his brother George ('our butt' as he always called him) bore the brunt of her frustrated rage. It was she who put him to butchering at the age of eleven, an offence for which he never forgave her but which earned her her nickname. To this day I don't know what she was really called, and I have never troubled to find out, but she was always referred to by all the Bennetts as the Gimmer, a gimmer a sheep that has no lambs and a nickname Dad must have brought home from the slaughterhouse in Oldfield Lane, where he was condemned to work. I can only just remember her, a figure in shiny black satin seemingly out of the depths of the nineteenth century but who must have died in the early forties. Shortly before her death she immortalised herself in the family by saying to my nine-year-old brother, Gordon, 'Get off that stool, you, or I'll kick you off.' Her funeral was an occasion of undiluted joy, sheer hysteria breaking out among the mourners when her coffin went down into the grave and Mam slipped and nearly went after it.

Grandad Bennett was as bald as an egg. He had worked at the gasworks in Wellington Road, the stench of which pervaded the acres of sooty red-brick streets around Armley Gaol. He had been in an explosion which perhaps literally or as the result of shock blew away all his hair, a cruel fate in our family, where the men all have thick and often un-greying hair. His second wife's piety must have infected him because in his old age he took to marching behind the Salvation Army band, his gleaming head jeered at by the unfeeling youths of Lower Wortley.

At some point when he was still a boy Dad took it into his head to learn the violin. Why he chose an instrument that in its initial stages is so unrewarding I don't know; it's one of the many questions I never got round to asking him. He got no help at home, where he could only practise in the freezing parlour, the Gimmer too mean even to let him have any light so that he had to manage with what there was from the gas lamp in the street outside. Whether he was born with perfect pitch I don't know but in later life he would play along to the hymns on the wireless, telling you the notes of the tune he was accompanying as easily as if he was spelling a word. In happier circumstances he would have been a professional violinist but there was never any hope of that and a butcher he remained, working firstly for the Co-op, before in 1946 buying a shop of his own, which he had to give up ten years later through ill health, then buying a smaller one and the same thing happening. With no money to speak of and the job having given him precious little satisfaction, he was never so happy as when in 1966 he was able to give up butchering for good.

Happy, that is, until 'this business with your Mam'. Driving backwards and forwards to Lancaster, I had never spent so much time with my father as then, and though there was no other revelation as startling as that to do with Grandad Peel, he talked more freely than he'd ever done about Mam and their life together, the car a kind of confessional. I was doing the driving and it helped that road safety precluded much eye contact, my own occasional embarrassment betrayed by abrupt bursts of speed as I suddenly put my foot down as if to get away as fast as I could from the past he was talking about.

The suicide, though, he could not be persuaded to discuss. Having let on to the fact, he still seemed to want to keep it hidden and would not be questioned about it, sensing perhaps that my interest in it was as drama and only one stage up from gossip. As a child I was clever and knew it, and when I showed off, as I often did, Dad would not trouble to hide his distaste. I detected a whiff of that still; he was probably wishing he'd kept his mouth shut and never mentioned the tragedy at all.

I did ask about his other revelation, 'the similar do' he had told Mr Parr that Mam had had just before they were married. Had that been to do with the suicide, I asked, as it must have been around the same time? Not really, said Dad. He thought it was more to do with their wedding.

It had never occurred to me as a child that there were no photographs of my parents' wedding. Along with the cut-glass fruit bowl, the stand of cork table mats and the lady leashing in her Alsatian, a wedding photograph was a component of the sideboard of every house of every friend or relative that I had been into. Typical was the wedding photograph of Uncle George and Aunty Flo, taken around 1925. Uncle George is in a suit, wing collar and spats, Aunty Flo in a white wedding-dress and veil, the folds of her dress carefully arranged to cascade down the sooty steps of St Mary of Bethany, Tong Road, where Uncle George sings in the choir, and watched off-camera by their respective families, the Rostrons and the Bennetts, and also by anybody who happens to be waiting this Saturday morning at the tram stop at the bottom of Fourteenth Avenue.

The absence of a similar photograph from our sideboard had never struck me. And if it was not on the sideboard nor was it in the top right-hand dressing-table drawer in Mam and Dad's bedroom where, along with a pot of wintergreen ointment and an old scent spray and the tuning fork for Dad's violin, the family photographic archive was kept. It was a slender collection, fitting easily into two or three tattered Kodak wallets and consisting chiefly of snaps of holidays at Morecambe or Filey: Mam stroking a baby donkey on the sands somewhere, Dad in a bathing costume holding Gordon up to the camera, the pair of us, me a baby, Gordon three, sitting on Grandma's knee on the wall at Gilpin Place. But no wedding.

The natural assumption by an imaginative child, particularly if he was a romancer as I was, would be that he was illegitimate or at any rate not his parents' child. Both possibilities had occurred to me, but I had seen their marriage certificate (also kept in the dressing-table drawer) and this disposed of the first possibility while a look in the mirror put paid to the second. There, depressingly, was the same pink face and long chin that all the Bennetts had. Grandma would sometimes take me with her when she went bowling at the Recreation Ground, her friends (black cloche hats, long duster coats) would look at me in the pushchair and say, 'Oh yes, Poll. He's a right Bennett.' It was never something I much wanted to be, until a year or two ago, unexpectedly coming across my cousin Geoff in a hotel car park in Wetherby, I saw both his father, Uncle George, in his face and my father too, and the grin neither of them was ever able quite to suppress, and I was not unhappy that I looked a bit like that too.

Had I given any thought to the missing photographs I would probably have taken this to be just another instance of our family never managing to be like other families, of which there were far more urgent and contentious instances than a mere unrecorded ceremony. There was never being allowed to wear an open-necked shirt, for instance, for fear we caught TB; there was never going without a cap lest we got sunstroke; never having a drink of cold water and it always having to be 'aired', and not being allowed to share a lemonade bottle with other boys (TB again); after Wolf Cubs most of my friends would have two-pennyworth of chips, but we weren't supposed to as they kept us awake, Mam even smelling our breath for vinegar just in case. Our family was no better or worse off than our neighbours but in all sorts of ways, that were no less weighty for being trivial, we never managed to be quite the same.

On the other hand, had there been a photograph of Mam and Dad's wedding it was likely to have been an early casualty of Mam's precocious interest in antiques, which led to a gradual purge of items like the fruit bowl, the table mats and the woodpecker calendar. Wedding presents though these items often were, the forties saw them gradually relegated to the attic to be replaced by her first tentative acquisitions from junk shops: a brass candlestick she bought in Ripon for 8s. 6d.; a green glass doorstop; a chipped lustre jug. To her credit she had never gone in for the lady and the Alsatian dog or (worse) the little boy holding a smockful of cherries who often kept her company. Both these items were unhesitatingly dubbed as 'common' by my mother, and she would be mortified today to see them on bric-à-brac stalls enjoying equal status with the lustre and the candlesticks, one as much sought after as the other, collectables all.

There was no question that Mam's liking for these ancient *objets trouvés* was entirely genuine, though in acquiring them she was also laying claim to a sort of refinement which was genuine too; it was hard to say where it came from, women's magazines, possibly and in particular Beverley Nichols's column in *Woman's Own*. Some of it, though, was instinctive if not inbred. She knew, for instance, without having read it anywhere, that the old-fashioned kitchen range that we had was preferable, had more 'character' than the tiled fireplaces everybody round about thought were the height of sophistication, and that the brass pot which held our fire irons was superior to the ceramic knight-in-armour wielding poker and tongs that stood sentinel on neighbouring hearthstones.

Desperate I think it now, and touching too, this faith she had in what constituted a better life. It couldn't be called a hobby, it was never systematic enough for that, though going through cupboards at home nowadays I'll still sometimes come across one of the many little notebooks she started, with wispy drawings of chair-backs labelled 'Sheraton' or 'Hepplewhite', and lists of pottery marks she copied out of library books; then there are some blank pages and another list, 'Bits of music I like': Chopin's Polonaise in A, Mendelssohn's *Italian Symphony*, *The Dream of Olwen*, the spelling all over the place.

Nowadays when 'bygones' are the stuff of half a dozen TV programmes, and nuggets of the more tuneful classics are trotted out to the banalities of disc jockeys who can scarcely pronounce the composers' names, such aspirations in a middle-aged working-class woman would not be particularly remarkable. But in Leeds in 1946 it was precocious if not eccentric, particularly since it hardly linked up with the way we lived, over a butcher's shop in a house with no hallway, the living room giving straight onto the street where Mam's painfully collected gentilities were periodically overwhelmed by the stench of fat being rendered in the cellar. Nothing she bought was ever worth much, her Staffordshire ornaments were always cracked, the 'Sheraton' chair an Edwardian reproduction and the turbanned Rockingham man smoking a pipe had lost his hand (a little mitten-like paw made of plasticine Mam's unconvincing prosthesis).

Still, her antiques, touching though they were in their inadequacy, were not an attempt to improve our social status. Though she herself would have said she liked 'old stuff' because it was 'classy', this definition had nothing to do with class, 'classy' in her vocabulary simply the opposite of 'common'. That was the real nub of it. Because if there was one consideration that determined my parents' conduct and defined their position in the world it was not to be (or to be thought) common.

Common, like camp (with which it shares a frontier), is not easy to define. At its simplest meaning vulgar or ostentatious, it is a more subtle and various disparagement than that, or was in our family anyway, taking in such widely disparate manifestations as tattoos, red paint, yellow gloves and two-tone cardigans, all entries in a catalogue of disapproval that ranged through fake leopard-skin coats and dyed (blonde) hair to slacks, cocktail cabinets, the aforementioned ladies with Alsatian dogs and boys with cherries, and umpteen other embellishments, domestic and personal.

The opposite of 'common' is not 'uncommon'; indeed an element of uncommonness in the ostentatious sense is part of being common – the dyed blonde hair and leopard-skin coat of Miss Fairey, the chemist's assistant at Armley Moor Top, or twenty years later the white Jaguar in which Russell Harty's parents would roll up to visit him in Oxford. So flaunting it (whatever 'it' was) and splashing money around were part of it. But so was having no aspirations at all or living in something approaching squalor while squandering money on gambling or drink; that was common too.

A dog could be common – a barbered poodle – but seldom a cat; colours like the red of paint (on a house) and purple (practically anywhere). 'Them's common curtains,' Mam's frequent observation from the top deck of a bus; it always had to be the top because Dad was a smoker and it served as a grandstand for a running commentary on the social scene. 'Tangerine! I wouldn't have tangerine curtains if you paid me. And look at that camel-hair coat. Makes him look like a bookie.' Haircuts were a dangerous area: if Dad had his cut too short he was thought to look 'right common'; cafés, too, particularly those doing too much fried stuff but omitting to serve toasted teacakes. These days shell suits would undoubtedly be condemned, as would walking down the street drinking from a can, and it would do as a definition of what's gone wrong with England in the last twenty years that it's got more common.

Such fastidious deprecations were invariably made privately and to each other, my parents too timid to think their views worth broadcasting or that they might be shared with anyone else, still less meet with general agreement; this reticence helping to reinforce the notion that we were a peculiar family and somehow set apart. Cheerful, rumbustious even within the security of the home, off their home ground they were shy and easily intimidated; there was an absence of swagger and they never, unlike my mother's self-confident sisters, 'had a lot off'. So when they stigmatised ostentatious behaviour as common it reaffirmed their natural preference not to want to attract attention and to get by unnoticed; they knew what they took to be their place, and kept to it.

Wanting to go unnoticed was what Mam's depression was about. Pressed to define why it was she found the village intimidating, she said, 'You don't understand. I'm the centrepiece here.' So it was hardly surprising that when Dad revealed that there had been something similar in the past it should have been on the eve of her wedding, an occasion when there could be no going unnoticed either: 'I'm the centrepiece here', which is a bride's boast, was my mother's dread. Was this why there were no photographs?

What was agitating her, and maybe it agitated him too, as he was in many ways more shy even than her, was the ceremony itself and the churchful of people it would inevitably involve. Marriage is a kind of going public, and I could see, as Dad couldn't or wouldn't, that coming to live in the village which had maybe brought on this second bout forty years later was a kind of going public too.

Not that the ceremony she was dreading was likely to be an elaborate one, as neither family can have had any money. A proper wedding, though, would have run to bridesmaids and they were there to hand in her two sisters, Kathleen and Myra, and this may well have been part of the trouble, as she had always felt overshadowed by them and something of a Cinderella. Unlike her they revelled in any kind of public show, edging into whatever limelight was going. Later in life they made far more of my brother's and my achievements than Mam and Dad did. When I got my degree at Oxford Dad wrote, 'We haven't let on to your aunties yet that you're getting your cap and gown. You won't be wanting a lot of splother' – splother Dad's word for the preening and fuss invariably attendant on the presence of the aunties.

The splother attendant upon the wedding was harder to get round, and Mam's fear of the occasion persisted until there came a point, Dad told me, when they nearly broke off their engagement because neither of them could see a way of ever getting over this first necessary hurdle. Eventually Dad sought the advice of the local vicar.

These days this would mean a cosy, even chummy chat with counselling the keynote. And why not? But Leeds in those days was the proving ground for many a future dean or bishop, some of the grandest Anglican dynasties – Hollises, Bickersteths, Vaughans – ministering to the slums of Hunslet and Holbeck. St Bartholomew's was a great slum parish too, its huge black church set on a hill above Armley and Wortley, and though the slums around it have gone, or at any rate changed their character, its heavy spire still dominates the south-western approaches to Leeds. The vicar in 1928 was the Reverend H. Lovell Clarke, subsequently Archdeacon of Leeds, and it was to him rather than to one of his several curates that Dad went.

It must have been hard to explain: all brides are nervous, after all; why should this Lilian Peel require special treatment? Public school and Cambridge, the vicar is just the kind of figure ('very better class') to make Dad nervous and tongue-tied. What he has come along to ask is whether the vicar will marry them at seven-thirty in the morning, with no fuss, no congregation and in time for Dad to get to work at Lower Wortley Co-op by eight-fifteen. Lovell Clarke says that this is out of the question; the law does not permit him to marry anyone before eight in the morning. However, he has no objection to performing the ceremony beginning at eight o'clock, and surely if he is getting married the Co-op won't mind if he is half an hour late for work? Dad enquires: the Co-op does mind; he has to be at work by eight-fifteen.

There are occasions in life, often not in the least momentous, which nail one's colours to the mast. There was the morning, ten days before the end of my National Service, when a sergeant in the Intelligence Corps at Maresfield made me scrub out a urinal with my bare hands; another when a consultant at the Radcliffe Infirmary discussed my naked body without reference to me with a class of smirking medical students; and though it occurred years before I was born, this moment in St Bartholomew's Vicarage when my father, baffled at every turn, tells Mr Lovell Clarke that he cannot get a quarter of an hour off work in order to get married is another. Logic, education, upbringing leave such moments unshifted and unforgotten. They are the self at its core.

My father, I suspect, gives up at this point but the vicar does not, and indeed comes up with a solution that is ingenious, even cheeky. To begin with the young couple will need a special licence from the Bishop of Ripon, dispensing with the need for the banns to be read, the vicar sensibly assuming that whatever plan he comes up with is better carried out quickly rather than waiting the three weeks that proclaiming the banns will involve. Then armed with the licence they are to present themselves at the church at seven-thirty the following morning, at which time the vicar will say the whole wedding service up to but not including the vows, thus complying with the law. On the stroke of eight the vows themselves can be said, the ring put on and this young butcher still have time to get to work by eight-fifteen. And on 28 September 1928 that is how it is done. Dad goes off to work, Mam goes home and in the evening, in lieu of a honeymoon, they get tickets for the Theatre Royal to see *The Desert Song.*

That was why there was no photograph on top of the sideboard or in the dressing-table drawer. At eight o'clock on a sooty September morning it would have been too dark; besides, a photograph would have taken time and would in any case have probably come under Dad's definition of 'splother'. But were I a poet I would write about those moments in that great empty church, the anxious groom in his working clothes with his tentative bride, and the urbane cleric, standing on the altar steps waiting for the clock to strike, the pause before the off. A former chaplain to nearby Armley Gaol, where prisoners used regularly to be hanged, Lovell Clarke must have waited many times for eight o'clock, the pause before a more terrible off. What he was like I have no idea, though I imagine him as a clergyman of the old school. But across seventy and more years, Herbert Lovell Clarke, I would like to shake your hand.

━━━━━━

In every other circumstance a man who hung back, follower not leader, visiting his wife in hospital my father was always in the front rank. The second the visiting bell went he would hurry down the ward ahead of the rest of the pack, always with a carrier or a parcel containing the vest he had washed or some of the Creamline toffees Mam liked and a few marigolds from the garden. And though he might have come thirty miles he was always on the dot, no second of the permitted time let go to waste.

Ferrying him to the hospital at Lancaster those first few nights I found his insistent punctuality irritating, particularly as there seemed to me nothing to be punctual *for*, so much of the visit passed in silence with Dad just sitting by the bed holding Mam's hand. They seemed even in misery such a self-contained couple that I thought he would have been happier coming alone. Their absorption in each other was total and almost wordless, a kind of anxious courting, and feeling spare I'd leave them to it, and wandering about the hospital or trailing glumly round the perimeter I

28

reflected that to have a mother who is deranged is bad enough, but that wasn't really why I was there; I was there because, alone among my contemporaries, I had a father who couldn't drive.

He had made at least two attempts. Twenty years before, in the late forties when he had had his first shop, he had invested in a second-hand motorbike and sidecar; except that it wasn't a sidecar but a large coffin-like box which Dad, never happier than when he had a brush in his hand, straight away painted green. The theory was that Dad would go round on this dilapidated combination delivering orders to his customers in Far Headingley, Cookridge and West Park. And perhaps this did happen once or twice, though since delivering necessarily involved a good deal of stopping and starting, and starting was not the bike's strong point, this mode of transport never became a regular routine or superseded the push-bike with its basket (*W. Bennett, High Class Meat Purveyors*) pedalled laboriously up the suburban drives and crescents of north Leeds by 'The Boy'.

I suspect the motorbike was bought as another means of escape, something to 'go off' on at weekends perhaps or for little evening runs round the lanes of Adel, Eccup and Arthington. It's hard to imagine, looking back, that Mam could ever have been persuaded to ride pillion, but though she was never keen ('too draughty for me') she was still game enough in those days to give it a try. Had crash helmets been obligatory then, that would have clinched it, as I cannot imagine either of them got up in the necessary gear. As it was, Mam would be in her usual clothes ('my little swagger coat and that turban thing') and Dad in his raincoat and trilby, making any concessions to what this mode of transport required thought by them to be pretending to be something they weren't . . . and they certainly weren't bikers. Sometimes even all four of us would go out, with Gordon and me laid on a bit of old curtain inside the closed box.

Dad had never got as far as a test and still had L-plates, and though helmets might not be obligatory it was already an offence for a learner driver to carry passengers. Thus it was that on one of our few outings as a whole family the bike was flagged down by a particularly pompous local policeman, PC Brownlow, who proceeded to lecture Dad on this point of law;

Mam presumably still sitting on the pillion clutching her eternal hand-bag, mortified at this public humiliation, particularly in a part as better class as Adel.

His lecture on the Highway Code completed, PC Brownlow lengthily puts away his pencil and adjusts his cape so that my brother and I, think-ing he's gone, choose this moment to open the lid of the box and reveal our presence, thus triggering a further lecture. Dad is ordered to drive home alone as Mam and my brother and I trail back to the tram terminus at Lawnswood, all of us knowing that the bike's days are now numbered.

Though it straight away took its place on the list of 'your Dad's crazes' (fretwork, fishing, home-made beer) the idea of a motorbike wasn't instantly extinguished, dwindling away via another short-lived invest-ment in a contraption called a Cyclemaster, whereby a motor was attached to the back wheel of a pedal cycle, and which came into play when climb-ing hills. Or didn't, as proved too often to be the case, so that it ended up like the fretsaw and the double bass advertised in the Miscellaneous Col-umn of the *Yorkshire Evening Post*. After this they stuck to the bus.

It wasn't until twenty years later, when Dad was over sixty and they knew they were about to leave Leeds, that Dad had some driving lessons and took his test in Harrogate. Always a considerate man, he had got it into his head that courtesy towards other drivers was on a par with the more basic requirements of the Highway Code. The result was that com-ing up to one of the town's many elaborately planted roundabouts he was so concerned to raise his hand to another driver who had given way to him (out of prudence, I should think) that he drove the wrong way round the Floral Clock and was failed instantly.

Harrogate had always been a favourite place with my parents, but the recollection of this humiliation was so keen that they seldom went there again and when he did take some more driving lessons it was in Skipton and he kept it a secret. The night of his test he telephoned me in London, but boasting was so foreign to him it was some time before he mentioned it. 'I took your Mam out in the car this afternoon.' 'Oh, that's nice,' I said, not catching the reference. 'I thought we'd have a run out. I passed my test.' For him it was as if he had joined the human race. Nothing that he had ever accomplished gave him so much pleasure or, I think, made him feel so much a man.

His first and only car was a khaki-coloured Mini which transformed their lives, put paid to hanging about in bus stations and set them free to range the countryside and visit places they had only read about. It affected my life, too, though in ways which, for them, were less welcome. Previously I had gone north at regular intervals really to chauffeur them around and give them a change of scene. Now I stayed longer and longer in London and saw them much less.

It meant, too, that when Dad rang to say 'I think your Mam's starting another depression do', there was not the same urgency to hurry home. He did not need me to ferry him the fifty miles round trip to the hospital. Now he could manage on his own, and manage he did, though Mam was often in hospital five or six weeks at a time. This was at Airedale, near Keighley, further than Lancaster it's true but modern and with better facilities. He drove there every day with no thought that he could do anything else, and in due course it was his conscientiousness and devotion to duty that killed him.

Love apart, what led my father to drive fifty miles a day to visit his wife in hospital was the conviction that no one knew her as he knew her, that if she were to regain the shore of sanity he must be there waiting for her; finding him she would find herself.

Years later I put this in my only play about madness, with Queen Charlotte as devoted to her husband, George III, as ever Dad was to Mam.

'It is the same with all the doctors,' the Queen says. 'None of them knows him. He is not himself. So how can they restore him to his proper self, not knowing what that self is.'

How could any doctor, seeing this wretched weeping woman, know that ordinarily she was loving and funny and full of life? Dad knew and felt that when she woke from this terrible dream he must be there to welcome her and assure her that she had found herself.

So together they trailed the long system-built corridors of the hospital, empty on those August afternoons – summer always her worst time; they sat by the unweeded flower beds, watched the comings and goings in the car park, had a cup of tea from the flask he had brought and a piece of the cake he had made. 'I think she's beginning to come round a bit,' he'd say on the phone. 'They say next week I can take her for a little run.'

The hospital where she was most often a patient was one of those designed by John Poulson, the corrupt architect who made his fortune in the sixties by deals done with city bosses all over the north. Architecturally undistinguished and structurally unsound – it was said to be slowly sliding down the hill – the hospital was still streets ahead of the ex-workhouse at Lancaster or the old St James's in Leeds, where Dad himself had all but died. 'Well, if Mr Poulson did one good thing in his life,' Dad would say when Mam was on the up and up, 'it was this hospital. It's a grand place.' And featureless though it was, it was indeed light, airy, cheerful and split up into small manageable units. The snag was that these units, colour-coded though they were, were all more or less identical. Even for those in their right minds this could be confusing, but for the patients who were already confused, like those on the psychiatric ward, it was doubly disorienting. Psychiatric was not far from Maternity, with the result that the unbalanced would wander into what looked to be their ward only to find what they took to be their bed was now occupied by, as Mam said, 'one of these gymslip mums. She didn't look more than fourteen,' her language and her humour discovered intact where she had abandoned them months before. 'She cracked out laughing this afternoon,' Dad said. 'They're going to let her come home for the weekend.'

Early on in her first bout of depression and not long after she had been transferred from Lancaster Moor to a smaller and less intimidating institution near Burley in Wharfedale, Mam was given electro-convulsive therapy. We had no thought then that ECT was particularly invasive, an interference with the mental make-up or a rearrangement of the personality, and I do not think this now more than thirty years later, when ECT is even more controversial and to some extent discredited. I do not, then or now, see it as torture or punishment and no more routinely decreed or callously administered than any other treatment, though these were the objections to it at the time as they are the objections to it now. So far as my mother is concerned, she does not show any alarm at the prospect, and talks about the procedure with curiosity but without apprehension.

This was the period when the fashionable analyst was R. D. Laing and madness, while not quite the mode, was certainly seen as an alternative view of things, the mad the truly sane a crude view of it. In practical terms (though it was never practical) enlightenment consisted in encouraging the mentally ill to work through their depression, schizophrenia or whatever to achieve a new balance and an enhanced sense of self; the most extreme case and often-quoted exemplar being Mary Barnes, who came to a revised perception of herself via a period in which she smeared the walls in excrement. I thought at the time that this was not on the cards for the average patient or for the unfortunate nurse or relative who eventually had to clean up after them, though this didn't seem to enter into the equation.

I had a similar difference of sympathy about the same time when at the long-gone Academy Cinema in Oxford Street I saw Ken Loach's film *Family Life*. It's about mental illness and includes a scene in which a doctor prescribes ECT for a patient, at which point the audience in the cinema roundly hissed the supposed villain. Unable to join in or share the general indignation, I felt rather out of it. Faced with a loved one who is mute with misery and immobilised by depression and despair, what was to be done? Hissing the doctor didn't seem to be the answer and I left the cinema (which wasn't the answer either).

ECT apart, much of the literature to do with mental and neurological illness irritated on a different level and still does. There is a snobbery about mental affliction beginning, I suspect, with Freud; there was little twisting of the cloth cap went on in Freud's consulting room, I'm sure, but it wasn't simply due to social snobbery. Like most writers on the subject, the great man concerned himself with the intellectual and the exotic, so that there was something of the freak show about many of his well-known case histories, with alleviation of suffering nowhere.

Depression, which is much the most common mental illness, doesn't even qualify as such and mustn't be so labelled, perhaps because it's routine and relatively unshowy; but maybe, too, because it's so widespread not calling depression mental illness helps to sidestep the stigma. A sufferer from it, though, might well regret that his or her condition is so common since a patient mindless with despair is such a regular occurrence as scarcely to be worthy of a proper physician's time.

Nothing excuses us from the obligation to divert our fellow creatures. We must not be boring. And since for the specialist most illnesses soon cease to intrigue, if you have to suffer choose a condition that is rare. Should you want to catch the doctor's eye, the trick is not to see no light at the end of the tunnel; anybody can do that. Rather mistake your wife for a hat and the doctor will never be away from your bedside.

To give them credit, Laing and his followers were not medically snobbish in this way, but what they seldom discussed was the effect an illness like depression had on the rest of the family, in this case my father. The reverse, the effect the family had on the patient, was much discussed and it was one of the central tenets of Laing's writing that mental illness was generally the work and the fault of the family. In the crowded family plot love, or at least relationships, cramped and warped the weak and ailing, with health only to be achieved by explaining how schizophrenia, say, had been a rational response to the constraints that other family members had imposed, this process of explanation invariably leaving the family, if not in the dock, at least a bit shamefaced.

But nothing that I read or saw at that time resembled the situation in our family, the sudden defection of a loved one, her normal personality wiped out with a total loss of nerve. In Laing and in Szasz the love that was on offer in the family was generally seen as rigid and repressive, with affection bartered for good behaviour. This didn't seem to me to have much to do with my father's affection for my mother, which, while not denying her faults, seemed as near selfless as one could get. There was no bargain here that I could see, just distress and loss on both sides. The books talked of the family working through its breakdown and coming to a new understanding, but when both parties were in their mid-sixties it seemed a bit late in the day for that. What Mam and Dad both wanted was the same going-on as they had had before, and if ECT was a short cut to that then they would take it.

We were told that following a few sessions of ECT Mam would be more herself, and progressively so as the treatment went on. In the event improvement was more dramatic. Given her first bout of ECT in the morning, by the afternoon Mam was walking and talking with my father as she hadn't for months. He saw it as a miracle, as I did too, and to hear on the phone the dull resignation gone from his voice and the old habitual cheerfulness back was like a miracle too.

Successive treatments consolidated the improvement and soon she was her old self, confused a little as to how this terrible visitation had come about and over what period, but that and other short-term memory loss could be put down to the treatment. Now for the first time she went back to the cottage for a trial weekend and was straight away on the phone, bubbling over with its charms and the beauty of the village and particularly how clean everything was.

My mother had fought a war against dirt all her life, as any conscientious housewife had to who lived in one of the industrial towns of the West Riding. To visit Halifax, where she grew up, was, my father always said, like going down into the mouth of hell, the bottom of the valley invisible in a haze of soot and smoke. Leeds was scarcely better, Armley, where we first lived, covered in a fine drizzle of grit from Kirkstall Power Station.

The campaign against this dirt produced its own elaborate weaponry, an armoury of Ewbanks, Hoovers, wringers, possers and mops in daily and wearisome use, items still familiar nowadays because sold in the humbler antique shops, everything in good time collectable. Besides these implements my mother maintained an elaborate hierarchy of cloths, buckets and dusters, to the Byzantine differences of which she alone was privy. Some cloths were dishcloths but not sink cloths; some were for the sink but not for the floor. There were dirty buckets and clean buckets, buckets for indoors, buckets for the flags outside. One mop had universal application, another a unique and terrible purpose and so had to be kept

35

outside hung on the wall. And however rinsed and clean these utensils were they remained polluted by their awful function.

In my television play *Afternoon Off* a husband is visiting his wife in hospital.

MRS BEEVERS: I bet the house is upside down.
MR BEEVERS: Nay, it never is. I did the kitchen floor this morning.
MRS BEEVERS: Which bucket did you use?
MR BEEVERS: The red one.
MRS BEEVERS: That's the outside bucket! I shall have it all to do again. Men, they make work.

Left to himself Dad, like the hapless Mr Beevers, would violate these taboos and use the first thing that came to hand to clean the hearth or wash the floor.

'It's all nowt,' he'd mutter, but when Mam was around he knew it saved time and temper to observe her order of things.

Latterly disposable cloths and kitchen rolls had tended to blur these ancient distinctions but the basic structure remained, perhaps the firmest part of the framework of her world.

When she became depressed the breakdown of this order was one of its first symptoms. She became incapable of cleaning the house herself, and stood by while Dad took over her duties. But however much he washed and tidied, the place was still 'upside down', dust and dirt an unstemmable tide, the house besieged by filth and chaos, its (imagined) squalor a talking point among the neighbours. So now when she came home from the hospital bright and better her first comment was how spotless the place looked. And not merely the house. She was taken up by the freshness of everything. It was as if the whole world and her existence in it had been rinsed clean.

But it did not last.

'I don't know what I've done wrong.'

'You've done nothing wrong.'

'Then why are you shouting at me?'

'I'm shouting at you to try and get it into your head.'

'They'll hear.'

'Who? There's nobody here.'

'Then what's that little car doing?'

'Having a nice time. Leading a normal life. Doing what we used to do.'

In the eight years between the onset of my mother's first depression and my father's death in 1974 there were half a dozen episodes, all of which ended up being what Dad called 'hospital dos' and in half of which she had ECT, other times just antidepressant drugs.

In no case was her recovery quite as dramatic as that first time. Perhaps it was that we were getting used to the sequence, but certainly with each successive visitation it became clear that in her case this wasn't an illness that was ever altogether going to go away, the likelihood of another attack there even in her most cheerful moments.

Still, there were long periods of remission, months, years even, when she was her old cheerful self, though Dad was now always on the lookout for any tell-tale signs and ready to head her off from any experience that might upset her. One night we were watching Jeremy Sandford's TV play *Edna, the Inebriate Woman*. Its elaborate depiction of irrational behaviour had nothing to do with Mam's depressive condition, and the connection never occurred to me, but while she was out of the room Dad quietly switched the television off.

'Oh, are we not watching that?' Mam said, coming back.

'Well,' said Dad, 'it was too far-fetched. You can't believe half the stuff that's on.'

Always there was the shame at the nature of the illness, something Mam was able to overcome or at least ignore when she was well but which became a burden whenever her spirits began to fall, the guilt attendant upon the depression one of the signals that it was returning. Self-consciousness, if not shame, was in such a small community understandable, but the longer my parents lived in the village the more I became aware that my mother was not alone in her condition. Several middle-aged women were similarly afflicted in different degrees, one stumping silently round the village every afternoon, another flitting anxiously into a friendly neighbour's, sometimes in tears, and both suffering from what was still called 'nerves' – a condition that goes largely unnoticed in cities as it cannot do in smaller communities.

'I haven't seen Mrs Bennett about? Is she alright?'

Except that after a while people learned not to ask. And while there were support groups for some identifiable disabilities like MS or muscular dystrophy, there were none for depression. As how could there be? Anyone suffering from it would be incapable of attending.

Insofar as I too kept it quiet when she was poorly, I shared in the shame, though it would have been callous to behave otherwise, as even when she was well Mam was always concerned with 'what folks would say' about every department of our lives. But once she was in hospital there could be no deception as Dad would be seen driving off on the dot of one and arriving back at six, day after day after day.

When Mam was ill the first time I used to wish that they both had had the education they always longed for, feeling, snobbishly perhaps, that mental affliction was more appropriate to, sat more suitably on, someone educated or higher up the social scale. It's a foolish assumption besides being statistically unfounded, which I'm sure I knew at the time though I felt it nevertheless. Education might at least have given them more insight into their predicament and diminished some of the self-consciousness they felt and which I felt too, though only in the village; among my own friends I made no secret of it. Still, if nothing else my mother's depression and the omissions and evasions that attended it made me appreciate more the shame that must have attached to my grandfather's drowning and how it was the episode had gone unspoken of for so long.

━━━━━━━

My father wore a suit every day of his life. He had two, 'my suit' and 'my other suit', 'my suit' being the one he wore every day, 'my other suit' his best. On the rare occasions when he invested in a new suit the suits moved up a place, 'my other suit' becoming 'my suit', the new suit becoming 'my other suit', with the old one just used for painting in or working in the shop. They were three-piece suits, generally navy, and he always wore black shoes and a collar and tie. This makes him seem formal or dressed like an accountant but he didn't give that impression because he never managed to be smart, his waistcoat ('weskit' as he pronounced it) generally unbuttoned and showing his braces, his sleeves rolled up, and when he was still butchering the suit would smell of meat, with the trousers and particularly the turn-ups greasy from the floor. He never had an overcoat, just a series of fawn or dark green gabardine raincoats, and he always wore a dark green trilby hat.

About clothes Dad must always have been conservative. There are photographs of him as a young man, sitting on the sands in a deck-chair in the 1920s, and he is in his three-piece suit, with dicky-bow and fly-collar and even a bowler hat, his only concession to the holiday spirit bare feet. Retirement, which often sanctions some sartorial indulgence, didn't alter this state of affairs, the regime of suit and other suit maintained as before. Or almost.

After he had learned to drive my parents would sometimes collect me off the train at Lancaster. Meeting them there one day in 1970, I came across the bridge to see my mother waiting at the barrier with a stranger, someone got up in a grey check sports coat, two-tone cardigan, brown trousers and what I suppose would be called loafers. I was deeply shocked. It was Dad in leisurewear, the only relic of the man he had always been his green trilby hat.

'What do you think of your Dad's new get-up?' Mam enquired as we were driving home. Not much was the truth of it but I didn't let on, and as Dad didn't say much either I took it to have been Mam's idea, confirmed when the experiment turned out to be short-lived; the sports coat and brown trousers soon demoted to the status of gardening clothes, and we were back on the regime of 'my suit' and 'my other suit'.

Dad's brief excursion into leisurewear wasn't an isolated occurrence but part of a process (Mam would have liked it to have been a programme) called 'branching out'. The aim of 'branching out' was to be more like other people, or like what Mam imagined other people to be, an idea she derived in the first instance from women's magazines and latterly from television. The world of coffee mornings, flower arrangement, fork lunches and having people round for drinks was never one my parents had been part of. Now that Mam was well again and Dad could drive, Mam's modest social ambitions, long dormant, started to revive and she began to entertain the possibility of 'being a bit more like other folks'. The possibility was all it was, though, and much to Dad's relief, all that it remained.

'It's your Dad,' Mam would complain. 'He won't mix. I'd like to, only he won't.'

And there was no sense in explaining to her that these occasions she read about in *Homes and Gardens* were not all that they were cracked up to be, or if it came to the point she'd be nonplussed in company. Other people did it, why couldn't we?

Drink would have helped but both my parents were teetotallers, though more from taste than conviction. Indeed alcohol had, for Mam at least, a certain romance, partly again to be put down to the cocktail parties she had read about in women's magazines. She had never been to, still less given, a cocktail party, which explains why she could never get the pronunciation of the actual word right, invariably laying the stress on the final syllable, cock*tail*. What a cock*tail* was I am sure she had no idea. Russell Harty used to tell how when he was at Oxford he had invited Vivien Leigh round for drinks and she had asked for pink gin. Only having the plain stuff Russell sent a friend out to the nearest off-licence for a bottle of the pink variety. Mam would not have understood there was a joke here, and had she ever got round to giving a cocktail party she would probably have tried to buy a bottle of cocktails.

The nearest my parents came to alcohol was at Holy Communion and they utterly overestimated its effects. However bad the weather, Dad never drove to church because Mam thought the sacrament might make him incapable on the return journey.

They did, however, gather that sherry was a generally acceptable drink, so once they were settled down in the village they invested in a bottle, as a first move in the 'branching out' campaign.

'Your Dad and me are going to start to mix,' Mam wrote. 'We've got some sherry in and we've got some peanuts too.'

Never having tasted the mysterious beverage, though, they lacked any notion of when it was appropriate and treated it as a round-the-clock facility. Thus the vicar, calling with the Free Will offering envelope, was startled to be offered a sweet sherry at 10 o'clock in the morning. They, of course, stuck to tea; or, when they were trying to fit in, Ribena.

'Well,' said Mam resignedly, 'it doesn't do for us. Our Kathleen used to put it in the trifle and it always rifted up on me.'

On another occasion when they had actually been asked out to drinks and gone in great trepidation Mam rang up in some excitement.

'Your Dad and me have found an alcoholic drink that we really like. It's called bitter lemon.'

Nor was it merely the drink at cocktail parties my mother found mysterious, but the food that was on offer there too – cocktail snacks, bits of cheese and pineapple, sausages-on-sticks, food that nowadays would come under the generic term of nibbles. Now sausages were not unknown in our house: my father had been a butcher after all, we took them in our stride. But a sausage had only to be hoisted onto a stick to become for my mother an emblem of impossible sophistication.

With these notions it's hardly surprising they never made the social round or lived the kind of model life my mother used to read about in magazines. They put it down, as they did most of their imagined shortcomings, to their not having been educated, education to them a passport to everything they lacked: self-confidence, social ease and above all the ability to be like other people. Every family has a secret and the secret is that it's not like other families. My mother imagined that every family in the kingdom except us sat down together to a cooked breakfast, that when the man of the house had gone off to work and the children to school there was an ordered programme of washing, cleaning, baking and other housewifely tasks, interspersed with coffee mornings and (higher up the social scale) cocktail parties. What my parents never really understood was that most families just rubbed along anyhow.

A kind of yearning underlay both their lives. Before they moved to the village, my father's dream was of a smallholding (always referred to as such). He saw himself keeping hens, a goat, and growing his own potatoes; an idyll of self-sufficiency.

I was in Holland not long ago, where along every railway line and on any spare bit of urban land were hundreds of neat plots, which were not allotments so much as enclosed gardens, each with a hut, a pavilion almost, outside which the largely elderly owners were sunbathing (some of them virtually naked). Dad would never have gone in for that, but I think, though less cheek by jowl, this was just what he meant by a small-holding. It was a dream, of course, of a generation older than his, a vision of the soldiers who survived the First World War, with Surrey, Essex and Kent full of rundown chicken farms, the sad relics of those days.

Dad had no social ambitions, such aspirations as he did have confined to playing his violin better. He read a good deal, though there was never a bookshelf in the living room and all the books in the house were kept in my room, Mam's view being that books not so much furnished a room as untidied it. What books they had of their own were kept in the sideboard, most of them even at this late stage in their lives to do with self-improve-ment: *How to Improve Your Memory Power, In Tune with the Infinite, Relax Your Way to Health!* After Dad died my brother and I went to collect his belongings from the hospital – his bus pass, a few toffees he'd had in his pocket, and in his wallet a cutting from a newspaper: 'Cure Bronchitis in a Week! Deep Breathing the Only Answer'.

> 'We're neither of us anything in the mixing line. We were when we were first married, but you lose the knack.'
>
> 'Anyway, I don't see what God has to do with mixing. Too much God and it puts the tin hat on it.'

This is an exchange from *Say Something Happened*, a TV play of mine about an oldish couple visited by a young social worker who is worried by their isolation. It never got to the social worker stage with Mam and Dad, but certainly they kept to themselves more and more as they got older and as Mam's depressions became more frequent. Besides, everything was social. They stopped going to church because all too often they got roped in after the service to take part in a discussion group.

'It was a talk on the Third World,' Dad wrote to me. 'Well, your Mam and me don't even know where the Third World is. Next week it's Buddhism. We're going to give it a miss.'

Small talk, Buddhism, sausages-on-sticks, like the second name he did not want Gordon to have, they were for other people, not for them.

With Mam, though, the dream of sociability persisted. When, after Dad died, she went to live with my brother, I was clearing out the kitchen cupboard, and there behind an old bottle of Goodall's Vanilla Essence and a half-empty packet of Be-Ro Self-Raising Flour I came across a sad little tube of cocktail sticks.

Put simply and as they themselves would have put it, both my parents were shy, a shortcoming they thought of as an affliction while at the same time enshrining it as a virtue. Better to be shy, however awkward it made you feel, than be too full of yourself and always shoving yourself forward.

It may have been shyness that drew my parents together in the first place; my mother was shy as her sisters were not and my father was the least outgoing of his brothers. The early morning wedding at St Bartholomew's, Armley, was a ceremony for a couple shy of ceremony, so it's not surprising if in the years that followed a premium was put on shy and it became our badge.

Half of Dad's morality came out of his shyness, reinforcing as it did the modesty of his expectations while resigning him to the superior enterprise and good fortune of others.

'Your Dad won't push himself forward,' Mam would say, 'that's his trouble.' That it was her trouble too was not the point; she was a woman, after all. Thus he seldom got angry and, too shy to tell anybody off, just 'felt sickened'. Regularly cheated or done down in business, he never became hardened to it or came by a philosophy to cope, other than doing imitations of the people he disliked, longing to give them 'Joe Fitton's remedy'* or just being funny generally. But he chafed against a temperament that made him much liked by everyone except himself, and it's not surprising that, suppressing his real feelings, he was a martyr to stomach trouble, a complaint, along with the shyness, he has bequeathed to me.

Shyness (which will keep cropping up in this book) is a soft word, foggy and woollen, and it throws its blanket over all sorts of behaviour. It covers a middle-aged son or neurasthenic daughter living at home with an elderly mother, through to some socially crippled and potentially dangerous creature incapable of human response; shy a spectrum that stretches from the wallflower to the psychopath. 'A bit of a loner' is how the tabloids put it after some shrinking wreck has ventured to approach or make off with a child or exposed himself in a park, 'shy' thought altogether too kindly a description. Because 'soft' comes near it, and 'timid', too, but without the compassion or understanding implicit in shy. That he or she is shy is an excuse or an extenuation that is made by others (mothers in particular) but seldom by the persons concerned. Because if you are shy then you're generally too shy to say so, 'I'm shy' a pretty bold thing to come out with.

Sheltering under shy, it was a long time before I understood that the self-effacing and the self-promoting, shy and its opposite, share a basic assumption, shy and forward the same. Everybody is looking at me, thinks the shy person (and I wish they weren't). Everybody is looking at me, thinks the self-confident (and quite right too). I learned this lesson in time to be able to point it out, probably rather sententiously, to my parents, but it was too late for them, and the other lesson I had learned, that to be shy was to be a bit of a bore, they knew already, to their cost. I assured them, falsely, that

---

* During the war Dad was a warden in the ARP, his companion on patrol a neighbour, Joe Fitton. Somebody aroused Joe's ire (a persistent failure to draw their blackout curtains, perhaps), and one night, having had to ring the bell and remonstrate yet again, Joe burst out, 'I'd like to give them a right kick up the arse.' This wasn't like Joe at all and turned into a family joke – and a useful one too, as Dad never swore, so to give somebody a kick up the arse became euphemistically known as 'Joe Fitton's remedy'. With Dad it even became a verb: 'I'd like to Joe Fitton him.'

everybody felt much as they did but that social ease was something that could and should be faked.

'Well, you can do that,' Dad would say, 'you've been educated,' adding how often he felt he had nothing to contribute. 'I'm boring, I think. I can't understand why anybody likes us. I wonder sometimes whether they do, really.'

I found this heartbreaking because it wasn't said with an eye to being told the opposite. It was genuinely how they thought of themselves.

Left out of this account are all their jokes and fun, the pleasure they got out of life and their sheer silliness. After retirement they both put on weight, and coming in one day I found them sitting side by side on the sofa. 'Here were are,' said Dad, 'Fat Pig One and Fat Pig Two.'

Dad had always been shy about sex, never talking about it directly and disapproving of any reference to it by us as children or even of Mam's occasional 'cheeky' remark. I was used to this and respected it, except that I was not immune to some of the modish stuff talked about mental illness in the seventies and at some point on one of the long drives to and from the hospital I heard myself asking my father if he touched my mother enough. He was too embarrassed to reply, 'Nay, Alan' all that he'd commit himself to, the implication being what business was it of mine. And he was quite right. Who was I to ask what amount of touching went on, who at that time had touched and was touching virtually no one at all? It might have been better, more acceptable as a question, had I said hugging rather than touching, but hugging as a manifestation of (often unfeeling) affection had not yet achieved the currency it did in the eighties and nineties when it often served to demonstrate that other loveless construct, caring. The thought of myself putting the question at all makes me wince in retrospect, but how should I ask about hugging when I knew, as he did, that none of our family were great huggers, though no less affectionate for that.

Dad would have been shy to have been seen embracing Mam, but when I put to him the unnecessary question about touching he could, unthinkably, have retorted that, though it was nothing to do with me, at seventy he still was actually touching Mam when and where it mattered. This emerged a year or two later, in 1974, when he was lying in Intensive Care in the same Airedale Hospital recovering, as we were assured, from a heart attack. Mam had only just been discharged from the same hospital and was at home coming round after yet another bout of depression. Dazed by her own illness and stunned by his, she lay in bed talking about Dad, sometimes, as was not uncommon when she was poorly, taking me for him. Out of the blue she suddenly said,

'He does very well, you know, your Dad.'

'Yes,' I said, taking this for a general statement.

'No. I mean for a fellow of seventy-one.'

Again I did not twig.

'Why?'

'Well, you know when we were in Leeds he had to have that little oper-ation to do with his water. Well, most fellers can't carry on much after that. But it didn't make any difference to your Dad. He does very well.'

Had I known it, the pity was all in the tense, since his doing, however well, was now almost done, and he died a few days later.

'It was only on Tuesday he drove us over to Morecambe,' said Mam. 'It was miserable all day, only it fined up at tea time so we thought we'd have a run-out. Will it be all the driving to the hospital that's done it?'

I said I didn't think so, though I did.

'We went up to the West End by the golf course. I wanted a bit of a walk on the sands but we'd only been going a minute when he said, "Nay, Mam, you'll have to stop. I can't go no further." It must have been com-ing on then.'

I knew exactly the place where they would have been walking. It was up towards Bare, the suburb of Morecambe always thought 'a bit more select'. We had walked on the same sands often, particularly during the war, when all our seaside holidays seemed to be taken at Morecambe. For Dad they were scarcely a holiday at all, as with no one to stand in for him at the Co-op he never managed more than a couple of days, a break so short it was always overshadowed by the grief-stricken leave-taking with which it invariably concluded. The sadness of these partings ought to have been comic, though it never seemed so. Having seen him off on the train the three of us would walk on the empty evening sands as the sun set across the bay, and Mam wept and wept. For what? They were only to be separated four or five days at the most, and Dad wasn't going back to the front but to dreary old Leeds, which seldom even ran to an air raid. It was love, I suppose, and the loneliness of a week with her two uncomforting boys.

So that these sands, where once she had wept so bitterly and grieved so needlessly, should now be the setting for their last walk together seems, if not fitting, then at least symmetrical, the disproportionate grief then finding its appropriate object forty years later, the equation complete.

Afterwards I came to think I might have been in some degree responsible, and that Dad's death was my doing if not my fault. Already written in 1974, though not filmed, was my second TV play, *Sunset Across the Bay*, where I had included a scene in which a retired couple say farewell to their son, who is going off to Australia. I set the goodbye on that same stretch of Morecambe sand before, in a later scene, killing off the father with a stroke in a seafront lavatory. The couple in the play have retired to Morecambe from Leeds and were not unlike my parents, except that whereas in the play their lives are lonely and unhappy and their expectations from retirement unfulfilled, Mam and Dad's retirement, even with Mam's depression, was one of the happiest times of their lives. We made the film that autumn, by which time Dad was three months dead, his first heart attack one Saturday morning in August 1974, the second a week later killing him.

Anyone who writes will be familiar with the element of involuntary prediction that informs the imagination; one writes about something, and if it does not exactly happen a version of it does. Sometimes, when one is writing about oneself, for instance, there is an objective explanation; it was only after writing a play that dealt, albeit farcically, with sexual inhibition that my own sex life picked up, the play a form of crude psychotherapy, 'getting it out of your system' (or 'off your chest') another way of putting it.

That by writing a play about the death of a father I brought on the death of my own is perhaps fanciful, though the thought certainly occurred. But there were other, less notional ways, too, in which I may have contributed to his dying.

The heart attack had not been without warning, but all attention, Dad's included, had been so concentrated on Mam's situation and her recurring depressions that his own failing health went unconsidered, at any rate by me, and he, typically, said nothing on the phone. Or did he? Maybe I didn't want to hear.

I had been taking the journey north less often than previously because I was acting in *Habeas Corpus* in the West End, the only way to get home to drive up on the Sunday and back on the Monday, so if I was neglecting my duties there was some excuse. Still, it was an excuse, and the truth was I was reluctant to be away from London even for a night because I was having a nice time, and what was more, knew it. I was 'living' as one of the characters in another play describes it, the play being *Intensive Care*, in which a father has a heart attack and his son sits at his hospital bedside in order to be with him when he dies, but at the crucial moment is not with his father but in bed with a nurse. I am not I and he is not he, but I could see where that play, written six years later, came from.

I had always been a late starter and aged forty, and in the nick of time as it seemed to me then, I had caught up with that sexual revolution which, so Philip Larkin (who was not a reliable witness) claimed, had begun a decade earlier. While sexual intercourse did not quite begin in 1974 it was certainly the year when sex was available pretty much for the asking . . . or maybe I had just learned the right way to ask. Whatever the reason, I suddenly seemed to be leading the kind of life I was told everybody else had been leading for years. I had at last, as they say, got it together. It was at this point my father died and I was summarily banished from London, where such things were possible, to live with my mother in Yorkshire, where they were not.

It was not quite as sudden as that, as a week intervened between his first attack and the second. I went up straight away to find him in Intensive Care, tired but said to be on the mend. *Habeas Corpus* had only half a dozen performances left so I was going back to London to finish the run, and also to resume my suddenly eventful existence, at least for as long as I was allowed to. On my way I called at the hospital to say good-bye and to tell him that I'd see him in a week's time. He was propped up in bed, his pyjama jacket open, the electrodes that monitored his heart attached to his chest. I don't think he ever sunbathed in his life or even wore an open-necked shirt and the line of his collar was sharp, his worn red face and neck like a helmet above the creamy whiteness of his chest.

We never kissed much in our family; I kissed my mother often but I don't ever recall kissing my father since I was a boy. Even when we were children Dad would make a joke of kissing, pulling a face and sticking his cheek out to indicate the exact spot on which this distasteful task had to be carried out. Seeing him less often than I did, my brother would shake hands, but I can't recall ever doing that either. Which is not to say that we were remote from each other, and indeed I felt much closer to him grown up than I ever did as a child when, smart and a show-off, I often felt myself an embarrassment and not the child he would have wanted.

So I sat for a while at his bedside and then stood up to say goodbye. And uniquely in my adulthood, kissed him on the cheek. Seeing the kiss com-ing he shifted slightly, and I saw a look of distant alarm in his eyes, on account not just of the kiss but of what it portended. I was kissing him, he clearly thought, because I did not expect to see him again. He knew it for what it was and so did I, because somebody had once done the same to me.[*] It was the kiss of death.

If I could wipe away that kiss and the memory of it I would do, though trusting in the doctor's prognosis I had no thought that Dad was likely to die. I fear what made me kiss him was again the fashionable nonsense about families being healthier for touching and showing affection, the same modish stuff that had made me ask him if he touched my mother. And it was something similar that made me ask after his death if I might see his body. It was death as the last taboo, death as much a part of life as birth, all the up-to-the-minute Sunday papers stuff. Less forgivably there was some

* See 'A Common Assault', p. 557.

notion that being a writer demanded an unflinching eye, to look on death part of the job. Besides, I was forty and the death of the father was one of the great formative experiences; I had a duty to make the most of it.

He had died on the Saturday morning when I was already on the train north, so when I saw his body on the Monday at Airedale Hospital he had been dead two days. The mortuary was somewhere at the back of the hospital; not a facility I suppose they wanted to make a show of, it was near the boiler room and the back doors of the kitchens. I was put into a curtained room (called the viewing room) where Dad lay under a terrible purple pall. There were two attendants, one of whom pulled back the shroud. It was a shocking sight. His face had shrunk and his teeth no longer fitted so that his mouth was set in a snarl, a look about as uncharacteristic of him as I could ever have imagined. It was the first time in his life (except that it wasn't in his life) that he can have looked fierce. I noticed that the attendants were looking at me, more interested in my reactions than in the corpse which to them must have been commonplace. Noting that at seventy-one he still had scarcely a grey hair, I nodded and they wheeled him out.

Back in London for a couple of days I mentioned my father's death to Miss Shepherd, the tramp on the street who, a few months before, had moved her van into my garden. She did not trouble to express any sympathy, never altogether crediting the misfortune of anyone but herself. Nor in this case.

'Yes. I knew he must have died. I saw him a few days ago. He was hovering over the convent at the top of the street. I think it was to warn you against the dangers of Communism.'

This vision was only slightly more implausible than its purported purpose. I could think of many reasons why my father might have been hovering around at the top of the street ('Try and be more patient with your Mam' for instance) but the Red Menace would have come very low down on the list.

My father's was not the only corpse I was to see that summer of 1974. Within a month I came across another body and in circumstances where even the terrible purple pall that covered my father would not have been unwelcome. But to tell that tale means going back to the forties and catching up on my aunties.

There were three aunties on my mother's side of the family, the Peels, which was the side of the family we saw most of. There were three aunties on my father's side too, the wives of his three Bennett brothers, but we saw much less of them. This was because, the Gimmer's fireside hardly being a welcoming one, no sooner had Dad started courting Mam than he was drawn into the far friendlier family of his fiancée. And this was the pattern for the rest of their lives, with us seeing far more of the Peels than we ever did of the Bennetts.

No one could have been less like the conventional mother-in-law than Grandma Peel and she was, for my father, very much the mother he had never had. Tall, dignified and straightforward, she was in every sense a big woman who had come through the tragedies of her life unembittered and with her sense of humour intact; she had seen two bankruptcies, her family reduced from relative affluence to abject poverty, the death of her only son in the trenches, and the never-spoken-of suicide of her husband which left her with three daughters to bring up on very little, and yet she remained a funny, self-sufficient, lively woman. Dad would never hear a word against her, so that when as a child I heard comedians making stock mother-in-law jokes I was mystified: who were these carping, cantankerous, fault-finding creatures, the bane of their sons-in-law's lives? I'd never come across one.

My mother's sisters were Kathleen and Lemira, both resident at Gilpin Place: Kathleen the oldest, Lemira the youngest, my mother, Lilian, the one in the middle. ('That was the trouble,' she used to say of her childhood, 'I got it from both sides.') Writing about them, I feel a twinge of snobbish regret that they were invariably called 'Aunty' and never 'Aunt'. Aunts, after all, are women to be taken seriously; they are, at the very least, middle class and come equipped with a long literary pedigree; aunties, on the other hand, have no lineage or standing at all. However you look at it, an aunty is an aunt cosified; even a literary dreadnought like Lady Bracknell would lose half her firepower were she Aunty Augusta. So the seriousness of a narrative like this in which my mother's sisters figure pretty continuously seems, as I say snobbishly, cheapened by calling them aunties. Best to forget the relationship altogether then; except that, brought up never to call grown-ups by anything so naked as their name, I could no more write plain Kathleen and Myra than I could have ever called them that to their faces. Moreover, shorn of their status such untitled creatures would not resemble the women I remember. No. Aunties it has to be.

We did have one aunt, though, Aunt Eveline, and she was preserved from diminishment into Aunty by her age – she was Grandma Peel's sister-in-law – by her demeanour, which was imposing, and by her build, which was stout. The word was hers, and it was dinned into my brother and me as children not only that we should never refer to Aunt Eveline in her presence as fat, which we would in any case have been unlikely to do, but – a much taller order – never even refer to anyone else in her presence as fat. This was particularly unfair because, had Aunt Eveline not thought of herself as fat, had fatness not been put on the agenda as it were, I'm sure it would never have occurred to us. She was just Aunt Eveline, her size (which was not exceptional) something we took for granted.

In retrospect I see that Aunt Eveline's problem was her large, undifferentiated bust, a bust that echoed the lid of the piano on which she was such an accomplished performer. It was this bust that until the brink of adolescence confused me about the female anatomy. Aunt Eveline's breasts were so large as to make the cleavage between them resemble a deep, damp-looking canyon, a shaft going down into the recesses of the body like the entrance to Gaping Ghyll. I knew vaguely about the shaft at the other end of the body, but there can be few boys who thought as I did, at the age of eleven, that the female anatomy includes a kind of pectoral vagina. And that the naked woman at the front of *Everybody's Home Doctor*, standing with her palms towards you 'showing all she'd got', displayed no trace of such an orifice, did not entirely dislodge the idea from my mind. Aunt Eveline was wont to screen the entrance to this mysterious shaft with an embroidered frontal not unlike the linen antimacassars on the back of the three-piece suite in the sitting room, between the backs of the easy chairs and Aunt Eveline's broad bust there not being much to choose.

Aunt Eveline was 'a lovely pianist' and had beautiful handwriting, her name and address in Pellon Lane, Halifax, written on the covers of all the music in the piano stool. She had had a brief career playing the piano in the silent cinema, then, when the talkies came in, had turned corsetière, a profession often embraced by ample ladies who could simultaneously model the product they were marketing. She still had a connection with corsets in the early forties but by this time she had turned housekeeper, looking after a Mr Wilson, a rich Bradford widower and former chairman of the Bradford Dyers' Association. Widower isn't a designation men would readily apply to themselves these days, and housekeeping as a profession seems to have gone out too. In those days, though, housekeeping covered a multitude of sins, but not, I think, in Aunt Eveline's case. Mr Wilson was well off and already had one fancy woman, whose doings and dresses would be scathingly described over high tea at Gilpin Place, together with the slights Aunt Eveline had suffered at this shameless creature's hands and what Aunt Eveline ('I was scrupulously polite') had rejoindered. Even aged ten I knew Aunt Eveline's hostility to this fancy woman owed less to outraged respectability than to Aunt Eveline's desire to be in her shoes, though it was hard to see why as on the only occasion we were led into her employer's presence ('Mr Wilson, may I introduce my great-nephews') I thought I had never seen anyone who looked more like a toad . . . or, as it might have occurred to me later, a character out of Priestley or John Braine. Oddly, his photo has ended up in the family archives, though Aunt Eveline's main bequest to us when she died in 1956 was her piano and the sheet music that came with it.

While Grandma is alive family Sunday evenings at Gilpin Place follow a settled routine, with the four of us coming over to Wortley from Headingley (Number 1 tram to City Square, Number 12 to Fourteenth

Avenue), where we would have high tea and then go to church at St Mary's. Dad would see his brother George, who sang in the choir, and afterwards they would adjourn to the sitting room at Gilpin Place.

There were always flowers in the sitting room, bought at Sleights, the greengrocer's at the corner of Green Lane and Tong Road; huge chrysanthemums (sixpence a bloom), carnations (threepence a spray) arranged in glass celery vases, and anemones in one of Grandma's many lustre jugs.

The chrysanthemums often had as backing another flower, which I never knew had a name and didn't much care for because it smelled to me of decay. I went to France first at the age of twenty and suddenly, hitchhiking near Cahors, I caught a whiff of it from a nearby field and realised it must be mimosa, for some a scent that means the Côte d'Azur but for me redolent of the front room of a sooty Leeds back-to-back.

The sitting room would also smell of smoke as the fire would have been lit by transferring a load of hot coals from the kitchen, a dramatic and dangerous proceeding, the children told to keep back as Grandma bore through the smoking shovel with one of the aunties following in her wake to retrieve any stray coals.

'Now then, Walter,' Aunt Eveline would say. 'What shall we give them?' though the truth was they were performing more for their own pleasure than for ours, particularly as the performance curtailed conversation. While Aunt Eveline was playing talking was out, a severe deprivation for Aunty Kathleen and Aunty Myra, who could only keep up an appearance of musical appreciation for so long before retreating to the kitchen to get on with their gabbing.

There was no self-consciousness about these musical evenings, and no sense that they were the last throes of a tradition that radio had dented but which within ten years television would put paid to altogether. Dad liked playing, Uncle George loved singing and Aunt Eveline, who seldom got a chance to play in company, came over from Bradford specially for the treat. As a child, of course, I found it all very boring, though it endowed me with a comprehensive knowledge of the works of Ivor Novello, Vivian Ellis and Gilbert and Sullivan, not to mention Edwardian favourites like

54

Albert Ketèlbey. I have only to hear 'I can give you the starlight, Love unchanging and true' or 'Fly home little heart' and I am back in the sitting room in 1949, crammed into the corner of the sofa, with Dad and his fiddle on one side of the piano, Uncle George and his beaming brick-red face on the other and in between Aunt Eveline's unmentionable bottom overflowing from the piano stool. Uncle George had his special party pieces, generally kicking off with 'Bless this House', which always found favour and which might sometimes provoke a few tears. Then there would be 'Did you not see my lady, go down the garden singing?' with no notion in any of our minds that this was by Handel and therefore a cut above 'In a Monastery Garden', say. There would be selections from Edward German, with Ivor Novello's 'Rose of England' another solo spot for Uncle George, and then Aunt Eveline would finish off with a medley from *HMS Pinafore* and perhaps a hymn or two. She would rise, flushed, from the piano stool and we'd all have a cup of tea and a bit of cake before she took herself off to Bradford and another week's housekeeping.

The aunties resident at Gilpin Place, Aunty Kathleen and Aunty Myra, were both what they were pleased to call career girls, which is to say shop assistants – Kathleen in Manfield's shoe shop on Commercial Street, Myra at White's Ladies' Mantles just across the road in Briggate. Kathleen was always said to be, said herself to be, the manageress of Manfield's, though I suspect this wasn't an official title but simply meant that she was the longest-serving of the women assistants. Longest-suffering too, as in those days buying shoes involved more what nowadays would be called interaction, the stock not laid out on racks for all to see and try on but secreted in banks of floor-to-ceiling boxes which were often accessible only on ladders, the assistants up and down them as nimble as sailors on the rigging. Customers, whatever their class, were deferentially treated ('Madam takes a broad fitting? Certainly') and off they would go up the ladder again.

It's a sign of my age that shoe shops seem nowadays to be staffed by sluts, indifferent, unhelpful and with none of that matronly dignity with which the selling of shoes and the buying of clothes were in those days conducted. It is a small loss, though buying shoes in a provincial town in Italy a few years ago I noted that none of the assistants was under forty, and all happy and helpful, and it made me remember Manfield's and realise such ladies are a loss, and that in some of what the papers call 'sections of the economy' the right age for a particular job (not that retailers will ever acknowledge it) is often middle age.

The personnel and politics of Manfield's are well known to us as after work Aunty Kathleen will often come up to Halliday Place and give us her regular bulletin on what has been happening at the shop, recounting the events of her day in Proustian detail. She has a characteristic way of talking, which has been developed as an almost Darwinian response to people's reluctance to listen to the lengthy and often formless narratives she likes to embark on. These are therefore punctuated by phrases like 'If you see what I mean, Lilian', 'If you follow me, Walter' or 'As it subsequently transpired', little verbal tags and tugs just to make sure the person she is talking to is still trotting at the heels of the interminable saga of what she said to the customer and what the customer said to her and what her friend, Miss Moore, said about it all afterwards. And when, after an evening dominated by these narratives, the door finally closes on her Dad blurts out, 'I wouldn't care, but you're no further on when she's done.'

'Yes, but Dad,' Mam chips in, 'she's very good-hearted.' Which indeed she was, but she was a marathon talker.

Unmarried though they are, Kathleen and Myra are hardly maiden aunts, literally or figuratively, and strait-laced is the last thing they want to seem. Less pretty than Mam, the aunties are in my brother's and my eyes much more glamorous, seeing themselves as dashing, adventuresome creatures, good sports and always on for what they see as a lark. They wear scent and camiknickers and have the occasional drink, which we are allowed to taste or are given a shandy instead. They even smoke if the occasion requires it and revel in the small sophistications of the single life. They see themselves as women of the world with Bette Davis as their model, over-polite sarcasm and a talent for putting someone in their place skills of which they are both proud. They are big fans of the Duke of

Windsor, Aunty Myra in particular giving the impression that, if things hadn't worked out well with Mrs Simpson, HRH could have done worse than marry her.

In those days aunties, particularly of the unmarried sort (and perhaps only if they are unmarried), serve in the family set-up as ladies of misrule. Untrammelled by domestic responsibilities with no husband whose line they have to toe, they are (or fancy themselves) freer spirits than their wifely sisters to whom, in turn, they are slightly suspect, blamed for 'putting ideas into the children's heads' or 'getting them all excited'. These sisters of subversion give their nephews and nieces forbidden foods, dismissing as 'fuss' well-founded parental prohibitions: 'Our Alan can't do with oatcakes, he comes out in heat spots' or 'They don't have fish and chips at night, it keeps them awake'.

In these dismal back streets the aunties' role is as exponents of a hard-won glamour that means wearing more lipstick then Mam ever wears, higher heels, having access to nylons, and if not, painting them on. They go to the second house at the pictures, which we never do, and the occasional dance at the Clock. They may even do things undreamed of with members of the armed forces and get airmail letters from distant parts to prove it. With their swept-up hair and peep-toe sling-backs, regularly consulting their powder compacts, repairing their lipstick and tapping out cigarettes, they are everything that mothers are not, agents of an approximate sophistication and a sooty, provincial chic that makes a sister like my mother who has managed 'to get herself a man' seem conventional and dull.

Renegades who do not subscribe to the grown-ups' pact that censors gossip in front of children, they let fall criticism of other grown-ups that Mam and Dad are careful to avoid when we're around. They even imply that parents themselves are not above criticism, and can be judged as other people are.

'Your mother was always one to carry on', 'They've always been worriers, your Mam and Dad' – judgements one didn't want to hear or wasn't ready to hear, parents still set apart and not subject to the shortcomings and disablements that diminished other people. Parents were the standard still.

Subversion could come in other forms, with an aunty picking up on a nephew or niece's aspirations that are overlooked at home, taking them to the theatre, say, or to 'A' pictures and even pictures in French. Though an aunty's own reading may not stretch much beyond *Rebecca* or the novels of Phyllis Bentley (read with a quarter of Quality Street to hand), it's enough to license her to preach the charms of the literary life and the glamour of those that lead it and to stamp her as a different sort of woman. Russell Harty had just such an aunty, Aunty Alice, who played a large part in his education. Widowed and with no children, she had friends in the choral society and took him to concerts and, if only implicitly, advertised the charms of a different way of life than he got at home, where both his parents worked on the market and never let him forget it.

My own aunties were never quite like this. True, Aunty Myra used to see herself as sensitive and poetry-loving, but since my parents were fond of reading and always liked music Aunty Myra used slyly to hint that these preoccupations, which she led you to believe came naturally to her but had been 'thwarted', were in my mother's case 'put on', casting Mam and Dad as parents who did not appreciate the potential of their own children. This must have been provoking to say the least but, as with the tedium attendant on Aunty Kathleen's footwear narratives, my parents kept their thoughts to themselves, only sharing them with us when we were old enough to sympathise and make the aunties' aspirations a family joke.

Both Aunty Kathleen and Aunty Myra have occasional boyfriends though none seem ever to be brought home, the only indication that something may be going on the frequency with which their names come up in conversation. There are stand-bys like Bill Walsh, a body-building young man who lives in the shadow of Armley Gaol and whose picture in a posing-pouch another that resides incongruously among the family photographs. He had been taken prisoner during the war and had been in a camp in Germany and, so Aunty Myra says, been put before a firing squad only for his name to be called out and him reprieved at the last moment.

'Well,' said Dad, 'the Germans must have known your aunties were running short of stuff to talk about.'

This, though, was a comment made long afterwards, and while we are children Dad keeps his misgivings to himself . . . or to Mam and himself. What galls him, and I suppose her, is that compared with their dashing, venturesome selves the aunties cast Mam as the sister who is timid and conventional. To some extent she is, though one of the conventions (and the one that galls them) is of course marriage, which neither of them has yet attained. My mother sees their contact with us, and particularly with my brother, who, less bookish and more boyish than me, is more in their line, as a continuation of the sisters' efforts to squash her, which had disfigured her childhood (and from which marriage had delivered her). But if my parents feel this they say nothing to my brother and me, the convention that adults and particularly adult relatives are not criticised in front of the children stronger than any resentment they are feeling. Besides, it is always unwise to let anything out in my presence as, show-off that I am, I am always ready to blab it out if I think it will bring me the limelight, however briefly. My aunties are less discreet than my parents, and I'm sure many an unconsidered remark about Mam when she was a girl or even Mam now is smugly reported back by me. During the war I often think how lucky I am to have been born in England and not to be living in an occupied country or even Germany itself. In fact it is my parents who are the lucky ones as I am the kind of child who, always attention-seeking, would quite happily betray them to the Gestapo if it meant getting centre stage.

For Aunty Myra the war comes as a godsend, and Mr Chamberlain has scarcely finished his broadcast when she is off like a pigeon from a coop. Enlisting in the WAAF, she is posted round the country to various enlistment and maintenance units so that we soon become familiar with the names of hitherto unheard-of places like Innsworth and Hednesford, Formby and Kidbrooke, until in 1943 she is posted to India, thus confirming her role as the adventurous one in the family.

One of the aunties' favourite films was *Now, Voyager* (1942). Mam liked it too but would have liked it more if Charles Boyer had been in it rather than Paul Henreid. I must have seen it at the time, probably at the Picturedrome on Wortley Road, though without caring for it much or even remembering it except as a film Aunty Kathleen and Aunty Myra went on about. But seeing it again recently I began to understand, as perhaps even they didn't, some of the reasons why it appealed to them, and I wrote about it in my diary.

Christmas Eve, 1996. Catch *Now, Voyager* on afternoon TV, watch part and record the rest. Bette Davis was always a favourite of Aunty Kathleen and Aunty Myra and this tale of a dowdy Boston spinster, Charlotte Vale, who finds herself on the high seas and falls into the arms of Paul Henreid seemed to them a promise of what life might hold in store. Perhaps my mother thought so too, though she was never as big a fan of Bette Davis as her sisters, and since she was married and had children she expected less of life.

For Aunty Myra the promise could be said to have come true, as it did for thousands of women who enlisted in the early forties. The first shot of Charlotte Vale is of her sensible-shoed feet and thick, stockinged legs coming hesitantly down the staircase of her tyrannical mother's grand house in Boston. It's echoed a little later in the film when we see another pair of legs, slim and silk-stockinged, stepping elegantly down a gangplank as the camera pans up to reveal a transformed Charlotte gazing from under a huge and glamorous hat, with what seems like poise but is actually shyness, at her fellow passengers on a cruise liner. Aunty Myra's mother, Grandma Peel, was anything but tyrannical and Aunty Myra neither hesitant nor shy, but a year or so after she would have seen *Now, Voyager* she made the same transition herself and exchanged the dark shiny-wallpapered stairs at Gilpin Place for the gangway of a cruise liner, stepping down her own gangplank to set foot on tropical shores when she disembarked at Bombay – though less elegantly than Bette Davis, and probably lugging her own kitbag as an LAC in the WAAF.

Christmas Day, 1996. Wake early as I always do these days, and in the absence of a newspaper watch the rest of *Now, Voyager*, finding more resonances this time than I had remembered. The shipboard romance with Paul Henreid over, Charlotte Vale, the ex-Aunt Charlotte, returns to Boston and revisits the sanatorium where her benevolent psychiatrist, Dr Jaquith, played by Claude Rains, had helped her to find herself. Seeing a miserable-looking child there she befriends her, the child, of course, turning out to be Tina, the daughter of Durrance, her shipboard lover. Seeing the child as her own once-unloved self, Charlotte takes over her treatment, virtually adopting her, becoming her aunt, until in the final scene the ex-lovers meet at a party at Charlotte's grand Boston home and dedicate their (for the time being) separate futures to the welfare of the now-blossoming child, the film ending with the line:

'And will you be happy, Charlotte?'

'Oh, Jerry. Don't let's ask for the moon. We have the stars.'

This relationship between Charlotte Vale, the ex-aunt and the child, Tina, mirrors the way Aunty Kathleen and Aunty Myra saw themselves, Miss Vale as Miss Peel, coming on as they both did as bolder and more fun-loving and at the same time more sensitive than their married sister, casting Mam and Dad as parents who did not appreciate their own children. This takes us back to *Now, Voyager* and the mysterious wife of Jerry Durrance who is spoken of but, like Daphne du Maurier's Rebecca, remains an off-screen presence though she, presumably, would have her own story to tell, and one in which Charlotte Vale might be less kindly regarded.

Aunty Kathleen probably longs to kick over the traces like her sister, but she is nearly forty when the war starts and unmarried, and as the breadwinner has to stay at home to look after Grandma. Her war service takes her no further than Armley Baths and her St John Ambulance Brigade classes; still, it's a uniform and that's what matters. Mam doesn't even get that far but then she has children and neither she nor Dad has any military ambitions, Dad only too relieved that his job as a butcher is a reserved occupation, thus making him immune from the call-up.

For a few years he is an air-raid warden, but raids on Leeds being relatively uncommon his duties are light: a short walk round the Hallidays to check the black-out and the rest of the evening spent playing billiards up at the wardens' post. Mam half-heartedly knits some lurid squares to be made into blankets and we occasionally trail over to the Ministry of Pensions hospital in Chapel Allerton to visit slightly mystified wounded soldiers, but otherwise hostilities scarcely impinge. War, peace, it makes no difference, our family never quite joining in, let alone joining up, and the camaraderie passes us by as camaraderie generally did.

In one sense Aunty Kathleen's membership of the Ambulance Brigade proves a disappointment to me. She is issued with a first-aid handbook which she seldom seems to consult and which with its black and silver lettering hangs about the sideboard at Gilpin Place for the rest of the war. Unlike other medical texts it proves to have little information about the relations between the sexes, not even the stylised nude drawing (the man with a loincloth) that formed the frontispiece of *Everybody's Home Doctor*. Of course on that point, according to Aunty Kathleen's as always overdetailed account, no instruction was needed. The sessions are held in Armley Baths, the big swimming bath boarded over for the duration and so available for functions. There is no thought in my mind that the bath will have been drained first and I imagine the water gleaming evilly in the darkness under the floor, as between the boards the sea did when we walked along Morecambe Pier to hear the concert party. Manfield's or Armley Baths, Dad has no time for either, but there is no escape as, with her usual 'If you follow me, Lilian' and 'As it went on to transpire', Kathleen tells the tale of these first-aid sessions, now and again shrieking with laughter, the wounded who were not wounded laid out on the beds all the better it seemed to be saucy.

'With all due respect,' says Mr Turnbull in *A Chip in the Sugar*, 'you're not supposed to move a person until it's been ascertained no bones are broken. I was in the St John Ambulance Brigade.'

'Yes,' said mother, 'and who did you learn your bandaging on?' And they both cracked out laughing.

That was what the war was like, in Armley anyway, peals of dirty laughter, middle-aged men in navy-blue battledress making jokes you didn't understand with women who weren't their wives, and nobody seeming to mind. For the duration: 1939, open brackets; 1945, close brackets.

━━━━━━

There is not much new furniture to be bought just after the war, all of it bearing the obligatory Utility stamp of two stylised Cs; what they stand for I never know or even wonder. Though some Utility furniture is well designed (and now probably ranks as collectable), Aunty Kathleen picks out an armchair that has no pretensions to style or beauty; it is squat and square with cushioned seat and back, and arms broad enough to conceal cupboards, one of which is intended to serve as a cocktail cabinet and the other as a receptacle for newspapers and magazines. There is even a drawer to hold a cigarette box.

Excitedly anticipating Aunty Myra's return from India in 1946, Kathleen demonstrates how Myra will be installed on this monstrous throne, which will slowly, to her demobbed surprise, yield up its secrets – the drawer filled with Craven A, the cupboard containing a bottle of milk stout (Grandma's not running to cocktails), and the magazine compartment with its copy of *Lilliput*. Thus, ceremonially enthroned in front of the kitchen fire, LAC/2 Peel will know that she has come home.

'What a common thing!' Mam said as soon as we are safely out of the house, a cocktail cabinet, even if it only housed milk stout, always a focus for my mother's contempt.

'Stout in a chair arm,' said Dad, 'whose cockeyed idea was that?'

What Aunty Myra thinks is not recorded. Not much, I would guess, as she's more taken up with her own gifts than anything given to her. Grandma, who has been quite happy with the old sossed-down chair this new Utility article has superseded, now takes it over as it's quite low and handy for sitting in front of the kitchen range with the toasting fork, or reading the *Evening Post* while she waits for her bread to bake, and it is in this chair she sits in recollection all through my childhood.

Meanwhile Aunty Myra blitzes the family with presents. Returning from India on HMS *Northway* in 1946, she brings with her all the spoils of the East. Even her suitcases are souvenirs. ('Natural pigskin, Walter. Hand stitched. I knocked him right down.') There are shawls, tray-cloths and no end of embroidery. ('All hand-done, Lilian. It's so intricate they go blind doing it, apparently. Just sat there in the street.') We are presented with a blood-red Buddha. ('I don't care if it is a God,' said Mam when we get it home, 'I am not having it on the sideboard with a belly-button that size.') The Buddha is just the tip of the iceberg and Myra regales us with gifts, very few of which we want; there are paper knives for the letters we seldom get, grotesquely carved salad servers for the salad we seldom serve, table mats, napkin rings, yet more accoutrements of that civilised life we never manage to lead, and so doomed to be consigned in due course to the bottom of the wardrobe and eventual wuthering by Dad.

There are also, as Dad puts it, 'cartloads of photographs', all neatly pasted up and labelled in a clutch of albums that pose a new boredom hazard.

'Don't let's get landed with the photographs,' Dad would warn as we trail up from Tong Road, but since they are invariably on hand to flesh out some anecdote of her military career that Aunty Myra is anxious to recount there is seldom any escape.

We soon become familiar with the sights of Bombay, Calcutta and Dehra Dunn. Here is Aunty and colleagues outside the 'WAAF-ery' at the Astoria Hotel; Aunty in a sari on the balcony of the YMCA; Aunty at the Taj Mahal; and photos of the entire staff of 305 Maintenance Unit gathered for Kiplingesque occasions like 'The Farewell to Wilson Barse'.

I am twelve when I first see these albums, which duly take their place, along with other family relics, in the sitting room dresser in which, while Grandma is dozing in the kitchen, I do my customary Saturday afternoon 'rooting'. One of the albums in particular fascinates me (and even today it falls open at the place): it has a photo, postcard size, of two Australian soldiers, 'Jordy' and 'Ossie', standing in bush hats and bathing trunks against a background of palm trees. 'Jordy' is unremarkable,

64

with a lascivious other-ranks sort of face. It is 'Ossie' who draws the eye, better-looking, with his arms folded and smiling, and with some reason, as he is weighed down, practically over-balanced, by what, even in the less than skimpy bathing trunks of the time, is a dick of enormous proportions, the bathing costume in effect just a hammock in which is lolling this colossal member. Underneath Aunty has written, roguishly:

'Yes, girls! It's all real!'

At some point, in deference I imagine to Grandma's sensibilities ('Nay, Myra'), this caption has been scratched out. Or perhaps it is an act of prudent censorship before aunty's marriage a year or two later. This takes her back into the RAF as her husband is a regular aircraftman, and henceforth her life is spent shuttling between bases in Singapore and Hong Kong and Kuala Lumpur.

Stan, Myra's husband, is ten years younger than she is, though to my adolescent eyes there doesn't seem much difference between them. Shortly after they are married we go to Grandma's for Christmas high tea. Meals at Gilpin Place are at the customary hour, dinner at noon, high tea around six, with a cup of tea and 'something to finish off with' around nine. Christmas, though, was harder to accommodate to this routine, though not at our house, where 'Dad has to watch his stomach and it doesn't do for him to wait', so with us the turkey would go in the night before, the smell of Christmas morning that of the turkey already cooked and waiting to be put on the table prompt at twelve.

This particular Christmas arrangements at Grandma's are in chaos. Our arrival is always deliberately timed to avoid the King's Speech, as both Myra and Kathleen are fervent patriots. A (literally) standing joke at Christmas is how to avoid being in the room when Aunty Kath jumps to her feet at the first note of the National Anthem – a reverent stance, head bowed, hands clasped, which Dad has been imitating at home for weeks beforehand.

The King's Speech is always a bit of a cliffhanger on account of his stutter, the conversation afterwards generally on the lines of 'How well he does, considering . . .' Having sidestepped all that, we arrive this year around four to find Grandma and Aunty Kath still clearing up after Christmas dinner, which has had to be put back because the newly-weds have been so late getting up. They have now retired upstairs again 'for a nap' so that high tea at six seems unlikely. It is scheduled for seven, but seven comes and then eight and still the middle-aged lovers have not come down. Aunt Eveline has gone through her entire repertoire twice, starting with 'Glamorous Night' and ending with 'Bless This House'. Dad dutifully accompanies her, with Mam urging him in view of his duodenal to 'have a biting-on', i.e. a snack.

I am thirteen or fourteen at this time but the significance of this elongated siesta is lost on me, as I keep asking why someone can't just go upstairs and wake them up.

'Nay, Alan,' Dad says with withering contempt, though had I shown any awareness of what was going on that would probably have earned his contempt too, sex with Dad always a difficult area. My brother presumably knows, but he has the sense to say nothing. Grandma is embarrassed by the whole business and it's only Aunty Kathleen, always having taken a vicarious pleasure in her younger sister's life, who plainly finds it highly exciting.

When, around nine, the two of them do eventually come downstairs it's not at all shamefacedly, though the meal has to be eaten hurriedly and with some strain, because no sooner is it over than we have to rush to catch the last tram from City Square back up to Headingley, with the ageing lovers, still famished for sex, going straight back upstairs.

As we grow up Aunty Myra in particular tries to stake more of a claim in both of us. That Gordon has chosen to go into the RAF for his National Service and, as Mam puts it, 'passed for a pilot' puts him firmly in Aunty Myra's territory, enabling her to have long discussions about RAF billets and postings in a jargon from which we are naturally excluded. 'Well,' says Mam resignedly, 'she was always a big Gordon fan.'

Even with me, 'the clever one', she tends to lasso my accomplishments to her, 'You get your brains from me' the crudest form of it, a claim never made for themselves by Mam or Dad, who didn't know where my brains came from and didn't much care either.

'Look, Walt,' said Aunty Myra, standing with Dad at the barrier in City Square waiting for a tram, 'just look at that girl with a wealth of auburn hair,' the 'wealth' and the 'auburn' both designed to impress Dad with the sensitivity of her observation and the breadth of her vocabulary, whereas all it did was depress him with the folly of her social pretension. But the phrase lives on and becomes another family joke.

In retrospect these disparagements seem petty and mean-minded, the aunties' splashy behaviour an occasion for fun and reminiscence now as it became a family joke then. For Dad, though, these disparagements are defensive, the response of a mild and unassertive man who feels such self-advertisement calls many of his innate assumptions into question. These are his wife's sisters, after all, but his wife is not like this, nor, if he can help it, are his children going to be. Showing off as a child, I often made him cringe, and though he never says it he probably thinks that that is my aunties 'coming out' in me and that Aunty Myra is right, I do take after them.

As I grow older I come to judge them myself from much the same standpoint as Mam and Dad, as embarrassed as Dad was by their pretensions, as mindful as Mam that it was the pair of them ('Well, you get it from both sides') who had made her so timid.

Still, as I see now, pretension takes pluck and both the aunties took on the world as Mam and Dad never quite did, somewhere finding the confidence to sail through life without being put down.

'Well, they have a lot off,' Mam would say.

So, despite the outside lav and the sheaf of newspapers hung behind the lav door, the bucket under the sink for the tea leaves and slops and (when caught short) pee, and the drizzle of soot from the railway notwithstanding, they yet contrived to think themselves a cut above the rest, their street a better street, their house a better house. ('Well, it's the end house, that's the difference.')

And so, hieratically vested in their cherished garments ('my little green costume', 'my fawn swagger coat', 'my Persian lamb with the fur bootees') and tricked out in bangles and brooches, bright lipstick and saucy little hats, smiling, as they fondly thought, vivaciously they would step out along those mean gas-smelling streets to catch a tram en route for the pictures at the Assembly Rooms or a dance at the Clock, making a little drama out of a trip to Harehills or a scene in the queue at the Crown. Generally genteel but vulgar if need be, they were sentimental, and with pluck and cheek besides, which if not quite virtues are not unconnected with courage.

Hung up in the back bedroom at Gilpin Place, Aunty Kathleen's shop assistant's black frock is slack and shiny, the pads under the arms stained and smelling of long-dead 4711. She is well into her forties now, cheerful, toothy but not, it is thought, likely to 'get off'. And how can she 'get off', since she has to look after Grandma? But in Manfield's 'on the floor', she still seems a commanding figure, the call 'Miss Peel!' implying a dignity and a rank, the 'Miss' giving her a status that 'Mrs' never quite gives to Mam.

As we grow older and begin to make our way, my brother and I both start to figure more in her conversation. Roundhay ladies wanting court shoes find themselves given an unsought bulletin on 'my nephew in Canada, a pilot in the RAF . . . does that feel easier, madam? . . . My other nephew's just won a scholarship to Oxford . . . Madam has a narrow foot, I'll see if we have something smaller.'

In another respect, too, I do my aunties an injustice. Starved though their lives are of drama, and ready on the thinnest excuse to see themselves in an interesting or tragic light, neither of them at any point indulges this taste for the theatrical by referring even obliquely to the biggest drama that can ever have happened to them, the suicide of their father. There is never the smallest hint of a secret sadness or of a tale that might be told. Loving mystery, in this regard they forgo it entirely. Their father died of a heart attack, here on the kitchen floor, and the conversation does not miss a beat. Though now I see this subterfuge as futile, mistaken, and the lie needless, there is no denying they carry it off superbly; the performances are impeccable. For Grandma and for my parents this is to be expected: to them reticence is second nature. For the aunties, though, not to tell the tale must always have been a sacrifice, and it's a measure of the disgrace attaching to the act that dwelling on it is thought to bring not sympathy but shame. And I see that, in this at least, we have been a united family.

With Myra and husband Stan back on the outskirts of Empire, life returns to its old ways. And there are musical evenings still at Gilpin Place, and Aunt Eveline comes over from Bradford, though now she plays medleys from *Bless the Bride* and *Oklahoma!* and Uncle George sings 'Oh What a Beautiful Morning' as well as 'Bless This House'.

But Grandma is not well, and sitting in the kitchen in the chair that had been bought against Aunty Myra's return she finds the cushion soaked in blood.

Dr Slaney is summoned, the Wolseley parked outside, and he and Aunty Kathleen in her best 'Miss Peel' manner have a hushed conversation in the sitting room. Briefly in hospital, Grandma comes home to the front bedroom at Gilpin Place, where the commode has been brought down from the attic and a fire lit in the tiny grate. She does not read or have the wireless on, but just lies there through the darkening days in that slum bedroom in Wortley, as behind the house the trains are shunted into Holbeck sidings and she waits for what is to come.

Grandma's death in 1950 takes us up to the grave in new Wortley Cemetery where, with St Bartholomew's on one side and Armley Gaol on the other, Grandad Peel had been buried. The grave is unmarked and has always been hard to find, the simple grass-covered mound so plain it seems almost prehistoric ('tump' would describe it), this raised mound the inverted shape of the long zinc baths some houses in Wortley still had hanging outside their back doors.

There is no stone, the only certain identification the withered remains of the flowers taken on our previous visit. This we know was Grandad's grave but that it is the grave of a suicide neither my brother nor I know, though that presumably is why it is unmarked. Putting flowers on it and occasionally on the more elaborate, marble-kerbed pebbled patch belonging to Grandad Bennett is one of the ways of passing Saturday afternoons, which we always spend at Grandma's. One of us threads our way across the cemetery with a jam jar, fills it at the cistern by the wall and bears it brimming back for the vase Mam has brought for the anemones. Sometimes we cut the grass with a pair of inadequate scissors.

Now the grave is open, the sides covered in the same green raffia matting Sleights the greengrocer's have in their window. The coffin being lowered into the hole has up to an hour ago been in the sitting room at Gilpin Place, and with the lid off so the mourners could be taken through by the aunties. ('Would you like to see her?') Dad, predictably, has refused but I am taken in, Kathleen and Myra stroking and kissing Grandma's impassive face. ('Doesn't she look beautiful, Alan?') I have never seen a dead person before, and though I've loved Grandma and liked her I find myself unable to cry or even be moved particularly, just feeling that with the quilted surround and the wimpled face she'd somehow found her way into a chocolate box.

Pretension, though, persists to the end, because as the coffin goes down one sees on the lid that Grandma is said to have died 'in her eightieth year'. This is strictly true as she was seventy-nine, but it doesn't escape what these days would be called Dad's shit-detector.

Nearly thirty years later I find myself filming just outside the gates of the cemetery, the location chosen without reference to me and entirely by chance because it provides a useful cul-de-sac with no passing traffic. In the lunch break I go looking for Grandma's (and Grandad's) grave. But the cemetery has long since been filled up and subsequently landscaped. There are lawns and seats and down-and-outs sleeping on them, together with rubbish and condoms and all the adornments of urban rurality. There are some graves, artfully disposed as features in the landscaping, but there is no grave of ours. Hard to find when I was a boy, now it has gone completely. Still overlooking the cemetery, though, are the black battlements of Armley Gaol. People are no longer buried in the cemetery, which is now a park; but the gaol is ever a gaol and men are still being buried there.

Regularly posted to the Far East, Hong Kong, Singapore, Kuala Lumpur, Aunty Myra resumes with delight the life she has tasted briefly during the war. Though husband Stan is only a warrant officer, now in the twilight of Empire they are entitled to amahs and houseboys and a standard of life way beyond anything they can ever have dreamed of down Tong Road. There are mess dances under the tropic night, beach parties on palm-fringed sands, trips up country and out to the islands, all the time waited on hand and foot by servants who, she is at pains to emphasise, adore her. These postings produce more sheaves of photographs, Aunty M. arm in arm with the devoted servants, beaming on balconies overlooking Hong Kong harbour or days out at Kowloon with Aunty holding armfuls of doubtful Chinese children, a resigned mother looking on.

Because it is children that she has always wanted and never had, believing herself more suited to their upbringing than my mother can ever be and wont to lay claim to a special understanding of their needs, though never grasping how much I certainly want to be left to myself, the fierceness of her regard, the ardour of her attention always making me cringe as a child.

In the intervals of service abroad this lately married couple are posted round England to what is even then only the scattered remnants of the defence establishment. They are stationed at Hednesford, Manston, Padgate or West Malling, airfields where one seldom sees a plane apart from the ceremonial Spitfire marooned among flower beds by the guard-house, a reminder of the great days when all that stood between the nation and its doom was the RAF.

Now the graceful trees of what was once a grand estate shelter Nissen huts and mean system-built houses where the paths are edged with whitewashed stones and the flowers look ready to stand by their beds. It's a suburb that's not quite a suburb, but billets and married quarters and an environment I feel faintly threatening from the days of my National Service, as if I could still be put to weed these beds and bull the kerbs as once I'd had to do in the army.

In a succession of these allotted accommodations Aunty Myra sets out the souvenirs of their tours overseas – an inlaid chest from Bombay, a nest of tables from Madras; there are bowls from Malaya, linen from Singapore and a painted scroll from Hong Kong. 'The writing means a blessing on this house. They do it while you wait. The boy who did it was crippled but he had a lovely face. Mind you, they're so poor they often cripple them themselves to make them more appealing.' Then Stan, her warrant officer husband, parks me in one of the bamboo armchairs and plies me with earnest questions about what I am doing at Oxford and what I am going to do with my medieval history afterwards. What use is it?

Stan being ten years younger than his wife, she naturally expects him to outlive her. But in 1964 he is flown home from Malaya suffering from inoperable cancer. He is taken first to the RAF Chest Unit which is part of the King Edward VII Hospital for Officers at Midhurst, a palatial mansion down a long drive flush with rhododendrons, with views across the manicured lawns to Chichester and the South Downs.

'It's a tip-top place,' said Aunty Myra. 'The surgeon looking after him is one of the first in the country,' and she gives me a long dramatised account of how this individual, an Air Vice-Marshal, had actually taken her by the arm and called her Mrs Rogerson before going on to explain the hopelessness of the situation.

My aunties were always like this, adducing a special status and reputation for any doctor assigned to them. 'Refined-looking fellow, has a big house at Alwoodley, his wife wears one of them sheepskin coats' is a version of it that's crept into one or two of my plays, though I don't suppose that on most occasions it is as purely snobbish as I make it appear. Perhaps Aunty Myra feels that attached to her often fanciful ascriptions of excellence and accomplishment is some shred of hope, as being a top man meant that he could defy the coming doom. (In Leeds it would have come out as 'You couldn't do better if he were in the Brotherton Wing'.) But the special smile, the squeeze of the arm, the recognition, so Aunty Myra sees it, of her natural breeding were also part of a desire to be different, to be marked out above the common ruck and to have a tale to tell.

But if in Aunty's eyes the top surgeon's concern singles her out, there is a high price to be paid for the touch of the Air Vice-Marshal's hand; it puts paid to hope, else why would he touch her at all? It also put paid to the rhododendrons, the lawns and that terrace which must once have had a grandstand view of the Battle of Britain. In its stead comes a poky Unit hospital in RAF Uxbridge, where, in more pain and discomfort than he need have had, Stan lengthily dies, the customary reluctance of hospitals to prescribe painkillers compounded in military establishments, I imagine, because part of their patients' profession is to be brave.

Deplorable though the place is as a hospital, I am interested in the camp because Uxbridge was where T. E. Lawrence, under the name of Shaw, had enlisted as an aircraftman in the early twenties, an account of which he gives in *The Mint*. This is 1964 but the corrugated-iron huts look scarcely to have changed, and as I wander about the camp in the intervals of sitting baffled by my uncle's bed there is a touch of 'And did those feet' about it. T. E. Lawrence figures in *Forty Years On*, and I see that literature is of as much moment to me as life, so that the death of this recently acquired and only occasionally encountered uncle doesn't really signify. Driving along the M40 today I still glance along the ridge to the tower of Uxbridge Church, in the shadow of which some of life's bleaker moments were spent. Though not as bleak as his, I hear a reproving voice. But I scarcely know him, with his red face and crinkly receding hair, and as an ex-National Serviceman I'm suspicious of 'a regular', even in something so innocuous and relatively wanting in bull as an RAF Maintenance Unit.

Stan having died on active service, he is entitled to a full military funeral and this, at Aunty's wish, he is duly given. It is thus that I find myself at the crematorium at Ruislip walking behind the RAF band (though trying not to be seen to march or even keep time) and led by an officer with a drawn sword between ranks of airmen presenting arms. It seems a bit excessive if, strictly speaking, appropriate, and I am ashamed by the ceremony and its insincerities to the extent that, far from being a comfort, I can scarcely be civil. I see the whole ceremony, much as Dad does, as a lot of splother, cringing at how unreluctantly Aunty is ready to take the limelight, a lone figure in black standing behind the coffin as the band plays.

'Bad acting' I think it, and grief no excuse, the more it shows the less it means my philosophy then, though I suppose I have come to appreciate how often a husband's funeral is the last chance most wives get to cut even a sombre dash or take the stage alone, and that they are not to be blamed if they get their teeth into it. This is her curtain call too. But though I hope I would feel less harshly towards Myra now than I did then, she was a woman who repelled sympathy. I have never come across grief that is transmuted so readily into anger, with no hint of resignation or philosophy. Though naïvely I am somehow expecting it to be all resignation. Try as I do to be more tolerant and understanding, I find myself tested by posthumous extravagances, of which the military funeral is one, the scattering of the ashes another.

Why I am chosen to accompany my aunty on this errand is something of a mystery. It's probably because at this date I'm the only one of the immediate family who can drive. Glum, unsympathetic and critical of the histrionic strain that runs through her grief, I make an unsatisfactory and unconsoling companion. 'She's putting it on,' I keep thinking, unmitigated by the thought that perhaps she's entitled to do so.

If as a dramatist I am offended by her bad acting, it's as a discerning tourist and seeker-out of unfrequented spots that I deplore the venue for the scattering. It is Ilkley Moor. For one of the various editions of *Beyond the Fringe* I had written a sketch about someone wanting their ashes scattered on the South Shore at Blackpool on August Bank Holiday; Aunty Myra's choice of venue seems not unlike. But it is Ilkley Moor where Aunty says they had their happiest times, and though I wish their enchantments had been less conventionally located (Bolton Abbey, say, or Fountains) it is to Ilkley Moor I drive her.

Having taken her to the edge of the moor, I don't even get out of the car, mumbling something about her doubtless wanting to be alone at a moment like this. Not that there is much chance of that. It is the first warm day of spring, and all over the chosen segment of moorland holidaymakers are taking the sun, even picnicking as presumably she and Stan had done in the happier times now being ultimately commemorated. It seems sensible to me to convey the urn and its contents to a stretch of heather that is less populous, and I diffidently suggest this. But the location is precise and seemingly sacred – it occurs to me now that sex may have marked the spot – and she is not to be shifted from her grim purpose by a few day-trippers.

In hat and gloves and wholly in black, Aunty cuts a distinctive figure as heedless of the sun-seekers she clambers over the rocks, unloading the contents of the urn as she goes. Prudence might have kept it, like a gas mask, in its cardboard box, but no, she brandishes the urn for all to see, this scattering literally her last fling as a loving wife and not a gesture she is prepared to muffle.

I sink lower and lower in the driving seat as she moves among the stunned sunbathers, shedding her load and heedless of the light breeze that whirls the ashes back in her face. Eventually, the urn emptied, she returns to the car: 'He didn't want to leave me,' she says tearfully, wiping a smut from her coat. It's a line of dialogue I might hesitate to wish onto an invented character on grounds of plausibility. But then I might make my character more plausible too, and certainly kinder than the unwilling, unfeeling chauffeur I am this afternoon, my sullen responses more to be censured than her inauthentic extravagances. What she wants is a decent audience, which is what I am determined not to be. Not for the first time on occasions requiring good manners, I think Gordon would have done it better and to hell with authenticity.

In the few years she has left to live Aunty Myra's life seems fuelled by pure anger – anger at the RAF, who had, as she sees it, taken her husband's life and refused her all but the most minimal pension, anger at fate, God even, that has dealt her this blow, anger at my mother, who has a husband and children and a cushioned life, anger above all at her other sister, Aunty Kathleen.

Kathleen has always in the past been Myra's companion and confidante, and Myra must have assumed that she would remain a lifelong spinster and so be always available for consolation and companionship. But to everyone's surprise, on the eve of her retirement from Manfield's, Kathleen is courted and briskly married by an elderly widower from Australia. It's a turn of events which takes Kathleen as much by surprise as it does everyone else, as her husband, a Mr Roach, is no more romantic than his name, plump, opinionated and small; Aunty Kathleen, never having expected to get married at all, can afford to have a detached view of these shortcomings. Exit Miss Peel; enter Mrs Roach.

The wedding ought to have been, like its predecessors, at St Mary's, Tong Road, but now there is grass growing between the paving stones there and the church like half the neighbourhood is on the brink of demolition. So at some church in Morecambe, where Bill has got them a little bungalow, there is the wedding of Mr William Roach and Miss Kathleen Elizabeth Peel, Aunty Kath flanked by Mam in gloves and 'that little maroon duster coat I had to Gordon's wedding', with Dad looking long-suffering in the back row. Dad dislikes being photographed, and faced with a camera his habitual geniality is replaced by a look of pained discomfort and boredom.

'Don't pull your jib, Dad,' Mam mutters, 'try and look natural.' But it is to no effect and in this mood there is no one he resembles so much as Somerset Maugham in his last days at the Villa Mauresque.

Happily, I do not have to go through this ordeal as I am in New York with *Beyond the Fringe*. Notably absent, too, is Aunty Myra, though she would probably have been looking as pained as Dad had she been on the church steps and not in one of the last outposts of the Empire, Kuala Lumpur possibly or Singapore. Having married late herself, to find her sister doing the same must have taken some of the shine off her own tardy nuptials. It was never on the cards that Aunty Kathleen would 'land a man', if only because she talks so much.

'I don't know how he managed to shut her up long enough to pop the question,' said Dad, though husband Bill was far from ungarrulous himself. This is one of Aunty Myra's complaints against him, that he talks a lot and that he bores her, but it is not the quality of his conversation that is the real issue: had Aunty Kathleen been marrying Isaiah Berlin it would have made no difference. No. The case against Bill is that he has disrupted the natural order of things.

Aunty Kathleen is the sister who stayed at home to look after her mother, and when that mother died stayed on as such dutiful daughters often did, living in the same house, guardian of the home where Myra and Stan could stay when they came on leave, and where we would still come for the ritual high tea on Christmas Day, though Grandma, who had given it fun and point, was now long since dead. Her death, though, does not change Kathleen's life one bit; she still works at Manfield's, keeps up with a vast network of friends and correspondents, writes innumerable letters, her job, her style, her way of talking unaltered since she and Myra went out to dances together in the twenties.

Now all that changes. Kathleen sells the house in Gilpin Place, and with it what is left of the grand furniture that came over from Halifax before the First War. Sold for a song is the huge oak kist that occupies the wall of one bedroom, and likewise a fruitwood sideboard the size of an altar, which all my childhood stood in the kitchen that its polished mellow wood reflected. In the little semi-detached bungalow at Bare on the outskirts of Morecambe that they had found for themselves and which backed, as did Gilpin Place, onto a railway, the sideboard would not even have got through the door.

Having followed in her sister's footsteps by making a late marriage, Aunty Kathleen continues the pattern when she and husband Bill take up globetrotting. When Aunty Myra brings her husband home to die, Aunty Kathleen and Bill are about to embark on a world cruise culminating in a visit to her new family in Australia. In the face of Myra's disapproval of both the marriage and the world cruise, it takes courage (plus the determination of her fierce Australian hamster of a husband) to persist. But off they go.

So now it is Kathleen's turn to send home photographs of herself in a rickshaw, or garlanded with flowers after some shipboard dinner dance, posed against the taffrail with Bill in his white dinner jacket, and even, as

77

Myra has done so often, brandishing some Oriental tot while its patient mother looks on. Letters come with hopes of better news of Stan, filled with accounts of their travels, the snaps enclosed. Meanwhile Stan fades and dies, and Aunty Myra crouches over her one-bar electric fire as through the letter box come the postcards of palm trees and koala bears.

Myra lives in a succession of briefly rented rooms, first in Midhurst, then Uxbridge, and finally at West Malling in Kent. These comfortless accommodations and the meals that go with them – or rather don't, as they seldom have cooking facilities, so have to be taken in cheap cafés serving spaghetti on toast or poached egg, tea and bread and butter – exude a particular sort of hopelessness quite separate from the sad circumstances which have brought her to them. Aunty Myra had too many sharp corners to be one of her characters, but they are the setting for many of the novels of Barbara Pym, and one of the reasons I find her books quite lowering to read. Eventually, though, Myra comes back north, choosing, as she thinks anyway, to face old age in a bungalow on a bleak little development at Wharton outside Lytham. Significantly, though this is not mentioned, it's across the road from an airfield.

Most of us, certainly as we get older, prefer it if our lives are played out against a permanent set and with a cast that is largely unaltered; we may change our own role and status (and partner), but it's better if friends and relations (the extras in our drama) remain fixed in their roles and the set-ups to which we have grown accustomed. The death of a close friend or, almost as distasteful, a divorce, alters our landscape; there is a distressing upheaval.

When Aunty Myra married and went abroad she not unreasonably expected that her sister would continue in the part which she had always played, the stay-at-home sister, unmarried and on call. After she'd tasted the joys of marriage with her Mr Roach, I've a feeling Aunty Kathleen may want this also but now it's too late.

Whether her husband wants a wife or not, he certainly wants a house-keeper, and he makes no secret of his desire to take her back to Australia. In the meantime they sit in their poky semi-detached bungalow by the railway at the back end of Morecambe, while thirty miles down the coast Aunty Myra sits in hers. Occasionally they meet, but the rift is never wholly healed. In a trashy novel, the little Australian would have died . . . and in a murder mystery in dubious circumstances; the sisters would have made it up, and life would have got back to normal, Stan made a saint and the distasteful episode of Kathleen's marriage never referred to. But it wasn't quite as tidy as that.

When it came to bringing comfort to the sick, no one was quicker off the mark than Kathleen or Myra. They both make a beeline for any bedside, the first hint of sickness fetching them round with Lucozade or calf's-foot jelly and a flow of enlivening chatter. Such visits were to be avoided at all costs, and so if there is illness in our family Dad prefers to keep it dark. ('Well, you get weary with them.') Mam's health has not been good for a few months and Aunty Myra has somehow got wind of it, and since she is now a widow she is a looser cannon than she was when married. Sure enough, she insists on coming over to stay.

'For Lilian's sake, Walter. You see,' Aunty Myra said, smiling her Bette Davis smile, 'I understand her.'

It also gives her an opportunity of demonstrating her home-making skills, taking over the cooking and generally playing the model housewife. It takes very little of this to bring about a rapid improvement in my mother's health, and on the night in question she and Dad have gone out to the pictures, leaving Aunty Myra at home with me.

For a while I try and talk to her but her grief, which shows no sign of abating, already bores me, and I am expected to corroborate the intense anger she is still feeling at the untimeliness of her husband's death and the unfeelingness of the RAF. Soon wearying of this I retire to the back room, the junk room as it's always called, where I am labouring over the series of sketches which will eventually turn into *Forty Years On*. While I struggle with this entirely literary piece in one room, in another Aunty Myra enacts a far more vivid scene that could come out of a play by D. H. Lawrence.

Not a reader, and too grief-stricken to want to watch television, Myra seeks solace in housework. The flat in Headingley where we are then living is bright and cosy, and Mam has set out her Staffordshire figures with their maimed hands and broken necks, the supposedly Sheraton table she has picked up at a sale and all the other purchases which make the place 'a bit more classy'. There is nothing to be done with any of these, which Aunty Myra doesn't have much time for anyway. Her concern is the gas oven, an ancient Belling that had come with the flat and is clean, so far as a gas oven is ever clean, but not in its inward parts.

Gas ovens can be readily dismantled for ease of cleaning, but ours has never been thus deconstructed until this evening, when Aunty Myra takes it in hand. And yes, it is to sublimate her grief and perhaps to help with the running of the household, but another interpretation is possible, having to do with Aunty Myra's superiority as a housewife and as a forces wife at that, one who knows how to keep a kitchen spotless and has had amahs and dhobi boys to do it. Now it is our turn, and while I labour in the back room our gas stove is split into its component parts and spread over the kitchen floor.

Unsurprisingly, the grease is caked on and proves more intractable than she had thought. In her scheme of things, of course, it would never have been allowed to get into such a state. She would have cleaned it – or supervised the cleaning of it – every week. So when in due course Mam and Dad return from the pictures it is to find Aunty Myra still sitting on the kitchen floor with the gas oven still unresolved around her.

Dad seldom loses his temper, and had I had to put words into his mouth I would have expected him only to say, 'Nay, Myra, what's all this?' But I had forgotten how such a ludicrous incident fitted into the undeclared war between the sisters, with Mam always portrayed as the silly, inefficient, unworldly one and Myra the new model housewife. There were tears from both sisters and, almost unheard of, shouting from my father, before all parties went to bed, the oven left in disarray.

To clean down in another woman's house, while ostensibly doing her a favour, is also to do her an injury and a disservice. Mam is house-proud but her pride begins with her little walnut work-box, her green glass doorstop and her blue and white plates. It doesn't extend to the dark recesses behind the Belling or the space between the top cupboard and the ceiling, the kind of areas only a sergeant major doing a kit inspection would ever dream of investigating.

But Aunty Myra has spent her life in camps where such fastidious probings were the norm, camps where whitened stones led up to the gates and where the formations on the square are echoed in the open order of the flowers in their beds. She has spent her evenings pressing her husband's uniform, blancoing his belt and even bulling his boots. Now he is dead she cleans the gas oven almost as an act of piety; she is doing what she has always done (or seen to be done) in his memory. None of this, of course, is appreciated by Mam and least of all by Dad and, bereaved or not, Myra leaves the next morning, the seriousness of this absurd incident reflected in the fact that it never becomes a family joke.

In the event Myra does not long survive her husband, her sojourn in her cold little bungalow bringing on pneumonia. She has so often contrasted her lonely situation and her toughness of spirit with my mother's more cosseted existence that at first I refuse to believe she is ill, taking it to be some sort of sideshow staged to divert attention from my mother, who has just come out of hospital after her first bout of depression. It's only when her letters start coming from the infirmary in Blackpool that I grudgingly acknowledge that there must be something in it. Dad has been similarly sceptical and it is only my brother, who has always felt less unkindly towards her, who takes it entirely seriously. Even so it is not at all plain what the matter is, the doctor diagnosing some sort of asthma, a condition from which she has never suffered.

So her death when it comes takes me by surprise. My brother telephones from the hospital, and I am in the middle of saying that even so I don't think it is as serious as all that when he tells me she has died. My parents had been at her bedside when she had taken my father's hand, scrabbling at her wrist to indicate he must have her watch. So Dad, who has always found her a difficult woman, is now as plagued with remorse as I am.

So entrenched, though, are my convictions about her character that even when she is in the grave it does not entirely undercut them, so that I catch myself feeling that her death was somehow not quite *sincere*: she had died just for effect. Aunty Kathleen keeps saying that she had never recovered from the death of her husband and that she has died of a broken heart. Ordinarily I would have made a joke of this, taken it as just another instance of the aunties' pretentiousness. But now I keep my thoughts to myself and Dad does too.

The funeral is at a featureless crematorium in Lytham St Annes. Afterwards we go for lunch to a roadhouse on the outskirts. I sit next to my grandmother's niece, Cousin Florence, who keeps a boarding house in Blackpool. A down-to-earth woman, she eats a large meal of lukewarm lasagne, then puts down her knife and fork and says, 'Well, that's the first time I've dined off brown plates.' Grief is not much in evidence, though with Cousin Florence it is hardly to be expected. Her husband's name was Frank, and six months before we had had a two-page letter filling us in on all her news. Halfway down the second page came the sentence: 'Frank died last week, haven't we been having some weather?' Seldom can a comma have borne such a burden.

In the bungalow that November afternoon, huddled in their coats against the cold that had killed their sister, Mam and Aunty Kathleen divide her possessions between them. Many of them are in tea chests from Singapore that have not been opened since she and her dying husband came back two years before. There are sheaves of tablecloths, bundles of napkins, sets of sheets and pillowcases, all of them stored up against the day when she and Stan would cease their globetrotting and settle down. Most of the linen has never been used, the cutlery still in its tissue paper. At one point Mam speaks up for a set of steak knives with bone handles, evidence that she is still dreaming of her own life being transformed and that she might one day branch out. They are still in their tissue paper twenty-five years later when she herself dies.

There are few family heirlooms. Mam gets Grandma's yew Windsor chair, which she has always wanted and which she partly credits with setting her off liking 'nice things'. I bag two pairs of steel shears that had been used to cut lino and oilcloth in Grandpa Peel's hardware shop in

Union Street, West Vale; fine, sensible objects shaped to fit the hand so that they are a physical pleasure to use, and come in handy for cutting paper. Back in 1966 I want them because they have a history which is also my history; but also because they are the kind of thing a writer has on his table. And they are on my table now as I write, the tools of my trade as they were the tools of my great grandfather's. Cut, cut, cut.

Though I do not speak up for them, it must have been then that Aunty Myra's photograph albums are given over to me on the assumption that, since I am the educated one, I should keep the family record, or a censored version of it as Grandad Peel's suicide is not yet out in the open. Still, there in the album is Ossie, lazily grinning on his tropical beach, the great sag of his dick as astonishing now as it had been when I was a boy, the page still scuffed where Aunty Myra had expunged her first roguish caption.

This sharing-out is a bizarre occasion, a kind of Christmas with endless presents to open, Mam and Aunty Kathleen by turns shrieking with laughter and then in floods of tears. Neither of them wants for much now; both have tea towels and sheets to last them all their days with tray cloths and napkins in their own bottom drawers that they are never going to use either. And more than the funeral itself or the bitter cold that grips the bungalow, it is this redundancy of possessions that makes them think of death.

Conscious that I have done Aunty Myra an injustice but knowing, too, that I would do exactly the same again, I try and write about her in my diary:

> She was a great maker of lists/inventories/lists of friends/lists of expenses/shopping lists/records of meter readings/contents of cases. It was a habit acquired in the Equipment Wing of RAF Innsworth, ticking off kit on lists on clipboards; lists of property which grew with every posting as she moved with her husband from station to station, and quarters to quarters. What is yours is what is signed for, and what is signed for must one day be accounted for, so a list must be made. And a check list in case the first list is lost. These are my possessions. I own these. I have these signatures.

On the day of her husband's death, she signed for his property: for the watch that still ticked on the dead wrist, the ring loose on the finger, the pyjamas in which he lay.

And when he was dead two years, and she was in a bungalow on the outskirts of nowhere in particular, she was still making lists: guy ropes for a life that didn't have much point, evidence of what she had and therefore what she was, and a sign that she was not settled there either, that soon she would up sticks and off. We found the lists, the packing cases still unopened: tea sets from Hong Kong, Pyrex won in raffles in a sergeants' mess in Kowloon in 1947, the sewing of amahs, the pictures of houseboys, her husband's uniform, his best BD and belt, all piled up in the back room of a bungalow on the outskirts of Lytham St Annes.

Aunty Kathleen holds up a pair of her husband's pyjama bottoms.

'See, Lilian,' she giggles, 'look at his little legs.' They are in the front bedroom at Morecambe while in the kitchen Bill, the husband in question, fills Dad in on the ins and outs of sanitary engineering in Western Australia.

It is Christmas Day early in the seventies, and Mam and Dad and me have driven over from home to the cheerless bungalow in Bare for Christmas dinner, a last faint echo of those communal gatherings twenty-odd years before. But now there is no Aunt Eveline to play the piano or Uncle George to sing, just this oddly married couple, half-strangers to one another still, a marriage of mutual convenience meant to keep one another company in their declining years.

With her regular gifts of shoe-trees Aunty Kath had hitherto held the record for boring Christmas presents, but Bill shows he is no slouch in this department either when he presents me with the history of some agricultural college in New South Wales (second volume only).

'You did history, Alan. This should interest you.' He has served in the First War and we spend much of Christmas afternoon leafing through the pages while he points out the names of the sons and grandsons of men in 'his mob' who have done time studying agriculture.

Quite what he is doing in England is not plain as he seldom misses an opportunity of running it down, along with blacks, Jews and, when Mam and Aunty Kathleen are out of the room, women generally. Dad, who has never enrolled in the sex war, lapses into Somerset Maugham mode, his face a picture of boredom and misery until the time comes when we can make our farewells and thankfully head off home in the Mini. Mam now tells us about the pyjama incident and becomes helpless with laughter, the mitigating 'But she's very good-hearted' which is always tacked onto any gossip involving Aunty Kathleen hard to employ where her husband is concerned, as good-hearted Bill plainly isn't.

Considering Morecambe is only three-quarters of an hour away from the village, Mam and Dad see the old newly marrieds relatively seldom as they are often abroad on trips, life in the bungalow by the railway enlivened by a visit to Switzerland, for instance, and a lengthy Pacific cruise culminating in a visit to Australia to meet her husband's family. It is tacitly assumed that this must be a prelude to them upping sticks and settling down there, but nothing is said. Instead, they come back and resume their life at Bare, slightly to Dad's dismay as it inevitably means more slides with Bill in his flowered shorts, Aunty Kathleen in a sarong; one way and another we'd been looking at pictures like this for nearly thirty years.

Scarcely, though, are they back from this odyssey when something begins to happen in Aunty Kathleen's head. She has always been intensely sociable, still with many friends in Leeds, and much of her time, home or away, is spent in keeping up with what she calls 'her correspondence' – scores of letters regularly fired off to friends and acquaintants, few of them of course known to her hubby, whom she may even press into running her over to Leeds to see them.

'I've half a dozen people who're always begging me to pop in,' says

Miss Prothero, 'one of them a chiropodist.' A character in an early play, hers is the unmistakable voice of Aunty Kath.

At some point, though, after their return from Australia her address book goes missing and with it half her life. Without this roster of names and addresses she is cut adrift. Mam doesn't think the address book has been lost at all and that Bill, in an effort to loosen her grip on the past and make sure she settles first in Morecambe, and eventually Australia, has himself deliberately mislaid this handbook to sociability.

True or not the effect is disastrous. Out of touch with her convoy of friends and acquaintances, she begins to drift aimlessly. Her discourse becomes wayward and Bill, who has several times remarked to Dad on how all the sisters could gab, now finds that her utterance accelerates, becomes garbled and impossible to follow. It doesn't take much of this before he commits her to a mental hospital, which is Lancaster Moor again. Indeed she is briefly in the same ward as Mam had been on her first admission a few years before, and there comes a time when Mam is in the psychiatric wing at Airedale Hospital and her sister in a similar wing at Lancaster.

Misconceiving where my father's loyalties lie, the little Australian makes no attempt at fellow-feeling, attributing both their misfortunes to the Peel family. Unsurprisingly Dad will have none of it; Mam's plight is not the same as her sister's, and that he might be thought to have anything in common with his coarse conceited brother-in-law is not even a joke.

Insofar as her condition is diagnosed at all, Kathleen is said to be suffering from arteriosclerosis of the brain: in a word, dementia. The catch-all term nowadays is Alzheimer's but that didn't have quite the same currency in the early seventies, or its current high profile. Insofar as it was futile to tell Aunty Kathleen anything and expect her to remember it for more than a moment, her condition was like that of an Alzheimer's patient, but the manner of her deterioration is not so simple as a mere forgetting. Not for her a listless, dull-eyed wordless decline; with her it is all rush, gabble, celerity.

She had always been a talker but now her dementia unleashes torrents of speech, monologues of continuous anecdote and dizzying complexity, one train of thought switching to another without signal or pause, rattling across points and through junctions at a rate no listener can follow.

Her speech, so imitable in the past, becomes impossible to reproduce, though now taking myself seriously as a writer and praised for 'an ear for dialogue' I dutifully try, making notes of these flights of speech as best I can, then when I get home trying to set them down but without success. Embarking on one story, she switches almost instantly to another and then another, and while her sentences still retain grammatical form they have no sequence or sense. Words pour out of her as they always have and with the same vivacity and hunger for your attention. But to listen to they are utterly bewildering, following the sense like trying to track a particular ripple in a pelting torrent of talk.

Still, despite this formless spate of loquacity she remains recognisably herself, discernible in the flood those immutable gentilities and components of her talk which have always characterised her (and been such a joke). 'If you follow me, Lilian . . .', 'As it transpired, Walter . . .', 'Ready to wend my way, if you take my meaning . . .' So that now, with no story to tell (or half a dozen), she must needs still tell it as genteelly as she has ever done but at five times the speed, her old worn politenesses detached from any narrative but still whole and hers, bobbing about in a ceaseless flood of unmeaning; demented, as she herself might have said, but very nicely spoken.

And as with her speech, so it is with her behaviour. Surrounded by the senile and by the wrecks of women as hopelessly, though differently, demented as she is, she still clings to the notion that she is somehow different and superior. Corseted in her immutable gentilities she still contrives to make something special out of her situation and her role in it.

'He'll always give me a smile,' she says of an impassive nurse who is handing out the tea. 'I'm his favourite.'

'This is my chair. They'll always put me here because this corner's that bit more select.'

Her life has been made meaningful by frail, fabricated connections, and now, when the proper connections in her brain are beginning to break down, it is this flimsy tissue of social niceties that still holds firm.

In this demented barracks she remains genteel, in circumstances where gentility is hardly appropriate: a man is wetting himself; a woman is howling.

'I'll just have a meander down,' says Aunty, stepping round the widening pool of piss. 'They've stood me in good stead, these shoes.'

The setting for this headlong fall from sense is the long-stay wing of the hospital: it's a nineteenth-century building, a fairly spectacular one at that, and in any other circumstances one might take pleasure in it as an example of the picturesque, in particular the vast Gothic hall which, with its few scattered figures, could be out of an Ackermann print. But the scattered figures are shaking with dementia or sunk in stupor and depression; it is Gothic, but the Gothic, too, of horror, madness and despair.

Of these surroundings Kathleen seems unaware, though her eyes sometimes fill with tears in a distress that cannot settle on its object, and should a nurse come by it is straight away replaced by the beaming smile, refined voice and all the trappings of the old Miss Peel. But the grimness of the institution, the plight of the patients and Kathleen's immunity to sense make her a distressing person to visit, and Dad is naturally reluctant to take Mam lest she sees her sister's condition as in any way reflecting her own. But when Mam is well enough and freed from her depression they go over to Lancaster regularly and conscientiously, and probably see more of Kathleen mad than they had lately seen of her sane.

She was never so touching as now when her brain is beginning to unravel.

'Give us a kiss, love,' she says when I am going. 'That's one thing I do like.' Then, as a nurse passes, 'Hello! Do you know my mother-in-law?' She smiles her toothy smiles as if this were just a slip of the tongue. 'No. I mean my father.' And she gives me another kiss.

Now, though, it is the summer of 1974. Mam is in and out of Airedale Hospital, Dad driving daily backwards and forwards in the loving routine that eventually, early in August, kills him.

It is perhaps because I am now forty, and am unappealingly conscious that the death of a father is one of the great unrepeatables and ought, if I am a proper writer, to be recorded, that about this time I begin to keep a more systematic diary, through which much of the rest of Aunty Kathleen's story can be told.

Sunday, 1 September 1974, Yorkshire. Drive down to Airedale to see Mam. For a while we sit outside in the hot sheltered sunshine, then go indoors and talk to another patient, Mary, who has been in hospital with Mam once before. Mam is more rational, slow and a bit distanced but collected, though able to talk more easily to Mary than to me. I drive back home and the telephone is going just as I am putting the key in the door and it's Gordon, who's ringing to say he's on his way north.

What has happened is that Aunty Kathleen has disappeared from Lancaster Moor, walking out of the ward in her summer frock last Wednesday afternoon and not having been seen since. The police begin looking on Thursday but find no trace of her. Now Gordon feels he must come up to search for her himself, and also to talk to her husband to see whether he can throw any light on her disappearance. He thinks he ought to visit her old haunts and suggests to me possible places where she might be, friends she might have gone to in Leeds, Morecambe and even Scarborough. This is someone who is incapable of keeping her mind or her discourse in one channel for more than ten seconds together, so I get slightly cross at these suggestions and try and persuade him not to come. I think I've succeeded and it's a relief when I can get the phone down, have a bath and go up to Dubb Syke for my supper.

When I get back around midnight it's to find Gordon waiting. There have been no further developments, except that the police seem to have been half-hearted in their searching, saying that with three mental hospitals in Lancaster disappearances are relatively common. I feel guilty that I have no feelings about it, but my case is that if Aunty Kathleen has had the wit to get any distance or to find someone to stay with then she should be left alone. Besides, if she is dead then she is probably better off. And if she is half-dead of exposure or whatever I am not sure that I would want to authorise desperate resuscitation measures to bring her round and put her back in that dismal fortress of a hospital. But in the night I hear the rain tippling down and think of her lying under a bush somewhere, bewildered as a child.

Monday, 2 September 1974. I work in the morning, then drive over to Lancaster to meet Gordon, who has been walking round fields and barns and a cemetery but found nothing. He has shown Aunty's photograph to bus conductors, as someone thinks she may have been seen on a bus. He has been to the hospital and talked to the orderlies, who do not think she can have gone far as she got into a panic if she thought she was going on a journey. One of the more lucid patients thinks she may have seen her getting into a Mini, and this raises the question whether Bill, who has a Mini, may have abducted her. When told of her disappearance he has said to the police, 'She will be found in water.'

This suggests that he had been told of the drowning of her father; the fact that such a recent recruit to the family should have been so readily told a secret that had been kept from us for forty years making me slightly resentful.

The thought, though, that her husband might have something to do with her disappearance is chilling, the more so since it's known he is anxious to get back to Australia but does not have the money to do so and (though this is unverified) does not have the disposal of what money Kathleen may have left; not much, I imagine, but maybe just enough. The police are not interested in any of this; to them it is just another disappearance.

Exhausted we drive back over the Pennines to Airedale to see Mam who is more rational than yesterday, discussing a little what is to happen when she comes out of hospital. Tomorrow Gordon goes to see Bill. A policewoman called at the bungalow and found on his door a notice saying 'Knock at your peril'. He had mentioned his Australian plans but then shut up about them quickly.

Unrecorded in my diary are the details of Gordon's visit to the bungalow in Bare, where he had in effect to ask Aunty Kathleen's husband whether he had done away with his wife. This is, to say the least, a difficult assignment and I could see no way of accomplishing it. But my brother, always more conscientious than I am, and anxious to do the right thing even when it might not be the right thing to do, feels he must make the attempt.

He gets nowhere of course but at least comes away convinced that Bill no more knows the whereabouts of Aunty Kathleen than we do. There is, though, a certain shiftiness about him, perhaps because, with his wife irretrievably demented, he may have decided to give her up as a bad job and decamp to Australia. But that is a different thing.

We enquire again whether she has been seen at the bus station, another dutiful but futile exercise; she can no longer have known what a bus was, let alone where it might be stationed. Capable of catching a bus she would not have been in hospital in the first place.

Tuesday, 3 September 1974. First we search on the other side of the road where the hospital borders the prison, two total institutions that blend seamlessly into one another with no evidence from the atmosphere or the architecture which is prison, which is hospital. We look in a long dyke bordering a rubbish dump, high in nettles. There are broken bits of surgical equipment, lavatory pans and big juicy evil-looking blackberries and the tall mulleins that grow in our own garden. We follow the filthy stream that runs along the bottom and come to furnace rooms and a smoking dump. A furnace man speaks out of the depths of a hut. Then there are nurses in clean rooms by a smooth lawn. We come back, Gordon saying that we would give it up soon but could we walk down the cinder track by Aunty's ward which leads eventually to the river? I think it pointless and am cross and ill-tempered because I want my lunch and it all seems so useless; in such surroundings she could be two feet away and we would not see her. But we go on looking and it's about half past one that we find her.

The wood runs from the cinder track to the edge of the motorway. I get over the wall into the wood a little way up the field, which has been newly sown with some winter crop. Gordon is ahead of me somewhere but I lose him when I get over the wall and start blundering about the wood. Someone has been here already as I can see the bracken and brambles trampled down, the police probably with their dogs, searching. Looking back on it now it seems as if I knew I must go to the end of the wood last, and only search by the wall at the finish. So I work along the hedge that borders the next field where I see now that Gordon is. Then I turn up towards the end of the wood where there seems to be a break in the wall which must lead up to the verge of the M6. The wood is full of terrible noise, the din of lorries passing, the traffic thundering ceaselessly by shaking the trees. I go towards the break in the wall and then I see her.

I see her legs. One red sandal off. Her summer frock. Her bright white hair, and if I look closely I think there is the yellow flesh of her face. She is lying face downwards, one arm stretched out. I stand there doing nothing with a mixture of feelings. Revulsion at this dead thing, which I do not want to look at closely. Exultation that I have found her and, shockingly, pleasure that it is me who has found her who had thought the whole search futile. But there is wonder, too, at the providence that has led us to this spot among the drenched undergrowth, the whole place heaving with noise, nature and not nature.

I go back through the wood a little and shout 'Gordon, Gordon' again and again. I must have shouted it twenty times until once the call happens to come in a break in the traffic, and he comes across from the field. He bends over her, touches the body as I have failed to do and says 'Such a little thing', and he puts his hand over his face. He says he thinks her nose has been bleeding. I see her outstretched arm, mushroom white, the flesh shrunk away from the bone, and still wonder how it is we have managed to come upon her and that it is solved and over. She has been there six days.

Then, all afternoon, we wait in the ward while the police are fetched who comb the wood for her other shoe, then fetch the body up to the mortuary. The coroner's assistant, a Scots policeman, comes and takes a statement from me as the one who discovered the body. Then we sit in the attendants' room off the old ladies' ward where Aunty has been this last year, odd bits of conversation filtering through.

'Are you my friend, Kitty?' says one of the nurses to an old girl who is braying with her spoon on the tray that fastens her in. 'Nay, Kitty. I thought you were my friend so why are you banging?'

Old ladies make endlessly for the door, only to be turned back. A woman walks about outside, one hand on her head, the other clasped to her cheek. From time to time nurses come in and talk, one saying how, though it had never happened before, Mr Blackburn, the charge nurse, had said it would happen if they could not lock the doors . . . as they can't under the current Mental Health Act, so half their time is spent fielding these lost and wandering creatures who are trying to reach the outside world or, like Aunty Kathleen, 'just having a meander down'. Mr Blackburn and his wife had searched and searched and now, having lost her, the atmosphere on the ward is terrible.

In the statement I give my profession as Company Director. There will be a post-mortem this evening and an inquest next week. We drive home, where I have a cold bath, then go off ten minutes later down to Airedale, where Mam is sleepy and slow but rational, talking of her life when she gets better. If she gets better, she says, and her eyes fill with tears.

Gordon is still concerned that the police did not begin searching until Thursday, a whole day after she disappeared and even then only looked half-heartedly. I am more philosophical about it, or lazier, Gordon seeing it as a situation which can be corrected if only it is pointed out whereas I see it as a reflection of the value we place on the old and think it useless to raise the matter.

A life varies in social importance. We set most value on the life of a child. Had a child been missing, the whole of the police force plus dozens of volunteers would have been systematically combing the waste ground where we wandered so aimlessly this morning. They

93

would have covered the area in wide sweeps from the hospital and in due course she would have been discovered, perhaps still alive; certainly she would have been found had she been a child, which in many senses she was, except that her life was behind not before her. Had she been a teenager they would probably not have looked, unless there was suspicion of foul play, and maybe if there had been any thought of foul play with Aunty Kathleen that would have fetched the police out too, though no willing volunteers such as turn out to look for someone young. Aunty Kathleen's life was at its lowest point of social valuation. She was seventy-three. She was senile. She was demented, and she was of no class or economic importance. When she was found concern centred not on her fate but on how it reflected on the staff of the hospital and the efficiency of the police force. Even in death she was of marginal importance as a person.

There is, too, under it all, the unspoken recognition that if such pathetic creatures escape – or 'wander off', since escape implies intention and she was long since incapable of that – then the death that they die, of exposure, hypothermia or heart failure, is better than the one they would otherwise have died: sitting vacantly in a chair year after year, fed by hand, soiling themselves, waiting without thought or feeling until the decay of the body catches up with the decay of the mind and they can cross the finishing line together. No, to die at the foot of a wall by the verge of the motorway is a better death than that.

Thursday, 12 September 1974. I drive over slowly to Lancaster Moor on a warm, misty day. So nervous of being late I had booked an alarm call for eight a.m. though the inquest is not until ten-thirty. Hanging over me for more than a week, I have almost come to think of it as a trial. I imagine the row, the hospital reprimanded for carelessness, the police for not conducting a rigorous search and the press wanting to know what I feel about it all.

We sit in a small room in the main building above the bowling green and the dreadful roaring motorway. Stand on the terrace of the hospital and you can see the trees in question. The copse even has a name, it is mentioned in evidence. Stockabank Wood.

Present are Nurse Blackburn, Bill – Aunty Kathleen's husband – and me, plus reporters, who do not seem like reporters at all, one a woman in thick glasses looking like a crafts instructor, the other an insurance agent.

It is not the coroner, but his deputy – and by the looks of him his grandfather, an old man in a bulky overcoat, sharp white stubble, glasses . . . and a manner reminiscent of Miles Malleson. He takes each witness through their statement, with very few questions asked. The pathologist, who looks as if he himself has died from exposure several days before, describes the post-mortem in a bored, blurred monotone . . . the lesions on the skin, the weight of the brain slightly lighter than average, the thickening of the arteries, several gallstones, many gastric ulcers. 'Would these be painful?' 'Not necessarily.' Heart in good condition; some emphysema. Death due to exposure aggravated by senile dementia.

The coroner records a verdict of misadventure almost before the words are out of the pathologist's mouth. Simpson, the coroner's officer, mutters to the two press about not mentioning my name, there is some handshaking and expressions of sympathy and I come away in the misty sunshine relieved and, for the first time in many weeks, happy. I have coffee in Lancaster, shop and drive back home. In the afternoon I blackberry up Crummock and a man passing up the lane says, 'I bet you're often mistaken for a television personality.'

Unrecorded is how all this week Mam has slowly been getting better, talking a little and taking a more measured view of what her life is to be. I arrive at the hospital at seven and she is already sitting in her blue raincoat and hat ready for our walk along the corridor for a cup of tea. On Tuesday I told her about Aunty Kathleen and how she had died in her sleep. She weeps a little . . . just as, coming into the house on Sunday, she wept remembering Dad. But it passes. And at least she weeps.

My anxiety that there should be no fuss and the word I had with the coroner's clerk which led him to take the reporters on one side were less to do with my own situation than with my mother's. In 1974 the tabloids were not so hungry for sensation as they are now, though even today 'Playwright Finds Aunt's Body' wouldn't be much of a circulation booster. What was bothering me was not the *Mirror* or the *Sun* but the local paper, the *Lancaster Guardian*, an old-fashioned weekly publication where inquests were a staple item, a whole page devoted exclusively to the proceedings of the coroner's court. The paper was read in the village, sold in the village shop, and though there was nothing to be ashamed of in my aunty's death or in the manner of her dying, my mother was about to come back home from the hospital and with the stigma of recurrent mental illness try to face life there alone. The last thing I wanted, or she would have wanted, was for it to be known that her sister too had ended up mentally deranged, dying tragically as a result. What kind of family was this, I imagined people saying, where two sisters were mentally unstable. No, the less said about Aunty Kathleen's death the better.

Vague as Mam was about recent events, including even Dad's death, it was not difficult to evade her questions about Kathleen. I told her that she had died in her sleep, and even the few relatives we had left in Leeds were not told the whole story. 'It's funny Kathleen going like that,' Mam would sometimes say. 'Because she was always a strong woman.'

It perhaps will seem strange and even hypocritical that my precautions against the circumstances of Aunty Kathleen's death becoming known did not then recall to me the similar precautions that had covered up the suicide of my grandfather and which I had found so shocking. That it did not was perhaps because I saw it not as my own shame or any reflection of prejudices that I held but as a necessary precaution to protect my mother against the prejudices of others. But perhaps that was how my grandmother had reasoned fifty years before? At any rate, the similarity (and the symmetry) never occurred to me at the time, and even had it done so I would not have acted differently. As it is I am so fearful of the news coming out I do not look in the *Lancaster Guardian* to see if the discovery of the body is reported or if there is a later account of the proceedings at the inquest, and if friends in the village see such reports no one ever mentions it to me.

Aunty Myra's cremation had been at Lytham St Annes; Aunty Kathleen's is at Morecambe, one as featureless as the other. Kathleen's husband then presumably takes himself off to Australia and is, I imagine, long since dead, as are all the Peels, though my mother perhaps because disencumbered of all her memories lives on into her nineties.

My mother never learns the true circumstances of her sister's death. My brother and I do not tell her, and even before her memory begins to slip away she seldom enquires. Whether Kathleen's disappearance and discovery were reported at the time I never know, and it's not until twenty years later when I am beginning to find out more of the circumstances of my grandfather's death that I eventually look in the archives of the *Lancaster Guardian* for what reports there had been.

The *Lancaster Guardian* is an old-fashioned newspaper with a splendidly parochial attitude to what constitutes news. 'Smelly Sow led to Rolling Pin Attack' is one item; 'Man Steals two Skirts Off Line' another. The paper for 6 September 1974 reports the finding of Aunty Kathleen's body under the heading:

FOUND DEAD

The body of a patient who had been at Lancaster Moor Hospital for the last six months was found in a small wood about a mile from the hospital at 2 p.m. on Tuesday September 3rd. She was Mrs Kathleen Elizabeth Roach (73) formerly of 26 Ruskin Drive, Bare, Morecambe. She was reported missing on Wednesday of last week and police with dogs have been searching since then. It is understood that the body was found by people walking in the wood. The coroner has been informed.

I look for the report of the inquest in the following week's paper. It is not even mentioned.

In 1985 I go over to Ypres in Belgium to search for the grave of Uncle Clarence, my mother's brother killed there in 1917.* I am fifty-one, which is about the age most people get interested in their origins, family history one of those enlivening occupations that these days take up the slack of early retirement. The sense that my own departure is not as distant as it has always seemed adds some mild urgency to the quest, but having found this grave, and having written about it, even then I don't go on to try and find out about the only remaining mystery in my family's history, the death of my grandfather.

However, in 1988 I make a documentary, *Dinner at Noon*, at the Crown Hotel in Harrogate. Without originally intending it to be autobiographical it turns out to be so, with reminiscences of some of the holidays we had had as children and my feelings about our failings as a family. It's perhaps in consequence of this that, stuck in Leeds one afternoon with a couple of hours to wait for a train, I go up to the Registrar's Office and get a copy of my grandfather's death certificate and now, furnished with the exact date of his death, 26 April 1925, I walk along the Headrow to the City Reference Library to see whether I can find out more.

It's a library I have known since I was a boy, when I used to go there in the evenings to do my homework and where I would often see sad old men consulting back numbers of the local papers, done up in a great swatch like a sagging piano accordion. Now it's my turn. However, expecting to be lumbered thus, I'm relieved to find that all the back numbers of newspapers are now on microfilm and so take my place in front of a screen, much as I used to do at a slightly later date but in the same library, on vacations from Oxford when I was reading the Memoranda Rolls of the medieval Exchequer. Now it is the death of my grandfather and I find it in the *Armley and Wortley News*, dated 1 May 1925, the item headed:

NEW WORTLEY MAN DROWNED AT CALVERLEY
Strange Conversation with Friendly Constable
The tragic story of how a policeman, after having been in conversation
with a friend who was depressed, noticed the strangeness of the lat-

* See 'Uncle Clarence' in *Writing Home*, p. 22.

ter's action and followed him only to find that he was dead, was told at an inquest at Calverley on Tuesday on William Peel (55) of 35 Bruce Street, New Wortley, who was found drowned in the canal at Calverley on Sunday.

Mary Ann Peel, wife of the deceased man, said that her husband was formerly a clothing shop manager. In October he became out of work and recently he acquired an empty shop in which to start on his own as a gentleman's outfitter. He had opened this shop last Tuesday and had been somewhat depressed, wondering if he would be a success. On Sunday last he left home just after noon. He did not say where he was going. Police Constable Goodison said that on Sunday last he boarded a Rodley tramcar in company with Peel. He inquired how the new shop in Wellington Road was getting along. Peel seemed rather depressed about it. When Goodison was leaving the tram at Cockshott Lane, Peel's parting words were, 'Goodbye old chap. I hope you make better headway than I have done.'

Constable Goodison left the car and was walking towards his home when, after thinking about what had been said, decided to go back and follow Peel.

'I caught the first available tram to Rodley terminus,' said Goodison. 'I made inquiries there, but failed to find any trace of him. I then searched along the canal bank in the direction of Calverley and when near the University boathouse I saw what appeared to be a stump in the water.'

He judged it to be the body of a man and went to obtain a boat hook. At 3.30 along with two other constables he recovered the body, which he at once identified as that of Mr Peel.

Mr Peel's hat, coat and stick were found on the canal bank, and three letters addressed to his wife, friends and relations were found in the coat pocket. In one of the letters was the passage 'I am going to Rodley by tram this afternoon, and my intention is to find a watery grave in the canal between Rodley and Apperley Bridge.'

A verdict that the deceased man drowned himself while suffering from depression was recorded.

(Interred New Wortley Cemetery.)

Some of the saddest circumstances were not reported at the inquest. When her father had gone out on his last errand Mam was not in the house as she and Dad had gone on a tram-ride themselves, out into the country, courting, but before he left the house that Sunday morning her father had kissed his wife and tried to kiss the other two daughters, but Kathleen would have none of it and as he was going out she said, 'Yes, go out . . . and come back a man,' words that she must have recalled without ever being able to call them back when later that day she had to identify him. But I hear in those words, too, harsh and melodramatic as they are, an echo of that same pent-up rage and frustration that my mother's depression came to induce in me.

Though I now know the precise location of the drowning, near the university boathouse, it's another year at least before I take myself along to look at the place – these involuntary intermissions such a feature of the unravelling of this mystery they call for an explanation. Hardly due to pressure of work or any conscious disinclination, these delays, I see now, are to do with appeasing the dead (the dead being my father as well as my grandfather) and shame at indulging a curiosity I still find unseemly.

My father would not have approved of it nor, I'm pretty sure, would my grandmother. As for my mother, she is by this time no longer in a state of mind where approval or disapproval means very much. How can she disapprove of a son whom she seldom recognises or have feelings about the death of a father she no longer recalls?

Still, while there is no doubt in my own mind that I will go and look at the place, and in due course write it up, these misgivings are enough to reinforce my reluctance. So that knowing I need to locate the spot on the canal that is near the university boathouse, when I find on the OS map for Rodley that there is no trace of a boathouse I am almost relieved, and put it off for another year. I have actually never heard of the university having a boat club, and whether it has one now I doubt. But in 1925 Leeds University is still young, the boat club perhaps a bid to hike what had hither-to been just the Yorkshire College up the scale a bit, rowing, after all, what proper university students do. So eventually I do the sensible thing and look up an older map, and finding that there is (or was) a boathouse after all, with no more excuse drive down to Leeds to find it.

The canal in question is the Leeds–Liverpool and running parallel with it across the valley is the railway, which in 1925 would have been the LMS going up to Keighley and Skipton. In between the canal and the railway is the river, the Aire. Though neither river nor dale has the same picturesque associations as the Wharfe, say, or the Nidd, the Aire is Charles Kingsley's river, the river in *The Water Babies*. Flowing clear out of Malham Cove, it is scarcely at Skipton ten miles away before it slows and thickens and starts to sidle its way through mud banks and the factories and tanneries of Keighley. Unswum and unfished, by the time it reaches Leeds it is as much a drain as it is a river, and at Kirkstall when I was a child it would sometimes steam as it slid through spears of blackened willow-herb past the soot-stained ruins of the abbey. It's hard to imagine that this spot had once been as idyllic and lost to the world as Fountains or Rievaulx, or fancy the monks fetching their sheep down this same valley from Skipton and Malham, where the lands of Kirkstall adjoin those of Fountains.

Rodley is beyond Kirkstall and on the way to Bingley. That trams came this far out of Leeds seems astonishing now, particularly as there is a long hill running down into Rodley, the haul up which must have been at the limit of the trams' capabilities. Down this hill in his Sunday suit and hat came my grandfather.

At Rodley today there is a marina of sorts and the lock has been done up and artful setts laid as part of some environmental scheme. A heritage trail begins or ends here and there are flower beds and whitened stones, much as there used to be outside the guardroom at Pontefract, where I started National Service, and that's what this looks like a bit, and prompts the reflection that some of what passes for care for the environment is just bulling-up, picking up the litter, weeding the cobbles, painting the kerbs . . . a prissy sort of neatness that panders to a sergeant major's feminine notion of what looks nice.

I walk along the canal away from the lock. There is a pub, haunt of the narrow-boat fraternity, I imagine, or a nice little run-out from Leeds; a rusty dredger; a small gasometer, not these days the blot on the landscape it must once have been, preserved and painted now as part of the environmental scheme. A retired couple march past in matching anoraks, walking a Labrador.

Here is a broad-planked swing bridge, for cattle to cross presumably. No boathouse, though, and I walk on, surprised at how far I have come from the lock and wondering at the persistence of Constable Goodison that Sunday afternoon, who didn't know but only suspected and who might, as he must have kept telling himself, running down the towpath and scanning the water, just have been imagining things. People often sound depressed, after all; he'd probably walked it off.

A train scuds past en route for Morecambe and another heading for Leeds: 'Shipley-joining tickets?' the conductor will be saying. Here the canal, the railway, the river and the road all run parallel, and just over the hill to the north is Leeds and Bradford Airport. It's like one of those fanciful landscapes in the boys' books of childhood in which one setting is made to comprehend transport in all its forms: a car, a train, a boat, a plane all going their separate ways as a man (giving the human scale) walks by the canal.

Across the valley is the factory of Sandoz Chemicals, which laces the spring breeze with the scent of lavatories; but look the other way and it is all fields still, the tower of Calverley Church on the horizon and the woods dropping steeply to the canal. And now there is a raised mound, set back from the bank where there are some stones and a tangle of silver birch and sycamore. I trample about in the undergrowth and see that there are foundations here and that this must be the place, only what was once a boathouse is now just a copse, a sinister word nowadays, a setting for sexual assault, the site of shallow graves: a copse is where bodies are found. Aunty Kathleen was in a copse.

On the other side of it and below the canal is the river, a better place to drown oneself perhaps as it's away from the path and with none to see. But there is a bank to be negotiated, mud to be waded through and the water like sludge. The canal is more wholesome; an element of fastidiousness discernible even in self-destruction. Besides, the bank is steep and the water deep, and it's likely Grandad Peel knew where he was coming. Fond of what was then called nature study, he must have taken the same tram-ride and walked this way before, past the boathouse and the water deep enough at the edge to take the boats. These days there would have been rowing on a Sunday but not then, nor many people about either, not straight after Sunday dinner. I imagine men in Sunday suits, dinner interrupted, running along the bank with boathooks. This, I think, is how one would begin it in a film: men in dark suits, running. But why should they run? He was past running for, given up as soon as he had stepped into the water, this man who could be mistaken for a tree stump.

I stand looking at the black water and I wonder whether Grandma ever came to look. Probably not, which makes it worse that I am here, tracking down the place where someone I never knew and about whom I know nothing did away with himself, long before I was born. Have I nothing better to do? Or rather, have I nothing better to write about? I think of the notes he left, the neatly folded coat, the hat and stick . . . the little pile that marked his grave.

Somebody is coming, a woman briskly walking her dog on a leash, and seeing her I am aware how odd and possibly threatening I must look, a middle-aged man standing staring into the water – and suddenly I am my grandfather. I turn and walk back, the dog straining towards me and growling as I pass.

━━━━━━━

'Dad. Dad.'

Mam calls down from her bedroom wanting me to go up and like a child she has to be sure she has my attention before she will deliver her message. Except that I cannot answer her, cannot even say 'Yes?' without confirming her assumption that I am my father. It's a delusion that comes in patches, so that when it passes she is left with a sense of ancient horror.

'We haven't done anything wrong, have we? Neither of us has done anything wrong?'

And the fear that something has happened 'between us' becomes another version of the shameful secret that the car waiting in the car park is on watch for, that the television is tuned to detect and the man hiding in the wardrobe ready to jump out and punish.

Saigon is much in the news and her delusions now begin to include helicopters and ladders at the window. She calls upstairs one morning to say that there is a pigeon outside with a message. At the third time of asking I abandon my attempt to work and wearily go down, telling her that she's imagining things. But there is a pigeon on the doorstep, a racer I suppose that has flown off course, and it does carry a message though it's only the name of the owner. On another occasion she struggles to convince me that there are three huge birds in the garden. I ridicule this but finally go into the garden with ill grace, and of course there they are: three peacocks from the Hall.

Liberal analysts, and in particular the followers of R. D. Laing, if there are still any such, would seize on these misunderstandings as demonstrating how families conspire to label one of their number deluded even when he or she is speaking the truth. Right about the racing pigeon and the peacocks, is she right, too, in thinking I want her out of the way?

Because that's how the descent into delusion always ends up, with Mam going yet again to hospital.

'I think we're on the hospital trail again,' says the cleaning woman in *Soldiering On*: that was always how Dad used to put it and now I do the same.

'You'll kill me if you go on in this way,' I say melodramatically, Mam having woken me up three times in the night. I am thinking of my father, and it takes some self-restraint not to say 'You'll kill me too', though that is what I mean. Of course the only way she is killing me is, in the way of women with men, not letting me have my own way, nor allowing me to lead the relatively liberated life I've lately discovered in London. No chance of any of that at home.

There are periods, though, almost of normality when we get along well enough and yet even then I can see, unreason apart, why it is she so easily conflates my father and myself, if only because I slip so naturally into what had been his retired routine: doing the shopping, much of the cooking and cleaning, and every afternoon taking her for a little run in the car.

One theory advanced, a little too readily I thought, by various of Mam's therapists over the years was that she had slipped into depression because when Dad retired she was deprived of her function in the household. This was to some extent true, as after Dad gave up work he did the baking and most of the cooking and cleaning so there was very little in the house for Mam to do. Her depressions, so the theory went, were called up to provide a reason for the sudden pointlessness of her life.

This has always seemed to me a little glib as Dad had always helped in the house all their married life. They shared the housework as they shared everything else. Retirement may have accentuated this, but the pattern was as it had always been.

On the draining board in the kitchen – which they still called the scullery – there would often be a pan of potatoes, peeled and ready for boiling, and a pan of sprouts and carrots likewise. Dad would have done them first thing that morning – or even the night before; with not enough to occupy his time jobs like this would get done earlier and earlier and long before they needed to be, one meal no sooner cleared than the next prepared.

I have seen similar premature preparations in the homes of other retired couples and it speaks of lives emptied of occupation and proper activity, so that squalor and slatternliness seem almost cheerful by comparison.

Two such pans would be a revealing shot in a documentary film. The two pans in the kitchen, the two people by the fire. Or one. Had he been alone, had Mam 'gone first', that would still have been Dad's way, though he was not without interests, reading, gardening, playing his violin. But excepting always when he had his hands full with my mother there was always time to spare. Had he been fonder of male company or she of company of any sort things might have been different. But they were, as they had always been, inseparable, 'your Dad and me', 'your Mam and me' always the phrases most often on their lips. Joining the Women's Institute when she came to the village, Mam would go off on their trips, but Dad would as often as not go too, utterly unembarrassed that he was the only man in the party.

As her depressions became more frequent such outings must have seemed almost unimaginable, the only outings Dad was now required to make his daily trek to the hospital.

Still, Mam's hankerings for society were not quite extinguished and after his death, in periods of remission, the social yearnings to which she had always been prone would tend to return. They were faltering a little by this time and the cocktail party, a long-standing ambition, was now firmly off the agenda. But television gave her aspirations a fresh direction as, tapping into a new potential audience, it began to preach the delights of retirement and the rolling back of the frontiers of old age through a more active use of leisure.

Trying to wean her off my company and making one of my many attempts to get her to stand on her own feet, I'd been to London for a couple of days, the first time she'd been alone in the house since my father died. When I came back I was encouraged when she said, 'I've started going to classes.'

'What in?'

'Pottery.'

'That's good. Didn't you once go to painting classes?'

'Did I? Oh yes. Only then he said it was for beginners whereas when I got there I found most of them could do it right well, they weren't beginners at all. I think that's what it is with classes, people just go to show off what they can do.'

'Well, it'll be a way of rubbing shoulders.'

And so for a while she went. 'Clay Night' she used to call it, and would come back as often as not with a Stone Age-type ashtray she had made . . . not that anybody in the house smoked.

At such times normality seemed within reach. I even thought she might learn to drive, and gave her one disastrous lesson. I smile to think of it now, but why is it still so inconceivable, I ask myself. I certainly asked myself then, and I'm sure lectured her on the subject, how other people's mothers learned to drive, went Old Tyme Dancing, did aerobics: a friend of mine's mother, not much younger than Mam, was Lord Mayor of Blackburn; what was it about our family that we were disqualified from normal social life, and which kept Dad out of the pub, Mam out of the WI and me, I suppose, out of the Garrick? Clay Night or no Clay Night, it isn't long before we are back sitting on the chair in the passage, lurking about the landing and never stirring out except to scuttle between the door and the car.

'There are lights on in the wood. I think there are people there.'

'It's the Children's Home.'

'No, besides that.'

'What do you want, Mam?'

'To be hung. You won't send me away, will you?'

'No.'

But as Laing and Co. might smugly note, 'No' meant 'Yes' and in due course she was back in hospital.

I knew the doctor in charge as we had been at school together in Leeds. Slightly older than me, he had played Canon Chasuble in *The Importance of Being Earnest* and I had played Cecily. Like me he had been very religious, and I wondered if he was as uneasy about his childhood self as I was about mine. Fortunately the subject didn't come up. I was always nervous of discussing anything but the matter in hand with my mother's various psychotherapists for fear they were taking notes on me too, and that whatever I said, however lightly, would be taken down and held in evidence against me; I was part of the equation.

And perhaps I was, and perhaps Dad was too; maybe we had both helped to make her into this helpless, cringing creature, though how I would find hard to say. She has made me timid too, I thought, hedging round our childhoods with all sorts of TB-fuelled fears and prohibitions that hung about well into middle age. But that is a long road to go down; she is seventy; better to patch her up (more tablets) and sit it out.

And in due course she begins to come round again, though whether this is thanks to the medication or the normal time span to these things I never know. Occasionally she will talk of Kathleen's death, wondering how she could go 'just like that. She was always such a bouncer. What was it exactly?'

'Her heart,' I would say, 'or else pneumonia.' But never, of course, the facts, so that now my secret matches hers, though that is not quite a secret any more and she will from time to time talk about her father and in particular of the Sunday when he died. But the reticence of forty years is hard to throw off, and she does not respond to questions and still feels that it is not a proper subject for conversation.

There are many opportunities for that now as I live at home in the village. It is only for six or eight months, though to me it seems much longer. I am trying to write a play about some contemporaries who every summer rent a villa abroad – the sort of holiday I used to go on myself before being saddled with my mother. Someone is killed in an air crash, who is, I suppose, my friend Francis Hope, who died in the Paris air crash in 1974. It isn't going well, so I don't suppose that with my depression about the play I am any easier to live with than Mam and her depression about practically everything else. I finish the play and it's turned down, a year's work, as I see it, wasted.

My brother and his wife, who are always more decent with my mother than I am, eventually shoulder the burden and Mam moves down to Bristol to live with them. There she stays, regularly hospitalised for depression, with even the periods in between tentative and precarious, never an unshadowed return to the cheerful, funny, affectionate woman she once had been.

Company seems to suit her, or so another hospital psychotherapist suggests, and so she graduates easily from one sort of institution to another, moving directly from the mental hospital to a series of old people's homes in Weston-super-Mare. In the home her memory begins to fail, and as it does so her depression lifts, leaving in its wake a vapid and generalised benevolence.

'This is my friend,' she says of any of the residents who happen to be in the room, and as often as not plants a kiss on the slightly startled cheek.

Going for a run in the car she is full of wonderment at the world, transformed as it is by her promiscuous magnanimity. 'What a lovely council estate,' she says of some grim new development. 'What charming houses.'

Except that now her language is beginning to go, and planted in front of a vast view over Somerset she laughs and says, 'Oh, what a lovely . . . lot of about.'

With my mother losing her memory I find myself wondering whether it can be put down to the ECT she has been given in the past, and so, therefore, if we are to some extent to blame. The stock answer to such questioning is that the memory loss associated with ECT is in the short term, particularly that period of confusion which follows immediately after the treatment, and that otherwise it has no measurable effect on the memory proper.

I am not wholly convinced of this, if only because the proponents of ECT must nowadays feel themselves so blamed and beleaguered that they are forced into demanding from its opponents evidence of its ill effects that is hard and fast and, in the nature of things, impossible to provide. What causes loss of memory? Nobody can be certain. It might be ECT in Mam's case, though her mother had begun to lose her memory at about the same age and would, no doubt, have lost it just as completely as her daughter had she not died in the interim. So both mother and daughter lost their memory; one had ECT, the other not.

Even had we been told that ECT would lead ultimately to a failure of memory in the long term I am not sure, given the circumstances, that we would have done anything differently. Unreachable in her despair Mam was unliveable with, her condition inspiring such strain in Dad that his health was as much a factor as hers.

In the end it was her disease that killed him long before it killed her, the strain of daily visiting over weeks and months and the fifty-mile drive they involved fetching on a heart attack. So, though licensing ECT may have been the wrong thing to do, I feel no remorse, and still think, as I did in that cinema in Oxford Street, when the controversy periodically surfaces that the opponents of ECT don't really know the half of it.

There are comic moments. After one visit I tell Miss Shepherd that Mam's memory is failing her and that I am not sure she knows who I am.

'Well, it's not surprising she doesn't remember you,' said Gloucester Crescent's resident moralist, 'she doesn't see you very often.'

A more common attempt at consolation was to say that, though her memory for the recent past might be failing, it would be compensated for by a more detailed recall of the remoter past. This proves not to be the case. As Mam slowly forgets my father so she forgets her mother and her two sisters, and even eventually who she is herself; the present goes and the past with it.

'Do you remember Dad?' I ask her.

'Oh yes. I remember your Dad.'

'What was he like?'

'Your Dad? Oh well,' and she studies a bit, 'well, he was a love.'

'And do you know who I am?'

'You're a love too,' and she laughs.

'But who am I?'

'Well, now then . . . you're my son, aren't you?'

'Yes. And what's my name?'

'Oh, I don't know *that*,' and she laughs again, as if this isn't a piece of information she could be reasonably expected to have, and moreover isn't in the least distressed not to have. She isn't seemingly distressed by anything much nowadays, even by the hip she broke sometime in 1986 and which has never healed properly. It's painful when she moves and I see her wince, but her memory span is so short it mitigates the discomfort and I'm not sure if without memory there can be such a thing as continuous pain. Sitting with her in the large hot bedroom overlooking the bay at Weston-super-Mare, I occupy myself with such vaguely philosophical speculations, watching as she smoothes the sheet with her thin, blue-veined hands, smoothing and stretching, stretching and smoothing all the weary afternoon.

She has long since ceased to wear her own clothes, which probably wouldn't fit her anyway since she's now so much thinner. These days she's kitted out from a pool of frocks and cardigans that the home must have accumulated and put into anything that's more or less her size.

To begin with we, or rather my brother, protest about this and insist that one of her original frocks be found, so long as it isn't actually adorning one of the other old ladies, which as often as not it is. In which case it's promised for 'next time' or 'when we change her'. Still, as Gordon argues, in a world where so much must seem strange, to be wearing a familiar frock may be a comfort.

As time goes on, though, this argument carries less weight. When she can't recognise her own children and doesn't even know what children are, how can she recall 'the little coatee I got at Richard Shops' all those years ago? Sometimes I'm not sure she's in her own glasses, and maybe her teeth would be a problem if they ever put them in; but then her mouth may have shrunk anyway, so perhaps like her clothes they don't fit either.

So when I go in I'm no longer surprised to find her sitting there in a fluorescent-orange cardigan she would in happier days have unhesitatingly labelled 'common'; or that the skirt she has hitched well above her scrawny knees is Tricel or Crimplene or some tufted material she wouldn't have been seen dead in.

And it isn't only the cardigan and the frock that aren't hers. She has even acquired someone else's name. The nurses, who are not really nurses but just jolly girls who don't mind this kind of job, aren't over-particular about names and call her Lily.

'Hello, Lily, how are we today? Let's lift you up, Lily. You're falling right over.'

'Her name's Lilian,' I venture.

'I know,' says the ministering angel, propping her back up, 'only we call her Lily, don't we, Lily? Give us a kiss.' And vacantly Mam smiles and gives her a kiss.

'You know what a kiss is, don't you, Lily?'

And she does, just, but it will be the next thing to go.

'She's with my brother,' I say if anyone asks who knew her in the village. 'It's down in Bristol.'

To admit she's in a home in Weston-super-Mare is itself a confession of failure, with the nowhereness of Weston a part of it, an acknowledgement that we have run out of patience, washed our hands of her and put her away in Weston, as it might be Reykjavik or Archangel, it seems so remote.

And if I do specify the location I'll often add, 'Except she's not there, you know. She's not anywhere,' and I explain that all her faculties have gone. It's then that people nod understandingly and say 'Alzheimer's'.

'Well,' I say, 'she's failing.' Or has failed, as she now can scarcely speak. But whether it's Alzheimer's I don't know, as she's never had a brain scan that would prove the point . . . though why is the point worth proving except for statistical purposes? But since for twenty-five years or so she's been in and out of institutions – hospitals, mental hospitals and homes – it wouldn't surprise me if her blankness now is partly the result and that she has become institutionalised. This would explain the decay of her powers of speech and her inability to walk just as plausibly as any specific disease.

But my vagueness (about her vagueness) has another, less creditable side. I'm reluctant to ascribe her situation to Alzheimer's because, without it being exactly modish or fashionable, it is a disease or a condition that gets a good deal of coverage as one of the scourges of our time. People are frightened of it; they make jokes about it; it's mainstream stuff. I don't mean that I'd prefer her to be suffering from, living with, dying from something a bit more *exclusive*, it's just that I wouldn't want anyone to think that by putting her situation down to Alzheimer's I was in any way jumping on a bandwagon.

A diagnosis, which is, essentially, a naming, puts someone in a category. Neither Mam nor Dad was ever a big joiner, 'not being able to mix' both their affliction and their boast. So now, faced with a choice of enrolling her in the ranks of those diagnosed and named as having Alzheimer's, I still prefer to keep my mother separate, so that she can die as she has lived, keeping herself to herself.

Except, of course, she does not die. Her bed is in a high bay-windowed room on the first floor, the house one of a row of granite mansions strung like battlements along the side of the hill that overlooks the bay. The prospect from the window is vast, taking in the town, the sands and the distant sea, and some hills beyond that I take to be Wales. The room, though, ignores the view, the plastic-covered chairs arranged in a row with their backs to the window so as to catch all of the place's diminishing life.

Here live four women, each with a high cream-painted hospital bed, a chair, a washbasin and a locker. All the women are incontinent and all are catheterised, a bottle of faint piss tilted under each chair. Cloyingly warm, the room has no particular smell (no smell of urine I suppose I mean), the air refreshed by frequent blasts of Woodland Glade or Ocean Breeze. That if anyone chose to open a window there could be a proper ocean breeze goes by the way.

On the top of the lockers are family snaps: the lurid single photographs of children, or rather grandchildren, of the sort that are routinely taken at primary school; photos of family outings, dead husbands, dead sons. 'Happier days'. There are birthday cards kept long after the big day: 'To the Best Mum in the World', 'To Nan from Toni, Michelle and little Christopher'.

With its broad landings and cavernous rooms, it's hard to think that this gaunt pile in Weston-super-Mare can ever have been a private house or imagine the family that lived in it. Everywhere is carpeted with the predominant colours orange and brown, and with the staircase wide enough to accommodate a chair lift.

'I've been on that thing,' Mam said in her early days here, then adding contemptuously, 'it's nowt.' It was as if it were the Big Dipper.

None of the residents are black yet, though there are one or two black nurses and several cleaners. When in due course blacks take their place among the patients here and in similar establishments it will, I suppose, signal a sort of victory, though hardly one to be rejoiced over as the price of it is a common enslavement to age and infirmity.

The residents are almost entirely women, the only man a voice from a distant room where he is presumably bedfast. I see a handyman occasionally, standing on a ladder changing light bulbs or dismantling a bed. He seldom speaks. There is the clash of a kitchen somewhere in the back, two trolleys outside a door, waiting.

The staff are young mainly and seldom stay long, the only attendant I recognise from the ten years or so I have been coming here now old herself. Doing less and less and with her help increasingly superfluous, she has gradually declined until now she is more nursed than nursing. Shedding her overall and wrapover pinny, she has taken her place among the rest, sitting in the bay window dozing and not looking at the view.

The shallow waves lap over the sands and at night ropes of lights prick out the promenade.

I sit by my mother's bed. She does not look at me or look at all, her eyes open but her gaze dull and unattached. I note her wild eyebrows, the coated tongue, the long lobes of her ears and the downy, crimped and slightly stained skin of her upper lip. A dispassionate inventory this, taken holding her slack hand, which I occasionally bend down and kiss.

She speaks infrequently, and when she does speak it makes less sense, with her words gradually becoming a babble. Second childhood in my mother's case is not just a phrase but a proper description of how skills learned in the first years of her life are gradually unlearned at its end and in reverse order: speech has come out of babble and now reverts to it.

A family drives onto the beach, lets out a romping dog, then arranges the canvas chairs. A man and a child set off barefooted across the sands to the distant sea, as on the promenade an ice-cream van sounds its glutinous unfinished song.

I have talked to only one of the women here besides Mam . . . Hilda, who in the days when she could talk told me she came from Darwen. Now, not knowing where she is, did she realise she had ended up in this unentrancing corner of Somerset she would be as puzzled as my mother whose own odyssey began in Leeds.

The turnover of residents is quite rapid since whoever is quartered in this room is generally in the later stages of dementia. But that is not what they die of. None of these lost women can feed herself and to feed them properly, to spoon in sufficient mince and mashed carrot topped off with rhubarb and custard to keep them going, demands the personal attention of a helper, in effect one helper per person. Lacking such one-to-one care, these helpless creatures slowly and quite respectably starve to death.

This is not something anybody acknowledges, not the matron or the relatives (if, as is rare, they visit), and not the doctor who makes out the death certificates. But it is so.

And if Mam has survived as long as she has it is because, though she can no longer feed herself, she nevertheless is anxious to eat; her appetite remains good and so she is easy (and satisfying) to feed. I spoon in the mince and carrot, catching the bits that dribble down her chin and letting her lick the spoon.

'Joined the clean plate club, Lily,' says the girl who is feeding Hilda, her neighbour. 'Aren't you a good girl?'

Hilda, grim, small-eyed and with a little curved nose and a face like a finch, is not a good girl, turning her head when the spoon approaches, keeping her teeth clamped shut with the spoon tapping to get in.

'Knock, knock,' says the girl.

Somewhere a phone rings. So, leaving the mince, the girl goes to answer it and does not come back. Ten minutes later comes a different girl who clears away the cold mince and carrot and substitutes rhubarb crumble.

While Mam polishes off hers, Hilda remains obdurate, beak closed.

'Don't want your sweet, Hilda?'

Hilda doesn't and it is left congealing on the tray while tea in lidded plastic beakers is taken round, which goes untouched also. So another mealtime passes and Hilda is quite caringly and with no malice or cruelty at all pushed one step nearer the grave.

Whose fault is it?

Her own, a little. Her relatives, if she has relatives. And the staff's, of course. But whereas a newspaper might make a horror story out of it, I can't.

Demented or not, if Hilda were a child there would be a story to tell and blame attaching. But Hilda is at the end of her life not the beginning. Even so, were she a Nobel Prize winner, or not a widow from Darwen but the last survivor of Bloomsbury, yes, then an effort might be made. As it is she is gradually slipping away, which is what this place is for.

The water creeps over the sands.

Coming back to London on the train, I am relieved that I have done my perfunctory duty and need not come again for a fortnight or three weeks; I am still uneasy, though, and would be however often I were to visit.

That there is something not right around homes for the elderly is evident in the language associated with them: it's swampy, terms do not quite fit and categories start to slip. A home is not a home but neither is it a hospital nor yet a hotel. What do we call the old people who live (and die) there? Are they residents? Patients? Inmates? No word altogether suits. And who looks after them? Nurses? Not really since very few of them are qualified. As Mam herself pointed out early in her residency:

'They're not nurses, these. Most of them are just lasses.'

And not knowing what to call them makes getting hold of one difficult, not least for the residents. In a hospital it would be 'Nurse!'. Here it tends to be 'Hello? Hello?', which said to nobody in particular and sometimes to an empty room already sounds deranged. Of course, calling them by name could be the answer, but though the staff all wear their name tags, names are what these lost women are not good at, not being good at names one of the things that has brought them here in the first place. And what do I call them, a visitor? Even if I cared for the word caring, 'Carer!' is not a word you can call down a corridor.

As it is, and feeling like one of those old-fashioned gentlemen who call every policeman 'Officer', I settle for 'Nurse', remembering at the same time Mrs Catchpole, Alan Bates's mother-in-law, who, incarcerated in the geriatric ward at the Royal Free, remarked bitterly of one such whom she called 'Bouncing Betty': 'She's not as highly qualified as she makes out. And she has very hard hands.'

These blurred classifications – a home that is not a home, a nurse who is not a nurse – arise because strictly speaking the people in homes are not ill; it is not sickness that has brought them here so much as incurable incompetence. They are not dying; they are just incapable of living, though capable of being long-lived nevertheless. My mother lives like this for fifteen years.

Now it is a year later or maybe two years. Nothing has changed except that there are new faces in the three other beds, all of them registering differing degrees of vacancy. None of them can talk, though one of them can shout.

I sit in the upstairs room and hold my mother's hand, the skin now just a translucent sheath for the bones, and a hand anyone who comes into the room is free to take and hold as Mam will not mind or even notice. And though there will be no replies forthcoming, having been told it is therapeutic I embark on a conversation.

'Gordon will have been, I expect.

'Set up with their new baby. Grandparents now. You're a great-grandmother. Takes after Ian, Rita says. Fair.

'They're going in for a new fridge apparently. One of those jumbo jobs.'

I have written conversations like this to point up the diminutive stature of our concerns and their persistence even into the jaws of death. But this conversation I now have to fabricate for real is as desultory and depressing as any of my fictions.

'They tell you to talk,' I had once written of a visitor talking to someone unconscious.

'I think it's got past that stage,' says the nurse.

And so it seems with Mam, as nothing I ever say provokes a response: no smile; no turn of the head even.

The staff do it differently; make a good deal more noise than I do for a start, and one of the maids now erupts into the room and seizes Mam's hand, stroking her face and kissing her lavishly.

'Isn't she a love!

'Aren't you a love!

'Aren't we pretty this morning!

'Who's going to give me a kiss?'

The dialogue makes me wince and the delivery of it seems so much bad acting better directed at a parrot or a Pekinese. But, irritatingly, Mam seems to enjoy it, this grotesque performance eliciting far more of a response than is achieved by my less condescending and altogether more tasteful contribution.

Mam's face twitches into a parody of a smile, her mouth opens in what she must think is a laugh and she waves her hand feebly in appreciation, all going to show, in my view, that taste and discrimination have gone along with everything else.

But then taste has always been my handicap, and so here when in this sponged and squeegeed bedroom with an audience of indifferent old women I do not care to unbend, call my mother 'chick', fetch my face close to hers and tell her or shout at her how much I love her and how we all love her and what a treasure she is.

Instead, smiling sadly, I lightly stroke her limp hand, so ungarish my display of affection I might be the curate, not the son.

The nurses (or whatever) have more sense. They know they are in a 'Carry On' film. I am playing it like it's *Brief Encounter*.

'Aren't you good, Lily? You've eaten all your mince.'

And Mam purses her lips over her toothless gums for a rewarding kiss. Twenty years ago she would have been as embarrassed by this affectation of affection as I am. But that person is dead, or forgotten anyway, living only in the memory of this morose middle-aged man who turns up every fortnight, if she's lucky, and sits there expecting his affection to be deduced from the way he occasionally takes her hand, stroking the almost transparent skin before putting it sensitively to his lips.

No. Now she is Lily who has eaten all her mince and polished off her Arctic Roll, and her eyes close, her mouth opens and her head falls sideways on the pillow.

'She's a real card is Lily. We always have a laugh.'

'Her name's actually Lilian,' I say primly.

'I know, but we call her Lily.'

The strip lights go on this winter afternoon and I get ready to leave.

I never come away but I think that this may be the last time I shall see her, and it's almost a superstition therefore that before I leave I should make eye contact with her. It's sometimes for the first time as she can spend the whole hour not looking at me or not seeing me if she does. Kissing does not make her see me nor stroking her hand. A loud shout may do so, though, and certainly if I were to squeeze her arm or cause her pain she would look at me then or even cry out. Otherwise, there is this settled indifference to my presence.

To make her see me is not easy. Sometimes it means bringing my head down, my cheek on the coverlet in order to intercept her eye line and obtrude on her gaze. In this absurd position, my head virtually in her lap, I say, 'Goodbye, Mam, goodbye,' trying as I say it (my head pressing into the candlewick) to picture her with Dad and print her face on my memory, Mam laughing on the sands at Filey with Gordon and me, Mam walking on the prom at Morecambe with Grandma. If this produces no satisfactory epiphany (a widening of the eyes, say, or a bit of a smile) I do it again, the spectacle of this middle-aged man knelt down with his head flat on the bed of no more interest to the other old women than it is to my mother.

Getting no response, I kiss her and go to the door, looking back for what I always think will be the last time. What I want to see is her gazing lovingly after me, her eyes brimming with tears or even just looking. But she has not noticed I've gone, and I might never have been in the room at all. I walk to the station.

'You have given the best,' says a hoarding advertising another home, 'now receive the best.' And in a film faintly would come the sound of the geriatric Horst Wessel, that sad and mendacious anthem, 'I am H-A-P-P-Y.'

Once her speech has unravelled, any further deterioration in her personality becomes hard for an onlooker to gauge (and we are all onlookers). Speechless and seemingly beyond reach, she dozes in the first-floor bedroom in the house above the bay, regularly fed and watered, her hair done every fortnight, oblivious of place and time and touch. In the other beds women come and go, or come and die, my mother outlasting them all. On the horizon ships pass and it is as if her own vessel, having sailed, now lies becalmed, anchored on its own horizon, life suspended, death waiting and in the meantime nothing: life holds her in its slack jaw and seems to doze.

So much of my childhood and youth was lived in dread of her death, never seeing that what would unsettle and unstitch my life much more would be the death of my father. It was his going that had cast the burden of care on my brother's family and myself and sent my mother stumbling into her long twilight.

In the event her death is as tranquil and unremarked as one of those shallow ripples licking over the sands that I had watched so many times from her window. All her life she has hoped to pass unnoticed and now she does.

As a boy I could not bear to contemplate her death. Now when it happens I almost shrug. She dies in 1995, I think. That I am not certain of the date and even the year and have to walk down to the graveyard to look at her gravestone to make sure is testimony to how long she has been waiting on the outskirts of mortality. My father's death on 3 August 1974 I never forget. There was before and after. With my mother nothing changes. Did she look at me the last time I took my leave? I can't remember.

Mindful of the snarl on my father's dead face I make no attempt to see my mother dead. Times are different anyway and in the self-loving nineties death is enjoying less of a vogue. Besides, there is little point in seeking out reminders of mortality. I am sixty myself now and my own reminder.

So while she rests at the undertaker's my brother and I consult our diaries and decide on a mutually acceptable date for the funeral, and I take the train to Weston-super-Mare for what I hope will be the last time now, though getting off at Nailsea, which is handier for the crematorium. It's a low-key affair, the congregation scarcely bigger than the only other public occasion in my mother's life, the wedding she had shrunk from more than sixty years before.

Of the four or five funerals in this book, only my father's is held in a proper church; the rest, though scattered across England, might all have been in the same place, so uniform is the setting of the municipal crematorium.

The building will be long and low, put up in the sixties, probably, when death begins to go secular. Set in country that is not quite country it looks like the reception area of a tasteful factory or the departure lounge of a small provincial airport confined to domestic flights. The style is contemporary but not eye-catchingly so; this is decorum-led architecture which does not draw attention even to its own merits. The long windows have a stylistic hint of tracery, denomination here a matter of hints, the plain statement of any sort of conviction very much to be avoided.

Related settings might be the waiting area of a motor showroom, the foyer of a small private hospital or a section of a department store selling modern furniture of inoffensive design: dead places. This is the architecture of reluctance, the furnishings of the functionally ill at ease, decor for a place you do not want to be.

It is neat with the neatness ill-omened; clutter means hope and there is none here, no children's drawings, no silly notices. There are flowers, yes, but never a Christmas tree and nothing that seems untidy. The whole function of the place, after all, is to do with tidying something away.

In the long low table a shallow well holds pot plants, African violets predominating, tended weekly by a firm that numbers among its clients a design consultancy, an Aids hospice, the boardroom of the local football club and a museum of industrial archaeology.

In the unechoing interior of the chapel soft music plays and grief too is muted, kept modest by the blond wood and oatmeal walls, the setting soft enough to make something so raw as grief seem out of place. It's harder to weep when there's a fitted carpet; at the altar (or furnace) end more blond wood, a table flanked by fins of some tawny-coloured hardwood set in a curved wall covered in blueish-greenish material, softly lit from below. No one lingers in these wings or makes an entrance through them, the priest presiding from a lectern or reading desk on the front of which is a (detachable) cross. A little more spectacular and it could be the setting for a TV game show. Above it all is a chandelier with many sprays of shaded lights which will dim when the coffin begins its journey.

Before that, though, there will be the faint dribble of a hymn, which is for the most part unsung by the men and only falteringly by the women. The deceased is unknown to the vicar, who in turn is a stranger to the mourners, the only participant on intimate terms with all concerned, the corpse included, being the undertaker. Unsolemn, hygienic and somehow retail, the service is so scant as to be scarcely a ceremony at all, and is not so much simple as inadequate. These clipboard send-offs have no swell to them, no tide, there is no launching for the soul, flung like Excalibur over the dark waters. How few lives now end full-throated to hymns soaring or bells pealing from the tower. How few escape a pinched suburban send-off, the last of a life, some half-known relatives strolling thankfully back to the car. Behind the boundary of dead rattling beech careful flower beds shelter from the wind, the pruned stumps of roses protruding from a bed of wood-chips.

My mother's funeral is all this, and her sisters' too; gruesome occasions, shamefaced even and followed by an unconvivial meal. Drink would help but our family has never been good at that, tea the most we ever run to with the best cups put out. Still, Mam's life does have a nice postscript when *en secondes funèbres* she is brought together with my father and her ashes put in his grave.

This takes place in the graveyard in the village where the vicar, the bluff straightforward bearded Mr Dalby, digs the little hole himself and puts together a makeshift service. Consolation is inappropriate as no one is grieving and, the prayers over, we are uncertain what to do. We stand there with the wind threshing the sycamores, wondering if that is all there is and if we can go now.

It ought to be me or my brother who takes charge, but after a moment or two's awkward waiting with wonderful inappropriateness it is my friend Anne, unrelated and now entirely unconnected with the family, who picks up some earth and throws it into the casket, whereupon we all follow suit.

'Well,' I can imagine my mother saying, as she did when excusing some lapse or discounting the gossip, 'well, she's right enough.'

Now we stroll back up to the village where she had come in such despair and anguish of mind twenty-five years before. I still live here with my partner, as the phrase is, who is fonder of the house and the village even than I am. He is thirty years younger than me and what the village makes of this I do not know and now at last I do not care. That, at least, my parents' lives have taught me.

Postscript

The church in our village is not one that Philip Larkin would have thought worth stopping for and I fancy he wouldn't even have bothered to take off his cycle clips. Rebuilt in the early nineteenth century, it's neither frowsty nor much-accoutred but barn it certainly is, a space that on the few occasions I've seen it full never seems so and even a large congregation in full voice sounds thin and inadequate.

I think of this church often these days as it will be where my funeral will doubtless be held and hymn-singing, though I seldom do it nowadays, has always been for me a great pleasure. But not in our village church and I feel sorry for the congregation that has to sing me out.

Nor, I'm afraid, is there much to divert the eye, with few monuments to muse on, no glass to speak of, no screen, just a plainness and lack of ornament that in a small church might be appealing but in a place the size of this seem frigid and bare.

There are, it's true, glimpses through the clear glass of the trees in the churchyard outside, and the churchyard is altogether pleasanter than the church it surrounds. Painted once by John Piper for Osbert Sitwell (his series of paintings of the village now at Renishaw), the churchyard is backed by trees with the beck on one side and a waterfall behind, and it looks over some cottages across the lane and down to the village below.

Not a bad place to end up, I think, except that I shan't, as the graveyard is full and burials nowadays are in the overflow cemetery on the other side of the bypass (built *circa* 1970) and en route for the station. To reach this graveyard means walking down to the end of the village and then, since the A65 is the main road to the Lake District and traffic incessant, taking the underpass put in specifically for cows and schoolchildren living south of the village. The tunnel also carries the beck which, if in spate, tends to flood the gate at the other end and so means wet feet.

None of which matters if coming by car (or hearse), though mourners should be prepared for a long wait at the bypass and an unhearselike scoot across when there's a rare break in the traffic. On the left as you go down the road is one of Coultherd's fields, which if it's a weekend will have its quota of caravans and the occasional camper.

The cemetery is small and surrounded by trees, sycamore mostly and horse chestnut but not the preferred beech. When we first came to the village in 1966 there was still a chapel of rest here, but that has gone, though a patch of red and buff tiles still marks the spot, some of which we bought from the parish and now form our kitchen floor. The only other building is a dilapidated shed in the south-eastern corner which also shelters the water butt.

The graves are in rows, some of them unmarked and very few of them with kerbs and plots, the graveyard largely laid to grass. My father's grave and my mother's ashes are on what is currently the last row on the eastern edge. He died in August 1974 aged seventy-one, and my mother nearly twenty years later when she was ninety-one. His neighbours in death are folks he may have known to say 'Good morning' to, most of the people buried here on those sort of terms, some of them families like Cross and Kay and Nelson who have been in the village for generations.

When I ordered the gravestone for my father I made some effort not to have one of the shiny marble jobs with gilt letters that most people seem to go in for. I wanted it plain, as plain as one of the war graves in France. And so it is, though not looking quite like that, as stained by damp and with too much in the way of lettering and so rather crowded.

On the grave is a kitchen storage jar which we use for flowers, anything more elaborate likely to be stolen. The flowers I periodically put there are from the garden, which Dad would have liked, though in the summer when the grass grows the place is a sea of dog daisies which he would have liked more, the whole graveyard a haven for wild flowers. One in particular grows here and is a favourite of mine, the water avens (*Geum rivale*), which Richard Mabey describes as having 'cup-shaped flowers, flushed with purple, pink and dull orange', which for some reason suggests strawberries though the strawberry flower is white. He also says it's 'a glamorous and secretive species', and in the cemetery it grows round the water butt where I fill the storage jar.

Filling the jar at the water butt reminds me of a similar watering place, a tap and an iron trough in New Wortley Cemetery down Tong Road, where I used to go with my grandmother as a child to tend that unmarked grass-covered tump that was my grandfather's grave. Because it was unmarked I was never certain of its precise location, and finding my way back there from the cistern, both hands gripped round a brimming vase, was never easy. Grandma is a tall woman, but she is likely to be bent down over the grave and invisible behind the gravestones. I dodge in and out among the graves, holding the heavy vase, trying to find a way through this sepulchral maze. I think I am lost and will never find it but then that is what I always think and suddenly, rounding an angel, I come upon Grandma on her knees snipping at the grass with her kitchen scissors.

The anemones she has bought at Sleights, the greengrocer on the corner of Green Lane, are put in the vase and we thread our way out, walking back hand in hand down the main avenue towards the cemetery gates with the battlements of Armley Gaol looming up behind us.

Sometimes as I'm standing by their grave I try and get a picture of my parents, Dad in his waistcoat and shirtsleeves, Mam in her blue coat and shiny straw hat. I even try and say a word or two in prayer, though what and to what I'd find it hard to say.

'Now then' is about all it amounts to. Or 'Very good, very good', which is what old men say when a transaction is completed.

Written on the Body

MATRON: I don't know what Mr Franklin will do without you.

HEADMASTER: Don't you? The first thing he will do is abolish corporal punishment, the second thing he will do is abolish compulsory games. And the third thing he will do is abolish the cadet corps. Those are the three things liberal schoolmasters always do, Matron, the first opportunity they get. They think it makes the sensitive boys happy. In my experience sensitive boys are never happy anyway, so what is the point?

(Forty Years On)

I sit at my desk in Form 4A, at thirteen just into long trousers, and noting, as he stumbles through some French translation, that since last week Ackroyd's voice seems to have broken. Stones across the aisle is growing out of his blazer, his head down on the desk, chin resting on one thick-wristed hand, the other out of sight somewhere beneath his desk. Stuart Jennings has shaved, I see, the faint moustache he has had for a month or two now gone, and even Simpson, nearly a year younger than me, is starting to fill out and, silhouetted against the window onto Otley Road, I note how thick his eyelashes have become.

The chief burden of my youth (and I do feel it as a burden) is that I take a long time growing up, and on that score feel myself set apart, stigmatised even. Boys matured later then than they do now, but none as late as I seem doomed to do when even at sixteen I am still a boy in a classroom of young men. They complain about acne; I long for it. They shave; I have no need to. In those days at the onset of puberty boys abandoned their fringe and 'put their hair back', a process which means enduring a few weeks of mockery while they look like hedgehogs before settling down to floppy adulthood. This hurdle, too, I fail to take, my hair at sixteen still the fringe it has always been and which it has remained ever since. So whereas my friends are no sooner out of the school gates before they thrust their school caps, the badge of boyhood, into their pockets, I don't bother. Why should I? I still look like a boy.

That I am going to lag behind other boys in growing up I have known since I was twelve, when it begins to happen for others in my class but not for me. And it is when I'm still immured in my impregnable boyhood that I begin to watch.

No matron ever charts the growth rate of her charges as sedulously as I do: half naked in PT, crucified twice weekly on the wall bars, I scrutinise the armpits of my classmates on the look-out for the first tell-tale graze of hair. I know the line of each neck, detecting the first bulge of an incipient Adam's apple even before its owner, and noting glumly not only that Hollis has respectable armpits but that a thin column of hair is now beginning to climb towards his navel.

Had Leeds Modern School been imbued with as much public school spirit as the headmaster fondly hoped, we would all have been herded into the showers after gym or games, thus rendering this furtive charting of my fellows' incipient manhood redundant: one glance at their pelvic regions would have told all. Fortunately, though, whether we take a shower is optional; after gym there is never the time and since I generally sidestep games the problem does not arise. But with, as it were, nothing to show throughout most of my adolescence, I live in fear of having to take my clothes off, managing somehow to avoid it during the whole of my schooldays and, more surprisingly, the entire two years I spend in the army. Occasionally I read of women who in the eighteenth and nineteenth centuries were able to serve as soldiers without their sex ever being discovered. It's no surprise to me, who, through school,

1 My father, aged twelve

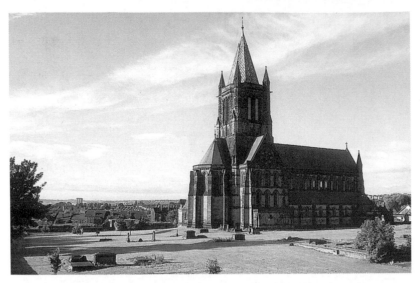

2 St Bartholomew's Church, Armley

3 & 4 My parents, shortly before they were married

5 Grandma Peel

6 Grandad Peel

7 Dad, on holiday as a young man

8 Mam and Gordon with Aunty Kathleen

9 Aunty Myra

10 Jordy and Ossie (see page 65)

11 Aunty Kathleen in manageress mode

12 Otley Road, 1950

13 Among the marigolds in Grandma's garden, Gilpin Place, 1947

14 Dad in the Otley Road shop

15 Mam on an outing with Somerset Maugham, 1952

16 Joint Services School for Linguists, Cambridge, 1953

17 With Mme Chernysheva in the garden of Salisbury Villas, Cambridge, 1953

18 Self-portrait, Oxford, 1955

National Service and university, am never caught with my pants down.

This elongated boyhood goes on, it seems to me, for years; furtive and ridden with guilt, a less carefree boy it would be hard to find. Not that I have much to be guilty about: it's true I discover wanking at the age of thirteen but in all my time at school I never touch or am touched by a single one of my schoolfellows, though in a provincial grammar school this is not unusual. It's also that, for all the prurient surveillance which I keep on my classmates, what action there is generally manages to escape my notice.

The best-looking boy in 4A is Ken Thomson, a greengrocer's son from Kirkstall. He is a sleepy kind of boy who sits in the second row of the class by the window, his back to the wall, surveying the class with a forgiving smile. He is an athlete and a good swimmer, broad-shouldered with a narrow waist and a body so perfect that in gym or the baths I find it hard to look at him. He is my age but unlike me is long past puberty. His nickname is Tommo. I have no nickname as there has never been any need for one.

Another boy in the class is Briggs, who is poor, quite shabby and not always very clean. With a cheeky face, wild hair and thin as a whippet, he, too, is good at games and nippy on the wing but with none of Tommo's slow Roman grace.

We are getting changed after swimming in the school baths. This is always hectic and hurried because Mr King, the PT master, invariably keeps us in the baths longer than he should and afterwards rampages up and down the aisles banging the doors of the cubicles and shouting at us to get a move on as the bell has long since gone. I am changing in a cubicle opposite Thomson, who is sharing with Briggs, and fearful of the displeasure of Mr King, who doesn't like me as I can only just swim and can't dive at all, I have dutifully hurried up, and so I'm almost dressed when I look over to the opposite cubicle where I can see that neither Thomson nor Briggs has even got his shirt on.

'Are you not ready yet?' I say, smugly. 'I'm dressed.' The two boys, who seem to be busy with something below the level of the cubicle door, look up slightly startled but also with a smile of both pity and contempt, and I can still feel the contempt fifty years later. They obviously know something I don't. At which point Mr King starts driving the class out, ready or not, and Thomson and Briggs hurry into their clothes and join the line-up outside, shirts hanging out and still half-dressed, and so get bollocked by Mr King, but only half-heartedly as they're both good swimmers.

It's only when we get back to the classroom that I realise that what they were looking at below the level of the door was each other, and what they were doing was tossing off, something which I've only just discovered how to do, and feel far from easy about, and needless to say mention to no one.

Why I remember so vividly an incident that I don't altogether understand at the time, I'm not sure. True, it makes me feel 'out of it', but plenty of things do that . . . chiefest, of course, that I am still a boy when most of the class are virtually men. But what puzzles me and makes a lasting impression is the disparity between the boys, one flawlessly handsome, the other nice enough but skinny and a bit of a runt. Sex, it seemed, didn't require equality between the participants or even parity of charm, just as in this case a cheerful and seemingly guiltless collaboration in its mischief.

This wasn't a lesson I was ever going to take to heart, or at any rate not until it was almost too late. Looking at old photographs of my school class then, I see that we all look untroubled and even happy, but I am filled with pity for myself, and at how little I know and how long it is going to take me to learn it. Thomson and Briggs know it already, and one component of that unforgotten look they give me across the wet corridor is that they share a secret I have not yet discovered, namely that there is no shame in this mischief, only pleasure, and that not to know this, as I plainly do not, is to be a fool.

There are plenty of boys in the class . . . Gedge, Stones, Maine . . . who, seeing it happening, would either have shouted encouragement or nipped across to have a look, even take part. But I am not that kind of boy. Or I am, but I can't let on. I think of their wet hair, the chlorine on the cold flesh, one body skinny and hard, the other smooth and classically proportioned. Both now in their seventies and this episode, so vivid for me still, by them buried or forgotten.

Two years after this incident nothing much has happened. I am still a boy, my anatomical clock seemingly stopped. Were it not for the prospect of National Service I might be easier in my mind about being so slow to grow, but my looming nightmare is that I shall still be in my unfledged state when, aged eighteen, I go for my army medical, so my last years at school turn into a race between puberty and the call-up. I know of no way of hastening the process, but I try. Somewhere I have read that it is the thyroid gland that controls growth and that one of its constituents is iodine. So I disinter our ancient bottle of iodine from the back of the bathroom cupboard; it is brown and ridged (and therefore poison) but I put it to my nose and deeply inhale, and even venture to lick the fatal cork.

That I do not achieve maturity until I am well past sixteen, though it blights my boyhood, I now regard as a blessing, this protracted pregnancy of puberty constituting an education more enduring and exclusive than any I receive courtesy of Leeds Modern School. It is an education in contraries: whereas in class and in anything to do with books I am always one of the leaders, in matters of the body I am among the last, the lessons in this parallel instruction written on the flesh. Or not written, that is the trouble. It is in those years from thirteen to seventeen that the conviction takes hold that, full membership having been denied me so long, I will never thereafter be a proper member of the human race, and will always to some extent be set apart. I am such a late starter it seems to me there is hardly any point in joining, still less catching up.

Thus it is that, though not ungregarious by nature, I have never since been a joiner, have avoided clubs and societies, and particularly those where women are not included; the absence of women, it seems to me, always bringing out the worst in men. Unfortunately until well into my twenties I regard sex as a club too, and one to which I have no hope of belonging. This begins at school, where sex seems an extension of organised games: the boys who are good at one are likely to be good at the other. So being excused games was also being excused life. There is always talk, of course, but skinny, fearful and prudish, I take no part in these discussions, partly because I haven't yet acquired the proper equipment, but also because I am 'religious' and 'not that kind of boy', and so am thought to disapprove. I think I disapprove, too, though I am careful to overhear what is being said, while not always appreciating what my classmates get up to. Innocent yet prurient, I am an unattractive youth.

In the plays that I have written characters often recur who are, in some respect or other, maimed: a boy with a club foot; a girl who, as they used to say, is not all there; a young man with mysterious eczema, and another who inflicts on himself a tattoo. They are individuals who are in various ways stigmatised. Having suffered nothing that could properly be regarded as a stigma (though the need to write sometimes seems so), that such characters so often smuggle themselves into my writing I put down to this period in my boyhood when I felt marked out. Marked out, because still unmarked.

I am conscious that to someone genuinely stigmatised – disfigured or crippled, say – such fictionalisations will seem both fanciful and exploitative, projected as they are from the experience of a boyhood protracted, which though it did not seem so when I was going through it was actually both brief and not uncommon. Still, a writer has to use whatever is to hand in the way of experience; he or she is in the business of making mountains out of molehills. I am not sure if the metaphor should come from vaccination or homeopathy, but it takes only a pinch of an experience to inform the imagination and body forth the whole.

So I have never regretted that time or the wretchedness that came from being a late developer. While looking in the mirror is not in itself an inducement to reflection, what we find there can be the beginning of wisdom. A boy sees acne, a girl small breasts, and another breasts that are too large; a small dick may look like an affliction but an over-large one may be an embarrassment too. We are self-stigmatised, our supposed shortcomings just one of the several educations of the heart.

As with many long-awaited occurrences, when puberty actually does arrive I hardly notice. I am seventeen, having a reluctant holiday with my mother, reluctant because I feel this is my father's job, not mine, but as usual he is unable to get away from the shop and I am her only available companion. And companion is exactly what I feel like; one of those downtrodden spinsterly attendants one saw then, but less often now, trailing after their employers at Harrogate or the seaside, buffers against loneliness. Actually almost anyone would be better company than me, who's sullen, moody and embarrassed at being too old to be on holiday with his mother. Which I am, though I don't look it.

It's Whitsuntide and we are staying in a suburban boarding house in Whitby. In the days after I'd found out about wanking I used to rush home from school at dinner time, get one in before the meal and then another before I went back to school. Those hectic, rapturous and guilt-laden times are long since gone, and my religious fervour has in any case put a brake on the self-abuse, sex and devotion thought to be more incompatible in 1951 than they are today. My body still seems to be on hold. There has been no progress on the pubic hair front that I can see, and on the watched-pot principle I've stopped checking.

It's early afternoon and my mother is waiting downstairs to go out so it's a far from ideal moment, but with nothing better to do and less out of desire than curiosity to see if anything's happened I lie on the bed in the boarding house back bedroom and pull myself off.

It's hardly the unstoppable gusher I might have hoped for but this time at least there is something. I'm going to be all right.

I don't know it at the time but there is an appropriateness in my first coming in the setting of a boarding-house bedroom; it had been in a boarding house that I was conceived sometime over the August Bank Holiday of 1933 at Morecambe or Filey. Not Whitby, though; that would be too neat.

But as the newly arrived young man descends the staircase before spending the afternoon on the sands with his mother, to whom I remember I was particularly foul that day, I feel for him only pity.

'If only I'd known.'

'Known what?'

'Oh, just known.'

Having made manhood as it seems to me just in time, when in August 1952 I go off to the York and Lancaster Regimental Depot at Pontefract Barracks to begin my National Service I am still far from adult. A puny boy, I have turned into a lanky young man, looking, in my khaki and beret, not unlike those underfed youths in outsize Wehrmacht uniforms, paraded before the Movietone cameras early in 1945 to demonstrate how far Nazi fortunes had sunk that the Fatherland must needs be defended by such children. Now it is my turn.

━━━━━━━

MRS HOPKINS: Anyroads, you seem to know a lot about them.

HOPKINS: Who, lesbians? Yes, well, I come across them in literature.

MRS HOPKINS: I hope it is in literature and not in Huddersfield. Course it's all right if you're educated. That makes it all carte-blanche. Well, I was the one that wanted you educated. You want to remember that when you're running your mother down.

HOPKINS: I don't.

MRS HOPKINS: And you're not, are you?

HOPKINS: What?

MRS HOPKINS: That?

HOPKINS: A lesbian?

MRS HOPKINS: No, the other.

HOPKINS: Mam, I'm nothing, Mam.

(*Me, I'm Afraid of Virginia Woolf*)

It is some time in 1950, while passing the First Church of Christian Science at the top of Headingley Lane, that I come to the conclusion that, all things considered, I am homosexual. The church has since moved to more modest premises and the imposing Portland stone temple that was witness to this boyish assessment is now an adjunct of Leeds Girls' High

School. It would have been evening and the chances are I was out for a walk. 'Going out for a walk, are you, love? Don't go anywhere lonely.' Mam is making a lampshade and Dad is playing along to the wireless on his violin. Television has not long been started; I have never even seen it and we still cling to the wireless, hoping it won't catch on.

Evenings are generally like this. I go out for a walk and visit the library on North Lane. Mam and Dad go to bed about nine, and when I come back I take them a cup of tea. My lonely patrols take me all over the still gaslit streets of Headingley, Woodhouse and Meanwood, the world to me at fifteen suddenly a place of inexpressible wonder. I marvel at the wind streaming through the beech trees on the edge of Beckett Park, the colours of the rain-washed flags, and the lights of Leeds laid out below Woodhouse Ridge. That is the way I will have gone on this particular evening. Down Wood Lane and along the path up to the Ridge, then cutting through one of the ginnels into North Hill Road or Cumberland Road, lined with the great mansions of nineteenth-century wool merchants, now hostels for the university or flats for lecturers. This brings me back into Headingley Lane, as off it run the Richmonds, and somewhere in Richmond Avenue is the reason I've taken to roaming these suburban streets on summer evenings: a boy, a couple of forms below me at school, with whom I am hopelessly infatuated, and to whom at this time I have scarcely spoken, and seldom do much, and he certainly never knows the part he plays in my life.

'There was a time when meadow, grove and stream,/ The earth, and every common sight, /To me did seem/ Apparelled in celestial light.' We had done Wordsworth for School Certificate, and at fifteen this seems to me not so much poetry as a statement of fact. Patrolling the streets on these 'rain-ceased evenings' it is just what I feel, though the cause of the world's transformation is plainer to me than it was to Wordsworth. It is love, as I have no hesitation in dubbing this feeling that sends me walking the streets; not to meet the loved one particularly, which I never actually do, still less anybody else (which I didn't know you did). It is just to look wide-eyed at the world.

Still, if love can transfigure Leeds, it isn't, it seems to me, just an adolescent phase. No. There is no doubt about it, and I cross the road to the
white Portland stone temple, I am homosexual.

Enlisting in the ranks of deviancy, though, has nothing to do with sex.
How can it, since I've never had any sex? It is as if someone who has never
been to a football match now decides which team he will support. With
me it is all looking, not doing, though the looking, I know, is always at my
own sex. It is a fate, too, a destiny, and one, it seems to me, that rules out
any possibility of happiness, which I think of not as a mood that comes
and goes, but as a goal, a place one arrives at . . . or in my case, not.

The problem, it seems to me then, is less an emotional than a mathemat-
ical one. If, as the papers sometimes say (and they say very little at this
time), one in ten men are homosexual; this means that the odds against one
meeting, falling for Mr Right, are ten times greater than if it's Miss Right
one is looking for. And the chances of Mr Right falling for me in return
make the odds against it astronomical. I see it all in terms of love and
romantic passion, the thought of sex with the loved one scarcely figuring –
and the thought of sex with anyone but the loved one not figuring at all.
Had it done so, I might have come to my senses – and that phrase exactly
describes it – much sooner. Where sex is concerned, what I find hard to
believe is that two people, boy and girl, or boy and boy (girl and girl never
occurs to me), can ever be of one mind. That one might desire the other,
that I understand since it's my permanent state of mind, from fifteen
onwards. But that that feeling might be returned, let alone acted upon, is
beyond my comprehension. The same sex, the other sex . . . whatever alterations are made to the parts, the equation seems to me impossible. How
can the desire of one person intersect with the desire of another? And produce the line, however long, they will never intersect; human beings are
parallels, never meeting, distinct, separate, each one moated and fortified,
on and on to infinity. It's this sense of impossibility that gives me, as knowing and lascivious as any other boy of that age, a seeming innocence.
Because I do not believe sex can happen, I seldom notice when it does, and
some of this incredulity has stayed with me all my life.

Fervently Christian though I am, it never occurs to me to think that my feelings are wrong, still less perverse, even though I am not at this time the least bit open-minded but illiberal and censorious rather. But how can a state of mind or heart that so transforms the world and vivifies it and makes each day count, painful though it is while filling me with melancholy and longing, how can this be other than good? And though there is no one in whom I can easily confide, I know instinctively that these unrequited affections, a succession of which will see me through my teens and, on and off, twenty years or so after, are the only education worth having. It isn't an education which I would have elected to undergo, but nor do I wish it away, then or now.

Still, the most bigoted clergyman would have been gratified by the degree to which I translate these longings into action, i.e. not at all. The objects of my affection are never aware of the place they hold in my heart, or that I am so primed with the details of their existence that I can at any moment of the day pinpoint their whereabouts. But so remote am I, and so aloof, they may not even think of me as a friend. None long to know me as I long to know them; all are normal, as I think of it; none, as I also think of it, are queer.

Though I know in my heart I am not mistaken, I still cling to the hope that these feelings (the feelings I have had for as long as I can remember) are 'just a phase', that this is a stage everybody goes through, and since at fifteen I am still technically a boy, not yet having achieved puberty, I kid myself there is still time.

What could trip the switch that will divert me from one sex to the other, I do not speculate. I try and pretend to myself there are girls I find attractive, but there aren't, and none find me attractive; but since our school is not co-educational, there's not much chance to find out.

The incentive, though, is always to be 'normal', or at least (as in so many other departments) like everyone else. Still, there is a part of me that takes pride in the fact that, for all its miseries, not being normal is to have been singled out, though for what, except continuing frustration and unhappiness, I find it hard to say.

I study as if they are code books the works of writers I have been told are homosexual, though of course they cannot at this time openly admit it. There is Stephen Spender, whose autobiography *World Within World* is on this score thought rather daring, though I am puzzled that he has subsequently got married. How could this be, homosexuality, as I see it, some sort of Devil's Island from which there is no escape? There is Auden, about whom I am not sure, though a careful study of the pronouns in the love poems seems to indicate that his affections might just go either way. There is Denton Welch, who is a little over-sensitive for my taste, and who, like me, seems only to gaze. Most satisfactorily, though, there is A. E. Housman, whose affections are unspoken (or spoken of as unspoken), which is what mine always are, and who regards love as a doomed enterprise, right from the start. Of his life and the object of his affections I know nothing, but as I roam the streets of Headingley in 1950 I feel he is the one I might tell it to, though what this 'it' was I would have been hard put to say.

As it is, I share my shameful secret with no one, though I have a friend at church, Robert Butterfield, who is older than I am, and who seems to take it for granted without being told, just as I know without being told that he is the same way. Did I not know, it would be hard to deduce from his demeanour, camp (at any rate in Leeds) not yet having been invented. Robert is so far from camp he's actually dangerous, prone to sudden rages and denunciations, scathing pronouncements on friends' characters that seem to me far too outspoken. Robert keeps a notebook and has unchanging, adult handwriting which I envy, mine large, obviously immature and changing from one day to the next. He has already done some of his National Service in the RAF, but has apparently been invalided out. He retains, though, a fondness for boots and heavy shoes which he keeps highly bulled. Religious, fond of music, and well read, he seems to have no job and lives at home, his brother and sister part of the same group of friends I belong to at St Michael's Church.

Far and away the most sophisticated and knowing member of our group, he is worldly, mocking and above all grown up. He has come to some conclusions about his character, decided what he is and where he is going. I like to think I am like that too, but only need to compare our handwriting to know this is not the case. Still, he seems to know what I am like and when he sums up my character, not always favourably, I am nevertheless flattered. A mystery to myself, sloppy and longing for definition, it pleases me that someone should have some notion of what I am like, because I don't.

We are both queer, that at least I do know, though I make him impatient because I am less resigned to it than he is, holding hands with the occasional girl (the furthest it ever gets), an effort at conformity he does not see the point of and which triggers off one of his rages.

Periodically he disappears, and it's only later I find these unexplained absences are time spent in a local mental hospital. It's not on this account, though, that we drift apart. I go into the army, and then am away at Oxford, so I see him very little. I am shocked, but somehow unsurprised, when in 1966 I hear that he has committed suicide.

It's Robert who gets me to read Denton Welch's journals, Stephen Spender's *World Within World* and the early novels of Mary Renault, books which, if you spotted them on someone's shelves, told you all you needed to know about their sexual proclivities. And told the police, too, though that might seem fanciful. But this is the 1950s, the period of the Montagu case and the suicide of the pianist Mewton-Wood, both casualties of the campaign against homosexuality conducted by the vicious and bigoted Home Secretary at the time, David Maxwell Fyfe. It's hardly surprising if to someone as timid as I am the very act of falling in love seemed to put you on the wrong side of the law.

The sight of such tell-tale books in someone's house ought then to signify safe ground: here at least there is no need for discretion. Perversely, never having chosen to be part of the homosexual club in the first place, I just wince at the implied complicity, and am bashful and ill at ease.

It's the same later on in life, where I find myself occasionally invited to all-male parties and where I resent the assumptions about my character and inclinations such an invitation implies, and find the uninhibited talk both tedious and embarrassing. This duly marks me out as stuffy and closeted, which may well be true (and was certainly true then), but since homosexuality is a differentness I've never been prepared wholly to accept in myself, why, I think, should it be so readily taken for granted by others, and I want nothing of their covert camaraderie.

As I am writing this I notice outside my window a man standing on the corner. It's nearly 1 o'clock, when the Hare Krishna van is due to park down the street in order to distribute free curry to the poor of the neighbourhood. Anticipating its arrival, a small crowd usually gathers, sitting on the edge of the pavement or lounging against the wall. The man on the corner obviously wants no part of this enforced conviviality, though he is as hungry and needy as the others. So now he waits, and when the van arrives and the queue subsides, having shown himself not too eager, and so set apart from the rest, he walks down the street to collect his lunch. That is me.

Whether my parents take note of these early torments, I never know. Nothing is ever said and I wonder if they even talk about it to each other. Only once does my father ask me outright if I am a homosexual, though not, it hardly needs to be said, in so many words, and in circumstances that now seem comic, though I do not think so then.

It is not until my first year in college that I become aware that there are fashions in clothes, a fact of life which, like other facts of life, the young nowadays seem aware of very much earlier than we were, the subtlest distinctions in footwear, for instance, now obvious to a ten-year-old.

With us, it is trousers. There had been no men's fashions that I know of until the fifties. Women have had the New Look but there was nothing comparable for men, suits or sports coat and flannels the general rule. There are variations in quality, certainly, but no discernible differences in style. By the time I go up to Oxford this has begun to change, particularly in the trouser department; narrow trousers now very much the vogue. Unable to afford a tailored version, I take mine along to the only place in Headingley which does alterations, the local dry cleaners, but this fashion not yet having reached Leeds, the motherly lady who does the sewing is not cognisant of the look I am after, so when the trousers come back they are narrowed but only at the ankle, so that had I worn them I would have looked like a West Indian immigrant or a circus clown.

Eventually I go to a proper alteration tailor but they are puritanical about it, refusing to take them in beyond a pretty conventional sixteen inches, when the least I am prepared to settle for is fifteen inches. It's odd, the relationship between fashion and morals; at this time I have just begun to study medieval history and in the fourteenth century it was very much an issue, and in Leeds, it seems, it still is.

Despairing of finding an understanding seamstress I decide to have a go myself, and painstakingly chalk out the necessary line, and sew along it, taking them down to under fourteen inches round the ankle. In these extraordinary trousers, which must have made me look like the late Max Wall, I parade before my wondering parents.

'You can't go out like that,' Mam said. 'People will think you're one of them.'

Whereupon Dad, who was even more shocked than she was, said (and the question must have had a long gestation), 'You're not one of them, are you?'

'Oh, Dad,' I think I replied, as if the question was absurd. 'Don't be daft.'

But I never wore the trousers.

To have lied like that ought to be shaming, even fifty years after the event. That it doesn't shame me is because to have said 'Yes, I am "one of them"', or in today's terms to have come out, would have made both of them deeply, and as I saw it needlessly, unhappy. Besides, if I am one of them, it is only in theory. Nothing has ever happened, except a persistent yearning for this friend or that. And had I said 'Yes', prey to the prejudices of their generation they would have assumed I hung around public lavatories, interfered with little boys, or even got done up in drag, none of which I ever have any inclination to do.

Whether my nonchalant and implied denial satisfied Dad or not, the subject was never raised again, not even much later in his life when I learned to talk to him more, and when, I suppose, it might have been possible. The incident, though, found its way into one of my TV plays, *Me, I'm Afraid of Virginia Woolf*, and the passage quoted at the head of this chapter, with Dad turned into Mam and me into Hopkins, a polytechnic lecturer, having tea together in the basement of Leeds Town Hall.

The irony is that, subject though my parents were to the prejudices of their own and succeeding generations, it didn't mean that when they met someone as exuberantly homosexual as Russell Harty they weren't captivated. He called them Walter and Lilian after just one meeting, the only one of my friends ever to use their first names; he played the piano while Dad accompanied him on the violin, and went round the house envying Mam her antiques and Staffordshire figures, and altogether delighting them both.

'He's grand, is that Russell,' Dad said.

'Well, he's one of them,' I ought to have said, but if I had they probably wouldn't have minded. It was only if it got into the family that there was cause for concern.

—

MAM: There's no sign of him getting off.

DAD: So? What you want to think is that it's better for us if he doesn't. Once he starts courting, there won't be any more of these little runs to Harrogate. He won't be fetching you flowers or following you round antique shops. Miss Right will put a stop to all that.

MAM: I wouldn't want him not getting married just because of us.

DAD: I didn't say it was because of us. I'm just saying, count your blessings.

Pause.

DAD: I wonder where he goes out on a night for these walks? Where does he go? Where is there to go?

(*Cocktail Sticks*)

In those days laden with smoke and dust, the skies over west Leeds produce dramatic sunsets, the lingering afterglow of which is often tinged with green. It is a spectacle that, in the early evening, will often draw me to the fringes of Beckett Park above the Aire Valley and a view that takes in the sky over Kirkstall and Armley. Which is what I try to do, too, take it in, though without knowing what it is I'm looking for, or why I feel the need to gaze.

Nor is it entirely wholehearted. I seldom look long enough, it seems to me, the impulse to stay or go never entirely resolved, and confronted with a mystery I cannot fathom or even adequately consider, my contemplation is impatient, insufficiently rapt and invariably curtailed. It's partly that, ever timid, I know that a young man (in a raincoat probably) hanging about in a park at dusk, is open to misinterpretation. And it is always dusk: at the going down of the sun, yes; in the morning, never.

Still, these half-hearted appointments with the sunset sky are the start of writing. If I can manage to put the sky into words, get it down on paper, then, as I see it, I will be released from the unrest it makes me feel. So I come home and scribble down phrases like 'hushed departure', 'sunset's cooling fires' or 'the embers of the day', wondering as I do if this, too, is just a phase as maybe love is. I show what I write to nobody.

It takes me years, though, to see that the heavens have no secret, at any rate for me, and that, however often I stand to for the sun's departure, the sky's sublimity will never be mine, and it's not until well into my thirties I begin to lower my sights to what's going on around me, and attend more to what I hear than what I see.

When I start to write, like Ruskin few of my thoughts are for my fellows, my teachers or the circumstances in which I find myself, none of which I attempt to describe.

> Oh, that someone had but told me in my youth, when all my heart seemed to be set on these colours and clouds, that appear for a little and then vanish away, how little my love of them would serve me, when the silence of the lawn and wood in the dews of morning should be completed [*sic*]; and all my thoughts should be of those whom, by neither, I was to meet more.*

* *The Works of John Ruskin*, Vol. XIII (1904), edited by E. T. Cook and A. Wedderburn.

It is the moon I look at, or the last of the sun, but as for people, how they seem, how they talk, how they behave, where writing is concerned none of this comes into it.

I do, on the other hand, notice the city. For all so much of Leeds is soot-covered and black there is an astonishing range of colour and texture in its brick and stone. The setts which pave so many of the streets (and, underneath the asphalt, still do) are for most of the time greasy and black, but after a storm glow with all the assorted colours of the stone, and even the acres of red brick and slate roof take on a richness and a shine.

Charles Ginner, who did many paintings of Leeds, catches both the colour and the grimness. The York stone pavements, now coveted, and indeed looted to grace southern patios and gardens, are another source of colour, and the eroded sandstone walls even more so. So in the evenings when I walk my lonely walks round Headingley and Woodhouse, dull though I think it all is and a place from which I long to be away, yet I can see this is a handsome and gracious city still, though not knowing then that I am seeing the last of it.

But the impulse to gaze never lets up. Oxford, Venice, New York at dusk, the line of the fells above Ribblesdale: 'Look at the light,' I say, but I don't, or not for long enough, anyway. And it persists. Driving through the outskirts of Leeds on Friday nights nowadays I often stop on Eccup Lane and look across to Cookridge, where the sun has just set. I am as I was fifty years ago, and in the same place, all my writing behind me and no nearer taking it in. And no nearer knowing what the 'it' is either.

━━━━━

ANDY: Have you ever thought what's happened to all the shy people?
    What became of them all of a sudden?
GEORGE: Right.
ANDY: Whatever happened to reserve, Dad, and self-consciousness?
    Was it your government that got rid of guilt? Tell me this, Dad.

How is it easier, how is it easier to reach out and touch someone for the first time? Why is it easier for me now than it was for you, then, whenever that was? Because that's the irreducible fact.

(Getting On)

'Our Alan's like us,' Mam would say. 'Shy.' And it is both boast and excuse, but with the pride uppermost, because though shyness is an elusive virtue there is no doubt in my mother's mind that it is a virtue, or at least has merit attaching to it.

So shy is passed on to me as it is not to my brother, as part of my inheritance. Nor do I question her assessment, seeing shy as she intends, as a mark of approval, a blessing on being blushing, bashful and diffident. That I may sometimes long to be none of these things hardly matters, as so do my parents, though they are able to blame their shyness as I never can on 'not having been educated'. I have nothing to blame it on at all, except possibly them. But that comes later. For the moment, shyness is the mark of a natural aristocracy to which I am deemed to belong, and though there is nothing socially superior about it (my father belongs to it after all) I take to the idea a bit too readily, happy to have my social shortcomings thus legitimised and my boyish character defined.

In Mam's vocabulary shy is adjacent to, and almost interchangeable with, sensitive . . . shy and sensitive belonging to a cluster of associated adjectives (refined, nicely spoken, unassuming) that she intends as high praise, though it's notable that none of them have masculinity to the fore, and with all of them saying 'No threat'.

They are qualities, though, that she detects in reassuringly high places; she thinks the King has a sensitive face, for instance (which perhaps explains his stammer), and also Anthony Eden (bullied by Churchill, though she is not to know that). 'He looks a sensitive feller,' she says of the Foreign Secretary, 'very refined,' which is what she will often say of someone, generally a man, who combines sensitivity with a bit of class. It means quiet, fastidious, educated probably (though not invariably) and generally with a degree of suffering etched on the face. Thus the actor

147

Robert Donat is thought of as sensitive (by virtue of his asthma), Ronald Colman refined, Laurence Olivier less so; Clark Gable, no; Leslie Howard, yes. Writers tend to be refined by dint of their profession, though some (Beverley Nichols) are more refined than others (J. B. Priestley). I suspect she may have thought my father refined when she first met him: quiet, violin-playing, and certainly not a typical butcher, besides being, as she always says, 'lovely looking when he was younger'.

Though like conscience it is something you might have been happier without, shyness saves you – and this is a big plus in my mother's eyes – saves you from being 'common', which is in many ways its antithesis, involving self-advertisement, self-display and a degree of groundless pushing yourself forward and attention-seeking that is the opposite of shy. Though what this disparagement of common doesn't take into account is that people who are common in my mother's terms are often funny and make you laugh, if only because they are readily on tap and don't have to be drawn out or made allowances for, and generally handled with care – the common Toad, I suppose, always more fun than the shy Badger.

Part of shy is 'always having your nose in a book', which in our house is no offence at all, though library books, which is generally what they are, are thought by my mother to carry contagion, TB and scarlet fever particularly, and so are not to be read in bed. But as time goes on I begin to see that the perils of books are the least of it, and that shyness has its own risks and its own incumbencies.

Shy at sixteen, for instance, means that I am happy (or prevailable, anyway) to accompany my mother on holiday long after my contemporaries are going off on expeditions of their own, or having tea and toasted teacakes in a café when I ought to have been venturing into pubs. Shy means taking Mam's arm as a surrogate Dad and being a makeshift companion.

'He's shy,' she would explain, 'but not with me.'

Or, as it later comes out (in *A Chip in the Sugar*):

'You're my boyfriend, aren't you, Graham?' Mam said, and she put her arm through mine.

Shy is also useful to someone shy of saying (or thinking) something else. Though my mother was the only girl my father ever went out with, and he her only boyfriend, and both are in that sense shy, the word when it is applied to me does not quite mean that. At a time when explanations are seldom sought, stigmas attached or categories imposed, shy is all that needs to be said; it means, is a nice way of saying, seemingly not interested in the opposite sex and being put off by girls; not shy of girls in general (I wasn't) but shy about them in one particular. So shy then is a cover, an excuse, a label that avoids saying something so unsayable (and shy-making) that Mam and particularly Dad prefer not even to think about it. In the event they do not have much to worry about because, though shy excludes me from the world of men (and therefore of women), it is not in itself a passport to the alternative: shy with one sex does not mean bold with the other. Nowadays, of course, when coming out is more common, shy is often just what such a boy is not, 'I wish he was bloody shy' a father's likely comment.

The perils of shyness are likely to persist, be lifelong . . . though happily not in my case. There is the risk of never managing to leave home, for instance, which I achieve finally at the age of thirty. Or if the father dies and the mother is left, the shy one, being unmarried, is the one likely to be called on as her companion. I am lucky in that I only come in for a year or so of that, the risk of being an unmarried son carrying the same penalties as being an unmarried daughter, the unmarriedness meaning that they must pay the price of not leaving home by being the companion and ending up a man of forty, who keeps his money in a purse, wears a raincoat too tightly belted and a neatly folded scarf, and who invariably writes out a shopping list. That is shy, careful, set in its ways, denizen of tea shops and haunter of libraries . . . a fate I see vividly as almost mine, and not always a fate either.

Shy is a gentle word – soft, blurred but sometimes murderous. I recall a film with Eric Portman as the loving son of a doting mother with whom he lives; his evenings (I think it had to do with the moon) given over to rape and murder. He is shy, though he keeps the newspaper cuttings to do with his crimes in his bedroom drawer, which his mother is shy of opening.

'He kept himself to himself' is what neighbours say of such figures, which is a way of saying shy after the event, the event all too often a murder or an abduction, a shattering of shy.

Shy has other, less dramatic, misprisions, particularly when you are young; it does not stop you being prurient, for instance, as I was, though you are thought the worse of should you be found out because being shy makes you seem like a hypocrite.

Shy means, too, that there are always people – and not merely PT instructors or drill sergeants – who see their role in life as shelling you from shy, the shelling both a bombardment and a splitting of your protective covering, to leave you blushing and exposed. It goes with a special kind of joviality. Doctors have it, a certain type of schoolmaster, and vicars even, coming at you with a heartiness that seems to me always without heart. They call it 'getting you out of your shell' and can mean it kindly, though it seldom works with me, my skin too thin, my shell too thick. Shyness invites interference, though, because it seems an evasion, an opacity with the real self occluded. It would have helped had I known all this at the time; instead of which, I think it's 'just me'. It would have helped, too, if I had seen the drawbacks of being shy earlier than I eventually do, and seen how it could mean missing out on a lot of fun – and I don't just mean sex (though I do mean sex).

It's another handicap when, just before I'm eighteen, I take to wearing glasses. Even at the time I know this is a kind of capitulation, an admission that I am or have settled for being a shy and spectacled sort of man. Glasses fit my face; they are an emblem, a tortoiseshell badge, a visible declaration that this is the kind of person I have decided to seem.

It isn't altogether a candid declaration, as a donnish figure in glasses isn't really what I feel like at all, and some of the next twenty-five years will be spent trying to unseem it. But my glasses are a defence and a disguise, an emplacement from behind which I can survey the world.

Actually I can see pretty well without them, except at the cinema or the theatre, and should have kept them exclusively for that. But I am lazy, and prescribed them only for distances I soon begin to wear them all the time so that they become part of me. Unless I'm wearing my glasses I scarcely seem to exist and my face falls apart. I note that on those pretty rare occasions when I go to bed with someone I take off all my clothes before finally I take off my glasses and become unspectacled again; the real nakedness comes last.

It is shortly after I start to wear glasses that I am called up, and though the next two years don't put paid to 'shy', I don't quite turn out to be the young man I thought I was going to be. Certainly as I get older I set less store by shyness and begin to see it as the burden it is, just as do my parents. In due course, too, their attitude broadens and the opposite of shy, namely common, invites less censure, with the judgement qualified or even quashed if being common happens to go with generosity and being good-hearted or even just a good laugh.

The comedienne, Hylda Baker, is common, hilariously so, overdressed, under-educated and unashamed of it, both on stage and off, pictured once in the *Evening Post* driving through Leeds in an open limousine with a monkey on a gold chain and a fetching young chauffeur in much the same position.

But of course Hylda Baker is safely on stage and it's in order for Mam and Dad to laugh at her. But they are the same about someone not unlike Hylda Baker, Russell Harty's mother Myrtle. Everything about the Harty family – dog, decorations, car, bath – is all dead-centre common, a natural hazard, I suppose, of successful greengrocery and a life spent in the covered market. But because she is kind and a good sort, and her torpid husband likewise, Myrtle's commonness does not enter into it, just as it never does with Russell himself, who can have Mam and Dad helpless with laughter at remarks which, coming from anyone else and myself in particular, would have been labelled 'cheeky' or 'suggestive' and had Dad in particular shrinking with embarrassment.

Russell's shock-horror exposure in the tabloids, and the so-called revelations about his sex life, come long after my father is dead and my mother is incapable, but if they'd still been around they might well have just shrugged it off. Dad certainly wouldn't have wanted him to stop coming round, as it would put an end to him playing his violin with Russell on the piano. But had there been similar revelations involving me, I could not have hoped to get off so lightly.

'We don't understand it. You've always been so shy.'

———

TOAD: Ratty, may I present the gaoler's daughter who single-handed effected my escape from prison.

GAOLER'S DAUGHTER: Oh Toady, you little love.

(*She kisses him. And just as Toad wanted to initiate Rat into the charms of caravanning, so now he wants to introduce him to the delights of kissing.*)

TOAD: Ratty kicked the weasels out of Toad Hall. I think he deserves a kiss, too.

RAT: No, no. Please. (*Rat is most reluctant but she manages to kiss him.*) Oh. I say. That's not unpleasant. I think my friend Mole might like that. Moley. Try this. (*So Mole gets a kiss too, and perhaps his kiss is longer and more lingering.*) What do you think?

MOLE: Mmmmm. Yes.

RAT: Yes. I think one could get quite used to it.

(*The Wind in the Willows*, stage adaptation)

And so it went on; I was generally in love, always unhappily, always with my own sex, and seldom with any physical outcome. I was still a medieval historian, not a profession, I imagine, with a high sexual strike rate. But by this time I was also in *Beyond the Fringe*, and whereas I might be quite near the sexual average for a medieval historian, for a performer in a smash hit West End show I must have been well below it. To translate the currency of theatrical success into sexual favours ought to have been easy (two of my colleagues did it with ease), but with me it remains strictly non-negotiable.

I have occasional flings, all of them straight, two of them with the same slightly depressing outcomes; shortly after going to bed with me, my partners announce their engagement (to someone else) and are briskly married. It is as if I had served as a reminder of the horrors of single life; properly marketed, I might have had a future bringing dithering girls to the point of matrimony.

It is said that blonds have more fun, and around the time I am stampeding these unfortunate girls into marriage David Hockney is dyeing his hair on that assumption. I have to say, though, that more fun was not, and has not been, my experience. To be tall is not a big plus either in my view, favourite, as lighting cameramen say, to be dark and of middle height.

All through my teens my dreams are seldom of happiness or fulfilment, but more often of transcendence. I never realistically expect that the loved one, if made aware of my affection, is likely to return it in kind, but I am comforted instead by some notion that I will rise above this and go on to greater things. Not vastly greater; the place I get at Cambridge in December 1951 comes in this category, as does the scholarship to Oxford two years later; the pride I take in both made keener because they must come to the chosen one's notice.

Making people laugh is another move in this game of transcendence, and sustains me through cabarets at Oxford and much of *Beyond the Fringe*, though my dwindling urge to perform thereafter coincides with the discovery that the satisfactions of sex, however sparse, are more worthwhile than the dubious rewards of rising above it.

I am now well into my twenties, not far off thirty in fact, and I feel I stand in much the same relation to the sexual life as Wilfred Thesiger did to the desert. Thesiger could traverse vast tracts of sand with little more than a swig of water and a few dates. In much the same way, I could go for months, years indeed, on virtually no dates at all. No quarter could have been emptier than my twenties.

Of course, to admit to sexual unsuccess, to admit to unsuccess of any sort perhaps, is to commend oneself to one's audience, at any rate in England. Philip Larkin's famous assertion that sexual intercourse began in

1963, and that this was just too late for him, did much to endear him to his readers. There can be few of us, after all, who don't feel that we were to some extent behind the door when sex was handed out, or that we have not had our proper ration, whatever that is. And if there was some disenchantment with Larkin after his death, or after the publication of his life, it was partly because it rapidly became plain that Larkin's poem, however true, was not frank and that far from missing the sexual boat in 1963, Larkin and his various girlfriends had been at it like knives on both sides of the year in question; and indeed had probably had a rather better time of it than many of his previously sympathetic readers.

Much of my sexual history is implicit in *Habeas Corpus* (1973), a farce which rings with cries (or wails) from the heart such as Canon Throbbing's:

> My life I squandered waiting
> Then let my chance go by.

But as often happens once put into words, the predicament alters. And after *Habeas Corpus* things take a turn for the better. Since it's a play about sexual liberation, this might be thought to be a case of life imitating art. And this does happen with plays, though often for the more down-to-earth reason that it helps to get things out into the open/off one's chest. Besides, the times were changing too, the seventies in my experience altogether easier in this regard than the more famous sixties.

If my sexual life looks up in what I see as the nick of time, it's partly too that as I get older I grow more light-minded. Having always thought of love as preceding sex, I now cease to care very much and so, I imagine, become easier to cope with. The young men I fall for are still straight, but sex in the seventies is not so particular about gender and boundaries, and so I find myself less often rebuffed and even having quite a nice time. And since one sex tends to lead to another, I also find myself being led back from the paths of deviancy to what becomes, in the eighties anyway, a pretty conventional life.

Such loving and long-lasting friendships that I have had have generally begun with sex and permutated (I do not say blossomed) into love. This was not the way I was told it would, or should, happen, the conventional model (as held up by vicars, schoolmasters and the better class of novel) having sex as the prize awarded to love, not the means of achieving it.

With sex, though, it's possible to think that you have both had less than your share and also more than you deserve.

There's an echo of this (unnoticed by me when I wrote it) in *The Madness of George III* when the Queen, his 'good little pudding', wonders whether, had he led a normal life, George III might not have gone mad.

KING: A normal life?

QUEEN: Other women, sir.

KING: Kicked over the traces, you mean, hey? No life is without its regrets. Yet none is without consolations. You are a good little woman, Mrs King. And we have been happy, have we not?

A refinement of regret comes to me occasionally nowadays when boys who were at school with me, now of course retired, write with their memories of school. They are boys, some of them, whom I often thought unapproachable at the time, and whom I longed to know. And now, when I can, it is fifty years too late. I reply but make no plans to meet.

If this account peters out just at the point when things are beginning to look up, this is not simply out of discretion or consideration for the other parties concerned, but because settling down, which is in effect what it was, is of less interest than the fairly parched route that took me there.

In 1989 Ian McKellen hosted a charity concert in support of the abolition of Clause 28, the section of the Local Government Bill barring the supposed promotion (which actually included the discussion) of homosexuality in schools. Various playwrights were represented, notably Wilde, Rattigan, Orton and myself, with Joan Plowright performing an extract from one of my monologues. Wilde, Rattigan, Orton and myself might be thought to have only one thing in common, but although I was quite happy to rally the troops, I did feel (not that anyone much cared) that this was oversimplifying my own situation.

I introduced the extract, saying that to enquire (as McKellen had done) if I was homosexual was like asking someone who had just crawled across the Sahara Desert whether they preferred Malvern or Perrier water. It was a good joke and got a big laugh, but at the time, at any rate, it seemed a fair statement of my situation.

Always a later starter, I must count myself blessed that, at a time in my fifties, when I expected to remain permanently unattached, I found, or was found by, a partner who, though much younger than I am, now shares my life. I can't quite boast that it's an ordinary life, or, my parents' ambition, a life like other people's. But it does for us.

Seeing Stars

In the 1940s within a mile or so of where we lived in Armley in Leeds there were at least half a dozen cinemas. Nearest was the Picturedrome on Wortley Road but others were just a walk or a tram-ride away – the Lyric down Tong Road, the Clifton at Bramley, the Palace off Stanningley Road and the Western a bit further on. And without ever being a dedicated film-goer I could have graded them all from fleapit upwards in their degree of comfort and sophistication just as, a little later, I would be able to grade the neighbourhood churches in terms of high and low, many of the churches and cinemas since sharing a common fate, conversion to carpet warehouses, second-hand furniture marts and, nowadays, health clubs.

Programmes changed twice a week and we generally went on a Monday and a Saturday. Comedies were best, particularly George Formby, but we took what was on offer, never knowing whether a film had any special merit. Some came with more of a reputation than others, *Mrs Miniver* for instance with Greer Garson, *Dangerous Moonlight* (with the Warsaw Concerto) and *Now, Voyager* with the famous cigarettes. But some didn't; I must have seen *Casablanca* on its first time round with no notion that this was a film of a different order from the usual twice-weekly fare. It was only towards the end of the war that more of a fuss started to be made over forthcoming films, so that I remember reading in *Picture Post* (and probably at the barber's) about *The Way to the Stars* with the young Jean Simmons, and the making of Michael Powell's *A Canterbury Tale*, and the first Royal Command Performance, another Powell film, *A Matter of Life and Death*.

Suburban cinemas were often pretty comfortless places. While the entrance could be quite imposing with the box office generally at the top of a flight of white marble steps, presumably to accommodate the rake, the auditorium itself was often not much more than a hangar, the aisle carpeted but the seats on lino or even bare concrete. Wartime meant there was no ice cream but en route to the cinema we would generally call at a sweet shop and get what Dad called 'some spice', provided, of course, we had the points, sweet rationing the most irksome of wartime restrictions and still in force as late as 1952 when I went in the army.

As a family we always went to the first house, which ended around 8.10 p.m., with the second-house queue waiting as we came out, scanning our faces for a clue to the experience we had just had, much as, I imagine, soldiers did when queuing outside a brothel. The second-house crowd seemed to me more loose-living than we were, raffish even. It certainly included more courting couples and folks who liked a drink (and who might even have had one already) and none of whom minded rolling home at the to us unheard-of hour of half past ten.

The waiting (and the Second World War involved a good deal of waiting in every department) was generally done up the side of the cinema in a grim open arcade that today would be drenched in urine but wasn't then. If the cinema was full and the performance continuous the commissionaire would come down the queue shouting: 'Two at 1s. 9d.', 'A single at 2s. 3d.' Or (very seldom), 'Seats in all parts.'

We always called it 'the pictures', seldom 'the cinema' and never 'the movies'. To this day I don't find it easy to say 'movies', 'going to the pictures' still the phrase that comes to me most naturally, though nowadays I'm not sure that 'the pictures', like 'the wireless', aren't among the self-consciously adopted emblems of fogeydom, the verbal equivalent of those smart Covent Garden establishments that do a line in old luggage. But calling the pictures 'the movies' went with calling cigarettes 'fags', beer 'booze' or girls 'birds'. It signalled a relaxed, unbuttoned approach to things, life led with more of a dash than I was ever going to manage.

Picture-going was generally a family affair, but when we were still quite young, at eight or nine, say, we were allowed to go to 'U' films by ourselves and (with a bit of nagging) to 'A' films too. Since the 'A' signi-fied that a child could only see the film when accompanied by an adult this meant hanging about outside the cinema accosting genial-looking cinema-goers, preferably women, with 'Can you take us in, please?' Warning us often, every time we left the house it almost seemed, against 'stopping with strange men', my mother never liked my brother and me to go to the pictures on our own but only once did I come to any harm and then not really.

In 1944 we moved, disastrously as it turned out, from Leeds to Guild-ford, where we stayed for a year, so at that time I would be ten, and had persuaded my mother one afternoon to let me go and see Errol Flynn in *The Sea Hawk*, which I'd seen in Armley but was now showing at The Plaza in Onslow Street (closed in 1956 to become a bingo hall and cur-rently a nightclub called The Drink). I hung about for a bit until a genial middle-aged man in glasses came along with one boy in tow already. This seemed to indicate respectability and I was about to ask him if he would take me in when he got in first, even taking my hand before shepherding us both past the box office; he may even have paid.

The film had already started, Errol Flynn flirting with Flora Robson as Queen Elizabeth while the usherette showed us down the aisle and before we had even sat down the man was pinching me and remarking on my nice chubby legs. This seemed fairly boring to me as, so far as I was concerned, they were just legs but I put up with it for the sake of Errol Flynn, who soon after we sat down was away on the Spanish Main. However, the clutching and the pinching was getting more urgent until, innocent though I was, it dawned on me that this must be what Mam's mysterious warnings had been about.

The sight of Errol Flynn now chained to an oar in the Spanish galley seemed to bring these claspings to a new pitch of urgency and I decided, as they moved higher up my legs, that I ought to make a break for it. So I got up and, foolishly, headed not up the aisle to the foyer but down the aisle to the Gents, where, not unsurprisingly, my admirer followed. Once there, I didn't hide in a cubicle but just stood waiting, not knowing what to do.

I see myself standing in that cinema lavatory and hearing the bang of the swing door as this kindly, bespectacled man, now suddenly sinister, comes through the door in pursuit. The entrance to the Gents was also the back door to the Exit and my admirer stood there for a second, obviously wondering if I had fled the cinema altogether. There was a moment, which in a film would hardly be credible, when he stood with his back to me trying to decide if I'd gone. Had he turned and looked down the steps to the lavatory he would have seen me. But he didn't turn, and obviously deciding it would be prudent to leave, he pushed the bar and went out through the Exit door.

I wish I could record that I went back and watched the finish of the film but I just hung about for a few minutes until the coast was clear, then (though nothing bad had happened to me) ran home in mild distress. I told my mother, who became satisfyingly hysterical, but Dad, a shy and fastidious man who I knew regarded me as a liar and a show-off, was just made angry, refusing even to believe anything had happened and, if it had, 'It was all nowt.' Certainly I hadn't been damaged, and if damage was done at all it was only in Dad's refusal to acknowledge the situation. As it was, the only lasting effect of the incident was to put paid to any further lone visits to the cinema and to teach me to keep quiet.

One's legs often got felt up as a child, though. Dad's old headmaster, Mr Alexander, used to give us lessons in algebra and he was a great stroker and clutcher, though only of the legs and not the parts appertaining. Vicars did it too, without seeming to want to take it further. It was something I came to expect, and just another of the ways in which grown-ups were boring.

The stars of the films seen in childhood had an unreality and a glamour that no stars have ever had since. It was inconceivable that their world should ever impinge on ours, though occasionally, almost miraculously, it did. That I can remember the deaths of both Leslie Howard and Carole Lombard chalked up on the newspaper-sellers' boards in City Square hardly counts. But there was the afternoon sometime in the 1940s when I was out shopping with Mam and we were walking up Thornton's Arcade and saw coming down a vast man with a much smaller friend in tow, like a whale and its pilot fish. He was wearing his coat slung around his shoulders just as I'm sure we'd seen him in the cinema when he was the Gestapo chief in *Pimpernel Smith* and, if it was in the late 1940s, we would have seen him as Mr Bumble in *Oliver Twist* and Jaggers in *Great Expectations*. It was Francis L. Sullivan, whose huge bulk must have been gracing the stage of the Grand that week, though we did not know it, thinking only that a creature from the celestial realms of film had materialised in, of all places, Leeds. We rushed home to tell Dad, who, predictably, was not much impressed.

Another brush with Hollywood came one morning in Manfield's shoe shop on Commercial Street, where Mam's older sister, Kathleen, was the (possibly self-appointed) manageress. An urbane figure slipped into the shop (and he, too, I think of with a camel-hair coat draped round his shoulders and even a cigarette-holder). Aunty (or 'Miss Peel', as she was known in the shop) takes charge, and I see her perched sideways on one of those low pentagonal stools on the sloping rubberised side of which the customer placed his or her foot, over which Aunty's head would be reverently bent about to unlace the shoe. Coyly she looks up. 'Have I,' she says in those exaggeratedly correct tones of which she was so proud and which mark her out as a professional woman: 'Have I the pleasure of serving Mr Ronald Colman?'

Whereupon Mr Ronald Colman (and God forgive him) looks most put out, says 'No' and strides out into Commercial Street. Of course had Aunty had more sense she would have waited until she had his shoe off, then his departure would have been necessarily less prompt. But there was no disguising the awfulness of the rebuff; it was so unmistakable that I'm surprised she was ready to retail the circumstances. But she had seen – and indeed touched – Ronald Colman and there was no gainsaying that. Still, I think even Dad, who was her sternest critic, felt a little sorry for her, believing that the Ronald Colman whom we had seen on the screen (in *Lost Horizon*, for instance, or *Random Harvest*) would have had more manners.

Except that now, telling the story, I can't be sure that it was Ronald Colman and not Robert Donat, who was certainly more likely to be in Leeds and indeed in England and who was known to be shy (and, as Mam said, 'a martyr to asthma') and therefore more likely to bolt from the shop.

Cherished and admired as a local boy was Eric Portman, who had made good while playing 'with the amateurs'. More robust than Donat, he was always said to have worked at a gents' outfitters in Bradford, where the aunties may even have claimed to have seen him behind the counter. Then he'd joined the Rep before becoming a star. James Mason was another local boy who had made good, though from rather posher beginnings in Huddersfield.

'Making good' meant getting out, as you would have to do if you were going to be a film star but which applied to literature too, the success of J. B. Priestley and, at a later date, John Braine evinced by their brisk departure from their Bradford birthplace. In this respect the Brontë sisters (Mam had seen the films, though she'd not read the books) were thought to be tragic figures, not on account of their bleak upbringing or their short lives, but because, so far as Mam knew anyway, they had never escaped from that terrible parsonage and stayed put in Haworth all their lives. For both Mam and Dad there was always a sense in which success could be summed up as a one-way ticket to King's Cross.

Film actors inevitably came trailing remnants of their previous roles, memories of other films in which they had figured and the inclinations of the characters they usually played. For a child at the cinema this was a help; there was not much ambiguity to be had and certainly with the masculine roles whether this was a goody or a baddy pretty soon became apparent, or was apparent already because the actor concerned had played more or less the same part in a film one had seen the previous week. Female roles were less easy to assess because love or passion was often a motivating factor and at the age of ten both were a bit of a mystery to me. Generally, though, where the actors stood on the moral scale was as plain as if they were characters out of a fairy story. We knew what they would do long before they did it, whatever the plot their roles in it fixed and immutable; they had no need to unpack their belongings: as soon as they showed their faces on the screen one knew what they had brought. There was a certain leeway in the details: the wicked but outwardly respectable businessman might be fond of art or dote on his pretty daughter, the lawyer be a bit of a dandy, the killer be fond of cats, but these were ornaments, decorations and in the fixed moral scheme of films in the 1930s and 1940s they did not alter the story but were just the accessories to costumes that were always off the same peg.

What puzzled me about villains was why, when they were masquerading as respectable citizens, their essential no-goodness wasn't as obvious to people on the screen as it was to me in the stalls. How could Pinocchio be so stupid as to be led astray by the patently wicked Fox, or Snow White not know the Queen was up to no good? Had the Queen been flesh and blood and not a cartoon she might well have been played by Joan Crawford, who was always something of an enigma to me. I never liked her, and with her gaunt face, protruding eyes and instinct for melodrama she seemed the embodiment of evil, yet she was often cast in the role of heroine. Even if she managed during the span of the film to convince me of her goodness and all ended happily, I felt it was only a matter of time before somewhere in the film's afterlife she would emerge in her true colours, grasping, selfish and (because she was like a man) a thoroughgoing rotter.

Claude Rains was another puzzle. He was determinedly silky and seldom unsmiling, sure signs that he was a baddy, though not always. There was the analyst in *Now, Voyager* or, more ambiguously, the Vichy police chief in *Casablanca*, ironic, twinkling and an advert for pragmatism. I wish the lesson I derived from these divergences from what I saw as the norm had been that people weren't always what they seemed, but probably I just wished they'd make their minds up.

Old Mother Riley apart, there weren't many funny women. I didn't go for Gracie Fields, nor did I understand why when she appeared everybody suddenly burst out singing – songs in films always something to be endured rather than enjoyed. Still, Gracie Fields in her Northern Mill epics and excursions to Blackpool was preferable to those gloomy, haunted heroines racked by passion and driven by concerns I didn't understand and who cropped up far too often for my taste. There was Ida Lupino, who always seemed to be either blind or confined to a wheelchair; Barbara Stanwyck, who seemed to want to be a man and certainly behaved like one; and the wholesome but plain Jane Wyman, who, on account of the plainness and wholesomeness, could be relied on in the end to get her man, homespun values always winning out against brittle sophistication.

The supreme exponent of brittle sophistication was Bette Davis, and for my aunties in particular she was someone to emulate. With her clipped tones, raised eyebrow and mocking smile Bette was a standard-bearer for shop assistants everywhere and in the 1940s you could find her presiding over the counters of the smarter shops – Marshall and Snelgrove, Matthias Robinson or, in my aunties' case, Manfield's shoe shop and White's Ladies' Mantles. The Davis manner, bored, sceptical, sarcastic, was particularly effective when 'chalking people off', as Mam called it. It was something she never had enough self-confidence to do herself but which her worldlier sisters saw as their professional duty, some sheepish Hunslet housewife trying to force her bunioned feet into a narrow 7 finding herself hardly helped by Aunty Kathleen doing her Manfield version of Bette Davis as Mrs Skeffington. When Aunty Myra joined the WAAF and went off to India she was Bette Davis too, a Leeds version of *Now, Voyager*, though I doubt that Aunty Myra ever had her Craven A lit by someone as refined at Paul Henreid, Australian lance corporals more her line of thing.

If not quite on the same footing as Davis or Crawford, there were a whole string of tall, elegant 'professional women' who were stars in their own right: Alexis Smith, Rosalind Russell, Eve Arden – women who could perch casually on the edge of an editorial desk, toss one long silk-stockinged leg over the other while lighting a cigarette or consulting a powder compact. Graceful and expensive as racehorses, they were amused, ironic and sceptical; they wrote newspaper columns in papers, edited magazines and were funny about love and romance with men just their playthings.

Mam can scarcely have thought she inhabited the same universe as these seen-twice-weekly stars and that any of us would ever come across them in the flesh was as unlikely as coming across Gulliver pegged out in Gott's Park or Horatio keeping the bridge over the Leeds–Liverpool canal. When, years later, I was playing in *Beyond the Fringe* on Broadway and wrote home to say I had actually met Rosalind Russell and Alexis Smith and a host of others besides, my weekly letters listing these occasions must have seemed like a reprise of those dark, wet wartime nights twenty years before when we all used to go to the pictures together.

Sometimes the setting of these encounters was backstage at the Golden Theatre on 45th Street, where *Beyond the Fringe* was lodged for its Broadway run, but more often than not it was the Central Park West apartment of Arnold Weissberger, partner in the firm of Weissberger and Frosch, showbiz lawyers and accountants. Aaron Frosch was the muscle in the firm (and looked it) whereas Arnold seemed to do nothing except throw parties, to which would be invited everybody currently appearing on Broadway or visiting New York from London or Hollywood. The cast was therefore staggering and I have never since been in rooms so stiff with celebrity.

What did one say to Henry Fonda or Joan Fontaine? How do you start a conversation with Judy Holliday and not mention *Born Yesterday* (an error I fell into)? How be casual with Katharine Hepburn or do anything but gaze at Steve McQueen?

My best plan, I found, was to make a mental note of who was there so that I could write home that night, then go and get some food at the vast buffet and gracefully retire. But it often turned out that the nicest people were at the buffet, or at any rate people who were more interested in eating than talking and who thus presented less of a social peril. Charles Boyer, for example, who was appearing next door to us on 45th Street in Rattigan's *Man and Boy*. With Leslie Howard he had been a particular heart-throb of Mam's. Now, napkin tucked under his chin and in that all too imitable accent in which he'd said farewell to Ingrid Bergman in *Arch of Triumph*, he pointed out which of the salads came up to scratch. Actually Ingrid Bergman was there, too, somewhere.

Such ancient icons, stars who might now be in decline but who had shone in the cinema of my childhood, were to me far more glamorous than their current counterparts. Here was Maureen O'Sullivan, whom I'd last seen as Tarzan's Jane in a skirt of palm leaves swinging through the jungly fronds in the arms of Johnny Weissmuller. Twenty years later, her star shone less brightly, though in reflected glory it would shortly rise again, for she was here with her daughter, a waif of extraordinary beauty wandering around the room as if somehow on offer; it was Mia Farrow, her mother therefore the mother-in-law to be of Frank Sinatra, and later still the tigerish adversary of Woody Allen.

Lauren Bacall, Gene Tierney, Laraine Day: here they all were in the un-cinematographic flesh, more worn perhaps than when we had first met in the ninepennies but still cool, still sceptical (and still smoking, very often), though they were grandmothers now as they piled their plates at the buffet table. How say I had last seen them aged eight at the Picture-drome on Wortley Road, though I fear I sometimes tried – to be met with a patient, practised smile.

Arnold Weissberger was a keen photographer, at any rate of celebrities. Indeed, he later published a book of photographs of the famous people in his life. You might hope to get away from the party unobserved but Arnold would have spotted you and followed you into the bedroom where the coats were left. Following him would come his tiny mother, who seldom left Arnold's side. And there, sometimes with his mother, he would snap you looking slightly startled and with the mountain of coats in the background. Thus it is I have a photograph of myself, just having put on my coat, and beside me is Joan Collins, though this was before she was Joan Collins and so not someone worth writing home about.

There were parties, too, when Arnold came to London, generally with his longtime partner Milton Goldman. They were held in the Savoy and were notorious for being graded according to reputation: the most famous or the eminently successful were invited on the A night, the less so on the B night and on the C night one could practically wander in from the street. I only once made the A night, shortly after *Forty Years On* had opened. The Burtons were there: it was not long after their marriage (or one of their marriages) and not seeing a chair handy Elizabeth Taylor, whom I had met in John Gielgud's dressing room at the theatre, perched briefly on my knee.

This was for me such an atypical situation that I find myself wondering whether I am recalling it correctly: did she sit on my knee or did I sit on hers? But this cannot have been (how would I have dared?), though I'm sure her knee would have been more comfortable than mine.

Oddly, this was not the first time I had figured in the Burton story and in a curiously similar capacity. When we had been in New York playing *Beyond the Fringe* we had got to know Burton's first (or at any rate current) wife, Sybil. She was jolly, domestic, very Welsh and living in a vast apartment on the West Side. One Sunday in 1963 she phoned and asked me if I would go with her to a film premiere at the 59th Street cinema.

Whatever partner she had been planning to go with must have cried off. I doubt it was Burton himself: he and Sybil were long past picture-going by this time. It would probably have been somebody Welsh, as the evening had a strong Celtic flavour, and in my memory the film was *The Criminal* with Stanley Baker. What I did not know, but presumably Sybil did, was that this was the day Burton had chosen to announce his divorce from Sybil. It followed that her companion had to be chosen with care, had not to be someone with whom Sybil could conceivably be thought of as conducting a liaison of her own.

Had I even the smallest liaison potential and certainly had I been something (or indeed anything) of a hunk, my presence would have been noted by the columnists who were in the audience and the photographers who were outside. As it was, nobody even noticed me: Sybil might have been there by herself. Nor was there any going on to supper or the party afterwards. I slipped away, leaving Sybil to Stanley Baker and other expatriate Celts.

In retrospect I see these two brushes with the Burtons as having a certain symmetry. One wife hitting on me as a suitably flavourless companion for the evening, the other sitting on me as a knee that would raise no eyebrows, both made me a prop in the drama of their lives far more interesting and celebrated than my own. I was, it should be said, an entirely willing prop, flattered to have had even such a small part to play in this legendary love story. Such brushes with the famous do have a name. That Elizabeth Taylor once sat on my knee is what in the Edwardian slang of the Baring family would have been called 'a Shelley plain' (after Browning's 'Ah, did you once see Shelley plain?'), an unlooked-for and even incongruous contact with the great.

However, that was not why the evening stuck in my memory, as I remember little of the film or of Sybil's mood or whether I even knew of the events in which I was playing a walk-on part. What made my heart beat faster was that while Sybil, the about to be ex-Mrs Burton, was sitting on my right, on my left was Myrna Loy.

I had no notion as a child that going to the pictures was a kind of education, or that I was absorbing a twice-weekly lesson in morality. The first film I remember being thought of as 'improving' was *Henry V*, which, during our brief sojourn in Guildford, was playing permanently at Studio 1 at the Marble Arch end of Oxford Street. I saw it, though, with my primary school at the local Odeon in Guildford, and that it was meant to be educational did not stop it being, for me, magical, particularly the transition from the confines and painted scenery of the Globe to the realities of the siege and battlefield in France. The reverse process had the same effect so that the final cut back to the Globe and the actors lining up for their call still gives me a thrill.

Seeing films one also saw – always saw – the newsreels, though only one remains in my memory. It would have been sometime in 1945 and it was at the Playhouse, a cinema down Guildford High Street. Before the newsreel began there was an announcement that scenes in it were unsuitable for children and that they should be taken out. None were; having already waited long enough in the queue nobody was prepared to give up their hard-won seat. It was, of course, the discovery of Belsen with the living corpses, the mass graves and the line-up of sullen guards. There were cries of horror in the cinema, though my recollection is that Mam and Dad were much more upset than my brother and me. Still, Belsen was not a name one ever forgot and became a place of horror long before Auschwitz.

The moral instruction to be had at the cinema was seldom as shocking as this: just a slow absorption of assumptions not so much about life as about lives, all of them far removed from one's own. There were cowboys' lives, for instance, where the dilemmas could be quite complex and moralities might compete: small-town morality v. the morality of the gunfighter with the latter more perilous and demanding of heroism, *High Noon* perhaps its ultimate demonstration. There was the lesson of standing up to the bully, a tale told in lots of guises: in westerns, obviously, but also in historical films – *Fire Over England*, *A Tale of Two Cities* and *The Young Mr Pitt* all told the same story of gallant little England squaring up to the might of France or Spain, for which, of course, read Germany.

Then there were the unofficial heroes: dedicated doctors, single-minded schoolteachers, or saints convinced of their vision (I am thinking particularly of *The Song of Bernadette*, a film that had me utterly terrified). Always in such films it was the official wisdom v. the lone voice and one knew five minutes into the film what the hero or heroine (star anyway) was going to be up against. I suppose one of the reasons *Casablanca* and *Citizen Kane* stand out above the rest is that their morality was less straightforward. William Empson never, I think, wrote about film but there are many the plot of which this describes:

> The web of European civilisation seems to have been strung between the ideas of Christianity and those of a half-secret rival, centring perhaps (if you made it a system) round honour: one that stresses pride rather than humility, self-realisation rather than self-denial, caste rather than either the communion of saints or the individual soul.

It was a dilemma I was familiar with because it was always cropping up at the Picturedrome.

Banal though the general run of films was, I learned, as one learned in fairy stories, about good and evil and how to spot them: the good where one would expect only degradation and squalor, and treachery and cowardice to be traced in the haunts of respectability. I learned about the occasional kindness of villains and the regular intransigence of saints but the abiding lesson had to do with the perils of prominence. I came out into Wortley Road grateful that, unlike Charles Boyer, we were not called on to stand up against the Nazi oppressor or battle like Jennifer Jones against the small-mindedness of nuns or like Cornel Wilde cough blood over the piano keys in order to liberate our country from the foreign yoke. Films taught you to be happy that you were ordinary.

Ordinary but not respectable, because in films respectable generally meant cowardly and there were other perils besides. One character who was always cropping up seemed the embodiment of respectability and was often played by the same actor. Not a star (I have had to look up his name), he was called Thurston Hall. With his bright white hair and substantial frame he looked not unlike the local doctors in Upper Wortley, Dr Monies and Dr Slaney, figures of some weight and even grandeur in the neighbourhood. Thurston Hall did play doctors from time to time but more often than not he was a businessman, highly thought of in the community, a person of unimpeachable morals who was ultimately revealed to be a crook. Kind to children, a president of orphanages, a donor of playing fields and a guarantor of symphony hall, he is prominent in every good cause. But the committee of charitable ladies who can always rely on him for a generous contribution would be surprised to learn that the money comes indirectly out of the pockets of their husbands, paid over to the many prostitutes of the city or in its poker dens and illicit drinking clubs behind all of which is this impeccably mannered immaculately suited villain.

That such a character in a film today would seem quite old-fashioned is the fault of the times. Villainy these days is more complicated and communities don't have pillars in quite the way they did. Two-faced respectability operates best in a setting of accepted values and that setting began to break up, so far as the cinema was concerned, sometime in the late 1950s, with one of its minor legacies for me a lifelong distrust of well-groomed, impressive middle-aged men. When I saw General Pinochet on one of his London jaunts I picked him out as a villain simply from the films I had seen in the 1940s.

To know that one is being taught a lesson or at any rate given a message leaves one free to reject it if only by dismissing plot or characters as clichés. But I had not realised how far the moral assumptions of film story-telling had sunk in, and how long they had stayed with me, until in 1974 I saw Louis Malle's film about the French Occupation, *Lacombe Lucien*. Lucien is a loutish, unappealing boy, recruited almost by accident into the French Fascist Milice. He falls in with and exploits a Jewish family, becoming involved with – it would be wrong to say falls in love with – the daughter, whom he helps to escape and with whom he lives. Then, as the Liberation draws near, he becomes himself a fugitive and is eventually, almost casually, shot.

The stock way to tell such a story would be to see the boy's experiences – witnessing torture and ill-treatment, falling for the Jewish girl – as a moral education in the same way, for example, that the Marlon Brando character is educated in *On the Waterfront*. That would be the convention and one I'd so much taken for granted that I kept looking in the Malle film for signs of this instruction in the school of life beginning to happen. But it doesn't. Largely untouched by the dramas he has passed through, Lucien is much the same at the end of the film as he is at the beginning, seemingly having learned nothing. To have quite unobtrusively resisted the tug of conventional tale-telling and the lure of resolution seemed to me honest in a way few films even attempt.

The Ginnel

Mam seldom came back from the pictures in those days without being desperate to empty her bladder, the diuretic effect of the proximity of home making the situation so urgent that my brother and I would be sent on ahead to unlock the door in readiness, thus saving her the last terrible moments bent double on the doorstep.

The urgency of her predicament was never more extreme, it seemed to me, than when we had been to the Palace, a cinema off Stanningley Road. It was a bleak place, having once been a skating rink; painted red, it had double seats for courting couples, and indeed my parents had done some of their courting at the Palace in the twenties, sitting in the raised seats along the sides which were known as the Deck. In those pre-talkie days there was a scratch orchestra which accompanied the films, the violin played by Dad's teacher, Norris Best, who, if he caught sight of him in the audience, would get Dad down into the pit to play another fiddle, a summary desertion which didn't please Mam at all. Those days were long gone and in my mind the Palace is associated particularly with George Formby films, and that we had all laughed so much might account for the acuteness of Mam's discomfort on the way home.

Off Stanningley Road on the left was and still is (in 1998 anyway) a narrow ginnel, only a few feet wide, one side of which backed onto a mill or factory, the other side forming the red-brick rear wall of the houses that make up Pasture View. Coming home from the Palace, when every minute saved was vital, we would go up this ginnel as it was a short cut to

Theaker Lane, hurrying along it in single file, then round the edge of the playground of our school, Upper Armley National, before going up by Christ Church across Ridge Road into the Hallidays and home.

Passing the end of this ginnel recently, where I can't have been for fifty years, I saw that whereas in the forties the passage was clean and uncluttered and did not smell (I know this because had it been in any way insalubrious Mam, ever fastidious, would have gritted her teeth and gone the long way round), now it was half-blocked with rubbish and loose stones, elders and buddleia had rooted on the mill wall and though I didn't investigate further I knew that it would stink. No one in their senses would nowadays use it as a thoroughfare or, if they did, would just by so doing become an object of suspicion.

Fifty years ago we used to trot up there and think nothing about it, a family on their way home from the pictures. It wasn't 'lonely'; it wasn't 'nasty' (i.e. people didn't piss in it); it was just a useful ginnel.

Inured as one is to change and destruction, the state of this narrow passage poses questions about life in cities that are regularly and routinely posed by weightier developments . . . motorways, out-of-town shopping centres, debates about violence and street crime and the unending debate about the sense of community and where it has gone.

When did this ginnel fall into disuse? When did it cease to be a short cut? Chart the clogging up of this passage and you will have anatomised urban decay in the second half of the twentieth century. Was it because of cars, people ceasing to walk this bleak stretch of Stanningley Road unless they had to? Was it the demolition of houses or the decay of public transport? At what point did the stones begin to fall from the wall and cease to be picked up? Because in the forties they must have been picked up, put back or to one side and the path kept clear.

Was it the fear of being 'attacked' that led to its decay? Because it would be a good place, as appropriate a setting for a filmed robbery or a rape as any locations manager could hope to find. I fancy once there was a lamppost at the top end but it isn't there now. I can't imagine anyone ever being responsible for this ginnel and its upkeep; it was kept up just by dint of being used. Old ladies would use it who'd been for a walk in Armley Park, children coming home from Armley Park school, courting couples.

Why the ginnel was there at all never occurred to me, as Leeds, or the Leeds of my childhood, was full of snickets and ginnels, passages behind and between houses, unadopted paths that went along the backs of gardens, preferred thoroughfares for us as children and with no logic to most of them, just cracks in the urban set-up that nobody'd bothered to fill in. The ginnel behind Pasture View, though, seemed older than most and it was only when reading about the history of Armley I found out why.

Like so many of the suburbs of Leeds, Armley had once been a village and in my childhood the lower reaches of Theaker Lane, which we thought of as slums and where we never willingly went, were made up of seventeenth- and eighteenth-century cottages, lived in originally by workers in the mills. Like many of the most interesting buildings in Leeds, they were pulled down in the fifties and sixties and now there are only high flats. And so it was in Holbeck and Wortley, Hunslet and Beeston and all the settlements Leeds swallowed up in its nineteenth-century expansion.

In those days the workers in the mills would often have to walk miles to their work and this ginnel off Stanningley Road turns out to be part of the old footpath from Wortley through Armley to the mills at Kirkstall, so that when the Pastures were built in the 1870s it had to be left open as an ancient right of way.

So what was for us just a short cut home from the pictures had once echoed at the beginning and end of the day to the rattle of clogs.

These days the mills are gone, Armley Mill now a museum and the Palace is gone too, or translated into the New Western Bingo and Social Club. The ginnel, though, is still there behind Pasture View, where, clogged with stones and rubbish, and wanting mill-workers and weak-bladdered cinema-goers or anyone heedless enough of the realities of street life in the last decade of the twentieth century as to be daft enough to use it, it will remain. 'Welcome to Leeds' the sign on the M1 used to say, 'Motorway City of the Seventies'.

Diaries 1996–2004

Every Christmas or New Year I publish extracts from my diary of the pre-ceding year in the *London Review of Books*. On a personal level these pub-lished diaries are pretty uninformative, not to say cagey, but they do give some indication of what work I was doing and where it took me, though more often than not nowadays this is no further than from the armchair to the desk.

Diaries lengthen the days. To read back over a year when nothing much seems to have happened is often to be nicely surprised, though I note how in earlier diaries much more of what I wrote down had to do with what I did whereas lately the entries are more often occasioned by what I've read or seen on television. I should get out more if only for the diary's sake.

A diary is undoubtedly a comfort. I feel better for having written it down, however hard the experience. I never enjoy, though, having to record set pieces and prefer to pick at incidents rather than try for a com-prehensive account. As I've noted before, my diary is often best when written in the intervals of other writing; it's a turning away, a place for asides. What I do always dislike is not having written anything for a while and then finding I have to catch up.

Where no place is specified the entry was written in Camden Town in London, where I have lived for the last forty years. Craven is the village in Yorkshire to which my parents retired and where we still have a house.

1996

3 January. To *Dynasties*, the exhibition of Tudor portraits at the Tate. There are some superb pictures but, with the sitters shortly to die or be executed, many of them seem ominous or doom-laden. New to me and to R. is Antonis Mor, whose portrait of Sir Thomas Gresham looks like an Edwardian tinted photograph, and with the sitter so eerily present not entirely pleasing. All art is tiring and these paintings in particular as they're crowded with detail and every dress and doublet draws you in to trace the embroidery or work out the folds and flourishes. The poster for the exhibition is Holbein's portrait of the Prince of Wales, later Edward VI; he's not the weed that he's normally pictured but a big solid bully of a baby, the image of his father. On the Underground R. says he's never known a poster so persistently defaced, the child's brutal look seeming to irritate people. One poster that he saw had UGLY written across the forehead and another SPAM.

27 January. To Leeds by the 9.10 train with snow flurries much of the way. We call at the British Epilepsy Association, where I have to sign some books as prizes in a writing competition. The premises are in Hanover Square up behind the Town Hall and beyond the Infirmary, and, when I was a boy, one of the grander squares in Leeds, where the posh doctors and surgeons from the Brotherton Wing had their consulting rooms. Nowadays the ring road makes the square difficult to get to and it's in a bad neighbourhood, not far from the Hyde Park street which is said to hold the record for the most burglaries in England. The British Epilepsy Association is offices only but has a steel door, having been broken into three times, one of them a ram-raid; so, coming away, I'm perhaps more conscious of vandalism and urban decay than I otherwise might be. The result is, when we see a starved-looking boy of ten and his sister, twelve or so, tugging at a bollard round some roadworks before sending it flying, I wind down the window and say primly: 'That's a pretty silly thing to do.'

This releases a torrent of abuse from the two Bisto kids, the girl cold and dirty and in a thin anorak, the boy with snot dribbling down from his pinched little nose. As we're driving off she gives me her parting shot: 'Get a *life*!' It's a ready-made cartoon for the *New Yorker*.

At Addingham we turn off to Bolton Abbey, deserted this cold bright afternoon with the paths down to the river covered in untrodden snow and the Wharfe winding black between the drifts. Building at the priory must have been going on until the very eve of the Dissolution, with the uncompleted west tower begun by Abbot Moon in 1520. The confidence such plans imply still surprises me as I've never quite got rid of the notion that the Dissolution of the Monasteries, and the Reformation altogether, was part of some general winding-down of the medieval Church. In fact, the future must have seemed bright, and when things did alter it was practically overnight.

10 February. When Stephen Fry took off last year I came in for one or two of the jobs he'd been contracted to do, notably a couple of voice-overs for children's cartoons. Telephoned by the same company last week I agree to do another in a Posy Simmonds animated film about a pig who acts as a theatrical dresser; this seems right up my street. Except I am called today to say that, unaware of my interest, the casting director has approached someone else and 'his agent is standing firm'. Clearly Stephen F. is back in the market.

11 February. Turn on the radio this evening to find Brahms's Second Piano Concerto just beginning, the unexpectedness of it taking me back to 1951, when I heard it for the first time. How lofty I thought my life was going to be then, just like this music; I saw myself modestly ascending shallow staircases to unspecified triumphs, with love disdained, or at any rate transcended, always a part of it.

It's a live performance on Classic FM, a concert by the Liverpool Phil. with someone coughing badly throughout and a rather wayward account by the soloist, who sometimes slows it down so much that it almost stops, the swooning second subject in the last movement well over the top. These days audiences know a work so well that soloists must find public performance more nerve-racking than it has ever been. To play one of the great concertos in the concert hall must be like an actor having to do 'To be or not to be' before an audience which knows the text as well as he does.

But I loathe Classic FM more and more for its cosiness, its safety and its wholehearted endorsement of the post-Thatcher world, with medical insurance and Saga holidays rammed down your throat between every item. Nor does the music get much respect; I'm frequently outraged when they play without acknowledgement or apology a sliced-up version of Beethoven's Ninth, filleted of all but the most tuneful bits. It's like a *Reader's Digest* condensation of the classics, defined on *Monty Python* once as 'Great Books got down to Pure'.

The only gramophone I had access to as a child was my grandma's – a red Rexene-covered wind-up job with metal needles, almost no amplification and few records to go with it. These included such oddities as 'Ain't it Grand to be Bloomin' Well Dead' (a possible signature tune for Kafka if not for Philip Larkin) and one of the chart-toppers of the time, 'Oh I lift up my finger and I say "Tweet tweet, Hush hush, Now now, Come come"'.

This somewhat sparse musical diet was supplemented from Hustwitt's Music shop up Tong Road, where there was an oddities box in which I found a 78 of Chopin's Polonaise in A, heard first in the film *A Song to Remember* with Cornel Wilde as Chopin and Merle Oberon as George Sand, and the never-to-be-forgotten scene when during an energetic sforzando the consumptive Chopin's blood spatters on the keys.

I also bought a record of Schubert's Unfinished Symphony, doubly unfinished in this case as I got only one record out of a set of three so it wasn't until years later I found out how it officially didn't finish. I played it so often then, though, that I've never cared for it since.

17 February. Catch part of BBC2's celebration of French cinema and note how much more nostalgic and redolent of the past are these French clips than those from British films of a similar period: *Les Enfants du Paradis*, for instance, the first French film I ever saw and which we were taken from school to see at the Tower in Upper Briggate in Leeds. Then when I was on the Russian course during National Service at Cambridge we used to see French films at the Arts cinema – *Une Partie de Campagne*, *Le Blé en Herbe*, films which were so much part of one's life then as to be almost commentaries on it. Perhaps their vividness now has to do with the fact that they combined reading (via the subtitles) with seeing, thus reinforcing the memory.

In an interview before reading *Doctor Dolittle* on Radio 4 last year I mentioned how mysterious a character I find the Cats' Meat Man, never having come across such a character as a child. Was the meat *from* cats, I wondered then, or for cats? I'd heard of dog meat but never cat meat. Since when I've had several letters telling me about real-life characters who used to sell such meat, generally on long skewers which were sometimes just put through the letter box, one telling me how, as a child, finding this forerunner of the kebab on the doormat she had scoffed the lot. I don't think there were such itinerant characters in Leeds, possibly because it wasn't affluent enough or because this was during the war when cats had to pull in their belts along with everyone else.

2 March, Venice. Fur much in evidence in Venice, where they plainly have no truck with animal rights, old ladies in their minks queuing along with everyone else to get on the vaporetto. One reason Venice feels like a real democracy is the absence of private transport. It's true there are taxis, but it's much harder to get down into a speedboat than to walk onto a water bus and as a result taxis are avoided by many of those rich enough to use them. Rich and poor in Venice rub shoulders with each other much more than we do and the city feels better for it.

A nice carrier bag from the Correr, red with yellow handles and on the front the signature of Leonardo da Vinci. There is a sticker inside saying 'Used by permission of Corbis Corporation and Bill Gates', to whom I suppose Leonardo, or his signature at least, now belongs.

Note the number of retired couples among the visitors, retirement more obvious in the British and the Americans than with the French, say (and where the Italians are concerned, utterly invisible).

In the basilica all the seats are now roped off so that one can't sit down and take it in (let alone pray) but just has to troop round, go with the flow, I suppose. Less magical now than once it seemed, the gold tawdry, the woodwork dusty, only the floors retaining their unfailing appeal. Nor is one any longer allowed along the marble-balustraded upstairs corridors that took you above the nave and much nearer to the mosaics. It's still possible, though, at this time of year, to find the piazza virtually empty at eleven in the evening, the floodlighting of the basilica not at all harshly done, so that St Mark's emerges from the gloom and seems to glow. And yet one gets a sense of the building sitting there like a spider, luring people in.

3 March, Venice. The Correr is an ideal museum, with just the right number of paintings, many of them superb, particularly the man in the red hat which I'd always thought by Carpaccio, but isn't now, and also the *Portrait of a Young Man* by Baldassare Estense. I don't care for Cosimo Tura, whom I usually find a sinister painter, the flesh and aspect of the living not much different from that of the dead; still I like his funny little *Pietà* with the Virgin looking at the wounds in Christ's hands as if he's making a bit of a fuss about nothing, while above them, in what I suppose is an apple tree and cocooned in a huge spider's web, is a tiny-headed devil. I'm puzzled by one painting of the Marriage at Cana where, hanging from the beams above the feast, are many rings with what seem to be labels fluttering from them. I ask the attendant, who comes over, looks at it glumly, shrugs and says: '*Non so.*' It's Madge H. who suggests, probably rightly, that the labels are flypapers.

10 March. I read the Sunday papers first thing, otherwise they hang about all day like an unmade bed. I find less and less in them to read and feel like somebody stood against a wall while a parade goes by. An article in *The Garden*, the journal of the Royal Horticultural Society: 'Making Sense of the Celandine'.

11 March. Depressed by an item glimpsed on TV last night revealing that Railtrack, to save itself money (and the problems of 'leaves on the line'), has sent in squads to cut down the woodland that grows along railway lines, a copse in Blackheath for instance sawn off level with the ground. Some of the squads for obvious reasons have begun their operations at four in the morning with any appeal to planning regulations of no avail as Railtrack claim public safety as a justification. If it happened to a wood that I was fond of I'd be inclined to find out the address of the local Railtrack manager, take along a chainsaw and do the same to his precious plot.

30 March. To Petersfield on a cold, blue day, the traffic thick over Hammersmith Bridge, where crowds are watching the crews practising for the Boat Race. Go via Midhurst to look at the Camoys tombs in St George's Church, Trotton. Lord Camoys was a veteran of Agincourt, where he commanded the left wing; he married Hotspur's widow and both of them are buried in a massive and inconveniently placed tomb at the east end of the centre aisle, smack in front of the altar. There's another much plainer tomb *c*.1478 on the north wall, carved with a symmetrically ruched frieze of draperies round the rim which seems very sophisticated for a village church, and more Italian than English.

Fragments of wall-paintings include one of *Clothing the Naked*, in which a man is taking off or putting on a shirt in a crude version of the man in Piero's *Baptism* in the National Gallery. Nosing about I see leaned up against the back wall near the vestry a dusty reproduction of Botticelli's *Mother and Child* from the National Gallery of Art in Washington. It's shielding a hole in the plaster and has an old label stuck on it: ' From Professor Joad. BBC.'

11 April, Wandsworth. What strikes you about a prison is not that it's unlike any other place you've ever been in, but that it's quite like all sorts of places you use quite regularly. It's not unlike a hospital, for instance, or a state school, a big post office or even one of the new universities. Here are the same harassed but well-meaning staff, short-handed, crippled by lack of funds, struggling to make the institution work despite all the curbs and cuts imposed by a penurious and ill-disposed government.

After umpteen TV series the look of the place is quite familiar too, though not as lofty as the prison in *Porridge*, and cosier altogether than the prisons in movies. But then this is the wing where most of the sex offenders are, or the prisoners who are likely to be attacked. Many of them are quite old, or seem so anyway; maybe they're just in their fifties. I look at them, bald, stooped, one of them only half there, and wonder what it is they've done, wishing that they carried a notice of their crime on their chests so that one could place them in some sort of spectrum, fit the face to the offence and so somehow make sense of it.

There's no particular smell but this wing is said to be the cleanest, with no slopping out, the remand wing the worst because there the inmates are certain they are going to get off so treat the place like a pigsty. Decent bearded art-school teachers is what one or two of them look like but whether these are prisoners or civilian staff I can't tell. Two gay men take me round the well-stocked library, dressers they could be on a film set or assistants in a provincial outfitters, opera buffs probably. There are two-tone walls, a century of paint over the bricks and lots of studded doors – cottage doors almost. Some dinky warders, in short-sleeved shirts, dark ties and epaulettes, not quite giving you the wink but certainly a cheeky stare.

Read and then answer questions though without feeling I do much good or do anything more than pass the time. I note, though, my presumptions, made out of sheer politeness rather than liberal prejudice, that most of my audience have been wrongly imprisoned and that I'm anxious not to be thought personally responsible for this.

26 April. To Holland for the Vermeer exhibition. Travel to Delft separately from the rest of the group, who make up a coach party. R. hopes that this expedition, which includes prominent bankers, lawyers and industrialists, all benefactors of the National Gallery, will nevertheless be overtaken by the ethos of rather different English coach parties abroad, chanting *"ere we go! 'ere we go! Ver-meer! Ver-meer!"* at the startled burghers of The Hague, while elderly connoisseurs moon out of the coach windows. One understands this did not happen.

With much of his life a mystery and the content of his paintings so simple and accessible, one reason for the popularity of Vermeer is that he eludes the art historians. With Vermeer expert knowledge doesn't take you far. There may be symbolic significance in a discarded broom, say, or an unemptied laundry basket, but that is not the point of the painting. The paintings are about women and about loving women, as he must surely have done; most of the men in differing degrees ninnies. Miracles of light, the paintings are also miracles of space as, for instance, *The Milkmaid*, where the space behind the stream of milk coming from the jug is almost palpable. I have a sense of vertigo, though, in the presence of great paintings, as when standing on a cliff and feeling oneself pulled to the edge. 'If I were to put my fist through this painting,' I think, 'things would be irrevocably changed and my whole life be seen as leading up to this act.'

The rooms adjoining the Vermeer exhibition contain part of the Maurits-huis's permanent collection, and passing from the presence of these few simple, utterly unassuming pictures into a room containing at least half a dozen Rembrandts, including *The Anatomy Lesson*, it's startling to find how clamorous these other masterpieces now seem to be. Though there is often something going on in the Vermeer paintings (a woman reading a love letter, or writing one, or just admiring herself in the glass), the inner peace of the pictures and the unassertiveness of the sitters, nearly all of them women, are so simple and direct that even two of Rembrandt's most famous self-portraits, one at either end of his life, seem almost coarse by comparison. I'm sure it's the tranquillity of the Vermeers rather than its small size, that makes it an untiring exhibition to see. And how small some of the pictures turn out to be, some of them scarcely larger than the postcards on sale in the museum shop.

27 *April, Delft*. A tangle of bicycles dredged up from the canal. Grey with mould and mud and with bright patches of rust, they are dumped on the quay where, surrounded by chic galleries and art establishments, one isn't certain that bicycles is all they are. Is this art?

The Dutch in the seventeenth century were famed for their neat houses and the orderliness of their lives, qualities celebrated not so much in Vermeer as in the paintings of his contemporaries, particularly de Hooch, which form a companion exhibition at Delft to the Vermeer show at The Hague. Though they're as bad at drink as we are (the carriage from Rotterdam to Brussels dominated by a group singing and shouting), and though they're as prone to graffiti, the Dutch are still noticeably neat in other aspects of their lives, as in the acres of carefully cultivated allotments which lie along the railway. The plots are quite modest, but all seem to come with a hut that is less of a garden shed than a summerhouse and outside which, this warm Friday afternoon, oldish couples in skimpy bathing costumes are taking the sun and one old man naked except for a G-string. I imagine the owners of these plots and pavilions live in the high flats nearby, though such a tempting display of civility and order would not long survive proximity to similar flats in England.

9 May. Vanity: my sixty-second birthday. Someone behind me in M&S says: 'Are you all right, young man?' I look round.

11 May. On the Leeds train the conductor announces: 'The trolley will shortly be coming through with a selection of hot and cold snacks, tea and coffee and other beverages. For your information, pushing the trolley this morning is Miss Castleford 1996.' And Miss Castleford duly comes through, though hardly the busty, brazen apparition one expected, but a rather quiet, shy-looking girl who, not surprisingly, is covered in confusion and fed up at having to cope with the jokes of the bolder passengers. Or customers, as we now are.

16 May. Classic FM continues to irritate. Tonight we have a recording of

Elgar's *Dream of Gerontius*, the gap between Parts One and Two filled with various promotions ('The haunting music of the Pan pipes'). Gerontius having achieved death, his soul begins its journey to judgement, lucky, I suppose, not to be seen off with a cheerful message from Henry Kelly. With it being *Gerontius* I'm surprised the whole thing isn't a plug for Saga's 'specialised insurance for those of fifty and over'.

Excepted from these strictures about Classic FM is Michael Mappin, who keeps the bad jokes to a minimum, isn't wearingly cheerful and has some specialised knowledge, lightly worn, i.e. he is like an announcer on Radio 3. Most of the others are scarcely past the stage where they snigger at foreign names.

17 May. Despite the vindication of the National Gallery in the filmed restoration of Holbein's *The Ambassadors*, the cleaning controversy rumbles on. One misconception that fogs the argument is to do with the nature of time. Michael Daley, the NG's chief critic, represents time as a benevolent mellowing process whereby paintings grow old gracefully, their colours maturing, the tints changing, but all at the same rate and in the same fashion, so that the composition arrives in the present day, veiled a little perhaps but still much as the artist intended. This is, of course, nonsense. Paintings more often than not have quite violent and eventful lives; they are loved, after all, and so naturally they get interfered with and touched up and, their admirers being fickle, when they get to seem a little old-fashioned they are dressed up a bit to suit the taste of the time. They limp into the present coated with centuries of make-up but still trying to keep body and soul together. 'Mellowing' is just not the word.

19 May. Come out this morning (still grey, still cold) to find smack in front of my door a fish – a wet fish actually, about nine inches long, still glistening as if just caught. Pinkish in parts (a mullet?) dropped by a seagull perhaps or hurled into the garden by a dissatisfied customer? Except that the wet fish shop in Camden High Street has long ago been ousted by yet another emporium selling leather jackets. Anyway, a fish. I leave it for a while to see if it catches a gull's eye, then put it in the bin.

24 May. Run into Frank Dickens the cartoonist walking down the stalled escalator at Camden Town tube. Says that in Bristow, his strip in the *Standard*, he's about to introduce the concept of Desk Rage, with frenzied attacks on other people in the office. About the same age as me, he still cycles but not as sedately as I do: Frank goes racing cycling and even wears Lycra shorts. He has several bikes, and when someone else in his club admired one of them and offered to buy it, Frank made him a present of it. When they were out cycling next, the young man to whom he had given the bike kept just behind him, mile after mile, until Frank slowed down and waved him on, whereupon the young man streaked away into the distance far faster than Frank could go. Afterwards he asked him why it had taken him so long to pass and the young man said: 'Well, I didn't feel it was right to pass you on your own bike.' The existence of such an unmapped social area and the delicacy required to negotiate it would have delighted Erving Goffman.

31 May, Chichester. The city has streets and streets of immaculate seventeenth- and eighteenth-century houses, particularly round Pallant House; they're manicured and swept clean and at night are as empty as a stage set. It's quiet too, except (and this is a feature of English country towns) in the distance one suddenly hears whooping and shouting and the sound of running feet as young drunks somewhere make their presence felt and kick out against this oppressive idyll.

1 June. When Jeremy Sams directed *Wind in the Willows* in Tokyo he had many practical problems, chief of which being that the actors did not trouble to make themselves heard. He was well into rehearsals before he found out that this was because they were all miked, as actors generally are in Japan. Another dilemma was almost philosophical: the cast were anxious to know about other characters like their own – other Moles, for instances, other Toads. 'But there are no others,' explained Jeremy. This the actors were unable to grasp or the fact that *Wind in the Willows* was not a type of English play and that there was no other with which it could be compared. All the plays in Japanese theatres are genre plays, variations on a theme or set of themes; the idea that a play might be unique seemed to them very strange indeed.

27 June, Chichester. Talking to Maggie Smith about the number of grey heads in the audience for *Talking Heads*, I compare them with a field of dandelion clocks. She says that she's read or been told that the Warwickshire folk name for these was 'chimney-sweeps' so that Shakespeare's 'Golden lads and girls all must,/As chimney-sweepers, come to dust' is thus explained. I had always taken chimney-sweepers to be a straightforward antithesis, poor and dirty boys and girls the opposite of clean and bronzed ones. This, of course, doesn't bear close examination, though what probably planted it in my mind was a nightmare I used regularly to have as a child in which a chimney-sweep or coalman rampaged through our spotless house. I look up chimney-sweeps in Geoffrey Grigson's *The Englishman's Flora* (shamefully out of print) and find that, the flowers being black and dusty, chimney-sweep and chimney-sweeper are Warwickshire slang for the plantain, particularly the ribwort, and that these were used to bind up sheaves of hay; children, whether golden or otherwise, used to play a game not unlike conkers with the flowers on their long stems, in the course of which, presumably, the flowers disintegrated, or came to dust.

1 July. Watch Stanley Kubrick's *Full Metal Jacket*, which was shot in England, the Isle of Dogs doubling for Vietnam. It's remarkable chiefly for the language of the Marine instructor, a wonderfully written and terrible part, which takes language into areas certainly undescribed in 1987, when it was made, and not often since. For example: 'You're the kind of guy who'd fuck someone up the ass and not do them the courtesy of a reach-around.'

3 July. Silly programme on *Timewatch* last night attempting to rehabilitate Haig. ('Acid-bath Haig?' 'No. Blood-bath Haig.') It was just historians playing see-saw with no new evidence forthcoming and no examination of the sources, his diaries, for instance, treated as trustworthy when it's pretty certain Haig rewrote them to fit in with his version of events. If the fact that he never visited the actual Front was the only count against him it would be sufficient to condemn him. But how like a man not wanting to see the suffering lest he be upset. People always complain about muck-raking biographers, saying: 'Leave us our heroes.' 'Leave us our villains' is just as important.

4 July. In the evening go across the road to the newly empty No. 55 for a kind of book fair. Francis Hope died in the Paris air-crash in 1974; pressed for space, his widow Mary Hope is now, twenty-two years later, disposing of his books and has asked some of his friends round for a glass of wine and to take away whatever they might want. It's an odd occasion, the sort of thing that might kick off a novel, with a group of middle-aged friends revisiting their youth and remembering some of the books they read then. There's Camus and Sartre, Colin Wilson and Lawrence Durrell – not quite the literary equivalent of flares but inducing something of the same incredulity: 'Did we really read/wear these?'

I miss the atlas I really wanted and come away with one or two biographies, including a memoir of David Winn, an Etonian contemporary of Francis who also died young.

26 August. Do not renew my subscription to the Friends of Regent's Park, one of whose aims seems to be to enforce the regulations against cycling in the Park. Ten years ago A. was fined £25 for riding her bike to the tennis courts at 7.30 in the morning, a piece of officiousness that could only happen in England. I have always thought that if the Prince of Wales or the Duke of Edinburgh meant what they say about the environment they'd long ago have put their weight behind a cycle track through the Park. Now it's out of their hands as the Park is run by some private concern which would, I'm sure, be only too happy to put a cycle track across the Park provided they could charge for the use of it.

1 October. I have just finished reading *A Passionate Prodigality* by Guy Chapman, one of the books belonging to Francis Hope that I picked up in the summer. From its less than snappy title it would be hard to guess what the book is about and this perhaps explains why, so far as I'm aware, it has no reputation. Originally published in 1933, it is Chapman's account of his experiences in the First War, when he served as a young subaltern from July 1915 right through until 1920, ending up in the Army of Occupation in Germany. It's one of the best accounts of the trenches I've read, with Chapman, despite himself, falling in love with his platoon and their life together much as Wilfred Owen did. He went on to become a professor of history at Leeds, where he married the novelist Storm Jameson, and thinking about it, I realise he must have taught the man who taught me history at school, H. H. Hill. So exhilarated have I been by the book, I find myself absurdly pleased at the connection.

17 October. Lunch in a restaurant in Chelsea with Maggie Smith and Beverley Cross. As Bev is paying the bill the proprietor murmurs that General Pinochet is lunching, as indeed he is, just round the corner from our table, though not quite within spitting distance. It's a table for eight or so, Pinochet with his back to the window, which might seem foolhardy except that in the first room of the restaurant there are three fairly obvious bodyguards, who scrutinise Bev and me carefully as we come out (and particularly, for some reason, my shoes). There's also a table nearby with four big young men, who might be heavies or might be businessmen, the fact that one can't tell maybe saying something about both. I cause the bodyguards some unease after Maggie comes out saying that sitting at an adjoining table had been Don Bachardy, so I go back in and have a word, last having seen him with Christopher Isherwood thirty-five years ago. Then he was an olive-skinned doe-eyed boy who came round and did a drawing of me. Now he looks exactly as

Isherwood did, even down to the little schoolboy sprout of hair at the back.

Apropos Pinochet, anybody brought up on Hollywood films of the forties would know instantly he was a villain. Distinguished, grey-haired and seemingly genial, he is the image of those crooked lawyers, ostensibly pillars of the community, who turned out to be the brains behind the local rackets and vice rings. They were played by actors like Edward Arnold, Thurston Hall or Otto Kruger; rich, kindly, avuncular figures, they deceived everyone in the film but nobody in the audience, who were not at all surprised to see them taken away at the end, snarling with impotent fury. Not so General Pinochet and his cronies, tucking into their fish this October afternoon, the murmur of polite conversation drowning the screams from the cellar.

25 *October*. A figure (often of fun) who keeps cropping up in memoirs of the Second War such as those of Nancy Mitford and James Lees-Milne is Stuart Preston, nicknamed the Sergeant, an American serviceman who came over to work at US HQ in London, later taking part in the invasion. He seems to have very rapidly become a feature of the upper-class English social scene, setting hearts of both sexes aflutter. Lees-Milne notes (Friday, 2 April 1943) how Preston once came to see him off at Euston; Lees-Milne was actually going to Preston but he doesn't make anything of the coincidence. What happened to the Sergeant? Did he go back to America? Is he still around? Certainly his memories of that period would be interesting.*

Being seen off for Preston by someone called Preston reminds me of a party given for Christopher Isherwood and Don Bachardy by Robin and Francis Hope in their flat in Goodge Street in the sixties. As the doorbell rang, Robin saw to his horror that there was on the table a bottle of Bacardi rum, which he whisked away just in time. It was only afterwards that he found himself unable to analyse or locate the faux pas that he thought he had narrowly avoided making. Why would it have mattered?

---

* Born in 1915, in 1996 he was very much alive (though hating his wartime nickname) and living in Paris. He died in 2005.

7 *November*. To Whitemoor High Security Prison near March in Cambridgeshire, March that fogbound halt where I used to change en route from Leeds to Cambridge forty-five years ago. That station has gone now and the prison is built over what once were the marshalling yards, the ground too saturated in mineral waste for much else. Not that this makes it very different from the surrounding countryside, as that's pretty thoroughly polluted too, all hedges gone, the soil soused in fertiliser, a real Fison's Fen. And it goes on: as I have my sandwiches by a raddled copse, two tractors in tandem ply up and down a vast field, conscientiously soaking the soil with yet another spray. From a distance the prison might be an out-of-town shopping mall, Texas Homecare, Do It All and Toys 'R' Us. There's a crèche at the gate and a Visitors' Centre, as it might be for Fountains Abbey or Stonehenge. Reasoning that I am a visitor myself, I battle across the windswept car park but when I put my head inside I find it full of visitors of a different sort, the wives and mothers (and very much the children) of the inmates, *Birds of a Feather* territory, I suppose. At the gate proper I'm frisked, X-rayed, my handprints taken, and am then taken through a series of barred gates and sliding doors every bit as intimidating as the institution in *The Silence of the Lambs*. The education officer says that this is just the outer prison and that at the heart of it is an even more secure compound, the one from which some IRA prisoners escaped a couple of years ago. It's oppressively bleak and intimidating, the odd flower bed or shrubbery emphasising how soulless it is. It could be a business park or a warehouse at an airport – Brinks Mat, I imagine, something like this.

While the prisoners are brought down I wait in a little common room with one or two instructors and interested parties: a blind boy who teaches maths; Anne Hunt, who has been seconded from UEA; and another teacher who has come over from Blundeston Prison near Lowestoft to hear the talk. Which is actually no talk at all, as the prisoners rather than be lectured at prefer to ask questions.

There are about two dozen, mostly in their twenties and thirties, the most interested and articulate a Glasgow boy with a deep scar on his left cheek, who did *Talking Heads* as an A-level set book last year and is counted one of their successes. He kicks off straight away with questions, which then come without any of the awkwardness or silences there were at Wandsworth. There's a sophisticated Indian with a vaguely American accent, one older man who from his questions has had something to do with the film industry and a young man in a tracksuit with a lovely lit-up face who seems unable to stop smiling. There's lots and lots of charm, which one detects as charm and so is wary of, being made to wonder what part charm has played in whatever crimes these men have committed; at the same time it's hard not to be touched by this strong desire to please.

The teachers, while gratified that their pupils are so responsive, are anxious that one doesn't think them angels. The young man with the scar is there for armed robbery, the smiling boy has been convicted of a particularly nasty murder. ('He was quite famous for a time,' says one of the teachers.) Afterwards I regret not asking the men more questions myself, particularly about why they're here, though aware that it's not the form to do so (not the form to ask about form). The predominant feeling is one of waste, that these men have been locked up and nothing is being done with them. With resources stretched to breaking point, these classes are the next target in the event of further cuts. And this is the other impression one comes away with: the universal hatred and contempt for Michael Howard*– prisoners, warders, teachers, everybody one speaks to complaining how he has stripped away from the service all those amenities which alleviate the lives of everyone cooped up here, warders and prisoners alike. Indeed one gets the feeling that the only thing that is holding the prison service together and making it for the moment work is this shared hatred for Michael Howard.

Confused and depressed, I have my handprints checked to ensure I am the same person now as the one who came here two hours ago; then I drive in high winds across the chemical countryside and down the A1, managing a quick bath before I bike down to the Comedy, where I'm filling in for Maggie Smith, who has laryngitis.

* Then Home Secretary.

9 November. To New York, travelling economy on British Airways as I generally do, though always in the hope (seldom realised) that I might be recognised and upgraded. It isn't that I can't afford the club-class fare but £2,000 seems a lot of money to pay for something I dislike as much as I do flying, even though the alternative is seven hours of discomfort. There's a Yorkshire dialect word that covers this feeling more succinctly than any phrase in standard English. When you can afford something but don't like to see the money go in that particular way you say: 'I can't *thoil* to pay it.' Which is exactly what I feel about club class. Most of my contemporaries seem to find organisations willing to pay their transatlantic fares for them, but I don't do very well here either and when Random House brought out *Writing Home* in the US last year they claimed their budget didn't run to flying me over for the occasion be it club class or economy.

17 November, New York. I sit in Dean and Delucca on Prince Street, reading how the men in brown coats have finally come to Westminster Abbey and carted off the Stone of Scone. No one in Scotland seems in the least impressed with John Major's imaginative gesture: they've got more sense, though with the relic up for grabs there was an undignified scramble between various venues wanting it for its commercial and tourist potential. In this sense it's very much in the tradition of all the other Tory sell-offs.

The return of the largely unwanted Stone was intended to buoy up the hapless Mr Forsyth, though any favour the government might have hoped to curry north of the border has since been wiped out by the aftermath of Dunblane. Sometimes feeling I am the last person in the country to believe in the monarchy, I am surprised the Queen didn't make more fuss. The Stone, if only by association, must be considered a part of the royal regalia over which the government, constitutionally, has no say at all. J. Major obviously didn't think of it as of much consequence, as the original decision was conveyed to the Dean of Westminster by some lowly official with a chitty. Whatever one expects from this government it's not a sense of history, and with a Japanese hotel opposite the Houses of

Parliament and a Ferris wheel dwarfing Big Ben, who cares that the shrine of Edward the Confessor has been robbed of its most ancient relic? As it is, the Coronation Chair is left looking like an empty commode. In view of the current state of the monarchy this may seem appropriate and please a lot of people, but not me.

1 December, New York. To the Brooklyn Museum to see *In the Light of Italy*, plein-air paintings by Thomas Jones, Valenciennes and the predecessors of Corot. It's a vast building with wide corridors and huge airy galleries, though without much atmosphere and no sense that the building itself might be of interest; the museum just a series of plain rooms within its shell. Take my canvas stool, which is a great talking point with other gallery-goers, mostly elderly and female and wanting the same.

On the way home we stop for some tea at Barnes and Noble on Union Square. All the Barnes and Noble bookshops have lately been transformed, turned into what are virtually free libraries. There are easy chairs in which people are encouraged to read the books on display; tables at which students are sitting, making notes from the books and, upstairs in the café, a huge rack of every conceivable magazine and newspaper which you are encouraged to take to your table to read with your tea, reading all that is required. Nor is it simply patronised by what one might think of as the reading public. A workman in overalls is sitting looking at a book on Chardin, the little black boy in Philip Roth's *Goodbye, Columbus* who came into the library to look at a book on Gauguin now grown up. But it doesn't have to be as worthy as that: the boy at the next table is leafing through a muscle mag. The feeling is overwhelmingly democratic and lifts the spirits. It's said that the experiment has improved business. I hope so, as it's inspiring to see and, as so often in America, one is shamed by a civic sense which, if we ever had it in England, we don't have now. Dutifully readers clear their tables, put the trash in the bin and the magazines back on the racks and behave in a way that is both more civilised and considerate and (this is where we would really fall down) unselfconscious than we could ever manage. God bless America.

1997

2 January. I'm sent a complimentary (*sic*) copy of Waterstone's Literary Diary which records the birthdays of various contemporary figures from the world of letters. Here is Dennis Potter on 17 May, Michael Frayn on 8 September, Edna O'Brien on 15 December, and so naturally I turn to my own birthday. May 9 is blank except for the note: 'The first British self-service launderette is opened on Queensway, London 1949.'

4 January. George F. tells me that when Andrew Lloyd Webber, the Lord Lloyd Webber, as we must now say, bought his Canaletto at Christie's he paid the £10 million bill by Access in order to earn the air miles – enough presumably to last him till the end of his days. Such lacing of extravagance with prudence has since become so common that Christie's has now suspended credit card payments altogether.

6 January, Yorkshire. Ring Mr Redhead, the coal-merchant in Ingleton.
    'Hello, Mr Redhead, this is Alan Bennett. I'm wanting some coal.'
    'Goodness me! I am consorting with higher beings!'
    Last time I rang Mr Redhead he said, 'Well, I don't care how celebrated you are, you'll never be a patch on your dad.' I remind him of this.
    'That's correct and I reiterate it.'

13 January. Liam Gallagher, the younger of the Oasis brothers, has the kind of eyes in which the pupils are half-hidden under the eyelids; as if the eyes had stopped between floors. Spike Lee has similar eyes, which I find attractive, maybe because they give a sense of inhabiting worlds other than this; they are, of course, irritating for exactly the same reason.
    A call from Barry Cryer, who claims to have heard a woman outside Liberty's saying to her husband: 'Remind me to tell Austin that there is no main verb in that sentence.'

15 January, Yorkshire. Trying to put my forty-year-old letters in order, I come across a diary for 1956–9. It's depressing to read as very little of it is factual and most of it to do with my slightly sickening obsession with, coupled with a lack of insight into, my own character. It's full of embarrassing resolutions about future conduct and exhortations to myself to do better. Love is treated very obliquely, passing fancies thought of as echoes of some Grand Passion.

My first inclination is to put it in the bin, though I probably won't. I can see why writers do, though, fearful that these commonplace beginnings might infect what comes after with their banality. In this sense Orton (and to some extent Larkin) are exceptional, Orton's early diaries written with the same peculiar slant on the world as his mature writing.

1957 was the year I should have come down from Oxford but didn't and one thing I think reading this tosh is that if I hadn't got a First (the circumstances undescribed in the diary) I would never have picked myself up to do much except possibly teach badly. It was the fairly spurious self-confidence I got from this fluke result, plus the breathing space it gave, that enabled me to go on doing silly turns, being funny and thus eventually to write.

20 January. Sheila J. up the road says that in last week's fog she came upon two Brent geese grounded outside No. 60. She rang the RSPCA, who said that since they were on the road they were the responsibility of the highways authority. Camden being Camden the highways department was unreachable and probably had better things to do anyway. So, remembering that in fairy stories goose-girls always carried a stick, Sheila got one from a garden; at which point Juliet C. emerged and the two of them herded the geese up the Crescent, eventually penning them in the garden of No. 70. One settled happily in the ornamental pond there, but the other, taking advantage of the not very long lawn, took off for home, presumably Regent's Park. In the morning its companion did the same.

26 January. Come back on an early train from Yorkshire to catch the last day of the National Art Collections Fund exhibition at Christie's. Expecting St James's to be empty, I find every street crammed with cars. Christie's, too, is crowded, full of art-lovers more specially earnest than the general run so that something about the show repels – the homogeneity of the art-lovers, perhaps, or their wholehearted worthiness and consistent middle-agedness. When I leave, the streets are full of disconsolate Roundheads and jubilant Cavaliers, the explanation for all the cars some mock battle in Green Park. Note how one passes these far from sheepish figures without a second glance; the kind of extraordinary feature of ordinary life that never gets into a film except as part of the plot.

In the evening read at St Mark's, Primrose Hill, in aid of the appeal against the demolition of the chapel of the old Boys' Home in Regent's Park Road and the construction of some frightful block of flats. Church packed, people standing at the back, and though the audience is a bit sticky to start with (heard it all before, I suspect), there is a good response at the end. I'd said no to an *Evening Standard* reporter who wanted to interview me and get a photograph. He'd been quite nice about it and gone away, but when I come out the photographer is still hanging about and asks me to pose with my bike. I say no, whereupon he starts snapping regardless. Even as I cycle off down Regent's Park Road he runs after me snapping away. Why? On spec, I suppose, but the real reason he wants a photograph is that he knows I don't. Whatever pictures he took would have me looking like a flustered turkey and presumably quite silly, so whether this is preferable to the Me and My Bike shot he wanted in the first place is debatable.

30 January. *Meats* is a form I don't care for, the proper plural of *meat* being *meat*. Perhaps *meats* (on a van: 'British Premium Meats') means cooked meats, though *meat* would still be acceptable there, too. *Meats* suggests to me something not only cooked but sliced, and already beginning to curl at the edges. Odd that one should have any feelings, let alone care, about such usages.

31 January. The limpid theme which introduces the Agnus Dei in Fauré's Requiem currently introduces the product in the Lurpak butter commercial.

Walk behind a tramp wearing no socks. Heels like turnips.

6 February. Alec G. asks for help with finding questions for a charity literary quiz. Suggest:

Q. Who thought the Venerable Bede was a woman?
A. Field Marshal Haig, who said so after musing for some time beside the Venerable Bede's tomb at Durham, presumably mixing up George Eliot and Adam Bede.
Q. Where in Oxford would you find a crucifix that had been gazed on by Pascal?
A. Campion Hall. (It is a Jansenist crucifix which comes from Port Royal.)
Q. What had A. E. Housman in common with the son of the author of *Wind in the Willows?*
A. A nickname: Mouse.

Tell the Bede story to Maggie Smith, who recalls some lines she had to sing in revue:

> Oh, I am the Venerable Bede
> I can scarcely write and just about read.

18 February. Listening to the last movement of Elgar's First Symphony I'm put in mind of some huge submerged mass coming to the surface. What is this great sunken thing that now heaves itself into view, the water sluicing off it? England, is it? Destiny? A sense of purpose? This is how I used to think when I was seventeen: that music showed you how to live your life.

As a boy, I was resigned though never reconciled to what I thought of as the back of beyondness, where I lived. Life in Leeds was desperately provincial and unexciting, so concerts in the Town Hall had another function in that they would sometimes bring to the city fabled creatures from the world of the wireless: Sargent, Barbirolli and even Beecham.

Still, so famished was I for fame I must be one of the few boys who could have seen Sir Adrian Boult as in any sense an exotic and even a glamorous figure. Not quite an Edwardian, which he certainly looked, Boult seemed of another age entirely, a contemporary (though he wasn't) of Elgar, whom with his walrus moustache he also resembled. Though what he also looked like was one of those inflexible generals (Sir Hubert Gough comes to mind) who had conducted the First War.

Boult eschewed any emotion on the podium, his impassive beat varied only by the occasional clenched fist. He was thus an early entrant into my (slightly priggish) pantheon of non-histrionics which included, in poetry A. E. Housman, in literature F. M. Forster, in philosophy J. L. Austin and in the matter of crossing deserts Wilfred Thesiger. I knew I could never live up to any of them: I talked too much.

20–21 February. Two days filming my TV parables programme *Heavenly Stories* at Dulwich College, the setting the Masters' Library, a galleried, High Victorian room adjoining the school hall, presumably where the masters foregather before assembly. Over the chimneypiece are two crude allegorical panels of Piety and Liberality, the ideals of Alleyn's foundation. There are plenty of nice books, many with a forties-ish feel, like *Enthusiasm* by Ronald Knox, one of the 'wider reading' books I swotted up for my scholarship.

Remembering Bruce McFarlane was at Dulwich, I wander into Charles Barry's huge hammer-beam hall, the walls lined with honours boards of distinctions at Oxford and Cambridge chiefly; though there's some mention of the army and the Indian Civil Service, there is none of any other universities or places of higher education. And here is Bruce's open scholarship to Exeter in 1922, his first-class degree three years later; his Senior Demyship at Magdalen in 1925 and the Bryce Studentship; then, in 1926, a fellowship at Magdalen. Unsurprisingly, he doesn't figure in any of the team photographs that line the corridors.

A woman is restoring some of the lettering on the honours board and she tells me that until a few years ago they were covered in varnish and thick wallpaper, the work of an aesthetically minded headmaster's wife. Now they are being restored and, as inaccuracies are uncovered (ex-pupils assigned to the wrong colleges), she is at work on corrections. She seems vaguely familiar and I start telling her about a woman I'd talked to a year or so ago, having gone into a church at Inglesham near Lechlade and found her restoring the wall-paintings there.

'Yes,' she says happily, 'it was me.' It seems an extraordinary coincidence. She tells me that the two paintings over the fireplace are far from being the daubs I thought they were but reputedly come from Queen Elizabeth I's state barge and may even have accompanied Drake round the world on the *Golden Hind*.

22 February. Jocelyn Herbert's eightieth birthday party at the Royal College of Art, the Senior Common Room packed with everyone Jocelyn has known or worked with. There is music that has been specially composed, and a poem by Tony Harrison, the theme of which is all the toasts he and Jocelyn have drunk together in all the various places where they have worked around the world. They're due to set off on Monday on another epic journey, the script, based on the Prometheus legend, about a gold statue transported from South Yorkshire (film of the demolition of some cooling towers near Barnsley) through Eastern Europe to Greece. Tony mentions in the poem her absent friends: George Devine, Ron Eyre, Tony Richardson, John and John (Dexter and Osborne), and at the conclusion a cake is brought in and Jocelyn is crowned with laurels. It could be thought pretentious but since Jocelyn is so far from pretentious it seems both fitting and moving.

I sit on a sofa with Alan Bates and Maggie Smith, thinking that no one would ever arrange such a do for me or get so many people to come. I turn to Maggie and she says: 'Don't say it. I know. I don't think I could even fill the kitchen.'

26 February. It's thought that most of the frocks that Princess Diana is selling off will end up in the wardrobes of transvestites. Were someone set to write a script which would persistently humiliate the Royal Family they could scarcely do better (or worse) than the one which circumstances have devised.

6 March. The eighty-five-year-old Sir Denis Mahon has been paying frequent visits to *Discovering the Italian Baroque*, the exhibition of his collection at the National Gallery, to which he has bequeathed many of the pictures that are on show. The other day a warder watched him for some time, then came up behind him and said: 'I've had my eye on you. You get too close to the pictures.' Sir Denis went to the Director and complimented him on the vigilance of his staff.

25 March, Yorkshire. Everybody else seems to have seen the comet, but though I've been up on the roof several times searching the northern sky like Herod, I have seen nothing. We're driving up from Leeds about eleven tonight when, without looking for it, I suddenly see it from the Addingham bypass, hovering, as it were, above Bolton Abbey. It dodges from side to side of the road all the way over into Airedale, then up to Settle and home. I can't get over the spread of its tail, a great shower of light flying behind it, and also that the thing itself doesn't look like a star but seems circular. In fact what is surprising is that a comet should look like the illustrations of comets. It's so bright it's as if there is a hole in the surface of the sky, a porthole through which the light is streaming from the shining world beyond. I look out again just before I go to bed and it's still tearing through the clear sky with its 60-million-mile train.

Maundy Thursday, Yorkshire. See on billboards in Leeds that HMQ has been in Bradford washing the feet of selected pensioners from the Bradford diocese, or rather paying in order not to. Interviewed, all the pensioners say they are overwhelmed at the honour done to the region; one says she knew the invitation was something out of the ordinary as the envelope wouldn't go through her letter box. When I get to the village I find that one of these pensioners was our ex-postman Maurice Brown. I ask him whether the Queen spoke to him. 'No. She only stopped at people who had something wrong with them. I haven't, so she just gave me the money.'

29 March, Yorkshire. Easter Saturday and an appropriately monastic day out, going first via traffic-choked Northallerton to Mount Grace, which I had thought a remote spot but which is within sight and sound of the busy A19 to Teesside. Envy the nice life a Carthusian monk must have had in the early fifteenth century: meals brought to the door, sitting room, study and bedroom looking out on a little garden with, at the end of the colonnade, the loo.

Then some delicious sandwiches (cold pheasant and stuffing) on the edge of a ploughed field near Masham, sun warm and the hawthorn just coming into leaf. We go down the hill to Well to look at the towering pinnacle of fretted wood over the font, 1352 and the second oldest in England. Then on to Jervaulx, one of the few monastic ruins not run by English Heritage or the National Trust but by its country-house owners, for whom it must once have been like an elaborate folly. The ruins are thatched with vegetation and herbaceous plants, and piled up round the grassy banks are great heaps of unlocated masonry. The plan of the abbey is quite clear, though, and I realise that any Cistercian monk could move from one abbey to another and not find himself puzzled as to his whereabouts. The component parts – cloisters, library, dormitory – might differ in scale, but the relationship between them would be much the same from one abbey to the next.

2 April, Yorkshire. Come across a thirty-year-old note from David Vaisey, at that time a postgraduate student at Bodley and subsequently its Librarian. The note just a crudely drawn swastika and the slogan: 'A.L. Raus'.

14 April. Pass two slightly cheeky-looking middle-aged businessmen in Hanover Square, one of whom is talking about 'the rodeo position'.

'Yes, what is that?' asks the other. 'I don't know what the rodeo position is.'

I take this to be a conversation about sex and it's only later that it occurs to me that if there's a company called Rodeo the discussion may well have been about a financial position rather than a sexual one.

16 April. Another day filming for the TV version of Anthony Powell's *Dance to the Music of Time*, the location a crumbling neo-Gothic pile at Sonning with a vast view over the Thames Valley. Built by a Victorian millionaire MP, it was only briefly inhabited before it became what it was obviously suited for – namely, an asylum. It's surrounded by various generations of outbuildings and Nissen huts but has a number of magnificent Gothic rooms, one of which is doing duty today as the House of Commons dining room.

I play Sillery, now eighty, though I can't say I adjust the acting to the age, a white wig doing most of the work. I am supposed to be entertaining, or being entertained by, a group of young MPs, my only line being: 'I will mention your name to the Italian Ambassador. I'm dining with him tomorrow night at Diana Cooper's.' Most of the time our table is 'background action' to a foreground scene of some talk at another table between John Standing, playing Nicholas Jenkins, and Jeremy Clyde, playing Roddie Cutts. Christopher Morahan wants our table to be having an animated and amusing conversation, with Sillery the life and soul of the party.

There is one problem with this and that is that the MPs are played by London extras, a notoriously difficult, uncooperative section of the profession and about as helpful as, I'm told, the chorus at Covent Garden. There are reasons for this unhelpfulness: though they're not badly paid, the extras are seldom given much encouragement by directors and often treated as not much more than movable scenery. Certainly on this occasion they resent having to talk at all and I am left animatedly chatting to these four unresponsive young men, one expressionless, light-eyed actor making me feel a particular fool. John Standing and Jeremy Clyde look across sympathetically, knowing exactly what the situation is. Eventually I try and force some response by asking them who is the worst director they've ever worked with or the most unpleasant actor. This at least elicits something, including the interesting fact that very often leading actors (Tom Cruise is mentioned and, down the scale a bit, Jimmy Nail) require that the extras do not look at them while they are performing as they find it off-putting.

One of the extras asks me what I am reading. I show him my book, some Alice Munro short stories, whereupon he says, 'I'm reading this,' and takes out a paperback of *My Secret Life*, the saga of the sexual adventures of a middle-class gentleman in Victorian London. It's a book with more sex per page than almost any other, and not a book I had thought that one reads, at least in any sequential way, as it's just one fuck after another, with no plot or progression, not even that short journey from the simple to the complex, the straight to the kinky, that characterises most pornography. The matter of fact way he brings out the book slightly surprises me but we talk about it and I explain, rather in the manner of the character I'm playing, the doubts that have been expressed about its authenticity and the light it throws on the street life and topography of Victorian London. But now they are ready to start the scene and I look again into the dead eyes of my impassive neighbour, who did three days last week on *The Bill*, and tell him that I will mention his name to the Italian Ambassador, with whom I will be dining tomorrow night at Diana Cooper's.

22 *April*. Filming again at Breakspears, the manor house near Harefield where last autumn we shot an earlier scene of *Dance to the Music of Time*. A Queen Anne house with later additions, it is now forlorn and neglected and has the CV of many too-large country houses, ending up as either a conference centre or an old people's home. This has been a home but has since been used for umpteen films, relics of which are scattered through its cold, damp and listed rooms. Judy Egerton at the National Gallery tells me that Breakspears was once the childhood home of Elizabeth Stephen, the bride of William Hallett, who together constitute Gainsborough's

Morning Walk, and that Reynolds's *Colonel Tarleton* used to hang in the house. *Colonel Tarleton* is one of the paintings (another being Millais's *Lorenzo and Isabella*) which would figure in a dream exhibition, 'Nice Legs' (or rather 'Nice Legs on Men').

1 May. Cast my vote early, the ballot paper longer than I ever remember and the party affiliations in very modest type. Though there are predictions of a Labour victory, even from the Tories, I am still nervous that factors like this will affect the result. Nor am I alone in my uncertainty. Go down to the National Gallery for a meeting of the Trustees, where Keith Thomas tells me that his polling booth in Oxford is next door to a pub in Merton Street and that, it being May morning, he had to fight his way in through crowds of drunken revellers, an ordeal he feels might deter tamer spirits. As a historian he speculates whether such considerations are too subtle to be picked up by the psephologists, among whom David Butler figures, as he has done in every election that I can ever recall.

2 May, Chicago. Sitting on my bag at O'Hare waiting for the other to come round on the carousel, I become aware of a small white terrier sniffing round me. Thinking it might slyly cock its leg, I shoo it away, only to find it's attached to a customs officer who politely asks me if I am carrying any prohibited merchandise. Having already declared on the form that I'm not, I suddenly remember two oranges I bought to eat on the plane and shamefacedly extract them. The customs officer examines them and says with no hint of reproach that he will have to confiscate the fruit but in return gives me a postcard with a picture of the dog and the compliments of the Beagle Brigade.

At the hotel, hoping to find some post-election coverage, I switch on CNN and indeed catch Tony Blair arriving at Downing Street (though not John Major leaving it, which I would quite like to have seen). However, it's the briefest flash and is put in perspective by the next item, a much more extensive piece about how Eddie Murphy invited a transvestite prostitute into his car with a view to putting him/her on the right road.

3 May. To the Chicago Art Institute, a relatively modest museum but with superb paintings. It's Saturday and very busy so I confine myself to rooms with benches and find myself sitting in front of a Cranach Crucifixion, notable because the Bad Thief is depicted as fat, a great beer gut sagging down from the Cross. Everyone – the Holy Family apart – is grotesque, while Christ himself is so idealised he belongs in a different painting, crucified against a blue and white sky that looks like a map of the world. His thighs are concealed by dancing draperies, and since I'm currently reading the new edition of Steinberg's *The Sexuality of Christ in Renaissance Art and Modern Oblivion*, I scan the floating linens for the erection Steinberg often manages to detect, though not, I think, here. In the crowd at the foot of the Cross is a child who looks up as its father points at the figure of Christ. There is a father and son of similar age looking at the picture, but here it is the child who is pointing while the father explains what is happening. It is such a neat coincidence I note it diffidently – one might easily be thought to have invented it.

The star of the gallery is Seurat's *La Grande Jatte*, which has a perpetual crowd, while ignored is a beautiful (and rather classical) self-portrait by Van Gogh, whom I don't always care for, and also the Degas Hat Shop, which was shown last year at the National Gallery.

6 May, New York. To the Frick, last visited in 1963. It hasn't changed much and can't change much, I imagine, by the terms of its endowment. What has changed is the number of visitors: in 1963 I was the only person there; today it's crowded out, a large proportion of the visitors for some reason French, including two droll-looking dikey, long-nosed ladies who might have run a bar or spirited away fallen flyers during the war. Few seats, or seats that can be sat on, so I end up in the picture gallery, where there are a couple of benches – and a couple of Rembrandts, too, and a brace of Turners, a Velázquez and a Vermeer, the arrangement, roughly, portrait–landscape–portrait–landscape all round this dark, glass-ceilinged room. None of the paintings is shown to advantage, most looking dull and hung so close to each other as to make them difficult to take in on their own. Thus there's a painting of Philip IV by Velázquez hung next to Vermeer's *Lady with Her Maid* and a self-portrait of Rembrandt in old age; none is lit, they don't complement one another, and together look like a trio of mud-coloured pictures.

It would be more sensible to arrange the collection chronologically: the way it is now, one is made more conscious of the fact that Frick had no particular taste and no eye for pictures, except the expensive ones, and that Duveen and Berenson and whoever else bought for him had no notion of putting together a group of paintings which, besides being masterpieces, were also a pleasure to live with. These were merely to be gloated over, so that Rembrandt and Van Dyck here seem vulgar and even Vermeer only just survives.

8 May, New York. The warders at the Metropolitan Museum are given no chairs and so are always on the move and, less mindful of the reverence due to art that pervades the National Gallery, hold lively conversations with the warder next door. 'I mean,' says one Hispanic warder, 'this is a woman who changes her hair colour three times a week. Where are you with a dame like that? You don't know.'

The names Americans visit on their children never cease to amaze me. One of Diana Ross's daughters labours under the name of Chudney.

12 May, New York. Sit looking out of the bedroom window into the back garden of a house on the next block where an idyll develops. An elderly couple are unhurriedly setting the table for brunch, beginning with a huge jar of buttercups, perhaps bought in yesterday's farmers' market in Union Square. Then as she brings out a bottle of white wine, the table setting is invaded and upset by a large Abyssinian cat, which has to be lifted off. Now comes lunch itself, omelette and salad, which he has prepared. The couple clink wine glasses before drinking, and, each with a book, eat their brunch. They seem straight out of a short story in the (old) *New Yorker*. Now a squirrel appears, running some urgent, necessary errand and slightly lame in its left paw. The wildlife in this garden

– sparrows, squirrels, a blackbird – all belongs to the third division, drab, tame, unexotic, the wildlife of my childhood. The vegetation is middle of the road too – ivy, sycamore, flowering currant and, of course, privet.

13 May, New York. Dining at Balthazar, Keith's new restaurant, we are across the aisle from Calvin Klein. I have half a mind to step across and say: 'I don't suppose you'd be interested, Mr Klein, and I don't want to intrude on your privacy, but we're both wearing your underpants.' Calvin Klein is sitting with Susan Sontag. Actually he isn't but if he were it would sum up what celebrity means in New York.

22 May. Watch the second programme in the BBC2 series *It's Not Unusual*, in which gays and lesbians, many in their seventies and eighties, recall their experiences in the Second World War and the lives they led. It's both droll and inspiring; the unselfconscious way these eighty-year-olds recall experiences in the WAAF or as seamen on the Western Approaches makes one want to raise a cheer, not for gay liberation particularly, but for toleration and common sense, and also for courage.

In tonight's programme there's an unlikely homosexual, a Doncaster miner, Fred Dyson; photographs show him as a merry-faced boy built like the proverbial brick shit-house, now recalled by the grey-haired monumental figure he has since become. Arrested for propositioning a policeman in a lavatory when he was in his early twenties, he was brought before a lady magistrate in Doncaster – this would be in the fifties – who asked him how long he had had 'these feelings'.

'All my life, Your Worship.'

'Have you ever thought of trying for a cure?'

'A cure? Listen, love. If there was a cure for this there'd be a queue miles long.'

He was fined £50, and because he'd spoken up the case was extensively reported in the local papers. He went to work next day (shots of miners soaping each other in the pit-head baths) and talked to a union official about whether he could go on working there, or show his face in the social club. The union official offered to go to the social club with him and they were standing at the bar when one of his fellow miners came up and shook his hand and after that it was all right.

31 May. A late birthday present from Mary-Kay Wilmers, a mug dated January 1889, commemorating the gift by Colonel North of the ruins of Kirkstall Abbey to the then borough of Leeds. There is a picture of Kirkstall and the inscription: 'Built in 1147. Destroyed by Oliver Cromwell in 1539.' This was what most people believed in Leeds when I was a boy, the notion that there could have been two iconoclasts both named Cromwell but a century apart too much of a coincidence for them to take. The idea that it was 'built in 1147' is equally silly.

Run into Edmund White, who tells me what a revelation *Beyond the Fringe* was when he saw it in New York in 1963, how sophisticated it seemed and how camp. He ends up by asking me, as Harold Wilson once did: 'Were you one of the original four?'

I wonder whether there were any shy, retiring Apostles: 'Were you one of the original twelve?'

14 July. I wish there had been rollerblades in my time (though I would probably have thought them 'not my kind of thing'). They seem the epitome of grace. Skateboarding, on the other hand, now looks clumsy and, however skilfully done, somehow desperate and without art.

25 July. Dubbing the kind of characters I write about – denizens of retirement homes, ageing aunties, old people on their last legs – I choose suitably solid, old-fashioned names: Frank, Harold, Arthur, Nora, names of their period. Just. Because, of course, the personnel of these designated scrap heaps is altering. Ranged in vacant rows or stood immobile by a radiator, these shrunken creatures still answer to Hannah, Arthur, Peggy and Bill. But soon it will be Melanie and Karen, Dean and Sandra Louise. Somewhere I wrote some half-heard dialogue on the edge of a scene outside an old people's home: as the middle-aged children of one deceased resident come away carrying his meagre possessions the matron is helping another old man out of the ambulance, saying: 'Hello! Welcome! You're our first Kevin!'

12 August. The BBC are planning some elite channel, and have written to Anthony Jones, my literary agent, saying that since I was so distinguished and award-winning etc. they would be happy to pay £3,500 for my entire oeuvre. What happens if you're not distinguished and award-winning, my agent wonders. Do you pay them?

Read an article suggesting that Giotto's frescoes in the Arena Chapel were largely done by another painter, Cavallini, now forgotten because, unlike Giotto, he was not singled out for mention by Vasari. I don't believe this, if only because the name Cavallini lacks substance. He sounds like a juggler or a conjuror appearing on the halls: The Great Cavallini.

14 August. From time to time, sitting in the garden chair outside my front door, I hear an audible thud and a fat, emerald-green caterpillar drops from one of the lime trees onto the car bonnet. Today one lands on the flags and is straight away assailed by a wasp which either bites or stings it so that the caterpillar wriggles in pain. I watch this process for a while, then stamp on the caterpillar to put it out of its misery. Later another caterpillar falls and is picked up by the resident blackbird, which pecks away at it. There is more flinching from the caterpillar but this I watch with no distaste at all, just glad that the blackbird has found a decent meal. The hen blackbird, which was rather stupid and which I thought the cats had got, is now about again.

31 August. An American woman who witnessed the accident to Princess Diana is interviewed on television and says that she noticed that the air bag was 'fully deployed'. An entirely correct usage, I'm sure, but who in England other than a technician would think to say it?

2 September. Hysteria over the death of Princess Diana continues, people 'from all walks of life' queuing down the Mall, not merely to sign the book but to sit there writing for up to fifteen minutes at a time. Others, presumably, just write 'Why?', which suggests a certain cosmic awareness besides having the merit of brevity.

'What a treasured possession these books will be for her two sons,' says the BBC commentator, which has echoes of Ernest Worthing and the Army Lists. It also summons up the last scene of *Raiders of the Lost Ark* and the thousands of tea chests in a dusty unvisited cellar. Apparently, similar volumes are to be opened all over the country and it will be possible to analyse regional differences in the degree of mourning.

3 September. The order of service is published for the funeral, the music to be played, Albinoni, Pachelbel and Elgar's 'Nimrod'. It's the apotheosis of Classic FM. The Dean: 'And now from Elgar's *Enigma Variations* "Nimrod", which is on page two of your Order of Service and No. 17 in this week's Classic Countdown.' The poor Queen is to be forced to go mournabout. I suppose it is a revolution but with Rosa Luxemburg played by Sharon and Tracy.

4 September. 'God created a blonde angel and called her Diana.' This is one of the cards on the flowers outside Kensington Palace that the BBC chooses to zoom in on. It purports to be from a child, though whether one is supposed to be touched by it or (as is my inclination) to throw up isn't plain.

HMQ to address the nation tomorrow. I'm only surprised Her Majesty hasn't had to submit to a phone-in.

5 September. HMQ gives an unconvincing broadcast: 'unconvincing' not because one doesn't believe that her sentiments are genuine (as to that there's no way of telling), but because she's not a good actress, indeed not an actress at all. What she should have been directed to do is to throw in a few pauses and seem to be searching for her words; then the speech would have been hailed as moving and heartfelt. As it is she reels her message off, as she always does. That is the difference between Princess Diana and the Queen: one could act, the other can't.

I remember, regretfully now, one of HMQ's lines in *A Question of Attribution* which, when we were looking for cuts, we took out: 'I don't like it when people clap me because there may come a time when they won't. Besides I'm *there*. It's like clapping Nelson's Column.'

After supper we go down to look at the scene in the Mall, which is full of people not particularly silent, no mood at all, really, just walking up and down as if coming away from an event, though it's also like a huge *passeggiata*. People crowd to the walls and hedges, where there are flowers and little candlelit shrines; flowers fixed to trees, poems, painted messages; a Union Jack and teddy bears (which always bode ill). Many are Asian and the populousness of it, as well as the random milling about, make me think that this is perhaps what India is like.

The evening is redeemed by an extraordinary sight. Despite the hundreds and hundreds of people trooping past, here, on the grass by the corner of Stable House Street, is a fox. It is just out of the light, slinking by with its head turned towards the parade of people passing, none of whom notice it. It's quite small, as much fawn as red, and is, I imagine, a vixen. It lopes unhurriedly along the verge before diving under the hedge into St James's Palace grounds. Besides us only one woman notices it, but that's probably just as well: such is the hysteria and general silliness it might have been hailed as the reincarnation of Princess Diana, another beautiful vixen, with whom lots of parallels suggest themselves. We walk back through Green Park where, set back from the Victoria Memorial, is a bright little bivouac, which I take to be people pitching camp and staking a claim for the procession tomorrow. In fact it's the HQ of British Telecom, half a dozen technicians squatting under their orange canopy, their interest focused on computer screens. It's the kind of subject Eric Ravilious would have picked out, or Ardizzone in the Western Desert.

Walk back through Shepherd Market, now smart and gentrified, cafés on pavements and all that. Except it hasn't altogether changed, as in one corner there's an open door, a lighted staircase and a notice: 'New Tasty Babe Upstairs'.

15 September, Yorkshire. Blackberrying up Black Bank, taking with me one of Miss Shepherd's old walking sticks. Huge clusters of berries so that one can gather them almost by the handful. Never so utterly at peace as when picking blackberries or looking for mushrooms, the spread of Ingleborough and Pen-y-ghent still sunny while black clouds gather over Morecambe. A flock of sheep comes up the road and won't pass me until I stand in the ditch. The pretty farm girl who is bringing up the rear seems almost as reluctant to pass as the sheep, just giving me a shy 'Hello' and running on. A mountain ash tree, weighed down with huge swags of crimson berries, catches the last of the sun. It's like something by Samuel Palmer; paint it as bright and glowing as it is and it would seem like a vision.

25 September. The *Bradford Telegraph and Argus* rings at about ten-thirty to say that Jonathan Silver has died. I last spoke to him in July, when he rang to say that I had been much in his mind since he was now wholly at the mercy of his doctors and so was feeling like George III. Some of their procedures (a baseball cap filled with ice worn for some hours to preserve his hair from radiotherapy) would not have been out of place in the eighteenth century. I am normally immune to enthusiasm and even recoil from it but Jonathan's was irresistible, and I admired the fact that he had created at Salt's Mill an arts centre, a bookshop, a restaurant and a gallery crammed with Hockneys, and that it wasn't simply pious or well intentioned but worked well on every level, artistic and commercial.

He was proud of the success of Salt's Mill and delighted to show it off, even taking one round the premises of the various firms whose rents made the running of the gallery possible. A look of patient indulgence would come over the faces of these northern executives, knowing that he was obsessive and bearing it patiently, because, had he not been so, the Mill would never have taken off.

In a way it's fitting that the setting for all this should have been Saltaire, the inspiration of the Nonconformist nineteenth-century mill owner and philanthropist Sir Titus Salt. Voluble, pony-tailed, brimming with enthusiasm, Jonathan Silver was his worthy successor.

26 September. Listen to a superb recording of *Tristram Shandy* read by John Moffatt, who manages to make sense in the reading of stuff that is almost incomprehensible on the page. John was once doing some Chekhov in Edinburgh and heard a lady coming away afterwards say: 'There was a lot of laughter at the end of the first act, but I soon put a stop to that.' He also played in Perth, where *The Cherry Orchard* was billed as *The Cheery Orchard*.

30 September. Read *The Birth of Shylock and the Death of Zero Mostel* by Arnold Wesker, an account of his attempts to get his play *Shylock* produced and how it flopped on Broadway. Much of it I find sympathetic, though the only lesson I can draw from it is that playwright and director should never correspond. The text is full of letters from Wesker to Peter Hall, from John Dexter to Wesker and from Wesker to anyone who would listen. The last letter I wrote concerning a production of one of my plays was in 1977, when I tried, with the permission of the director, to change the performance of one of the actors in *The Old Country*. It didn't work, as letters in my experience never do work; however larded with praise, they almost invariably cause offence. You can say what you think or not, but never write it down.

6 October. Rowse dies, the obituary in the *Independent* by Jack Simmons much kinder than one might have expected. I only met him a few times, first in 1973 at All Souls, when he was so pleased with himself and so concerned to strike the 'me me me' note that he was untalkable to. When I used to see him as an undergraduate I was always struck by his massive forehead, a feature that doesn't come out in photographs. Bruce McFarlane, while he made fun of him, says somewhere in his letters that there was another side to him, one of great kindness and consideration. There must have been more than met the later eye because as he got older he was a terrible bore, one reason he was passed over for honours for so long presumably being that the great and the good who decide such things had been given too many earfuls when dining at All Souls.

He was a compulsive diarist, Bruce saying that when he was out walking Rowse often fell behind in order to write down one of his remarks. It's said in the obituaries that Eliot liked his poems but this doesn't accord with Charles Monteith's story of coming into Eliot's office at Faber's one morning and finding him pacing the room, groaning. 'More poems from Leslie Rowse. Oh God.'

He came up to Oxford (as he never tired of telling you) as a scholarship boy from Cornwall, the son of working-class parents and with what was presumably a broad Cornish accent. What I've always wanted to know is when exactly his native tones gave way to the exaggerated Oxford accent he always affected. Was it a sudden change or did it happen gradually? It's one of the many questions I should have asked McFarlane but never got round to.

24 October. Headline in the *Observer*: 'Boy, six, raped by girl of 14'. This is the main front-page headline and presumably what the *Observer* thinks is the most important item of news this weekend.

7 November. Isaiah Berlin dies. I've never understood (as he claims he never understood) why he should have been held in such high intellectual esteem. His writing is windy and verbose and the only one of his books I've managed to get through is *The Hedgehog and the Fox*, read when I was twenty. He was the darling of the *New York Review of Books*, which in the eighties seemed to carry pieces about him in virtually every issue.

I'm currently reading *Errata*, the intellectual autobiography of George Steiner. I wish it wasn't quite so intellectual, as the purely autobiographical sections – e.g. his early days at the University of Chicago – are fascinating. Steiner, in contrast to Berlin, never fails to embroil you in his language, making the reader feel that his thoughts have been hewn from the living flesh, as Kafka and Wittgenstein felt they should be. But again in contrast to Berlin, Steiner has not had much luck in commending himself to the English, partly because he's awkward and, I imagine, touchy; and as he himself admits, the breadth of his approach, and not being modest or self-conscious about his intellectual equipment, have provoked 'distaste, professional suspicion and marginalisation'. Berlin and Steiner would make good protagonists in a play, the two Jews, both supremely intellectual but one modest, self-deprecating and social, the other chippy, difficult and wholly unassimilable, so never given his due.

Apropos Steiner, there was a time in the early seventies when some friends and their families, including Brian Wenham, Derrick Amoore and Francis Hope (all dead before their time), used to rent a villa on the Mediterranean every summer. One year they were most excited to learn that Steiner was due to rent the villa next door. All of them, particularly Francis, were mettlesome intellects and they looked forward to the advent of Steiner and some off-the-cuff seminars.

Steiner duly arrived but turned out to be Steiner the hairdresser.

9 November. Cool and showery but on the M40 going towards Oxford we drive out of the rain into a perfect autumn day, windy and cold with the sky swept clean of clouds. First to Easington, a remote church by a farmyard. I last came here twenty years ago, and since then the roof has been almost blown off and restored, but though there's a new and brutal farm building within a few yards of the south wall it's still a delightful place. Driving back over the hill to the road we see two huge birds with a wingspan of three or four feet, much larger than hawks and certainly not herons, which are clumsy fliers and trail their legs, whereas these bank and soar and circle and eventually make off across the fields. We turn into a field to have our sandwiches and there they are again, about a quarter of a mile away, swooping over a ploughed field and occasionally alighting, once coming close enough for us to see the white bars under their wings.

Then on to Great Milton to see the Dormer tomb. The church is locked, and when we get the key from a nearby cottage the woman tells us that it's because the helm and sword of Sir Michael Dormer, which have hung above his tomb for nearly four hundred years, were stolen two weeks ago. This makes me feel murderous, but it's a superb tomb, a double-decker repositioned in the nineteenth century so that the feet of Sir Michael, Dorothea his lady and Ambrose his father are all turned firmly towards the altar. Wonderful though it is, it's not quite in the same class as the Fettiplace tombs at Swinbrook, where the effigies are stacked one on top of the other as if in a sepulchral couchette.

10 November. I tell my agent Rosalind Chatto about seeing the huge birds and ten minutes later her partner, Michael Linnit, rings to say that what we saw were red kites. He lives on top of the Chilterns and often sees them and has even had them on his lawn. A few years ago a pair migrated or were brought from Wales, their only surviving habitat, and flourished in their new surroundings to the extent that there are now five or six pairs. They take voles and pigeons even, and are fearless in the presence of humans, their only enemy nowadays egg collectors.

16 November, Yorkshire. I watch two unlisted and unadvertised programmes on BBC2 in which Isaiah Berlin is interviewed by Michael Ignatieff. Never having seen Berlin or heard him (except in frequent imitation), I fall straight away for his charm and see how one would want to think that here was a good man living the true life of the mind.

It had occurred to me that Berlin was the antithesis of Wittgenstein and that Berlin in spate, as it were, would have been intolerable to a philosopher who was, to say the least, somewhat more terse. It transpires that they did once meet and that even Wittgenstein succumbed to the spell, not much caring for what Berlin said, but welcoming the honesty with which he said it. Though his writing is often inflated his mode of utterance is endlessly fascinating. Down the road from here is a spring called the Ebbing and Flowing Well, which bubbles up and falls back much as Berlin does, words overflowing from his mouth rather like a baby bringing back its food. He would have been almost impossible to dislike and I find myself greatly cheered.

4 December. To the funeral at St Dunstan's, Canterbury, of John Williams, whom I have known since we were at Oxford and whose character is summed up in an incident during his National Service. Entered for officer selection, he found himself pitted against another candidate on an obstacle course. Arriving at a hanging rope at the same time as the other man, John stood back politely and said: 'After you.' Which would have been all right except that a major general who was observing the proceedings went purple in the face and immediately put an end to John's prospects.

I am early for the service and wander round the church, ancient-looking on the outside but heavily Victorianised within and seemingly without much of interest. However, in the south aisle are a couple of sixteenth-century tombs, beneath which is the vault of the Roper family. William Roper was the son-in-law of Sir Thomas More, and after More's execution in 1535, his daughter Margaret, who was married to William, bribed someone to remove the parboiled head from London Bridge and kept it in spices for the rest of her life. Investigations in the nineteenth century revealed a grille in the Roper vault behind which was a skull, thought to be that of Sir Thomas, St Thomas as he now is, so the chapel in this undistinguished-seeming church is a place of Catholic pilgrimage. None of which has much to do with John Williams, whose coffin now waits in the porch. The church is full of his friends, few of whom know each other. Were he here (which he is and he isn't) he would have been going round the pews apologising to the congregation that they had had to go to the trouble of attending his funeral.

'We've got a stone hot-water bottle,' John wrote to me in 1959. 'Mother uses it for airing the beds. I have filled it with flowers – it makes a good vase – at least, quite a good one and anyway it's nice to think that the hot-water bottle is being admired for what it is rather than for what it does. I really think it is grateful, though this must sound very silly in a letter.' This catches some of the qualities that were peculiar to him: his odd angle on the world and sympathy for both people and things that were unregarded in it; his ability to see form and beauty in the most mundane objects and which one saw again and again in his house, in the furniture he restored and the tools which he almost obsessively collected. It catches, too, a divine silliness about him which struck me forcibly when he was a young man at Oxford, though it was a quality he happily retained all his life.

He was a craftsman of a kind that has nowadays disappeared. Largely self-taught, he knew the nature of the materials with which he worked and lavished care and affection on them. He haunted car-boot sales and couldn't resist rescuing old tools, of which he eventually had a vast collection and which now happily is to go to the National Trust. The V&A has some of his leather work as do a dozen great houses – and once he made a guitar sling for Paul McCartney.

Coming away from the gathering afterwards, I find that just as there isn't an object in his house I wouldn't want, so there isn't a person I've talked to whom I haven't liked. Trying to extract some sort of message from his life, I think it's something to do with privacy and diversity and the persistence in an increasingly homogeneous world of rarity, individuality and character. John was like someone out of the nineteenth century, out of Dickens in particular, so much was he his own man.[*]

1998

10 January. Listen to a tape Ariel Crittall has made about her life at the request of the Imperial War Museum. She remembers meeting Unity and Diana Mitford off the train in Munich on the morning of the Night of the Long Knives and Diana saying: 'What bliss. The first time I've been on a train without a nanny or a husband!'

---

[*] Many of John Williams's tools and the diapered boards he painted on which to hang them are now in the carpenter's shop at the entrance to Erddig, the National Trust house in North Wales.

Ariel's language is a joy. About meeting Hitler she remarks: 'I was pregnant at the time so I wasn't feeling very . . . *brisk*. Hitler said, "I only have four words in a foreign language, the four words being: *Vous êtes mon prisonnier*."'

24 January. Note the hairstyle of two of the Catholic boys carrying the coffin of their father or their brother, murdered by the UVF in an effort to disrupt the talks. The hair is cut short at the front but selected locks are left a little longer to dangle over the forehead in an attenuated fringe. Somehow to see them both with these carefully considered haircuts makes the scene even more touching.

6 February. I am reading a history of the Yorkshire Dales by Robert White, one of a series, *Landscape through Time*, published by English Heritage. During the enclosures of the eighteenth and nineteenth centuries, most of the land enclosed was added to existing farms, but in 1890 John Hulton used the land allotted to him from the enclosure of Marske Moor in Swaledale to create a new farm, Cordilleras. The farm and most of the fields round about were named after places in South America: Valparaiso, Cotopaxi, Sierra Pedragosa and so on. Today the farm, with its echoes of the pampas, has been swallowed up by the Ministry of Defence's Training Area and so is now the playground of those upright and blameless young men recently corrupted by the shameless women of Catterick.

15 February. The train from Leeds comes to a halt somewhere outside Wakefield, where it waits for ten minutes. Then, when we have got going again, there is a crash from the front of the train as if something colossal has fallen over. At Doncaster it is announced that the first delay was on account of a family sitting on the line trying to commit suicide, and then, in an unrelated incident, some youths had hurled a brick through one of the windows. The window is replaced and so is the driver, who is presumably shocked (or 'in shock' as we are supposed to say).

On the train is a judge whom I know slightly from fifty years ago when we both used to do our homework in the City Reference Library. When the announcement is made about the attempted family suicide and the hooliganism that follows I notice that he does not even raise his eyes from his papers, behaviour of this nature being presumably what his job has led him to expect.

15 March, Yorkshire. Having seen there was a Bronze Age stone circle (more accurately the remains of a barrow) at Yockenthwaite I look at the map and see what I take to be a narrow and presumably little-used road over from Hawes. It's a spectacular day with deep snowdrifts still on the tops where we stop to look at the Roman road snaking over Cam Fell and down to Bainbridge. Then through Oughtershaw and along Langstrothdale by what is called Oughtershaw Beck but is in fact the Wharfe, both the Wharfe and the Ribble rising in these hills, one flowing south, the other west. The stone circle is small and hard to find and the search is made harder because all down the beck cars are parked on the verge and the supposedly unfrequented road up the valley very busy. I had forgotten, but it's always been like this in the Wharfe Valley from Otley and Ilkley northward, no stretch of it remote or unvisited – Bolton Abbey, Burnsall, Kettlewell, Buckden, nowhere now too desolate or far-flung.

So we go down to Hubberholme to look at the rood loft, one of only two remaining in Yorkshire (the other at Flamborough). And it is a loft proper, not just a screen with a top on it, three feet or so wide and with a slatted floor as if it might be a loft for hay, the screen and loft said to have been brought over the tops from Coverham Abbey after the Dissolution. As we're looking round two women come in and what interests them isn't the rood loft or the pews carved and dated 1641. They are on the trail of Thompson, the woodworker of Kilburn who always carved a mouse on his handiwork. Some of the pews are his, done in the forties or fifties, so somewhere here will be a mouse and they scuttle along the pews looking for it. Rather a silly quest, I think, condescendingly, though with as much point and pleasure in it as the two of us marvelling at the ancient loft or noting the memorial plaque to J. B. Priestley, whose ashes were scattered in the churchyard.

19 March. All day at Twickenham recording 'Nights in the Gardens of Spain' with Penelope Wilton, directed by Tristram Powell. She does it beautifully and Tristram keeps it simple and static, which is exactly right. [Predictably, when it comes to be transmitted it is this monologue, the simplest in form and entirely perfect in execution, which the sad creatures who preview TV programmes generally disparage.]

At lunchtime I walk by the river opposite Eel Pie Island, then sit for a while in the gardens of Orleans House, the octagon by James Gibbs *c.*1720, and all that remains of the house lived and entertained in by Caroline of Ansbach. The garden has some tall trees, the upper branches of which are alive with bright green and yellow birds which twitter like hawks. I look them up when I come back and decide, rather doubtfully, that they must have been golden orioles. However, Kate M. tells me that they were probably parakeets, which are spreading rapidly in London (a large colony at Sunbury apparently) and may one day oust the pigeons.

29 March, Yorkshire. The conductor on the GNER train to Leeds is now styled Customer Operations Leader and announces himself as such, though (and it's to his credit) he stumbles several times when he has to broadcast this absurdity.

4 April. Asked to read *The Good Companions* for a possible production I find I can only get as far as the end of Act I. It's interesting, though, in that it's Priestley on one of his favourite themes, that of escape and escape from the north particularly. Act I, Scene I, ends like this:

LEONARD: Where yer going?
OAKROYD (*at door*): Down south.
Exit to triumphant music from the gramophone.

And earlier:

> OAKROYD: I'd like to go down south again. I'd like to see . . . yer know
> . . . some of them places . . . Bedfordshire.
> OGLETHORPE: I nivver heard tell much o'that place; is there owt
> special i'Bedfordshire?
> OAKROYD: I don't know but it's summat to see.

Which was my attitude exactly when I was sixteen. And my father's in 1944, when the family upped sticks and migrated disastrously from Leeds to Guildford for a year. In the end Oakroyd goes off to Canada, between Bedfordshire and Canada there not being much to choose.

Easter Monday. Watch two programmes on Noël Coward, wishing now I'd agreed to be interviewed for them. I'd said no on the grounds that my acquaintance with him was so slight, but Wesker appears whose connection was even slighter.

I saw Coward first in New York in 1962 at one of the regular parties given by Arnold Weissberger, a show-business accountant. The party was, as ever, stiff with celebrities, the most glamorous to me being the now slightly faded film stars I had queued as a boy to see at the Picturedrome on Wortley Road. Here was Alexis Smith, Eve Arden, Charles Boyer, and Tarzan's Jane (and Mia Farrow's mother) Maureen O'Sullivan. The four of us from *Beyond the Fringe* had been invited as a unit and Dudley Moore had been prevailed on (may even have volunteered) to play the piano. With Coward in the room this was perhaps foolhardy and having watched him for a while Coward turned away, saying: 'What a clever young man. He can play on the black notes as well as the white.'

The second time I saw him must have been a few years later at the Mermaid Theatre at a performance of Peter Luke's play *Hadrian VII* with Alec McCowen. Then it was his characteristic walk that I noticed: he tripped down the aisle after the designer, Gladys Calthrop, his hands, fingers pressed together, half slipped into his trouser pockets – 'shucked' I think would have been the word – and gave the impression of someone who moved as neatly and with as much forethought and consideration as he talked.

I actually met Coward for the first time when he came to the penultimate preview of *Forty Years On*, where he bolstered the confidence of the still uncertain John Gielgud. Later in the run he took me out to supper with Cole Lesley and Graham Payn to the Savoy, where we had sausages and mash. Alas, I have no memories of his conversation on either occasion, remembering only how he put me at my ease and seemed much kinder and nicer than I'd been led to expect.

14 April. Watch *Grammar School Days* (BBC2), a documentary about the eleven-plus, and after, with reminiscences by various advertisements for the system, including Kenneth Clarke, David Puttnam and Barry Hines. Listening to their recollections of taking and passing the eleven-plus makes me wonder whether I ever took it at all. I had jumped one or two classes at my primary school so by July 1944, when I left to go to secondary school, I was only ten, my most vivid memory of that time not any examination but that my friend Albert Benson, who was regularly top of the class, wasn't going on to the high school because he would have to go out to work at the earliest opportunity.

Ironically, of those taking part the one whose experience is closest to mine is Kenneth Clarke. Like me he took exams in his stride and just assumed, as I did, that he would go on to grammar school as a matter of course. The most interesting of the participants was Harry Ognall, now a judge, who is pictured going through the old buildings of the empty (because translated to the outskirts) Leeds Grammar School and remarking that he thinks there is less class distinction at the school than there was in his day. My brief visit to LGS in the eighties to open their theatre suggested the opposite, with lots of silly public-school flummery (braided gowns, tassels on caps), public school as filtered through the pages of *Hotspur* and *Wizard*, the only encouraging feature the number of clever Asian boys, who obviously now rival the Jewish boys as the intellectual elite.

Several of those taking part say, as I would have done, how desperate the lesser grammar schools were to hike themselves up the social scale and be considered public schools. To this end the headmaster of my own school, Leeds Modern, changed the school over from soccer to rugger, pushed more and more boys towards Oxford and Cambridge and even briefly got himself invited to the Headmasters' Conference. It was all to no purpose as in a few years the school went comprehensive, lost its identity and was merged with the girls' school next door.

Hard to fit myself into any of the categories represented except (again like Kenneth Clarke) I feel I had a great deal of luck, not least when I was aged eight and went in for the entrance examination to Leeds Grammar School and happily failed. One of the questions was 'Who was Job?' This mystified me.

'Who *was* Job?' I came home and asked, not even knowing it was a name and pronouncing it the same as in a job of work. 'I've never heard of Job.' And a good job I hadn't.

25 April. Graffiti in the lift at the Middlesex Hospital: Love. Sex. Salt. An Arab, presumably, pining for the desert.

20 May. Listen to a CD of Elgar's *Dream of Gerontius*. It's a piece I know well, first heard, like most of what I thought of then as 'good music', at one of the concerts in Leeds Town Hall 1950–52. By mistake I put on the second disc first, and so hear not the slow introduction but a section of the recitative by the soul of Gerontius on seeing the angel at the start of Part 2.

> It is a member of that family of wondrous beings who, ere the world was made, millions of years back, have stood around the Throne of God. I will address him. Mighty one, my Lord, my Guardian Spirit, all hail.

Hearing it unexpectedly I can't think what it is this reminds me of until Gerontius gets to 'I will address him', and I realise it's Gilbert and Sullivan, or Gilbert at any rate, the period of Newman's poem roughly contemporary and the diction every bit as unintentionally arch as Gilbert's is deliberately so. It's conducted by Barbirolli, the thought of him affecting still: that frail physique, the unkempt hair and the style, histrionic but not self-choreographed; and the concert over, going home in his old raincoat through the fogs of fifties Manchester.

4 June. In one of the new *Talking Heads* monologues, *Playing Sandwiches*, I give the five- or six-year-old Samantha studs in her ears, while at the same time thinking that this is a little excessive, because it weights the scales against her mother. This morning in M&S I see a child with earrings who cannot be more than two.

20 June. Watch some of Hitchcock's *To Catch a Thief* on TV, more for Jessie Royce Landis's performance as Grace Kelly's mother than for either Grace Kelly or Cary Grant. One scene is now unintentionally funny: Cary Grant, as the reformed cat burglar, invites the Lloyd's insurance agent (John Williams) to have lunch at his villa overlooking the Mediterranean. Grant's housekeeper serves a delicious meal, the first course of which is a tart with ham, herbs and eggs. 'It's a local speciality,' says Grant, looking immensely sophisticated. 'They call it quiche lorraine.'

29 June. A letter from my Italian translator telling me of a wonderful afternoon in Milan 'spent talking about your work and listening to some of your minologue plays'.

12 July. On this Sunday morning when the fate of Northern Ireland hangs in the balance at Drumcree the *Observer* gives it one small paragraph on the front page, the rest all to do with the lobbying scandal the *Observer* is so proud of having unearthed. It's only after nine whole pages to do with the paper's 'exclusive' that it manages to get its head out of its own arse to start talking about Northern Ireland.

19 July. Watch two good programmes about Henry Moore, one of whose works, a *Reclining Figure* bought for the city, could still raise a storm of protest in Leeds as late as 1951. Now of course the city is home to the Henry Moore Institute. Moore has no trace, even early on, of what must have been quite a thick Yorkshire accent; he was the son of a Castleford coal miner after all. The accent could have gone through rubbing shoulders as a young man with the more well-spoken Ben Nicholson, say, or Kenneth Clark. But I would have thought that in the thirties he needed to get rid of it (or at least knock the edges off it) in order to be taken seriously, whereas thirty years later, in Hockney's day, a sculptor from a similar background would have been well advised to keep it. The contrast is most noticeable when one of his early girlfriends is interviewed: she's a delightful woman, now eighty-odd, called Edna 'Gin' Coxon who is still quite definitely Yorkshire and sounds it. She says Moore wanted to go to bed with her but she wouldn't because she had a boyfriend already and to do it with Moore would have been unfaithful. 'You shouldn't do it with two. You can do it with ten but not with two.'

24 July. It's announced this morning that the three hundred or so soldiers shot for cowardice during the First World War are not to be pardoned, though in a speech later described as 'deeply felt' the Armed Forces Minister, Dr Reid, says that their names can now be inscribed on war memorials and that they will be pardoned in our hearts etc. The official reason they cannot be pardoned is that there is now (as there no doubt was then) little evidence as to who were genuinely cowards, poor wretches, and who were innocent and that it would never do to pardon the guilty with the innocent. Why not? If among the three hundred there was one man who was innocent (and there were many more) then his innocence should procure the pardon of them all. Or so Simone Weil would have said. But Simone Weil doesn't have much clout in the Ministry of Defence, this decision bearing all the marks of over-cautious civil servants whom the Minister has it in his power to disregard. I write to Frank Dobson, my MP, saying, intemperately, that John Reid is more of a coward than many of the men who were executed.

15 August, Yorkshire. To Pateley Bridge on a lovely afternoon of flashing sunshine and rushing clouds, the drive over from Settle to Hetton going past the house of Cromwell's general, Lambert, who ought to have been buried at Malham but as a regicide died in captivity and is buried at Plymouth. Tea in Pateley, then up the hill above the high street to look at Pateley old church, roofless now but restored by English Heritage. It's a bare interior with a primitive Gothic east window, a tower and plenty of odd doors and openings, which is somehow Scottish and feels like a set for *Hamlet*.

Then back via Burnsall to look at the Saxon hog-back tombstones in the churchyard. These are a bit of a disappointment, just huge hunks of stone which could be gateposts from the end of any drystone wall, and I imagine that is where other similar tombstones have ended up. Much more interesting is the lychgate (restored *c.*1989): a single broad gate, attached by a bar and chain to an ancient pulley in the thickness of the wall. If you push against the right-hand side of the gate it opens inwards with the left-hand side opening outwards, the pulley then closing the gate. It's the kind of thing Lutyens would have delighted in and incorporated into one of his country houses.

17 August. Some time this last week a bearded man in a frock strolled through the National Gallery, observed by warders, though not accosted by them until he reached the room with the Rembrandts. In front of Rembrandt's *Self-Portrait at the Age of 63* he suddenly whips off the frock (the marvels of Velcro) to reveal that he is stark naked with, strapped to his leg, a tube of yellow acrylic. He daubs the beginning of a £ sign on the portrait before he is wrestled to the ground by a warder and a helpful member of the public and bundled away. The police are called, but before they can forbid anything to be touched the conservation department are on the scene, remove the painting and wash off the acrylic while it is still wet: had it dried the process would have been much more complicated. The upshot is that the painting is back on view the next day, Rembrandt doubtless looking even more pissed off than he normally looks in that particular self-portrait.

What interests me about the incident is what happened after the young man had been overpowered – a case of conflicting pruderies as the warders would not want to escort a naked man through the gallery but at the same time might be reluctant to re-dress a naked (and bearded) man in a frock.*

20 August, Toulouse. A new twist in hotel pornography is that the dirty channels are largely, but not completely, blocked out by a card announcing that they can be viewed only if paid for by pressing such and such a number, the card allowing an intriguing glimpse of what is going on to be shown round its edges: a man's leg in this instance, his thrown-up arm, and what might be an armpit or, there again, not. I can imagine a taste so refined that it would find such marginal glimpses more exciting than the whole scene.

21 August, L'Espiessac. At ten o'clock this morning we are still trying to get out of Toulouse, driving round and round the new suburbs of Blagnac (one of the streets the avenue Albert Camus: '*voie sans issue*'). Eventually we cut across on virtually empty D roads, stopping for coffee at Beaumont-de-Lomagne, an ordinary enough little town, the size of Otley, say, and with no pretensions at all, though seemingly from a street name the birthplace of Fermat of Theorem fame.

The square is taken up almost entirely by a huge open-timbered market hall which is, I suppose, seventeenth or eighteenth century, a vast edifice with a roof like a cathedral. We sit outside the local pool-hall café and watch the comings and goings. Were such a building in Otley and not the Garonne it would be high on the English tourist trail; here, thank goodness, no one bothers. And of course this is Europe and more stained by history than England ever is. These beams will have seen ropes flung over them for hurried hangings in the Terror and the White Terror that

---

* When the case comes up in the magistrates' court and the young man is in the dock, he manages, despite being flanked by two policemen, to get naked again and to streak across Parliament Square, generally displaying such a facility in stripping off that it's hard not to feel that's where his future lies. He turns out to be from Coventry, which is, of course, a place with some tradition of public nudity.

followed, and the Occupation and the retribution that followed that, dark shapes swinging among the beams. So it is not like Otley, which just nurtured Thomas Chippendale, who made chairs. No, we are not a serious people, as how should we be?

26 August, L'Espiessac. After years of sniggering English tourists having themselves photographed next to the town sign, the burghers of Condom have at last woken up to the fact that they are sitting on a gold mine. So now, though there is some doubt whether the town has any connection with prophylaxis at all, a Musée des Préservatifs has opened and the decent old-fashioned sepia postcards of this fairly ordinary provincial town have been banished in favour of highly coloured jokey views: a landscape in which the poplars are green condoms, the clouds white ones; monks have condoms as cowls and even the chaste tower of the twelfth-century cathedral has been sheathed in a condom.

None of which would matter much had not some enterprising mayor decided that the town could do other things besides exploiting its eponymous connection, so the decent little square in front of the cathedral now boasts half a dozen gleaming steel flagpoles, with the flags, I suppose, of all condom-using nations. Still, one must be grateful they are flags and not themselves condoms. Worse, there is a 'water feature', a pool from which water overflows down a ramp of artificial stone crossed by a shallow steel bridge which tourists are encouraged to think of as an ideal photo opportunity. In due course someone will throw a coin in the pool and all that will start. It's almost English in its vulgarity.

Apropos the cathedral (and French churches in general): I never understand why they are so dull. There are generally no monuments, no ancient clutter, just sickly nineteenth-century statuary, virulent stained glass and bits of modish ecumenicalism. Why there is no evidence of society in the shape of tombstones, plaques and inscriptions no one seems satisfactorily to explain. I suppose it's the Revolution, but how was it so comprehensive as to leave not even a paving stone to bear witness to the society it displaced?

31 August. Drive by back roads to Leeds, avoiding the Bank Holiday traffic and stopping en route to look at a church at Broughton near Skipton. The vicar comes over to open the door, a bit dishevelled as he's just back from a car-boot sale to raise funds to restore the bells so that they can ring in the millennium. At first sight it's quite a plain church, though with some good fourteenth- and fifteenth-century woodwork round the family pew of the Tempests, the local gentry who were (and are) Catholic. This helps to explain a tomb cover propped against the wall which is a communal gravestone for those who died in the Pilgrimage of Grace, the northern rebellion against the Dissolution of the Monasteries in 1537. Mutilated around the same time are two effigies of the Virgin and Child, the head of the Virgin knocked off one, the head of the Child knocked off the other and both found buried outside the north wall sometime in the nineteenth century.

The guidebook implies that burying the statues was a further stage in the iconoclasm which knocked the heads off, but it might equally well have been done out of reverence and to preserve what was left, this neatly exemplifying one of the current controversies in sixteenth-century historiography: the degree of persistence of Catholic belief after the break with Rome.

A leaflet explains how the red sandstone from the tower came from the foundations of the Roman fort in nearby Elslack, some of the stones still blackened from when the Scots attacked the church after Bannockburn in 1314. Near the gate of the churchyard is the tomb of Enoch Hall, who was one of the escorts accompanying Napoleon to St Helena and who stayed there ten years before coming home to Broughton to be thirty years the local schoolmaster.

We sit outside listening to the wind streaming through a huge copper beech and talk about this ordinary enough church which has been bound up with great events in the nation's history: a conventional thought, though one which would have excited me when I was fifteen and first took to visiting churches and which excites me still, fifty years later, when, thanks to Rupert, I've taken to visiting them again.

Then over the deserted moors and down into Keighley, an empty Leeds and the train to King's Cross.

10 September. Watch some of a programme about Dennis Potter, but the assumptions it makes about the relationship between art and life are so naïve and wide-eyed and scarcely above the tabloid level that I don't persist. It takes Potter at his own self-valuation (always high) when there was a good deal of indifferent stuff which was skated over. One of his best plays, *Where Adam Stood*, an adaptation of Edmund Gosse's *Father and Son*, is not mentioned, as it seldom is. The programme also interviews some of Potter's heroines, and once the actors start talking about what they see as the significance of the words they're required to speak there's no telling what nonsense comes out, some of it very solemn.

13 September. Wake early on Sunday morning and short of something to read find a copy of the *Torrington Diaries: Tours through England 1781–94 of Hon. John Byng*, and this passage:

> Oh that a critical tourist had minutely described, before the Civil War, the state of the castles, and of the religious remains and of the mode of living of the nobility and gentry, e'er the former were dismantled, the monuments of religion demolish'd; and that the entrance of folly, by high roads, and a general society, had introduced one universal set of manners, of luxury and expence.

There are echoes of Aubrey here but also, in the comments on roads and 'a general society', of almost anybody writing about the state of England any time in the last forty years; one just needs to substitute 'TV' for 'a general society' and it's a contemporary cliché.

30 September. Finish reading *The Guest from the Future* by György Dalos, an account of Isaiah Berlin's visit to Anna Akhmatova in Moscow in November 1945 and its disastrous repercussions on Akhmatova's career, or, at any rate, on her relations with the authorities. Neither the poet nor the philosopher comes out of it particularly well, though right at the start I have a problem with Akhmatova, who is universally acknowledged as a great poet but whose poetry, of which snatches are printed here, seems in translation commonplace and banal. This is thanks, no doubt, to the shortcomings of the translation, as I remember feeling much the same about Pushkin when I was in the army on the Russian course, my rudimentary Russian never sufficient for me to appreciate him in the original. So one has to take the greatness of the poetry on trust, which is what Akhmatova does herself, her conviction of her own greatness another stumbling block. Indeed both she and Berlin take for granted their role at the centre of history, which again is unappealing. What they both lack, Akhmatova in particular, is a touch of Kafka.

Had I known about this meeting twenty years ago I might have thought of making it a companion piece (or a pendant, as they say in art history) for *An Englishman Abroad*, an account of another Moscow visit, though the Berlin–Akhmatova encounter furnishes fewer jokes other than the comic (but portentous) appearance in the courtyard of Akhmatova's apartment house of the drunken Randolph Churchill.

Run into David Storey in M&S. Never in high spirits, he always cheers me up. Today he is trailing round the store a couple whom he has spotted shoplifting. He often does this apparently, I suppose because he is a novelist, and says the shoplifters' technique is always the same. Those intending to pinch go into the store, find the security guard and ask the whereabouts of, say, soup or sandwiches. The guard shows them and then, since they have established themselves as bona fide customers, takes no further notice of them. David S. says he has never reported anyone, though, like me, he's tempted to do so when they shoplift so blatantly as to insult the intelligence of anybody who might be watching.

6 October. I have been reading, courtesy of Keith Thomas, *Bare Ruined Choirs*, Dom David Knowles's account of the Dissolution of the Monasteries. Four hundred and fifty years after the event I find myself actively depressed by the destruction and vandalism it involved, so when R. says to me this morning, 'You seem a bit low,' it's not because my mind has been on Kosovo but on how the King's Commissioners even grubbed up the floor tiles at Fountains in 1538 in order to sell them off in the chapter-house as architectural salvage. And like Randolph Churchill reading the Bible and saying, 'God, isn't God a shit!' so have I never quite taken in the full horror of Henry VIII (whom, typically, the English just think of as a joke).

Knowles, of course, is a Catholic historian but he's hardly propagandist, not bothering to bring out some ironies I would have found it hard to resist. Latimer, for instance, one of the Oxford martyrs burned by Mary, was himself present and preached at the much more savage burning of a friar, John Forest, in 1538. I had always thought both Ridley and Latimer saintly figures but Latimer seems to have been pretty coarse-grained and a clown and was lucky to have friends who made sure he had a quicker end than he gave Friar Forest. Conversely there is Thomas More, venerated as a saint but himself a burner and harrier of heretics, though that is not dwelled on by Knowles or, more lately, by P. Ackroyd. So it's not inappropriate this morning that I sign an appeal by the National Secular Society on behalf of Peter Tatchell, charged under some ecclesiastical nonsense Act of 1860 with indecent behaviour (i.e. demonstrating) in Canterbury Cathedral.

It occurs to me that there is something *rollicking* about many Protestant divines in the sixteenth century and which comes from indulging in constant controversy. It's the same coarsening detectable nowadays when bishops are too much on television.

19 October. Alan Clark and Kenneth Clarke resurrected this lunchtime to comment on the arrest of Pinochet. Both routinely acknowledge Pinochet's crimes, although Clark A. is careful to refer to them as 'alleged', probably because he didn't actually hear the screams of the tortured himself. Both have that built-in shrug characteristic of eighties Conservatism, electrodes on the testicles a small price to pay when economic recovery's at stake. They both talk contemptuously of gesture politics as if Lady Thatcher having tea with the General isn't gesture politics too, the gesture in question being two fingers to humanity.

25 October. At Broadcasting House I run into Richard Wortley, now a distinguished drama producer and who was at Oxford with me, where we both had digs in Summertown with a Mrs Munsey. Mrs Munsey had a middle-aged daughter, Dulcie, who was excessively shy and who bolted noisily into the back room if she ever heard one coming. There was also a large old cat which used to crap in the bath. In the way of things when one is young, none of this seemed at all strange to me.

Mrs Munsey was a good soul, every morning providing a huge cooked breakfast brought up on a tray by Dulcie and laid reverently outside the bedroom door. All I want in a morning is a cup of tea and a bit of toast, but perhaps sensing that this huge breakfast was a source of pride to Mrs Munsey I never had the heart to point this out, leaving me with the daily problem of disposing of a fried egg, two rashers of bacon, baked beans and a slice of fried bread. I eventually evolved a routine whereby I parcelled the lot up in yesterday's *Times* (stolen from the JCR), which I deposited in the used-ticket receptacle at the bus stop in Banbury Road. So skilled did I become at this daily deposition that I could punt the parcel in as I cycled by without even slowing down, and I can see myself doing this the hot Whitsuntide morning at the start of Final Schools in 1957 (when such a breakfast was particularly unwelcome), never thinking that I would remember this silly moment all my life.

1 November. Lord Tebbit writes to the *Times* saying that homosexuals should be banned from sensitive cabinet posts lest they be in a position to do each other favours. This is taken to be just an eccentricity on the part of the noble lord, though exactly the same argument used to be advanced, and with about as much substance, against Jews. Tebbit, of course, has always gone out of his way to be unsympathetic, the single moment he achieved pathos when he was being dug out of the wreckage of the bombed Brighton hotel in his pyjamas and was weakly trying to shield his balls from the waiting cameras.

By chance I am reading *French and Germans, Germans and French*, Richard Cobb's book on France under occupation in the First and Second

World Wars, and, on the same day as Tebbit's letter, come across this: 'Perhaps homosexuals will always welcome some dramatic turn in national fortunes or misfortunes as an opportunity to move in and secure the best jobs.' Cobb doesn't offer much evidence for this unexpected statement other than the fondness of the French Right for youth organisations with bare knees. Generally a superb historian (and very readable), Cobb is sometimes a little too pleased with himself for not making moral judgements – torturing for the Milice, for instance, and selling nylons on the black market just different points on the same scale. It's the reluctance to condemn which makes his assertion of gay opportunism seem so startling. It's not a subject on which there can be a sensible or a productive argument, but it would be just as true to say that in a crisis homosexuals would welcome some dramatic turn in national fortunes in order to put themselves in positions of great personal danger, and that the late Bunny Rogers, who used the opportunity of a fierce German bombardment to touch up his eyeliner, is just as typical as any knee-fancying collaborator.

6 November. Some Essex police officers convicted of ill-treating (and in one case killing) police dogs. They are said to be likely to lose their jobs, which makes a nice change. Had it been blacks they had been ill-treating (or indeed killing) they would be returned to duty as a matter of course.

17 November. I'm looking forward to a quiet morning's work when out of the blue [*sic*] a letter comes from Oxford offering an honorary degree. This distinction is what Larkin called 'the big one' and when he got his letter he uncharacteristically bounded up the stairs to tell Monica Jones the good news. I sit looking at mine and wondering about it for most of the morning, wishing I could just say 'Delighted' and have done with it. But ever since the establishment of the Rupert Murdoch Chair in Language and Communication I've felt disaffected with the University. I'm aware of the arguments about bad money being put to good uses but I still think that Murdoch's is not a name with which Oxford should have associated itself. So, eventually, I write back saying no and explaining why.

Of course I am aware that writing (and publishing) this may be sneered at as showing off, and that if one does turn something down it's proper to keep quiet about it. But this refusal isn't for my own private moral satisfaction: Murdoch is a bully and should be stood up to publicly and so, however puny the gesture, it needs to be in the open.

One disappointment about the proposal is that it comes on ordinary paper. My first contact with Oxford took place nearly fifty years ago when, as a schoolboy, I sent off for the prospectuses of the scholarships and exhibitions given by the various groups of colleges. These were printed on quarto sheets of thick rough-edged paper, rag paper perhaps it was, the texture so fleecy and absorbent it was practically blotting paper. Peppered with phrases I had never come across like '*viva voce*', '*pro hac vice*' and 'Founder's kin', these sheets I took as evidence of the grandeur and antiquity of the institution I was hoping to enter; one could imagine them peeled off the stone and hung up to dry. I wonder this morning when such prospectuses fell into disuse and the University's correspondence ceased to be conducted in such an antique mode. Certainly today's letter, apart from its contents, is just like any other.

I wish I could say that this refusal leaves me with a warm feeling of having done the right thing, but not a bit of it. I end up, as so often when I have tried to get it right, feeling I've slightly made a fool of myself, so that I wonder whether after more momentous refusals martyrs ever went to their deaths not in the strong confidence of virtue but just feeling that they had somehow muffed it.

7 December, Venice. The size of the place apart, there's not much difference between landing at Venice and at JFK. There's the same grey lagoon with industry on the horizon, the same sparsely inhabited islands of cold brown grass with channels in between and, once you're out, the same thrill to be had in both places from the first glimpse of the towers of the city.

It's always said that one should arrive in Venice by boat, which, if you come by air, you generally do. But I think rail is best. The first time I came was by train and at night and, not knowing what to expect, was amazed to find that the canals weren't sequestered in a quarter of their own but were part of the city itself and that, with the water lapping the steps, Venice began right outside the station. And that still astonishes.

8 December, Venice. I used to feel badly that I didn't care for the inside of St Mark's (tatty, no vistas and too much gold) but once written off or regarded as a collection of superior bric-à-brac it's full of separate pleasures, particularly the floor, though what takes my eye this morning is an intricate little stretch of Gothic arcading in brown and white marble on the right of the steps behind the lectern. I would like to parcel it up and take it home, just as, like so much else in the church, it was presumably parcelled up and brought home here by the Venetians, who plundered it in the first place.

We climb the steps to the outside loggia, empty this cold bright morning. The horses overlooking the Piazza are now replicas, the Greek or Roman originals these days stabled in a room behind. Here they can be seen face on and in close-up as they can seldom have been seen before in their long history. It is as if they are in conversation with each other and, at first glance, it seems from their expressions that two are clearly female, two male. But move round them and the genders shift, so that each animal can be seen to partake of both. The patina is a sumptuous blend of green and gold, the remnants of the harness still hiding the joints in the casting. But they are not much visited now, or not on this particular morning anyway, though they must be the most extraordinary and certainly the most appealing sculptures in Venice.

9 December, Venice. The Scuola San Giorgio behind the Riva degli Schiavoni is never easy to locate so when we've managed to track it down it's a keener disappointment to find it (and its collection of Carpaccios) closed. A handwritten note on the door promises that it will be open on Wednesday at ten, but today is Wednesday and it's after eleven and there's no sign of life, just a handful of disconsolate Carpaccio-lovers hanging about on the Calle Furlani.

I first came across these Carpaccios by accident late one Saturday afternoon in 1970, a couple of hours before my train left. The caretaker was about to lock up and he waited while I put in my 200-lire coin to turn on the light in what seemed on that hurried visit like a dark parish room which just happened to house these extraordinary pictures.

Being a particularly human painter with quite a limited output, Carpaccio is an artist, unlike Titian, say, or Veronese, who has fans. His grave, long-nosed elegantly turned-out young persons people a Venice that is still walkable-through today, though the picture here I would most have liked to see again isn't of Venice at all but of the monks thrown into a panic by the arrival of St Jerome's lion.

10 December, Venice. Walking back to the Accademia from the Rialto, we come through the Campo Santa Margherita, a long, irregular-shaped space surrounded mostly by two-storey houses. J. G. Links's *Venice for Pleasure* directs us to what is reputedly the oldest house in Venice, which, except for a marble well-head built into a garden wall, isn't very interesting. But coming out again into the Campo I realise that this was where we lodged when I first came to Venice in the summer of 1957. I was with Russell Harty and two other undergraduates from my college and we had digs in one of these little low houses. In those days I only needed to shave once or twice a week, the process always painful and never achieved without a cut or two. Shaving one morning, I had an accident and was mystified as to what to do. None of us spoke Italian but Russell, always the man of the world, went out into the Campo and bought a large bunch of flowers which he presented to the beaming but baffled landlady while I tried to explain (the phrase not occurring in any of the phrase books) that I had dropped my styptic pencil down the plughole.

24 December. I watch the Service of Nine Lessons and Carols from King's with the familiar words, as particularly with carols, coming unbidden and with them the same odd associations. 'Word of the Father, now in flesh appearing', for instance, has always seemed to me like theatrical billing – and without thinking I've taken it as meaning that, until this afternoon the daftness of it comes home.

27 *December, Yorkshire*. A wet dark day as it has been all through Christmas. Train late into Leeds, where we pick up a car and drive out through Garforth and Castleford to Methley. The church (noted from Pevsner) is locked and when we go to the vicarage for the key the vicar, a woman, asks me for some identification. When I show her my railcard she glances at it briefly and says, 'Yes, I thought it was you' (which isn't quite what identification means).

The church is well worth the detour, though, crammed with monuments, many of them in the Waterton chantry, which has a painted, coffered ceiling and two superb fifteenth-century alabaster tombs with that of Lord Welles (killed at Towton in 1461) particularly fine – the features (broken nose, big chin, pudding-basin haircut) make it seem a definite portrait, though the church leaflet says not. Waterton's own tomb is even bolder and more individual but the most striking monument is to a seventeenth-century Savile and his son and daughter-in-law, done by Maximilian Colt, who sculpted Elizabeth I's monument in Westminster Abbey.

Elsewhere in the church are two faceless reclining figures and, acting as corbels, some huge grotesque stone heads. I don't take much notice of these but it turns out that these carvings are why the church is famous as they are among the earliest subjects of Henry Moore who, visiting his aunt at Methley as a boy of nine, used to come to the church and draw. Which is a link with Blake, whose first experience as an artist was also drawing tombs, in his case in Westminster Abbey when he was apprenticed to an engraver.

The church as a whole is fascinating (though rather snubbingly dismissed in Pevsner as 'over-restored') and full of curiosities, with oddest of all in the vestry a rather watery crucifixion done by Robert Medley, the schoolboy friend of Auden who first turned him on to poetry. I mean to ask the vicar how it got here but when we return the key she is so keen to tell us how, apropos Henry Moore, the church has its own website that I forget.

It's dark when we get to the village, where the beck is high, the moon almost full and snow on the tops. We fetch in some logs, light the fire and have cheese on toast.

1999

12 January. A New York producer sends me *Waiting in the Wings*, Noël Coward's play about a theatrical retirement home – Denville Hall, I suppose it is. He wants me to update it, though lest I should think this kind of thing beneath me what he says he wants is 'a new perspective on the play'.

The perspective will have to be a pretty distant one as it now seems a creaking piece all round, the only character not requiring updating (or a new perspective) is an old actress, Sarita Myrtle, who's gone completely doolally, and so still seems contemporary. The most startling revelation is that it includes a character called Alan Bennet (*sic*) who is described as 'in his late forties. He is neatly dressed but there is an indefinable quality of failure about him.'

Coward's play was staged in September 1960, a month after *Beyond the Fringe*, and a year after I had appeared on stage for the first time with the Oxford Theatre Group. (I am just thinking how the name might have lodged in Coward's mind.) Nobody has ever noticed it before – not even Nora Nicholson, who played Sarita Myrtle and was with me in *Forty Years On*.

13 January. Humphrey Carpenter comes round to do some fact-checking for his forthcoming book on satire and after. He asks me if we ever had any alternative titles to *Beyond the Fringe*, which was Robert Ponsonby's contribution and not popular with us at the time. I can't think of any but J. Miller later remembers 'At the Drop of a Brick', a reference to Flanders and Swann's *At the Drop of a Hat* and Peter Cook's suggestion that we call it 'Quite the best revue I've seen for some time. Bernard Levin', the point being that whatever the notices this could go up at the front of the house.

27 January. A woman writes to me saying that having read a piece I'd written about him, she has tried to read Kafka but without success. For the same reason she asked at the library for something on Larkin but seeing his photograph gave the book straight back: 'He looked too much like Sergeant Bilko.'

28 January. I switch on the *Antiques Roadshow* where someone is showing an expert a drawing by E. H. Shepard, the illustrator of *Winnie the Pooh*. It's a cartoon or an illustration dated 1942, entitled 'Gobbling Market' and meant as a satire on black marketeers. It was for *Punch* but it could just as easily have been for *Der Stürmer*, as all the black marketeers are strongly Semitic in features, some as demonic as the worst Nazi propaganda. The expert makes no reference to this, except to say: 'It's very strong.' When the owner bought the drawing he'd had the chance of getting a *Winnie the Pooh* cartoon instead: that would have appreciated in value a good deal but 'Gobbling Market' not at all, which is encouraging.

9 February. Yesterday evening to the National Gallery's Ingres exhibition. Some glowing early portraits . . . the earliest like Fabre or Géricault and the best an extraordinary painting of his friend J. B. Desdéban. Red-haired, orange-jacketed and against a russet background, he's not unlike the Chicago Degas of the woman having her hair brushed, which is another exercise in red. Ingres is supposed to have said it was the best thing he ever did and it could be taken for an early Picasso. Lynn points out how bony and articulated the hands are in the drawings whereas in the paintings the hands become fat, boneless and almost claw-like.

Dame Iris Murdoch dies and gets excellent reviews, all saying how (morally) good she was, though hers was not goodness that seemed to require much effort, just a grace she had been given: so she was plump and she was also good, both attributes she had been born with and didn't trouble herself over. I wonder if it's easier to be good if you don't care whether you're wearing knickers or mind, as Wittgenstein didn't, living on porridge; goodness more accessible if you're what my mother used to call 'a sluppers'.

Nobody explains (or seems to think an explanation required) how this unworldly woman managed to be made a dame by Mrs Thatcher and was laden with honorary degrees; sheer inadvertence perhaps.

In a later obituary it's said that she approved of the Falklands War and one begins to see that for all her goodness and mild appeal she may have trod the same path as her contemporaries Amis and Larkin. Masked though she was in kindliness and general benevolence, she may have ended up as far from her radical beginnings as they did, Dame Iris's spiritual journey not all that different from Paul Johnson's.

10 February. At Christmas G. and R. gave me a subscription to *This England* ('Britain's Loveliest Magazine'), which at first seemed a conventional magazine of the countryside with thatched cottages, country houses and even Patience Strong. Closer examination shows it to be more sinister: it is seemingly the house magazine of the Society of Saint George and dedicated to the preservation of the English identity. A second number comes today, more virulent than the last with columns of correspondence all fervently opposed to the European connection, denouncing Labour (and half the Conservatives) as traitors. It's the usual stuff, except to find a magazine ostensibly devoted to singing the praises of the countryside but peddling such rot is quite disturbing. And of course not a black face to be seen. It's the kind of publication one laughs about, but go a thousand miles across Europe and sentiments no more rancid and parochial are inspiring neighbours to slit each other's throats.

12 March. Reading P. Ackroyd's *Thomas More*, which I finish today, leaves me in two minds, the tolerance and scepticism of the author of *Utopia* and the dogmatism and heresy-hunting of the lawyer never adding up and not short of hypocrisy. It's hard not to feel there is something specifically English about this two-mindedness (More's, not mine). Ackroyd writes how during his time in prison More was tormented by fears of torture and the barbarities of his possible punishment, without it seeming to occur to him (or Ackroyd) that the torments he had himself visited on heretics were just as terrible. Nor did these have a dogmatic justification as intended to save the victims from the pains of hell; More rejoiced in the cruelties since they gave the poor souls a foretaste of eternal fire. However noble his conduct in the face of death it's difficult to feel much sympathy with him. Henry VIII is a devil but that doesn't make More a saint.

In the afternoon to Kendal and the Abbot Hall Gallery, notable for its collection of Romneys (Romney died in Kendal). Less taken by the finished portraits, which are staid and wooden, than by his preliminary sketches, some of them so rough and full of energy they're reminiscent of Frank Auerbach, though none of this dash survives into the finished portraits. Occasionally funny, too, particularly a sketch of *Two Lovers Startled by a Young Person*, a child gazing at a snogging couple.

22 March. Good example of journalistic spite last week when I was rung by the *Independent* (journalist's name forgotten) wanting my comments on a movement for Yorkshire independence. I say I have none. 'What, none at all?' 'No,' and I put the phone down. In the item the next day it is recorded that I have no comment despite having written such 'treacly' plays about the region. An untreacly (and incorrect) joke about Yorkshire via George Melly:

A driver lost near Leeds stops to ask a local the way.

'Excuse me. Do you know the Bradford turn-off?'

'I should do. I married her.'

7 April. I call at the Regent Bookshop in Parkway to find Peter the proprietor's mother there with a bundle of papers she's brought in for him to photocopy. She is from Vienna, which she left in 1938 at the age of twenty, her parents having managed to find someone in England who would employ her and her two sisters as domestics and so procure them visas.

Here is her passport stamped with a large red J and the letters she wrote after the war trying to find out what happened to her parents, both dead in a camp. I come away thinking about the supposed shame stamped on the passport and the grudging visa that had saved her life. The issues then all seem so clear and much more shocking than what now happens every day on the borders of Yugoslavia. Easier to be indignant about, too, with, sixty years ago, the rights and wrongs so unquestionable. Whereas nowadays one says: 'Well, they've always been at each other's throats,' and 'If the Serbs weren't doing it to them they would be doing it to the Serbs.' And so I often don't read any of the five or six pages the papers devote every morning to Kosovo, as maybe I wouldn't have read about the Jews clamouring to get out of Germany and Austria in 1938.

13 April. Watching *Great Expectations* on TV, I found it lacked (and rather prided itself on lacking) the element of the grotesque that Dickens needs, one reason being the costume design. Most costume dramas, whether on stage or film, tend to assume that fashions came and went in the past much as they do today. But it's only in the last fifty or sixty years that there've been large retail outlets like Burton's or M&S which have homogenised fashion. Before that, the latest thing must have impinged on ordinary lives much less, so that there would be characters in 1830 still going around in the fashions of 1800, say. My grandmother in 1949 was still wearing the long duster coats she had worn in 1920 and Queen Mary looked like an Edwardian lady all her life: dying in the fifties, she still dressed as she had in 1910. Look at Ford Madox Brown's *Work*: only the middle and upper classes are dressed in a contemporary way; the work-men, the flower seller and the poorer characters are dressed in what comes to hand – fashion doesn't enter into it. Portraits, too, are deceptive as the sitters generally choose to be in their Sunday best.

Apropos of which, one of the many pleasures of Judy Egerton's National Gallery catalogue of *The British School* is her dissection of the hunting gear worn by Lord Ribblesdale in Sargent's famous portrait. Though he seems the epitome of high fashion, in this as in much else he isn't typical and certainly isn't wearing what the well-dressed Master of Foxhounds might have chosen but an assemblage of favourite garments that are no less striking for being utterly individual.

16 April. Foul young businessman on the train making arrangements for the evening with a girlfriend via his mobile phone. 'Save some for me,' he says, and as he signs off: 'Be kissed.'

1 May, Oxford. Outside the Museum of Natural History in Parks Road is a large stone disc curved, faceted and looking like a giant turtle shell. The label says it's a 'septarian concretion', consisting of limestone formed 165 million years ago and found in the Bicester clay in 1984. Similar limestone concretions, though more the size of tortoise shells, are in various gardens and borders in our village in Yorkshire, having been found in the bed of the village beck, where they're unsurprisingly not called 'septarian concretions' but 'pudding stones'.

We look round the Museum, much more spick and span than it was when I was last here as an undergraduate, when the cast-iron roof and elaborate arcading were less well thought of and more of a piece with the dusty dinosaur skeletons down below. Wanting to ask about porphyry, I spot a middle-aged man rearranging one of the showcases and ask him if he knows anything about stones. 'I should do,' he says. 'I'm one of the curators.' I tell him about visiting Chastleton, the seventeenth-century house near Chipping Norton newly restored by the National Trust, and it turns out he was the expert called in to advise on the conservation of the stonework. The Trust was anxious to know where the stone had originally been quarried. He told them to walk across the field opposite the house and when they came to a dip in the ground and the house disappeared from view that would be where the stone came from. And so it was.

12 May. I go to the post office for my bus pass. The woman behind the counter leans over and says confidentially: 'Is it your first time?' It's as if I'm going to a brothel. Except that in a brothel they don't require proof of residence or identity and I'm sent home to get them.

14 May. A piece in the *Independent* about David Blunkett tackling failing standards in education. I am pictured, though whether as evidence of decline or hope for the future I can't make out. Either would please me.

Judging from newspaper reports, the congregation at Ted Hughes's memorial service in Westminster Abbey was an odd mixture, with a surprising number of old aristocratic biddies (the oldest being the Queen Mother), and society (the dead poets society, I suppose) well represented. It's no secret that the Laureate had put it about a bit, which, of course, isn't mentioned in the tributes, though there is some comment afterwards that the service had more of Hughes than it did of God and that it was altogether too free-form. I rather wish it had been more so, and done on the lines of Graham Norton's current TV show, so that the priest in charge could have said: 'All sit . . . but *remain standing* those who had any sort of fling with the deceased.'

15 May. Finish reading *A Pacifist's War* by Frances Partridge and start reading *Stalingrad* by Antony Beevor, both books covering the same period though from different angles, foxholes at Ham Spray and foxholes at Stalingrad hardly the same. *Stalingrad* is unsurprisingly a bestseller, the course of the conflict making it compulsive reading and almost Homeric, the two vain and wilful leaders like the gods meddling with and frustrating the best efforts of their generals, and the troops on both sides suffering unimaginable hardships. So, though I'm feeling quite low this morning, I look round my cosy book-lined room and think: 'Well, at least it's not Stalingrad: it's warm and I don't have lice.'

The struggle in the ruins of Stalingrad I think I knew about as a boy from a series in *Hotspur* or *Wizard*; there was certainly a storyline set in the tunnels under Odessa and I think Stalingrad, too. This can't have been much later than 1943, the war I suppose a godsend to comics whose writers kept up with its progress. The setting of ruined cities, though, may have eventually got monotonous or confusing; I'm not sure now, for instance, that I'm not mixing up Stalingrad with a slightly later series of stories set in the ruins of Monte Cassino.

11 June. Watching them Beating the Retreat on TV last night, I remember how, when I was doing basic training at the start of National Service, against all my inclinations and instincts I came to enjoy drill and how (had I played the trumpet) I might have been quite happy as a military bandsman.

8 July. It seemed unlikely that Classic FM could get worse but it has. I switched on briefly yesterday to hear an announcer (all of whom feel it necessary to have a smile in their voices) saying: 'That was the very catchy third movement of Sibelius's Violin Concerto.' Still, one should no doubt be grateful their pronunciation has improved. I was startled in its earlier days to hear a presenter announce the ballet music from 'The Female Guardee'. This turned out to be *La Fille mal gardée*.

Actually a ballet called 'The Female Guardee' might be quite interesting. Better than *Giselle* anyway.

24 July. Wake this Sunday morning with what seemed in my dream a superb title for a play: 'The Fun to be Had with Models of Dubious Sensibility'.

30 July. Jessye Norman has been appearing at the Barbican. She is touchy about her size and, having difficulty getting into a small aeroplane, is supposed to have been told by the air hostess to try getting in sideways. 'Lady,' she is said to have remarked, 'I ain't got no sideways.'

It would be a nice joke if she had ever made it, which she hotly denies and seemingly rightly as today I came across the same joke in a nineteenth-century *Punch* cartoon by L. Ravenhill, the vehicle the lady was trying to get into then a horse-drawn omnibus.

10 August. Any war that is fought these days, in the Falklands, the Gulf, the Balkans or wherever, must as a matter of course become straight away the subject of tactical analysis, seminars at Sandhurst and a general post-operational picking to pieces. This is for the benefit of both the military and the armaments manufacturers and it is not new. I am reading *Alabaster Tombs* by Arthur Gardner, who, discussing the representations of fifteenth-century armour on church monuments, writes: 'It is record-ed that after a battle the squires and armourers held a sort of inquest over the bodies of the slain in order to discuss how best to prevent or ward off the blows that had proved fatal in the fray.' So among the camp followers finishing off the dying and stripping the dead there would be a more pur-poseful and professional group making notes. And as with the increasing-ly sophisticated developments in today's armaments, so the adjustments consequent on these medieval inquests were a mixed blessing: 'The results of their conclusions were not always satisfactory as armour became so heavy that in some fighting the knights were found dead from exhaus-tion without any sign of blow or wound.'

Gardner's book was sent to the publishers in November 1939, and like the excavation at Sutton Hoo earlier that year must have seemed an almost quixotic gesture of faith in permanence and continuity at a time when general destruction was in prospect and alabaster tombs and Saxon burial ships were hardly top priorities.

26 August. Switch on the radio after supper and catch most of Elgar's First Symphony, music which invariably transports me back to boyhood and walking up Headingley Lane on a summer evening after a concert in Leeds Town Hall. The evocative power of music is, I suppose, greatest when heard in live performance. This is a recording but it still casts a spell because I have come on it by accident. Had I put on the recording myself the spell would have been nowhere near as powerful because self-induced. Why this should be I can't think, though doubtless Proust would know.

7 September. Alan Clark dies. I never met him, though I saw him once in the street, noting then that he shared a walk with Denis Healey, both of them swinging their arms laterally as they walked in the manner of Soviet soldiery. Except I fancy Clark swung his arms more slowly than Healey, this putting him in a slightly King of the Apes mode.

10 September. Catch part of the revamped *Round Britain Quiz*, none of the contestants a patch on the team of Eric Korn and Irene Thomas with their personalised and often over-informative answers. There is a question on the *trivium*, the discipline of the Latin schoolmen, which takes in Oedipus. Had Eric Korn been on the team I'm sure he would have been the one to point out that the earliest recorded victim of road rage must have been Laius, Oedipus' father.

15 September. Having finished the rewrites on the dramatisation of *The Lady in the Van*, I begin reading through Larkin for a selection of his poems I have agreed to do for Faber. Instantly I feel like hanging up my pen. Even in the turgid and sometimes incomprehensible early poems phrases demand to be noted ('even slovenly grief', 'the dingy hospital of snow') so that one's tempted to include the whole poem, if only to preserve the phrase. Not that Larkin would thank one for saying so (or saying anything), the awareness of his contempt, even though it's posthumous, a real deterrent.

Cars abandoned by the road nowadays often bear a notice saying 'Police Aware'. Maybe one could slap 'Poet Aware' on a beauty spot or even on some particularly touching vagrant.

1 October. Finish reading *The Jew of Linz* by Kimberley Cornish, 'an investigation of what may prove to be the century's most significant coincidence, the hitherto overlooked fact that its most evil politician (Hitler) and its most brilliant philosopher (Wittgenstein) were at school together'. Not overlooked by me, as it occurs in *Kafka's Dick* (1986), where it's almost thrown away since I assumed, I'm sure rightly, that this wasn't much of a revelation.

More controversial is Cornish's assertion that Hitler and Wittgenstein were actual classmates at the Linz Realschule *c.*1904. This may have been true, but even if they weren't and were just in the school at the same time it seems likely that Hitler would have heard of the philosopher-to-be, whose schooldays sound to have been pretty disastrous. Socially and intellectually he was a cut above his fellows, while being unhappy for the conventional reasons, not being good at games and so on, and it seems probable that the 'one Jewish boy' mentioned early on in *Mein Kampf* was, as Cornish asserts, Ludwig Wittgenstein. The trouble is Cornish makes his case in such a tendentious and overheated fashion, and utterly without humour, that he invites scepticism. To add to all his other problems the young Wittgenstein had a double rupture so if Hitler really did only have one ball it's tempting to think of the pair of them behind the bike sheds comparing notes.

Cornish goes on to suggest that (while at Cambridge) Wittgenstein may have been the master spy who recruited for the Soviets, this line of reasoning having much to do with Wittgenstein's homosexuality. So we have lists of Trinity men who were Apostles, which of them were homosexual and so on, Cornish dodgily assuming, as did Andrew Boyle and John Costello before him, that homosexuality is itself a bond and that if two men can be shown to be homosexual the likelihood is that they're sleeping together. So we trail down that road looking for cliques and coteries with even G. M. Trevelyan's sexual credentials called into question because he happens to have recommended the homosexual Guy Burgess for a job at the BBC.

I wonder apropos of this whether hunting the spies would have taken the same turn if it had not been for Lewis Namier. His work on the eighteenth-century Parliament pioneered the study of friendship and connection as the building blocks of eighteenth-century Parliamentary politics, a method that was quickly taken up and adapted for other periods, the fourteenth and fifteenth centuries included. Sussing out who slept with whom in the thirties, sex and friendship as a preliminary to recruitment, looks like the Namier method debased, less spy mania than spy Namier.

It's hard to believe that the author of the *Tractatus* was a master spy, though not much harder than accommodating to the known fact that he was a big fan of Betty Hutton and Carmen Miranda (Judy Garland one would have understood). And even though Wittgenstein was never big on small talk, he must have been tempted in those dark days of the war to drop the name of his former schoolmate, which he never seems to have done – or not to anyone who mattered. But who knows? Say, when Wittgenstein is doing his stint as a hospital porter at Guy's and he's wheeling some wretched casualty of the Blitz back from the operating theatre. Still dozy from the anaesthetic the patient comes round and is alarmed to find the frail porter with the burning eyes bending over him.

'Air raids nothing,' he whispers. 'What do you expect from that Adolf? I used to see him in the playground and he was Mr No-Good then already. Still' – he spies Matron approaching – 'whereof one cannot speak, thereof one must be silent.'

11 October. The Larkin selection falls through, a casualty of Larkin's early connection with George Hartley and the Marvell Press, which originally published *The Less Deceived*, the rights in which Hartley has understandably hung onto ever since. Sometimes he gives permission for the poems to be reproduced, sometimes not: this time not.

Writing an introduction has forced me, reluctantly, to think about Larkin again. His gloom has to be faced and sometimes, I've come to think, faced down. It gets under the skin as Hardy's never does. Though this may be because he's our contemporary, it's also that where melancholy is concerned Larkin is such a missionary. It's not enough that he sees the world as he does: we must see it, too, and feel as depressed about it.

My perspective on this is of someone who has had to stand on the stage and read the poems, when it becomes a predicament. Declaiming lines like 'Life is first boredom then fear' or 'Courage is no good/ It means not scaring others' and sensing an audience happily concurring, I feel a tart: it's just giving them a cheap thrill. The despair is too easy.

24 October. In an interview for the *Observer* this morning Robert

McCrum congratulates Michael Frayn on being more of a free spirit than others of his generation, 'Michael Winner and Alan Bennett being prisoners of their own celebrity'.

Prisoners possibly but I hope we're not in the same cell.

14 November. Watch part of the Remembrance Day ceremony with the usual mixed feelings, hating the seven-foot-tall, never-cheating, never-doubting generals stalking onto the parade (the Army always harder to take than the Navy) and the hard-faced high-ranking veteran (younger than me, I note) who marches out on behalf of the British Legion. Untelevised is the planting of pink triangles on behalf of the gay dead, the consequence, it seems, of a refusal by both the British Legion and the MoD to allow surviving same-sex partners of the dead to take part in the parade. I find myself out of sympathy with both sides, though more angered by the intransigence of the old guard from whom only a small effort of the imagination is required. The dead would have more sense, a great posthumous shrug the proper answer. (And a shout from somewhere in the ranks of 'What the fuck does it matter now, anyway?')

Untelevised, too, is the protest of Mr John Hipkiss, a dedicated Geordie pensioner who is, shamefully, having to campaign for the pardon of those shot for cowardice on the Western Front, and in particular for the boy soldiers who were executed, some as young as sixteen. Shown in tonight's *Everyman* programme is Dr John Reid, the Armed Forces Minister who is still managing to pretend that there was some justice in these executions, no doubt because one of the seven-foot-tall generals in the MoD has bullied him into compliance. So Dr Reid presumably knows more about cowardice than some of the boys who were shot. Shown on the programme is one of the death sentences passed by a court martial on a seventeen-year-old carrying with it a recommendation of mercy. Except that the recommendation is personally countermanded by Field Marshal Earl Haig, that old brute whose descendants are still (despite his earldom, his country estate and a grateful nation's pension) complaining how unfairly history has treated their papa.

18 November. In one of the scenes in *The Lady in the Van* Nicholas Farrell, playing me, is briefly interviewed at home by a visiting journalist, the scene beginning with her returning from the loo and saying: 'Pictures in the lavatory! That to me spells civilisation!'

Watching today's dress rehearsal at the Queen's through a haze of flu, I think I hear: 'Victor's in the lavatory! That to me spells civilisation!'

Well, I fluily think, it could have been, as this was in 1974 and at the time V. S. Pritchett was living round the corner and I suppose the presence of our leading literary critic and short-story writer in one's loo would testify to some degree of sophistication. Or, I doze, perhaps there's no apostrophe and it's 'Victors in the lavatory!' – a successful skirmish in the war against constipation, a war Miss Shepherd fought virtually on my doorstep.

Meanwhile the play has moved on and Maggie Smith as Miss Shepherd is now driving the van onto the stage and as it were into my garden. That I can't actually recall this happening I put down to my assumption that it was only going to be for three months. Had I known at the time that it would be for fifteen years the moment must surely have etched itself on my memory.

25 November. Multiplied on the stage I now seem to be multiplying in life. At rehearsal today Ben Aris, who plays Miss Shepherd's brother, asks me about my time as a chorister at King's, Cambridge, some of my memories of which are printed in December's *Gramophone*. He shows me the magazine and there is my photograph and an account of my time as a chorister (and indeed senior chorister) from 1937 to 1941 when, nothing if not precocious, I would have been all of three years old. It turns out to be a mix-up between words and pictures: there is an Alan Bennett, an ex-chorister whose reminiscences these are, and seeing the name, the picture editor has slapped on my photograph. I imagine the singing Alan Bennett gets more grief from his name than I do but it does leave me with a small regret as I would have liked to have taken part in the ceremony of the Nine Lessons and Carols during the darkest days of the war along with Dadie Rylands, perhaps, E. M. Forster and Maynard Keynes. As it was, come 1941 and all I was doing was giving my shepherd abiding in the fields in the Upper Armley National School nativity play.

27 November. The wife of Nicholas Farrell is having a baby and it had been agreed before rehearsals started that he should have time off to attend the birth. This ought to have been a fortnight ago, well before the start of previews, but the baby is overdue and labour began last night and looks like going on throughout the afternoon. His understudy has had no chance to rehearse and I therefore go on with the book at the matinee and play myself.

It's a salutary experience. I tend to underestimate the energy required by acting, my own efforts on the stage fitting well with Gerald du Maurier's definition of acting as 'overpaid casual labour'. I stand at the van door, a foot or so from Maggie Smith, who is in full flow, her face working, her eyes popping, grimy hands clenching and unclenching, and the force and energy coming off her so palpable that were I not required to stand there in the script I would certainly move back out of range. I am thankful I have the book to shield me and let me occasionally look away from this fierce, demented, deluded woman.

In other respects the performance seems gentler than normal with Kevin McNally, who plays my other half, often putting his hand on my shoulder or stroking my back. This is an illusion. The arm round my shoulder grips me with fingers of steel and steers me to where I should be standing on the stage and the stroking of the back firmly pushes me out of the way.

Luckily it is not an experience I have to repeat as Baby Farrell has been born just as the curtain goes up for the matinee and her proud father is back on stage for the evening performance.

11 December. Tidy my desk, going through piles of paper accumulated during the rewrites and rehearsals of *The Lady in the Van* and feeling, as I often do when a play has been mounted, that it's slightly to the side of the play I wanted to write and that, now it's on, here among the cuts and alterations is the real play.

There are odd lines I have forgotten to include. 'I know the difference between urine and honeysuckle' (my anguished retort when Miss S. attributed the smell from the van to the creeper on my neighbour's wall) and a remark of my mother's: 'By, you've had some script out of me!' I find a note about my fear of Catholic churches as a boy, which I always entered warily and with some sense of a spell cast. They were exotic places, tasteless and vulgar, the incense and images and explicit devotion making me nervous of stopping long in such an idolatrous lair.

'Try and get some silliness in' is another note.

And a vision of Miss Shepherd on some dream outing, stood sentinel by her van on top of the Sussex Downs. The light shafts through the clouds and she gazes across the Channel like a figure from a Shell poster in the pioneer days of motoring.

2000

5 January. A lorry delivers some stone lintels at No. 61. The driver is a stocky, heavy-shouldered, neatly coiffed woman of around sixty. While she doesn't actually do the unloading, she humps pallets up and down the lorry and does everything a male (and younger) lorry driver would do, with only a certain doggedness to her actions an indication of her gender. One or two passers-by look twice and a neighbour posting a letter stops to talk – and what enables him to break the ice is that she is a woman doing a man's job.

8 January. By train to Cambridge on a day of blinding sunshine and bitter cold. We eat our sandwiches on the train, a busy, bucketing electric job that scampers through Shepreth and Foxton and very different from the plodding little steam train I used to take into Cambridge when I was doing National Service. These days, the populousness of the place apart, the big difference is not being able to wander at will, 'The college is closed to visitors' always on the gate. By luck we manage to get into Trinity and Trinity Great Court, which R. has never seen and which still seems to me one of the sights of Europe. The chapel is notable chiefly for Roubiliac's statue of Newton 'voyaging through strange seas of thought, alone'; Newton a young man and unwigged so that his head seems quite small and (appropriately) apple-like.

We buy a luminous blue and white Victorian tile at Gabor Cossa which one of the partners thinks is William de Morgan but isn't and then cross the road to the Fitzwilliam. I take in a chance selection of pictures, dictated by which happen to be in range of available banquettes, and in particular the Van Dyck portrait of Archbishop Laud. It's hung beside one of his voluptuous court ladies, compared to which it's almost a sketch with Laud looking tetchy and impatient, as if resentful of having to spend time on such fripperies. He looks entirely humourless and more administrator than cleric with no hint of the beauty of holiness. But scrappy and almost unfinished, it's a superb character study; why it wasn't in the recent RA exhibition is hard to understand.

17 January. The Prince of Wales and Mrs Parker Bowles come to *The Lady in the Van*. Normally royalty is guaranteed to put a frost on an audience but their presence peps things up and it's a very good house. This is because, unlike most royal persons, the Prince of Wales actually laughs and loudly too and so gets the audience going. Their arrival at the theatre comes shortly after that of Barry Manilow, who is puzzled to find press and paparazzi abruptly deserting him as they go in pursuit of grander quarry. The Prince is very enthusiastic about the play when he goes round afterwards, though I'd have thought the chances of him persuading his mamma to come are pretty slim. John Gielgud was once telling me about Mrs Simpson and how smart she was. 'Mind you,' he said 'she'd have made a disastrous queen. Didn't go to the theatre at all.'

19 January. I know very little opera, the few operas I have seen, mostly when I was a boy, consisting of those productions that occasionally turned up at Leeds Grand Theatre when put on by the touring company of Covent Garden or the Carl Rosa. Thus in one week in 1951 I saw Walton's *Troilus and Cressida*, Vaughan Williams's *Pilgrim's Progress* and *La Bohème*. None of these bowled me over, but standing in the gallery at the Grand again in 1951 I heard *Der Rosenkavalier* for the first time (and saw it for the only time) and I felt I had known the music all my life. It was so hot at the top of the theatre that the gold paint from the guard rail came off on my hands.

But I was an odd unfinished boy and came to many things backwards. At seventeen I knew all about the final act of *Der Rosenkavalier* where the Marschallin (sung in this instance by Sylvia Fisher) renounces her love for the young Octavian and graciously gives way to Sophie. I knew already that my lot in life would be cast with the General's wife, renunciation the rule: it was already my story. But the first act which opens in the morning with Octavian and the Marschallin in her bedroom was lost on me. It never occurred to me what Octavian might have been doing there or that he had stopped the night: I just thought he'd popped round for breakfast.

22 January. Take Richard Buckle's autobiography, *The Most Upsetting Woman*, out of the London Library in order to refresh my memory of the Diaghilev exhibition in 1954. Buckle had organised it and put it on first at the Edinburgh Festival (a much smarter venue then than it is now) from which it later transferred to London. I must have seen it in my first vacation from Oxford in January 1955 and in memory had put it somewhere north of Oxford Street, Portman Square possibly. In fact it was in Forbes House in Belgrave Square: not knowing London, I took Knightsbridge to be Oxford Street.

Of the exhibition I recall only the two huge blackamoors at the foot of the staircase in the entrance and the music that was playing throughout (the notion of music in an exhibition then thought quite daring), though I remember, too, coveting some of the portraits and drawings of the

Diaghilev troupe and finding the wild colour exciting. The exhibition had been sponsored by the *Observer*, at that time peopled with fabled beings like Kenneth Tynan, Edward Crankshaw and C. A. Lejeune, a socially and intellectually glamorous world, particularly to Michael Frayn, one of a group of us who went to the exhibition. But, of course, London itself was beginning to seem glamorous then – the Coffee House in Northumberland Avenue, the Soup Kitchen in Chandos Place, films at the Academy on Oxford Street and suppers at Schmidts in Charlotte Street or Romano Santi's in Soho.

No glamour today, I think as I stand at the lights at Wardour Street waiting to cycle up past the Queen's, though maybe some young man down from Oxford for the weekend finds it as exciting now as I did then, but probably not. Too much going on in the world for that.

31 January. Further to Richard Buckle (family from Warcop in Westmorland): he served in the war in the Scots Guards, a brave if bumbling officer who took part in the gruelling campaign that preceded the capture of Monte Cassino. The rigours of the fighting were mitigated by a ready supply of willing Italian boys and on one occasion Buckle bounced into the mess announcing: 'I've just slept with a cardinal's nephew!' Nor was he alone, a brother officer referring to his Military Cross as 'my new brooch'.

For all that, morale seems to have been impeccable so that I wonder what the senior army officer who has recently resigned because of the tolerance now legally extended to gays in the armed forces would make of this passage (referring to Buckle's scavenging activities on behalf of the mess) taken from the official Scots Guards regimental history: 'Eggs were not the sole commodity Lieutenant Buckle collected; a brother officer alleged that he "walked over to the German lines in daylight, rummaged at will, and usually returned with old curious books, abstruse and pornographic. One day he came back with a bridal dress which he wore for dinner in the evening."'

10 February. In one of the many pieces on Austria's Mr Haider it's said that he's 'wickedly funny'. As wickedly funny, presumably, as the SS guards whose honour and camaraderie he so much admires and who, when a prisoner escaped from a concentration camp and was recaptured, paraded him round the camp with a placard say: 'Hurrah! I'm back.'

12 February, Yorkshire. It's a sad fact but it has to be acknowledged that whatever the sublimity and splendour of our great abbeys (we are visiting Rievaulx), to the droves of often apathetic visitors the monastic life only comes alive when contemplating its toilet arrangements. Not monks stumbling down the night stairs at three in the morning to sing the first office of the day; not the round of prayer and praise unceasing sent heavenwards from altar and cell: what fires the popular imagination is stuff from the reredorter plopping twenty feet into the drains. The soaring buttresses of the Chapel of the Nine Altars at Fountains count for nothing beside what remains of a fifteen-stall latrine.

The past is also a place of punishment and were there relics of that they would also entertain, but disappointingly these are cells of the wrong sort. I once heard a child at Chatsworth ask where the torture chambers were.

Another thought occurs apropos the monastic life: what is it about music that encourages the non-performance of its duties? Musicians are notoriously unreliable and think nothing of sending someone else along to take their place. And so it has always been, apparently. Quite early in their history the monks wearied of getting up in the middle of the night and were putting in deputies to sing the offices.

13 February. The few archaeologists I have come across in life were shy, retiring and mildly eccentric. The archaeologists on television are loud, unprepossessing and extrovert – their loudness and overenthusiasm to be accounted for, I suppose, by the need to inject some immediacy into a process which, if properly undertaken, is slow, painstaking and, more often than not, dull. Sir Mortimer Wheeler probably started the rot and then there was Glyn Daniel and his bow ties and today it's Tony Robinson capering about professing huge excitement because of the uncovering of the (entirely predictable) foundations of a Benedictine priory at Coventry. His enthusiasm is anything but infectious and almost reconciles one to the bulldozer.

And there's always a spurious time limit, thus making it another version of *Ground Force*, where a transformation has to be wrought in the space of three days. The timetable of the Resurrection would just have suited the programme-makers; the angel appearing to Mary Magdalene in the garden was probably Alan Titchmarsh.

17 February. Though she complains about having to put on so much make-up and even more about the bore of taking it all off, Maggie Smith seems to enjoy transforming herself into Miss Shepherd, today showing me her grey mottled legs as if they are a newly completed landscape. She's particularly pleased with the ulcers she has incorporated into the decorative scheme, displaying them with the relish of a beggar on the streets of Calcutta. In her body stocking and headband she looks like a downtrodden Beatrice Lillie.

19 February. 'Police killing was lawful' says inquest. What police killing isn't? I can't recall any that has been censured and none certainly without the policeman concerned being hurriedly retired on medical grounds. There's an instance of that in the paper this morning, one of the officers criticised in the Lawrence inquiry off to pastures new with his pension and his hurt feelings. It's also reported this morning that two of the presumably incriminating rifles used in the Bloody Sunday shootings and supposedly in the safe keeping of the Ministry of Defence have been 'destroyed'. The mystery on mornings like this is how one can still persist in thinking that this is a decent society whichever government we live under.

20 February, Yorkshire. Via Mallerstang to Kirkby Stephen and Barnard Castle, the tops still veined with snow and in the late afternoon bathed in a rich tawny light, the valleys in shadow with the hills still catching the sun. We have tea at Muker, where we look in the church, which is dull and scraped, how dull one can see from an old photograph of the way it was before it was done up in the nineteenth century – galleried with a three-decker pulpit and looking (as Whitby still does) like some dreamlike marine interior, crooked, bargeboarded, a church out of *Alice* or Kafka. Now it is subdued to a rigid ecclesiastical geometry – even the sixteenth-century font recarved and thus deprived of its original design.

22 February. Noel Annan dies and gets good notices. He was one of the models for Duff, the best or certainly the most enjoyable character in *The Old Country* (1977). I always felt kindly towards him after learning that he would not stay in the same room as Paul Johnson.

15 March. There is generally a beggar sitting outside the back door of M&S (and likely to be one at the front as well). I will sometimes give them my change as I'm coming out, though I'm irritated at being asked for money as I'm padlocking my bike before going in. Today I see the young man who's begging furtively reading a newspaper and I find myself not giving him anything for that reason. It's as if, having grudgingly accepted that begging is an occupation, I expect it to be carried out with a proper degree of diligence, and if someone is going to beg half-heartedly I am not willing to contribute.

I wish I were one of those people who say 'I never give to beggars', as it must make life so much simpler. Sometimes I do, sometimes I don't. When I do it'll often be out of superstition or wanting a bit of luck; when I don't it's because the beggar has a mean face, looks a crook or, as today, because he's not doing a good job.

21 March. Read the hitherto unpublished extracts from Sylvia Plath's diaries without much interest. I hadn't known about Hughes's homophobia – though I'm not sure that antipathy to Truman Capote can be so subsumed, Capote really deserving a phobia to himself. As usual, I'm repelled by how 'poetic' it all is – their fierce quarrels and affections and all the fish, blood and bone of the verse. If there had been jokes, I suppose, the spell might have been broken.

2 *April*. Remember the device advertised in comics sixty years or so ago called, I think, a Seebackroscope. It was a small funnel in black Bakelite containing a tilted mirror about the size of a sixpence; this device you were meant to hold to your eye or screw into your eye socket in order to check that you weren't being followed. It was intended, presumably, as part of the equipment of the schoolboy sleuth (invisible ink similarly) and my brother even sent off for one. When it came we were swiftly disillusioned, the mirror never reflecting anything useful or even in focus. It was a definite stage in that process of discovering that things were never as good as advertisements cracked them up to be.

7 *April*. After filming *An Englishman Abroad* Coral Browne gave the extravagant fur coat she wore in the film to the National Theatre, partly for sentimental reasons but partly, too, because times were changing and it was getting almost unwearable. Hoping to be able to use it in their current production, the West Yorkshire Playhouse wrote to the NT to see if they could borrow it, only to find it has been disposed of. This was not due to shortage of space (the NT has a large warehouse for costumes) but because it was natural fur and therefore disapproved of. I'd like to have heard Coral herself confronting whichever apparatchik it was that made this decision.

26 *April, New York*. A middle-aged woman on the bus; a man sitting behind her opens his paper rather noisily and the woman turns round.

WOMAN: I don't like your paper in my hair.
MAN: I don't like your hair in my paper.

At this point the bus passes an anti-Castro demonstration on behalf of Elian Gonzalez and an argument breaks out in which the whole bus takes part, the (quite sensible) conclusion being that there wouldn't have been any fuss at all if it had been his mother claiming the boy not his father.

7 May. I'm coming to the end of *Ravelstein*, Saul Bellow's novel supposedly based on his friend and associate Allan Bloom. I'm never entirely comfortable with (and never unaware of) Bellow's style, which puts an almost treacly patina on the prose – designer prose it is, good, tasteful and self-evidently rich. In this book he writes about the rich too, Ravelstein suddenly a multi-millionaire from the success of his book (Bloom's original book called *The Closing of the American Mind*). I'm perhaps behind the times here but I would have thought it unlikely for such a book (even when widely translated) to make its author a multi-millionaire (and certainly not if he or she is with Faber and Faber).

Bellow has a good time detailing the evidence for and display of this newly gotten wealth – a suite at the Crillon in Paris, neckties from Hermès, shirts from Turnbull and Asser and a mink thrown on the bed. Though Chick, the teller of the tale, is in a more modest way of things, I'm not sure these evidences are volunteered with an eye to their vulgarity, and there is an Ian Fleming-like knowingness about him – the best place to stay, the shop to buy shirts, etc. Bellow's presentation of vulgarity itself vulgar. But maybe I'm missing something here and it's all part of Bellow's take on Bloom.

In the past it's Bellow's women I've found trying, generally heavy-breasted, a touch exotic and very much in control. The woman most closely scrutinised in *Ravelstein* is rather different. This is Vela, Chick's Serbian first wife – slim, fastidious and over-discriminating. To viewers of *Cheers* or *Frasier* she will not be unfamiliar, as she sounds very like Frasier's ex-wife Lilith, and Niles's ex-wife, Maris.

14 May. A group of women, care-workers or probation officers, white and black, are coming out of the resettlement centre on the corner of Arlington Road. 'Hello!' says one to a new arrival whom she kisses. 'Hello, you motherfucker.' This is said in such lazy affectionate tones, with 'Hello, you old cunt' I suppose once the equivalent but these days not permitted.

20 May. Nick Hytner is in the second week of rehearsals of Tennessee Williams's *Orpheus Descending* at the Donmar. We chat in Maggie Smith's dressing-room in the interval of *The Lady in the Van*, Maggie saying that Tennessee Williams had a distinctive laugh and when she was playing Hedda Gabler at the Old Vic she kept hearing him chuckling in the stalls at wholly inappropriate moments, Hedda's predicament seeming to him a huge joke. Similarly footage of thousands made homeless by typhoons could reduce him to helpless laughter.

21 May. Gielgud dies. Asked to appear on various programmes, including the Nine O'Clock News, but say no. Reluctant to jump on the bandwagon, particularly when the bandwagon is a hearse. Some notes:

Despite the umpteen programmes of reminiscence Gielgud did on both radio and television there was always more and I never felt he had been sufficiently debriefed. Anyone of any distinction at all should, on reaching a certain age, be taken away for a weekend at the state's expense, formally interviewed and stripped of all their recollections.

It was hard to tell if he liked someone, only that he didn't dislike them. I think I came in the latter category. I went round to see him after *Home* and he said how much he liked David Storey. 'He's the ideal author . . . never says a word!'

In *Chariots of Fire* he shared a scene with Lindsay Anderson, both of them playing Cambridge dons. Lindsay was uncharacteristically nervous but having directed John G. in *Home* felt able to ask his help, saying that if he felt Lindsay was doing too much or had any other tips he was to tell him. Gielgud was appalled: 'Oh no, no. I can't do that. I shall be far too busy thinking about myself!'

The last time I saw him was when we were filming an episode of the TV adaptation of *A Dance to the Music of Time*. We were supposedly talking to one another but the speeches were separately recorded and intercut. His speech was haltingly delivered (but then so had mine been) and we did several takes. At the end he was given a round of applause by cast and crew, which I felt had not much to do with the quality of the speech itself so much as his having stayed alive long enough to deliver it. I imagine this kind of thing happened on most of the jobs he did (and he did a good many) in his nineties, and it was probably one of the things he hated about being old as there was inevitably some condescension to the applause. But he would just smile, do his funny snuffle and say that people were awfully kind.

23 May. Watch the *Omnibus* tribute to John G. in which *Oedipus* and *Forty Years On,* which came after it, both go unmentioned, though much is made of *Prospero's Books,* largely because he took his clothes off in it (not, incidentally, for the first time, as he did so in Bob Guccione's *Caligula;* this too goes unmentioned, though more out of kindness, I would have thought). To some extent the omissions simply reflect the material that is available – the programme is archive-led. The BBC did have film of *Forty Years On* but lost it or wiped it or certainly made no effort to preserve it, though I would have thought that even in 1968 it was plain that any film or tape of Gielgud needed to be set aside. Thirty years and more later, I doubt the situation has improved much and it remains a scandal that a public corporation should still have no foolproof archive system.[*]

Letters from Gielgud were always unmistakable because of the one-in-five slope of his handwriting, the text sliding off the page. I always felt it was slightly unfriendly that I'd never been invited down to Buckinghamshire but then I reread a letter he wrote me after I'd reviewed one of his books and in it I find an open invitation to lunch any time, with telephone number, directions, and how to get from the station. So now, of course, I feel mortified.

---

[*] I later discovered that some of the film of *Forty Years On* had survived, though by accident; what is kept and what is scrapped still being hit and miss.

31 May. Carnations are an unregarded flower nowadays, on sale at garages and supermarkets, packaged and mass-produced and utterly without scent. A young man, a boy still really, going into Cambridge on Saturday afternoons and fancying himself a bit of a dandy, I used to buy a carnation for my buttonhole and it would scent the day – musty, rich and, as I thought, sophisticated. I buy them still in Yorkshire because the garden is over-supplied with lady's mantle, *Alchemilla mollis*, and in early summer particularly the red carnations and the sharp fresh green of the alchemilla light up the room.

13 June. At supper Alec Guinness tells a curious story apropos a BBC documentary on Anthony Eden last night. In pre-war days Eden used to see a good deal of the theatre director Glen Byam Shaw and when he was contemplating resignation over Abyssinia in 1938 he sought Byam Shaw's advice. Byam Shaw said that his advice wasn't worth having as he knew nothing of politics, but Eden said that wasn't what he wanted. He needed to know how ordinary people would react: who would know that? Whereupon Byam Shaw took him round to Lord North Street, where the impresario Binkie Beaumont lived, and they put the question to him. 'Resign,' said Binkie promptly. And so he did. Binkie Beaumont as voice of the people sounds odd and indeed alarming and A.G. isn't always a reliable witness or when he's been told a story will often get it wrong. But this one is so peculiar as to seem not unlikely.

Whenever I see anyone with a shaven head, a boy particularly, I still think of them as poor, as such boys generally were when I was young. I even thought it of Beckham yesterday, sullenly leaving the pitch in Eindhoven.

17 June, Yorkshire. In the morning I find a bee trapped under a cloth in the house and revive it by giving it a blob of honey into which it sticks its tongue or nozzle or whatever, greedily sucking it up so that it soon gets back its buzz and flies away. Contrast this with the evening when I go out with my salt pot and ruthlessly track down slugs and snails, the awful cocktail of salt and slime now waiting by the garden window to be emptied.

18 June. Halted at Doncaster this evening by an electrical fault, we are eventually turned out onto the platform to wait for the next train. It's a blessing, though, as it's around 7 o'clock and the platform bathed in sunshine still. Fifty years later, and still a sucker for summer evenings, I remember the hours spent waiting on country platforms in 1948 or 1949 when I had a Runabout ticket and went all over the North and East Ridings. The mood persists when we get back on the train so that the landscape seems taken back in time: the fields as plush and waist-deep in corn as they ever were, embankments thick with blossom-laden elders and in the hedgerows even, it seems, elms still – all suspended in amber evening light.

All this is much better put in John Cheever's *The Wapshot Scandal*:

> She went to the window to see the twilight, wondering why the last light of day demanded from her similes and resolutions. Why, all the days of her life, had she compared its colours to apples, to the pages of old books, to lighted tents, to sapphires and sere ashes? Why had she always stood up to the evening light as if it could instruct her in decency and courage?

12 July. I don't hear many sermons nowadays but they don't seem to have changed much – viz. the Archbishop of Canterbury at yesterday's service for the Queen Mother: 'She is someone who can help us to travel that country we call life.'

24 July. The *News of the World* publishes photographs of dozens of paedophiles whom it labels beasts and wants 'nailing'. I wonder if in the seminar room of Oxford's Rupert Murdoch Professor of Communications such tactics are the subject of academic discussion: 'Naming and Shaming: Rebekah Wade on Circulation Boosting, Its Postures and Properties'.

5 August. I saw Alec Guinness two days before he died. Though the papers say he had been ill for some time he had not been seriously incommoded until the last few weeks and had no notion that he was dying.

Almost the last thing he said to me as I was going was to ask where I was getting the train.

'Petersfield.'

'Liss is better. It takes ten minutes off the journey.'

This bending you to his will, gently though he did it, was entirely characteristic and the way he had always been, particularly on the hundreds of occasions he took me out to supper.

'What are you having?' he would ask.

'I thought I'd try the bream.'

'Oh, the bream? Are you sure?'

'Yes, I rather fancied some fish.'

'Sure you don't want the lamb? It's very good here.'

I hesitate.

'No, I think I'd prefer the bream.'

'Would you? Oh.'

He seemed disappointed so I would relent.

'Oh, all right. I'll have the lamb.'

'You don't have to. Have the bream by all means.'

And so we would go on in a ritual with which all his dining companions were familiar: part of a procedure designed to make sure you weren't just choosing something because it was cheap (this, except at the Connaught, seldom entering my head) or to please him, though pleasing him and endorsing his choice were often the quickest way of terminating the discussion. So on this last occasion I should have said I'll go via Liss but don't, and this time he is too weak to argue.

His bed has been brought down to the corner of the living room so that when he lies down, a handkerchief over his head against the sun, he is effectively turning his face to the wall. Still I come away with no notion that this is the last time I shall see him. People keep ringing up to console me. It's like being consoled for the destruction of a view or the disappearance of a part of the landscape.

8 August. To the Cottesloe in the evening to talk to Humphrey Carpenter about his book *That Was Satire That Was* and answer questions from the audience. It goes well enough though I feel only slightly less inarticulate than I was in the period we are discussing. At one point Humphrey asks me about the end of satire and what I feel about it now. It's another question I don't satisfactorily answer and wake in the night wishing I'd thought to recall my last satirical fling, sometime in the early 1980s at Drury Lane in an Amnesty concert, *The Secret Policeman's Other Ball*, and a sketch I did with John Fortune.

Two upper-class figures are comparing notes about sex, one of them picking up lorry drivers (or what he fondly imagines to be lorry drivers) in the lavatories of Notting Hill, the other claiming to have exuberant sex with his wife. The best line comes when the gay one asks, re some straight-sex marathon:

'How long did it go on?'

'Well, if you include the foreplay and the wind-down afterwards, I don't suppose we had much change from three hours.'

'*Three hours?* Good God! you could be in Leeds in that time!'

The audience, which had come expecting to chant the *Python* parrot sketch, didn't like all this talk of sex one bit (didn't like anything, I suspect, that they hadn't heard fourteen times before) and we came off to virtual silence, the other performers, as is usual on such occasions, gathered in the wings to watch, now drawing back from us in a very New York fashion lest our lack of success be somehow infectious. That was the end of satire for me and also, I'm happy to say, the end of appearing in those mammoth charity shows which always turn out overlong, slyly competitive and never the least bit heart-warming.

10 August. Appalling scenes on the Portsmouth housing estate which is conducting a witch hunt against suspected paedophiles and the nation is treated to the spectacle of a tattooed mother with a fag dangling from her lips and a baby in her arms proclaiming how concerned she is for her kiddies.

The joy of being a mob, particularly these days, is that it's probably the first time the people on this estate have found common cause on anything; it's 'the community' they've been told so much about and for the first time in their lives each day seems purposeful and exciting.

11 August. En route for Petersfield and A.G.'s funeral I turn off the A3 to look at Ockham church and eat my sandwich lunch in the churchyard. It's locked but a rather grand woman who's working in the churchyard opens it up. It's the church of William of Ockham and Ockham's razor (in Latin) is inscribed on mugs for sale at the bookstall. Coming out, I thank the woman and she says I'm lucky because she wouldn't normally be around but they've been having trouble with the myrrh. The church hadn't seemed to be particularly ritualistic so this puzzles me.

'The myrrh?' I say.

'Yes'.

'You mean the incense?'

'No, no. The *myrrh*. For the grass. It's broken down.'

At Petersfield we go down to the church in a people-carrier. It belongs to Sally, Alec's granddaughter, and probably wouldn't have suited him at all but it seats everybody nicely, and as it doesn't look at all funereal none of the waiting photographers takes a second look. The note of 'Alec wouldn't like this' keeps recurring and is perhaps the most vivid way in which he is recalled.

The coffin is borne in and on it a cushion with his decorations. When he was given the CH he thought it unlikely that he'd ever get to wear it, having no tails now that would fit him, and that the only time it might be seen would be on his coffin. This is remembered in the nick of time and it's disinterred from the bottom of the wardrobe or wherever and pinned to a cushion which Merula, his widow, had embroidered years ago with a flowing tapestry of Walter, A.G.'s favourite dog. Once when A.G. was appearing in the West End Walter was run over by a milk float and slightly injured. The dog was so loved that this news had to be kept from Alec lest he be unable to take the stage.

The service is simple and being Catholic to me is utterly mysterious, as I never understand how they get the Mass over with quite so quickly, Holy Communion in the Anglican service more of a journey. Nowadays there's the handshake in common which, even though today I know everybody, I still don't find easy and it's quite hard to see how someone as fastidious as A.G. managed it all these years; Merula would have been one of his neighbours so perhaps he always sat on the aisle.

At the cemetery I talk to Michael and Henrietta Gough.

MICHAEL: Who's that woman over there who looks like Eileen Atkins?
ME: Eileen Atkins.
MICHAEL: That would account for it.

The undertaker retrieves Walter's cushion and the CH from the grave and we go back to the house which, when it was built *c.*1950, was in the depths of the country. Now it is within 200 yards of the M3, the roar of which was never absent in this last decade of their lives.

14 August. Listen to the last programme in Charles Wheeler's Radio 4 series on National Service, a discussion with, among others, Neal Ascherson, Michael Mates and Arnold Wesker. Though my own experiences (basic training in the Infantry, then the Joint Services Russian Course) were hardly typical, I find myself more in agreement with Wesker and indeed Michael Mates than I do with Ascherson.

Wesker admits that for all its miseries and boredom he enjoyed himself, as I did, and not merely when I was learning Russian. I enjoyed drill once I'd got used to it, the sense of being part of a group wheeling and counter-wheeling on the square not much different, I imagine, from the joys of the chorus line. Ascherson and also Paul Foot seemed to consider the two years as time wasted but I suspect that part of their impatience can be put down to their having been at public school, Ascherson at Eton, Foot at Shrewsbury. Part of the pleasure I had in National Service was that it represented delayed schooling, and that for the first time in my life I was away from home. No politician would dare suggest it but six months or a year of National Service nowadays, provided the time was well used, would seem to me to do little harm and have many advantages.

There were many bad moments during my two-year conscription, the worst entirely of my own making. En route for breakfast about a week after I began basic training I went for a pee and in the process dropped my knife, fork and spoon in the communal trough. I then had to retrieve them, rinse them off and go in and use them for breakfast. Still, since some of my fellows went on to be killed in Korea this hardly counts as an ordeal. Best were moments of intense lyrical delight I've seldom experienced since. South Yorkshire is hardly an area of outstanding natural beauty but having finished reassembling my Bren and ordered to take five, a soldier lying in the long grass, I would be enraptured.

A biker delivers a letter from the BBC: 'Alan Bennett? Can I shake your hand? The trouble is I sold all your plays for a gram of speed about five years ago.'

23 August, L'Espiessac. Sitting in the shade of the cherry tree outside the *pigeonnier* in a rough, warm wind that snatches at the paper as I write. Over the door is the date 22 mai 1816, a year after Waterloo and the departure of Napoleon, when this farmhouse was supposedly a nunnery.

Packed and waiting for the cab yesterday, I catch a Radio 3 repeat of a 1949 broadcast from the Edinburgh Festival of Kathleen Ferrier singing some Brahms songs. It's preceded by five minutes of her talking about her career, working with Bruno Walter and plans for the future she wasn't going to have. I've never heard her speak before and it's a voice as careful and considered and indeed tragic as many of the *lieder* that she sings. Though there's no trace of the Blackburn telephonist she had been only a few years before, the accent isn't in any way 'put on' – low, sad and yet full of hope, as if the words themselves were lyrics and deserving of the same care in phrasing and pronunciation. When she sings the voice is at the same time austere and yet rich and with none of that unctuousness that some contraltos have. It's her voice in *The Song of the Earth* and the

Strauss *Four Last Songs* and Brahms's *Alto Rhapsody* that I hear still as their proper tone, with no one else to touch her.

Before she was really famous – it must have been *c.*1947 – she came to Leeds to sing at Brunswick Chapel. Uncle George made Mam and Dad go with him to hear her, and though they weren't big ones for singing, they came back full of this young woman they had heard who turned out to be Kathleen Ferrier. What makes music inviolable still for me, and preserves it from the poisonous flippancies of Classic FM, are scenes like that, a Methodist chapel in the slums of Leeds lit up and packed with people on a winter night in 1947 and the voice of Kathleen Ferrier drifting out over the grimy snow.

27 August, L'Espiessac. Remember as I labour up and down the pool in the late afternoon the old lady in Gstaad who had always wanted a swimming pool of her own but her husband wouldn't have it. He then died and having dug one hole for him she dug a much bigger hole for herself and when we called one morning in 1971 she was chugging up and down the pool like a little water beetle, never happier in her life.

28 August, L'Espiessac. Pick out from this holiday bookcase *As They Were*, a book of travel pieces by M. F. K. Fisher, and read 'About Looking Alone at a Place', an account of a winter visit to Arles in 1971. I am shamed by its exactitude of expression and, though the language is simple, her ability to hit on a phrase. She's like Richard Cobb in finding out the ordinary rhythms of a place, its habits and the flavour of the small lives lived there – waiters (and the *shoes* of the waiters), hotel receptionists, attendants in museums. Born 1908 and now presumably dead. I have never heard of her.

2 September. In a piece in the *LRB* on Buñuel Michael Wood mentions among 'a number of startling and now famous images' in *Viridiana* 'a small crucifix that flicks open to become a menacing knife'.

The film came out in 1961 but I didn't see it until sometime in the 1970s after Buñuel's much more popular films like *Belle de Jour* and *The*

Discreet Charm of the Bourgeoisie. However, on the BBC's *Not So Much a Programme* in 1965 I played a pipe-smoking vicar with on his desk a crucifix that doubled as a pipe rack – a small blasphemy that provoked a question in Parliament.

The difference between the images is revealing: Buñuel's resonant and bold, Catholic and dangerous, mine Anglican, cosy and not threatening at all. Lindsay Anderson was a great admirer of (and borrower from) Buñuel and in the comparison of the two images he would have found all that was wrong with England.

2 *October*. Finish Peter Nichols's *Diaries*, a good read and hard to put down. He's blessed, as Osborne was, with droves of relatives to whom he seems far more attentive and considerate than ever I managed to be to my few. Still, they repay the attention and are a good source of material. I may not be the one to talk but with Nichols the vestibule between Life and Art is quite short and nobody lingers in it long.

Also reading Eamon Duffy's *The Stripping of the Altars*, which is hard going but full of interesting stuff about the ceremonial life of the late medieval church and its systematic dismantling under Edward VI and Elizabeth. I hadn't realised that the Elizabethan Settlement also meant the end of the mystery plays, which were pretty well forgotten by 1580. It shames me that I am more outraged by these events of nearly five hundred years ago (particularly by the iconoclasm) than I am by anything that's currently happening (and to flesh and blood) in Yugoslavia or Sierra Leone.

25 *October*. In the obituaries that I saw of Alec Guinness not much mention was made of his wife of sixty years, Merula Salaman, who was treated as if she was just an appendage to him. Now, when she too has died, would have been the time to make amends but death hasn't brought her out of his shadow, with no one giving a proper account of Merula herself as distinct from Lady Guinness. That wasn't a role she particularly wanted to play, especially in the late 1940s when Alec became a film star and felt he had to

lead a film star's life. Even when she was dying she talked with horror of those days, of the number of frocks she was required to have, the amount of changing that went on and the difficulties of dining in gloves.

Brought up as a wild country child in a large eccentric family (which deserves its own chronicler), she was happy as soon as the opportunity occurred to leave the high life to Alec and spend most of her time in the house that her architect brother had designed in Hampshire. Here she was surrounded by dogs, kept goats, had a donkey in the field and painted in a style that was vaguely Russian but which only came into its own when she took up needlework. Her needlework pictures are glowing with colour and intricate in texture, medieval in their richness. It was only in the last ten years or so that she had the confidence to exhibit them, Alec always nervous she would show him up or show herself up. They sold immediately and I bought several only to have Alec thank me as if I were doing it as a favour to him.

This was nothing new. Merula was, for instance, a superb cook and when I first stayed at Kettlebrook would produce delicious meals which Alec would apologise for – behaviour which she took in her stride, knowing it would pass. And when I'd been there two or three times (and always had second and even third helpings) he stopped apologising. The truth was that she made him a nicer, less awkward, more accessible person but even after sixty years of marriage she still found it odd that they got on and that she could cope with his fussing and over-propriety. But her affection for him didn't waver and only a few days before she died, when she scarcely had the strength to hold a pen, she wrote a poem praying that they would soon be reunited and this was read at her funeral.

She had faced death with her usual lack of fuss, writing to me in August: 'I have taken to my bed hence perculiar [*sic*] writing. I wish Alec were here to read that bit' – her spelling always caused him pain – 'I think I shall stay in my bed now for the duration. It saves a lot of trouble.'

She made it, as she had wanted, to her eighty-sixth birthday. It was two days before she died and with the dogs strewn across her bed she raised a glass of champagne, saying, 'Chin, chin.'

28 October. Cutting across from the M40 to Chipping Norton, we find ourselves passing the road to Rousham. Surprisingly this wet Saturday the gardens are open though apart from a young Japanese couple, who look to be honeymooners, we are the only visitors. We find a summer house by the bowling green, where we eat our sandwiches, then wander round the kitchen garden. The house itself is quite bleak and the garden front, grey and sash-windowed, and altered in the nineteenth century, almost institutional. The gardens are by William Kent but what delights is less the design than the beautiful cambered yew hedges (and hedges inside hedges and doors in walls that open onto hedges). In another kitchen garden is a pigeon house dated 1683, with an espaliered pear growing round it and doves and pigeons still in residence.

14 November. Alan Tyson has died. Of his work in psychoanalysis and musicology I know nothing and even his jokes and his silliness only by report. But he was good value and known to be. Once in the 1980s he rang the *LRB* and, passing on the call, someone said: 'How long before he makes his first pun?' It was in the first sentence. 'Hello! And what is it this morning, *belles lettres* or *Belgrano*?'

18 November. Various letters about *Telling Tales*, some of them chiding me for putting Francis L. Sullivan alongside Leslie Howard in *Escape to Happiness* when it should have been in *Pimpernel Smith*. It might as well have been *49th Parallel* so far as my memory is concerned as all the escape films of the early 1940s have run together in my mind. I had mentioned that I once saw Sullivan walking down Thornton's Arcade in Leeds some time during the war, a progress that was of necessity stately on account of his bulk and made more impressive by a camel-hair overcoat slung over his shoulders. The coat as cloak (and particularly a camel-hair coat) was standard dress, at any rate in the provinces, for anyone who wished to come on as 'artistic'. I seem to remember Anton Walbrook similarly garbed as the impresario in *The Red Shoes*, though I'll probably be deluged with letters telling me it was in *Dangerous Moonlight*.

1 December, New York. We go up to the Dakota to look at Sydney W.'s apartment. A group of middle-aged tourists on the other side of the street are being talked through the Dakota's history.

'Too old for John Lennon,' I think, whose anniversary is coming up, but of course these dumpy middle-aged women in their plastic rainhoods and their pork-pie-hatted husbands are his contemporaries. Not a speck of dust on the immaculate driveway on this building that I last went into nearly forty years ago for a party given for Judy Garland. She obligingly performed, to be followed after she had left by a drunken Shelley Winters, who lurched to her feet saying, 'I'm now going to sing ya all the songs Judy *never* sang', and launched into some striptease numbers. The saddest person there was Judy Holliday whom I tried to talk to but could think of nothing else to say other than how much I'd loved her in *Born Yesterday*, which was one of the reasons, presumably, why she was sad in the first place.

3 December, New York. I had forgotten how bleak American theatres are, the auditoriums seldom carpeted or even warm, the lobbies grey and functional and with none of that gilded Edwardian extravagance that frames the theatrical experience in England. One reason Americans go on about English theatre is just that it's comfier. It's a ballet we're seeing and to piped music, the dancers doing a good deal of running about as much to keep warm as anything else as I can't see a lot of artistry to it and with not even a smile. At the first interval we escape and join the crowds strolling down Fifth Avenue looking at the lights this Saturday night. The open-air skating rink is crowded. Most of the skaters are proficient except for one young businessman, who looks as if he's come straight from the office (carrying his briefcase): he knows how to skate but not how to stop so just has to sail straight for the barrier, thereby causing havoc. It's bitterly cold but the atmosphere is friendly and festive as it wouldn't be, I'm sure, on Oxford Street; people's faces are lit up and excited with no evidence of the famous surliness of New Yorkers, only pleasure and, I suppose, pride. Besides which nobody is drunk or even drinking.

I notice this again on Sunday when we cut through the main hall of Grand Central en route for Brooks Bros. The coved ceiling has been rigged for a Christmas laser show and travellers are standing about the vast hall gazing up at the lights flickering and dancing across the roof. And again there is that sense of fun and occasion so seldom generated in London except when licensed by the passage of royalty.

10 December. Watch the last of Richard Eyre's *Changing Stages,* which readily concedes that the stage for most people nowadays is big musicals and that whatever the magic of theatre might be for Peter Brook, say, to the average theatre-goer it's *Cats* or *Phantom of the Opera.*

I don't have many theories about what theatre is or what a play should be, never having got much beyond the notion of a play as a journey, even if it's only from A to B. And it would be comforting to be able to grade plays in terms of the distance travelled, particularly if at the lower end of the scale were the plays and musicals on in the West End and at the top end productions at the subsidised theatre and on the fringe.

But this is far from being the case and an audience at Edward Bond can sometimes travel no further in its head than the audience at *Cats.* Last year I went to a matinee of Theatre de Complicite's *Street of Crocodiles* where the audience were all fans and a journey that should have taken place in the theatre that afternoon had happened long before.

In part this comes about because the role of the audience has altered in the last twenty years and been infected by the pop concert. There the fans make themselves part of the event, helping to create the experience they have come to see. And so it is more and more with the theatre. Which is fine if you're in that particular club but if you're not (as I wasn't at *Street of Crocodiles*) and have just come to see the play it can be pretty depressing.

Peter Brook thinks, I imagine, that he is immune from such tendencies, and that his audience is a blank canvas; that he purveys a purer theatre. I doubt this or that his audience comes with fewer preconceptions than go to other productions. Give him an audience that thinks it's going to see Ray Cooney and he would be put to the test. As it is, an audience goes to

Brook expecting magic and gets it – just as a different audience does from Andrew Lloyd Webber. I'd just like to see those audiences switched round; that would be real theatre.

23 December. A good documentary on Channel 4 about Humphrey Jennings in which one of the conclusions is that Jennings's work deserves consideration because at a time when we are uncertain of our identity it helps to tell us who we are (or were).

Over the credits the next programme is announced, self-examination as it has since become: yet another round-up of the *Big Brother* series. No irony, I imagine, is intended.

2001

8 January. Note how personalised and peopled the material world is at a level almost beneath scrutiny. I'm thinking of the cutlery in the drawer or the crockery I every morning empty from the dishwasher. Some wooden spoons, for instance, I like, think of as friendly; others are impersonal or without character. Some bowls are favourites; others I have no feeling for at all. There is a friendly fork, a bad knife and a blue and white plate that is thicker than the others which I think of as taking the kick if I discriminate against it by using it less.

Set down this seems close to insanity but it goes back to childhood when the entire household was populated with friends and not-friends and few objects were altogether inanimate, particularly knives and forks. Both shoe brushes had characters, the bad brush with which the polish was put on, the good brush that brought out the shine. This was true of clothes, too, with a patchwork blouse I had to wear as a toddler thought of as unfriendly and which I always disliked. Sticks had characters, too, and cushions. Sixty years later more traces of this animistic world persist than I would like, making a mockery of reason and sense.

23 February. To look at a house in Sharpleshall Street. It isn't right but, empty though it is, still has lots of interesting books lying about which I have to resist looking at. There is some furniture, too, heavy William IV stuff, and dominating the ground-floor front room (which might once have been a shop) is a huge formal portrait of Lord Thurlow, the Lord Chancellor who plays a part in *The Madness of George III*. It's in a frame with a coronet built into it which suggests it may have been one of a series or hung once in the Inns of Court. When we were making the film of *George III* there was some thought that Alec Guinness might play Thurlow and as part of the wooing process that one always had to go through with Alec we went to Windsor to look at the Lawrence portrait of Thurlow in the Royal Collection. It wasn't nearly as powerful as this less 'artistic' one which might have taken A.G.'s fancy as the Lawrence portrait didn't. Still, it's odd to find Thurlow installed in this empty house so close to where Nicholas Hytner and myself both live. I ask David Burkett, the estate agent, how it comes to be there and he thinks it may have been an ex-stage prop from the Old Vic. Thurlow isn't someone I'd want to import into my front room. House priced at £1m.

24 February. Larkin's companion, Monica Jones, dies; met once, the only time I met Larkin, at his sixtieth birthday party at Faber. I cut out her obituary and 'tip it', as booksellers say, into Andrew Motion's biography of Larkin, reflecting that 'Tipping In' would be a good title for a Larkin poem, with its implications of a life completed and reduced to a few columns of newsprint, the sort of subject he might have picked up on. While, of course, resenting that you would think this was the sort of subject he might have picked up on. To be tipped into a life of Larkin, though, was what Monica Jones feared her fate was always likely to be.

Condemning some unfortunate for a sex crime yesterday, a judge uses the word 'loins' . . . 'with lust in your loins', I think it was. I'd have him off the bench for that alone. Bad language, I suppose.

25 February. To Yarnton on the outskirts of Oxford. Have our sandwiches in the warm sunshine on the edge of an empty undulating road running over to Woodstock, with the primroses already out. Yarnton Church is at the gates of what was Colonel Kolkhorst's manor house, which is a little too neat now and with more of the conference centre about it than it presumably had when Betjeman used to come here as an undergraduate.

The church itself is a delight, seemingly the pet project of the eighteenth-century Oxford antiquarian Alderman Fletcher, who is buried here in a tomb rescued from the ruins of Godstow Priory. He filled the windows with his collection of medieval glass, some of it superb, including one window with fragments of medieval birds straight out of Edward Lear. There are other artefacts including a series of fine Nottingham alabaster panels disinterred from St Peter in the East; no traces of colour left but the detail of the carving sharp and fresh down to the points of the Magi's crown and the fold of the donkey's ears. Almost uniquely for me I experience a warmth towards this Alderman Fletcher of whom I've never heard and dead now 200 years, whose eccentric enthusiasm preserved all this to give us such pleasure this sunny February afternoon.

6 March. Catch Sean Rafferty on Radio 3 talking to the 101-year-old Mary Ellis, Ivor Novello's leading lady (Novello dead fifty years ago today). She's bright as a button with brisk, common-sense opinions and is, as she points out herself, entirely unimpressed by glamour, of which, of course, Novello had a hefty dose. But she points out how it was the combination of Novello's looks and his tunefulness that got him underestimated so that he became a joke, as she says, almost to his face when he was much more of an artist than he was ever given credit for.

9 March, Venice, Palazzo S. Justina. We arrive in torrential rain, all the bells having rung half an hour before to warn of rapidly rising water so that the taxi bringing us from the airport cannot get under the bridges and leaves us in the Campo S. Justina huddled under umbrellas. Here Luigi, a lovely elegant English-sports-coated and flannelled Italian young man rescues us and takes us to the Palazzo . . . which is indeed a Palazzo and not the glorified boarding house I feared it might be. In the courtyard indeed is an arcaded staircase like the Ca D'Oro, broad shallow steps leading up to the piano nobile, where in the warm dining room are set out rice and meatballs, a takeaway from Harry's Bar. And it's cosy, comfortable and friendly and all the things I'd feared its grandeur would preclude.

10 March. R. is doing a recce for a feature on a creeper-covered house built in the fifties next to the Salute, but first we go to what is not much more than a cottage in an alley near the Palazzo Grassi. This belongs to the Sitwells and houses some of the furniture from Montegufoni, Sir George Sitwell's Tuscan castello that features in Osbert Sitwell's autobiography. And house the furniture is about all it manages to do as it's a tiny place, the furniture vastly too large for the rooms so that one wonders how they managed to cram it all in. There are huge gilt four-poster beds, caissons and sideboards in these odd up and down little rooms which I suppose are part of some holiday home but which exude gloom. I've never seen R. in action, as it were, and it's interesting that, though he doesn't care for it himself, he looks for ways in which an article can be made out of it . . . close-up shots of the elaborate beds, for instance, with some sort of view through an open door behind; details of some marquetry; a view of the tiny roof garden. Still, it's a relief when we finish and are cruising back down the Grand Canal to the Salute.

Marvel at the Viking graffiti on the flanks of the left-hand lion outside the Arsenal, looted by the Venetians complete with graffiti from Athens in the seventeenth century. The graffiti were only recognised for what they were (and translated) by some visiting Danish dignitaries in the nineteenth century. I hope the left-hand lion is the right one as the graffiti is very blurred and more graffiti has been added since, notably a painted D on the chest. But it's the right-hand lion that looks the most ancient and the most Greek (or Cretan anyway). Still, I run my hands over the supposed runes and marvel.

Spend Saturday morning scouring Venice for a shop where R. can buy the chocolate-brown Wellington boots he sees everybody wearing. ('How do I say, Do you have a pair with the little yellow stripe?')

While in Venice read Simon Gray's *Enter a Fox*, his account of how his plays get (or don't get) produced. He sent *The Late Middle Classes* to Trevor Nunn at the National when after a lengthy delay he got a letter back in which Nunn explained his reasons for turning the play down, in spite of his having enjoyed reading it. No, not in spite of . . . that was actually his reason for turning it down, that he'd enjoyed reading it – indeed so enjoyed reading it that he was convinced it didn't need 'the production environment of the National'. This was approximately the same letter I had thirty-odd years ago from the National (or the Old Vic as it was still) from Kenneth Tynan. I suspect it's a stock excuse for the subsidised theatres and one that comes readily to hand. 'You don't realise what a good play it is you've written! It's commercial!' Whereas if it was truly commercial the National would snap it up straight away.

17 March. The *OED* is appealing for help in finding the earliest use of, among others, phrases like 'I could murder a curry', the earliest date they have at the moment being 1986.

I don't know about curry but 'I could murder a (whatever)' was a phrase certainly current in Blackburn in the late sixties and early seventies. On holiday in Bardolino in 1972 a group of us made an expedition to Padua which proved barren of tea shops, my friend Madge Hindle (who is from Blackburn) scouring its ancient precincts saying, 'I could murder a Kunzle cake.' There may be some hesitation about including this as a reference point in the *OED* as it might involve explaining what a Kunzle cake was, namely what in the north is called 'a fancy' . . . a small rectangular individual iced cake, plentifully layered with cream. Kunzle cakes were wrapped in cellophane to make them long-life versions of fancies and were thought rather superior and on sale, for instance, at Fuller's tea shops alongside their (much more delicious) walnut cake. Who or what Kunzle was I have no idea but the cakes (and Fuller's) disappeared *c.*1980, or maybe earlier. They were certainly not to be had in Padua in 1972. The *OED* is welcome to this information.

24 March, Inverary. Sophistication hasn't reached this corner of Scotland. At Inverary, a pretty and, I imagine, fairly tourist-ridden place, we go into one of the half-dozen or so cafés. Gourmets should not make a beeline for the Paddle Wheel where there is a blackboard advertising the menu, which includes toast and (a separate item) baked beans. I ask for baked beans on toast. 'We don't do baked beans on toast,' says the unsmiling girl. 'But you do baked beans?' 'Yes.' 'And toast?' 'Yes.' 'But not baked beans on toast?' 'No.' I can't help laughing but she doesn't see this as a joke. There are two courses open . . . to order toast and baked beans and combine them under one's own steam, as it were, or to take our custom elsewhere, which we do, ending up in an equally dispiriting establishment trying to eat a toasted cheese and tomato sandwich. 'Could I have it on brown bread?' 'No brown bread. All white.' So much for Inverary.

27 March, Ardkinglas. Books in our bedroom at this Scottish country house. *My Memoirs of Six Reigns* by Princess Marie Louise; novels by Ian Hay, George A. Birmingham and John Buchan, the covers all bleached to the same shade, which is hardly a colour even but is characteristic of all the bookshelves I've ever liked and which I've never managed to achieve on stage or on film. *Getting On*, *The Old Country* and *An Englishman Abroad* all had bookshelves which ended up looking like caravan sites, not the faded sun-bleached greyish-brownish hue I'd specified in the script.

The architect of this wonderful house is Lorimer, who designed many houses in Scotland, chiefly for the newly rich magnates of Glasgow and Dundee, but south of the border seems largely to have confined himself to war memorials.

10 April. Going through the Public School Hymn Book today looking for a title for my memorial service short story, I read through 'Glorious Things of Thee Are Spoken' (No. 385) and come to the line 'Fading is the worldling's pleasure'. I must have sung this line thousands of times and have always unthinkingly taken this to be a disparagement of the worldling's languid approach to things, so that even when it came to pleasure the worldling couldn't go at it wholeheartedly but gave it up halfway through. It's only now, aged sixty-six, that I see that it's the pleasure that's meant to be fading and which doesn't last. This isn't half as subtle as my mistaken version and also tells you less about the aristocracy, which is what I've always taken these worldlings to be.

11 April. Foot and mouth. One of the drunks down the market pauses before he puts his can to his lips. 'Well,' he says, 'there's no outbreak in South Tyrone,' as if this were a good reason for drinking Strongbow at eight-thirty in the morning in Inverness Street market.

A gay driving instructor who rather than tapping the windscreen with his clipboard finds he gets better emergency stops by putting his hand on his pupil's knee.

12 May. Watching five minutes at the conclusion of the Cup Final (to the outcome of which I am utterly indifferent), I wonder whether the girlfriend of Michael Owen, who scores the winning goal, will be thinking that any love they might make later on this evening will stand no comparison with the ecstasy induced by the goal, and what she feels about this.

13 May. Somewhere I've always imagined living (and it pre-dates the Lyttelton–Hart-Davis letters where Hart-Davis's Kisdon cottage is such a place) is a house on the southern-facing slopes of Wensleydale or Swaledale, a long house with barns attached and built into the hillside with a terrace in front that looks across the valley. Wilsill, where we were evacuated, was such a house, though quite low down in the Nidd valley. Now I gather from watching Aubrey Manning's BBC2 series *Talking Landscapes* that such sites were not just my dream but a stock location for settlement since the Iron Age . . . some of them, of course, still inhabited sites but others abandoned, as he describes them, like a half-closed eye, a half-circle on the side of the hill where once a hut stood and behind it the banked earth, excavated for the platform. Even though we're so happy where we are, I always dream of such a place, and of sitting in a chair outside the back door catching the last of the sun, the Proms on the radio, watching the few doings in the dale.

18 May. Last week was Charlotte next door's birthday and we give her a little *Oxford Dictionary of Quotations*. It's divided into subjects . . . Family, Age, Morals, etc. and I figure in several departments, though with the same lumbering extracts that are in the larger dictionary, few of which I would have thought memorable at all. Somewhere in Larkin's interviews he speculates about the lines for which he will be remembered: 'Sexual intercourse began in 1963' of course; 'Books are a load of crap'; 'Nothing like something happens anywhere'; and of course 'What will survive of us is love', though he professes to think most of what he's written isn't particularly memorable.

I feel much the same, though I compiled a list a few years ago of what I thought was worth quoting and look it out to see what I think of it now, and though I don't find any of them imprint themselves on the mind, they're better than the ones in the *ODQ*.

> Legs always leave something to be desired, do they not? It is part of their function and all of their charm. (Wilde parody, *Forty Years On*)
> A butterfly is an event. (*Forty Years On*)
> That awkward gap between the cradle and the grave. (*Getting On*)
> When we are on our best behaviour we are not always at our best.
> (*A Question of Attribution*)
> Life is generally something that happens elsewhere. (*Writing Home*)
> (Also said by Milan Kundera, though not cribbed by me.)
> There is no such thing as false modesty. All modesty is false otherwise it's not modesty. (Not included in anything so far.)
> Cheek, though not quite a virtue, belongs in the other ranks of courage. (Obituary of Russell Harty, 1988.)
> The good is better than the best or what does society mean.
> (*The Old Country*)

If you have a secret there's no point in making a secret of it.

(*The Old Country*)

Sooner or later in life everything turns into work, including work. (One of the prefaces to the plays, I think.)

One of the functions of women is to bring an element of trouble into the otherwise tranquil lives of men. (*The Lady in the Van*)

In England age wipes the slate clean. If you live to be ninety in England and can still eat a boiled egg they think you deserve the Nobel Prize. (*Single Spies*)

Still, my favourite lines, though, are ones which while having an internal consistency in the play in which they occur, when taken out of context appear utterly absurd, e.g.:

'You can't knit bootees for the Nicene Creed', a line spoken by the Virgin Mary in *Kafka's Dick*.

And from the same play:

MAX BROD: I need to go to the toilet.

SYDNEY: Well, for God's sake don't do it over the goldfish or we'll be entertaining the Brontë sisters.

19 May, Yorkshire. Going into Settle this morning we pass a lorry at Austwick loaded with the carcasses of slaughtered sheep and find the main car park now given over to vehicles, bulldozers and all the paraphernalia of this dreadful travelling circus. Though for the soldiers and the slaughtermen the work must now be just a wearisome routine, cars still slow to watch the mounds of carcasses slither down the ramps and it's hard not to think it's but a step from this to the more terrible slaughters that go on in Eastern Europe. To date it has not quite come to our village, the cows on our two farms still unaffected, though a convoy goes through early this afternoon to start picking sheep off the fells.

30 May. It's a little life, my mother would say as my father killed a wasp or even an ant. Left to herself she was more predisposed in favour of some insects than others. To lift a plant pot and find it boiling with woodlice made her shudder, but to come across one on a solitary and hazardous trek across the fleecy rug was hardly a matter for revulsion and she would coax it onto a piece of paper before chucking it out of the door.

A similar rescue operation would be mounted whenever she found a daddy-long-legs. These insects, both ungainly and unthreatening, somehow commended themselves to her and she would strive to catch them in her cupped hands before releasing them into the unwelcoming street, her capture and subsequent liberation of them sometimes involving the loss of at least one of their elaborate limbs so that Dad growled unhelpfully: 'By the time she's finished saving their lives they're dead.'

14 June, Yorkshire. Much in the local papers about how the 'hefted' sheep will not be easily restocked, having been born on the fells and thus bred up to know its ways and its weather. They keep (and teach their lambs to keep) to their own patch and do not wander at will. They lamb every year by the same sheltered wall, come lower down when they sense the cold is coming or a storm expected and all in all these sheep know a good deal and the farmers know that they know it. I wonder, though, if there are other things the sheep know which the farmers do not acknowledge. Do they know that their male lambs will be taken away a few months after they are born? Do they know or do they wonder where they are being taken on the vast two- and three-tier lorries that ship them halfway across the country to market? If they know so much by instinct perhaps that is not all that they know and they perhaps deserve to be treated differently on that account. In fifty years' time I am sure that we will not handle animals the way we do now and to succeeding generations our behaviour will seem as barbarous as bear-baiting.

The beginning of a film: a boy and a girl collecting branches in seventeenth-century costume, the day idyllic, the pair of them in love, possibly.

'Here's a good one.'

'Here's a beauty.'

They collect an armful of branches each and then hand them over to a

jovial good-natured man who is stockpiling wood. It is for a public burning, the wood green to make it burn more slowly. The victim is already on
the pyre. The boy and girl settle down to watch.

26 June. En route home from the National we drive up Drury Lane and
then on towards Camden Town. Waiting at the lights in Bloomsbury
Square R. spots a fox, gaunt, grey and long-legged, seemingly waiting for
the lights too. It then trots unhurriedly across. A tall elegant creature, old
I would have thought, its delicacy and silence making it seem almost wolf-
like as it turns down a side street and vanishes into Holborn.

1 July. Listen to Nick Hytner on *Private Passions*, Michael Berkeley's
always excellent programme, a superior and more interesting *Desert Island
Discs* without its tiresome conventions. Most of Nick's musical choices are
quite spare (or 'transparent' as Nick calls them), not caring for music as a
warm bath, which is generally where my musical appreciation stops. So
there's Handel, Janácek, Sondheim, Haydn and Britten and ending with a
wonderfully slow and sexy rendering of 'Bewitched' by Ella Fitzgerald,
with the words 'I'll sing to him, each spring to him/ And worship the
trousers that cling to him.'

Nick doesn't mention the stories of singing as a boy in the choir with
the Hallé under Barbirolli or how he was winkled out of Jewish prayers to
bolster the singing of the Christian hymns, at Manchester Grammar
School. But it reminds me of the stories as Nick told them to me and how
vivid and touching they were, so after the programme I make notes to see
if I can turn these anecdotes into a film.*

9 July, Yorkshire. With there being so few visitors to the village and no
walking in the countryside generally, even in this comparatively short
space of time nature has reasserted herself. I've seen a deer bounding off
the fell below Buckhaw Brow and A. has seen a couple. A heron comes to

---

* This turns out to be the beginning of *The History Boys*, which I write and Nick directs three
years later.

the garden now and W., who occasionally mows the lawn, has three times seen a kingfisher below the bridge. Meanwhile, uncropped and ungrazed, the fields look more and more unkempt and every gathering of cattle inspires dread. The vast mechanised farm just before the Skipton bypass is now silent so I imagine their stock has been culled. It's such an ugly sprawling place with huge piles of tyres and rows of system-built hangars that it's not easy to feel much regret. It's more like a factory than a farm and hard to locate the actual farmhouse or to think there may be a family grieving there. Or not; the amounts of possible compensation said to be colossal.

12 July. I'm brushing my teeth in the bathroom this morning when a little school passes – or a class anyway – on an outing, to the zoo probably. Ethnically mixed with Muslim women in headscarves in attendance, a couple of tired-looking teachers and young fathers too, one with a rucksack on and a child in either hand. A poor school by the looks of it as distinct from the two other schools in the neighbourhood (green-uniformed children delivered by four-wheel drives). But the simplicity of this little column, the tired goodness of it, reaffirms . . . what? A belief in common decency, is it, and hope, as the green uniforms and four-wheel drives do not? Though it's hard not to think that against this trusting little column the four-wheel drives and the green uniforms will prevail.

A mad letter forwarded by the BBC apropos one of my *Telling Tales* programmes. 'I was intrigued by your references to certain Sexual Experiments which took place in your street-located Air Raid Shelter (but you didn't mention the opposite sex?) Was it MB? Fellatio or Cunilingus (*sic*) . . . please put me out of my misery on the subject. But it turned me on. I had to MB.' Odd to think of an old man wanking at the memory of an innocent short-trousered little boy playing in an air-raid shelter sixty-odd years ago.

'She is frail but it's deceptive: get her behind a supermarket trolley and she turns into Von Rundstedt.'

16 August. It occurs to me at Brian Brindley's funeral that one thing about the Catholic Mass is that it attracts and is open to anybody who just happens to be passing. There's almost an 'Ah, Bisto!' aspect to it so that even at the smartest requiems there are these oddities who, not having anything better to do, have just wandered in. And that way, maybe, salvation lies.

Another thought: the first requirement in any assembly is *to be heard*. I come home and tell Nora, my cleaning lady, about the Mass. 'Oh, that's a nice thing. I'll always go to Mass myself. And I do believe in God and all that so that people would say I was very devout. But when you're dead I think it's a case of Bob's your uncle.'

3 September. Very much enjoy Mark Ravenhill's *Mother Clapp's Molly House* at the NT. It has frequent references to 'wandering' . . . I suppose in the play it means cruising, though the simple boy in the first act seems to wander without knowing why or to what it might lead. This is like I was in my teens, wandering the streets of Headingley at night though without anything ever coming of it.

Then I come across an article about Roger Mayne, the photographer, of whom it was said, 'His eyes were wide open but he was a shy young man. It is the shy boy, not the streetwise, who goes wandering.'

11 September. Working rather disconsolately when Tom M. rings to tell me to switch on the television as the Twin Towers have been attacked. Not long after I switch on one of the towers collapses, an unbearable sight, like a huge plumed beast plunging earthwards. I go to put the kettle on and in that moment the other tower collapses.

15 September. Lynn in New York says that people in the city so want to be together they stand outside so that though New York is quiet there are many people on the streets, the atmosphere kindly and unthreatening, everyone courteous and not at all like New York. She had gone down to the Odeon when the first tower was hit and found the restaurant turned into a dressing station. She was out on the street when the second tower fell and had to flee the dust cloud, not stopping or looking behind her until she got to Canal Street.

1 October. Meet on Leeds Station Brian P., to whose home in Cookridge I used to deliver meat as a boy. He and his brother went to the Grammar School but we knew each other at the Crusaders Bible class, where I was even more conscious of my lowly status as delivery boy. We talk of battling through the snow in 1947 and he remembers how the canyon through the snow on Cookridge Heights was cut by German POWs. The height of the chasm was that of a double-decker bus and along this towering passage the POWs cut out embrasures for seats, grottoes almost, for the good people of Cookridge. He pats me on the shoulder and says how much he has enjoyed my work, a pat which had it been administered when I was thirteen would have made my day.

2 October. An obituary in today's *Guardian* of the novelist and poet Amy Witting who taught her classes French by writing the words of Charles Trenet's *La Mer* on the blackboard and getting the class to sing it. I see her . . . or a teacher in a play . . . pointing to a boy to take a line and maybe a young black boy whose voice hasn't broken singing it perfectly.*

4 October. To Robinsfield, the primary school in St John's Wood where I sometimes go to read. I do some *Winnie the Pooh* but the poem they really like is Michael Rosen's 'Don't' (with the line 'Don't put mustard in the custard'). They spontaneously ask questions afterwards, where did I buy the book I'm reading from? What was the first book I ever read? What was the first book I wrote? A multi-racial school, the children so friendly and attentive to one another and so gentle it's hard to see anyone even of the most extreme views withstanding such serious innocence. The teachers are plagued by the requirements of inspection and assessment, a party due round this very morning, the same time-wasting bureaucracy that

---

* This is *The History Boys* again.

clogs every institution in the country be it the National Gallery or a tiny primary school in north London. As I'm leaving one boy of mixed race who's maybe five or six runs after me and asks if I have heard of a play called *A Midsummer Night's Dream* and what is it about?

10 October. A poor day ends badly when I take the rubbish out to find the dustbin slopping around with half a dozen turds which had dissolved in the rain of the last three days to make a kind of shit soup. To actually shit in the dustbin must take some skill or maybe it's a dog owner whose social responsibility stretches to picking up the mess but not to putting it in their own bin.

Anyway I empty the water as best I can and manoeuvre the turds into a bag then change and wash every stitch of clothing I'm wearing. My mother, on the other hand, would have moved house.

From this unsavoury episode I salvage an etymological distinction: shit I think of as the self-contained shapes; shite as what's smeared round the sides of the bin.

16 October. A lesson from life: when the dying want to give you something, take it.

Gardening woman (to someone planting bulbs): 'Can I say one word? Drifts. Drifts.'

Coming up the escalator at Camden Town one catches its authentic smell: piss and chips.

19 October. Reading, in bed chiefly, Larkin's *Oxford Book of Twentieth Century English Verse* (1973) bought along with a dozen or so other copies as presents on the first night of *Habeas Corpus* in 1973.

Some of the poems chosen reflect his own concerns, e.g. E. Nesbit's 'The Things That Matter':

> I know so many little things,
> And now the Angels will make haste

To dust it all away with wings!
O God, you made me like to know,
You kept the things straight in my head,
Please God, if you can make it so,
Let me know *something* when I'm dead.

The Oxford anthology came out a few years before Larkin's 'Aubade', which has the lines:

. . . no sight or sound,
No touch or taste or smell, nothing to think with,
Nothing to love or link with . . .

2 November. The car gets a flat tyre, out of sheer boredom, I imagine, as it gets driven so seldom. I take it to Chalk Farm Tyres opposite the Roundhouse where a boy runs out, assesses the damage then jacks up the car while a bald Alfred Drayton-like man finds the split and decides it needs a new tyre. This is put on and it is all over and done with in ten minutes. I feel I want to ask them home so that they can take charge of my life.

16 November. I am reading Paul Bailey's *Three Queer Lives*, one of whom is Naomi Jacob. Eccentric though she was (and what Mam used to call 'one of those men-women'), she did represent the attraction, the glamour and certainly the possibilities of escape, of the literary life. This was partly because she was Yorkshire-born (Ripon) and thus often in the local papers but she was also one of a breed of popular writers . . . others would be Godfrey Wynn, Beverley Nichols, Phyllis Bentley and even (though he would have scorned such company) J. B. Priestley . . . who impinged on our lives as more celebrated literary practitioners, Virginia Woolf, say, or Evelyn Waugh, never did.

So absurd though Naomi Jacob was . . . and without ever having read a word that she wrote . . . I feel she made it easier for others starting off down the literary path and I wonder whether she was ever read by John Braine, who in his way was as absurd a figure as she was but equally talismanic.

I imagine human beings have always seen faces in fires and foliage or in the play of sun and shadow. So, lying on my bed, I fancy I can see a girl's face composed of the reflections of the bookshelf in the mirror. It's not a naturalistic face and were it reproduced on paper or canvas would look almost abstract. So when with Cubism (is it?) painters start making faces out of awkward angular shapes it's really only a setting down of what most people . . . an old lady looking into the fire, a child staring at a tree through the bedroom window . . . do as a matter of course and without thinking.

So abstract art, to begin with, isn't very abstract at all and as a figurative way of seeing is surely pretty general.

30 November. More Larkin parallels, this time with an indifferent poem by Belloc: 'The world's a stage . . .' – life as a play.

> The only part about it I enjoy
> Is what they call in English the Foyay.
> There will I stand apart awhile and toy
> With thought, and set my cigarette alight;
> And then – without returning to the play –
> On with my coat and out into the night.

This mirrors Larkin's own account of how when he was an undergraduate he went to see *The Playboy of the Western World* at the Oxford Playhouse. At the interval he asked himself whether he was enjoying it, decided he'd seldom had to listen to so much balls so had another drink and didn't go back for the second half . . . a decision he found immensely liberating. Which is okay but hardly earns Belloc's poem its place.

9 December. Page 4 of today's *Observer* is taken up with a large photograph of me and extensive coverage of the supposedly riveting news that I have writer's block. Below is a list of other writers who have suffered from this dreadful affliction. On the opposite page is a picture of Osama Bin Laden (writer's block not his problem). The piece stems from the Q and A session I did last week at the Queen Elizabeth Hall, where on being asked what I was doing at the moment, I said I wasn't doing anything very much, and that I was a bit stuck. But the phrase writer's block was not used (I never do use it) and the tone of my reply was sceptical and ironic. This has passed the reporter by and she reports the exchange so that it appears I have gone to the *Observer* and wept on its caring shoulder.

This is a technique perfected by the *Mail* but which (particularly in the week of David Astor's death) ought not to disgrace the *Observer*. However, as R. says, who reads the papers?

10 December. Well, lots of people seems to be the answer as I have had letters from *Observer* readers recommending various remedies for my sad situation and my supposed writer's block: remedies psychological, remedies physical and indeed remedies herbal. Since I always acknowledge letters, though seldom pursue a correspondence, this has increased my workload considerably. One letter is actually from the *Mail on Sunday* wondering if I would consider being interviewed about 'my problem'.

15 December. Words only used at Christmas: Tidings. Abiding. Swaddling. Lo! Abhors.

Carols are also full of titles for bad novels:

This Happy Morning
The Son of Earth
The King of Angels

A card from Victor Lewis-Smith with a sanctimonious picture of Jesus and printed underneath:

Jesus loves everyone, except you, you cunt.

This makes me laugh helplessly.

Isabelle McN. is twelve and her end of term assignment is 'The Most Outstanding Personality of the Twentieth Century'. She chooses Martin

Luther King but having been writing for five minutes she switches to Joan Crawford.

26 December. Nigel Hawthorne dies. A heart attack, though presumably related to the pancreatic cancer he'd had for the last eighteen months and which was discovered quite by chance in the course of another investigation entirely. Courteous, grand, a man of the world and superb at what he did, with his technique never so obvious as to become familiar as, say, Olivier's did or Alec Guinness's. No one could have played George III as well, even though his superb performance sometimes cast the play itself into the shade. He was a delight to watch, as I imagine a superb batsman is, touching the ball to the boundary with no effort at all; a dancer, little flicks and glances, the raising of an eyebrow, techniques honed, I imagine, in the umpteen small parts he played until middle age when *Yes, Minister* made him famous.

He owed me something but I probably owed him more. *George III* would have been half the play it was without his performance, a performance that I was able to write around as I saw it evolving in rehearsal, thus benefiting both him and the play.

27 December. Still ploughing through Larkin's *Oxford Book of Twentieth Century Verse*. It's full of poets I've never heard of and rather than organising little trips to Larkin's parents' grave and any other spots the poet may have known or visited, the Larkin Society would do better putting together a companion to this particular Oxford book. It would tell you more about Larkin and about these out-of-the-way poets he discovered and would, I should think, commend itself to him far more than their brackish trips down memory lane.

The poems he chose continue to chime in with poems of his own (which would also bear investigating), e.g. poems about horses or jockeys (nos. 240, 302), a country fair, the 'Fair at Windgap' (no. 293) as it might be his 'Show Saturday'. And there are other prescient notes.

The old couple in the brand new bungalow,
Drugged with the milk of municipal kindness,
Fumble their way to bed.

This from 'The Old Couple' by F. Pratt Green, and a foreshadowing of the old age Larkin and Monica Jones were not to have.

29 December. Snow in the night and when we stop for our sandwiches on the road to Garsdale Head, Dentdale is in immaculate relief with the Howgills ghostly beyond. They're Christmas sandwiches (cold pheasant, apple sauce, Cumberland sauce and lettuce, followed by mince pies), then we go on down Mallerstang to Kirkby Stephen where we buy a curtain pole and two storage jars at Mrs Hill's and then in another shop a couple of country elm chairs ('Hepplewhite' the label has it) which are only £65 and which we buy to use in the kitchen. Plain, bleached and nicely bowed, they could well be out of Kettle's Yard, and really need a similarly spacious white-painted interior such as we don't have.

'No stopping J. K. Rowling,' says this morning's *Independent*.

'No stopping Marcel Proust' either, not that any paper said so at the time. But then he didn't make any money.

'No stopping J. K. Rowling coining it' is what the *Independent* means.

2002

4 January. A Christmas letter from Cami Elbow, wife of Peter Elbow, an American college friend who teaches English at Amherst:

Life in Amherst is very placid. Even grammatically correct. In December the town decided to encourage shoppers to patronise the downtown stores with free parking. They ordered plastic bags to cover up the parking meters but the bags arrived with the message wrongly punctuated: 'Season's Greeting's'. When the bag company refused to replace them staffers at the Town Hall spent hours pasting little pieces of adhesive tape over every offending apostrophe. My contradictory husband, who is sometimes known in his field as Write-it-Wrong Elbow, liberated a few of the apostrophes by pulling off the adhesive tape.

13 January. The canonisation of Dame Iris proceeds apace and the BBC are now preparing to show on *Omnibus* extracts from a video taken from an interview carried out by an eminent neurologist, Professor John Hodges, and presumably taped for research purposes. It's sanctioned, one imagines, by John Bayley, whose efforts on behalf of his late wife and her reputation make Max Clifford seem timid and retiring.

One lesson of this deplorable business is never to sanction the shooting of any video, however lofty its purpose, because once shot it will be shown. Professor Hodges seems to have arrived at his diagnosis of Alzheimer's by, among other things, asking Dame Iris to recall which of her many books won the Booker Prize. This was *The Sea, The Sea*, the winner in 1978, a triumph the ailing author could not recall, but since the Booker Prize in 1978 was not the over-publicised proto-Oscars it tries to be today, this is hardly surprising. Still, that an artist's state of mind should be assessed by his or her recollection of awards won adds a new terror to success. The test used to be recalling the name of the prime minister or counting backwards from 10 to 1. Now it's whether you can remember winning the *Evening Standard* Award or something similar at BAFTA. These sorry occasions have always been best forgotten; now their memory must be kept green against the possible arrival of the men in white coats.

19 January. Watch a video of Michael Powell's *A Matter of Life and Death* (1946), the first time, I think, that I have watched it all the way through since I saw it as a child at a cinema in Guildford. Then its particular interest was that the village scenes featuring the local doctor (Roger Livesey) had been shot at Shere, a picturesque hamlet below Newlands Corner, where we'd sometimes go on walks. Livesey watches the goings-on in the village via a camera obscura, though why he does this isn't explained, or the workings of the device either, which must have mystified most people at the time. The notion of eavesdropping keeps coming up in Powell's work until with *Peeping Tom* it virtually ended his career.

Other oddities in *AMOLAD* are the naked goatherd playing the flute, an unlikely sight on the Norfolk sands, I would have thought, even in 1946, and a man with wild red hair (looking like Léonide Massine in *The Red Shoes*) who brings Livesey and David Niven tea in the country house where some amateurs are rehearsing *A Midsummer Night's Dream*.

This house seems to be set on a series of steps which, though the film was shot in the studio, relates it to Hardwick Hall and also to the dream sequences that follow with a stairway to heaven. The steps, coincidentally, chime in with a poem by the recently dead Ian Hamilton printed in the *LRB*.

> We are on a kind of stair. The world below
> Will never be regained; was never there
> Perhaps. And yet it seems
> We've climbed to where we are
> With diligence, as if told long ago
> How high the highest rung.

23 January. To Sotheby's, where I'm reminded of a lunch given for Alec Guinness in 1989 when I sat next to Lord Charteris, the Provost of Eton and previously the Queen's Private Secretary. Talking of *A Question of Attribution*, then playing at the National, he remarked: 'Of course, the question everybody asks is whether the Queen knew and whether Blunt know the Queen knew. The truth of the matter is they *both* knew – but, of course, that's not to be said.'

At the time I remember thinking this was sensationally indiscreet (and it would certainly have made the newspapers). Now it's tame stuff. But thinking about Charteris, who was a funny man, one realises that it's much harder if you have a sense of humour not to be indiscreet; the temptation to hang discretion and make jokes or be witty is too great. Secrets are best kept by those with no sense of humour.

2 February. A letter from a reader comparing her experiences of evacuation with mine. She was sent to Grantham and says that Alderman

Roberts, Mrs Thatcher's father, was thought to be in the black market and that Maggie used to hang out of her bedroom window and spit on the other children.

12 February. A shoddy programme about the conviction of Jonathan King for offences against young men dating back twenty-five years and more. While it features some of the police involved, it manages not to ask the pertinent question: if these fifteen-year-old boys had been fifteen-year-old girls and romping round in Rolls-Royces even more famous than those of Jonathan King, the Beatles' say, or the Rolling Stones', would the police have been quite so zealous in trawling for the supposed victims from a quarter of a century ago? King does himself no favours but I prefer his defiance and want of remorse to the odiously caring voice of the man who presents the programme. As it is, a succession of sad middle-aged men are encouraged to blame their failure in life on these ancient wanks, a service for which the state will now reward them far more munificently than King ever did.

16 February. Man on a mobile opposite takes a piss by the wall, talking throughout. I wonder whether he tells the person he is talking to that he's currently having a piss and, if it's a woman, if this is some sort of come-on.

28 February. Spike Milligan dies and the nation's laughter-makers queue up to testify to what it was that made his talents unique, how irreplaceable is his inspired lunacy, and how they personally have benefited from his instructive anarchy. All of which is, I suppose, true, though comedians are never reluctant to provide such posthumous attestations of one another's genius. It happened when Peter Cook died and with the same maudlin affection. 'Dear Cooky'. 'Dear Spike'. The necessary element of suffering, the cost always sought for in the deaths of comics, and which in Peter's case came with the drink, is here supplied by mental illness ('No less than 12 nervous breakdowns', 'the price he had to pay').

There is no doubt that Milligan was very funny and inspired, particularly in the *Q5* TV programmes he did in the 1970s, though his verbal dexterities I found less engaging and with unfortunate effects on some of his disciples, e.g. John Lennon's *In His Own Write*. The disciples were always the problem, *The Goon Show* was very funny, the people who liked it (and knew it by heart) less so.

16 March. In the afternoon to the new British Galleries at the V&A, particularly to look at one of the surviving copes from the set of vestments given to Westminster Abbey by Henry VII. Anthony Symondson has written about its subsequent history in a piece in the *Catholic Herald* and how, via a seventeenth-century second-hand dealer in London and the Catholic college at St Omer, the cope eventually ended up at Stonyhurst. The vestments were designed apparently by Torrigiano, though this is not said on the label nor is a link made with the bust of Henry VII, also by Torrigiano, in a neighbouring showcase. Even the most limited imagination would find this cope evocative, though; worn presumably at Henry VII's funeral and possibly, too, at the coronation of Henry VIII, it then went with the young King to the Field of the Cloth of Gold. Smuggled out to Flanders in the seventeenth century, whence it eventually came back to Stonyhurst, it must have been seen if not worn by Gerard Manley Hopkins, who taught there.

Apropos Henry VII, what happened between 1485 and 1500? How did bold Harry Tudor of Bosworth Field turn into the crabbed penny-pinching accountant that is his usual representation?

24 March. A film beginning with a man being shepherded through a darkened hall; glimpses of paintings, a shaft of light on a plaster ceiling, the gleam of armour but so dark (lines of light around the shutters) that it's hard to see anyone's face. A distant murmur of sound. Odd muttered directions. 'Steady, a step here,' the man steered round sheeted furniture and up uncarpeted stairs. Then the group comes to a stop. Someone knocks on the shutter and it is thrown open, light floods in, there is the sudden roar of the crowd. Charles I steps out onto the scaffold.

30 March. Obituary of Dudley M. in yesterday's *Independent* by Harry Thompson, the biographer of Peter Cook, whose side one might therefore expect him to take. Instead Thompson very much takes Dudley's line on himself: namely, that he was only brought into *Beyond the Fringe* as a musical afterthought. In fact he came as the acknowledged star of the Oxford cabaret circuit, and right through the run of *Beyond the Fringe* remained the darling of the audience. Cheerful, extrovert and on his own musical ground very sure of himself, he only started to play up the melancholy and portray himself as a tortured clown, a line journalists are always happy to encourage, after he'd teamed up with Peter and subsequently gone into analysis or psychotherapy.

Obviously Dudley did get sadder as he got older and coping with Peter's drunkenness can have been no joke. But portraying himself as shy, put-upon and intimidated by Jonathan, Peter and to a lesser extent myself was a construction that came later. On and off the stage during *Beyond the Fringe* he was sunny, social and effortlessly successful. A sad clown he wasn't.

5 April. I persevere with Sebald but the contrivance of it, particularly his un-peopling of the landscape, never fails to irritate. 'It was already afternoon, six in the evening when I reached the outskirts of Lowestoft. Not a living soul was about in the long street.' In Southwold 'everybody who had been out for an evening stroll was gone. I felt as if I were in a deserted theatre.' Maybe East Anglia is like this (or more like it than West Yorkshire, say) but Sebald seems to stage-manage both the landscape and the weather to suit his (seldom cheerful) mood. Kafka has been invoked in this connection, but Kafka dealt with the world as he found it and didn't dress it up (or down) to suit him.

'The heights of epiphanic beauty normally only encountered in the likes of Proust' is another comparison, and equally unwarranted because there is no one more grounded in the everything that is the case than Proust. Once noticed, Sebald's technique seems almost comic. 'Never yet on my many visits . . . have I found anyone about.' The fact is, in Sebald nobody is ever about. This may be poetic but it seems to me a short cut to significance.

6 April, Yorkshire. The new organic shop in the village continues to do well, the walk down the lane to the Nissen hut always a pleasure even in the bitterest weather. There are sheep in the adjoining field, the occasional bull and (despite the bypass) a lovely feeling of open country. The shop has fresh-picked salad with more to be gathered while you wait, three or four kinds of apple plus sprouts on the stalk that look so sculpted and swag-like they could have inspired Grinling Gibbons. Today there are one or two customers in the shop. Everyone speaks, a little too readily for me sometimes, this friendliness engendered by the nature of the enterprise. It's a kind of *camaraderie biologique*. In the same way, halted on my bike at traffic lights I will occasionally chat to another cyclist, cycling a similar undertaking with a creed and an agenda and its own *esprit de corps de vélos*.

9 April. The Queen Mother interred.

Scene: Windsor. A vault. A dusty coffin. A flagstone in the roof is drawn back and a new coffin is slowly lowered down beside it. The flagstone is replaced and there is silence. Voice from old coffin: 'Y-y-y-you've t-t-taken y-y-your t-t-time.'

5 May, Yorkshire. Michael Bryant has died, who I'd known was ill but had never enquired after, from superstition largely, hoping he would pull through. Sardonic, sceptical, tough, he was not an easy man to praise and so much a staple of National Theatre productions and so consistently good that when it came to honours, national or theatrical, he was overlooked. True, he got the CBE in 1988, but not the knighthood he deserved because he was too unshowy. As a young actor (e.g. with Judi Dench in John Hopkins's *Talking to a Stranger*) I thought him dull but he got better and better, though it would have been hard to say so to his face. Not – emphatically not – a university actor like Jacobi or McKellen, he used to call me (not to my face) 'College' Bennett. His was a non-commissioned life and, of course, a straight one. The list of roles he took on and the productions he was part of are a history of the Old Vic and the National Theatre over the last forty years and the quality and sheer volume of his work bestowed on him a mantle of wisdom and experience no one else at the NT could touch.

25 *May*. Thinking about Dudley M. since his death, I'm struck by how little was said at the time of his musical abilities. In particular his talents as a jazz pianist. This would have come as no surprise to him as his success as a comedian and subsequently as a movie star put his musical accomplishment in the shade; jazz became marginal.

Something of a prodigy when young but with no specialist musical background, Dudley landed what I imagine was a strongly contested organ scholarship at Magdalen. He was a working-class boy but there was no trace of it in his voice or indeed of any class at all, though the fact that his parents had kitted him out with three Christian names may indicate their ambitions for him. This was a time, with boys anyway, when two initials were the standard, boys equipped with three more likely to be from a public school or one of the grander grammar schools. But he was D. S. J. Moore and without it being the least bit 'put on' there was nothing in his voice to betray that he was from Dagenham. This may well have helped at Magdalen, which was at that time socially quite smart as well as being academically grand, and though in later life he tended to represent his time at Oxford as uneasy and not altogether happy, he was popular and gregarious, taking part in college and university drama productions as both actor and musician.

Modest and unassuming, he was immensely appealing and, of course, always very funny but with regard to his area of expertise never very forthcoming. Presumably he talked to fellow musicians about jazz and its techniques but it was not a subject that came up much when he teamed up with the rest of us in *Beyond the Fringe*. We all professed to like jazz, though it was not as modish as it had been for the generation of Larkin and Amis a few years before. Jazz was no longer the anthem of youth and disaffection. Now there was Elvis, Bill Haley and even our own Cliff Richard. Still, we would go along to hear Dudley play, particularly when Peter Cook's The Establishment opened in New York, where Dudley alternated at the piano with Teddy ('Fly Me to the Moon') Wilson. But knowing nothing of its history or development and never having listened to it much, I was baffled and bored by jazz, while Jonathan Miller's experience of it didn't stretch much beyond undergraduate hops where it served as a background to his vigorous though uncoordinated attempts to jive.

Perhaps because he was the youngest of the four of us, Peter's lack of interest in jazz was the most obvious, though he would later have heard a good deal more of Dudley's playing than Jonathan or I did. When in old clips of *Not Only . . . But Also* Dudley is seen playing or parodying jazz as the play-out at the finish, Peter will sometimes be standing by the piano with a sophisticated smile, clicking his fingers to what he hopes may be the beat. This was both a pose and a piss-take but it came closer to the reality than Peter would perhaps have liked to admit. Despite their long working relationship, he continued to know nothing of jazz and, like the condescending figure at the piano, always slightly disparaged it. His music was pop not jazz; he would have liked to have been a pop singer and fancied himself as such, hence his truly dreadful imitation of Elvis Presley.

None of which is of much interest except to make plain that whatever the public's appreciation of his musical talent, Dudley was nevertheless corralled for four years with three other performers who didn't share his enthusiasm and then for ten or a dozen years more with Peter, who regarded his music as at best an interlude between the comedy. So when later in life with that slightly aggrieved air with which he discussed his early career Dudley complained of being unappreciated by his colleagues in *Beyond the Fringe*, this was partly what it was about. He was a very funny instinctive comedian but he was not a writer and, no good at one sort of language, he found that music, the language he was good at, was largely discounted. And when on chat shows and interviews he gave his always defensive account of himself, complaining of the inferior status he had been accorded, particularly by Peter, music was at the heart of it.

Of course, words and music are not the only languages and at this time, when we were all in our twenties, what ranked him above the rest of us and indeed anyone I've ever come across since, was his sexual success. This, unlike his musical accomplishment, was the subject of constant discussion and enquiry and it was a topic on which, while not boastful, Dudley was always frank, informative and very funny.

That Dudley, given the chance, could talk illuminatingly about music was brought home to me in almost the only conversation I had with him about jazz, when he explained the difference, as he saw it, between a good and an average performance. It had to do with the musical beat, which he told me to think of not as a brief and indivisible moment but as an interval with a discernible length, and a beginning, a middle and an end. The art of playing good jazz, he explained, was to try and hit the beat as near as possible to its ending.

To musicians this may well be a truism but I had never come across the notion before, and it linked, as Dudley then linked it, with comedy timing in the theatre, where the same applies and which I did understand and practised, though instinctively.

This conversation would have taken place in New York sometime in 1963 in the apartment which he was then subletting on Washington Square and where he also taught me to add a spoonful of water to the mixture of the scrambled eggs we invariably had for lunch. It was there too that, possibly in order to wean me off Elgar, he played me the long sinuous romantic theme that begins Bruckner's Seventh Symphony. Though I always add the water when scrambling eggs, I have never got much further with Bruckner and the opening of the Seventh is still all I know.

1 June, Yorkshire. I try out my new slug killer: a cane with a sponge tied to the end with which, dipped in a strong solution of salt and water, I douse the slugs. I'm not sure if it works as this morning there's no trace of any of the dead. This may mean they've crawled home to lick their wounds or their corpses may have been eaten by the early birds. Another device is a big darning needle fixed to the end of a cane on which I impale the blameless creatures.

11 June. Make notes for the Tate Britain sound guide, my chosen picture Millais's *Christ in the House of His Parents* (or 'The Carpenter's Shop', as I think of it). It's one of those paintings – Holman Hunt's *Shadow of Death* is another – when Jesus's childhood or youth skids to a halt at some rather vulgar prefiguring of what is in store, in this case the boy Jesus snagging his hand on a nail and blood dripping onto his foot. What's always struck me particularly about the picture is the glum boy on the right fetching in a bowl of water. He's John the Baptist but I've always thought of him as like 'the lad' in my father's butcher's shop who was already working for his living while I was, like Jesus, a namby-pamby figure in a nightdress who had plainly never done a stroke of work in his life. Dickens disliked this Jesus figure, too, apparently, though with less justification as he was always inventing boys like this himself. As with so many Pre-Raphaelite paintings the feeling is one of impending doom with even Joseph a slightly sinister figure.

4 July. The Home Secretary announces that because of 'public concern' (which probably means one article in the *Daily Mail*) he has decided to make it known that Dr Shipman will remain in prison for the rest of his life. This is not more than anyone, including Dr Shipman, can have expected but why announce it? Who benefits? All it does is satisfy the desire for revenge of the public (or the public as imagined by the *Daily Mail*). It seems sheer sadism and not for the first time I wonder if Blunkett would be a more liberal man if he were not blind.

22 July, L'Espiessac. I did not think my hearing had deteriorated at all but at some relatively refined level it has, as at nights here I can no longer catch the sound of crickets. It is the sound most evocative of the South or any warm climate and on our first night I put down its absence to the usual suspects – mechanised farming, fertilisers, the decline of nature. But standing at the top of the steps yesterday night, R. asks me if I can hear the crickets and cannot believe that, the night tingling with the sound, I am deaf to it. I strain to hear . . . and I can catch the bark of a distant dog, a car on the road to Nérac and the dishwasher still going in the kitchen. But crickets, no.

23 July, L'Espiessac. Hornets are building a nest in a tiny hole in the wall bordering the window frame of the *pigeonnier* where we sleep. And it is a nest, too, with the hornet and/or a colleague bringing pieces of straw which it draws into the hole and presumably incorporates into the fabric of the nest. I have never seen insects do this (except ants possibly), imagining that wasps and such creatures somehow extruded the materials for their nests as bees do for their hives. I have a strong impulse to disrupt the process, even stop up the hole with chewing gum but resist it. Another sunny warm day but with a strong wind that ruffles the lavender (and makes landing for the hornets tricky).

1 August. Apropos Jeffrey Archer, I am rereading the Lyttelton–Hart-Davis letters and come across this remark by George Lyttelton: 'Sprinters always try to beat the pistol, therefore are essentially unscrupulous and unreliable.'

30 August. A commercial for Carte d'Or ice cream I would have been very pleased to have written. A family which includes the aged grandmother is having Sunday dinner. 'Pass your father the potatoes,' the mother says to the grown-up son. 'He's not your father,' snaps the grandmother. 'We never knew who your father was.' There is an awkward silence, then the mother ushers the grandmother from the table saying: 'Come along, mother, I'll take you upstairs.' On the way out of the room the old lady passes an open piano on which (this is the stroke of genius) she suddenly hits a petulant discord. The scene lasts all of a minute and is worth pages of dialogue. Why it's advertising ice cream I'm not sure.

26 September. A call from Channel 4 wanting to know if I'd like to be one of the participants in *Celebrity Big Brother*. In view of the status of previous participants I suppose this indicates that in celebrity terms I'm pretty low grade so I don't say no immediately but ask my agent, Ros Chatto, to find out who else they have in mind. They smell a rat, of course, and won't let on, promising only 'someone quite high up in the music business'. (This turns out to be an ex-member of Take That, who eventually triumphs.)

30 September, Yorkshire. Glimpsed in Crosshills, en route for Leeds: a young man in a wheelchair with a girl (-friend, possibly) on his knee, giving her a lift – the wheelchair playing the same role as the crossbar of a bike. I've never seen this before and find it cheering.

1 October. I am reading Geoffrey Moorhouse's book on the Pilgrimage of Grace and have reached the point in October 1536 when Robert Aske and the huge rebel host are at Doncaster waiting to move south, virtually unopposed. It's a campaign that would surely have changed the course of history and might even have deposed Henry VIII, though this was not the rebels' aim. They hesitated, and the chapter in question will presumably explain why. I can scarcely bear to read it and put the book to one side. Meanwhile Bush edges daily closer to war and I can't bear to read about that either.

2 October. The bin men in Camden come on Mondays and Thursdays and on Mondays too comes the recycling lorry, taking away the weekly hoard of paper and glass. Ludicrously I assumed that these recycling men would (because greener) be a cut above the ordinary bin men. In fact it's the reverse. The traditional crew is jolly, know me by name and call out if they see me in the street. They also close the gate and don't leave any mess. The green men are unsmiling, wanting in any obvious conviviality, shove the crate back any old how and don't close the gate. Green, in Camden anyway, isn't necessarily nice.

15 October. Insofar as Bush (and therefore Blair) have any strategy within Iraq it is to depress the condition of the people to the point where they rise up against their leader. It's a deplorable policy on humanitarian grounds but it's also historically unsound. Revolutions happen not when people are at their most desperate but when conditions are just beginning to improve. The best way to topple Saddam would be to send Iraq aid.

24 October, Yorkshire. To Fountains on a day of tearing wind and sudden storms with skies periodically swept to a clear Mediterranean blue. The tower at Fountains never fails to surprise, the last two stages so tall that they stand clear above the top of the valley, and so look like a rather squat parish church surrounded by trees. Avoiding the Visitors' Centre, we go in at the bottom gate where the bus from Ripon first deposited my mother and me *c*.1947. It's half-term and the outer court is full of children and family parties, though never as busy as it must have been in its medieval heyday. In the slype, the passage next to the chapterhouse, we find traces of the original paint. (I am actually rather pleased that I know the word 'slype' – a slip, I suppose it means, or a short cut.) The passage doubled as sacristy and library and, having been protected from the weather, some of the stone is still painted the original greyish white that once covered most of the masonry. This is overlaid with black decorative lines that impose a pattern of painted blocks irrespective of and unrelated to the stonework underneath. It feels glossy, almost waxy and the thought that this is just as it was at the Dissolution nearly 500 years ago I find absurdly satisfying. As I'm stroking this paint I become aware of a small child cowering in an alcove, playing hide-and-seek, who obviously thinks I am mad.

On the hill south of the main buildings is the Applegarth, where there are two yew trees, unvisited by any tourists but survivors of a group of seven such trees that had long been growing here in the twelfth century when a band of monks from St Mary's at York camped out on this hillside before founding the abbey. That the yews have survived both the building of Fountains and its dissolution and all that has happened since makes them more objects of wonder than the abbey itself. Since they are not highlighted or on any 'trail' I suppose my wonder has a touch of snobbery to it, too.

31 October, New York. Upgraded to first on American Airlines, I am early down to Immigration, to be met by a large emerald-green bird, fully feathered and with an orange beak. It flaps its wings and motions me onwards. I take the creature, just discernible as a middle-aged woman, to be a loony and, always nervous at Immigration, remain firmly behind the yellow line. The bird gets extremely agitated, flaps both its wings and indicates that I should proceed through one of the few gates that are manned. I now realise it's Halloween, though the festive spirit doesn't extend to the guy in the booth, who is mean-faced, unwelcoming and possibly more pissed off than he usually is because he has had a whole day in the company of this demented barnyard fowl, which is now clucking up and down the waiting line of jaded travellers, all of them as mystified as I was. Still, compared with others I see later that evening in New York she's a fairly low-level eccentric; there's a man with a pan on his head, another dressed in (or as) a condom, hand in hand with two of the sperms he has presumably frustrated. None of them, though, seems much in party mood, the festivity almost an obligation.

'Foreigners,' says the cab driver of some other (normally dressed) group. 'Europeans. Do you know how ya tell? They're *smoking*.'

Promotion to first class gives me my first experience of a pod, the extendable seat which is supposed to make sleep possible. In fact it's about a foot too short for me and my feet hang off the end, the whole contraption not unlike a stationary version of the fairground Waltzer.

'Would you like hot nuts?' asks the stewardess.

The purpose of this very much flying visit, paid for by Random House, is to do a five-minute 'segment' on the *Today* show, the book club of which has selected (or had selected for them) *The Lady in the Van* and *The Clothes They Stood Up In* as their this month's read. It's actually the choice of Helen Fielding, whom I'd imagined utterly metropolitan but turns out to be from Morley, though now living in Los Angeles presumably on the proceeds of her two bestsellers. After the segment we have tea in the Pierre and talk about Leeds, and I walk down the corridor where forty years ago Dudley Moore and I saw Stravinsky.

I avoid downtown and notice how, in the car to the airport, I don't look back to take in the view of the towers of Manhattan. It's something I'd always done as a kind of farewell every time I came away from New York. Not today. Brooklyn cemetery on the right, Queens on the left, Manhattan maimed so not to be stared at.

5 November. To the British Library to record an edition of Radio 4's *Bookclub* in which a panel of readers, chaired by James Naughtie, questions me about my stuff, some of which figures in a little exhibition laid on by the Library, including the original script of *Beyond the Fringe* and another of *Forty Years On*, both now part of the Lord Chamberlain's Office archive. Back in 1960 the reader pencilled a note on the *Beyond the Fringe* MS that it was 'full of silly pseudo-intellectual jokes'. *Forty Years On* maybe deserved a similar comment but as censorship was abolished while it was still waiting to be read it is unmarked. More thrilling by far is Anne Boleyn's copy of Tyndale's English Bible, a compact and handy volume along the fore-edge of which she has written in red 'Regina Angliae'. I am allowed to hold this Bible, as she must often have held it, and wonder if it's the Bible she had with her in the Tower or on the scaffold.

11 November. Much talk of republicanism, recalling Brooklyn-born Joan Panzer's remark twenty years ago: 'England without the Royal Family? Never. It would be like Fire Island without the gays.'

13 November. Apropos the Queen's Speech, Andrew Marr on *The World at One* talks of the future saying, 'If the war with Iraq goes well . . .', the conditional to do not with the likelihood of war but only with its conduct. No one demurs. But Bush is extraordinary. Seldom can there have been a leader of a modern democratic nation who showed such unfeigned eagerness and enthusiasm for war. He must be Saddam Hussein's biggest asset.

22 November, New York. I am reading *Wittgenstein's Poker*, an account of the events leading up to the clash between Wittgenstein and Karl Popper at a meeting of the Moral Sciences Club in Cambridge in 1946. It's fascinating but as with all accounts of philosophy I can never get my mind round the questions at issue – Popper the general, Wittgenstein the particular is how I make sense of it. Both were bullies and in a gender-specific way: I can't imagine two women going head to head like this or being so single- (and so bloody-) minded. I had not known that Wittgenstein's attitude to his wealth (or his ex-wealth) was as ambiguous as it appears to have been, or of the high-level negotiations that bartered much of the Wittgenstein fortune for the lives of his two sisters, who remained in Vienna throughout the war. With both philosophers holding forth to their respective circles and riding roughshod over any opposition, I long for some bold student to stand up and say that this way of teaching philosophy defeats it own purpose and isn't worth the bruised feelings and human diminishment arguing with Wittgenstein and Popper seems to have involved.

It's encouraging, though, to find that Wittgenstein's mature (but coded) thoughts about being in love seem scarcely above my own sixteen-year-old level. One of his last unrequited passions was a medical student, Ben Richards, who is pictured in the book looking remarkably like Ted Hughes – who was almost Wittgenstein's contemporary at Cambridge. Wittgenstein died in 1951; had he survived a year or two to coincide with Hughes it would have been an interesting conjunction. One anachronism (I think) is that the authors imagine Wittgenstein buying tomato sandwiches from Woolworth's. If there was a café in Woolworth's in Cambridge he might well have bought sandwiches to eat on the premises but I don't think in 1946 Woolworth's were doing takeaways. (More reports please.)

23 November, New York. Back for another 'segment' on the *Today* show, I stop and talk to a handful of peace protestors who have unfurled their home-made banners around the statue of Lincoln on the north side of Union Square. They are standing in the middle of the farmers' market and are of a muchness with most of the stallholders: worthy, decent, unmetropolitan figures in late middle age, muffled up against the biting wind but not chanting or speechmaking, just a group of twenty or so standing there in silence. I ask a woman if they have come in for much abuse. 'No. Not here. This is a liberal neighbourhood, you see.' She has a petition which I offer to sign but since I'm not resident there is no point. I say, rather futilely, that many if not most people in England feel the same and wish them luck. Like dissidents seen once in Moscow they make me feel both comfort-loving and inadequate.

3 December. My old school, Leeds Modern (subsequently Lawnswood) School, is about to be demolished, new premises having been built on the playing fields in front of it. The new school doesn't look much of a building, whereas the old school is a handsome example of its period (*c.*1930). Its demolition illustrates almost to the minute what Brendan Gill, late of the *New Yorker*, christened the 'Gordon Curve' after the preservationist Douglas Gordon of Baltimore. 'This posits that a building is at its maximum moment of approbation when it is brand new, that it then goes steadily downhill and at 70 reaches its nadir. If you can get a building past that sticky moment, then the curve begins to go up again very rapidly until at 100 it is back where it was in year one. A 100-year-old building is much more likely to be saved than a 70-year-old one.'

Nowadays presenting itself as sensitive to its surroundings and careful of its inheritance, Leeds has been happily demolishing decent architecture for most of my life. Still, all it will mean now is that in order to avoid passing the scene of the crime I'll not take the Otley road out of Leeds but instead go past Kirkstall Abbey, which Leeds would probably have demolished too had Thomas Cromwell not saved them the trouble.

5 December. My fears as to my celebrity rating earlier in the year are happily allayed this morning by an invitation to appear on *Through the Keyhole*, Sir David Frost and Paradine Productions' series for BBC1. This is not, the letter assures me, Sir David in interrogatory mode. Gravitas has been laid aside and when he comes through the keyhole in the person of his proxy, Loyd Grossman, it's 'just a bit of fun and promotion'. Though previous guests have included Eartha Kitt, Gloria Gaynor and Neil Sedaka, I have to say no and write explaining how, as so often happens in our wacky showbiz world, in the same post came another offer, the chance of some temping as a tripe dresser in Hull. Showcase though *Through the Keyhole* surely is, most reasonable people would, I think, agree that the latter is a more tempting proposition. I send my regards to Sir David and to Mr Grossman, whom I have never met but whose sauces often enliven my lonely dish of spaghetti.

2003

1 January. A Christmas card from Eric Korn:

> This is the one about Jesus
> And his father who constantly sees us
> Like CCTV from above
> But they call it heavenly love;
> And the other a spook or a bird
> Or possible merely a Word.
> Rejoice! We are ruled thru' infinity
> By this highly dysfunctional Trinity!

10 January. In George Lyttelton's *Commonplace Book* it's recorded that Yeats told Peter Warlock that after being invited to hear 'The Lake Isle of Innisfree' (a solitary man's expression of longing for still greater solitude) sung by a thousand Boy Scouts he set up a rigid censorship to prevent anything like that ever happening again. This is presumably the origin of Larkin's remark that before he died he fully expected to hear 'They fuck you up, your mum and dad' recited by a thousand Girl Guides in the Royal Albert Hall.

12 January. Read *Macbeth* for maybe the second time in my life (and I don't think I've ever seen it). Much of the language is as opaque as I generally find in Shakespeare but I'm struck by how soon he gets down to business, so that within a scene the play is at full gallop. No messing about with Lady M. either. No sooner does she learn Duncan is going to visit than she decides on the murder. Oddities are Macduff's abandonment of wife and family in order, seemingly, to save his own skin, though the scene in which his wife is discussing this with Ross is unbearably tense, the audience knowing she is about to be murdered. The ending is as abrupt as the beginning, with not much in the way of a dying fall from Malcolm, who's straight away off to Scone for his coronation. Most relevant bit:

> . . . Alas, poor country,
> Almost afraid to know itself . . .
> . . . where violent sorrow seems
> A modern ecstasy.

14 January. When I am occasionally stumped on a grammatical point, having no English grammar, I consult a copy of Kennedy's Latin primer, filched more than thirty years ago from Giggleswick School. It's only today that I notice that some schoolboy half a lifetime ago has painstakingly converted *The Revised Latin Primer* into 'The Revised Man Eating Primer'. Perhaps it is the same boy who has inscribed across one of the pages: 'G. H. Williams, Lancs and England'.

22 January. Watching *Footballers' Wives*, I see among the production credits the name Sue de Beauvoir.

I do hope she's a relation.

19 *The Drinking Party*, BBC TV, 1966
(left to right: Roddy Maude-Roxby, AB, John Fortune, Leo McKern, Barry Justice, Michael Gough)

20 With Dudley Moore and Joan Collins in Arnold Weissberger's bedroom, 1963

21 With Dudley Moore, Peter Cook and Jonathan Miller, *Beyond the Fringe*, 1962

22 Yorkshire

23 Photographed by Christopher Fry in his garden, 1992

24 With Rupert Thomas and Madge Hindle, Venice, 1996

25 L'Espiessac, 1997

26 L'Espiessac, 1997

27 With Harry McNally, New York, 1985

28 With Lynn Wagenknecht, 1987

29 Rupert, Fountains Abbey, 1999

30 Palazzo S. Justina, Venice, 2001

1 February, Yorkshire. Last time we visited Kirkby Stephen we were in Mrs H.'s shop when a clock chimed. I've never wanted a clock and this one was pretty dull, made in the 1950s probably and very plain. But the chime, a full Westminster chime, was so appealing that we talked about it on the way home and later asked Mrs H. to put it on one side. Today we collect it and it looks every bit as dull as we remember, but now on the table behind the living-room door it seems very much at home. And the sound is of such celestial sweetness that when it does chime it's hard not to smile.

9 February. To Widford in the Windrush valley near Burford for a second look at the church built on the site of a Roman villa, the mosaic floor (now covered over) once the floor of the chancel. There are box pews, aged down to a silvery grey, a three-decker pulpit, Jacobean altar rails and the remains of whitewash-blurred medieval wall-paintings. It's an immensely appealing place, not unlike Lead in Yorkshire or Heath near Ludlow. Good graves on the north side, some for a family called Secker, who seem to live in the manor house across the field, a romantic rambling house that looks unrestored and has oddly in its grounds an ornate seaside-looking Edwardian clock tower.

The Windrush tumbles through the weir on this mild winter morning, but the idyll is deceptive as once, at least, the river has seen slaughter. It was in 1388 that Richard II's favourite, Robert Vere, led his army floundering along this flooded valley, desperate to escape his baronial pursuers, who eventually caught up and cut most of them down a little upstream at Radcot Bridge.

15 February. R. and I go down to Leicester Square at noon, the tube as crowded as the rush hour, then walk up Charing Cross Road to where the anti-war march is streaming across Cambridge Circus. There seems no structure to it, ahead of us some SWP banners but marching, or rather strolling, beside them the Surrey Heath Liberal Democrats. Scattered among the more seasoned marchers are many unlikely figures, two women in front of us in fur hats and bootees looking as if they're just off to the WI. I'm an unlikely figure, too, of course, as the last march I went on was in 1956 and that was an accident: I was standing in Broad Street in Oxford watching the Suez demonstration go by when a friend pulled me in.

Today it's bitterly cold, particularly since the march keeps stopping or is stopped by the police, who seem bored that they've got so little to do, the mood of the march overwhelmingly friendly and domestic and hardly political at all. I'd have quite liked something to march to, even (however inappropriately) 'Onward Christian Soldiers', but the nearest we get is (to the tune of 'Yellow Submarine') 'We all live in a terrorist regime', which isn't a chant I feel entirely able to endorse. At Albemarle Street we split off and go and have lunch at Fenwick's, having, I suppose, walked a third of the route.

On the TV news the police estimate the numbers at 750,000, the organisers at two million, the true figure presumably somewhere in between. Whether anyone has ever nailed the police on why they routinely overestimate the numbers for demonstrations they approve of (like the so-called Liberty and Livelihood March) while marking down more dissident movements, I don't know. They would presumably deny it as vigorously as their not infrequent throttling of black suspects.

26 February. For much of last year the post in Gloucester Crescent was delivered by a delightful French girl, Stephanie Tunc; blonde and pretty, she was chatty, funny and also very efficient. Unique among the French of my acquaintance, she didn't like France one bit and pulled a face if you told her you were going on holiday there. Before Christmas she and her sister took off for South America and this last week the market men in Inverness Street got a postcard from Stephanie in Peru, which they pinned up on one of the stalls.

Then yesterday the new postman told us that having run out of money in Peru she and her sister had come back from South America to Miami. Sunbathing on the beach they had been run over by a police car, which had then reversed over them. Stephanie was dead and her sister in a critical condition.

'Add something,' I note as I transcribe this entry. But there is nothing to add. A lovely, lively girl is senselessly dead. That's all.

8 March. A phrase often in the mouth of Bush and Blair is 'Our patience is exhausted.' It's a phrase that is seldom used by anyone who had much patience in the first place; Hitler was quite fond of it.

14 March. To Oxford to vote for the chancellor, though it doesn't seem very long since I did the same for Roy Jenkins. At Bodley I'm overtaken by A. N. Wilson, who's brought his gown in a Sainsbury's bag, though it's part of Roy Jenkins's legacy that gowns are no longer required on such occasions. This doesn't stop many of the voters swishing about in them for the benefit of their families, who are then left at the door of the Divinity Schools while the graduates go in to participate in the mystery.

Not much of a mystery now, though, as in another of Jenkins's reforms there is no ceremony at all and certainly no vice-chancellor enthroned in Convocation waiting to take your voting paper and lift his hat as Patrick Neill tipped his twenty years ago. Now Neill is himself a candidate in what feels more like a local council election, with trestle tables, ushers and the proctors taking the votes. One of Tom Bingham's proposers, I vote for him and no one else, the single transferable vote (another Jenkins inspiration) likely, it's thought, to favour Bingham's chief rival, Chris Patten. At the table I hand in my paper to one of the junior proctors, a weary-looking don who, in what is perhaps a ritual humiliation, demands some evidence of identification. I hand over my Camden bus pass, which he scrutinises as grimly as an Albanian border guard, even checking the likeness. Andrew Wilson sails through unchallenged.

I walk back through the streets of Oxford and as always I have a sense of being shut out and that there is something going on here that I'm not a part of; not that I was a part of it even when I was a part of it.

16 March. One of the lowest moments this year was Tony Blair and Jack Straw misrepresenting the French and German position on Iraq in order to encourage xenophobia and get more support from the Murdoch papers.

17 March. A Bin Laden associate reported as being 'quizzed' by American agents in Pakistan. Were suspects 'quizzed' by the Gestapo, I wonder. Other people torture; we quiz.

19 March. What is particularly bitter is to hear one's own moderate, pragmatic and indeed patriotic sentiments in the mouth of the Foreign Minister of Germany, Joschka Fischer, while our own prime minister parrots the American line, a case, I suppose, of Speak for England, Joschka. Meanwhile the troops get ready to 'rock and roll', as they call it this time; last time it was 'shooting fish in a barrel'.

21 March. The first soldiers killed. If our army had been made up of conscripts no one would have tolerated this war for a moment. However much these are 'our boys' , the war can only be waged because the US and the UK have armies of mercenaries.

24 March. G. was on the bus en route for Camden when a woman opposite leaned across and said: 'I suppose you think I've got this sore throat because I've had a cock in my mouth? Actually I've been in Germany, but I wasn't going to let them rearrange my face.'

6 April. All of Rupert Murdoch's 175 papers are in favour of the war, though he always claims that his editors are independent and decide for themselves. I wonder whether the Rupert Murdoch Professorship at Oxford maintains the same fiction. I know I'm a bore on the subject and thought to be an unworldly fool, but so long as it bears his name this grubby appointment is a continuing stain on the reputation of the university that solicited it.

10 April. George Fenton has been in Berlin talking to some of the Berlin Philharmonic, with whom he is due to record and conduct his *Blue Planet* music. They go out to supper in a restaurant in what was East Berlin, a vast converted warehouse where the food is superb. The Germans are all very nice and hugely taken with recent events: 'The world has turned upside down. The best golfer in the world is black; the best rapper in the world is white; and now there is a war and, guess what, Germany doesn't want to be in it.'

The sense of impotence is what one never gets used to, of being led into ignominy and not being able to do anything about it except march and, one day, vote.

22 April, Yorkshire. Drive up towards Kirkby Lonsdale then along Wandales Lane, the old Roman road from Burrow to Sedbergh. Walking down one of the green lanes below the fells we come across a fold with a stone stile and in the centre of the fold a boulder so huge it looks like an ancient feature of the landscape, walled for its own protection; an erratic perhaps, carried down and deposited here by the melting glaciers of the Ice Age and then become the centre of some ancient ritual.

It's a lovely day and strolling along the lane towards Leck we find a similar fold with another boulder and a hundred yards along a third and a fourth. All are neat, grazed by sheep which have access through a cattle creep under the wall, and all have stiles. They seem ancient, fit snugly into the landscape and are immensely pleasing to look at, some of the pleasure admittedly being in their discovery and their mystery. Are the boulders prehistoric? Or stations along what is plainly an ancient track, some of which is banked up and possibly Roman?

We turn back and drive down to the nursery at Brownthwaite, which is attached to an old-fashioned farm where there are hens and their chickens scuttering about, sheep and today a huge turkey. It's a farm out of a children's story, kept by a nice oldish woman and her son, both expert gardeners, their nursery full of rare plants, and ending in a gate to their own garden, which overlooks the valley.

We ask the son about the sheepfolds and the son smiles indulgently at the thought that they might be ancient monuments. They're actually part of an installation or a series of installations by Andy Goldsworthy, who put up a hundred or so similar folds as Cumbria's Millennium Project. It was an expensive do, costing £500,000 or so, and involved shifting the boulders down from the fells with earthmovers besides building the folds that surrounded them. An additional burden, I would have thought, was likely to have been the scepticism of the local communities that were home to these 'sculptures', though nobody could object that they're not wholly in the tradition of the countryside in which they've been sited. However the only criticism our market gardener has is that Goldsworthy refused to allow any guide to be printed to the location of the folds, the public meant to come across them by accident just as we did and presumably to ask the same kind of questions – who made them, what for and when?

28 April, Yorkshire. Our clock has been losing time, so this morning we pack it up ready to go to Settle to be overhauled. Like a dog being taken to the vet it seems to know where it's going and as soon as it's in the box begins to chime, chimes all the way down in the car and only stops when we find that Mr Barraclough, whose retirement job it is, doesn't have a clock surgery today. So now it's back home, though still in its box, sulking perhaps, but occasionally giving a plaintive chime.

3 May, Yorkshire. The cherry tree that my father planted just by the back door some thirty years ago is now not much more than a stump. It was radically pruned a few years back in an effort to cure the blackfly that annually infested it, making the leaves clumped and scorched like burned fists. Even then, with so few leaves, it still got infested, though it was the only tree in the garden that I was ever driven to spray. A few years ago, in desperation, I planted a vine (*Vitis coignetiae*) just over the wall in A.'s garden (and so in full sun) and began to train it over what was left of the cherry tree. It flourished, so much so that it has covered the stump with its broad heart-shaped leaves, the cherry is virtually obliterated and the tree now looks like a mop-headed catalpa. It's one of my few ventures into creative gardening and the only time I've had foresight enough to devise a remedy for a problem and the patience to see it carried through.

One drawback is that with so few leaves there is very little cherry blossom, but this year the *coignetiae* has compensated for that, too, as its newly emergent leaves are a darkish pink on the front and white at the back so that they look as much like blossom as leaves. It reminds me of a Claude Rogers painting I once tried to buy and now here it is outside the back door.

15 May. After supper we go down to look at the Titian exhibition, now in its last few days at the National Gallery. It's ten-fifteen and the doors have only just closed so that the rooms still smell of the hordes that have been passing through; there are screwed-up tickets and abandoned programmes on the floor with, a few feet above the clutter, these sublime paintings.

As usual in galleries I feel inadequate and somehow ungiving and am quicker through the rooms than R., like a child wanting to see what's next, though this means, too, that I can keep having a sit down as I wait for him to catch up. Some of the wonder the paintings inspire is at Titian's technical accomplishment: his rendering of *stuff*, the fur and the fabric and the raised and knotted embroideries on the fabric, all of which melt into a brown mess on close examination, and only achieve form when one steps back. Oddly favourite is a portrait of the (unappealing) Pope Paul III in a faded rose-coloured cape enthroned on a worn velvet chair, the supreme pontiff just a lay figure there to demonstrate the painter's skill with his materials. Next to him the irresistible portrait of the twelve-year-old Ranuccio Farnese and another of Clarissa Strozzi that could almost be a Goya.

Least impressive is the much advertised reconstruction of Alfonso d'Este's *camerino* which doesn't work because a) the room is too large and b) certain elements are missing and c) the NG's *Bacchus and Ariadne* apart, I don't altogether like the paintings. I don't care for his last pictures much either, while recognising how (in every sense) far-sighted they are. *The Flaying of Marsyas* is a disturbing picture, the detachment of the satyrs watching the torture of their fellow creature chilling; Marsyas' upended eye, blank with a horror beyond feeling or fixed in death, is done with a single dot of white paint, a dot I'd like to see enlarged or in detail.

Now it's a quarter of an hour before midnight and we walk back through the dark and deserted gallery, the feeling of privilege we had when we were first able to do this ten years ago never lost; it's the greatest and most tangible honour I have ever been given.

Lying in bed, though, I think of the time I invited Alec Guinness to go round with me. Having given him careful instructions which door to come to, I waited in the lobby until well past the appointed time. Never late, he eventually arrived cross and out of sorts, claiming I had sent him to the wrong door. I hadn't, but I should have known that any attempt to return his always munificent hospitality would end in tears. He so disliked being beholden to anyone that he was bound to fuck things up if you ever tried to give him a treat. Though whether he knew this (or knew it about himself) was never plain.

26 May, Yorkshire. A dullish day, though fine enough to garden, which we do until, around five, we take some rubbish down to the dump in Settle. It used to be on the edge of a disused quarry and reminded me of the place where the Virgin Mary appeared to St Bernadette at Lourdes, as seen in *The Song of Bernadette*, a film which terrified me as a child. Now it's in Settle itself, an immaculately kept installation below the railway with a series of skips all lined up and with steps and a platform as for the launching of a ship rather than the filling of a skip. The man in charge has a commodious hut, where he may very well live, and is cheerful and helpful and this, plus the fact that disencumbering oneself of rubbish always lifts the heart, makes most people come away in a cheerful frame of mind. It isn't all rubbish, though, and today as I junk some of the mysterious accoutrements that always come with a vacuum cleaner I spot some quite ancient-looking decorated wood. Alas, one of the rules of the establishment (displayed on a painted board) is that one cannot go through the contents of the skip, so I have to leave my fancied medieval panels to their fate.

Afterwards we go the back way along the Feizor road, stopping to walk up the green lane towards the Celtic wall. The lane is lined with patches of water avens, the dusky purples and pinks in its strawberryish flower growing in among the spokes of yellow wood spurge, an arrangement more effective than anything you'd get at Pulbrook and Gould.

29 May. That Tony Blair (as today talking to troops in Basra) will often say 'I honestly believe' rather than just 'I believe' says all that needs to be said. 'To be honest' another of his frank-seeming phrases.

11 June. Why isn't more fuss made over Charles Causley? Looking through his *Collected Poems* to copy out his 'Ten Types of Hospital Visitor', I dip into some of his other poems, so many of them vivid and memorable. Well into his eighties, he must be one of the most distinguished poets writing today (if he still is). But why does nobody say so and celebrate him while he's still around? Hurrah for Charles Causley is what I say.*

23 June. The woollen hats worn by boys nowadays often take the form of medieval basinets or such helmets as soldiers wear in a French Book of Hours. A boy comes by this morning with just such a helmet looking as if he might be coming off duty from the foot of the Cross.

25 July. John Schlesinger dies. The obituaries are more measured than he would have liked, the many undistinguished films he made later in life set against *A Kind of Loving* and *Sunday, Bloody Sunday*. He wasn't by nature

* Too late. He dies 4 November.

a journeyman film-maker, taking whatever came along, but was forced into this way of working by having three houses to keep up, one of them in Hollywood, and always leading quite an expensive life. What none of the obituaries says is what a joy he was to work with, though no one had a shorter fuse, besides being wonderfully funny, particularly about his sex life.

Short, solid and fat, John looked like the screen Nazi he had once or twice played in his early days as an actor; he was a scaled-down Francis L. Sullivan, managing nevertheless to be surprisingly successful in finding partners. Not invariably, though. Sometime in the 1970s he was in a New York bath house where the practice was for someone wanting a partner to leave the cubicle door open. This Schlesinger accordingly did and lay monumentally on the table under his towel waiting for someone to pass by. A youth duly did and indeed ventured in, but seeing this mound of flesh laid out on the slab recoiled, saying: 'Oh, please. I couldn't. You've got to be kidding.' Schlesinger closed his eyes and said primly: 'A simple "No" will suffice.'

6 August. Driving along the back road from Muker to Kirkby Stephen, we spot down in the valley another of Andy Goldsworthy's circular sheep-folds and a mile or two further on a complex of folds that at first we take to be a development of his art but which on closer examination turns out to be the real thing: a series of three or four walled enclosures set round a one-chamber single-storey cottage used for dipping and shearing sheep. And still used, seemingly, the long stone-lined pit brimming with evil-looking oily dip, a ragged fleece hanging by the wall and the ground carpeted in flocks and curds of wool. It's a sinister place and much as it must always have been, an old board blocking one of the cattle creeps hinged with scraps of ancient leather. That it can at first sight be mistaken for one of Goldsworthy's installations says much for the authenticity of his work.

14 August. Another death: Cedric Price, for many years the partner of Eleanor Bron and an inspirational figure to many architects. He was a figure of eighteenth-century exuberance with views on conservation that were shockingly at variance with received wisdom. Cedric didn't believe in preserving buildings that had outlived their usefulness; he would have made a good character in a modern-day Ibsen play. At Cambridge as an undergraduate he was once in the Rex cinema when the adverts came on, including one for Kellogg's Ricicles. 'Rice is nice,' went the jingle, 'but Ricicles are twicicles as nicicles.' Whereupon Cedric boomed out: 'But testicles are besticles.'

By their jokes ye shall know them.

The elegance of the black building crew up the street is a constant delight. Today one comes down the street in a lemon-coloured shirt, his head wrapped in a bandanna of matching shade and a white dust mask pushed up above his forehead. He is like a wonderfully exotic rhinoceros, but with a grace and self-assurance that wouldn't be out of place on the catwalk.

24 August. Our GNER train from Leeds stops at Retford, where passengers are bussed down the AI to Grantham, the line between being under repair. It's around seven and the clouds are beginning to break up and the journey is redeemed by a vision on the eastern horizon of the towers of Lincoln Cathedral, caught in the late light of the setting sun. It's the kind of thing that would have immensely excited me as a boy (and quite excites me now). I've driven up and down this road hundreds of times and never seen it before, but that's because in a coach you're hoisted above the hedge and given an artist's prospect of the countryside.

28 August. T. Blair claims to the Hutton Inquiry that if the BBC had been right and the Iraq dossier had been 'sexed up' he would have resigned. This is presumably intended to pre-empt any calls for his resignation at the conclusion of the Inquiry, which, whether it reports so or not, has conclusively shown that this is exactly what happened to the Iraq dossier. I suppose 'sexed up' is a euphemism for 'hardened up' ('stiffened up' even), fastidiousness about language not being one of the characteristics of Blair and Co.; one of the many distasteful aspects of the whole affair is that anyone (Lord Hutton included) engaging with the issues has to do so in the language dictated by Number 10.

14 September. Finish reading *Toast*, Nigel Slater's memoir of his childhood. It's such an enjoyable book I regret reading it so quickly, bolting it in fact, the metaphor appropriate. Food apart, it's also a very sexy book. The young Nigel must have had some sort of glint in his eye because he's always getting shown a bit of the action until at fourteen he starts spending his evenings hanging round the local lay-by spying on couples having it away. Life finally takes off when he fucks a girl-friend with his best friend watching from the other bed. An idyllic childhood I would have said. The rest is history. Or cookery.

25 September. To Folkestone to speak at the Saga-sponsored literary festival. We have tea at the seafront hotel and sitting on the balcony in the warm sunshine I reflect on how seldom it is that I see the sea. The tide is in and the waves are breaking only a yard or two from the road and although it's quite busy there is something restorative about sitting here, watching the brown waves edge up the narrow beach. On the horizon to the south is the power station at Dungeness and beyond it, I imagine, Derek Jarman's now much visited cottage, trips to it one of the features of the festival. There are three or four ships motionless on the horizon, putting one in mind of Larkin's 'To the Sea', though there is no 'miniature gaiety of seasides' here, just the occasional grim jogger toiling along the front.

Saga itself turns out to be a tall modern block set in a steep park above the sea and alongside the offices an even more modern auditorium up to which several senior citizens are already labouring. The lavishness of the set-up – the vast terrace outside the auditorium above the sea, the spacious park and the many-storeyed office block – combine to make it slightly sinister, as if the ostensible purpose of the organisation, the interests and welfare of old(er) people, is just a front as it would be in a Bond film, say, a cover for international criminality with a hatch opening in the cliff-side parkland to reveal a hangar humming with the mechanism of some project that will take over the world. And all the thousands of employees are old. As the audience certainly are at my meeting, though very amiable and jolly. At the finish I am presented with a stick of Folkestone rock the size of a barber's pole, sign books for an hour and then get the train back; home by ten-thirty.

30 September. A memorial service for John Schlesinger. It's in the synagogue opposite Lord's and though it's Liberal Jewish I don't feel it's quite liberal enough for me to tell the bath-house story. Still, there are a lot of laughs in the other speeches, so I do feel able to give John's own account of his investiture with the CBE. John was so aware of his sexuality that he managed to detect a corresponding awareness in the unlikeliest of places. On this occasion HMQ had a momentary difficulty getting the ribbon round his sizeable neck, whereupon she said, 'Now, Mr Schlesinger, we must try and get this *straight*,' the emphasis according to John very much hers and which he chose to take as both a coded acknowledgement of his situation and a seal of royal approval.

4 October. To Ely to look at the cathedral, last visited all of twenty-five years ago when the town was still a lost place like Beverley or Cartmel. Nowadays, like so much of East Anglia, it thrives and today is the Harvest Festival. At the west end of the nave is a pen of sheep and a few roosters crowing their heads off and in odd corners all over the cathedral little heaps of baked beans, cling peaches and custard powder, the staples of such occasions, and which, as Clive James noted, will later be distributed among the poor and devout old ladies who contributed them in the first place. A truer symbol of the locality's harvest would, I suppose, be a sheaf of emails or a roll of print-outs, electronics round here more profitable than agriculture.

The sheep attracting most of the visitors, the rest of the cathedral is blessedly quiet and there is much to see. Our favourites are a little eccentric, with mine the late fifteenth-century cloister arcades outside the south door, bricked up presumably at the Dissolution, and R.'s a fragment of wooden tracery from the prior's study and the framework of a door that once housed the library cupboard for the monks. But there's much more spectacular stuff, even though the methodical iconoclasm of East Anglian puritanism is more in evidence here than in York, say, with even the little fragment of glass preserved and restored in one of the cloister windows having the Virgin's face scratched out. Every statue and saint is headless or faceless, with the mutilations in the Lady Chapel looking so fresh they might have been done by the vandals of today.

The shop is doing a brisk trade in tea towels, table mats and all the merchandise that were I Jesus I'd be overturning. And, as always, no decent postcards, the want of a proper series of black and white repro-ductions of architectural details such as you find in French cathedrals an indictment of . . . whom? The cathedral chapter? The dean? Un-enterprising photographers? Or just, as Lindsay Anderson would say, 'England!'

Why the west tower is not one of the wonders of European architecture I don't understand. It's as extraordinary and asymmetrical as Gaudí and a staggering achievement for its time, every bit as astonishing as Pisa, which its arcades recall, though lacking the lean that would put it in the big league and have people gawping (which of course I wouldn't want any-way). 'Oh, grumble, grumble,' says R.

15 October. The Earl of Pembroke, Henry Herbert, has died. I met him only once in July 1974 when I had to do a Kilvert recital in the Double Cube room at Wilton. He was charming and easy but it didn't go well for all sorts of reasons, some sad, some comic. The evening was to have been introduced by Cecil Beaton, but earlier that week he had had a stroke and this overshadowed the proceedings. Princess Alexandra was the guest of honour but being Kilvert there was quite a bit about little girls' bottoms and suchlike so HRH put rather a damper on things as royalty often does, or did in those days anyway. I was wearing a new velvet suit and it was only afterwards I found that my flies had been open throughout. 'Never mind,' said the lighting assistant. 'The spot was on your face.'

The story wouldn't be worth telling except that nearly twenty years later when *The Madness of George III* was playing at the National, Henry Herbert wrote to me about the Lady Pembroke who figures in the play. This was a lady of mature years to whom in his derangement George III takes a fancy; she was a woman of some dignity who did not in the least reciprocate his attentions, which were something of a joke at Court. Herbert's letter filled in the family tradition about this ancestor with an anecdote told him by his father:

> Lady Pembroke's husband, Henry, was charming but he was also a shit and the King was so incensed by the Earl's behaviour towards his wife that he demanded to know what possible excuse he had for treating her so badly. To which the Earl replied: 'Sire, if you had a wife whose cunt was as cold as a greyhound's nostril, you would have done the same.'

Twenty years after the Kilvert recital we went back to Wilton to film part of *The Madness of King George*, by which time Richenda Carey, who had played Lady Pembroke on the stage, had had to give way to the less matronly Amanda Donohoe, star of *Castaway* and more what Hollywood thought audiences were entitled to expect in a fancy woman, and one unlikely to be suffering from her historical counterpart's genital hypothermia.

19 October. Watch the second part of ITV's *Henry VIII* with Ray Winstone as the much married monarch. It's no better than the first half and as wilfully inaccurate, the Dissolution of the Monasteries presented as if it were some Viking raid, with troops riding down the fleeing monks, hacking them to death as they try to rescue the monastic treasures. It's a far cry from the peaceful retirement on a small pension that was the lot of most of the monks and nuns, with the actual dismantling of the fabric and selling off of the furnishings far more interesting (and far more interesting to watch) than these silly melodramatics.

Aske, the leader of the Pilgrimage of Grace (played by Sean Bean), is pictured being hauled up outside Clifford's Tower in York, with the wicked Duke of Norfolk ordering that he be left to hang for three days, presumably to die of exposure. This is picturesque nonsense. Aske was sentenced to be hanged, drawn and quartered and though there's seldom much to be said for Henry VIII in the clemency department he did at least agree to Aske's request that he be hanged and allowed to die before the rest of the sentence was carried out.*

In the same programme Thomas Cromwell is pictured being inexpertly despatched by a novice executioner, Cromwell's face contorted in agony as the first two blows fall, his head only cut off by the third. This, too, is fanciful. Certainly there must have been many botched beheadings, but Cromwell's was not one of them, the executioner (whose name is known) taking off his head at a stroke.

In a programme as poor as this it might seem pedantic to be concerned about such details. But there is more than enough savagery in the reign of Henry VIII without adding to it.

4 November. Passing through Cambridge, we pay a ritual visit to Kettle's Yard. It's a house that never fails to delight and though there are features I don't like, it's a place I could happily live in. The attendants are mostly elderly and many of them seem to have known Jim Ede, whose house it was and who gave it and its art collection to the University in the 1970s.

One particularly sparky old lady recommends a video display running in the big room downstairs. At first it simply seems to be a slightly blurred record of a domestic interior: a kitchen, a sitting room with on the floor some toys including a couple of model planes. Suddenly one of these planes takes off, then another lands and soon the kitchen and dining room have turned into a busy international airport, planes crossing the room, landing on tables, taking off from work surfaces and all in total silence. They negotiate the narrow chasm of a slightly open door, deftly avoid a light fitting or a bowl of fruit and it's so absurd and silly I find myself grin-

---

* Except that it has also been suggested that Henry VIII had Aske hung in chains, thus condemning him to an even more lingering death, an incident that forms part of H. F. M. Prescott's fine historical novel *Man on a Donkey*.

ning like a child. The artist, whose name I forget to write down, is Japanese and it's the last thing I'd ever have chosen to watch or expected to find in the austere surroundings of a house like this, but it's a delight.

15 November. Around nine I go out to put some rubbish in the bin to find someone curled up on the doorstep. I say someone because, swathed in an anorak, it's impossible to tell whether it's a man or a woman; he/she doesn't speak and when shaken just moans a little. He/she is surrounded by half a dozen plastic bags, most of them empty and not the carefully transported possessions of the usual bag lady, if it is a lady. So, having talked about it, we eventually ring 999, where the Scotland Yard operator is quite helpful and within ten minutes (on a Saturday night) a squad car comes round with two policemen. They're sensible and firm with what turns out to be a young man. He's filthy, his hands so black he might have been shifting coal, and is no help when they try to get him on his feet, moaning still and saying he has an abscess.

Now an ambulance arrives, and it's this that seems to bring the young man round. He plainly doesn't want to go to hospital and, abandoning whatever possessions he has on our doorstep, vanishes into the night. One of the policemen comes back and explains that, because among the rubbish is a squeezed-out lemon, he is likely to be an addict, the juice used to purify the drugs. He counsels caution when we're clearing up the mess lest there be any needles about and then says, 'Actually I can do it,' goes to the car for some gloves and tidies everything away himself and in such a sensible, straightforward way it seems genuine goodness.

It makes me ashamed of my habitual prejudice against the police when here is one dealing with what for him is presumably a regular occurrence and going out of his way just to be helpful. I think what a dispiriting job it must be night after night coping with the thieves and addicts of Camden Town and how hard it must be not to despise respectable folk who call them in to solve what for us is just a problem of hygiene. With a final instruction to swill down the flags, he goes off in the squad car, I go up and have my bath and then we sit down to our shepherd's pie.

Among the contents of the bags that constitute the young man's possessions were part of a safety belt, presumably used as a tourniquet, a candlestick with a stub of a candle, a packet of Yorkshire puddings and, unaccountably, some rosemary.

21 November. I see from the paper this morning that while I was trudging up Whitehall past the end of Downing Street on the second anti-war march Tom Stoppard was in Downing Street having lunch with Mrs Bush. While she was there, apparently, they watched some children doing Shakespeare. I would have felt uncomfortable about this for various reasons, not least because it comes so close to a playbill done the night before at the Royal Court. This included an extract from Tony Kushner's next play in which Mrs Bush visits a school and talks to the children about literature and (slightly improbably) about Dostoevsky. As she chats to them she slowly realises that all the children are dead. In the same programme there's another playlet, *Advice to Iraqi Women* by Martin Crimp. I'd dearly love to have written both of them and it would have done more good, I'm sure, than going on the march.

15 December. As I'm correcting the proofs of this diary the news breaks of the arrest of Saddam Hussein. It ought to matter, and maybe does matter in Iraq; it certainly matters in America. But here? Whatever is said it does not affect the issue. We should not have gone to war.

It has been a shameful year.

2004

3 January. Alan Bates dies on 27 December and we break the journey from Yorkshire at Derby in order to go to his funeral. It's at Bradbourne, a tiny village the taxi driver has never heard of, and he and his Asian colleagues have a map session before we eventually head off into the Derbyshire hills. The cab is old and draughty, it's beginning to snow and as we drive through this landscape of lost villages and frostbitten fields it gets more and more foggy and like a journey out of *Le Grand Meaulnes*.

It's all of an hour before we reach the church and everyone has gone in, the undertakers with a policeman looking on just shouldering the coffin. Since the bill is £40 I feel I need a receipt but while the driver ransacks his cab for pad and pencil the policeman saunters over: 'The body is waiting to go in, sir.'

We make an undignified dash for the church where, hearing the door open, the congregation begin to rise, thinking we're the coffin, then sink back disappointed as, laden down with bags and both with backpacks on, we are ushered down the centre aisle to seats in the chancel. It looks like the most upstaging of showbiz entrances, the only consolation being that the deceased would have been the first to laugh.

It's a rather wandering service with plenty of time to reflect that, as always, it will be the jokes one will most miss and how at the regular suppers we used to have at L'Etoile we always told each other the same stories. They were generally of Alan's romantic escapades or of other people's bad behaviour, a favourite being how, after a performance in John Osborne's *A Patriot for Me* at Chichester for which he had been much praised, Alan was sitting in his dressing-room when there was a knock on the door. It was Alec Guinness. He shook Alan's hand, said, 'You must be very tired,' and left.

Alan's languid phone calls were often to do with professional humiliation. In the 1999 production of *Antony and Cleopatra* at Stratford the curtain rose with Antony on his knees pleasuring the Egyptian queen of Frances de la Tour. Even the jaded eyebrows of Stratford went up a bit at this and just before it transferred to the Barbican Alan rang and began without preamble: 'I'm sure you will be relieved to learn that for our London debut the director has elbowed the offending cunnilingus and replaced it with a walk-down in kingly garb. While this might seem a radical change it is, I suppose, only the difference between coming down and going down, though there's no doubt which one the audience prefers. Goodbye.'

We sit in on a history class of thirteen-year-olds, who are well behaved, alert and attentive, though not always getting it right. They are doing the changeover from the domestic system to factory working in the Industrial Revolution: 'If they couldn't get enough money from work at home,' asks the teacher, 'what did they do?'

Up goes a hand. 'Take in lodgers?'

Next is an English class of fifteen-year-olds, all of them past puberty and so less submissive, more anarchic and all over the place, though there is one self-contained boy who is neat, smart and prematurely sophisticated, a boy out of Saki.

Finally the sixth form: half a dozen boys and one girl. Except not boys: one has a full-grown beard and though destined for Cambridge looks less like an undergraduate than a fully fledged lecturer; another, ignoring us completely as they all do, sits working by himself and could be a young broker from the City. Their history teacher talks about them quietly and the problems she and they have, particularly non-attendance, and it all seems a long way from the sixth form that I've written.

1 March. In the accounts I have seen of Sir Andrew Turnbull's reproving letter to Clare Short for breaching cabinet confidence, nobody has commented on his use of the word 'disappointed'. The head of the Civil Service wasn't dismayed by Ms Short's revelations nor was he disconcerted; he didn't say he disapproved (though he did); no, he was disappointed. It's a headmasterly word implying a falling short (I know) and a failure to live up to standards that shouldn't have to be spelled out, and thus very much a word of the establishment.

This would hardly be worth saying did not Sir Andrew advertise his emancipation from the establishment by, among other things, chairing meetings in his shirtsleeves. But shirtsleeves only take you so far (the prime minister is often in them, after all). No, Sir Andrew needs to take the jacket off his language, too. Were I not on Clare Short's side already, to read that the head of the Civil Service is disappointed in her would be enough to make up my mind.

6 March. A young man passes wearing a close-fitting leather cap meant to strap under the chin, the strap unfastened and dangling loose. He looks like 1) a racing driver at Brooklands in the 1930s; 2) someone out of Brueghel about to torment Christ. Neither, I would have thought, is the look he is aiming for.

13 March. The last of the History Boys to be cast is Russell Tovey, who is in the NT company and who took part in the first reading of the play. He reads Rudge, the athletic and supposedly stupid boy, effortlessly, but isn't sure it's what he really wants to do, having set his sights on playing the more glamorous part of Dakin. This makes me think again about Rudge and I rewrite the part to accommodate some of the actor's aspirations in the character, which both suits him and improves the play. This is one of the pleasures of writing plays which I can't see writing novels or poems ever providing.

After the train bombs in Madrid T. Blair commends the Spanish for turning out in their millions to demonstrate against terrorism. These are the same people who thronged the streets in Madrid and in London also in their millions to demonstrate against the war but this is not said by the prime minister. Our fearless leader is a democrat only as and when it suits him.

20 March. Nicholas Hytner has shown the script of *The History Boys* to one of his former teachers at Manchester Grammar School, who says that teaching these days is so circumscribed that many traditional tools of the trade are now impermissible. Sarcasm, for instance, is out, pupils are never touched and there are often viewing panels in the doors.

31 March. We place a different value on the lives of Iraqi combatants, with the dead not even numbered or named. Our view of the Iraqis is not far off Falstaff's view of his company: 'They'll fill a pit as well as better. Tush, man, mortal men, mortal men.'

22 April. An absurd direction from the ENO management requesting all employees at the Coliseum to cease from calling each other 'darling' and indeed from touching one another at all or using other terms of endearment.

News of this is gleefully received at the National Theatre, where copies of the directive are given to everybody arriving at the stage door and announcements over the tannoy take on a husky intimacy. 'Sweethearts. Could we have two of those delightful electricians to the stage of the Cottesloe. Hurry, hurry, hurry. *A bientôt.*'

27 April. R. and I drive over to Rievaulx, where they are to video the titles of Irwin's TV history series, *Heroes or Villains?*, in the sequence which opens the second act of the play. En route we stop and have our sandwiches at Byland, where we are the only visitors this cold and cloudy morning. As an abbey it's always more peaceful because less dramatically situated than either Rievaulx or Fountains, on a flat and boggy plain backed by woods and often quite hard to find. A notable feature is an alleyway of reading carrels backing the cloister, together with many surviving stretches of medieval tiled floor, but much the most numinous object is a green earthenware inkwell found in the chapterhouse during excavations and now in the abbey museum; it was presumably used, possibly for the last time, to sign the deed of surrender handing the abbey over to Henry VIII's commissioners.

Over at Rievaulx we film in the rain and in the cavernous latrine below the monks' dormitory. With a lighting cameraman this would have taken most of the day, but brought up in the brisker school of music video Ben Taylor, who looks not long out of school himself, polishes off the whole sequence in a couple of hours.

10 May. Filling a pot with water to take a huge bunch of peonies L. has sent for my birthday I slip on the wet flags and fall down three or four stone steps into the area. It's a fall long enough for me to think, 'This is quite serious,' as it's going on, but when I get up I find I'm all right and it's only when I've had a bath and am having a lie-down that I realise that this is one of those accidents that usually occur on or around my birthday, previous experience showing that I'd be well advised to spend the whole octave of that festival in bed and out of harm's way.

18 May. We sit in the stalls of the Lyttelton having a last notes session before the press night. There are no nerves as we've had a week of enthusiastic and sometimes tumultuous previews, the theatre is sold out for the whole of the first booking period and the play will run on word of mouth regardless of what the reviews are like. This is no guarantee of good notices, though, and Nick H. explains this to the cast, particularly the boys, few of whom have had a first night before. He also says how he's never had such a good time with a play. I say the same, though with more melancholy, as my part in it is almost over.

Afterwards I sit on the terrace outside the Lyttelton, reading my messages, and watch the audience begin to arrive. It's only when I go inside for a dutiful drink with the sponsors that Bob Crowley tells me that the theatre is in chaos.

One of the recurrent themes of the play is the unpredictability of things or, as Rudge puts it, history is just one fucking thing after another – a point made in the play by the death of Hector on his motorbike and the crippling of Irwin, his unlooked for passenger. And all the time we were sitting joking in the stalls thinking it was all sewn up and everything taken care of, a fire was smouldering in the flies. An hour before curtain, with the theatre empty and the stage management on their break, the flame sets off the sprinklers, and when next someone steps onto the stage it's ankle-deep in water.

There is no light at all as the power has immediately to be switched off and when I go into the auditorium (the first-night audience now waiting in the foyer ready for the start) there are dim figures moving about the sodden stage, torches flashing in the gloom and firemen clambering up the rig. It's all very theatrical, though not quite theatre as we'd planned it.

Not all the firemen have found the supposed blaze. Backstage the

347

various auditoriums for the National are notoriously difficult to locate and when I go through I come upon a helmeted fireman, axe at the ready, wandering down a dressing-room corridor and who asks me to point him in the direction of 'this Lyttelton Theatre'.

Eventually all the stage crews from the other theatres are mobilised to mop the stage and the curtain goes up an hour late. The actors are dribbled on throughout the performance but the audience, possibly because of the free drinks they've been given while they've been waiting, are happy and responsive and the play goes well.

21 May. Give a talk at the London Review Bookshop and answer questions, in the course of which I mention how, when I was seventeen and hitchhiking through the Llanberis pass in Wales, I was rather ineffectually touched up on the back of a motorbike much as Hector's pupils are in the play. The *Sunday Times* must have been lurking in the audience and a reporter rings the NT press office the next day asking them to confirm that a master touched me up as a boy, thus blighting my schooldays. They don't confirm it, and emphasise how trivial the incident was. No matter. The *Sunday Times* prints the story exactly as it wants it to be, making the whole play some sort of expiation. I often read Anthony Powell's *Journals*, where a recurring theme is the stupidity and bad behaviour of journalists by whose crassness Powell was always unsurprised. So no change there.

26 May. Do a question-and-answer session at Warwick Arts Centre. The talk is preceded by a book signing at which, having had her book signed, a woman leans low over the table to confide in me: 'I'd like to be buried in a little grave right next to yours.'

When I say I hope this won't be quite yet she says, 'Well, I'm the same age as you,' as if this somehow made our posthumous propinquity more of a likelihood.

27 May. Ashcroft, the US Attorney General, applies for the extradition of Abu Hamza, the radical Muslim cleric. No friend to freedom and from the extremity of his utterances not an attractive figure, Hamza is additionally demonised by the hook he has instead of a hand, so that his fellow prisoners at Belmarsh hang a sheet out of the window inscribed 'Sling Your Hook'. At which point I suppose the Home Secretary pours himself another drink.

Under its current administration I would not extradite a dog to the United States, whatever the crime. In a country where the rule of law can be set aside by executive decree, prisoners kept outside the law and imprisoned without trial or legal representation, Hamza is likely to disappear without trace. If there is evidence against him he should be tried here and if he's found guilty, imprisoned here too.

The case comes up on BBC1's *Question Time* later on, when the sleek and suited Peter Hain, now Leader of the House of Commons, maintains that Hamza should be handed over to face justice (*sic*) in the United States, the same sort of justice (though nobody is indelicate enough to say this) as there used to be in South Africa at a time when Hain saw things rather differently.

Nor does anyone point out that while Hamza is an extreme Muslim fundamentalist the evangelical Ashcroft is his precise Christian equivalent, only Ashcroft wears a suit and is surrounded by young men in suits rather than disciples in djellabas and, having no hooks for hands, is the voice of respectability.

1 June. Success (like death) brings letters and I spend most of the morning trying to clear my table. Then, just as I'm putting stamps on a score or so of envelopes, the letter box goes and another jorum of mail cascades over the doormat. It's a scene from a Frank Randle film I saw as a child when Frank is in the army, doing fatigues and peeling potatoes. He is just peeling the last spud with the shed all clean and bare when a trapdoor in the roof opens and another ton of potatoes comes cascading down.

10 June. Were I a schoolmaster like Irwin in the play, instructing pupils about the Dissolution of the Monasteries, I would begin with the ancient

349

oak tree still standing at the crossroads at Caton on the Kirkby Lonsdale–Lancaster road. It was at this tree that the monks of Cockersands Abbey on the Lune estuary would sell their fish, the fish said to have been hung from its branches. One day in 1536 or so the fish-monks didn't turn up, so for the people of Caton in the Lune Valley the Dissolution of the Monasteries simply meant no more fresh fish. Caton, though it has some good houses, is now a dormitory village of Lancaster. It's also on the Lune, just as Cockersands is on the estuary, so perhaps it was that the monks brought up the fish by boat, sailing up on the incoming tide. Easier anyway than humping it round Lancaster over the heights of Quernmore.

Apropos *The History Boys*, I have been thinking about dons. When I was at school I never quite knew what the word meant, associating it (the Spanish flavour and the gown, I suppose) with that cloaked and mysterious figure who used to advertise Sandeman's port.

Most dons at my own college were shy in some degree, except for the Senior Tutor, Dacre Balsdon, but not being a squash player, a Rhodes Scholar or someone of a refreshingly extrovert temperament, I never really took his eye. It was partly his exaggerated utterance that put me off (he was the Brian Sewell of his day), meeting him always a hazard of going round the front quad. I was dull and he made me feel even duller.

Far and away the most distinguished of the Fellows in my time at Exeter was Sir Cyril Hinshelwood. A Nobel Laureate, he was President of the Royal Society, President of the Classical Association and had the Order of Merit and honorary degrees galore. He spoke half a dozen languages and it was said he could learn a new one in a fortnight. He was not a sociable man, the only person allowed in his room said to be Cantwell, one of the older scouts, who reported that Hinshelwood was also an accomplished painter. Like Dacre Balsdon he was a bachelor and lived in College but no two dons could seemingly be less alike, Balsdon sociable, expansive but not a distinguished scholar, Hinshelwood shy, introverted but a great figure in the world.

One afternoon around tea time I came out of the JCR and went over to the buttery to get my tea, and saw Hinshelwood hovering about at the foot of the JCR staircase. He was still there when I came back and it was only when I was sitting in the window having my tea that I saw, like a scene out of Proust, what it was that was happening. On the other side of the quad on the ground floor were the rooms of Watkins, one of the chemistry scholars, and as I watched he came out and went over to the buttery to get his tea. Hinshelwood waited a moment then hurried over to the buttery too. Five minutes later they came back together, Hinshelwood's not entirely accidental arrival in the buttery at the same time having enabled him to ask the young man up to his rooms to share his tea. Furtive though it seemed it was of course entirely innocent, the kind of thing Balsdon would have had no need to engineer, just shouting his invitation across the quad ('Tea, dear fellow? Oh how delightful!'). Still, Hinshelwood and Balsdon were more like each other than either would have wanted, which was another reason for the rumoured antipathy between them.

What lesson I learned from this incident it would be hard to say, though it should be something to do with solitariness and futility.

20 June. Sent a postcard this morning of a painting I've never seen reproduced by an artist I've never heard of. It's Napoleon in hell. He's wearing the usual hat and has his arms folded in the customary way and is looking very stern as wild women wave in front of him the severed limbs of their loved ones, presumably slain in his wars. The painting by Antoine Wiertz (1806–65) is in the Musée des Beaux Arts in Brussels, and though Wiertz is hardly an old master, about suffering he wasn't wrong either.

25 June. As I leave Robin Hope's birthday party at the Old Sessions House in Clerkenwell Square someone says that England scored in the first minute against Portugal. The pubs I pass seem oddly subdued, with none of the usual crowds spilling out onto the pavement or the roars from within, so I take it the match is all over, shouting included. It's only when I get home to Camden Town and switch on the TV that I find it's still going on, with a penalty shoot-out in progress. I catch Postiga's elegant deception of the goalkeeper, who jumps the wrong way so that the Portuguese can just tap the ball in. It's like an expert squash player who, after everybody else has been banging and smashing, casually trickles the winning shot down the back wall. As always, having dreaded an English victory I am mortified by their defeat; the truth is I want them neither to win nor to lose, though the frenzy after the first goal is a reminder of how intolerable we would have been in victory.

14 July. There seems scarcely a mention of President Bush in the Butler Report though there is no doubt that he did the original mischief and persuaded our blameless prime minister that he ought to make war. Nothing that I've read about the report alters the obvious verdict that, having decided on war, Blair then looked round for reasons to justify it. And had everybody else looking, too. Once he'd let it be known what his will was (the whole country knew) and government being what it is, there were plenty of people in the cabinet and outside it ready to help the prime minister along. And so much *nodding*, and from Jack Straw in particular, still nodding on the front bench today like a dog in the back window of a Fiesta. The newspapers fall for Butler's smooth speaking even when they know how specious it is. One of his predecessors as master of University College Oxford was another smooth operator, Lord Redcliffe-Maud, smoothness something of a University College tradition.

27 July. In good time, as I think, for Paul Foot's funeral, I get to Golders Green to find outside the station what seems like a political rally in progress, with trade-union banners and a steel band just leading off towards the crematorium. The crowd entirely fills the Finchley Road and as we trudge along in the hot sunshine the march, ragged, unceremonious and heartfelt, is almost Indian in its disorganisation and spontaneity, with people coming out of houses and leaning from cars to ask who it is who's died.

I see no one I know and they're an odd mixture. 'He would have been pleased by the turn-out,' says a voice behind me. 'Possibly,' says a tall, stately old man, who sounds as if he's from the East End, 'but I am of the opinion the dead can't see us anyway.'

At the crematorium, the mourners separate into those with cards and those (like me) without. I see the coffin in then go into the loggia, where there's another huge gathering listening to the relay, some sitting on the grass, others squatting down by the pillars or crowded round the relay screen. I manage to find a sort of golf cart and enthroned on that hear the proceedings in more comfort than if I'd been inside.

I never knew Foot well, though occasionally I would write to congratulate him after some vindication (and if one waited long enough he was generally vindicated and so often got things right). I'd last spoken to him when I was writing *The History Boys* apropos 'Kek', F. McEachran, the charismatic schoolmaster who had taught him and some of the *Private Eye* people at Shrewsbury. What was almost unique about Foot was that he was a crusader who never lost his sense of humour so that he could get the (often very conservative) audience of *Any Questions* on his radical side simply by being funny and running rings round the other speakers. He had a kind of moral charm which made one want his approval.

Now it's the 'Internationale' and I get down from the golf cart and stand, a little self-consciously, astonished how many of this mild, unmilitant gathering raise their right arm in a clenched fist as they sing: a young man in front with a baby on one arm raises the other, and old husbands and wives clasp hands and raise arms together, and two boys, like Julian Bell and John Cornford, who've been lying out on the lawn get to their feet and sing – and moreover know the words.

30 July. In the week that Paul Foot is buried the Court of Appeal orders that the Hickeys, acquitted after being wrongly imprisoned for eighteen years for the murder of Carl Bridgewater, and for whose innocence Foot campaigned, must now effectively pay board and lodging for the years they have spent in gaol. It's the kind of joke the SS would have played on a prisoner lucky enough to be released from a concentration camp, presenting him at the gates with the bill. We ought to know the name of the official who dreamed up this little wheeze so as to watch out for him in a forthcoming Honours List. As it is we can only be grateful that Nelson Mandela wasn't imprisoned in England or he would have been bankrupted on his release.*

12 August. While it ought to be a pleasant place to shop, Marylebone High Street is spoiled by the people who shop there, who are often pushy and heedless so single-minded are they about getting just what they want. As a result it's a pretty graceless place and it's noticeable today even in the hushed precincts of Daunt's bookshop, where a man is talking on his mobile about some euros and so loudly it's embarrassing. Villandry, which is on the other edge of Marylebone, has some of the same rich, pushy atmosphere, though diluted by the number of office workers who now use it.

Biking back I stop for a pee at the London Clinic, where half a dozen hoods are hanging about the door. And that is what they are, not chauffeurs, not (certainly not) concerned relations, but bodyguards and hoods, possibly Russian, with dark glasses and grim unsmiling faces. I go past them, cycle clips always a passport, though even so I half expect someone to want to go through my bag. Having had a pee I come away slightly cheered, if only to have managed something free at the most expensive hospital in London. But I am in a bad temper and biking through Regent's Park with cars coming uncomfortably close I start writing letters in my head as to why there is no provision for cyclists in the park, no cycle lanes in the Inner or Outer Circle, no designated cycle path through the park, nothing, only a vigilant police force ready to fine any biker they can catch. Why? Is this the case in all the royal parks or in all the parks in London? Dogs shit here. People fuck here. They even play football and put on plays. But no cycling.

---

* A reader (though not, I think, a well-wisher) wrote to the *LRB* to point out that the Hickeys were only having to repay money that had been wrongly awarded to them for board and lodging. Possibly, though, it's a pity the Courts didn't show the same zeal for justice in the first instance as they did for financial regularity in the last.

16 August. The best films on TV are often in the middle of the day and at lunch time. Today it's *The Stars Look Down* (1939) with Michael Redgrave, which I would have seen in 1940 in one of Armley's half a dozen picture houses. Like *How Green Was My Valley* (1941) and Emlyn Williams's *The Corn is Green* (1945), it's the story of a working-class boy bettering himself through education and outgrowing his roots. They were none of them great films but they should figure in any account of the origins of the Welfare State as powerful myth-makers, particularly in our household where their message was taken for gospel, the value of education as a means of rising above one's circumstances never questioned. So, trailing back from the Picturedrome in that first year of the war, we thought Michael Redgrave and Roddy McDowall were real heroes in whose footsteps my parents hoped my brother and I would one day tread.

7 September. Watch a documentary about Wodehouse, geared to the publication of the new McCrum biography. Though there's some private newsreel footage there's nothing that hasn't been in previous programmes nor does it come to any different conclusions – namely, that Wodehouse was an innocent, unworldly figure who behaved foolishly over the famous broadcasts but no more than that. This was the verdict of an official inquiry which, had it been published at the time (*c.*1949), would have cleared his name and he would have been rehabilitated much earlier than he was. Or so the programme claims.

I'm not so sure. His famous innocence must have been pretty impregnable not to know by 1940 that there was more to Nazi Germany than a lot of bores dressing up in uniform and going round saluting one another. Did his wife, the notoriously canny Ethel, not read the papers either? Their unawareness doesn't hold up even as the programme proclaims it, since it shows the Wodehouses making attempts to get away from their home in Le Touquet but turning back because of the number of refugees on the road, the columns dive-bombed by Stukas. Did the Wodehouses witness this or is it just stock programme padding? If they did it must have come home even to them that this was serious stuff.

I start off, though, at a disadvantage in that, inspired though his language is, I can never take more than ten pages of the novels at a time, their relentless flippancy wearing and tedious. I am put off, too, by the Wodehouse fans, particularly since they're pretty much identical with the cricketing tendency. Waugh is entitled to call Wodehouse a genius but even with Waugh there's some feeling of self-congratulation at being the one to point it out. Nor does it help that Muggeridge was such a fan and the general chappishness of it all.

No, I'm not an impartial judge, though in the actual business of recording broadcasts for American listeners and then finding that they've been broadcast to England Wodehouse seems scarcely culpable at all. Newspapers pull that sort of trick all the time.

16 September. Some of my irritation with the Commons pro-hunting protestors is antiquarian: that these callow young men should have been the first to invade the floor of the House of Commons since Charles I seems vandalism not so much of the Commons itself as of tradition, the more so because it's in aid of such an ignoble cause. Though I feel much the same about another vandal, Lord Falconer, and the scrambled abolition of the office of Lord Chancellor.

About the sport itself Nancy Mitford, no opponent of hunting, was both perceptive and unsentimental:

> The next day we all went out hunting. The Radletts loved animals, they loved foxes, they risked dreadful beating to unstop the earths, they read and cried over *Reynard the Fox*, in summer they got up at four to go and see the cubs playing in the pale green light of the woods; nevertheless more than anything in the world, they loved hunting. It was in their blood and bones and in my blood and bones, and nothing could eradicate it, though we knew it for a kind of original sin. For three hours that day I forgot everything except my body and my pony's body . . . That must be the great hold hunting has over people, especially stupid people; it enforces absolute concentration, both mental and physical. (*The Pursuit of Love*)

The most sensible approach would have been to ban stag hunting and hare coursing as soon as Labour got into power. Both are barbarous and indefensible, except if you're Clarissa Dickson Wright, who presumably feels her casserole threatened. But what a feast of humbug it is in every department. 'We do what we like. We always have and always will. That's democracy.'

20 September. I am having my lunch outside the front door (salad of lettuce, beetroot, tomato and brown bread spread with olive paste) when Jonathan Miller passes en route for rehearsals at Covent Garden. He asks me what I'm reading. It's actually re-rereading, and telling him he would hate every page I show him James Lees-Milne's *Through Wood and Dale*. I ask him what he is reading and he shows me *The Origins of the Final Solution*. Both are unsuitable books and, as I say to him, we would each of us derive more benefit if I were reading his book and he mine. My book is cosy, comforting and I know everything in it; his book is just as familiar and, though hardly cosy, is consoling, too, both of us happiest reading what we know already.

11 October. Stephen Page (Faber) and Andrew Franklin (Profile Books) come round to take delivery of the MS of *Untold Stories*, a collection of diaries and other memoirs which they are to publish jointly next September. It's in a big box file with some of the stuff in manuscript and the rest as printed in the *LRB*. Opening the box, Andrew remarks that it's a long time since he's seen one of these, manuscripts nowadays generally coming in the form of a floppy disk. For my part I hope they don't notice the smear of jam on the box, the odd grease spot and even the faint odour of old milk, a consequence of the manuscript being put regularly in the fridge for safe-keeping whenever we go away. I used to keep my manuscripts in boxes on the floor of the kitchen but about twenty years or so ago I had a burst boiler which flooded the kitchen and ruined half of them. I told Miss Shepherd, then living in her van, of this disaster. 'Oh dear,' she said mustering what she could in the way of fellow-feeling. 'What a waste of water.'

16 October. Three former NatWest bankers in court over charges to do with the collapse of Enron and due to be extradited for trial in Texas. This doesn't get much coverage in the papers, with none at all in the *Independent* and in the *Guardian* confined to the business pages. Nor, I imagine, will they receive much sympathy generally, bankers, whether innocent or guilty, not having much appeal. But that we now have regulations that allow the United States to bundle away whomsoever it chooses for trial in America without needing to show any cause at all or even set out the evidence seems a monstrous erosion of civil liberties and one that has passed into law virtually unnoticed. That such a procedure, designed to expedite action against supposed terrorists, should straight away be used against defendants who are not terrorists at all points up its dangers. The legislation is, of course, not reciprocal, British courts having no such rights in the United States.

20 October. Memorial services apart, it's quite seldom that I see other writers, authorship not a particularly convivial profession. This does mean, though, that it still retains some of the glamour with which I invested it when I was young.

When I first got a room in college at Oxford it was on the staircase where a Professor Dawkins was in residence. Now old and crippled, as a young man he had known and been duped by Frederick Rolfe, Baron Corvo, the author of *Hadrian VII*, a book which in 1955 I had just read. I knew even then that it would be inappropriate ('not cool' I think would be today's term) to mention this to Professor Dawkins when I overtook him labouring up the stairs but I regarded him with awe.

Nevill Coghill was a Fellow of Exeter and he was dining in one night with a guest when I happened to be sitting low down on the scholars' table and so quite near the dons. I could hear every word of a (fairly one-sided) conversation the guest, a man with a harsh, quacking voice, was having with Nevill. It was Auden, still fairly smooth-faced, though already in carpet slippers and in Oxford to deliver his inaugural lecture as Professor of Poetry.

These literary connections will seem commonplace today but I was still young enough then not quite to believe that authors inhabited the same world as ordinary mortals, still less secondary school boys from Leeds, and so in this respect I did find Oxford immensely glamorous. Around this time I got talking to an Old Exonian, Joel Sayre, who had known Scott and Zelda Fitzgerald – as of course it was perfectly possible to have done in terms of time, Fitzgerald only having died fifteen or so years before. But it was worlds apart, not years, and I couldn't believe that the world of the author of *The Great Gatsby* could conceivably overlap with mine. And though I'm more sophisticated now some of this wonder happily remains, a persistent pleasure in life, even at seventy the feeling that one is still a small boy seeing giants.

21 October. This evening to Camden Town Hall for a meeting of the planning committee which will decide whether the new Kentish Town Health Centre gets the go-ahead. My doctor, Roy Macgregor, whose vision it is and who has spent the last ten years getting the scheme to this point, feels it may now fall at the last fence. Certainly he's at the end of his tether, though the public gallery is full of staff and patients like me, all of whom wish the scheme well. It's a crowded agenda and though the meeting starts at seven we don't reach the Health Centre project until after half past nine, the previous proceedings of mind-numbing tedium, leaving one both wondering why these councillors choose this as a way of occupying their time and grateful that they do. Eventually a planning officer presents our scheme but it's virtually inaudible; the opposition to it, chiefly from some local residents, is articulate and straightforward, so that though Roy makes a good and passionate speech it seems we shall lose. But when eventually at twenty past ten the vote is taken, against all expectations the building is accepted and we come out jubilant.

At one point I nearly blot my copybook when a councillor claims that the model is an inaccurate representation of the development because the trees are shown as too tall. 'But trees *grow*, haven't you heard?' I mutter far too loudly, wondering how Repton or Capability Brown would have fared before Camden Planning Committee. 'When will the trees reach this height, Mr Brown? In fifty years' time? That's an optimistic perspective surely?'

25 October. Due to go to Venice and Bologna for a week's holiday I damage an Achilles tendon which makes walking difficult and Venice impossible. Instead we take a slow and stopping journey northwards, calling first at Burford in Oxfordshire to look at the church. I must have been before but have no recollection of it, particularly the unexpected Romanesque core of the building which from its Perpendicular exterior seems like a typical fifteenth-century wool church.

At first the heart sinks to find the nave has lost its pews and is now filled with blue upholstered conference chairs arranged in a tell-tale semicircle. That churches should show any interest in God at all always puts R. off but there's plenty here to outweigh any children's cornery, particularly the early seventeenth-century Tanfield tomb where the free-standing angels above the columns are perched on pediments that are in fact breasts (nipple downwards). The memorial tablet to Edmund Harman, Henry VIII's doctor, is even more extraordinary, with figures in relief which are among the first representations of Native Americans but which seem less of the sixteenth than the early twentieth century and could well be mistaken for sculptures by Eric Gill.

27 October. We call at Stokesay Castle. It's an English Heritage property, as one might deduce from the sheet of paper torn from an exercise book and stuck on the gate of the car park: 'Closed today and tomorrow'. It's exactly the same at a later stopping point, English Heritage's Haughmond Abbey, only this time the torn sheet of paper reads: 'Closed till next April'. English Heritage curators are an eccentric lot, which I don't mind except that they seem to open and close their properties on a whim, 'Well, it's half-term' the probable excuse.

Still there are compensations, as denied access both to Stokesay Castle and Stokesay Church we wander round the graveyard and come upon the war memorial. It's of a soldier, solid and even squat, looking as much

French as English, and though it's strictly representational it has something of Vorticism about it, like a three-dimensional version of the figures that populate the paintings of William Roberts. There's a reluctance about the soldier, too, the heaviness of the figure more to do with resignation than any eager embracing of the military calling. One of my fellow conscripts in the army used to maintain that the pose of soldiers on war memorials only made sense if you thought of them as just having been caught skiving. And certainly this soldier hardly looks keen and definitely not noble. I've often wished there was a comprehensive study of war memorials even if it were only in the form of a register; they go largely unnoticed in guidebooks and I've never seen this stocky little squaddy reproduced. It's anonymous, too, with what seems like the name of the sculptor carved on the side of the plinth more probably an overflow from the list of the dead that fills the front.*

8 November. Sitting in the barber's chair this afternoon I wonder whether there were barbers in Auschwitz, Jews who were put aside before being killed to cut the hair not of the other Jews but of the officers and guards, and what such a barber's might have been like. One could see a film opening like this, a man in the chair covered by a sheet while a thin, nervous barber puts the finishing touches to his hair, holds up the mirror, dusts the back of his neck, then takes the sheet off to reveal someone in SS uniform.

These thoughts are occasioned by my barber, who is Moroccan or Algerian, not Jewish, but is thin and delicate and quite nervous, too, but much to be preferred to his two colleagues because he has very little English and so does not expect me to talk.

Also in the barber's chair I think about Alec Guinness. I don't know where he had his hair cut but it was probably somewhere in Mayfair, Trumper's possibly, or wherever smart, upper-class men go these days. Knowing Alec I imagine there would be a large tip, over-tipping his way

---

* A reader of the *LRB* subsequently wrote in to say that what is also remarkable about the memorial is that on the back, facing the hedge, is a list of those who returned safely from the war.

of coping with his social unease. The tip would be so large and Alec so bald it would probably have been possible to put a price on each individual hair.

14 November. Appropriately for Remembrance Day I am reading *Assault Division* by Norman Scarfe, a history of the 3rd Division from D-Day to the surrender of Germany, first published in 1947 and here reissued (Spellmount, £20).

Norman, now eighty and our leading local historian, particularly of East Anglia, was at the time of writing not much more than a schoolboy. He'd spent a year at Oxford before he was called up and at twenty found himself a gunnery officer attached to the 3rd Division in the first wave of landings on D-Day, firing his guns as the incoming tide lapped around his boots. He stayed with the division all that last year of the war, then went back to Oxford, where he wrote this book in the intervals of doing undergraduate essays on medieval history.

Military history so soon after the war was more tight-lipped than it subsequently became but the young Scarfe's exuberance keeps breaking in and with his jokes and digs and exclamation marks he's like a new old boy writing back to his school magazine. It's a humbling book, though, and an inspiring one, some of it unbearable to read, particularly the action on the first few days: Sherman tanks up-ended in the waves, drowning their helpless crews, and the beach raked by machine-gun fire from the shabby seaside promenade. Who now would willingly walk into such a hail of bullets and without recrimination?

I've always thought acting and soldiering had much in common though I hadn't realised it ran to a common interest in the reviews. Some units (and whole armies) were persistently unsung, with journalists then as now incapable of the proper ascription of credit, opting for the showy (e.g. Lord Lovat's arrival with his piper) rather than the death-defying slog that preceded it. This youthful book is both magnanimous and fair but later histories and memoirs were not so understanding and there would be much hoovering up of credit, not least by Montgomery himself.

It was this second Second World War, the fighting as seen through the prism of the 1950s and the films and clichés that came with it, that we were satirising in *Beyond the Fringe*. By that time the understatement that comes naturally to Norman Scarfe and the earliest chroniclers had turned into a trope, a specious and self-deprecating gloss applied to the many movies made about the war, and which nowadays seem comic.

With death everywhere this dry, factual book brings back the reality, as Remembrance Day and its attendant commemorations never entirely do, the sentiments attaching to these solemnities enlisted in whatever conflict we're engaged in. This year both Blair and the fox-hunters are keen to dabble us in the long-spilled blood. 'This was the freedom they died for.' No, it wasn't.

15 December. Handy hints: a garage I go to occasionally in Ilkley has a box of coppers by the till. If you're short of a penny or two you take some from the box and, though there's no obligation, if you get the odd penny in change you put it back. I am as happy getting rid of the odd penny as taking one since the end result is the same, reducing the amount of copper in one's pocket. With many bottles of unused coppers at home I wish this practice was more widespread.

Apropos shopping, I note that this year Sainsbury's profits have fallen. I have played a small part in this as I am increasingly reluctant to visit their Camden Town store, a grey, dingy steel and glass structure designed by Nicholas Grimshaw, who, in order to make room for his little bit of Danzig, demolished a pleasing and easily convertible Art Deco bakery that was previously on the site. Visiting the store has always been lowering to the spirit, though alleviated somewhat by an old-fashioned flower stall outside the back door, kept by a mother and daughter and where one could always buy posies of anemones. It persisted for some years until Sainsbury's itself decided to sell flowers (though not anemones), the mother and daughter lost their pitch, I lost any incentive to shop there and Sainsbury's profits fell accordingly. Did I know about economics, all this could probably be expressed in the form of an equation.

16 December. As I'm correcting the proofs of this diary the news comes of David Blunkett's resignation. It's hard not to welcome his departure, while at the same time deploring the manner of it: anyone hounded by the newspapers has my sympathy, even though in Blunkett's case the leaders of the pack were the very papers he had courted. Scarcely has he cleared his desk when the judges in the Lords condemn the indefinite detention of foreign nationals as unlawful, a judgement which, it's to be hoped, signals some sort of turning of the tide. Santa may call at Belmarsh if not at Guantánamo Bay.

Theatre and Plays

The Lady in the Van

After Miss Shepherd drove her van into my garden in 1974 friends used to ask me if I was planning to write a play about her. I wasn't, but twenty-five years later I have. There are plenty of reasons for the time lag, the most obvious being that it would have been very difficult to write about her when she was alive and, as it were, on site.

'How can I write about her?' says one of the Alan Bennetts in the play. 'She's *there*.' And although the line was later cut it remains true.

Miss Shepherd's presence in the garden didn't, of course, stop me jotting things down, making notes on her activities and chronicling her various comic encounters. Indeed, in my bleaker moments it sometimes seemed that this was all there was to note down since nothing else was happening to me, hence, I suppose, the plaintive denials that make up the last speech in the play.

Still, there was no question of writing or publishing anything about her until she was dead or gone from the garden, and as time passed the two came to seem the same thing. Occasionally newspapers took an interest and tried to blow the situation up into a jolly news item, but again, as is said in the play, the ramparts of privacy were more impregnable in those pre-Murdoch days and she was generally left to herself. Even journalists who came to interview me were often too polite to ask what an (increasingly whiffy) old van was doing parked a few feet from my door. If they did enquire I would explain, while asking them to keep it to themselves, which they invariably did. I can't think that these days there would be similar discretion.

Miss Shepherd helped, of course, lying low if anybody came to my door, and at night straight away switching off her light whenever she heard a foot-step. But though she was undoubtedly a recluse ('Is she', a neighbour once asked, 'a genuine eccentric?'), Miss Shepherd was not averse to the occasional bout of celebrity. I came back one day to find her posing beside the van for a woman columnist (gender did count with Miss S.) who had somehow sweet-talked her into giving an interview, Miss Shepherd managing in the process to imply that I had over the years systematically stifled her voice. If she has since achieved any fame or notoriety through my having written about her, I suspect that she would think it no more than her due and that her position as writer of pamphlets and political commentator entitled her to public recognition or, as she says in the play, 'the freedom of the land'.

It was this imaginary celebrity – I think the psychological term for it is 'delusion of reference' – that made her assume with every IRA bomb that she was next on the list. A disastrous fire in the Isle of Man meant, she was certain, that the culprit would now target her, and had she been alive at the time of Princess Diana's death she would have taken it as a personal warning to avoid travelling (in the van as distinct from a high-powered Mercedes) under the Pont d'Alma. In the first (and much longer) draft of the play this obsession was examined in more detail:

MISS SHEPHERD: Mr Bennett. Will you look under the van?

A. BENNETT: What for?

MISS SHEPHERD: One of these explosive devices. There was another bomb last night and I think I may be the next on the list.

A. BENNETT: Why you?

MISS SHEPHERD: Because of the Fidelis Party. The IRA may have got wind of it with a view to thwarting of reconciliation attempts, possibly. Look under the van.

A. BENNETT: I can't see anything because of all your plastic bags.

MISS SHEPHERD: Yes and the explosive's plastic so it wouldn't show, possibly. Are there any wires? The wireless tells you to look for wires. Nothing that looks like a timing device?

A. BENNETT: There's an old biscuit tin.

MISS SHEPHERD: No. That's not a bomb. It's just something that was on offer at FineFare. I ought to have special protection with being a party leader, increased risk through subverting of democracy, possibly.

A. BENNETT: Nobody knows you're leader of a party.

MISS SHEPHERD Well, it was on an anonymous footing but somebody may have spilled the beans. No organisation is watertight.

It's said of Robert Lowell that when he regularly went off his head it took the form of thinking he could rub shoulders with Beethoven, Voltaire and other all-time greats, with whom he considered himself to be on equal terms. (Actually Isaiah Berlin, about whose sanity there was no doubt, made exactly the same assumption, but that's by the way.) The Virgin Mary excepted, Miss Shepherd's sights were set rather lower. Her assumed equals were Harold Wilson, Mr Heath and (as she always called him) 'Enoch' and I was constantly being badgered to find out their private addresses so that they could be sent the latest copy of *True View*. Atypically for someone unbalanced, Miss Shepherd never seemed to take much interest in the Royal Family, the Queen and the Duke of Edinburgh never thought of as potential readers. This did not mean, though, that she was a disloyal subject and on the occasion of the Queen's Jubilee in 1977 there was only one flag to be seen in our well-to-do socialist street and that was in the back window of the van where only I could see it.

To begin with I wrote the play in three acts, knowing, though, that these days this is not a popular format. Still, that's how Miss Shepherd's story seemed to present itself, the first act consisting of her life in the street and culminating with her driving the van into the garden; the second act was life in the garden (all fifteen years of it); and the third act the events leading to her death and departure. The trouble with this way of telling the story was that whereas there was movement built into the first act (the lead-up to her arrival) and movement in the third (her decline and death), Act Two simply consisted of her being there, parked in the garden and going nowhere, the only movement me occasionally going up the wall.

A second draft condensed the material into two acts, and though the passage of time within the play was perhaps not as clear, the passage of time within the theatre was altogether more acceptable, an hour each way quite enough for me. As Churchill said, the mind cannot take in more than the seat will endure.

Telling the truth crops up quite a bit in the play, what Miss Shepherd did or didn't do a subject of some disagreement between 'the boys', as I tended to think of the two Alan Bennetts. They call not telling the truth 'lying', but 'the imagination' would be a kinder way of putting it, with Alan Bennett the writer finally winning through to make Miss Shepherd talk of her past (as she never actually did) and even to bring her back from the dead in order to take her bodily up to heaven (also imaginary).

These departures from the facts were genuinely hard won and took some coming to, causing me to reflect, not for the first time, that the biggest handicap for a writer is to have had a decent upbringing. Brought up not to lie or show off, I was temperamentally inclined to do both, particularly as a small child, and though reining me in perhaps improved my character, it was no help in my future profession where lying, or romancing anyway, is the essence of it.

Nor did my education help. One of the difficulties I had in writing *The Madness of George III* was that, having been educated as a historian, I found it hard ever to take leave of the facts. With George III's first bout of madness the facts needed scarcely any alteration to make them dramatic and only a little tweaking was required, but even that I found hard to do. It was still harder to play around with the facts of Miss Shepherd's life, although the only person to know how much I may have doctored her history is me. And actually, while I've obviously had to compress a good deal, I haven't had to alter much at all. It's true, though, that a lengthier account of the events leading up to her moving into the garden with the van would make this development less dramatic, and less of a turning point.

What happened was that one night several of the van's windows were broken by two drunks, an incident that occurs in the play. This meant that Miss Shepherd was now much more at the mercy of the elements, the faded cretonne curtains which covered one or two of the windows her only protection from the weather and from prying eyes. I had a lean-to down some steps at the side of my house and now ran an electric lead out to this hut, so that on cold nights she could go in there to keep warm. Inevitably she began to spend the night there on a regular basis, the van becoming part office, part wardrobe, a repository for her pamphlets and her clothes and the place where she would spend what she saw as her working day.

As I write I see Michael Frayn walking up the street en route from his home to his office nearby, where he writes. Miss Shepherd's routine was not very different, in this instance as in others mentioned in the play her life not as dissimilar from that of her neighbours as they would have liked to think. They had offices to go to and so did she. They had second homes and, having acquired a Robin Reliant, so did she, a parallel which Miss Ferris, the irritatingly patient (and somewhat jargon-ridden) social worker in the play, is not slow to point out. But with Miss Shepherd going to and from her sleeping quarters in the hut to her office in the van it meant that I got used to her crossing the garden in front of my window, so that when she did finally move in, bags and all, it was neither the surprise nor the life-changing decision (for both of us) that the play perhaps implies.

Over the years Miss Shepherd was visited by a succession of social workers, so Miss Ferris is a composite figure. To begin with the social workers got short shrift, their only function in Miss Shepherd's view to procure her concessions from the council: another walking stick, an additional wheelchair 'in case this one conks out, possibly' and (a dream she never attained) the electrified chair in which she saw herself moving regally through the streets of Camden Town.

A composite, too, are the neighbours, Pauline and Rufus, though I have made Rufus a publisher in remembrance of my neighbour, the late Colin

Haycraft, the proprietor of Duckworth's. Married to the novelist Alice Thomas Ellis, he regarded Miss Shepherd with a sceptical eye, never moderating his (not unpenetrating) voice when he was discussing her, though she might well be in the van only a few feet away. He, I'm sure, thought I was mad to let her stay. Still, he came to her funeral and as the coffin was slid into the hearse he remarked loudly as ever, 'Well, it's a cut above her previous vehicle.'

Like Rufus in the play, Colin had little time for feminism. I once asked him if he was jealous of his wife's literary success. 'Good God, no. One couldn't be jealous of a woman, surely?'

Though the character of Underwood is a fiction, invented in order to hint at something unexplained in Miss Shepherd's past (and ultimately to explain it), he had, certainly as regards his appearance, a basis in fact. When the van was still parked in the street the late Nicholas Tomalin and I had been mobilised by Miss Shepherd to push it forward a few yards to a fresh location. I wrote in my diary:

> As we are poised for the move another Camden Town eccentric mater-
> ialises, a tall, elderly figure in a long overcoat and Homburg hat with a
> distinguished grey moustache and in his buttonhole a flag for the
> Primrose League. Removing a grubby canary glove he leans a shaking
> hand against the rear of the van in a token gesture of assistance and
> when we have moved it the few statutory feet he puts the glove on
> again, saying grandly, 'If you should need me in the future, I'm just
> around the corner' – i.e. in Arlington House.

For all the doubts I voice about tramps in the play, when one comes across such a fugitive from *Godot* it's hard not to think that Beckett's role as social observer has been underestimated.

I have allowed myself a little leeway in speculating about Miss Shepherd's concert career, though if, as her brother said, she had studied with Cortot she must have been a pianist of some ability. Cortot was the leading French pianist between the wars, Miss Shepherd presumably studying with him at the height of his fame. Continuing to give concerts throughout the Occupation, he finished the war under a cloud and it was perhaps this that sent him on a concert tour to England, where I remember seeing his photograph on posters sometime in the late forties. Perhaps Miss Shepherd saw it too, though by this time her hopes of a concert career must have been fading, a vocation as a nun already her goal.

Her war had been spent driving ambulances, a job for which she had presumably enlisted and been trained and which marked the beginning of her lifelong fascination with anything on wheels. Comically she figures in my mind alongside the Queen, who as Princess Elizabeth also did war service and as an ATS recruit was filmed in a famous piece of wartime propaganda changing the wheel on an army lorry, a vehicle my mother fondly believed HRH drove for the duration of hostilities.

What with land girls, nurses, WAAFs, the ATS and Wrens, these were years of cheerful, confident, seemingly carefree women and I'd like to think of Miss Shepherd as briefly one of them, having the time of her life: accompanying a singsong in the NAAFI perhaps, snatching a meal in a British restaurant, then going to the pictures to see Leslie Howard or Joan Fontaine. It was maybe this taste of wartime independence that later unsuited her for the veil, or it may be, as her brother suggested, that she suffered shellshock after a bomb exploded near her ambulance. At any rate she was invalided out and this was when her troubles began, with, in her brother's view, the call of the convent a part of it.

I would have liked her concert career to have outlasted the war or to have resumed after the duration, when the notion of a woman playing the piano against psychological odds was the theme of the film *The Seventh Veil* (1945), with Ann Todd as the pianist Francesca and James Mason her tyrannical stick-wielding Svengali. Enormously popular at the time (and with it the Grieg Piano Concerto), the film set the tone for a generation of glamorous pianists, best known of whom was Eileen Joyce, who was reputed to change her frock between movements.

The Seventh Veil was subsequently adapted for the stage and I still have the programme of the matinee I saw at the Grand Theatre in Leeds in March 1951. The Grieg Concerto had by this time been replaced by

Rachmaninov Number Two and James Mason by Leo Genn, but it was still Ann Todd, her guardian as ever bringing his stick down across her fingers as she cowered at the keyboard.

If Miss Shepherd had ever made it to the concert circuit this would be when I might have seen her, as I was by now going every week to symphony concerts in Leeds Town Hall where Miss Shepherd would have taken her place alongside Daphne Spottiswoode or Phyllis Sellick, Moura Lympany, Valda Aveling and Gina Bachauer – artistes with their décolleté, shawl-collared gowns as glamorous and imposing in my fourteen-year-old eyes as fashion models, Barbara Goalens of the keyboard, brought to their feet by the conductor to acknowledge the applause then sinking in a curtsy to receive the obligatory flowers just as, in memory anyway, Miss Shepherd does in the play.

When I wrote the original account I glossed over the fact that Miss Shepherd's death occurred the same night that, washed and in clean things, she returned from the day centre. I chose not to make this plain because for Miss Shepherd to die then seemed so handy and convenient, just when a writer would (if a little obviously) have chosen for her to die. So I note that I was nervous not only of altering the facts to suit the drama but of even seeming to have altered them. But that night or in the early hours of the morning was when she did die, the nurse who took her to the day centre (who wasn't the social worker) saying that she had come across several cases when someone who had lived rough had seemed somehow to know that death was imminent and had made preparations accordingly, in Miss Shepherd's case not merely seeing that she was washed and made more presentable but the previous week struggling to confession and Mass.

A year or so earlier when Miss Shepherd had been ill I'd tried to get some help from what remained of the convent at the top of the street. I got nowhere but the visit confirmed me in my low opinion of nuns, or this particular order anyway. Another cut:

A. BENNETT 2: Nuns, it seems to me, took the wrong turning at the
same point as British Rail. Around the time that porters were

forced to forsake their black serge waistcoats, monkey jackets and oilcloth caps, so some monastic Dr Beeching decreed that nuns lose their billowing wimpled innocence and come on like prison wardresses in grey Tricel twinsets.

WOMAN: Yes?

A. BENNETT: I live down the street.

WOMAN: You do. I've seen you. It's you that has the van.

A. BENNETT: Yes.

WOMAN: Difficult woman.

A. BENNETT: A Catholic.

WOMAN: One of the sisters remembers her. You're not Catholic?

A. BENNETT: No.

WOMAN: A novice. It may have been twice. Had two stabs at it. It takes a special type.

A. BENNETT 2: Cold brown lino on the floor, dimpled from being so often polished. Room spotless and uncomforting, the only ornament a crucifix.

WOMAN: It's not an ornament at all.

A. BENNETT: I've been told she was very argumentative.

WOMAN: Disputatious she was. I've had her pointed out to me on that account. Chalking on the pavement and so on.

A. BENNETT: That's all in the past. Did she play the piano?

WOMAN: She did not. This is a house of God. There is no piano here. Anyway what is it you want?

A. BENNETT: She's ill.

WOMAN: Who? The woman?

A. BENNETT: I wondered if there was a nun available who could talk to her, do her some shopping.

WOMAN: We don't have shopping nuns. It's a strict order.

A. BENNETT: I've seen them shopping. I saw one yesterday in Marks and Spencer. She was buying meringues.

WOMAN: The Bishop may have been coming.

A. BENNETT: Does he like meringues?

WOMAN: What business is it of yours what the Monsignor likes? Who are you, coming round asking if the Bishop likes meringues? Are you a Communist?

A. BENNETT: I just thought there must be nuns with time on their hands.

WOMAN: They don't have time on their hands. That's what prayer is for.

A. BENNETT: But she's ill. She's a Catholic. I think she may be dying.

WOMAN: They can pray for her, only you'll have to fill in a form. She'll probably pull her socks up once your back is turned. That's been my experience where invalids are concerned.

I make no apology for the fact that Miss Shepherd makes great play with place names: St Albans, Bodmin, Hounslow, Staines. Since the oddity of place names is a staple of English comedy I might be accused of introducing Dunstable, say, for an easy laugh. I was once taken to task by a critic for using Burgess Hill in a play, a name devoid of comic overtones for me but thought by the critic to be a sure indicator of my triviality of mind. I'd actually just been hard put to think of a place and asked the actor who had the line (it was Valentine Dyall) where he lived, hence Burgess Hill. But with Miss Shepherd the extended landscape of places she had known was very real to this now largely stationary wanderer and they were still vivid in her mind as the objects of journeys she was always planning (and sometimes threatening) to make.

When our paths first crossed in the late sixties there was much less dereliction on the streets of London than there is today. Camden Town had its resident company of tramps and eccentrics, it's true, by no means all of them homeless or beggars, but they were as an aristocracy compared with the dozens of young poor and homeless that nowadays sleep in its doorways and beg on its streets. Several of these ancient archetypal figures were long-time residents of Arlington House, among the last of the Rowton Houses that provided cheap accommodation for working men in London, the one in Camden Town still happily functioning today. Nowadays, though, the windows of its individual cubicles look across to spacious executive apartments and over the restaurants, clubs and all the tawdry chaos of Camden Lock, which to my mind is far more offensive and destructive of the area than the beggars have ever been.

Another speech cut from the play:

> There is a community in dereliction even though it may not amount to much more than passing round a bottle. This seems especially apparent in Camden Town, where the doorway of the periodically defunct Odeon or the steps of the drop-in centre opposite are home to a band of social dysfuncts notable for their indiscriminate conviviality and sudden antipathies. Itinerant in that they periodically move on, or are made to do so, they do not go far, the premises of any enterprise that shows signs of faltering ('Shocking Discounts', 'Everything Must Go') likely to be immediately roosted by this crew of slurred and contentious intoxicates.

Miss Shepherd, though, never thought of herself as a tramp. As a potential prime minister, how could she?

A. BENNETT 2: Our neighbourhood is peopled by several commanding widows and wives: there is Lady Pritchett, the wife of Sir Victor; there is Mrs Vaughan Williams, the widow of the composer; and occasionally to be seen is Elizabeth Jane Howard, the novelist and sometime wife of Kingsley Amis. All tall, grand roost-ruling women possessed of great self-confidence and assured of their position in the world. It is of this substantial sisterhood that Miss Shepherd sees herself as a natural member.

After Miss Shepherd died in April 1989 I had no immediate plans to write about her or any idea of the kind of thing I wanted to write, but it was coming up to the tenth anniversary of the *London Review of Books* and I had promised Mary-Kay Wilmers that I would contribute something. So I put together an account of Miss Shepherd, using some of the material from my diaries and quoting from the pamphlets of hers that I had saved

377

or rescued from the van. After this account had been published I had one or two stabs at turning it into a play but without success. Miss Shepherd's story was not difficult to tell; it was my own story over the same period that defeated me. Not that there was a great deal to be said, but somehow the two stories had to interconnect. It was only when I had the notion of splitting myself into two that the problem seemed to solve itself.

Still, very little of my own life is revealed, too little for one of the Alan Bennetts who, having brought the play to a conclusion, breaks back to speak directly to the audience (a function he's previously left to his partner):

> Look. This has been one path through my life . . . me and Miss
> Shepherd. Just one track. I wrote things; people used to come and
> stay the night, and of both sexes. What I mean to say is, it's not as if
> it's the whole picture. Lots of other stuff happened. No end of things.

The device of having two actors playing me isn't just a bit of theatrical showing off and does, however crudely, correspond to the reality. There was one bit of me (often irritated and resentful) that had to deal with this unwelcome guest camped literally on my doorstep, but there was another bit of me that was amused by how cross this eccentric lodger made me and that took pleasure in Miss Shepherd's absurdities and her outrageous demands.

There is no satisfactory way of dubbing these two parts (I would not call them halves) of my personality, and even if 'the writer' would do for one, what is the other? The person? The householder? Or (a phrase from the courts) 'the responsible adult'? As I wrote them first they were like an old married couple, complaining and finding fault with one another, nothing one thought or said a surprise to the other. I then started to find more fun in their relationship, made it teasing and even flirtatious, a line that the actors Nicholas Farrell and Kevin McNally made more of in rehearsal.

Alan Bennett the author then became definitely more mischievous, more amoral, than the Alan Bennett who goes out dutifully in his Marigold gloves in order to scoop his unsavoury lodger's poop, so that in some sense the division between them illustrates Kafka's remark that to write is to do the devil's work. Of course Kafka doesn't imply the converse, that scooping the poop (or fetching Miss Shepherd her sherbet lemons) is God's work. I never felt it so and resented neighbours or well-wishers who cast me in the saintly role, preferring to be thought of as a fool. Still, there was no way of ducking these attributions of goodness, as the more I rebutted them the more selfless I seemed. 'Kind is so tame,' says Kevin McNally in the play, and that at least comes from the heart.

In one particular instance, I wish the part of me Kevin McNally plays had in life been more venturesome. The cheap commercialisation of Camden High Street was just getting into its stride in 1989 when Miss Shepherd died but it was already far enough advanced for fliers about new boutiques and cafés to be put regularly through my door. At that time I let slip several opportunities that someone of a more mischievous temper than mine might well have taken up. Being on the electoral roll, Miss Shepherd was sent as many circulars as I was, including several from restaurants offering a free dinner (generally candlelit) to potential customers. I didn't avail myself of any of these offers but I regret now that I didn't pass on her vouchers to Miss Shepherd, as I would quite like to have seen the scene in such a restaurant with Miss Shepherd scowling and slurping (and smelling), surrounded by the appalled residents of Primrose Hill.

We were fortunate with the play to have a long rehearsal period (five and a half weeks) plus two weeks of previews, a time in which the anticipated difficulties of getting the van onto the stage and hoisting it off could be dealt with. In the event there were few problems with the van or the Robin Reliant, which also does a tour of the stage. What took up the time was the text, in particular the presentation of the two selves. Should they be dressed alike, for instance, in sports coat, M&S corduroys, suede shoes, the clothes I like to think I just happened to be wearing when the designer, Mark Thompson, paid me a visit, but near enough, I suppose, to what I wear every day? But are these the proper garments of my inner voice? Should the other self be put into something more sophisticated and metropolitan, black trousers, perhaps, a black polo neck?

In the end we decided that would be simplistic and so the two selves were dressed alike, and though this means that some of the audience are a bit slow to understand what is going on, it is probably better and sillier (which I like) to make them Tweedledum and Tweedledee. They were luckier than Maggie Smith, who as Miss Shepherd had to deck herself out in a variety of outfits, many of them quick changes, which had to be achieved in the cramped interior of the van.

Over the years Miss Shepherd had four or five vans, of which in the stage production we see two: the one (donated by Lady Wiggin) which she drives onto the stage halfway through the first act, and another, supposedly the same, on which the curtain rises for Act Two, but since this is several years later now transformed by Miss Shepherd's usual coat of scrambled egg or badly made custard. Miss Shepherd's fascination with any aid to locomotion meant that she over-supplied herself not only with vans but even with walking sticks, of which she had many, one of which Maggie Smith uses in the play. It still bears traces of Miss Shepherd's characteristic yellow paint, evidence of her last painting job done on the three-wheeler which she parked outside my gate, where (another relic) the kerb still shows a few tell-tale yellow spots.

The three-wheeler had a predecessor, a battered Mini, but this was stolen only a month or two after Miss Shepherd acquired it and was later found abandoned in the basement of the council flats in Maiden Lane near King's Cross. Like the Reliant, its chief function had been as a supplementary wardrobe and it was thus heavily pervaded by Miss Shepherd's characteristic odour. I felt slightly sorry for the thieves (who were never, of course, caught), imagining them making off with the vehicle and only as they sped illicitly through Camden Town being hit by the awfulness of what it contained, this realisation signalled by expressions of vernacular fastidiousness such as 'Do me a favour!', 'Cor, strike a light!' or, as the scent took hold, 'Jesus wept!' So that when, having gone to Maiden Lane to recover some of her papers from the car, I found it bearing a Police Aware notice, I felt that it had, in this case, a heightened significance.

I have always spelled her name Shepherd but I think the correct spelling, if an assumed name can have a correct spelling, was Sheppard, the difference, I suppose, distinguishing between the character whom I knew and the one I have written about. At one early stage, out of a courtesy which was probably even then old-fashioned, I called her Mrs Shepherd, a designation which she did not immediately correct. Nowadays, of course, such delicacy seems misplaced, and also fanciful, because if she was Mrs Shepherd there must have been a Mr Shepherd and he would be very hard to imagine.

Miss Shepherd was solipsistic to a degree, and in her persistent refusal to take into account the concerns or feelings of anyone else except herself and her inability to see the world and what happened in it except as it affected her, she behaved more like a man than a woman. I took this undeviating selfishness to have something to do with staying alive. Gratitude, humility, forgiveness or fellow feelings were foreign to her nature or had become so over the years, but had she been otherwise she might not have survived as long as she did. She hated noise, though she made plenty, particularly when sitting in her three-wheeler on a Sunday morning revving the engine to recharge the battery. She hated children. Reluctant to have the police called when the van's window had been broken and herself hurt, she would want the law summoning if there were children playing in the street and making what she considered too much noise or indeed any noise at all.

She inhabited a different world from ordinary humanity, a world in which the Virgin Mary could be encountered outside the post office in Parkway and Mr Khrushchev higher up the street; a world in which her advice was welcomed by world leaders and the College of Cardinals took note of her opinion. Seeing herself as the centre of this world, she had great faith in the power of the individual voice, even though it could only be heard through pamphlets photocopied at Prontaprint or read on the pavement outside Williams and Glyns Bank.

Though I never questioned Miss Shepherd on the subject, what intrigued me about the regular appearances put in by the Virgin Mary was that she seldom turned up in her traditional habiliments; no sky-blue veil for her, still less a halo. Before leaving heaven for earth the BVM always seemed to go through the dressing-up box so that she could come down as Queen Victoria, say, or dressed in what sounded very much like a sari. And not only her. One of my father's posthumous appearances was as a Victorian statesman, and an old tramp, grey-haired and not undistinguished, was confidently identified as St Joseph (though minus his donkey), just as I was taken briefly for St John.

With their fancy dress and a good deal of gliding about, it was hard not to find Miss Shepherd's visions comic, but they were evidence of a faith that manifestly sustained her and a component of her daily and difficult life. In one of her pamphlets she mentions the poet Francis Thompson, who was as Catholic as she was (and who lived in similar squalor). Her vision of the intermingling of this world and the next was not unlike his:

> But (when so sad thou canst not sadder)
> Cry: – and upon thy so sore loss
> Shall shine the traffic of Jacob's ladder
> Pitched betwixt Heaven and Charing Cross.
>
> Yea, in the night, my Soul, my daughter,
> Cry, – clinging Heaven by the hems;
> And lo, Christ walking on the water
> Not of Gennesareth, but Thames!

It's now ten years since Miss Shepherd died, but hearing a van door slide shut will still take me back to the time when she was in the garden. For Marcel, the narrator in Proust's *Remembrance of Things Past*, the sound that took him back was that of the gate of his aunt's idyllic garden; with me it's the door of a broken-down Commer van. The discrepancy is depressing but then most writers discover quite early on that they're not going to be Proust. Besides, I couldn't have heard my own garden gate because in order to deaden the (to her) irritating noise Miss Shepherd had insisted on me putting a piece of chewing gum on the latch.

The National Theatre

The first time I ever set foot on the stage at the National was in November 1987 at the Cottesloe. It was an inauspicious debut. Patrick Garland had put together an evening of Philip Larkin's poetry and prose entitled *Down Cemetery Road*, done as a two-hander with Alan Bates as Larkin. This was then revived at short notice for some extra performances but Alan wasn't available and I agreed to substitute. The change of cast hadn't been advertised and many of the audience, having come along expecting to see Alan Bates, must just have thought he'd gone downhill a bit since they last saw him wrestling naked on a rug with Oliver Reed.

I was also in the middle of some extensive dentistry, which involved the removal of several bridges and, though the dentist had assured me that the effects of the anaesthetic would have worn off long before the evening's performance, I often took the stage feeling as if large sections of my mouth were coned off. The anaesthetic did indeed wear off during the course of the performance so that when I hit a suddenly tender spot there was the occasional agonised yelp uncatered for in Larkin's muted verse. Even at the best of times the poet didn't care for the public performance of his works so it was perhaps fortunate he had died two years previously.

What the audience felt I tried not to think though I remember coming off at the interval and en route for my dressing-room meeting Judi Dench and her attendants bound for the Olivier stage. 'Not many laughs tonight,' I said. 'None at all with us,' she replied, but since she was appearing in *Antony and Cleopatra* this was hardly surprising. They had one unscheduled laugh one night, though, as it was while she was giving her Cleopatra that Judi was made a dame. On the evening in question Michael Bryant, playing Enobarbus, turned upstage and muttered en passant, 'Well, I suppose a fuck's *quite* out of the question now', an extra-textual remark, such is Michael's never other than immaculate diction, that was heard by the first ten rows.

About the NT building itself I've always had reservations. It's better inside than out with the foyers, in particular, interesting and lively and even living up to those fanciful illustrations in which architects populate their constructions with idly gossiping creatures who seem to have all the time in the world. They always have oval heads and are wholly intent on using the space the architect has so thoughtfully provided. Oval heads apart, the foyer of the National is a bit like that and works, just as Denys Lasdun envisaged it should.

Nor are the three theatres too bad, with the Olivier, to my mind, the best. From an actor's point of view (or that of someone with a weak bladder) the huge central block of seats of the Lyttelton is daunting. The Olivier is more broken up, though that, too, has its drawbacks and it's said that Michael Gambon got so accustomed to playing the vast space that even in private conversation he would still slowly move through the necessary arc.

The outside of the building, though, I've never much cared for, which is harder to admit since I was impressed by Denys Lasdun talking about it on television not long before he died. The first truly modern architecture I saw as a boy in 1951 was the Royal Festival Hall, which I've always found exciting, light, airy and playful, which the National isn't at all. I don't like stacked horizontals, which Denys Lasdun plainly did as they figure in the National and in his Royal College of Physicians building in Regent's Park. Moreover the back parts of the theatre seem to me both depressing and inadequate. Actors are used to slumming it, particularly in the West End, but there was no excuse for treating the backstage as if it were the servants' quarters.

That said, though, I've no doubt that the building will grow in the public's affections. The appeal of most modern buildings slowly diminishes over a period of fifty or sixty years at which low point they stand in greatest danger of demolition or substantial alteration. If they survive that then they begin to acquire a period charm and their future is assured and so, I imagine, it will be with the NT.

A few years after the building had opened the late Ronald Eyre, having directed one or two productions here, said that it would be better for all concerned if the National Theatre could straight away close again and be converted into an ice rink and/or dance hall . . . the Olivier, I suppose most suited for the ice rink, the Lyttelton for the *palais de danse*. Then, after twenty years or so, when the corners had been rubbed off the building and it had acquired its own shabby and disreputable history, all the cultural stuffing long since knocked out of it and every breath of Art dispersed, it would be time for it to be reclaimed for the theatre. As it was it was too much of a temple for him and altogether too worthy; somewhere ordinary was what he wanted and with no pretensions.

It's certainly true that audiences (and critics in particular) come to the National Theatre in a different frame of mind from when they go to see a play on Shaftesbury Avenue. They're more reverential, more inclined to invest what they're seeing with significance (or deplore its absence). It's all in capital letters: Art, Theatre; it's never just a play. I first noticed this twenty-five years ago in the Lyttelton. It was the second night of the opening week and the play was John Osborne's *Watch It Come Down*. It wasn't one of his best but as always with Osborne even when I disliked the play I found his tone sympathetic. I was in a minority. To give a flavour of the audience, Edward Heath was sitting in front, Alec Douglas-Home behind and the rest looked as if they'd come on reluctantly after the Lord Mayor's Banquet. Of course, audiences were bound to get better and broader and they have but there's still a feeling that this is Something Special; it's not yet the community-minded place that subsidised theatres (those that survive) manage to be in the provinces.

Nor is it particularly comforting. When I was acting in *Single Spies* I never got over the nightly walk along the corridor from my dressing-room, pushing through the swing doors and suddenly being hit by the amplified roar of the audience. They were just chatting before curtain up but to me they sounded like the crowd at the Colosseum waiting for the massacre to begin.

Mind you, this is not peculiar to the National Theatre. All theatre is theatre of blood. I once had to give a talk at the West Yorkshire Playhouse and was accosted on my way in by two sabre-toothed pensioners:

'It had better be good,' warned one of them. 'We're big fans of yours.'

Still, whatever its shortcomings or the fear that stalks its corridors, the bleakness of the building has always been compensated for by the cheerfulness of the staff and I have never felt other than welcome here. This is particularly true at the stage door and in the visiting directors' office, run in my time by Ghita Cohen and Sharon Duckworth. It was a cosy spot where you could always drop in for gossip and a not always loyal verdict on current productions. Royal visit nothing, Ghita's retirement party last year was one of the most distinguished occasions the theatre has seen in all its twenty-five years.

Ghita could always procure house seats even for the most sought-after shows though one didn't always need them. One of the inestimable privileges enjoyed when working at the National is the use of the directors' boxes at the back of the stalls of both the Lyttelton and the Olivier. Both are entered not through the auditorium so that one can slip in and see an act of a play then slip out again, much as one could at a Victorian music hall. As a playwright I perhaps ought to deplore such bite-size theatre but it suits me no end. The boxes are also soundproof so one can even groan aloud.

With all my grumblings, I am thankful to have had a small part in the National's history. *The Wind in the Willows* and *The Madness of George III*, both directed by Nicholas Hytner, were two of the happiest plays I've worked on and when I recall the ending of the first part of *Wind in the Willows* with the snow coming down and the mice singing 'In the Bleak Midwinter' and the wonderful bravura opening of *The Madness of George*

III when the whole cast comes over the crest of the hill and down onto the stage, I am glad to have been at least the occasion for such spectacle.

Of *Single Spies* my memories are only less fond because the cast was quite small and looming up at the end of rehearsal there was the awful prospect of having to go on stage and do it. Also, though the technical side of it wasn't particularly complicated, things did tend to go wrong. In the scene in Buckingham Palace where the Queen comes upon Anthony Blunt hanging a picture, there were two console tables trucked in from stage left and stage right. On the tables were various *objets d'art* which the Queen would pick up and comment on as she chatted to her Keeper of Pictures. These tables had a life of their own, only occasionally trucking on submissively as they were meant to do, but more often coming on, taking one look at the audience then retreating shyly into the wings. This meant that Prunella Scales, playing the Queen, instead of idly fingering an object and discoursing on its origins ('This ostrich egg was a present from the people of Zambia') had instead to dive off stage, locate the item in question and fetch it on for Sir Anthony to admire, so that she looked less like the Monarch than one of those beady ladies queuing up with their treasures on the *Antiques Roadshow*.

The History Boys

I have generally done well in examinations and not been intimidated by them. Back in 1948, when I took my O levels – or School Certificate, as it was then called – I was made fun of by the other boys in the class because on the morning of the first paper I turned up in a suit. It was my only suit and already too small, but to wear it didn't seem silly to me then as I thought the examination was an occasion and that I must rise to it accordingly.

Ten years or so later I took my Finals at Oxford and dressed up again. This time, though, nobody laughed as we were all dressed up in the suit, white tie, mortar board and gown that were obligatory for the occasion. This was, I suppose, the last and most significant examination in my life, and it was in this examination that I cheated, just as I had cheated a few years before to get the scholarship that took me to Oxford in the first place.

I was not dishonest; I kept to the rules and didn't crib, and nobody else would have called it cheating, then or now, but it has always seemed so to me. False pretences, anyway.

I was educated at Leeds Modern School, a state school which in the forties and early fifties regularly sent boys on to Leeds University but seldom to Oxford or Cambridge. I don't recall the sixth form in my year being considered outstandingly clever but in 1951, for the first time, the headmaster, who had been at Cambridge himself, made an effort to push some of his university entrants towards the older universities. Snobbery was part of it, I imagine, and by the same token he switched the school from playing soccer to rugger, though since I avoided both this had little impact on me. However, there were about eight of us sixth-formers who went up for the examinations and we all managed to get in, and some even to be awarded scholarships.

Though that's a situation which seems to mirror that of *The History Boys*, the play has nothing to do with my contemporaries, only a couple of whom were historians anyway, but it does draw on some of the pains and the excitement of working for a scholarship at a time when Oxford and Cambridge were as daunting and mysterious to me as to any of the boys in the play.

The first hurdle, more intimidating to me than any examination, was having to go up to Cambridge and stay in the college for the weekend. I had seldom been away from home and was not equipped for travel. I fancy a sponge bag had to be bought, but since at seventeen I still didn't shave, there wasn't much to go in it; my mother probably invested in some better pyjamas for me, but that was it. A stock vision of an undergraduate then (gleaned from movies like Robert Taylor in *A Yank at Oxford*) was of a young man in dressing gown and slippers, a towel round his neck, en route for the distant baths. I didn't run to a dressing gown and slippers either: 'Nobody'll mind if you just wear your raincoat,' my mother reassuringly said. I wasn't reassured but there was a limit to what my parents could afford.

It all seems absurd now, but not then. For all I knew someone who went to the baths in a raincoat and his ordinary shoes might not be the sort of undergraduate the college was looking for. And droll though these misgivings seem, then they were more real than any worries about the examination itself, and they persisted long after examinations were over, my social and class self-consciousness not entirely shed until years after my education proper was finished.

December 1951 was sunny but bitterly cold, and though there was no snow the Cam was frozen and the lawns and quadrangles white with frost; coming to it from the soot and grime of the West Riding, I had never seen or imagined a place of such beauty. And even today the only place that has enchanted me as much as Cambridge did then is Venice.

It was out of term, the university had gone down and apart from candidates like myself who had come up for the examination there was nobody about. But then that was true of most English country towns in the early 1950s, when tourism was not yet an option. I walked through King's, past Clare, Trinity Hall and Caius, and then through the back gate of Trinity and out into Trinity Great Court, and thought that this was how all cities should be. Nothing disconcerted this wondering boy, and I even managed to find the smell of old dinner that clung to the screens passage in the college halls somehow romantic and redolent of the past. And in those days one could just wander at will, go into any chapel or library, so that long after dusk I was still patrolling this enchanted place. Starved for antiquity, Hector says of himself in the play, and that was certainly true of me.

Gothick rather than Gothic, Sidney Sussex, the college of my choice, wasn't quite my taste in buildings, but I was realistic about what I was entitled to expect both architecturally and academically, and (with Balliol the exception) the nastier a college looked the lower seemed to be its social and academic status. You had to be cleverer than I was or from higher up the social scale to have the real pick of the architecture.

It was unnerving to be interviewed by dons who had actually written books one had read. At Sidney it was the historian David Thomson, with whose face I was familiar from the back of his Penguin. What surprised me, though, was the geniality of everyone and their kindness, though I'm familiar with it now, even as recently as this play. Being interviewed for Cambridge is not unlike being auditioned, only now my role is reversed. I hope I am just as genial and twinkling with our would-be performers as David Thomson and R. C. Smail were with me.

If the dons were genial, some of my fellow candidates were less so. That weekend was the first time I had ever come across public schoolboys in the mass, and I was appalled. They were loud, self-confident and all seemed to know one another, shouting down the table to prove it while also being shockingly greedy.

I had always found eating in public a nervous business, the way one was supposed to eat, like the way one was supposed to speak, a delicate area. I had only just learned, for instance, that the polite way when finishing your soup was to tip the plate away from you. I soon realised that this careful manoeuvre was not a refinement that was going to take me very far, not in this company anyway. Unabashed by the imposing surroundings in which they found themselves or (another first for me) being waited on by men, these boys hogged the bread, they slurped the soup and bolted whatever was put on their plates with medieval abandon. Public school they might be, but they were louts. Seated at long refectory tables, the walls hung with armorial escutcheons and the mellow portraits of Tudor and Stuart grandees, neat, timorous and genteel, we grammar schoolboys were the interlopers; these slobs, as they seemed to me, the party in possession.

Like Scripps in the play, on Sunday morning I went to Communion in the college chapel, and in the same self-serving frame of mind, though in those days I would go to Communion every Sunday anyway and sometimes mid-week too. Asked in the interview what I was intending to do with my life, I think I probably said I planned to take Holy Orders. This was true, though I'm glad to say none of the dons thought to probe the nature of my faith, or they would have found it to be pretty shallow. And clichéd too, which Scripps's faith is not, besides being far more detached and sceptical than mine ever managed to be.

On the foggy way home I changed trains at Doncaster, where in a junk shop I bought my mother a little Rowlandson print of Dr Syntax pursued by bees. It was 7s. 6d. and is probably not worth much more now, but it still hangs in the passage at home in Yorkshire, a reminder of that memorable weekend. A few days later I got a letter offering me a place at Sidney Sussex after I'd done my two years' National Service. It didn't work out like that, but at the time it all seemed very satisfactory. I was going to Cambridge.

At school I never had a teacher like Hector or like Irwin. My own history master was solid and dependable, his approach factual and down to earth, much as Mrs Lintott's. What drew me to him, though, was a hint of some secret sorrow. Mr Hill – H. H. Hill, the alliteration also a plus – was rumoured to have had some Housman-like breakdown at university when, having been expected to get a First, he had scarcely passed at all. That was as far as the Housman comparison would stretch, though, as he was happily married and fond of golf. An ironic and undemonstrative man, he was not temperamentally suited to the role of mentor or sage; still, he never made me feel a fool, which is high praise.

With other masters the secret sorrow was probably just that of middle-aged teachers in a not particularly good school with nothing to look forward to but retirement. Huddled at the bus stop waiting for the four-fifteen to Horsforth, they looked a sad and shabby lot.

Once in a slack period of the afternoon when we were being particularly un-bright, the French master put his head down on the desk and wailed, 'Why am I wasting my life in this godforsaken school?' It was not a question to which he expected an answer, and there was an embarrassed silence and a snigger from one of the less sensitive boys, much as there is in the play when Hector does the same. The incident stuck in my mind, I suppose, because it was a revelation to me at the time – I was fourteen or so – that masters had inner lives (or lives at all). Teaching French, he looked French in a rather M. Hulot-like way, but was far from being an apostle of Continental abandon. Not long before he had shepherded the class to a school showing of Marcel Carné's *Les Enfants du Paradis*, one of the earliest French films to be shown in Leeds after the war. Mystifying to me, it had deeply shocked him, and he had warned the class that those who led lives like the circus people in the film (fat chance) were likely to end up blind or riddled with disease. This just made me want to go back and see the film again, as I felt there must have been something that I'd missed.

That there were schoolmasters who were larger than life, whose pupils considered themselves set apart, only came home to me after I'd left school and was doing National Service. It was then, too, that I began to mix with boys who were much cleverer than I was and who had been better taught, all of us having ended up learning Russian at the Joint Services

School. This, delightfully, was based at Cambridge, and while we officer cadets didn't quite lead the lives of undergraduates, service discipline was kept to a minimum in order to facilitate our Slavonic studies; we did not have to wear uniform or take part in parades, and in lots of ways it was a more easeful and idyllic existence than I was eventually to enjoy at university proper.

It was a heady atmosphere. Many of the others on the course were disconcertingly clever, particularly, I remember, a group of boys from Christ's Hospital – boys whose schools had been a world as mine never was; and when they talked of their schooldays there was often in the background a master whose teaching had been memorable and about whom they told anecdotes, and whose sayings they remembered: teachers, I remember thinking bitterly, who had presumably played a part in getting them the scholarships most of them had at Oxford and Cambridge. To me this just seemed unfair. I had never had such a teacher and had had to make my own way, which may be one of the reasons why I've been prompted to write such a teacher now.

As the months passed I began to feel that since I could hold my own with these boys in Russian maybe I ought to have another shot at getting a scholarship myself. Besides, I was at Cambridge already; perhaps, rather than come back there after National Service, I would be better (more rounded I fear I thought of it) going to Oxford. This first occurred to me in October 1953, and having written off for the prospectuses I found that I could take the scholarship examination at Exeter College, Oxford, in the following January.

There was no practical advantage to getting a scholarship. It carried more prestige, certainly, but no more money; there was the gown, of course, as at Oxford scholars wore a longer gown than commoners and in those days, though it pains me to say so, I aspired to be a natty dresser. A commoner's gown, resembling as it did a sleeveless cardigan or an uninflated life-jacket, was flattering to no one. It's true that scholars had an extra year in college rather than in digs but the gown was really why I wanted a scholarship; I wanted something with a swing to it. It was sheer vanity.

Or not quite. I had fallen for one of my colleagues with a passion as hopeless and unrequited as Posner's for Dakin. This boy was going to Oxford on a scholarship, so naturally (or unnaturally as it was then) I wanted to do the same, and with some silly notion, again like Posner, that if I did manage to get a scholarship he would think more of me in consequence. Such illusions and the disillusions that inevitably came with them were, I see now, as significant as any examinations I did or did not take, and a sign that underneath my formal education a more useful course of instruction was meanwhile in process.

If I was to take the examination at Exeter I didn't have much time. My history was rusty, and studying Russian during the day meant that the only time I had to myself was in the evenings, which I generally spent in the Cambridge Public Library. In the meantime I reduced everything I knew to a set of notes with answers to possible questions and odd, eye-catching quotations all written out on a series of forty or fifty correspondence cards, a handful of which I carried in my pocket wherever I went. I learned them in class while ostensibly doing Russian, on the bus coming into Cambridge in the mornings, and in any odd moment that presented itself.

When I went on Christmas leave just before the examination, I happened to find in Leeds Reference Library a complete set of *Horizon*, Cyril Connolly's wartime magazine which had ceased publication only a year or two previously, but of which I had never heard. It opened my eyes to all sorts of cultural developments like existentialism which were then current and fashionable. I didn't understand them altogether, but these, too, got reduced to minced morsels on my cards in order to serve as fodder for the General Paper.

Come the examination, everything tumbled out: facts, quotations, all the stuff I'd laboriously committed to memory over the previous three months, my only problem being lack of time. At the interview I still said, as I had at Cambridge, that I would probably end up taking Holy Orders, though in view of the existentialism I spewed out it seemed increasingly unlikely.

When the letter came saying I'd won a scholarship I thought life was never going to be the same again, though it quite soon was, of course. The object of my affections was predictably unimpressed, and after my initial joy and surprise I began to feel the whole exercise had been a con on my part. I was a promising something, maybe, but certainly it wasn't a scholar.

Cut to three years later, when I'm two terms away from my final examinations in history. I hadn't had a notable university career either socially or academically, and I'd never had the same sense of life opening out as I'd had in the army. Now it was nearly over. I'd no idea what I wanted to do. Just as once I'd thought to become a vicar for no better reason than that I looked like one, so now it occurred to me I might become a don on the same principle. But to do that I had to perform much better in finals than I or my tutors expected me to do.

Whatever had seemed unusual or promising about me when I'd been given a scholarship had long since worn off. I never deceived myself that I was that unappealing entity 'a first-class mind'. I no more had a first-class mind than I had a first-class body (which I would at that time much have preferred). I worked hard, it's true, and took copious notes but for most of my undergraduate career never had the first idea how to organise them into an essay. I must have been a dull pupil to teach, tutorials tentative and awkward affairs, punctuated by long silences – exactly the kind of tutorials I was later to give myself when I taught pupils as a postgraduate. In other colleges one met undergraduates of stunning self-assurance and intellectual maturity (or that premature middle age that often passes for such). They saw themselves, particularly those reading Greats, as destined for the First Class, the degree simply a certificate waiting in a pigeonhole with their name already on it: all they had to do was go through a few tedious days at the Examination Schools before collecting it. But not me. I was a safe, plodding Second. I knew it and my college knew it too.

It was then that I remembered how I'd got the scholarship three years before, and as I began to cram for finals I adopted the same technique, reducing everything I knew to fit on cards which I carried everywhere, just as I'd done before. There were more cards this time but the contents were much the same: handy arguments, quotations, an examination kit in fact.

I also twigged what somebody ought to have taught me but never had, namely that there was a journalistic side to answering an examination question; that going for the wrong end of the stick was more attention-grabbing than a more conventional approach, however balanced. Nobody had ever tutored me in examination techniques or conceded that such techniques existed, this omission I suspect to be put down to sheer snobbery or the notion (here ascribed to Hector) that all such considerations were practically indecent.

What we were supposed to be doing in the Final Schools was writing dry scholarly answers to academic questions. It's Mrs Lintott's method, with at Oxford a model answer often compared to a *Times* leader. In my case there wasn't much hope of that, with the alternative journalism of a lowlier sort, the question argued in brisk generalities flavoured with sufficient facts and quotations to engage the examiner's interest and disguise my basic ignorance. This is the Irwin method.

Once I'd got into the way of turning a question on its head in the way Irwin describes I began to get pleasure out of the technique itself, much as Dakin does, sketching out skeleton answers to all sorts of questions and using the same facts, for instance, to argue opposite points of view, all seasoned with a wide variety of references and quotations. I knew it wasn't scholarship, and in the Final Honours schools it would only take me so far, but it was my only hope.

I duly took the examination in scorching weather, two three-hour papers a day and the most gruelling five days of my life. At the finish I'd no idea how I had done and was so exhausted I didn't care and went to the cinema every afternoon for a week.

The results came out about six weeks later, after a viva voce examination. In those days everyone was viva'd, coming before the examining board even if it was only for half a minute, with a longer viva meaning that you were on the edge of a class and so likely to go up or down. Mine lasted half an hour and went, I thought, badly. I could see a couple of examiners were on my side and endeavouring to be kind; the others weren't interested. I went back home to Leeds in low spirits.

A friend who was in Oxford when the list went up sent me a postcard. It came on Monday morning when I was working at Tetleys Brewery, rolling barrels. My father was ill and out of work, and he and my mother brought this card to the lodge at the brewery gates, where I was sent for from the cellars. They weren't sure what a First was.

'Does it mean you've come top?' asked my mother, not particularly surprised, as from their point of view that's what I'd always done ever since elementary school.

I went back to pushing the barrels around, hardly able to believe my luck. It was one of the great days of my life, but it was luck. I was right: I hadn't done well in the viva, but another candidate had and with approximately the same results as mine had been put in the First Class so I had to be included too. It was a narrow squeak.

With a First, a research grant was a formality, so I stayed on at Oxford and for a time even convinced myself I was a scholar, coming up twice a week to read manuscripts at the Public Records Office, then still in Chancery Lane. But I was more a copyist than a scholar, since that was all I did, copying out medieval records with no notion what to do with them, and the longer I did it – for five years after taking my degree – the more dissatisfied with myself and the bigger fraud I felt. The truth was not in me.

However, in addition to my so-called research I did some college teaching, and though I wasn't much good at that either (and in today's more demanding conditions would soon have been stopped), I did at least try and teach my pupils the technique of answering essay questions and the strategy for passing examinations – techniques which I'd had to discover for myself and in the nick of time: journalism, in fact.

So *The History Boys* is in some sense an outcome of those two crucial examinations and the play both a confession and an expiation. I have no nostalgia for my Oxford days at all and am happy never to have to sit an examination again. In playwriting there are no examinations unless, that is, you count the viva voce the audience puts the actors through every night.

What sort of school is it that can send eight boys to sit for history scholarships at Oxford and Cambridge? Not a state school, surely, even in the 1980s? I wanted it to be, partly because that's how I'd imagined it, setting the action in my mind's eye as taking place in my own school, Leeds Modern School as was.

This last year while I was writing the play I used regularly to pass what had been the Modern School, now known as Lawnswood School. It was, almost symbolically I felt, in process of demolition, and the more I wrote of the play the less there was of the building. Now it has completely gone and been replaced by a new school built directly in front of the old site.

The process of demolition was protracted because, put up in 1930, the building contained asbestos. This meant I couldn't pop in for one last look or to refresh my memory, until by chance *Look North* arranged to film me there a week or two before it was finally pulled down. I went along expecting it to seem smaller, which it duly did, but in memory it had a shine to it which had utterly vanished. Once there had been polished parquet floors, the woodwork was of bright chestnut varnish, and particularly in the late afternoon (as was at one point mentioned in the play), the place took on a wonderful glow. Not now. It was shabby and dull and run-down.

The headmaster, whom I had in my mind somehow blamed for the abandonment of the building, turned out to be helpful and understanding while not surprisingly being anxious to get out of what he saw as shabby and restrictive surroundings. I had no reason for nostalgia as the time I had spent in the school had been pretty dull and unmemorable, but still, it was a good building, and the façade should certainly have been incorporated in whatever replaced it. Had it survived another ten or fifteen years it would certainly have been listed and preserved. Standing on the northern boundary of Leeds, it was always a handsome and decent piece of thirties architecture, designed in the Municipal Architect's Department, which in the thirties was one of the best in the country. I don't know who designed its replacement, but it has none of the old building's dignity and (this is the nub of it) none of its confidence. In 1930 the future of state education seemed assured. Now, who knows?

On the stage the school is vaguely taken to be in Sheffield, and in my head I called it Cutlers' and though there isn't a Cutlers' Grammar School in Sheffield I feel there ought to have been. I made it a grammar school only because a comprehensive school would be unlikely to be fielding Oxbridge candidates in such numbers. Unlikely, I subsequently found, to be fielding Oxbridge candidates at all, or at least not in the way I'd imagined.

When I was writing *The History Boys* I didn't pay much heed to when it was supposed to be set. While not timeless (though one always hopes), its period didn't seem important. It seemed to me to be about two sorts of teaching – or two teachers, anyway (characters always more important than themes), who were teaching more or less in the present; I could decide when precisely after I'd finished the play.

My own memories of sitting the Cambridge scholarship examination were so vivid that they coloured the writing of the play, with Oxford and Cambridge still held up to my sixth-formers as citadels to be taken just as they were to me and my schoolfellows fifty years ago. I knew things had changed, of course, but I assumed that candidates for the scholarship examination spent two or three days at whichever university, staying in the college of their first choice, sitting a few examination papers and being interviewed; after which they would go back to Leeds or Blackburn or wherever to await the results ten days or so later. That was what had happened to me in December 1951, and it was a time I had never forgotten.

I was well on with the play when I mentioned it to a friend who had actually sat next to me in one of the scholarship examinations. He told me that I was hopelessly out of date, and that scholarship examinations such as we'd both experienced were a thing of the past, and even that scholarships themselves were not what they were. What had replaced the system he wasn't sure, but he thought that candidates no longer took scholarship examinations while they were at school, but at the end of their first year in college, when awards were made on course work.

I was shocked and didn't want to know, not because this invalidated the play (it is a play, after all, and not a white paper), but because what had been such a memorable episode in my life was now wholly confined to history. What had happened so unforgettably to me couldn't happen any more; it was as outmoded as maypole dancing or the tram. And as for the now stay-at-home examinees, I just felt sorry for them. No romantic weekend for them, threading the frosted Backs or sliding over the cobbles of Trinity; no Evensong in King's; life, as in so many other respects, duller than once it was. I don't imagine the candidates themselves felt much deprived, and from the colleges' point of view it simply meant that they had another weekend available for conferences.

However, I now had to decide if I should adapt the play to present-day circumstances, but decided I shouldn't, as much for practical reasons as any concern for the facts. The current system of assessment, whatever its merits, is no help to the playwright. Graduated assessment is no use at all. The test, the examination, the ordeal, unfair though they may be, are at least dramatic.

Accordingly I set the play in the 1980s, just before the time people seemed to think the system had changed. It's significant that without looking it up nobody I spoke to could quite remember the sequence, which testifies to the truth of Irwin's remark about the remoteness of the recent past but is also an instance of how formless the history of institutions becomes once its public procedures are meddled with. Fairer, more decent and catering to the individual the new system may be, but memorable and even ceremonious, no, and that is a loss, though these days not an uncommon one.

Luckily the eighties were a period with no special sartorial stamp, no wince-making flares, for instance, or tie 'n' dye. Mrs Thatcher was more of an obtruding presence then than she is in the play, but that particular omission will, I hope, be forgiven me.

The school is not a fee-paying grammar school such as Leeds or Manchester, which are both represented at the Headmasters' Conference and count as public schools. This, though, is what Mr Armstrong, the headmaster in the play, would aspire to, just as my own headteacher did all those years ago. I'm old-fashioned enough to believe that private education should long since have been abolished and that Britain has paid too high a price in social inequality for its public schools. At the same time, I can't see that public schools could be abolished (even if there was the will) without an enormous amount of social disruption. The proper way forward would be for state education to reach such a standard that private schools would be undersubscribed, but there's fat chance of that, particularly under the present administration. The same hope, of course, ought to animate the National Health Service, but the future for that seems equally bleak.

These days getting into Oxford or Cambridge or indeed any university is only the beginning of the story. Money has to be found, earned, donated by parents, borrowed from the bank or wherever student loans currently come from. It's a sizeable hurdle, and one my generation were happy to be without, if we ever gave it a thought. At that time acceptance by a university or any institution of higher learning automatically brought with it a grant from the state or the local authority. The names of the recipients of such grants would be printed in the local paper, occasionally with their photographs, the underlying assumption being that the names of these students should be known because they had done the state or the county some service and would now go on to do more. There was genuine pride in such achievements and in the free education that had made them possible – particularly perhaps in Leeds, which had an outstanding Education Department.

I am told that I am naïve or unrealistic, but I do not understand why we cannot afford such a system today. As a nation we are poorer for the lack of it, the latest round in that lost fight the bullying through of the bill on top-up fees with this so-called Labour government stamping on the grave of what it was once thought to stand for. Though there is much that is called education nowadays that is nothing of the sort and doesn't deserve subsidy, yet I still hold to the belief that a proper education should be free at the point of entry and the point of exit.

Some of these views can be put down to the circumstances of my own education but also to a book which made a great impression on me as a young man. This was Richard Hoggart's *The Uses of Literacy* (1955), and in particular his account of growing up in the slums of Leeds, going to Cockburn High School, and eventually to Leeds University, where he was taught by Bonamy Dobrée. It was a harder childhood than mine (and an earlier one) but it was reading Hoggart forty years ago that made me feel that my life, dull though it was, might be made the stuff of literature. *The Uses of Literacy* spawned a series of books, one of which, *Education and the Working Class* by Brian Jackson and Dennis Marsden, included a study of sixth form boys who had made it to university but not done well there, the conclusion being that the effort of getting to university often took so much out of working-class boys that once there they were exhausted. This is one of Posner's complaints in the play.

'The scholarship boy,' writes Hoggart, 'has been equipped for hurdle-jumping, so he merely thinks of getting on, but somehow not in the world's way . . . He has left his class, at least in spirit, by being in certain ways unusual, and he is still unusual in another class, too tense and over-wound.' I had forgotten this passage until I found it quoted in *Injury Time*, one of the commonplace books of D. J. Enright, who must also have found it relevant to his own case.

Things have changed since Hoggart was writing, and the boys in the play are more privileged than Hoggart, Enright or me, but I suspect hurdle-jumping hasn't much changed, or the strain it engenders, though maybe it shows itself less in terms of class.

At Oxford in the late fifties some of the teaching I did was for Magdalen (which explains why it is occasionally mentioned in the text). One year I was also drafted in to help mark and interview candidates for the history scholarships. It didn't seem all that long since I had been interviewed myself, and I was nervous lest my marks should differ from those of my more experienced colleagues by whom I was every bit as intimidated as the candidates were.

I needn't have worried, though, as apart from the papers of authentic

Wykehamist brilliance, the other promising candidates were virtually self-selecting, one's attention always caught by oddity, extremity and flair just as Irwin foresees. Whether these candidates were genuine originals or (like the boys in the play) coached into seeming so, the interview was meant to show up, but I'm not sure it always did. It was the triumph of Irwin.

Candidates do well in examinations for various reasons, some from genuine ability, obviously, but others because doing well in examinations is what they do well; they can put on a show. Maybe it doesn't work like that now that course work is taken into consideration and more weight is given to solider virtues. But it has always struck me that some of the flashier historians, particularly on television, are just grown-up versions of the wised-up schoolboys who generally got the scholarships (myself included). Here is R. W. Johnson, himself a historian, reviewing Niall Ferguson's *The Pity of War*:

> Both *The Pity of War* and the reception it has enjoyed illustrate aspects of British culture about which one can only feel ambivalent. Anyone who has been a victim, let alone a perpetrator, of the Oxbridge system will recognise Niall Ferguson's book for what it is: an extended and argumentative tutorial from a self-consciously clever, confrontational young don, determined to stand everything on its head and argue with vehemence against what he sees as the conventional wisdom – or worse still, the fashion – of the time. The idea is to teach the young to think and argue, and the real past masters at it (Harry Weldon [Senior Tutor at Magdalen] was always held up as an example to me) were those who first argued undergraduates out of their received opinions, then turned around after a time and argued them out of their new-found radicalism, leaving them mystified as to what they believed and suspended in a free-floating state of cleverness.
>
> (*London Review of Books*, 18 February 1999)

I had friends at Magdalen who went through this dialectical debriefing in their first year and it used to worry me that nothing remotely similar happened at Exeter. Nothing much happened at all until my third year, when in the nick of time I began to get to grips with it myself. Still, I never thought of this as a proper education, just a way of getting through the examinations.

These considerations have acquired a general interest as history has become more popular both on the page and on the screen. The doyen of TV historians, Simon Schama, is in a league of his own, and his political viewpoint is not in the forefront, but the new breed of historians – Niall Ferguson, Andrew Roberts and Norman Stone – all came to prominence under Mrs Thatcher and share some of her characteristics. Having found that taking the contrary view pays dividends, they seem to make this the tone of their customary discourse. A sneer is never far away and there's a persistently jeering note, perhaps bred by the habit of contention. David Starkey sneers too, but I feel this is more cosmetic.

None of this posing, though, is altogether new. A. J. P. Taylor was its original exponent, certainly on television, and was every bit as pleased with himself as the new breed of history boys. Still, with nothing else to put in the frame but his own personality and with no graphics and no film, he had perhaps more excuse for hamming it up a bit. His pleasure at his own technique, the flawless delivery (no autocue) and the winding-up of the lecture to the very second allotted were reasons enough for watching him, regardless of whatever history it was he was purveying. Even with him, though, the paradoxes and the contrariousness could get wearisome, certainly in the lecture hall, where I remember nodding off during one of his Ford Lectures.

Irwin's career path might seem odd. Schoolmaster to TV don is plausible enough, but from lecturing about the Dissolution of the Monasteries to government spokesperson is a bit of a leap, though there are odder episodes in the early career of Alastair Campbell. No subject was further from my mind when I began to write the play, and it was only as I sat in on Irwin's classes, as it were, that I saw that teaching history or teaching the self-presentation involved with the examination of history was not unrelated to presentation in general.

The rehearsals for the plays were unusual in that the eight young actors playing the sixth-formers had to learn not only the parts they had to act but also what they meant. The play is stiff with literary and historical references, many of which, at first reading anyway, meant little to the actors.

The early stages of rehearsal were therefore more like proper school than a stage version of it.

They read and talked about Auden, a favourite of Hector's in the play (though not of Mrs Lintott). Auden keeps being quoted, so we read and discussed some of his poems and the circumstances of his life. Hardy was another subject for tutorials, leading on to Larkin much as happens in the last scene of Act One. The First and Second Wars figure largely in the play, as they seemed to do on the classroom walls of the schools we visited to get some local colour before rehearsals started, so the period 1914–45 was also much discussed. I normally get impatient when there's a lot of talking before rehearsals proper start, but with this play it was essential.

Maybe too, it says something about the status of the actor. Half a lifetime ago my first play, *Forty Years On*, though about a very different sort of school, was as full of buried quotations and historical allusion as *The History Boys*. Back in 1968, though, there was never any question of educating the score or so boys that made up Albion House School. We never, that I recall, filled them in on who Virginia Woolf was or put them in the picture about Lady Ottoline Morrell, Sapper, Buchan, Osbert Sitwell – to the boys these must have been names only, familiar to the principal players, John Gielgud and Paul Eddington, but as remote to the rest of the cast as historical figures in Shakespeare. This omission was partly because with only four weeks to rehearse there wasn't time to tell them more, but also because in those days actors were treated with less consideration than they are now, at any rate at the National Theatre.

But these early rehearsals with Nicholas Hytner taking the class were a reminder that good directors are often good teachers (Ronald Eyre is another example) and that theatre is often at its most absorbing when it's school.

Always beneath the play you write is the play you meant to write; changed but not abandoned and, with luck, not betrayed, but shadowing still the play that has come to be.

It is to Nicholas Hytner that I owe, among so much else, the idea for the original play, the one I didn't quite write, as it first came to me when I was listening to him being interviewed by Michael Berkeley on BBC Radio 3's *Private Passions*. Nick had earlier told me of his schooldays at Manchester Grammar School and how, having a good singing voice, he had sung in a boys' choir with the Hallé under Barbirolli. I was expecting him to talk about this on *Private Passions*, but rather to my disappointment he didn't. However, one of the records he chose was Ella Fitzgerald singing 'Bewitched' with its original Lorenz Hart lyrics, and it occurred to me at the time how theatrical this would sound sung by a boy with an unbroken voice.

This in turn took me back to my own childhood when, though I was no singer, I had been very slow to grow up, my voice still unbroken when I was well past sixteen. So one of the history boys as first written was a boy much as I had been, a child in a class of young men. Nick (whose own voice broke at twelve) thought that these days a sixteen-year-old boy with an unbroken voice was both unlikely and impossible to cast. This I could appreciate, though at the time I abandoned the notion with some regret.

The casting difficulty I can understand, but I don't entirely agree that such late development no longer occurs. It's true that today most children develop earlier, but the few who don't suffer more acutely in consequence, and it certainly still happens. I knew one boy, the son of a friend, who matured every bit as late as I did, though he coped with it much better than me. Looking back, I see those years from fourteen to sixteen as determining so much that I would later wish away, particularly a sense of being shut out that I have never entirely lost.

As it is, Posner is the heir to the character I never quite wrote, a boy who is young for his age and whose physical immaturity engenders a premature disillusion. Watching Sam Barnett playing the part, I wince to hear my own voice at sixteen.

Radio and TV

Hymn

In 2001 the Medici Quartet commissioned the composer George Fenton to write them a piece commemorating their thirtieth anniversary. George Fenton appeared in my first play Forty Years On *and has written music for many of my plays since, and he asked me to collaborate on the commission.* Hymn *was the result. First performed at the Harrogate Festival in August 2001, it's a series of memoirs with music. Besides purely instrumental passages for the quartet, many of the speeches are under-scored, incorporating some of the hymns and music I remember from my childhood and youth. The text is printed here but not the musical directions.*

> And so through all the length of days,
> Thy goodness faileth never.
> Good shepherd may I sing thy praise
> Within thy house forever.

Up the words come, unbidden, known but never learned. Some of that weightless baggage carried down the years, not from piety or belief, and more credentials than creed, a testimonial that I am one of those boys state-educated in the forties and fifties who came by the words of *Hymns Ancient and Modern* through singing them day in day out at school every morning in assembly.

It's a dwindling band; old-fashioned and of a certain age, you can pick us out at funerals and memorial services, because we can sing the hymns without the book.

> Alleluia alleluia,
> Hearts to heaven and voices raised,
> Sing to God a hymn of gladness
> Sing to God a hymn of praise.

With me, there are hymns at home, too, because my father is an amateur violinist and on Sunday nights plays along to the music on the wireless, warming up with Albert Sandler and his Palm Court Orchestra then taking off with the hymn singing on *Sunday Half Hour*.

So hymns are him playing his fiddle. At one period Dad's thoughts turn to something larger than the violin and he invests in a double bass, thinking to augment his butcher's wages by working nights as a player in a dance band. One of the several burdens of wives are the hare-brained schemes of husbands, and my mother was never other than sceptical of my father's money-making enterprises. Another had been the manufacture of home-made herb beer. This was referred to by Mam as 'taking on Tetleys' and the double bass period as 'your Dad's Geraldo phase'.

It means, though, that as a change from *Sunday Half Hour* the family are now mustered round the wireless and made to listen to Henry Hall and the Andrews Sisters.

> Mares eat oats and does eat oats and little lambs eat ivy,
> A kid'll eat ivy too, wouldn't you? Pom pom.

'Did you hear that?' Dad would say. 'That's the bass giving the beat! That'll be me!' It was difficult to enthuse.

To no one's surprise, he never got far with the bass. Quite literally, as they often wouldn't let him even put it on the tram. And just as the home-made beer saga had ended in the explosion of half a dozen bottles that practically wrecked the scullery, so the double bass era ended with a succession of rows with tram conductors after which Dad reverted to the violin.

Praise to the holiest in the height
And in the depths be praise.
In all his works most wonderful,
Most sure in all his ways.

The words are those of Cardinal Newman's hymn but they are also part of Elgar's *Dream of Gerontius,* heard first in Leeds Town Hall in 1952. I thought Elgar had missed a trick by not using the familiar tune and at its first outing in 1900 the audience had thought so too, and the general feeling then that this sublime work was a bit of a dud.

Most of my musical education was in Leeds Town Hall at weekly concerts by the short-lived (but to me always memorable) Yorkshire Symphony Orchestra. They excelled in English music – Delius particularly whom I was astonished to find had been born in Bradford. And George Butterworth, too, from York who died on the Somme in 1916.

The cheapest seats and the school seats were behind the orchestra and here the double bass raises its ponderous voice again as our chosen perch was behind the basses. It was rather like watching the circus from behind the elephants. Hardly a lyrical instrument, the bass tends to attract players of a like disposition, dogged and even disenchanted with a robust no-nonsense approach to performance. Indifferent to applause, if we go on too long at the end of a concert, the principal, a Mr Campbell, turns round and says 'Have you no homes to go to?'

At that age, though, we find this work-a-day attitude to music-making infectious. Sitting looking down on the conductor, we fifteen-year-olds are alert to pretension and subject the sometimes eminent musicians to our sceptical schoolboy scrutiny, grading them by the degree of their self-regard.

It isn't just a matter of histrionics with the baton, as both Barbirolli and Sargent, for instance, go in for a good deal of that but they are not the same. Urbane, Brylcreemed and always with a carnation in his buttonhole and a wolfish smile, Sir Malcolm is an obvious showman. Sir John, unkempt and in a rumpled tail-coat with his bow tie on the skew and sometimes without his bottom teeth, seems entirely unselfconscious but he is a showman too – both of them putting on a performance. For me, always a sucker for the unassuming, it is Barbirolli who touches the heart and serves the music, unlike Sargent, who merely presents it.

So it is not just music that I learn, sitting on those harsh benches, Saturday by Saturday. Music in the concert hall is also a moral education, and watching the musicians at close quarters I realise that it is not just ecstasy and inspiration but that there is drudge to it too. Sometimes, the players would be on the same tram coming home, and I see that they are just like everybody else – shabby, in dirty raincoats and sometimes with tab ends in their mouths; ordinary people who, half an hour ago, were artists and agents of the sublime.

———————

That music had nothing to do with showing off was, I see now, one of the lessons my father had been wanting me to learn when I was ten years old when he tried to teach me the violin. He knew instinctively that art has not much to do with artistic, and that there was no need for a lot of carry-on, or, as Dad always put it, 'a lot of splother'.

His violin case is deceptively ordinary, battered even, and kept in my parents' bedroom, which is where my father generally does his practice. Having made sure that he is out, I lay the case on the bed, unflip its two catches and open the lid to reveal, snugly couched in velvet, this glowing tawny thing. It is like coming on a newly fallen horse chestnut, the neat housing split to reveal the conker's wet gleam. I stroke the coved back, grained as if with spine and ribs, hold the scrolled head in my hand and feel its weight, running my fingers round the piped and scalloped edge and peering through the S-shaped holes into its dark interior.

Mounted on the underside of the lid is the bow and that too is finely done, the handle inlaid with mother-of-pearl, the end tipped with ivory; so pampered this instrument seems to me to be, so lavishly appointed, with nothing spared for its protection and comfort, that even my looking has to be hurried and furtive knowing that if my father catches me at it, I shall be in trouble. 'It's not a toy.' But I don't think of it as a toy either. It is the most luxurious object in the house, and sensitive to the spell it casts, I see myself playing it – even pretend to, in front of the dressing-table mirror.

So I ask to learn. I'm a clever boy. I am sure it will not be hard.

'To begin with, you don't hold it like that, you hold it like this.' He takes the bow out of my ten-year-old hand. 'Just do it naturally.' He bends my fingers round the handle of the bow, covering my hands with his big butcher's hands, standing there in his shirtsleeves and shop trousers and smelling of meat. We are in the hot attic under the roof with the half-size violin I have to learn on, nothing like as glamorous as his, a chipped, unpolished brown little thing that looks as though it can't produce a note.

'You're holding the bow wrong again. Nobody holds it like that. People will laugh at you.' He purses my fingers again round the bow handle, his own violin held casually under his chin, jutting out from his shoulder as he tightens the silky hair of the bow. Even at ten, I know this is showing off, 'Look! No hands!' the kindest labelling of it. But holding this scrolled extension of himself is also him being a man and doing something that with my puny neck and chin I know I can't do now and probably ever.

'I've written you on the notes: E, G, B, D, F. What do they stand for?' This, at least, I know. Every Good Boy Deserves Favour. I know it too, because this favoured boy is not just an aid to memory but to me almost a creature of flesh and blood. It is as if the very structure of the stave has been rigged against me and this good boy deserving of favour is all the things I am not – capable, modest and quiet, who holds the bow with his small fingers just as my father does in his big ones and does not scrape it agonisingly across the strings as I do, but extracts from this unpromising almost plywood fiddle something sweet and tuneful. This good boy, who is not me, deserves favour from my father, as I never shall.

Violin still jutting, Dad puts a sheet of music on the gunmetal stand. 'Now the Day is Over', copied out from *Hymns Ancient and Modern* in a hand as square and blunt as his fingers.

Now the day is over,
Night is drawing nigh.
Shadows of the evening
Steal across the sky.

I start on the first note, dragging the bow across the strings.

'Nay, Alan! Frame yourself. Look at your fingers!' Once again, his big butcher's hands come over mine, gripping the bow for me, so that now it is he who is playing the tune, not me. I let go of the violin and it falls on the floor.

'You dateless article! What is the point?' At first, I think that he is going to hit me, but, golden violin in one hand and bow in the other, he can't, and instead he charges off down the attic steps. I know that I am a disappointment to my father and that this disappointment will outlast the violin and my childhood and go down into the grave.

The attic door bangs shut. Through the open skylight I hear the trams hurtling down Otley Road and the bell-ringers over at St Chad's beginning their practice. I climb up on the chair and look out at the evening sky.

———

I've always liked looking in churches and though I'm not quite one of those who, in Philip Larkin's words, 'tap and jot and know what rood lofts were' I do know what rood lofts were and it has brought me to Hubberholme at the top of Wharfedale and the very tip of the West Riding.

The church is broad and low, like its liturgy, I imagine, but unique in the West Riding – its rood loft survives. Put up in 1558, it was perhaps salvaged from Coverham Abbey and brought over the tops on a farm cart. But they were behind the times at Hubberholme. They did not know in 1558 that Catholic Queen Mary was dead and that, as they were putting up their loft, everywhere else the lofts were coming down. But amazingly, it survives and is still here and a proper loft it is too, slatted as it could be for hay and straw as much as for candles and the cross.

Centuries pass – births, marriages and deaths – the church's next moment in history recorded in a picture frame hung slightly askew on one of the pillars – a roll of honour with the names and, unusually for England, the photographs of the young men of the parish who died in the First War.

The harvest in, they go off on a farm cart, too, probably, down the dale to join those queuing to enlist outside Skipton Town Hall. And four years later, in Wilfred Owen's words:

> A few, a few, too few for drums and yells,
>
> May creep back, silent, to village wells,
> Up half-known roads.

One who does come back from that war, and years later has his ashes scattered here, is J. B. Priestley, and on another pillar is a plaque to say so.

The rood, the roll of honour, the ashes of a writer – the remnants of history, the random trig points of time.

I have never found it easy to belong. So much repels. Hymns help. They blur. And here among the tombs and tablets and vases of dead flowers, and lists of the fallen, it is less hard to feel, at least, tacked on to church and country.

Amen. Or, with that lilting interrogation with which young people nowadays cast doubt on any certainty, Amen?

Cheeky Chappies

Brought up during the Second War I am a child of the BBC Home Service, listened to, at the beginning of the war anyway, on a wireless that still requires an accumulator. This is a heavy glass battery, the shape not unlike that of a miniature police box as was, though that too has long since disappeared and is remembered now only as the original of the Tardis in *Doctor Who*.

The accumulator has to be regularly recharged, a process that involves me or my brother lugging it (the metal handle cutting into one's fingers) along the path by the Recreation Ground and across Moorfield Road to an electrician's grimy workshop somewhere in the perilous Edinburghs, which are poorer streets than ours and infested with wild boys and slummy girls and urchins with a permanent rivulet of snot running from their noses.

With the accumulator the wireless takes a long time to warm up, a phrase that later becomes one of the standard jokes in the wartime comedy show *Much Binding in the Marsh*, with Kenneth Horne and Richard Murdoch. We blame it, too, for our often poor reception so it's a relief when Dad invests in another wireless, a Philco, bought second-hand through the Miscellaneous column of the *Yorkshire Evening Post*. Domed and in brown Bakelite, according to Dad this is a better set than our previous one not only because it runs off the mains but because it lights up.

Television had briefly begun in the 1930s before the war put paid to it, but though I must have heard of it, it was one of those many things that happened Down South and certainly not in Leeds, and none of us had ever seen it. Still, the notion of it must have been there because Dad having promised us a wireless that will light up, it is a disappointment to find that that is all it does . . . no faces, no figures, just an illuminated dial and a knob with which to scan Hilversum, Droitwich, Dortmund and all the other faraway places of which we know nothing, the only two stations we ever tune in to the Home Service and the Light Programme.

In common with virtually every family in the country at that time we settle down every week to listen to *ITMA – It's That Man Again –* a title which I take to refer to Hitler, about whom there are constant jokes, but is more likely to be the show's compère and anchorman (and the most popular comedian of the day) Tommy Handley. Relentlessly cheerful and with an unstoppable flow of wisecracks and repartee, Tommy Handley presides over a regular cast of characters, Mrs Mopp, the charwoman, Colonel Chinstrap, the drunk, Funf, the German spy, and half a dozen others, all kitted out with their particular catchphrases. With Mrs Mopp it's 'Can I do you now, sir?', for Colonel Chinstrap 'I don't mind if I do', the mere repetition of which is enough to have the audience and the nation in stitches. But not me.

Tommy Handley's unquenchable high spirits come to stand for the spirit of the Blitz and in his time (and for long afterwards) he is an iconic figure who is beyond criticism. But as a child I know that he is not funny, ranking in my book with those equally unfunny uncles whose idea of humour is to throw you up in the air, hard-hearted mirthless jokers on the family stage.

I see Tommy Handley as the essential cheeky chappie, a type I have disliked ever since. There is Tommy Trinder too, who also shelters under the banner of the Blitz, harsh, male and, one suspects, not very nice and never raising a smile with me the whole of his long life. There is Ted Ray and Arthur Askey, both from the north it's true but like Dickie Henderson, unmistakeable cheeky chappies. A child of the north, I don't care for cockneys or their much-advertised Blitz-defeating cheerfulness: all that knees-up, thumbs in the lapels down at the old Bull and Bush cockney sparrerdom has always left me cold.

Even Max Miller, though regarded by some writers (notably John Osborne) as a secular saint and reverenced for his anarchic spirit and the subversiveness of his sexual innuendo, still has too much of a permanent grin on his face for me. Besides, those violent check suits he goes in for seem to me quite definitely common. Like the fox in Pinocchio, he is plainly up to no good.

Cheeky chappies are not gender-specific: Two Ton Tessie O'Shea is a cheeky chappie, for instance (and massively unfunny). So to a lesser extent are Elsie and Doris Waters, sisters to Jack Warner, who started off as a cheeky chappie before ending up as the respected desk sergeant of television's *Dixon of Dock Green*. Generally, though, cheeky chappieness was overwhelmingly male and there is not a breath of camp to it. It's perky, aggressive, wisecracking and a routine. It's seldom subversive and it caters to prejudice rather than running counter to it, its current exponents Bernard Manning and Jim Davidson.

Happily, though, there aren't as many cheeky chappies now as there once were; they began to peter out in the wastes of Dickie Henderson and *Sunday Night at the London Palladium*, where, once the native supply of cheeky chappies began to dry up they could be imported from America. Sammy Davis Jr was a cheeky chappie and Bob Hope, too, gag merchants whose art cost them only what they paid their gag-writers.

Because cheeky chappies are practitioners and professionals. There's no mining of their own lives and no undermining of them either. They do not put themselves down, make themselves the butt of their own jokes, as, say, Jack Benny used to do or Frankie Howerd. They are not their own subjects and comedy costs them nothing. And above all, of course, they are cheerful, repellently so, so that even as a child what I feel these comedians lack is a sense of humour.

Having disparaged *ITMA*, it's only fair to add that if I have a preference for the lugubrious in comedy that may be due to *ITMA*, too, as one of the regular characters was Mona Lott (catchphrase: 'It's being so cheerful as keeps me going'). She was certainly more up my street, more up our actual social street in fact, than Tommy Handley; more, too, than Jack Train's Colonel Chinstrap, the programme's resident drunk, whose jokes often meant nothing to me, brought up in a teetotal family with never a drink in the house. Mona Lott, though, was not too distantly related to those headscarved women who, though seldom so determinedly morose, populated my wartime childhood.

Familiar too were the characters I saw portrayed on the stage in our annual visit to the theatre to see the pantomime at the Theatre Royal in Leeds. Here comedians like Norman Evans, Frank Randle and Albert Modley would play the dame in *Mother Goose* or *Babes in the Wood* though they could hardly be said to be in drag. A skirt, a wig, a battered straw hat were about as far as cross-dressing was allowed to go with any implication of effeminacy countered by a defiant pair of hobnailed boots.

These comedians generally incorporated into the proceedings a version of their regular music-hall act. In Norman Evans's case this was *Over the Garden Wall* (an act later revivified on television by Les Dawson). It may seem fanciful to claim that remarks like 'Leave that cat alone! Do you know, I could taste it in t'custard' were closer to real life than the gags purveyed by Tommy Handley, but so it was and I thought the Dame hilarious. And though *Cinderella* was hardly social realism it came much closer to my life than ever *ITMA* did, particularly as every pantomime would include a slapstick routine based on some household chore . . . wallpapering, say, or making pastry or doing the washing, procedures with which I was familiar and so found very funny. It was a lesson, though I didn't realise it at the time, that comedy and real life were in some relation.

Norman Evans (always minus his teeth) talked as northern women talked and, I fancy, carried over his act into a brief radio series in the late forties. Then came Al Read (catchphrase: 'I thought, Right monkey!'), whose humour was even more rooted in everyday life, this development in radio comedy preceding by several years and without credit a similar revolution in the theatre. Radio was at the kitchen sink long before Arnold Wesker.

Then there was Hylda Baker, who presented a different sort of north-ern woman, Edith Piaf without the voice or the love life, a little sparrow of a thing with a six-foot straight man (Eli Woods in drag). Again it may seem perverse to maintain that Hylda Baker and the lofty Cynthia were in any sense a representation of ordinary life but they certainly rang familiar bells with me. Hylda Baker and Wittgenstein can seldom have been men-tioned in the same breath but certainly she was closer to everything that is the case than Tommy Trinder ever was.

Life apart, the other thing that has always made me laugh is sheer silli-ness. Silly daftness is what my father called it. It was what was funny about George Formby, the only comedian who has ever made me fall off my seat laughing (at the Palace, Stanningley Road, it would have been). Arthur Askey was undoubtedly a cheeky chappie but he was redeemed by a streak of inspired daftness, as when he was doing his bumblebee routine; Tommy Cooper, Eric Morecambe and Ken Dodd were all silly as cheeky chappies seldom are. Silliness is surreal and without reason and to indulge in it is not without risk, a kind of balancing act, and risk is some-thing cheeky chappies don't like, hence their reliance on gags.

In the forties, radio comedians lived on long after the programmes that had brought them fame went off the air. This was on account of *Radio Fun*, a children's comic the cartoon characters in which had all figured on the wireless. But when I must have started reading it in 1940 I had never heard of any of them. Who was Lupino Lane, for instance? Or Revnell and West ('The Long and the Short of It') and if there had ever been a radio series featuring Jack Warner saying 'Mind my bike', as he did in *Radio Fun*, it had long since passed from memory.

The fame of all these comedians had to be taken on trust and no one seemed ever to make it to the pages of the comic until long after their hey-day was over. I doubt if the editors of *Radio Fun* had heard of Hegel but if one wanted proof of Hegel's dictum that 'The owl of Minerva takes her flight only when the shades of light are already failing' the pages of *Radio Fun* would provide it.

Comedians are supposed to have sad lives, though this isn't a cliché I entirely endorse, the sad clown not a type I've ever come across whereas the mean clown, the selfish clown and the downright unpleasant clown are commonplace. Northern comedians were sad only in the sense that they generally ended up at Morecambe or the better end of Blackpool, retired to seafront homes presided over by wives every bit as formidable as the battleaxes they were wont to complain of in their acts, George Formby and his prison wardress of a wife, Beryl, the most famous example.

Equally daunting, if only in appearance, was Mrs Albert Modley. Albert Modley was a northern comic who, unlike Norman Evans, had never quite acquired a national reputation but was well liked around the music halls of the north and never out of work in the pantomime season. I came across him only after his retirement when in 1974 we were making *Sunset Across the Bay*, a BBC TV film set in Morecambe, where he now lived.

Included in the script was a scene in which two old men chat outside the hut on the Leeds allotment which one of them is having to abandon before retiring to the seaside. It was a nice scene and the director, Stephen Frears, thought to cast Albert Modley, though he'd never seen him on the stage as I had.

When it came to the shot Albert turned out to be none too sure of the words, covering up his uncertainty just as he'd done all those years ago on the stage of the Theatre Royal with a good deal of laughing and stock phrases like, 'By! It's a beggar is this,' or 'By shots, this is a funny do. Hee hee.'

Still, hesitant though he was, it seemed entirely authentic. He certainly sounded like the genuine article and looked it, too, in an old raincoat and cap, and we were all ready to shoot when Mrs Modley, who had been hovering in the background, suddenly came forward with a large hatbox.

'He's never wearing that old cap,' said Mrs Modley. 'Folks won't recognise him in that fiddling thing,' and she opened the hatbox to reveal a cap of truly epic proportions. It was the cap he had worn on the halls.

'He has to wear his own cap,' insisted Mrs Modley. 'They won't recognise him without The Cap.'

It was a difficult moment, with Mrs Modley insisting and even threatening and Albert in no mood to resist her. It was solved by the cameraman, who suggested that Albert should save The Cap for the shot and that Mrs Modley should take charge of it while he supposedly rehearsed with headgear of normal dimensions.

When, having done several takes, The Cap came out of its hatbox and was put on Albert's head ('By shots, that feels better. This is more like it, hee hee') and he proceeded to act his socks off, there was actually no film in the camera.

The Last of the Sun

At Thora Hird's Memorial Service in Westminster Abbey, a joyous occasion which unaccountably went unrecorded by the BBC, I began by saying how scrupulous she was about the text and instanced her performance in *A Kind of Loving* made in 1962. Forty years later when we recorded *The Last of the Sun* and the last work she did, any diversion from the text was still making her distressed and unhappy.

'No, I said that wrong,' she would say, though by now she was sometimes so frail and breathless the wonder was that she could say anything at all.

Age and incapacity had also robbed her of any notion of recording technique so that when she did get it wrong, or didn't say a line to her own satisfaction, she didn't wait for another cue but simply gave the line again, until eventually the producer, Colin Smith, found it easier to keep the tape running without interruption.

Fortunately with us in the studio was Thora's daughter, Janette Scott-Rademakers, who was licensed to be more brusque with her mother than either Colin or I would have dared or wanted to be and so managed to cajole and bully and sometimes laugh her into something like her old self and a recollection of her abilities. I think amanuensis would be the word to describe it; certainly Thora could not have done it without her.

It's true that Thora is sometimes almost inaudible and finds, for instance, passages of description hard to put over. But once she gets into her 'I said to her . . . she said to me' mode she hits her stride. This, after all, had been the structure of her normal discourse for most of her life and it did not fail her now.

Tears, though, were never far away, though it wasn't always clear what Thora was weeping for. Sometimes it was the character she was playing; sometimes it was for herself playing the character; and sometimes, I'm sure, without it ever being specifically acknowledged, she wept because she knew she had come to the end of her work and was coming to the end of her life.

The play was recorded in the BBC7 Studio at Broadcasting House, the only studio which at that time had proper and indeed somewhat ceremonial wheelchair access. No stranger to chairlifts on this, her last ride, Thora achieved something of an apotheosis. Wheeled onto the upper level of the apparatus, she was then borne slowly and serenely downwards to studio level. Done up to the nines and every inch a star, she looked like Katharine Hepburn descending in the lift in the film of *Suddenly Last Summer* and as regal and commanding as a woman should whose career had begun ninety years before when she was brought onto stage as a two-month-old baby at the Royalty Theatre, Morecambe.

Her elegance, though, was characteristic. Few actors these days would dress up for a rehearsal, let alone a rehearsal on radio. But Thora belonged to a generation where to be seen at all in public was a performance in itself and part of the job.

I had caught what I thought was the tail end of this tradition in 1978 when working with Jill Bennett and Rachel Roberts who came to rehearsals in competing mink coats. Then in 1982 I went with Coral Browne for a fitting at Nathan's and saw all the dressers come out and watch in acknowledgement that such unashamed glamour was now almost an anachronism.

Thora was of the same generation even though glamour to her was a white trouser suit and a bright yellow beret, an outfit that she claimed made her look like a poached egg. Still, her smartness was somewhat unexpected, as so thoroughly did she inhabit her roles her public was mildly surprised that she didn't turn up dressed in her natural rig-out of headscarf and wrap-around pinny.

For all her frailty in gaps in the recording Thora keeps up an unstoppable flow of anecdote about her life in the theatre and her childhood in Morecambe.

The figure that most vividly emerges from these tales is always her father, the manager of the Royalty Theatre and director of many of the shows put on there. Today in the studio she remembers how she was sacked from Brundreth's, a posh drapers in Morecambe where she worked as an assistant and was sent home having been wrongly accused of stealing sixpence.

Mrs Hird senior embraces her wronged child, playing the scene for all its worth, and when Mr Hird returns home later there is a second performance with him slipping naturally into his role of the stern but righteous father determined to clear his daughter's name. Thora's family sound like a scaled-down version of the family of Judith Bliss in Coward's *Hay Fever*, reaching for any excuse to play out one of the melodramas they have all in their time acted in and now can get their teeth into in real life.

She said of the second monologue that I wrote for her, *Waiting for the Telegram*, that she would never have got past the first paragraph if it hadn't have been mine and that she'd never have said a swear word for anyone else. I took this as the compliment it was meant to be, though this was in 1999 and since the word in question was 'penis' the percentage of the population regarding it as a swear word must have been small, but still it seemed so to Thora. She had her audience on *Songs of Praise* to think about.

It was a delicate issue in the play as Violet, the character she played, didn't actually have to say the word herself but since this was a monologue she had to report other people – the matron, the social worker – saying it, which they persisted in doing with some relish. But I was the author and she had given me her trust and I count it not the least of my accomplishments that I got Dame Thora Hird, aged eighty-seven, to say penis with pride.

Still, it was one of her strengths that she believed, along with so many of the characters she played, that there were appearances to be kept up, susceptibilities to be considered and a line to be drawn if not in art then certainly in life.

I once saw her on *Parkinson* when she was the second guest. The first was Jim Davidson. It seemed an unlikely pairing and certainly the conversation between Parky and Davidson was, as Thora would have put it, quite suggestive. When she came on they both looked suitably shamefaced: it was as if an aunt had unexpectedly arrived from Lytham and they hastily put away the stout and brought out the lemonade.

Considerations of taste came up again when I was writing *The Last of the Sun*. Despite the title I didn't want this to be yet another heart-rending account of a woman descending into forgetfulness and dementia so I did deliberately endeavour to think the unthinkable and imagine what the public would least expect (or even want) Thora to be doing, with a spot of geriatric heavy petting coming out top.

Even so, the saga of Dolly and Mr Pilling isn't all that far from some of the scenarios dreamed up for Thora and myself by the genial myth-makers of *Dead Ringers*. While these always made me laugh I never found the dialogue attributed to me quite as witty as I'd have liked, nor was our association ever as close and continuous as the parody demanded. *Spitting Image* had once had us tucked up in bed together and in *Dead Ringers* we were always in one another's pockets: as the brains behind an international drugs ring was one I particularly liked.

The truth, unsurprisingly, was more ordinary. Thora and I worked together only half a dozen times in thirty years. Though each collaboration was memorable, it never seemed to me that I wrote a great deal for Thora; rather I feel now I didn't write nearly enough. Nor did we see each other socially. We were always going to have lunch but never did, which is another regret, and though we'd occasionally chat on the phone, if I ever walked over the awkward cobbles to her crowded flat in Leinster Mews it would be to talk about work.

The myth, of course, is funnier but it did present a real dilemma when I started to think about writing what turned out to be our final fling. Is there any point, I wondered, now that we're both such a joke? If we bring an indulgent smile so readily to the face of the public why not just leave it there? The sight of Thora helpless in her wheelchair, still very much herself but rusting away for want of employment made these considerations seem trivial and self-serving so I put together this short final piece.

The Last of the Sun could be said to be about the persistence of desire, which isn't an entirely respectable subject and not something the young or even the middle-aged are prepared to contemplate, let alone acknowledge, still wanting it at eighty the stuff of seaside postcards.

Dignify such longings with the word 'needs' and they would these day be more acceptable, 'sexual needs' just another earnest box to be ticked off on a social services list. But 'needs' hasn't ever quite made it into my vocabulary and I am happy still to think of them as wants, desires or even cravings.

Maybe all that can be said for Mr Pilling's fumblings with his old ladies is that they make a change and that, as the shadows lengthen, to be mildly interfered with might occasionally be preferable to *Countdown*. But that the old ladies should allow such liberties on a weekly (and eventually twice-weekly) basis might stretch credulity. Or it may shock; it may hearten. And at least Mr Pilling has found his niche. The monologue might even be thought to be about tolerance.

Originally I thought of the story concluding with the disgraced Mr Pilling banished from the home and even imprisoned, with Dolly and her friend Blanche left to contemplate what future there was unenlivened by his furtive attentions. Deprived of these ancient heavy pettings what did life have in store for either of these ladies except a straight run to the grave? Another dying fall, in fact.

And that would have been the approved way to end it and – though I'm not keen on the phrase (or what it describes) – the politically correct way.

In the meantime I wasn't sure the plot I was constructing might not be beyond Thora. It hinges on the current law that a house left by a parent to his or her children seven years or more before the parent's death thereby escapes estate duty.

I need not have worried. Thora had made just such an arrangement herself, as indeed had that other old lady, Thora's only rival in the public's affections, the Queen Mother. Neither arrangement had resulted in the bitterness and recrimination that occur in the play where Vera, the daughter, is concerned only that her mother stay alive long enough to save them the tax. It works. Vera (and indeed the Queen) are the lucky ones, their parent having successfully disencumbered themselves (or been disencumbered) of a substantial asset, thus saving the children a packet when death duties have to be paid.

Others less canny face a situation in which the family home the children might justifiably see as their nest egg has to be sold in order to finance the upkeep of the aged parent now living in a home. The parent lives on, the capital from the sale dwindles, the children's future narrows in consequence. In such circumstances, and particularly when the old person has lost touch with reality and may not even know them, it must be hard for the offspring (themselves in their sixties already) not to long for their parent's speedy departure.

The law, so sedulous in its protection of children at the beginning of life, in their second childhood abandons them to the harsh disciplines of the market. So much for caring, so called.

'We would like closure,' say the children, their language fashionable even when the bedspread is not.

It's difficult to end a play set in an old people's home on an upbeat note and, as I say, to begin with I went along with the convention. Mr Pilling was duly disgraced and banned from the premises, and Dolly and Blanche were left to face their shortening days deprived of his attentions. The triumph of Vera, in fact. A candlewick farewell.

But knowing this was likely to be the last work that Thora would do, I wanted her to go out with a bang and certainly with a laugh, even if it was a dirty one. The Veras of this world must not be allowed to get their own way. Dolly should triumph. And so, though it perhaps makes the play more of a fable than a story, I let Mr Pilling off the hook, doubled his fiddling time and installed Dolly and Blanche in a room of their own where they can really enjoy it.

And so at the finish Thora goes down with all her flags flying, game to the last.

The song she then sings was a song she sang when she was in *Our Miss Gibbs* at the Royalty Theatre, Morecambe. She was sixteen then but more than seventy years later she was still word perfect.

The Last of the Sun

An old lady, Dolly, in bed or possibly lying on the bed in her clothes. There are three other beds in the room but we do not see them. (We don't see them also because Thora was too frail to do the piece on television but only on radio.)

I love Tuesdays.

We get our hair done in the morning. We have bilberry tart to our dinner and Mr Pilling comes in the afternoon.

I said to Blanche, 'I wouldn't care if every day was a Tuesday. It's grand.'

I didn't use to like the Bible, only Mr Pilling gives it such feeling. Widower. Retired. Had a little gents' outfitters over at Rawdon. Blanche'll put on her lipstick when he comes.

Pause.

Our Vera came this morning and all. Paid us a state visit. Her and . . . Neville, is it? . . . the feller she's married to now. Member of the boating fraternity. Blazer. Little cap. Weighing anchor at Tadcaster so they thought they could pop in en route.

I said, 'How's my house?'

She said, 'We've put in a conservatory.'

I said, 'Am I allowed to die yet?'

She said, 'Don't be silly, mother.'

She counts on her fingers.

It'll be six years now.

End of section. Go to black.

Bindra's just been round with the air freshener when Mr Pilling arrives. Raincoat always neatly folded. Puts it down on the bed. Holds up the Bible. Lovely fingernails. I complimented him on them once and he said 'Well, it's not something I would want broadcasting, Mrs Walker, but I have them manicured. Kelly does them at Salon Snippets and I count it money well spent.' Never looks at you when he's doing it. Just concentrates on the words of the New Testament.

Down goes the raincoat, up comes the Bible and away we go.

There's four of us in the room and he'll generally kick off with Annie or Lois because they're both confused. Then Blanche, then me. 'My two princesses' is what he calls us.

And this afternoon he's just got started down at the daft end when who should turn up again but our Vera.

I thought, 'Oh stink.'

I said, 'I know why you've come. You're bothered I might peg out. It's that fiddle you did over my house.'

I reckoned to give it to her to save tax, but I had to last another seven years and it must be coming up to the seven now.

She said, 'Oh, is it? I haven't been counting. Only it's not a fiddle. The Queen Mother did it so it must be all right.'

I said, 'Yes, only her daughter didn't put her in a home.'

By this time, Mr Pilling's on with Blanche.

I said to Vera, 'I'm next, so you'd better be off or he'll be reading the Bible to you.'

That does the trick and she suddenly remembers she's got a stint at Age Concern.

And I said, 'There's no need to keep coming. I'm not going to die out of spite.'

Only she doesn't hear and I see she's watching Mr Pilling.

I said, 'My daughter's going now, Mr Pilling.'

He just nods but doesn't stop reading, then (*she mimes withdrawing movement*) waves his other hand.

When it's my turn, Mr Pilling says, 'A grand-looking woman, your daughter.'

I said, 'You're not alone in that opinion.'

'Why,' he says, 'who else thinks so?'

I said, 'She does.'

He smiled.

'I'm going to read from St Paul's Epistle to the Ephesians.'

431

And he pats my leg.
End of section.

You wouldn't credit it, but on the following Tuesday our Vera's here again.
I thought, 'If you want to see me that badly, why did you put me in a
home in the first place?'
Mr Pilling's already reading to Annie, who's banging her tray most of
the time but it doesn't bother him, just reads.
Vera enthrones herself by my bed but she's naught to say and I must
have dozed off because when I come round she's gone.
I said to Blanche, 'Did our Vera go?'
'No, mother,' she whispers, 'I'm here.' And for some reason she's hiding
behind the bed.
I said, 'What are you doing there? Come sit down.'
Meanwhile, Mr Pilling's come over to Blanche.
Our Vera's sat with her back to him and she still hasn't got much to say.
I said, 'How's the navy?'
She said, 'What?'
I said, 'The round-the-world yachtsman? *Neville?*'
She doesn't say anything and when I look I see it's because she's glued to
my washbasin mirror.
I call out to Blanche.
'Our Vera can see you in the mirror, Blanche. Give her a wave, Mr
Pilling. There you are, Vera, he's waving.'
Vera looks right mad.
'Funny name, Blanche, for somebody that age. What's his name?'
I said, 'Arthur.' Only we never call him that. We're not on such familiar
terms.
Mr Pilling comes over in a bit and says 'I'm afraid, Mrs Walker, I'm
going to have to curtail my visit. Rain wasn't forecast and I foolishly
ventured out without my umbrella.'
He folds his scarf, puts his little gloves on. '*A bientôt*. Don't the daffodils
look a picture?'

When he's gone, Vera says, 'Presumably they're all confused except you.'

I said, 'Who?'

She said, 'The other women.'

I said, 'Blanche isn't confused. They took her on a trip to Harewood House.'

Vera said, 'What's she doing blonde? At her age? Does she dye it?'

I said, 'Well, they dye it for her.'

She said, 'Yes, but she must give them the green light. A name like Blanche. Anybody'd know they were on an easy wicket. No wonder he gets his hands under the bedclothes. He knows he's assured of a warm welcome.'

She takes both my hands.

'Oh, mother, mother. You've had such a narrow escape.'

I said, 'Have I?'

End of section.

Lovely ears this lad had. He kept asking me these questions and blushing, and his ears blushed as well. I've never seen that before.

He said did I know what the word 'traumatised' meant, and had a list of things I might feel.

Did I feel: annoyed

angry

injured

assaulted

damaged

polluted

violated?

I said, 'No.'

He said, 'What then?'

So I told him.

He wasn't the police. I don't think it's got that far. I think he's just a lad from the solicitors.

It's all our Vera.

433

She said to me, 'Oh, mother. To think, mother, if you'd been that bit
younger he might have tried it on with you.'

I said, 'Yes, I'm lucky.'

She said, 'Little glasses, raincoat. The Bible was just a smokescreen. He
was an animal.

'Anyway, it's over.

'You won't be wanting to stay here, I can understand that. And I don't
blame you. I don't want you living in a place where they turn a blind
eye to sexual molestation.

'We'll find you somewhere else. I've heard very good reports of a place
over at Cawood.'

I said, 'Cawood? There's nothing at Cawood. I get few enough visitors as
it is. Nobody's going to pole over to Cawood.'

She said, 'We would, mother, and that's all you want.'

I said, 'You mean it's handy for the boat?'

She said, 'Well, we can't let you stay here. And once we've put in the
claim for compensation, they won't let you.'

I said, 'How do you mean, compensation?'

She said, 'Mother, the home has a duty of care. He was interfering with
people. Fortunately, not you; you're too old. But your friend, Blanche,
and the other two . . . I saw him.'

I said, 'So what's going to happen to Mr Pilling?'

She said, 'Well, for obvious reasons the home isn't anxious to prosecute,
but he'll never show his face again here, I can tell you.'

She said, 'Shall you want counselling?'

I said, 'Yes, I bloody well do want counselling. *If* he stops.'

She said, 'What?'

I said, 'I used to look forward to his visits. I lived for Tuesdays. We all did.'

She said, 'Mother, you disgust me.'

I said, 'Not as much as you disgust me. And always have, you po-faced
article. Not to put too fine a point on it, I like having the tops of my
legs stroked, even at my age, and so does Blanche and if there's a
gentleman like Mr Pilling willing to undertake the task and derive

434

pleasure from it then I prefer to think of that not as something disgusting but as God moving in his mysterious way.

'That or else he deserves the Duke of Edinburgh's Award.'

And I said, 'I'm not moving from this home. It's not ideal but it's better than the last dump you put me in.

'I shall tell them it was all done of my own free will. We were consenting adults.

'So you can kiss goodbye to your flaming compensation.'

Bindra comes in with the air freshener.

I said 'Bindra. I think Mrs Turnbull wants a tissue.'

End of section.

It's lovely Blanche and me having our own room.

We've got a TV that we can switch off and we don't have Radio 1 blaring out all the time, or Lois banging her tray. We've each got one of these cassette things and we can have the window open if we want.

The home were so grateful I didn't want any compensation, they put us in here at a discount. Vera still wanted to shift me somewhere else but the rate was so reasonable Neville wouldn't hear of it. So boat or no boat, he turns out to have more sense than she does.

Mr Pilling still comes over on Tuesdays and sometimes Thursdays as well, or Arthur as we now call him. We can't wean him off the religion but as I said to Blanche, without the Bible in one hand he doesn't seem to be able to function with the other.

We're on the Epistle of Timothy at the moment.

It's all very . . . 'civilised' would I think be the word. And we've got a nice outlook. You can see the planes coming in to Leeds and Bradford airport and there's a view of the reservoir and sometimes I kid myself it's the sea.

I look out of the window on an evening, watching the last of the sun and I know it's daft, but sometimes I'll wave at it. (*She waves.*) Bye-bye, sun. See you tomorrow.

End.

Thora Hird

1911–2003

One of Thora's many merits as an actress – and I shall call her that rather than the currently more correct actor because Thora would have called herself an actress and not thought it demeaning to do so – one of Thora's many merits as an actress was that she was scrupulous about the text. Always word perfect, she knew if she'd said an 'and' when you'd written a 'but' and almost shamed you by the respect she accorded to the words you had written and her anxiety to reproduce them perfectly.

It's ironic, then, that her first memorable performance for me should have been to some extent improvised. This was in John Schlesinger's 1962 film of Stan Barstow's *A Kind of Loving*, in which she played the sour-faced Mrs Rothwell, straitlaced, house-proud and watchful mother of the beautiful Ingrid. Woken late one night, she comes downstairs to find Alan Bates's Vic drunk and snogging the matchless Ingrid in the parlour. Bates is about to apologise when he is abruptly and copiously sick behind the sofa.

Thora's reaction to this, as written, was 'You filthy, disgusting pig', a line tailor-made to her talents. However, it had to cover a good deal of action, Bates, for instance, throwing up at least twice, and so Schlesinger told her to improvise . . . not a technique Thora had ever had any occasion to acquire; her job was to say the words not make them up. Still she did her best and having a basic text, 'You filthy disgusting pig', she proceeded to play variations on it.

'You pig,' glaring at the cowering Bates.

436

'You're filthy, you. Disgusting.'

Then, forcing herself to look at the sick behind the sofa:

'You . . . you're a pig.'

Schlesinger, with what in every sense was gay abandon, kept the camera rolling until Thora had given every possible variation of the four words the script had allowed her, her frustration both at her own lack of invention and the sadism of the director transmuted into a memorable performance on the screen.

Lear grieving over the corpse of Cordelia was not more grief-stricken than Mrs Rothwell over her polluted parlour.

Long before this, of course, she had become a favourite on television, in films and in the theatre and all her life she never stopped working. On the Yorkshire novelist Winifred Holtby's gravestone there is the inscription:

> God give me work
> Till my life shall end
> And life
> Till my work is done.

Few lives can have seen that prayer so fully answered as Thora's, who played her first part on the stage of the Royalty Theatre, Morecambe at two months old and who was still working ninety-one years later in Studio 5 at Portland Place a few months before she died.

Until she was quite late on in life the parts she played were generally comic and so were underrated and it was only in late middle age when she began to play the occasional serious role that her talent was properly acknowledged. There are not many artists who reach a peak in their seventies and eighties but Thora did. She lived long enough to be taken seriously.

She never took herself seriously, though no one was more dedicated to the job in hand, coached in her words by Scotty, her devoted husband, and after he died by Jan, their daughter, her family's devotion not the least element in Thora's success.

And she knew she was loved and it delighted her, people calling out to her in the street knowing they'd always get a smile or a wave. It's a sort of appreciation that can be dangerous to an artist, but loved though she was, whether her fans would approve of her in a part came quite low down on her list.

Doris, the part she played in *A Cream Cracker Under the Settee*, is not a particularly nice woman, narrow, censorious, preferring concrete in the garden to grass and disliking trees because they drop leaves everywhere. As in the course of rehearsal the harsh nature of this woman began to come home Thora took me on one side.

'You couldn't give me a line somewhere, love, that would show that even if I'm not nice now, I may have been once upon a time?'

I didn't manage to think of one, partly because I didn't really want to, and there are many performers in that situation who would, as it were, have tipped the audience the wink off their own bat, softening a line, perhaps, or giving the occasional sad smile. Thora didn't. If harsh was what you'd written that was the way she'd play it.

And she won your heart as a writer because, unusually in our profession, she trusted the words more than she did the director.

She was never difficult with directors but there'd been so many of them that she'd long since ceased to bother to learn their names, referring to them all to their faces by the generic name 'Mr de Grunwald', presumably after Anatole de Grunwald, with whom she'd worked in her early days in films.

Her expectations of a director were not high. She was once singing to me the praises of a director with whom she'd worked on television, saying how she'd had this difficult scene to play on location:

'And you could tell he was a good director, love, because he put me against the most beautiful lamppost you've ever seen.'

It's not a notion of directing that would commend itself to Peter Brook.

And she got better as she got older and in ways that her father, always her sternest critic, would have approved. She got simpler and, given the chance, relied less on her familiar tricks, letting her own personality show through and steering closer to herself as the best acting demands.

At the finish she sometimes found it hard to tell the difference, taking the frail and immobilised creatures whom she played both in my plays and in Deric Longden's *Lost for Words* as versions of herself; she was acting out her own demise. They were on the last lap and so was she.

Peter Cook and Dudley Moore used to be able to make the band laugh. Thora could make the cameraman cry and the whole crew sometimes and when she finished the scene in *Waiting for the Telegram* in which she recalled the departure of her First War sweetheart it was a minute or two in the studio before anybody trusted themselves to speak. Then it was Thora:

'I think I got one of the words wrong. Will you be wanting to go again?'

Most of the time between takes would be filled with Thora talking about the past, her only rival in relentless reminiscence in my experience being John Gielgud. But whereas the stuff of Gielgud's recollections was theatre in the West End, Larry and Gertie and Noël, Thora's memories were of poky gas-lit dressing-rooms in the provinces, playing to a rowdy second house on a Saturday night, the meanness of some of the comedians she'd worked with and the backstage antics of the Crazy Gang and the punishing routine of three performances daily at the height of the Blackpool season.

For all her success on television and in films, it was this now vanished world that had been her foundation and her home. It was only in the last few months of her life that she ceased to manage on her own and had to be taken into care, at which point she had a choice . . . between Denville Hall, the home for retired actors, and Brinsley House, the Variety Artists' Home at Twickenham. That she opted for the latter shows, I think, that for all the awards she had won and the acclaim her acting had been accorded she was still at heart the local lass who could do a turn before the front cloth at the Winter Gardens, Morecambe, or a number like 'I'm so silly when the moon comes out' from *Our Miss Gibbs*, which she did there when she was sixteen and hadn't forgotten the words when she sang it in a BBC studio only a few months before she died.

She was blessed at the finish in that her decline was both short and painless, though even in this she could not help but be funny. Still living on her own in her mews flat, she would sometimes become confused and on one occasion telephoned her daughter Jan, complaining bitterly.

'I'm in the studio, love. I'm doing this film with John Wayne only he's gone out and left me and everybody else has gone out and I'm stuck here on my own.'

Jan said, 'Mum, you're not in the studio, you're in the flat in the mews.'

She said, 'I am not. I'm in the studio with John Wayne and the beggar's gone out and left me.'

Jan said, 'Mum. You're in the flat. Now look out of the window, is that the mews?'

Pause.

'Well, it looks like the mews . . . but they can do wonders with scenery nowadays.'

Thora only once played in Shakespeare, the Nurse in *Romeo and Juliet*. And she could never have thought to play Cleopatra. But Charmian's lament for the dead Cleopatra is a proper epitaph for this droll-faced northern girl, who in the course of a long and happy life took her place among the best that we have.

'Now boast thee, death. In thy possession lies a lass unparallel'd.'

Lindsay Anderson

1923–94

At the drabber moments of my life (swilling some excrement from the steps, for instance, or rooting with a bent coat-hanger down a blocked sink) thoughts occur like 'I bet Tom Stoppard doesn't have to do this' or 'There is no doubt David Hare would have deputed this to an underling.'

So I was happy to read in Gavin Lambert's *Mainly about Lindsay Anderson* that Lindsay harboured similar thoughts about such self-imposed menialities. On the eve of filming *O Lucky Man* Lindsay has his ailing mother to stay in his flat in Swiss Cottage. Before she arrives he cleans up the kitchen and bathroom and is just tackling the fireplace in his mother's room when the doorbell rings and it's the studio driver.

He confides to his diary:

> Thinks: at 48, turning 49, this leading British director on his knees at a dirty grate with a plastic bucket and detergent. Possibly from the outside this looks admirably humble and determinedly individual. To me it feels just a desperate rearguard action. Nobody realises what a mess of loneliness and inadequacy I am inside.

The last sentence apart, those are my sentiments exactly.

I worked with Lindsay only once, when he directed my TV play *The Old Crowd* for LWT in 1978, some account of which I gave (and Lindsay gave too) in the published version of the play. I hadn't realised why my script should so readily have appealed to him until I read Lambert's quote from Lindsay's contribution to *Declaration*, an anthology of protest pieces by the so-called Angry Young Men.

Coming back to Britain is, in many respects, like going back to the nursery. The outside world, the dangerous world, is shut away; it sounds muffled. Cretonne curtains are drawn, with a pretty pattern on them of the Queen and her fairytale Prince, riding to Westminster in a golden coach. Nanny lights the fire and sits herself down with a nice cup of tea and yesterday's *Daily Express*, but she keeps half an eye on us too, as we bring out our trophies from abroad, the books and pictures we have managed to get past the customs. (Nanny has a pair of scissors handy, to cut out anything it wouldn't be right for children to see.) The clock ticks on. The servants are all downstairs, watching TV. Mummy and Daddy have gone to the new Noël Coward at the Globe. Sometimes there is a bang from the street outside – backfire, says Nanny. Sometimes there's a scream from the cellar – Nanny's lips tighten, but she doesn't say anything . . . Is it to be wondered at that, from time to time, a window is found open, and the family is diminished by one? We hear of him later sometimes, living in a penthouse in New York, or a dacha near Moscow.

This was written in 1958 but when, twenty years later, I worked with Lindsay it was still his view of England, down to the bang in the street outside and the open window, both of which he inserted into the original draft of *The Old Crowd*.

As soon as we started working on the script it was plain that Lindsay needed a villain. In feature films and for understandable reasons this role was generally played by the producer or 'the money' but there were often lesser villains, too, closer at hand and almost haphazardly decided on: a costume designer, for instance, and more often a woman than a man. Sometimes, unforgivably (though she forgave him), it was his frequent collaborator, the designer Jocelyn Herbert. The nominal producer of *The Old Crowd* was Stephen Frears, but in real terms it was LWT and its then head of programmes, Michael Grade. Used as I was to the BBC and to my regular producer, Innes Lloyd, I found LWT entirely well-meaning but awkward to work with only because it wasn't an organisation geared to producing drama. Michael Grade, though, was unwavering in his support and when Lindsay fell behind on the shooting schedule Grade sanctioned extension after extension; when the studio finally broke it was half past three in the morning.

Inured to the duplicity and stubbornness of the front office, Lindsay, I think, found these accommodations a bit of a disappointment. Cartooned, he would be Old Mother Riley, rolling up her sleeves and with an elaborate display of pugilistics squaring up to an entirely imaginary opponent.

In his films, too, Lindsay believed in confrontation, fetching an audience up short, shocking them into recognition. In *Is That All There Is?*, a TV film that turned out to be virtually an obituary, he intercuts newsreel shots of starving Somalian children with supermarket shelves and shopping carts laden with food. It's possible Lindsay wanted to chastise his audience, in which case such juxtapositions are permissible if clichéd. But if his intention was to make an audience think or to touch its conscience the technique is just too crude and more likely to elicit groans than guilt.

Lindsay thought more subtle approaches were timid (and, of course, 'English'). At the start of my career I might have agreed, but even when I was in *Beyond the Fringe* (which I'm sure he didn't much care for) it seemed to me that laughter had to come into the equation. And however manfully Gavin Lambert defends him, it very seldom did: so much of *Britannia Hospital*, for instance, just isn't funny.

One reason Lindsay persistently underestimated the sophistication of his audience was that he didn't watch much television. He never appreciated the regular diet of not always mild subversion and social criticism that was still the staple of television drama; police brutality or municipal corruption were taken for granted by a TV audience (or were certainly nothing fresh) so they were not easy to shock as Lindsay wanted to shock them. But it wasn't because they were jaded, just more discriminating than he gave them credit for. He thought he was saying something bold and new in *Britannia Hospital* but even in 1982 he wasn't – not in England anyway. One of his Polish friends said: 'It's the best Polish film I've seen in a long time.'

Of course his films provoked and when *Britannia Hospital* was shown at the Cannes Festival during the Falklands War the British delegation staged a walk-out. But quite over what it would be hard to say. There's a scene in the film where, during a strike of hospital workers, an ambulance is allowed through the picket lines but hospital porters insist on taking their tea break at that point, thus condemning the patient to die in the lobby. 'Oh, it couldn't happen,' one is meant to say (and some critics no doubt did say). But Lindsay could show you chapter and verse in a news item culled by his scriptwriter, David Sherwin.

Still, that wasn't quite the point. One felt bullied, lectured, remonstrated with, as I'm sure some people felt bullied by the (altogether sillier) *Old Crowd*. And had Lindsay been lecturing and bullying on behalf of the poor and underprivileged some critics would have given him credit for that, as they give credit to Ken Loach. But in Lindsay's view class wasn't the issue but humanity in general.

He affected to despise the press, whatever its complexion, his daily paper generally the *Telegraph*. But, as Tony Richardson said, 'he was a sublime and sometimes pugnacious publicist' and could never resist an interview or an opportunity to sound off, particularly when common sense dictated otherwise. During *The Old Crowd*, for instance, he was shadowed by Tom Sutcliffe of the *Guardian*, to whom he held forth on what he saw as the significance of the piece and the shortcomings of television. One article in the lead-up to the showing was entitled 'The Master at Work'. Had I been a disinterested reader it would certainly have put my back up; as it was, it just filled me with foreboding. Of course, Dennis Potter did the same but he was more skilful at it than Lindsay. So after the pretentious pre-publicity the howls of outrage that greeted *The Old Crowd* were predictable, though Lindsay wasn't at all contrite, blaming affronted national pride: 'The English like to think they like to laugh at themselves. This may have been true once when there was no apprehension that the Sun might one day Set. But it is not true today. The good ship Britannia is waterlogged in a shark-infested sea. Don't rock the boat.'

I think now, as I thought then, that this was well over the top, even though the play had the bad luck to be screened during the so-called winter of discontent. Still, it was a much better piece than was generally allowed (Clive James and Richard Ingrams making particular fools of themselves), but it wasn't what viewers had come to expect from me and so was unfamiliar, or too unfamiliar anyway, a little unfamiliarity often an ingredient of success at any rate with critics, as it enables them to buff up on their role as guides to the less discerning public.

None of this, though, takes into account his sheer fun and his pleasure in (and exasperation with) actors. In *The Old Crowd* the middle-aged couple are determined to hold their house-warming party, come what may. Their furniture has been delayed in transit so dinner has to be eaten off an old trestle table. Without warning the actors, Lindsay had the table jacked-up eighteen inches so that on the actual take Rachel Roberts, Jill Bennett and Co. found themselves trying to behave normally although the dining-table was practically under their chins.

On the other hand, as with the Royal Family, it did have to be *his* fun. He had no time for the occasional giggles and private jokes that occur when a group of actors are working together for any length of time. Then he was the schoolmaster, once even clambering onto the stage during a performance to stop some silliness of which he disapproved.

Lambert's book is a memoir of Lindsay, not a full-scale biography, and doesn't, for instance, go into Lindsay's finances. I have always understood that he enjoyed an income from one of his aunts, a Miss Bell of Bell's Whisky (and I sometimes bought it on that account). Certainly there must have been money beyond what he earned in films and in the theatre, which (certainly in today's terms) amounted to very little. Not that he enjoyed an extravagant lifestyle. His flat was comfortable but plain, over-crowded and shabby. He wasn't interested in clothes or possessions and meals out consisted in popping down the road to the Cosmo on the Finchley Road. 'This is good,' Lindsay would say, tucking into some leathery veal. 'Nothing fancy about it.'

Where the money went was on supporting a resident cast of lame ducks. Sandy, his schizophrenic nephew; Patsy Healey, who had acted in his short film *The White Bus* and been depressed ever since. There was his mother

445

and, for a while, his brother's wife, and he was always on call to counsel and very often to subsidise needy friends and actors who had lost their way. I have had some credit because I gave room in my garden to one social inadequate. Lindsay played host to half a dozen with no credit at all nor, I imagine, much thanks. And he made nothing of it. He was a good, compassionate man presenting to the public a face that was scornful and reproving and hungry for publicity while doing untold acts of private goodness. And if this shows nothing else it proves he can't have much liked being alone, as he seldom was – how he worked on his scripts in the middle of such domestic chaos is a mystery.

'I imagine,' I begin, but 'I imagine', 'I suppose', 'possibly', 'slightly' and the kind of qualification that peppers (or unpeppers) everything I write, Lindsay would want struck out. Bold, clear statement was his chosen mode, which perhaps (*sic*) explains his failure with Chekhov; Lindsay's preferred ending to *Three Sisters*: 'We're going to Moscow and there's no perhaps about it!'

Still, David Storey's *Home* is nothing if not tentative and he did that superbly. *Home* is so nebulous on the page that at the time I couldn't see how Gielgud in particular would ever manage to learn the lines (or the half lines). But it was a wonderful production, as were all Lindsay's collaborations with Storey, *Home*, *The Contractor*, *The Changing Room* and *Life Class* still not accorded their due; though the ease with which Storey seemed to write his plays filled me at the time, I remember, with envy and despair.

As he disliked tentativeness and ambiguity so Lindsay also had no time for irony, which he saw as a compromise, a means of having it both ways and thus dear to the English heart. And maybe we do overdose on it, but with more irony (or even some) *Britannia Hospital* would have seemed less crass and been easier to swallow. (A voice from a French lakeside: 'But, my dear Alan, why should it be easy to swallow? I didn't want it to be "easy to swallow" as you put it.')

There are odd surprises in Lambert's book. That Lindsay should have had a stab at transcendental meditation and even been given a mantra is understandable because it was done to please Frank Grimes, whom he loved, but that he not only experimented with but appears to have relied on the *I Ching* seems unlike the man I knew.

Lambert reveals that at Oxford he himself had a fling with Peter Brook, whom I had thought a model of heterosexuality but who seduced Lambert via a silk dressing-gown and Chopin nocturnes on the gramophone. It's something to be remembered nowadays when the sage of the modern theatre is taking himself too seriously (i.e. quite often), though one can see how turning his back on such fripperies might lead, as with Wittgenstein, to a life of punishing rigour ending up, as it did with Brook and the *Mahabharata*, literally in the desert. Lambert also reminds us that Barbara Cartland, that calcified gay icon (and dead this very day), did not in the 1950s think pink, and in between writing one novel per fortnight found time to be a harrier of deviants or, as she called them, 'ghouls of perverted sex'.

Lambert was urged to write this book by Jocelyn Herbert and Anthony Page, even though he misdates Page's production of Ben Travers's *A Cuckoo in the Nest* to 1974 and calls it a success. It was actually done in 1964 and a disaster. I know as I acted in it, lured by the distinction of a cast that included Beatrix Lehmann, Arthur Lowe, Nicol Williamson and John Osborne. Nicol Williamson, who played the lead, was no farceur and seldom wrung a laugh from the audience, whom he chose to intimidate rather than entertain. Very shaky on the words, he would pause lengthily, snarl 'Yes?' and stare malevolently at the stalls until the prompt came.

I suppose Lindsay must have seen it (Arthur Lowe was one of his favourite actors) but it would have been with a good deal of heavy sighing, looks of despair to his neighbours and even groans, a visit to the theatre with Lindsay generally something of a pantomime.

In the light of Lindsay's unrequited affections, I wanted to know if he liked the look of himself. Lambert doesn't say, though it's probably in Lindsay's diary, from which he only sparingly quotes. I would guess that he didn't, and so not expecting anyone else to either. The great loves of his life map out his career: Richard Harris (*This Sporting Life*), Albert Finney (*Billy Liar*), Malcolm McDowell (*If . . .*) and Frank Grimes. None of them seems to have come across (if that, indeed, was what he wanted). They were all incorrigibly male and not all were over-blessed with imagination.

Reading this, to me, overwhelmingly sad memoir, I was grateful for Gavin Lambert's parallel (and much happier) experiences which thread through it. Without them the frustrations of Lindsay's life would have been unbearable to read. He was like Rattigan's schoolmaster Crocker-Harris, armoured against feeling and taken to be so by many of his associates but underneath emotionally raw and a lifetime romantic, 'Can this be love?' a recurring question. He never seems to have become inured to passion or grown a thicker skin, his last love for Grimes as strong and compulsive (and futile) as his first for Serge Reggiani. Love, as he said himself, was not feasible. Sex might have made it easier, but there's some doubt if there was much of that. The theatre ought to have made it easier, too. It's a good production in my experience when people start to fall for one another, director included, but Lindsay tended to fall in love first then do the film or play afterwards, which is rather different.

The fact that all the men Lindsay fell for were straight should have been less of a problem in the supposedly permissive 1960s and 1970s, but it would have been a remarkable young man who could have got past the sarcasm and the banter and the picking you up on every word, actually to dare to lay a hand on him. A remarkable young man or, of course, a rented one, which was still a possibility in the 1970s and, pre-Aids and pre-Murdoch, quite safe, prostitution then a profession with some standards and not, as it became in the 1980s, a subsidiary of tabloid journalism. But with Lindsay such an inveterate romantic it was no more feasible than love, though one could write the scene – his pretended indifference and verbal sparring met with the boy's professional incomprehension, the shy man's reserve gradually breaking down as the master becomes the pupil.

That was one way his life might have been better, or at any rate different; the loss of his private income would have been another, if only because the security it offered allowed him to be too choosy. There are theatre and TV directors who do productions on the cab-rank principle, taking whatever turns up next and without making too much of a fuss about it. Lindsay emphatically wasn't such a director, though some of his choices, William Douglas Home's *The Kingfisher*, for instance, might suggest otherwise. Playwrights, for their part, like to think of their plays as events and, if not looming as large in the lives and careers of their directors as their own, nevertheless constituting more than just a job of work or a way of bringing home the bacon.

The plays and films that Lindsay directed were never just jobs; often, as with the productions of *Hamlet* that he did with Frank Grimes, they were outcrops of his inner life. Even *The Old Crowd* he made part of his own story by casting old friends like Rachel Roberts and Jill Bennett, and by expanding the script to give more scope to Frank Grimes – none of which was to its detriment.

Still, it's hard not to feel that had he been directing in the 1940s, say, or under the studio system in Hollywood, he would have had to make two or three films a year, perhaps one of which might have been good. Instead, so much of his life was spent waiting around for films to be set up, working on futile development deals, with years wasted in the process. Had he been making films in the 1940s, too, they might have been war movies, which he revelled in. *Das Boot*, the submarine epic, he liked very much ('no shit about it'), and it was one of the videos that lined the shelves in his flat which he was always ready to take down and play, often with a running commentary – MacArthur's departure in *They Were Expendable* I got once after asking what 'epic' meant.

He wasn't magnanimous. He was often unwilling to recognise the talents of others, particularly if they were recognised already, and especially if they were English. But he was always wonderfully, uncompromisingly himself. Gavin Lambert ends this sad, loving book with some afterwords, one of which is from Karel Reisz:

> One day a man came up to Lindsay and myself in the street and congratulated us on *This Sporting Life*. He praised it effusively and called it the most

important British film in years etc., etc. We thanked him, and then he said, 'But there's a scene near the end that I don't think . . .' and got no further. 'Fuck off!' Lindsay said, and walked on.

Art, Architecture and Authors

Going to the Pictures

In 1993 I was made a Trustee of the National Gallery at a time when free entry to the nation's museums and galleries was still a contentious issue, as I hope it no longer is today. While I was a Trustee I gave two lectures: Going to the Pictures, *which is about my experience of pictures and galleries in general, and* Spoiled for Choice, *a lecture to accompany Sainsbury's Paintings in Schools scheme, when I had to choose four paintings from any gallery in Great Britain. The lectures suffer from want of all the illustrations they had in the lecture theatre but I hope they are of some interest nevertheless.*

The Wilton Diptych

The first time I set foot in the National Gallery must have been early in 1957, and I came in to look at this picture, the Wilton Diptych – the two panels painted by an unknown artist in the late fourteenth century for Richard II, who kneels in the left-hand panel, accompanied by a trio of

453

saints: Edmund, King and Martyr; Edward the Confessor and John the Baptist, who together sponsor him into the presence of the Virgin, whose angels in a show of celestial solidarity encouragingly sport Richard II's badge of the white hart.

It was probably a portable altarpiece and in 1957 it was the only painting in the gallery that I knew anything about. This wasn't because I had any knowledge or interest in art history, which in 1957 was still something of an academic backwater, frequented so far as undergraduate Oxford was concerned chiefly by Firbankian inadequates and boys from Stowe. I knew about the Wilton Diptych because I was in my last year reading history with Richard II my special subject, and when later that year I took my degree I stayed on to do research, again into Richard II.

The research came to nothing, though humiliating memories of it return on occasions like this when I'm required to lecture. Lecturing is not a natural activity for a playwright, accustomed as one is to diffuse responsibility for one's words among one's characters, so that the audience is never quite sure you mean what you say, or you mean what they say. I only ever gave one lecture on Richard II and it was to an historical society in Oxford, the audience a mixture of dons and undergraduates. At the conclusion of this less than exciting paper I asked if there were any questions. There was an endless silence until finally one timid undergraduate at the back put up his hand.

'Could you tell me where you bought your shoes?'

It was shortly after this I abandoned history and went on the stage.

Dissolve to Boston a few years later where I was on tour with *Beyond the Fringe* and went one free afternoon to Fenway Court, the museum and former home of the Boston heiress Isabella Stewart Gardner, famously seen in Sargent's portrait. The house had been kept much as it was in Mrs Gardner's lifetime and I remember it as being rather dowdy. It may have altered since – I was last there in 1975 – but I hope not, as it's the kind of museum one felt should be in a museum, as being very much of its time.

Much of Mrs Gardner's art collection had been put together and bought for Mrs Gardner by the expatriate American – expatriate Boston-ian in fact – the art historian and connoisseur Bernard Berenson. Mrs Gardner had died in 1924 but in 1962, when I went round the museum, Berenson himself was not long dead and biographies, diaries and commonplace books were being regularly brought out. So I got rather interested in Berenson, which, in retrospect, I wish I hadn't, as some of my anxieties about art, which is what a lot of this lecture is about, date back to that time.

Though Berenson later put together a large library of photographs, his study and listing of Italian paintings began before photographic reproductions were widely available. This to some extent dictated his method, though I suspect that with or without photographs Berenson's method would have been the same. This was, quite simply, to look and look and look, and he would stand in front of a painting by the hour together until every detail of it was committed to memory.

At some point in the course of this confrontation Berenson would experience a sense of rapture very like, I imagine, what far more people experience when listening to music. And in this connection it's no accident that Berenson's mentor when he came as a young man from Harvard to Oxford was Walter Pater, whose most famous dictum, I suppose, is that 'All art aspires towards the condition of music.'

I have to confess that I've never had a sensation of rapture, or any physical sensation in fact, standing in front of a painting except maybe aching legs or, to quote Nathaniel Hawthorne, 'That icy demon of weariness who haunts great picture galleries.' But it does happen; paintings do affect people. Take George Eliot in 1858:

> I sat on a sofa in the Dresden Picture Gallery opposite the picture (it was Raphael's *Sistine Madonna*) and a sort of awe, as if I was suddenly in the presence of some glorious being, made my heart swell too much for me to remain comfortably and we hurried out of the room.

Well, it hasn't happened to me, and having read about Berenson I took that to mean that I was lacking something, even if it was only the patience or the stamina to stand long enough looking. And though I later found that in my unfeelingness I was in distinguished company – Bertrand

Russell, for instance, Berenson's brother-in-law, complaining that pictures never made his stomach turn over either – nevertheless I felt I was failing some sort of sensitivity test and I invariably came out of galleries dissatisfied with myself.

It was not unlike the feeling I used to have coming out of church. As a boy I'd been very religious and my failure to respond to paintings on an emotional level was like my failure to respond to God: one was supposed to love Him but I didn't know what that meant. Thankfully all that was long since over, but here I was back in the same boat, only now it was Art.

Reading about Berenson engendered social anxieties too. Increasingly as he grew older the sage held court at his Florentine villa of I Tatti, where he was visited not merely by friends from the world of art but by anybody who was anybody who was passing through. No Nobel Prizewinner was ever turned away.

All his visitors were constrained seemingly without protest to fall in with his careful self-presentation and inflexible routine; few of them ever demurred, seeming to take this privileged mode of life as some sort of saintly dedication to art, with which, as I see now, it had very little to do.

That I must have been troubled about Berenson and about art, I realise in retrospect because at the time I wrote something about him. When I first started writing, in the early sixties, most of my stuff came out of being in two minds, the play or the sketch or whatever an attempt to achieve a kind of resolution. So when in 1964 I wrote a parody of an account of a visit to Berenson called *Ta Ta I Tatti* it came out of being dubious about this social sanctification of art.

In retrospect I don't know why I bothered. Re-reading about Berenson for this lecture I found him both intolerable and silly. How can you take seriously someone who had a correspondence with Ernest Hemingway about sex and wrote of himself that 'He had loved much but copulated little, although with the appreciation one would bring to a fine champagne.'

Besides being pretentious Berenson could also be a bit of a rogue. For much of his life he was on a retainer from the art dealer Duveen, which meant that some of his attributions were more self-serving than scholarly. He bulks more largely in the history of American museums and galleries than he does here, though he figures in a complicated saga to do with the acquisition of Titian's *La Schiavona*, which came to the National Gallery in 1942 and which Berenson originally thought was a copy of a lost Giorgione.

He was also indirectly involved in the purchase of the group of paintings by Sassetta now in the Sainsbury Wing, which Kenneth Clark bought when he was Director, probably for an inflated sum and again through Duveen, who was also a trustee. Trust, it has to be said, was not Duveen's strong suit.

If as a young man I'd had to put into words what my response was to pictures I'd have said I liked paintings that had what I thought of as a *glow* to them. That is what drew me across a room to a picture and (I say this slightly shamefacedly) made me want to take the picture home. It never came to that, but around this time I did buy one or two early nineteenth-century glass paintings which, whatever their artistic merits, do have, as does all painting on glass, a translucent glow.

It's only too easy to demonstrate what I thought of – still think of, I suppose – as this glow. Chosen almost at random there is Bellini's *Agony in the Garden*, the glow there coming, I suppose, from the approach of dawn, just as in Giorgione's *Il Tramonto* it's the light of sunset; whereas in this *Portrait of a Young Man* by Catena it could be thought to be the glow of youth.

Then there's the rather cosy glow of Antonello's *St Jerome in his Study*. Because its flesh was not supposed to decay the peacock was a symbol of immortality and resurrection. Less well known is the fact that it was supposed to scream at the sight of its own feet, not recognising them as its own – a predicament with which one sympathises more and more as one gets older.

Technically, particularly with Venetian pictures, the glow is often to do with glazes and the accumulation of glazes which give depth to the painting. Sometimes, too, it has to do with the colour tones being close together but, whatever it is, all I can say is that I know it when I see it, which is of course intellectually not very respectable or communicable. So it was fortunate that around this time, the late sixties, I began to be aware that pictures had another aspect and so began to take an interest in art history.

Of course I wasn't alone in this, as it was in the late sixties that the boom in art history really began to take off. The history of the history of art in England in the second half of the twentieth century would make a fascinating study as it would have to take in, be a sidelong look at, all sorts of other developments – the beginning of the colour supplements, for instance, and the expansion of newspapers and illustration, the ungentrification of Sotheby's and Christie's, the notion of the heritage and even, though one winces to say so, the *Antiques Roadshow*.

Crucial to the development of art history in this country was the arrival here in the thirties of refugee art historians from Nazi Germany, many of them iconographers. Now Berenson had had little time for iconography, being more taken up with what a painting looked like than with what it might mean. This seems pretty obviously short-sighted as one of the bonuses of iconography, of unpacking the meanings within a picture, is that you are detained longer in front of it; like sleeping policemen, iconography slows you down and you have to dwell on the picture with a particular purpose in mind and then, as a side effect (and side effect is exactly the right word because it's something that happens out of the corner of the eye), the beauty of the painting, which is hard to confront directly, begins to be unwittingly taken in. As E. M. Forster says, 'Only what is seen sideways sinks deep.'*

To find, though, that paintings could be decoded, that they were intellectual as well as aesthetic experiences, was something of a relief because it straight away put them in a familiar and much more English context if only because a lot of iconography, saying who's who and what's what in a painting, could be taken as a higher form of that very English preoccupation, gossip.

---

* Though I think Emily Dickinson had the same thought.

Emmanuel de Witte, *Adriana van Heusden and Her Daughter*
at the New Fishmarket in Amsterdam

Take the portrait of *Adriana van Heusden and Her Daughter at the New Fishmarket in Amsterdam* by the seventeenth-century Dutch painter Emmanuel de Witte. Now it helps to know the gossip about this picture which is that when he painted it de Witte was on his beam ends, and that by an undertaking he'd entered into with his landlord everything he painted was to belong to him in return for board and lodging. And that Adriana van Heusden, who looks pretty formidable even over the squid and skate, was his landlord's wife.

Or look at Veronese's wonderful panorama of *The Family of Darius before Alexander*. Darius, the King of Persia, had been defeated by Alexander at the battle of Issus and had fled the field, rather caddishly leaving his mother, wife and children to face his conqueror. There's always been some dispute as to which of the two young men standing right of centre is Alexander and which his friend Hephaestion. And this of course is also the subject of the painting, as Darius's mother Sysygambis addresses her pleas to the wrong man. Now Plutarch says that Alexander could get quite smelly so it's been conjectured that the figure on the left in red is more likely to be Alexander because, unlike the figure in black, he's not in armour; knowing he's going to be meeting the Darius family and mindful of his problems with personal hygiene, Alexander has had a quick shower and changed. Which is art history, but it's also gossip.

Veronese, *The Family of Darius before Alexander*

Knowing the saints and their stories is another source of gossip and here I find it hard sometimes to suppress my sense of the ridiculous, though it took me time to realise that appreciating pictures didn't rule out laughing at them. Saints and their attributes always seem to me to have a droll side to them though some more than others.

Having struck it lucky once with Jesus, it's understandable that Mary Magdalene should thereafter never go anywhere without her pot of ointment, so when she's reading, in the painting by Roger van der Weyden, she has the pot ready just in case there are more unexpected feet to anoint. And approaching the sepulchre in Savvoldo's painting, once again she is taking no chances, and the pot doesn't jar because it's generally quite discreet.

San Rocco, the patron saint of the plague, is more difficult to take however well he's painted because he must always be hitching up his skirt to show you his boil, which is unfortunately placed at the top of his thigh. In the painting by Crivelli which is in the Wallace Collection you half expect him to be wearing suspenders.

Almost any painting of the martyrdom of St Sebastian hovers between pornography and the ridiculous without it ever being quite a martyrdom as the saint didn't die from his wounds but was nursed back to health by some holy ladies, only to get himself battered to death in less picturesque circumstances. So the real martyrdom of St Sebastian never gets depicted. Invariably his response to the arrows is quite inadequate, no more than wincing as yet another bolt finds it mark, as if to say, 'Oh, really. Must you?'

Then too there's the mixture of nudity and decorum as in the version attributed to Antonello at Bergamo. His private parts are so neatly packaged they look like an uncooked apple turnover. Scarcely any of which applies to the National Gallery's Pollaiuolo with the superb archers in the foreground and the spreading landscape behind. Though again I feel it's the saint who lets it down a bit.

Perhaps the hardest saint to take seriously is St Peter Martyr. He had had a holy life, beginning when as a seven-year-old child, according to the *Golden Legend*, he came home from school to find his uncle reeking of heresy and promptly gave him a good talking-to, thereby setting the tone for the rest of his life . . . in the course of which by laying his hands over his chest he cured a nobleman, who thereupon vomited a worm with two heads and covered with thick hairs. *Alien* has nothing to teach the *Golden Legend*.

St Peter Martyr is seldom represented without an axe buried Excalibur-like in his head, though in fact he wasn't killed with an axe. While he was being murdered, as in the painting in the Gallery by Bellini, it happened that woodmen were chopping down some trees nearby so the axe somehow went to his head.

But the fact that the saints can never be separated from the instruments of their martyrdom but must always cart them along to whatever picture they're appearing in seems to indicate a highly developed degree of social inadequacy. Unless she trundles in her wheel St Catherine thinks nobody will recognise her, as indeed they won't. And what Peter Martyr is saying is, 'Hello, everybody. [*Pointing to the axe in his head:*] Remember me?'

Of course it's not only saints who have their attributes, and there are modern equivalents. I once did a film in the north that included a scene with two old men talking on an allotment, one of them played by the old music hall comedian Albert Modley. Albert Modley's trademark, his attribute, was an outsize cloth cap, and it happened that in the scene we were doing he was supposed to wear a cap, though not of the cosmic proportions of his music-hall one. He was quite happy to discard the large cap for the smaller version, but not so Mrs Modley, who said, 'Oh no. Albert has to wear his big cap or else the public won't know who he is.' I imagine St Lawrence's mother kicking up a similar fuss if he came on without his barbecue.

Similarly I once did a disastrous production of one of my plays in America with among the cast the actress Celeste Holm. It was a comedy and, though I say it myself, she had some good lines but she got very little response from the audience. She put this down not to her own inadequacy but to the fact that the audience didn't know who she was and needed reminding. She had made her debut many years before as Annie in *Annie Get Your Gun* so she had the inspired notion that it would recall her to the audience's memory if she came on at her first entrance and fired off a shotgun. It didn't, nor did it endear her to the rest of the cast, and since the play was set in a suburban drawing room the gesture was, to say the least, opaque.

But San Rocco with his boil, Mary Magdalene with her pot of ointment, Albert Modley with his cap, Celeste Holm with her shotgun . . . they are all attributes.

Somewhere in the Gallery I'd like there to be a notice saying, 'You don't have to like everything.' When you're appointed a Trustee here Neil MacGregor takes you round on an introductory tour. Mine was at nine in the morning, when I find it hard to look the milkman in the eye let alone a Titian, but we were passing through the North Wing, I remember, and Neil was about to take me into one of the rooms when I said, 'Oh, I don't like Dutch pictures' – thereby seeming to dismiss Vermeer, De Hooch and indeed Rembrandt. And I saw a look of brief alarm pass over his face, as if to say, 'Who is this joker we've appointed?'

But of course I didn't quite mean that. By Dutch paintings I meant (and this will be just as shocking to the curator, Christopher Brown)

Dutch landscape and marine paintings. Pictures like Jan van de Cappelle's *A River Scene*, for instance, or *A Moonlit View* by Aert van der Neer. And feeling foolish about it afterwards, I asked myself why I didn't like them, and realised it was because as a child I'd been given far too many pictures like them to do as jigsaws. So much sky and so many browns: they may be masterpieces, but as jigsaws they are a bugger.

Besides the Dutch landscapes, which I was exposed to too young, there were other casualties of inept or promiscuous reproduction. I don't like *The Haywain* because it featured on a table mat at home. Gainsborough had a narrow escape, too, due to *The Blue Boy* regularly featuring on old biscuit tins and at one point was, I believe, a brand of toffee.

Then there was *Mrs Siddons*, though Gainsborough's portrait of her was confused in my child's mind with the lady in the lunette at the start of Gainsborough Films. This was a British company operating in the forties and fifties, and the lady posed as if she were a painting, then, just before the film began, turned and inclined her head graciously to the cinema audience. The fact that American films as often as not began with a lion that roared and British films with a lady who bowed could, I suppose, be thought to signify something about our national vitality, but somehow Gainsborough the painter got the blame for this genteel tastefulness.

It wasn't until much later when I saw what I think of as the much gawkier (because earlier) Gainsboroughs, particularly *Mr and Mrs Andrews*, that I changed my opinion. I particularly like the bad temper of

Thomas Gainsborough, *Mr and Mrs Andrews*

Mrs Andrews, who even if she doesn't quite have a drop on her nose certainly looks as if she'd be better off indoors. I like too the recently acquired early *Self-portrait of Gainsborough with His Family*, done before he got into his full fashionable stride.

In those unillustrated days just after the war when so much of English life was on hold my mother would take magazines like *My Home* and *Ideal Home*, which sometimes included flower prints, and Mam with her yearning for gentility would cut them out, put a frame round them made out of passepartout and hang them above the sideboard, thereby so far as I was concerned knocking another school of painting for six. In the Spanish Still Life exhibition I loved the first couple of rooms, particularly Cotan's hanging cabbages, but when I got to the flower paintings, thanks to *Ideal Home* forty years ago, I swept straight through.

What is hard to recall about growing up in the forties and fifties is that while one did not feel deprived there was a kind of illustrative famine, a rationing of reproduction, particularly in colour, which really only ended in the early sixties. I don't recall art galleries selling posters, for instance, and the range of postcards was very limited. One of the pleasures of going abroad then – I first went to Italy in 1957 – was to see not merely the pictures in the galleries but the postcards that were on sale there too and which seemed to me, partly because they were so glossy but also because they were bled off, that's to say they had no margin, the picture taking up the whole card . . . they seemed truly glamorous. This was Art, it seemed to me, certainly when contrasted with their English counterpart: poorly printed, undetailed and always set within a timid white margin.

Even today, though reproduction is so much improved, the margins persist and still represent to me drabness, austerity and everything that abroad wasn't. I believe I differ with the director on this, who prefers margins and who has, I'm sure, cogent arguments in their favour, but were he fifteen years older he would understand. A postcard with a margin is to me part of a world that includes nylon shirts, custard powder and thick Utility socks. I recoil from it with the same shudder that young people today reserve for flared trousers.

If one can find an explanation like the jigsaws for one's dislikes and blind spots, it's reassuring, makes one feel taste isn't just an arbitrary business. Of course the greater the artists the more timid one is about voicing one's opinions. I have to say, for instance, that I don't much care for the paintings of Leonardo, though I dislike some more than others, with *St John the Baptist*, from the Ashmolean, particularly unsympathetic. It's the smile I find hard to take, though I suppose smiles in paintings are quite unusual at this date, but this one's so knowing it's practically 'Won't you come up and see me sometime?'

Of course if he or she is too shamefaced to avow an opinion, a writer has a remedy or a resource not available to other people: writers simply displace their uncertainties and put their opinions into the mouths of their characters. When I did this in 1988 in a play about Anthony Blunt, *A Question of Attribution*, I can see that, like the sketch about Berenson, this too was a flag of distress about art. There were three voices in the play: Blunt's voice which, not altogether successfully, I tried to make authentic, the voice of Chubb, a fictional officer from MI5 and the third voice that of Her Majesty the Queen . . . with the policeman and to some extent the Queen bearing the burden of my doubts and uncertainties about art.

'What am I supposed to feel?' asks the policeman about going into the National Gallery.

'What do you feel?' asks Blunt.

'Baffled,' says Chubb, 'and also knackered' . . . this last remark very much from the heart.

Blunt, though he's exasperated, can't resist instructing his tormentor, aware, though, that the policeman's naïvety may be a ruse to entrap him or soften him up. He tries to explain that the history of art shouldn't be seen as simply a progress towards accurate or naturalistic representation.

'Do we say Giotto isn't a patch on Michelangelo because his figures are less lifelike?'

'Michelangelo?' says Chubb. 'I don't think his figures are lifelike frankly. The women aren't. They're just like men with tits. And the tits

look as if they've been put on with an ice cream scoop. Has nobody pointed that out?'

'Not in quite those terms.'

And I suppose that is what I feel about Michelangelo's women, though
I don't like to say so. Husky, I suppose the word for them – steroidal
almost. I don't think any of them would be allowed in the 100-metre dash
without giving at least one urine sample.

In *A Question of Attribution* the Queen is made to have some doubts
about paintings of the Annunciation.

'There are quite a lot of them,' says the Queen. 'When we visited Florence we were taken round the art gallery there and well . . . I won't say
Annunciations were two a penny but they were certainly quite thick on
the ground. And not all of them very convincing. My husband remarked
that one of them looked to him like the messenger arriving from Little-
wood's Pools. And that the Virgin was protesting that she had put a cross
for no publicity.'

This last remark, though given to the Duke of Edinburgh, was actually another flag of distress, stemming from my unsuccessful attempts to
assimilate and remember an article about the various positions of the
Virgin's hands, which are a careful semaphore of her feelings . . . a semaphore instantly understandable to contemporaries but, short of elaborate
exposition, lost on us today. It's a pretty out of the way corner of art history but it leads me on to another question and another worry.

Floundering through some unreadable work on art history, I've sometimes allowed myself the philistine thought that these intricate exposi-
tions, gestures echoing other gestures, one picture calling up another and
all underpinned with classical myth . . . that surely contemporaries could
not have had all this at their fingertips or grasp by instinct what we can
only attain by painstaking study and explication, and that this is pictures
being given what's been called 'over meaning'. What made me repent,
though, was when I started to think about my childhood and going to a
different kind of pictures, the cinema.

When I was a boy we went to the pictures at least twice a week, as most families did then, regardless of the merits of the film. To me *Citizen Kane* was more boring but otherwise no different from a film by George Formby, say, or Will Hay. And going to the pictures like this, taking what was on offer week in week out was, I can see now, a sort of education, an induction into the subtle and complicated and not always conventional moral scheme that prevailed in the world of the cinema then, and which persisted with very little change until the early sixties.

I've been trying recently to write about some of the stock characters of films of that period and I'll talk about two in particular in the hope that I can relate one sort of pictures to the other.

A regular figure in films of that time was a middle-aged businessman, a pillar of the community, genial, avuncular, with bright white hair, and the older ones among you will know immediately the kind of character I mean if I show you this actor. His name is Thurston Hall, and this is another actor, Edward Arnold. Their names are unimportant but they were at that time instantly recognisable.[*] I certainly knew at the age of eight that as soon as this character or this type of character put in an appearance he was up to no good.

The character speaks:

> I am not an elaborate villain, nor is my spirit particularly tormented; crime in my case is not a substitute for art. It is just that my silver hair and general benevolence, invariably supplemented by a double-breasted suit, give me the appearance of an honest man. In the movies honest men do not look like honest men and suave is just another way of saying suspect. Bad men wear good suits; honest men wear raincoats, and so untiring are they in the pursuit of evil that they sometimes forget to shave.

The converse of this character, though he is seldom in the same film, would be the man who has been respectable himself once but who has made one big mistake in his life – a gun-fighter, say, who has killed an innocent man, a doctor who bungled an operation – and who by virtue of his misdemeanour (and the drink he takes to forget it) has put himself outside society.

[*] See *Seeing Stars*, p. 157.

Thomas Mitchell was such a doctor in John Ford's *Stagecoach*, and though such lost souls are more often come across in westerns they turn up in the tropics too, their frequent location the back of beyond.

The character speaks:

> In westerns I will generally team up with the tough wise-cracking no-nonsense lady who runs the saloon, who in her turn, inhabits the audience's presuppositions about her character. They know that a life spent in incessant and lucrative sexual activity has not dulled her moral perceptions one bit. They remember Jesus had a soft spot for such women, and so do they.
>
> I am frequently a doctor, in particular a doctor who at a crucial turn of events has to be sobered up to deliver the heroine's baby or to save a child dying of diphtheria. Rusty though my skills are, I find they have not entirely deserted me and I am assisted in the operation by my friend the proprietress of the saloon. She is tough and unsqueamish and together we pull the patient through, and having performed a deft tracheotomy my success is signalled when I come downstairs and say, 'She is sleeping now.'

He concludes:

> But though I rise to the occasion as and when the plot requires it, there is never any suggestion that I am going to mend my ways in any permanent fashion. Delivering the baby, flying the plane, shooting the villain . . . none of this heralds a return to respectability, still less sobriety. I go on much as ever down the path to self-destruction. I know I cannot change so I do not try. A scoundrel but never a villain, I know redemption is not for me. It is this that redeems me.

Now though this analysis may seem a bit drawn out, the point I am making is that the twentieth-century audience had only to see one of these characters on the screen to know instinctively what moral luggage they were carrying, the past they had had, the future they could expect. And this was after, if one includes the silent films, not more than thirty years of going to the pictures. In the sixteenth century the audience or congregation would have been going to the pictures for 500 years at least, so how much more instinctive and instantaneous would their responses have been, how readily and unthinkingly they would have been able to decode their pictures – just as, as a not very precocious child of eight, I could decode mine.

468

And while it's not yet true that the films of the thirties and forties would need decoding for a child of the present day, nevertheless that time may come; the period of settled morality and accepted beliefs which produced such films is as much over now as is the set of beliefs and assumptions that produced a painting as complicated and difficult, for us at any rate, as Bronzino's *Allegory of Venus and Cupid.*

Looking at pictures is an odd mixture of the public and the private. It is public but it is not communal as, say, the theatre is. We are happy when we go to the theatre to find it full, but we prefer a gallery to be if not empty then not crowded. This is because though the setting is public the experience is private; other people do not contribute to it as they do in the theatre or the cinema. One is not part of an audience or a congregation. And though it adds to the pleasure to have someone to share the pictures with and talk them over, one doesn't really want it to go beyond that. So that when arrangements are made because they have to be made for the experience to be communal – as at the Rijksmuseum in Amsterdam, for instance, where Rembrandt's *Night Watch* is in a kind of auditorium – I feel (though always grateful to sit down) that there's something wrong.

In his autobiography John Pope-Hennessy talks about discovering painting in Italy when he was a young man in the thirties, and how 'one's impressions of works of art become more vivid in the ratio of the trouble one takes to see them'. Of course he didn't realise how lucky he was. Nowadays everything is trailed and signposted to such an extent that the chances of genuine discovery are very slim; what is hard to find, in Europe at any rate, is something that is hard to find. Still, I can see that, while one is occasionally irritated by children scouting round the gallery on some trail or other, what the education department is trying to do for them, even artificially, is give them some sense of discovery about paintings.

Seeing them sitting round their teachers on the floor of the gallery I wonder whether they'll ask the questions that really puzzle them. It always used to bother me as a child, for instance, that the crucifixion of Christ was always depicted as more decorous than that of the thieves, their agonies much more graphic and protracted than his, who ought to be their superior in suffering as he was in everything else.

Jesus' crucifixion was also much more attended too . . . and I wondered why one of the Holy Family couldn't occasionally walk over and pay one of the other crosses a visit. The thieves after all never had any family with them, and it's what we always did if we went to see someone in hospital and there was someone on the ward with no visitors. Joseph, too, I used to feel, was unregarded, always elbowed out of the way by the Wise Men and never even getting to hold the baby. Then there was Judas.

I've always had a sneaking sympathy for Judas, partly because without him Christianity would never have got off the ground and also because since one of its central tenets is the forgiveness of sins then Judas ought to be right up there at the top of the forgiveness list. Judas is the real test of Christianity. He's the T-shirt that's been soaked in oil and ketchup and I don't know what else and yet, washed in the blood of a lamb, ought to come out whiter than white. Instead of which he's never mentioned; like Trotsky under Stalin, he's a non-person.

In paintings he's generally presented as such a stage villain, red-haired, pointy-eared and with a treacherous cat under his chair that a child at any rate might think Jesus must have been a bit of a fool to choose him in the

Caravaggio, *The Taking of Christ*

first place. This is partly what makes for me the newly discovered Caravaggio in Dublin so impressive. Here Judas doesn't seem to me much of a villain at all; he seems genuinely puzzled and can't look Christ in the face. I certainly don't see much villainy there, what's happening to him as terrible as what's happening to Christ, who's quite passive and, because he's looking down, almost abstracted from the scene.

It must be harder, though, for many children coming into the Gallery these days than it was, say, thirty years ago, simply because their knowledge of Christianity is much patchier now than it was then, not to mention of course their knowledge of classical myths. Still, even a little knowledge has its drawbacks and multiplies the opportunities for error. The turn of the century novelist Samuel Butler wrote in his notebook how he had come into the Gallery with his Aunt Worsley:

> We were before Van Eyck's picture of John Arnolfini and his wife. My Aunt mistook it for an Annunciation and said, 'Dear, dear. What a funny notion . . . to put the Holy Ghost in a hat!'

But almost any reaction in front of a picture is better than none. Confronted with the *Grotesque Old Woman* attributed to Quintin Massys, a lady who remarks 'Well, to me she has a look of Mrs Ridsdale' may seem to be missing the point, ignoring as this does the picture's past as a drawing by Leonardo and its future as the model for Tenniel's Ugly Duchess in *Alice in Wonderland*. But if it is Mrs Ridsdale that fixes it in the mind, no matter.

The portrait of *Alexander Mornauer* only came into the collection in 1991, but had it been here twenty years ago a child might have been struck by its resemblance to the TV actor Raymond Burr portraying the detective Perry Mason. And that of course is not the kind of remark that would have gone down well at I Tatti or, I imagine, with Sir John Pope-Hennessy, but it doesn't matter. You've got to start somewhere, and anything that hooks you onto a picture and makes you look again at it is better than nothing. And certainly more helpful than being told, 'You should look at this. It's a masterpiece.'

Sometimes when one's reading a book, a novel say, you come across a thought or a feeling which you've had yourself and, thinking it peculiar to yourself, you haven't expressed it or communicated it . . . and now here it is set down by someone else. And it's as if a hand has come out and taken yours.

It's a sentiment I later put into the mouth of Hector, the eccentric schoolmaster in *The History Boys*, but something similar, which one might call evidences of humanity, happens in pictures. The most notable example in one of the most popular paintings in the Gallery is in the Piero *Baptism* . . . and it's the man taking off his shirt. There's something obscurely comforting in the fact that they took their shirts off 500 years ago much as we do now, this piece of naturalism more vivid for its contrast with the hieratic figures of Christ and the Baptist in the foreground who are, of course, like all the figures in Piero's pictures, stern and unsmiling. They wouldn't get far advertising toothpaste, Piero's people.

In Piero's *Nativity*, another favourite picture, there's an oddly modern piece of observation where Joseph is relaxing in the background, one leg

Piero della Francesca, *The Baptism of Christ*

472

resting on the other and showing the sole of his foot. In view of this relaxed behaviour one might be forgiven for thinking that Joseph is celebrating the birth of the baby by smoking a large cigar. But that's an illusion, and not the kind of illusion Sir Ernst Gombrich specialises in.

Paradoxically, animals are often there in paintings to introduce the human touch. In Catena's *A Warrior Adoring the Infant Christ* it's a little dog. In Hogarth's *The Graham Children* the cat has maybe jumped up to get at the bird, but it's also for the sheer pleasure of clawing the upholstery. In Veronese's *The Family of Darius* a monkey is distracting one of the little girls, or maybe alarming her, as it's quite a sizeable creature.

Cats and monkeys enable me to say that the *News of the World* used to have on its masthead, if it could be called a masthead, the motto 'All human life is there'. I shouldn't think anybody on the paper knew the source of the quotation, which in full reads 'Cats and monkeys, monkeys and cats, all human life is there.' And the author – about the most unlikely person one would think of in connection with the *News of the World* – is Henry James.

Piero della Francesca, *The Nativity*

473

Staying with Veronese, the most affecting touch in the painting isn't the children, though, or the monkey, it's Alexander himself. He's portrayed as a very young man, and here is someone who is the master of the known world but who still can't quite manage to grow a satisfactory beard. I find that very human.

In Titian's *The Vendramin Family* the children are generally what strikes one as most human, especially the little boy with the dog, but the most appealing figure is Leonardo Vendramin, who seems much less impressive than his father or his uncle, a bit weak, simple almost, and the only one in the picture whose entire attention is fixed on the relic on the altar, which is what the picture is ostensibly about. He's like one of the weaker brothers in *The Godfather* who you know will end up getting bumped off.

Titian, *The Vendramin Family*

Finally in this catalogue of human touches, *The Mantelpiece* by Vuillard, whom I think of rather perversely as a French Harold Gilman – simply because Leeds Art Gallery, where I first discovered paintings, has a very good collection of Camden Town paintings which I got to know long before I ever saw any French paintings of the same date. This could be in Camden Town. I love the mantelpiece; I love the wallpaper; I wish it were my mantelpiece and my picture.

I was going to end on a rather clichéd note by saying that we shouldn't take the National Gallery for granted. But of course the opposite is true;

the more institutions and freedoms and benefits one can take for granted – of which in my view free state-supported galleries and museums come high on the list – the more civilised a society is. Free public libraries are another, but we certainly can't take them for granted. Around the time I was beginning to write this lecture I read a piece by Madsen Pirie, the Director of the Adam Smith Institute, dismissing public libraries as simply providing free entertainment for the middle classes. When such views can be so unabashedly expressed and taken seriously by government a free National Gallery can't be taken for granted at all.

Not having to pay to come into the Gallery doesn't mean that one doesn't value it. One of the most rampant misapprehensions of the last fifteen years has been the notion that we only value what we pay for, and that to be given something – even when what is supposedly being given is actually our own, as these pictures are – means that we set no store by it. All my experience, and in particular my education, for which my parents never had to pay a penny, belies that.

In my view we should put no obstacle, financial or otherwise, between the people and their pictures. They belong as much to a boy or girl sleeping in a doorway in the Strand as they do to the benefactors whose names are emblazoned on these walls. With its lectures and educational programmes what has been created here in the National Gallery, particularly over the last ten years and in the teeth of the prevailing orthodoxy, is a free university of art, free and to a high standard. It does a wonderful job.

But like most public institutions today the Gallery is required not merely to do its job but also to prove that it is doing its job. It is an exercise that is at the same time self-defeating and self-fulfilling. The current orthodoxy assumes that public servants will only do their job as well as they can if they are required to prove that they are doing their job as well as they can. But this proving takes time, and the time spent preparing annual reports and corporate plans showing one is doing the job is taken out of the time one would otherwise spend doing it . . . thus ensuring that the institution is indeed less efficient than would otherwise be the case. Which is the point the Treasury is trying to prove in the first place. And every public institution now is involved in this futile time-wasting merry-go-round.

Necessary to this merry-go-round is another misapprehension, namely that everything is quantifiable, that what visitors to the Gallery come away with can be assessed by means of questionnaires and so on. Well, maybe 20 per cent of it can, and maybe 20 per cent of all these efficiency-inducing exercises are worthwhile, or worth the hours and hours of time and form-filling they take up. And yes, one can gauge from a questionnaire how quick the service is in the café or how clean the lavatories are, but it cannot be said too often that the heart of what goes on here, the experience of someone in front of a painting, cannot be assessed and remains a mystery even, very often, to them.

Another contributory misapprehension is that people always know what they want from the Gallery. It's not condescending to say that they don't. If most of the visitors here were single-minded and coming in just to look at the pictures the Gallery would be a much emptier place.

The truth is people come in for all sorts of reasons, some of them just to take the weight off their feet or to get out of the rain, to look at the pictures perhaps, or to look at other people looking at the pictures. And the hope is, the faith is, that the paintings will somehow get to them and that they'll take away something they weren't expecting and couldn't predict.

So I'll end with a tired shopper or someone coming home from work with half an hour to spare before catching the train at Charing Cross. Not really looking at anything in particular, and maybe not far from the entrance, they come across a picture of some towels drying on a balcony in Naples in 1782. It was painted by Thomas Jones and is scarcely a picture at all, more like a fragment of a building, the kind of thing you see out of the corner of the eye. And maybe that's how the tired commuter sees it. But I've got great faith in the corner of the eye and with that remark of E. M. Forster that I quoted earlier: 'Only what is seen sideways sinks deep.'

Spoiled for Choice

Four paintings for schools

When I was at school in the late forties there were two sorts of paintings on the walls. Most classrooms hosted a couple of pictures scarcely above the Highland-cattle level that had been discarded by the City Art Gallery and palmed off on the Education Committee, which then sent them round to schools. These uninspired canvases didn't so much encourage an appreciation of art as a proficiency at darts. However, there was another category of picture occasionally to be seen: reproductions on board of work by modern British painters – Ravilious, Paul Nash, Henry Moore, Pasmore. These, I think, were put out by Shell and turn up occasionally nowadays at auction, though not quite at Sotheby's. That I've always liked – and found no effort in liking – British paintings of the forties and fifties I partly put down to my early exposure to these well-chosen reproductions. So it was my own largely unwitting experience that made me welcome the Sainsbury scheme whereby every year four selected paintings are reproduced, framed and sent round with an information pack to schools local to Sainsbury's stores.

To be asked to choose four paintings from any of the galleries in the British Isles feels, I imagine, not unlike taking part in that dreadful TV game in which contestants are each given a trolley and the run of a supermarket and, dashing frantically between the cling peaches and the minced morsels, end up with far more Jeyes Fluid than any sane person could reasonably want. The supermarket, I hasten to add, not Sainsbury's.

As a Trustee I felt that one of my paintings should be from the National

477

Gallery and I originally wanted *The Good Samaritan* by Bassano. It may seem, in view of its much more spectacular neighbours like Veronese's *The Family of Darius before Alexander* or Titian's *Bacchus and Ariadne*, to be a dull choice. Indeed this rather intimate picture is an exception for Bassano himself, who produced much more spectacular paintings, one of which, a tumultuous *Nativity* in the National Gallery of Scotland, at one point I had it in mind to choose.

The Good Samaritan is quite low key, the Samaritan caught just as he's trying to heave the injured man onto his horse; it's an awkward movement because the man is either unconscious or unable to do much to help and the tension of the effort runs right across the picture. In the background the priest and the Levite, having chosen not to see the injured man, are making off. In the distance is the town where the Samaritan will pay for the man to be lodged until he recovers, the town thought to be a representation of the painter's home, Bassano near Venice.

So many paintings in galleries are populated by the beautiful and the perfectly proportioned that it's a relief to find one of this date (mid-sixteenth century) where the characters are so downright ordinary. These are no gods, or athletes even: just one balding, middle-aged man helping another, their bodies worn and slack and past their best. That seemed to me to be something that a child could learn from – apart, of course, from the relevance of the parable itself, and particularly the fact that Samaritans were rather looked down on in their day, which points up the contrast between the priest and the Levite, who ought, if they were sincere in their beliefs, to have lent a hand, and the despised figure who actually did help. It's as if you've broken down on the M6 and the only person who bothers to stop and help is a Hell's Angel.

Having decided this was one of the paintings I wanted, I was told that it wouldn't reproduce well, so I had to look elsewhere.

An obvious choice was the spectacular painting of St George and the Dragon by the Spanish painter Bermejo, which the National Gallery acquired a couple of years ago. Wherever you look in this painting there is something that delights: in particular, the vivacious and many-mouthed dragon – it even has mouths in its elbows. St George looks a little baby-faced but his armour makes up for it, particularly the reflections in his breastplate, which are said to represent the Heavenly City but look not unlike All Souls College, Oxford. Having chosen this painting, I was looking forward to the umpteen papier-mâché versions of the dragon – with or without egg boxes – that the children would inevitably construct. But again my choice was thwarted. The painting is long and thin and I was told it would be difficult to reproduce without a vast border of white – and since borders are something I hate I had to look elsewhere.

I finally chose *The Adoration of the Kings* by Gossaert, also called Mabuse, which hangs in Room 12 of the Gallery. There's such a lot going on in it that it's hard to take it all in: the Holy Family below, confronted by rich visitors and attendants plus a crowd of onlookers, the sky above buzzing with a flotilla of angels. The picture is painted in extraordinary detail, every bit of it in focus – which is partly why it seems so crowded

Jan Gossaert, *The Adoration of the Kings*

479

and confusing. Caspar is offering the Christ child a gold chalice filled with coins, the lid of the chalice lying on the floor. Balthazar on the left is identified by an inscription on his crown, and Gossaert has painted his own name below it (and again on the neck ornament of Balthazar's black servant). On the right, Melchior is waiting with his presentation rather precariously balanced in his limp hand. The detail is such that one can distinguish the hairs on the mole on Caspar's cheek. Above the scene, and in another order of things, the angels crowd the sky, where the star that led the Wise Men to the manger is still shining. A dove representing the Holy Spirit descends from the star.

Gossaert was an artist from near Antwerp, painting in the first quarter of the sixteenth century, and this picture was done as an altarpiece for the Abbey of Grammont in Flanders around 1510. Somewhere on the painting the restorers at the National Gallery have found Gossaert's own fingerprints.

It's a painting that cries out to be made into an Advent calendar, though there would be an insufficiency of windows to display all its wonderful detail. And yet I always feel that it's with the Adoration of the Kings that the Christian story begins to go wrong; that the unlooked-for display of material wealth and the shower of gifts, for all their emblematic significance, are a foretaste of the wealth and worldliness that were to ensnare the medieval Church; and while the Virgin, always the perfect hostess, takes it all in her stride, even in this painting, accepting the chalice of coins proffered by Caspar, it nevertheless bodes ill for the future.

As is generally the case with the Adoration, it's the animals who get it right, even though, as here, they scarcely figure, shouldered out of the way by the Kings and their arrogant followers, the young man on the left, for instance, the picture of boredom and superciliousness. In the Bassano *Nativity* the animals scarcely manage to get their noses in the painting at all. Here they do a bit better, as the ox keeps company with Gossaert himself, just peeping into his own painting, while the ass is at the back of the picture, where the sightseers are gazing over the ramshackle fence. The dogs, being dogs, get more of a look-in than the ox and the ass. They seem to be quite posh dogs and probably came with the Kings, both having distinguished pedigrees, the one on the left taken from Schongauer's engraving of *The Adoration of the Kings*, the other from Dürer's *St Eustace*.

One way of looking at this extraordinary painting is as an advertisement for the Flanders Tourist Board, or as the equivalent of one of those airport bazaars where all the products of the locality are on sale. Embroidery, millinery, jewellery, leather, fancy goods – it's all here. On this view, the Three Kings in their elaborate apparel could be seen as fugitives from the catwalk – and like anyone dressed at the very height of fashion, startling and not unridiculous.

This way of looking at the painting isn't entirely a joke, though, because if one wants a prime site from which to advertise, what better place than the altar?

The character and situation of Joseph interest me partly because in most paintings of this period, and until the end of the sixteenth century, he has to take a back seat, particularly in paintings of the Adoration. He's often so much in the background that one wonders if his role in the Holy Family, which is in any case ambiguous, isn't made more so by his persistence in keeping out of the limelight. It must have been very puzzling. One can imagine a conversation between the Wise Men:

'Who's the guy with the grey hair?'

'That's the *husband*.'

'Oh my God!'

And so it must often have been with Joseph, his situation not helped by his always being represented as getting on in years. This is possibly because he's not mentioned in the New Testament after the Presentation of Jesus in the Temple, Jesus then being twelve, and so is presumed to have died before Jesus' ministry began.

Even when Joseph is not depicted as old he is often made into such a pathetic and eccentric figure as almost to reflect discredit on the Virgin, who picked him out in the first place. But I suppose that to portray him as an old man or a bit of a fool bolsters the doctrine of the Virgin Birth. After all, there is a sense in which Joseph is cuckolded by the Holy Ghost, a notion which is easier to accept if he fulfils the familiar role of the elderly and foolish husband of a much younger wife. Indeed, in some mystery plays he was presented as a cuckold.

It's hardly fair and one feels that he's rightly a saint, if only because, having to play second fiddle, he needs to be. It's a situation one sometimes comes across in show business, the famous actress with the supportive spouse; and while Joseph hasn't quite had to sacrifice carpentry to the demands of his wife's career, he's definitely No. 2 in this marriage, a male wife in fact.

In Gossaert's *Adoration* he shrinks into the background as usual, but it's nice occasionally to find a painting in which he doesn't and where the Wise Men pay him a proper degree of attention. There is, for instance, an *Adoration* by Giovanni di Paolo in the Linsky Collection at the Metropolitan Museum in New York, in which one of the Wise Men has his arm round Joseph's shoulder and is also holding his hand, perhaps saying: 'Well, I know what it's like to be woken up in the middle of the night. I've got children of my own.' Nice, too, when Joseph so seldom gets to hold the baby, to find him in a painting from the Paris Hours of René of Anjou, helping to bathe the baby and, in a fifteenth-century Book of Hours from Besançon, sitting by the fire, airing Jesus' nappy.

Looking at the extraordinary gifts brought by the Three Kings, a child might well wonder what happened to them while Jesus was growing up. The myrrh is traditionally said to have been used to anoint Christ's body after the Crucifixion. But what of the cup? Did it foreshadow the cup from which he drank at the Last Supper? Did Mary and Joseph ever take it down from its shelf, unwrap the cloth in which it was kept and think back to that extraordinary time when kings and their retinues paid them court and pitched camp around their stable? Which, in Gossaert's painting, isn't a stable at all but a derelict palace, the run-down building a symbol of the teachings of the Old Testament, which Christ would now supersede and make new and so build his own temple.

Painters of this period never get the baby right. He's always far too big, as he is here, and frequently looks as if he knows exactly what's going on, the problem for the painter being that, if he is the personification of God, he would know what was going on, and how do you represent that? But almost all of the babies depicted in paintings of the Nativity, sometimes spindly, sometimes gross, were they taken along to a baby clinic today would arouse concern. A paediatrician would have to ask Mary some very searching questions.

The National Gallery is particularly rich in Gossaert's work, not all of which I like, but none of his other paintings is as spectacular as the *Adoration*. One recent addition to the canon is a *Virgin and Child*, previously thought to be a seventeenth-century copy but which, when cleaned, was shown to be the genuine article. What to me is remarkable about this painting is that if you glance back at it from the door of Room 12 the illusion of it being three-dimensional is so strong that the Virgin looks as if she is a wax figure. It's as startling an effect as the anamorphic skull in Holbein's *The Ambassadors* or the perspective tricks of the Hoogstraten Box. As a painting, though, I'm not particularly keen on it because the Virgin looks as if she is enthroned in a Victorian fireplace.

Hanging next to Gossaert's *Adoration of the Kings* is *Portrait of a Man aged 38* by Lucas van Leyden, painted around 1521. The age of the sitter is written on the scroll that he's holding and, given his somewhat doleful countenance, if it said forty rather than thirty-eight it would be rather funny. I find it hard to say why I like the painting so much. It's partly the austerity, which brings to mind some of Lucian Freud's early portraits, while the sitter reminds me of Max von Sydow in *The Seventh Seal*. When I go through Room 12 it's the painting I always glance at as if it were a friend. I haven't got anything more to say about it than that, though, and I couldn't choose it as one of my four pictures because it, too, must seem rather dull. But I love it and I think it's a reminder – and not one that all art historians would welcome – that about some paintings there isn't all that much to be said.

In much the same category as the Lucas van Leyden, a painting I find ravishing but can't find much to say about is John Sell Cotman's *Greta Bridge*, a watercolour in the British Museum. I was brought up on Cotman, in that they have a very good collection of his work in Leeds, most of it bequeathed by Sidney Kitson, who was so fond of the artist he was said to suffer from Cotmania. Understandably in my view, as I've yet to see a Cotman I didn't like. But that just about says it all. It's true one could find things to say about Greta Bridge itself, which has a dramatic history, and when I was a boy was the subject of a *Children's Hour* serial. But nothing I could say would add much to the appeal of the painting, and if there is nothing to be said one should have the sense not to say it.

My second choice, *Hambletonian, Rubbing Down*, by George Stubbs, was painted in 1800. It hangs at Mount Stewart, a National Trust property in Northern Ireland. Hambletonian was one of a string of racehorses belonging to Sir Henry Vane Tempest, a landowner from County Durham. Having already won some important races, the horse was matched at Newmarket in 1799 against a much-fancied rival, Diamond. The race was exceptionally dramatic, both horses being cruelly whipped and goaded with the spur until, utterly exhausted, Hambletonian managed to pull ahead and win the race by half a neck. Though he went on to win other races, the horse never wholly recovered from his ordeal and was eventually retired to Wynyard Park in County Durham, where he is buried under a large oak tree.

George Stubbs, *Hambletonian, Rubbing Down*

Stubbs was an old man of seventy-five when he painted *Hambletonian*, one of his last pictures, but the drawings he made of the skeletons and muscles of horses years before show that he knew horses literally inside out. For a long time this didn't help his reputation, as he was thought of as just an animal painter. It's only in the last thirty years that he has come to be recognised as one of the greatest English painters, a landmark in this process the exhibition at the Tate in 1985, curated by Judy Egerton, from whose magnificent catalogue I'm cribbing most of what I am saying.

The background of Stubbs's painting hints at the scene of Hambletonian's triumph, as we can see the pavilions and the winning post of the course over which his famous race was run. There's no sign of the piteous state the horse must have been in at the conclusion of the race, no weals from the whip or blood from the spurs. Nor do the groom and boy who have charge of the horse show any emotions. It's obviously not 'The Triumph of Hambletonian', which may well have been the kind of painting the owner wanted. Certainly Stubbs had a great deal of trouble getting paid for his commission.

Both groom and boy look quite stern and self-possessed, and though both are the owner's servants they seem anything but servile, and are so indifferent to our regard as to appear almost arrogant. The reason may be that they have a skill that we do not share. They know about horses and this horse in particular, and they look down on us, who are watching them, because we don't. Groundsmen and coaches have a similar attitude to spectators: they are professionals – we are just fans.

I can't decide whether Stubbs has made the boy's right arm longer than it could possibly have been in order to have it reach over the horse's neck. One would like to see a reverse angle on the scene in order to be sure. Mind you, I'm no authority. As a boy I was hopeless at drawing horses and thought there was something almost magical about other children who could. There were more horses about then, of course (though not like Hambletonian). Coal was delivered by horse and cart, as was milk, and when I was evacuated during the war – though I find this hard to believe now – I went to Ripon market by horse and cart. On the other hand, I have never been to a horse race.

Stubbs was born and brought up in Liverpool, then moved to York, and then beyond York to an area even more remote than the one inhabited by his contemporary, the clergyman Sydney Smith, who complained that he was so remote from civilisation he was twenty miles from a lemon. An absence of lemons wouldn't have bothered Stubbs, who shut himself up in a farmhouse at Hawkstow in north Lincolnshire, in what's now Humberside, where he dissected and drew the corpses of horses, only abandoning the cadaver when it stank so much as to be intolerable.

My third choice is *Lorenzo and Isabella* by Sir John Millais, painted in 1849 and now in the Walker Art Gallery, Liverpool. Millais's picture was inspired by Keats's 'Isabella; or, The Pot of Basil', a story retold from Boccaccio. Lorenzo is in love with his master's daughter, Isabella, and this arouses the resentment of her three brothers, who lure him into the forest and murder him, leaving Isabella to think that he has abandoned her. Lorenzo then appears to Isabella in a dream and reveals the whereabouts of his forest grave: she digs him up and brings home his head, which she keeps in a pot on her window sill in which she grows herbs.

It's a macabre tale which, in Millais's painting, is just beginning, Lorenzo handing Isabella half an orange while the brothers look on. The most brutish brother teases his sister's dog with his foot, while the eldest brother looks as if he is already making plans to do away with the upstart. On the window sill a pot of herbs hints at the story's dreadful conclusion. Most of the people in the painting, even the unsympathetic brothers, are portraits of Millais's friends and family; for instance, the old man delicately touching his napkin to his lips (in a gesture I had hitherto associated with northern ladies in teashops) is a portrait of Millais' father.

Many Pre-Raphaelite paintings, this one included, I find to some degree sinister or disturbing, peopled with characters who seem fearful or haunted, like the flower-seller in Ford Madox Brown's *Work* or the potboy in the same picture, or the young John the Baptist in Millais's *Christ in the*

Carpenter's Shop. They all look as if something dreadful is about to happen, which in Lorenzo's case is no less than the truth.

On one side of the table are the brothers, three in Boccaccio, two in Keats and it could be two or three in Millais – the young man at the rear looks less evil-minded than the other two. It's a deliberate configuration and confrontation, but slightly awkward, as the rest of the party have to budge up on the other side of the table – though their sober dress suggests they are all inferior members of the household anyway and so not entitled to much comfort. The dogs, incidentally, don't do at all well here, one getting teased by the probing foot, the other quite likely to have its paw or tail crushed when the awful brother puts his chair back.

John Everett Millais, *Lorenzo and Isabella*

I suppose the brothers would defend themselves by saying that they are concerned for their sister's virtue but I don't believe it, the young men's obligation to keep their sister pure having more to do with their own frustrated desires than with any concern for morality. Besides, they don't want her marrying Lorenzo because, however capable he might be, her destiny is to marry into the aristocracy, thus improving the family's status. This element – and the mercantile activities of the family – is stressed by Keats, and Millais was very much aware of it.

The painting had originated as one of a series of etchings planned by Millais and Holman Hunt in the first flush of Pre-Raphaelite enthusiasm and there is a drawing by Holman Hunt, *Lorenzo at Work Supervising the Brothers' Warehouse*, which strikes the same note. The initials of the Pre-Raphaelite Brotherhood, incidentally, are visible on Isabella's stool. Millais was not yet twenty when he painted the picture and its technical accomplishment is astonishing, Ford Madox Brown saying that the modelling of the napkin carried by the servant was the painting's supreme achievement.

It was exhibited at the Academy in May 1849 and sold for £150 to three tailors in Bond Street who were making a start in picture-dealing. The tailors beat Millais down from his original price but threw in a suit of clothes as compensation. People disliked the painting so much, however, that they got rid of it for the £150 they had paid and lost the suit of clothes into the bargain. It passed through one or two pairs of hands before coming to the Walker Art Gallery as early as 1884.

What always makes me remember the painting is the bully's wonderful, terrible leg, arrogant, perfectly proportioned and up to no good. Here teasing the greyhound, today it might be flung loutishly across the aisle of a bus or shoved on a spare seat in the train, a hurdle one has to take (stepping over it or asking for it to be removed) if one is to retain one's self-esteem.

It's the leg of a ballet dancer – Nureyev's leg, if you like. I only saw Nureyev dance once, in *Manon* at Covent Garden. He was partnered by Anthony Dowell, who is much more delicately made. There was nothing delicate about Nureyev. He had legs, like the leg in the painting, that were not so much legs as hindquarters. Nureyev was often compared to Nijinsky and the comparison is apt. He was like Nijinsky, but it was Nijinsky the horse.

The last of my four paintings comes from the art gallery at Aberdeen, which has a particularly good collection of modern British paintings, and from which I was hoping to choose Eric Ravilious's *Train Landscape*. It's a painting redolent of all the journeys by train that I remember, particularly in my teens and during my National Service, when it was still possible to explore the English countryside by rail, a period that the foolishness of Dr Beeching put an end to. I then found that I'd been forestalled and that this particular Ravilious had already figured in Sainsbury's Pictures for Schools. Aberdeen has others, though, and appropriately, as so much of Ravilious's work was done in the north of Scotland. He was a war artist and painted the convoys waiting in Scapa Flow to depart on the gruelling voyage to Murmansk. It was on one such trip that Ravilious himself died, killed off Iceland in 1942.

Two other paintings of his that I like very much are *Farmhouse Bedroom* (1939), which is in the V&A, and one of England before the war called *Tea at Furlongs*. It's seemingly a very peaceful scene but its emptiness is ominous and I think it could equally be called 'Munich, 1938'. I might well have chosen it but it turns out to be in a private collection and so doesn't qualify.

I ended up plumping for another of Aberdeen's pictures, a beach scene by Stanley Spencer, *Southwold 1937*. In my childhood, holidays at the seaside were often quite doleful affairs. It rained or was cold and if we weren't cringing in the shelter of some breakwater, as they're doing in the

Stanley Spencer, *Southwold 1937*

489

picture, we were probably trailing up and down the seafront until we were allowed to go back to the boarding house (which was strictly off-limits between meals). That was Morecambe or Cleveleys on the north-west coast, whereas this is Southwold in Suffolk, but the sea looks much the same. Stanley Spencer described it as 'dirty washing water colour . . . splashed by homely aunties' legs' and the air of Southwold as 'full of suburban seaside abandonment'. He's right about the sea, though Southwold looks more sedate than he describes, no aunties paddling at the moment and scarcely a child that I can see. It's certainly not Blackpool.

Stanley Spencer painted this lovely, blustery picture 'before the war', as I tend to think of it, because within two years beaches like this would be cordoned off, the shore strewn with tank traps and the sea unreachable behind rolls of barbed wire. That was what the seaside was like when I first saw it, so this painting is for me a carefree vision of what holidays were like between the wars.

In 1925 Spencer had married his wife Hilda in a village not far from Southwold, but in 1937 the marriage had broken up and Spencer came back to Southwold in great distress of mind. None of this sadness finds its way into the picture, painting as much an escape for the artist as the holiday is an escape for the people in the deck-chairs.

Stanley Spencer didn't quite play the artist in the manner, say, of Augustus John; but his odd personality has tended to get in the way of his professional reputation and has somewhat diminished it, much as Lowry's did, both of them too easily caricatured as the artist as eccentric. It's a way the newspapers have of making art palatable, of showing how unpretentious we English are, but it's not much more useful or informative than a view of French art which has the painter wearing a smock and beret and living in a garret. There's no doubt that Spencer was eccentric. His cousin said that he didn't look fit to take a sheep down the street and he was a gift to magazines like *Picture Post*, one minute pottering round Cookham with his paints in a pram, the next doing his stint as a war artist in the Glasgow shipyards.

One is so used to allegory in Spencer's work that when it's absent, as it is here, one feels a little uneasy, as if the painting is perhaps a detail from something much larger – 'Christ and the Miraculous Draught of Fishes', say, with the fishing boat just off the top of the canvas. Or perhaps it's the 'Calling of the Disciples', Christ skirting the shoreline off to the right with some of these determined sunbathers blissfully unaware that they're about to be enlisted among the Twelve. But Southwold is not Galilee, just a select, rather refined seaside place which retains much of its gentility today.

The towels deserve a word. I know this kind of towel from childhood, thin, ribbed, the nap long since gone, and only just big enough to do the job. It's the kind of towel, brisk, bracing and comfortless, that would have commended itself to Baden-Powell. Towels for me have always been strong indicators of class, the often smelly towel that hung behind the kitchen door when I was a child firmly putting us in our social place, a pile of thick fleecy towels in the airing cupboard signifying luxury and something that I've never quite attained. When I first went to America in 1962 the first present I sent home were some huge bath towels from Bloomingdale's, the sort of towels I'd always hankered after. Typically, my parents never put them in the airing cupboard, but left them in their cellophane wrappers, feeling they were too good to use. The other thing to be said about towels – and these towels in particular – is that when one used to go swimming as a child to the beach or, more generally, to the municipal baths, one carried the towel under one's arm in a kind of Swiss roll with one's cossy in the centre. Children don't do that now. Why? What happened and when?

Looking at the four paintings I ended up choosing, I can see that three of them have to do with my own childhood, most obviously the Stanley Spencer with its echoes of pre-war summers I was too young to remember. *Lorenzo and Isabella* is also to do with school, where I was quite late growing up, and I was always very conscious of how big some of my schoolfellows were, making the young man with the perfect leg both a bully to be avoided and also someone whose physique I would have envied. Stubbs's *Hambletonian, Rubbing Down* is childhood too, and the feeling I always had of being shut out of sports and the expertise that went with sports. Only *The Adoration of the Kings* is unconnected with anything I recognise or remember, though it's also the most bewitching painting from a child's point of view.

This is not to say, though, that these are my 'favourite' paintings. I'd find it hard (and not very useful) to determine what my 'favourite' paintings were. Making lists of this kind – the Hundred Best Paintings, the Hundred Best Classics – is a silly game that newspapers and radio stations play. Of course, it's easier to do with music, but I'm sure that if there was a way of putting paintings into some sort of league table, radio and television would not hesitate to do so. So just as one is supposed to wait with breathless excitement to find out whether '*Vissi d'arte*' has dislodged Samuel Barber's Adagio from its position at No. 18 in the Classic Countdown, no doubt with paintings we would be expected to catch our breath on hearing that Paris Bordone has made a surprise entry at No. 47.

Who would have thought that one would one day groan at the name of Albinoni? God forbid that paintings should share such a jaded fate. Art is not a race. And there often is – and probably should be – something clandestine about it. When I was at school, art was a soft option for games and was in consequence looked down on. These days there's nothing so respectable as art, which is fine, except that it makes art somehow official.

All masterpieces are eloquent: not all of them are articulate. And of course it is, rightfully, one of the functions of art history to try and make a painting articulate: to demonstrate its virtues, inform you of its background and history and put it in its context. Some paintings have to be cajoled into speaking when they may have very little to say in words. There's not a lot to be said about the self-portraits of Rembrandt, for instance. 'I am' is what they say. Or 'Here I am again.' In fact, there are two voices: Rembrandt saying 'I am' and the painting saying 'I am.' Of the paintings I have chosen, the most eloquent and the least articulate is *Hambletonian, Rubbing Down*. The National Gallery has recently acquired Stubbs's *Whistlejacket* and that's another wonderfully eloquent but wholly inarticulate picture. And though there's lots to be said about both these paintings, what can be said about a work of art can never outsay what a work of art says about itself.

Sometimes – and I don't mean to disparage art history, which I've always found fascinating – it's as if paintings were being doorstepped, art historians crowding in on them like reporters from the *Mirror* or the *Mail*, pestering some inarticulate unfortunate about 'What they really feel', teasing out an inappropriate and inadequate response when the person interviewed would sensibly prefer to say nothing at all. And maybe, hearing what is said about them, some paintings might shrug, saying: 'Well, if you say so.' The Mona Lisa's smile is the smile of art.

Portrait or Bust

These notes arise out of a TV documentary, Portrait or Bust, *which Jonathan Stedall and I made about Leeds City Art Gallery in December 1993 and which was first transmitted on BBC2 in April 1994.*

Other than 'These are the paintings I like' I'm not sure I've much else of consequence to say about the actual paintings. What I did in the programme was to advertise my own ignorance in the hope that it would encourage people with similar feelings of inadequacy where art is concerned to come into the Gallery nevertheless. Leeds after all is not an intimidating collection. To begin with it's relatively small, you're not outfaced by it and anyone with two hours to spare can see most of it. Watercolours apart, it's weighted towards the twentieth century and has some of the best modern British paintings to be seen anywhere in the provinces.

The Gallery is friendly too and (not the least of its virtues) has plenty of seats, often with quite odd or eccentric characters sitting in them. This is all to the good. It bears repeating that people come into an art gallery for all sorts of reasons; some, it's true, because they like paintings, but with a lot of visitors, looking at the pictures is quite low on the list. They come in out of the rain, to keep warm maybe, or to take the weight off their feet; perhaps they're early for a meeting or they're on the look-out for a meeting and have come in hoping to pick somebody up – all of which are perfectly proper and legitimate reasons for being here. An art gallery, after all, is not unlike a park. But the hope is – the *faith* is – that the art will rub

494

off, be taken in out of the corner of the eye. Because the corner of the eye is a good short cut to the back of the mind.

When I was a boy I used to do my homework in the Reference Library next door, and I'd come down to the Gallery not because I wanted to look at the pictures but because I wanted a break. I got to know the pictures by accident, by osmosis almost; I just absorbed them. And I can see that it's from this experience that I derive my attitude to television, believing as I do that a lot of people switch on at random and with no definite idea of the programme they want to watch, just as they come in here at random and for a variety of reasons; but given good comedy, good drama, good documentaries, they can be diverted and elevated, just as they can be by good paintings.

My appreciation of painting is quite shallow. I find it hard to divorce appreciation from possession, so I know I like a picture only when I'm tempted to walk out with it under my raincoat. However much I like a painting I seldom hang about in front of it, but go and get a postcard instead. Art is hard on the feet. I loathe standing, and get more speedily exhausted in a gallery than anywhere else, except perhaps a second-hand bookshop.

My ideal gallery would be traversed by a narrow-gauge railway where one could be shunted into a siding in front of the pictures one likes. How Bernard Berenson could stand in front of a painting for hours at a stretch, just taking it in, beats me. Give me a postcard any day.

The first visit I paid to the Art Gallery was early in the Second World War when I was aged eight. There was very little to see in the way of art as, in the expectation of air raids, most of the city's pictures had been evacuated to a place of safety. Frantic operations of a similar kind went on all over the country in the early months of the war and famously in London, where the precious contents of the National Gallery were crated up and taken off, to end up eventually in a slate quarry in Wales, there to be hidden in caves.

Lacking metropolitan masterpieces, Leeds chose a handier refuge, Temple Newsam. I like to think the pictures were loaded onto a tram and

495

taken the little ride along York Road, through Halton and up that leafy incline by the municipal golf course to Temple Newsam House. It was a trip I'd done several times with my grandma. The contrast, though, was revealing: in London a get-away in the nick of time to a remote and romantic haven; in Leeds a twopenny-halfpenny tram-ride. From as early as I can remember, life – or at any rate life in Leeds – never quite came up to scratch.

But now we are in the Art Gallery sometime in 1942 and Standard 3 from Upper Armley National School has been brought into town by our teacher, Miss Timpson, to see an exhibition to do with Ark Royal Week. Miss Timpson is a thin, severe woman with grey hair in a bun and the kind of old lady's legs that seem to have gone out now, which begin at the far corners of the skirt and converge on the ankles. We have looked at the fund-raising thermometer on the Town Hall steps and now Miss Timpson has shepherded us into the back of a crowded hall in the Gallery where a choir of orphans from the Boys' Home and press-ganged into the Sea Scouts are singing and whistling 'Pedro the Fisherman'.

Entertainment was scarce in those early days of the war but even I knew that this performance was no crowd-puller and it's not long before the attention of Standard 3 begins to wander. Except that there's not much else to look at, just one large picture that hasn't been evacuated, because either it's too big or is of no artistic merit. Merit not really at the top of their list, two of the bolder boys in the class, Rowland Ellis and John Marston, have gone over to take a closer look.

It's a vast work, acres of paint varnished to an over-all brown, and it depicts the aftermath of some great battle, the kind of battle that's always being described in the Bible with mountains of dead and piteous and imploring wounded. Night is coming on and women wander over the field comforting the wounded and searching for their loved ones. Prominent among these is a striking figure (what my mother would have called 'a big woman') – bold, scornful, with her many bangles proclaiming her a person of some consequence. She stands astride a wounded warrior, possibly her consort and certainly someone with whom she is on familiar terms, because she has torn aside her bodice and, standing back from the prostrate figure, displays an ample breast.

Some of the boys in Standard 3 (not me) have begun to nudge and snigger. But I am thought to be a shy child (sly would be nearer the truth) so I hedge my bets, keeping one eye on Miss Timpson while stealing looks at this extraordinary canvas.

The sight of a breast so insolently displayed was, even in the hygienic context of art, not a common sight in 1942 so it was hardly surprising that Standard 3 had started to smirk. But the gallery was gloomy and the picture was gloomy too, so it was only gradually one made out what it was this brazen woman was doing with the breast, and as it became plain Standard 3's mirth turned to awe.

Seemingly without shame, the lady, who may have been Boadicea (though she also bore some resemblance to Mrs Hutchinson, the vicar's wife), was squeezing the contents of her breast into the (presumably) parched mouth of the injured warrior. Novel though this procedure was, what really staggered Standard 3 was the accuracy of her aim. The range was at least three yards. Of course she may have been all over the place before she got it right but certainly at the moment of depiction her perfect lactic parabola was dead on target.

Perhaps I was less surprised at this achievement than the others. I knew boys who could spit as accurately as that and I took this to be a possible female equivalent. I could not spit, at any rate over any distance, and had none of that copious supply of saliva that the more brutish boys seemed always to carry in readiness. I think I knew, even at the age of eight, that not being able to spit would mean not being able to do a lot of other things too (dive, throw a cricket ball, piss in public, catch the barman's eye), that not being able to spit was only the tip of an iceberg so vast that it would float beside and under me all the length of my life. However.

A hiatus before the choir struck up with Bobby Shaftoe brought us back to Miss Timpson's attention and she suddenly caught sight of her class, myself included, clustered round the picture. Now, whereas Miss Timpson would expect nothing better of boys like Rowland Ellis and

UNTOLD STORIES

John Marston (both of whom could of course spit) than to be found sniggering at rude pictures, this had never been my role. I was not that sort
of boy and here I was about to be tarred with the same prurient brush as
the rest. But I was a precocious child and no sooner did I perceive the
danger than I retrieved the situation.

'Miss,' I asked innocently, 'is that what they mean by succouring the
wounded?'

'No, Alan,' said Miss Timpson crisply, 'it is what they mean by smut.
But very good. Do any of you others know the word "succour"? And what
are you smirking about, Rowland Ellis, perhaps you can spell it?'

'S-U-C-K-E-R,' says Rowland Ellis proudly, and is mystified to get a
clip over the ear.

'Come along, children,' says Miss Timpson. 'Next door there are some
ladies demonstrating how to knit sea-socks. We may pick up a few tips.
And pay attention all of you, I shall want you to write a composition about
this when we get back to school.'

Where that 'After the Battle' painting is now I've no idea and nor has
the Gallery. So utterly has it disappeared that I began to think I had imagined it; but my brother remembers it, several viewers remember it and the
Chairman of the Cultural Services Committee, Bernard Atha, remembers
it, so I'm not just romancing. Still, I suspect it's no loss to art, or even to
memory, because if it did turn up it would probably seem much milder
now than it seemed to our eight-year-old eyes then.

For all Miss Timpson's strictures, one of the earliest lessons a child
learns in a gallery is the propriety of art, that art and antiquity make it
quite proper to peep.

'It's all right if it's art.' I was once in the Hayward Gallery at an exhibition of Indian painting, *Tantra*, and there was one panel on which a god-
dess, I suppose, was having everything possible done to her through every
conceivable orifice by half a dozen strapping young men and enjoying it
no end. Looking at this were two very proper middle-aged, middle-class
ladies. Eventually one of them spoke:

'Goodness! She's a busy lady!'

498

WILLIAM HOLMAN HUNT, *The Shadow of Death*, 1870

This painting is perhaps the most famous in the Gallery, Holman Hunt's *The Shadow of Death*, in which Mary sees Jesus' death prefigured. There's a larger version of the painting in Manchester but this one was the original, slightly smaller than the other versions so that Hunt could carry it around with him and make alterations as he went.

He painted the picture on location in Palestine and went to elaborate lengths to get the background and fittings right. The body of Christ belonged to one model, the head to another, who was not at all Christ-like, a notorious villain in fact and on one occasion before he painted him Hunt had to go to the local gaol and bail him out.

It's not at all plain what Jesus is supposed to be doing, apart from casting the appropriate shadow; I suppose he's meant to be stretching after a hard day's work, but it hardly looks like that. What always used to puzzle me as a child was that apart from the hair on his head Jesus (I mean not merely this Jesus, but any Jesus) never had a stitch of hair anywhere else. Never a whisper of hair on that always angular chest; God seemed to have sent his only begotten son into the world with no hair whatsoever under his arms. This rang a bell with me, though, because I was a late developer

499

and at fifteen was longing for puberty. So Jesus' pose here is exactly how I felt, crucified on the wall bars during PE, displaying to my much more hirsute classmates my still-unsullied armpits.

St Cyril and St Justin thought that Christ must have been (or should have been) mean and disgusting, 'the most hideous of the sons of men'. This cut no ice with the powers that be. Louis B. Mayer had nothing on the Early Fathers. They knew that someone with billing and his name above the title couldn't be a slob. So never a fat Jesus or a small Jesus even, and always a dish, though of course we must not say so.

And so serious. Scour the art galleries of the world and you will not find a picture of Jesus grinning. Jesus enjoying a joke. A God who rarely smiled, a man who never sniggered. Did he see jokes, one wonders? And were they ever on him?

There aren't many pictures of Jesus in the Gallery, which suits me as my threshold for Jesus pictures is quite low. The later they get the harder I find them to take, so that by the time we get to the nineteenth century Jesus is uncomfortably close to the only slightly sicklier versions we were given to stick in our books at Sunday School.

REMBRANDT VAN RIJN,
Christ Returning from the Temple with His Parents, 1654

Excepted from these irreverences is the Rembrandt etching *Christ Returning from the Temple with His Parents*, who don't look like the Holy

Family at all but peasants out for a walk complete with dog. He's one of Rembrandt's frisky and utterly non-symbolic dogs. Maybe that's why he's frisky, because he knows he doesn't have to represent fidelity or trust or anything at all from Hall's *Dictionary of Subjects and Symbols*. He's just happy to be All Dog.

ATKINSON GRIMSHAW, *Park Row, Leeds, by Moonlight*, 1882

Anyone who knows Leeds will find this painting, *Park Row* by Atkinson Grimshaw, almost a documentary record (the church apart) of how the street looked as late as 1960, which was when the city fell to greed and mediocrity.

Some silly people on the right nowadays wish the sixties hadn't happened because that was when people discovered sex and pot-smoking. I wish the sixties hadn't happened because that was when avarice and stupidity got to the wheel of the bulldozer. They called it enterprise and still do, but the real enterprise would have been if someone in 1960 had had the clout and the imagination to say, 'Let us leave this city much as it is, convert it perhaps, replumb it, but nothing else.'

If they had, Leeds today would have been one of the architectural showplaces of the kingdom, a Victorian Genoa or Florence, on the buildings of which many of its banks and commercial properties (like the one in the right foreground) were modelled. Instead it's now like anywhere else.

ANTONIO CANOVA, *The Hope of Venus, c.*1818–20

I've included this sculpture by Canova simply as a reminder. In all the fuss there was earlier this year about retaining his *Three Graces* in this country I saw no mention of this or other sculptures by him that were already in public galleries here and which were comparatively unregarded. Now it's true that Leeds has only one lady not three, but whereas the *Three Graces* are in a bit of a huddle here you can at least see Venus in the round.

PATRICK WILLIAM ADAM, *Interior, Rutland Lodge, Potternewton*, 1920
Interior, Rutland Lodge: vista through open doors, 1920
GEORGE CLAUSEN, *A Girl in Black*, 1913

The name Sam Wilson suggests some bluff mill owner standing four-square on the hearthrug with his thumbs in his waistcoat, holding forth about the shortcomings of the workers and generally laying down the law. In fact Sam Wilson seems to have been a discerning, if rather conservative collector and his house at Potternewton must have been crowded out with the pictures he left to the Art Gallery in 1915.

I've chosen three, two which I remember from childhood and the third, by George Clausen, because it appeals to me now. The two pictures of his house by Patrick William Adam aren't remarkable as paintings but I used to look at them and think that this was the kind of house I would one day like to live in – a place of hushed, handsome rooms, and rooms that gave onto other rooms and rooms beyond them, all bathed in a subdued aqueous light and the setting for a life of great elegance. Nothing could be further removed from our homely (but entirely comfortable) kitchen–living room in Otley Road.

This vision of gracious living remains a vision (and now an unwanted one) though the sense of long views through a house still gives me pleasure when I walk through the upper floors at Temple Newsam.

JOHN SELL COTMAN, *On the River Yare*, 1807–8
Refectory of Walsingham Priory, 1807–8
A Ploughed Field, c.1808

I can see that in aesthetic terms my liking for Cotman's watercolours is related to my fondness for the Camden Town school of painting. With both the colour range is quite narrow, the closeness of the tones imparting a kind of glow to the paper or canvas and which, more than subject, line or setting, draws me to it.

I can say nothing about the composition of these wonderful works though even I can see that the man's red cap at the centre of *On the River*

Yare is an inspired touch. Part of the pleasure, I'm sure, is nostalgic, a longing for England as it once was – or perhaps never quite was, as Cotman creates as well as records a world.

On a more prosaic note, the crow that hangs from the stick in *A Ploughed Field* is a feature of the countryside that has always puzzled me. Displaying the carcasses of crows (and also moles) is (or used to be) a favourite device of gamekeepers though quite to what end I'm not sure. Perhaps the farmer or gamekeeper is simply advertising his skill as a killer of crows and catcher of moles. But it seems to me that the unfortunate creatures were also strung up as an Awful Warning. The unshot crows and unsnared moles were meant to take note of the carcasses of their unlucky fellows and take the lesson to heart: in future they must Mend Their Ways (i.e. not behave like crows or moles). It seems flippant when spelled out but there is some unthought-out notion like this at the back of such displays, deriving, I suppose, from the assumption that potential human wrongdoers would be deterred by the bodies of thieves left hanging on gibbets.

LUCIEN PISSARRO, *Wells Farm Railway Bridge, Acton,* 1907
ANDRÉ DERAIN, *Barges on the Thames,* about 1906

I remember thinking as a boy, and without knowing anything about *Les Fauves,* that this was quite a fierce picture and being rather pleased with myself that I liked it. The colours were so bold and uncompromising and, literal-minded as I was then, I knew that they were untrue and that the much muddier Camden Town version of London on view elsewhere in the Gallery was closer to the real thing.

I like the unashamed way the blue crane turns red when it's crossing the line of the blue bridge and the cheeky toy train in what, I suppose, is a version of Southern Railways green, puffing across to Broad Street. A nice exhibition (I'm sure there's been one) would be the English scene through French eyes. It would include Derain, Monet, Pissarro (of which Leeds has a good example) and Agasse, two of whose slightly sinister paintings were in a recent exhibition at the National Gallery.

Derain had a sad end. He behaved rather disreputably during the Second War and was one of several artists, including Vlaminck, who went on a sponsored tour of Germany and at the Liberation was denounced by Picasso. Tall and burly, he was a boxer in his youth; he died in 1954 after being run over. When asked if there was anything he wanted his last words were: 'A bicycle and a piece of sky.'

WALTER RICHARD SICKERT, *The New Bedford*, 1916–17
MALCOLM DRUMMOND, *The Coconut Shy*, *c.*1920
HAROLD GILMAN, *Mrs Mounter*, 1916–17
In Sickert's House, *c.*1907

Portrait of Spencer Frederick Gore, 1906–7
JEAN EDOUARD VUILLARD, *Mlle Nathanson in the Artist's Studio*,
*c.*1912
SPENCER FREDERICK GORE, *In Berkshire*, 1912
Interior with Nude, *c.*1907

It's said that when people come to London they settle near the station where they first arrive. Thus north of Euston (the station for Liverpool) one finds the Irish; Southall (near to Heathrow) is the centre of the Asian community; and even the Australians in Earls Court fit into the theory because once upon a time British Airways had its passenger terminal there.

I conform to the theory myself: King's Cross was the station I arrived at and for thirty years I've lived not far away in Camden Town.

Though the dreadful Camden Lock and its attendant touristification has driven out anything resembling normal life from large areas there are still parts of Camden Town that haven't changed since Sickert, Gilman and Gore were painting here at the turn of the last century.

Sickert lived all over the place, and briefly in the street where I live now, but his blue plaque is in Mornington Crescent. Spencer Gore was nearby, though his lodgings were demolished in the thirties to make way for the

Black Cat cigarette factory, itself an Art Deco monument but stripped in the 1960s of everything that made it distinctive.

When I first moved here part of the New Bedford music hall was still standing, and the site is vacant even today. I like Sickert's painting of it though the picture of his I would have chosen was of the front of St Mark's in Venice. This used to hang in the Gallery in the 1950s but it was only on loan and has now been reclaimed.

I came backwards to French painting. I like Vuillard's interiors but it was Harold Gilman's I knew first so that I came to Paris via Camden Town. There is no patriotism involved but I think it's a pity that so many modern English painters are ranked a poor second to their French contemporaries. The reasons are as much commercial as artistic; their prices remain relatively modest because few Americans know much about English twentieth-century painting, though a notable exception was Vincent Price, who had several Camden Town pictures, picked up for what in international terms was a song. Leeds owes most of its splendid Camden Town pictures to the taste and foresight of Frank Rutter, who was Director here from 1912 to 1924 and who said of Gore, 'He was the most lovable man it has been my privilege to know.' In some ways the most refined painter of the group, Gore died quite young from pneumonia just when his paintings were beginning to be flooded with sun and light.

GWEN JOHN, *Portrait of Chloe Boughton-Leigh*, 1910–14

Gwen John was the sister of Augustus John – or perhaps one should say that Augustus was the brother of Gwen, because whereas since her death in 1939 her reputation has continued to grow, his is now rather patchy. She was the opposite of her brother in almost every respect, by nature diffident and retiring and painting with restraint and delicacy but with great strength. She was a friend of Rodin and an admirer of Whistler and a few years ago she was vividly (and bravely) portrayed on television by Anna Massey.

In her dedication and asceticism and her lack of concern for her reputation (she seldom exhibited her work) Gwen John conforms to one notion of what an artist should be just as her more flamboyant bohemian brother conforms to another.

ROGER FRY, *Portrait of Virginia Woolf*, *c*.1910
Portrait of Nina Hamnett, 1917
DUNCAN GRANT, *Still-Life*, 1930

Roger Fry is represented in the collection by a small and not very interesting landscape. He was more influential as an aesthetic theorist than as a painter but I've always found his portraits particularly satisfying. The portrait of Nina Hamnett which is in the University of Leeds' art collection is an excellent example.

The portrait of Virginia Woolf is on loan to the Gallery and must have been painted about 1910. The strained expression and hunched shoulders suggest that it may have been done on the verge of one of her frequent breakdowns. But she didn't like having her portrait painted so maybe that's where the tension arose.

Duncan Grant was married to Vanessa Bell, Virginia Woolf's sister, and this still-life was painted in 1930.

Painters seem an altogether nicer class of person than writers, though they often make good writers themselves. They're less envious of each other, less competitive and with more of a sense that they are all engaged on the same enterprise. I once met Duncan Grant when he was very old and asked him if he was envious of other painters. There was a pause, then he said, 'Titian, sometimes.' It was a good remark because besides being a joke it was also a rebuke to me for being so shallow-minded.

Seeing the little boy when we were making *Portrait or Bust* laboriously spelling out the label under Barbara Hepworth's *Dual Form* then looking up at it, grinning and saying, 'It's good is that!' makes me realise that there comes a point, particularly in music and the visual arts, where one's taste stops developing – or at any rate falters. Thus in English music I never got much beyond Walton and Vaughan Williams, and in English painting, though I don't quite stop, I certainly slow down in the late 1950s and begin to settle for what I know already. Thus I like the smoother, suppler forms of Henry Moore and dislike (or don't feel easy with) the pointy-headed figures that come later. And, unlike the little boy, don't go much for Barbara Hepworth.

JACOB KRAMER, *The Day of Atonement*, 1919
JACOB EPSTEIN, *Bust of Jacob Kramer*, *c.* 1921

Tramps are, I suppose, an occupational hazard of art galleries, particularly these days, but I should be sorry to see them turned away, their right to look at the pictures (or not look at them) every bit as inalienable as mine.

Still, I can see they can pose problems. I wrote a television play once in which there was a scene in a provincial art gallery with a conversation between a down-to-earth attendant and a casual visitor:

VISITOR: Now then, Neville. Not busy?
ATTENDANT: Ay. Run off us feet. (*The gallery is empty*)
VISITOR: I could do with your job.
ATTENDANT: It carries its own burdens. We get that much rubbish
   traipsing through here I feel like a social worker. This is one of their

regular ports of call, you know. Here and the social security. Mind you, they don't come in for the pictures.

VISITOR: No?

ATTENDANT: No. They come in for the central heating. Genuine art lovers you can tell them a mile off. They're looking at a picture and what they're looking for are the effects of light. The brush strokes. Economy of effect. But not the lot we get. Riff-raff. Rubbish. Human flotsam. The detritus of a sick society. Shove up half a dozen Rembrandts and they'd never come near. Turn the Dimplex up three degrees and it's packed out.

(*He stops another visitor*)

You're not looking for the Turner?

VISITOR 2: Sorry?

ATTENDANT: No. Beg pardon. That's generally what they all want to see. Anybody who has any idea. 'Where's the Turner?' Flaming Turner. I can't see anything in it. Looks as if it's been left out in the rain. We had Kenneth Clark in here once. Same old story. 'Where's the Turner?' I've never seen a suit like it. Tweed! It was just like silk. Then some of them come in just because we have a better class of urinal. See the Turner, use the urinal and then off. And who pays? Right. The ratepayer.

(*Afternoon Off*, 1979)

There was often a tramp in here in the late forties, hanging about the gallery or slumped over an art book in the corner of the Reference Library. Except that he wasn't a tramp; he was quite a distinguished painter, Jacob Kramer, and his bust by Epstein is one of the most powerful pieces of sculpture in the Gallery. Kramer was Jewish, his family from the Ukraine, one of many thousands of Jewish families who came to Leeds at the end of the nineteenth century. As a young man he was a Vorticist and an associate of Wyndham Lewis and William Roberts. I'd find it hard to say what Vorticism is; I think of it as the jagged school of painting, Cubism with an English slant, but both Kramer's Jewishness and his Vorticism can be seen in his *The Day of Atonement*, which was unveiled in the Gallery in 1920 to a storm of anti-Semitic protest.

There was still a lot of anti-Semitism in Leeds even after the Second War, and I can remember Jewish boys in my school being regularly bullied, one boy in particular, Alan Harris, always coming in for it. The masters used to turn a blind eye and even collaborate, one master catching him a terrific slap across the face for very little reason. Years later when I was in Harrogate I ran across this master, now tranquilly retired, in a tea shop and as he came up to me I thought, Oh yes, you're the one who hit the Jew. Nowadays Asians have replaced the Jews in the front line, living where the Jews used to live, the difference being that nowadays we talk about prejudice, whereas in those days one never mentioned it.

Kramer himself died in 1962 indistinguishable from a lot of the tramps whom you'll see outside. Except that in 1966 Leeds College of Art was, briefly, renamed after him, so he was more respectable in death than he ever was in life.

Though the collection is particularly strong on twentieth-century British pictures there are inevitably gaps. There are only two watercolours by Eric Ravilious, for instance, one of my favourite painters, who caught the atmosphere of wartime Britain better than anyone. Though there are two paintings by Duncan Grant there's nothing of any great interest by his long-time associate, Vanessa Bell.

Another absentee is Hockney (except for several etchings), though with the glut of his paintings at Saltaire the region isn't exactly going short. Perhaps some of the ancient rivalry between Leeds and Bradford still persists. I'm sure one of his paintings would be better placed here than on the wall of some Californian millionaire.

In the documentary *Portrait or Bust* I told the story of how I was mistaken for Hockney in a tea shop in Arezzo. It continues to happen. A few months after the programme went out I was marooned in Nice airport with two or three hours to wait for a plane. Unless I'm being paid for I travel economy but my travel agent, who has an exalted view of my status, has VIP put on my tickets, a largely futile gesture which seldom ever gets me upgraded. However, rather than sit on a hard bench for three hours I thought I'd use my notional status to wangle my way into the Club Lounge.

A stone-faced stewardess barred my way and I laboriously stated my case, whereupon she grudgingly undertook to make a telephone call. As she was phoning there was a tap on my shoulder. It was an English woman who, judging by her luggage and general demeanour, had a hereditary right to be in the Club Lounge and had been in Club Lounges from the cradle. 'Could I', she said kindly, 'congratulate you on your designs for the *Rake's Progress?*'

At which point the stewardess put the phone down and said, 'No. You can't come in here.'

The English have never been entirely comfortable with art and are happiest thinking of pictures as decor; I certainly prefer paintings in settings, feel easier with a picture in a room than when faced with it on a blank wall. Twentieth-century paintings in particular benefit from a domestic surrounding. I liked the mixture of paintings and furniture in the recent exhibition about Herbert Read, for instance, and the intimate galleries at Kettle's Yard in Cambridge carry that mixture further. The paintings can benefit too, and the shortcomings of the Bloomsbury painters become virtues when one sees their pictures as part of a comprehensive (if haphazard) decorative scheme as one does at Charleston. And of course this applies to much grander artists too. How many old master paintings, now seen in splendid isolation in galleries, were once part of rich and complex decorative and devotional schemes that we can now scarcely imagine?

Which makes me feel less frivolous five centuries later for liking to see a vase of flowers, say, beside or even in front of a painting.

The focus of this selection has been unashamedly retrospective, concentrating on the pictures I got to know in this Gallery when I was young. What my generation had then, which I think has weakened since, was a powerful sense of the city. I've mentioned that Atkinson Grimshaw's painting of Park Row reminded me of Genoa or Florence. I don't think it's fanciful to take that further and say that in the forties and fifties one had a sense of belonging to Leeds that can't have been unlike the feelings of someone growing up in a fifteenth-century Italian city-state.

There were the arms of the city for a start. Everywhere in Leeds in those days one was confronted with the owls and the lamb in the sling and the motto '*Pro Rege et Lege*'. One could not escape those arms. They were on my schoolbooks and they were at the tram stop; they were on the market; they were over the entrance to the Central Library (where, rather battered, they still survive). At every turn there was this reminder that you were a son or daughter of the city.

Its relics persist and in unexpected places. Staying at the Metropole Hotel while we were making the TV programme on which this selection is based, I happened to go down the side of the hotel and there, for no particular reason and seemingly over the kitchen door, was the familiar coat of arms, the stamp of Leeds.

I'm sure this sense of place survives but in a different form. The West Yorkshire Playhouse will centre some people's sense of identity. Leeds United (never much of a team when I was a boy) will centre others'. And I would not be so foolish as to say things were altogether better then or worse; they were different. Of one thing, though, I am sure.

My affection for this collection began in the late 1940s and it's coupled in my memory with other formative experiences of that time, with the books I borrowed from the public library next door, for instance, or with the concerts by the Yorkshire Symphony Orchestra that I heard every Saturday night in the Town Hall. The pictures were free, the library was free and the concerts (at 6d a time) were virtually free. And I was being educated at Leeds Modern School, which was, naturally, free and in due course went off to university, at first on a scholarship from Leeds, then on one from my college, free again.

Now if the assumptions – I would not call them a philosophy – that have informed government and public life over the last fifteen years are true, I would not set much store by the paintings I saw here, the books I read next door, the music I heard over the road, or the education I had up at Lawnswood. I had not had them to pay for and nor had my parents, so because they were free I am assumed to have taken them for granted. Only if I had to pay my way would I really appreciate them. Or so the libertarian argument goes.

Nothing is further from the truth.

I valued then as I value now what I was given in Leeds, as I'm sure most of my generation did and do.

But what am I on about, you say? The Art Gallery is still free, and though the suburban branches have been cut back the libraries are still free. Which is true. But they are not free, as once they were, because they are every citizen's birthright. I am not even sure we have a birthright now. No, they are only free because the government has not been able to devise a legal method of stealing them from the public for short-term financial gain and putting them out to private tender. If, as seems likely, we are now going to have to pay to die, why should we not also have to pay to look and to read?

Here is a picture of a boy looking up at a Barbara Hepworth.* I see myself fifty years ago and I know that through no fault of his own he is going to have a harder time of it than I had. And I think that is wrong.

* In the BBC film of *Portrait or Bust*.

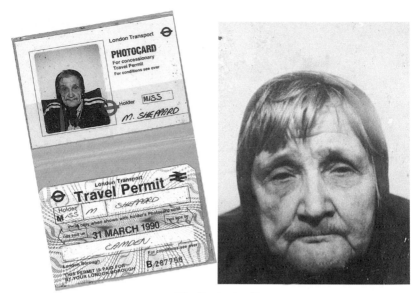

31 Miss Shepherd, 1989

32 *The Lady in the Van, 1999*
(left to right: Kevin McNally, Maggie Smith, Nicholas Farrell)

33 Leeds Modern School, 1952

34 J.S.S.L., Bodmin, 1954
(left to right: AB, Michael Frayn, David Thompson, P. B. Naylor)

35 *The History Boys*, 2004 (left to right: Jamie Parker, Dominic Cooper, Samuel Barnett, James Corden, AB, Andrew Knott, Samuel Anderson, Sacha Dhawan, Russell Tovey)

36 Richard Griffiths and Frances de la Tour in rehearsal

37 Exeter College, Oxford Staircase 5:6

38 Exeter College, Oxford Staircase 9:11

39 Leeds Town Hall

40 George Fenton (and one of Miss Shepherd's vans), 1974

41 Mam and Dad, 1970

42 County Arcade, Leeds

43 The Masons' Loft, York Minster

44 Templets (*sic*) in the loft

Bennett, A.

45 1953

Making York Minster

It is a morning in May and York Minster is already thronged with visitors. In the vast octagon of ancient glass that is the chapterhouse we sidestep the crowds gazing up at the windows and slip unnoticed behind one of the great iron-bound thirteenth-century doors.

Here there is another door set in the thickness of the wall and a narrow spiral staircase that takes us high up above the vestibule of the chapterhouse to the door of what is in effect an attic. It's a cold, dark, dusty loft and as I scramble thankfully across the threshold and look around the dim interior it appears as if we have come into some sort of cloakroom, with racks and racks of what seem to be stiffened remnants hanging in bundles from the rails. Or, with no two pieces the same, the shapes could almost be pelts and this a kind of curing place.

It is tall and narrow with windows set low in the wall and above them an elaborately beamed roof, the timbers so fresh and sharp they recall Philip Larkin's lines in *Church Going*:

> From where I stand, the roof looks almost new –
> Cleaned, or restored? Someone would know: I don't

The someone who does know is my companion, Louise Hampson, the cathedral archivist, who tells me it's a scissor-beam roof, dating like the rest of the room from the fourteenth century, and that this is the masons' loft, put up almost as an afterthought on top of the chapterhouse vestibule to serve in effect as the drawing office of the medieval Minster.

Like the vestibule, it's L-shaped, with the long arm of the L taken up with racks not of remnants, still less pelts, but shapes of wood and blackened zinc, the patterns for some of the countless architectural features of this vast building.

At first glance the other half of the room seems empty; it's just a long stretch of dusty grey floor covered in a layer of crumbling plaster. Only when you scrutinise the floor more carefully do you see that there are shapes in this dust, outlines of mouldings, arches even, and that it is not a floor at all but a vast drawing board.

It was on this floor, thinly washed with lime plaster or gesso, that were traced the designs for crucial pieces of construction in the building of the Minster, the earliest of the designs still detectable that of some window tracery in the retro-choir, known to have been put up in 1356. The loft itself was probably constructed thirty years or so earlier as a drawing space needed for the rebuilding of the Minster's west end.

Not all features would need to be traced out here. A standard arch, for instance, that presented no difficulties could be put up on the spot. It was more complex constructions, two or three arches springing from the same pillar at different angles, for instance, that would need preparatory drawings and a tracing on the floor that could be made into a templet. This would then be taken down to the site, either in one piece or in sections, and used when shaping the stone. I would have called it a template but as John David, the current master mason, points out, this is a nineteenth-century spelling; templet is what the medieval masons would have called it. So the spelling (along with the templets themselves) is here preserved.

This is not just out of piety. The templets that remain are mostly from the early nineteenth century, when the master mason was William Shout, and are still used, or at least referred to, when some tricky design problem has to be sorted out. There is information in these scraps of wood and discoloured zinc that could not be stored on a computer. The fabric of a centuries-old cathedral is more like a body than a building, odd, asymmetrical, hunched, sometimes awkwardly, into the place it has occupied for over a thousand years and thus resistant to computerised planning or adjustment. The job of the master mason now does not differ in essentials from the job of William of Colchester, say, master mason in 1404, and though John David's 8-by-13-foot drawing table may have replaced this lime-washed floor its function is the same.

With a pair of medieval dividers, which are still in use in the Minster, John David demonstrates on a piece of modern concrete how simple it is to score out a design so when the floor became overcrowded with old material it would only need the thinnest wash of lime or gesso to provide a clean unbroken surface. It would be as easy as cleaning a blackboard.

How many men worked on the fabric of the Minster would presumably depend on what work was being done, but the records of their names, the hours they put in and how much they earned are preserved in the master masons' rolls in the Minster archives. The tracing floor itself is undocumented and in England only one other, at Wells, has survived. There are similar installations, though, on the Continent, and there must once have been many more here. A building of the size and complexity of Fountains Abbey, for instance, must have had some sort of drawing office; one only has to think of the fan vaulting at Gloucester or Westminster Abbey to realise that they couldn't have been put up simply by rule of thumb. Such installations as there were may have been more provisional than this at York, and once they had served their purpose there was likely to be no reason to preserve them. But even had their function and historical significance been recognised, the evidence for such drawing floors would have been easy to overlook, as they must often have seemed, as this one does, just like a crumbling surface crying out for renewal.

As paper became cheaper and more readily available, the floor as a draughtsman's board must have fallen into disuse. There was a disastrous fire at York in 1829 and it was perhaps then that the loft became a storeroom and its original purpose forgotten. The templets were piled in heaps across the floor, thus preserving the traces of the original drawings. It was only in the sixties, when they were cleared out and catalogued, that the diagrams were rediscovered and the function of the room recalled.

There are other treasures here besides the floor. Since the loft was built on top of the vestibule and a little later than the main building, it abutted on and obscured part of what had been the external wall, thus taking in the top of one of the windows. Protected from the elements for more than six centuries, the moulding and the two heads that form the capitals are as crisp and unweathered as when they were first put up. I'm disconcerted, though, that their very freshness makes me not care for them; they look crude and sentimental and not all that different from the Victorian Gothic that abounds in the churches and chapels of the West Riding. The Tadcaster stone of which York is built is so luminously white it adds to this effect, though when they were put up these carvings, like the rest of the Minster, were likely to have been boldly painted (and so might have seemed crude in a different way).

As a workplace the loft can never have been cosy. Today is warm but it's chilly up here under the roof, and it would once have been chillier as the windows were only glazed in the nineteenth century, what protection there was against the wind and cold coming from crude wooden shutters which, 600 years on, are still hanging here. But there is a fireplace and a loo, a one-seater that, primitive though it is, hardly looks to have seen the bottoms of centuries and which debouches down the outside of the vestibule wall.

Always fastidious in this respect, I ask Louise Hampson if the cubicle had a door. She thinks not, a curtain more likely (which wouldn't have suited me at all). Already empathising with some shy fourteenth-century apprentice with the squits, I am absurdly pleased as I run my hand round the door opening to discover the iron staples on which must once have hung the door that would have saved his blushes. In a previous life I was a medieval historian but the discovery of these door hooks is more of a contribution than I ever made through my study of the archives.

Thinking about the loo, though, I wonder that there are no graffiti here, but I suppose it's less surprising when one reflects that the masons who sat here were making their mark elsewhere in the building where some of their signatures do survive, carved in the stone in the form of mason's marks.

I have known York Minster since I was a boy, when in the late forties I toiled over here from Leeds on my bike. York and Ripon were the only cathedrals I had seen until I was sixteen, both of them, I used to think then, plain no-nonsense places. This was only partly because the glass had yet to be put back after the war; I didn't go much for glass in those days. Anyway what I was really missing was any mystery or romance. In our school library was a copy of an early Thames & Hudson book, *English Cathedrals*, with magnificent photographs by Martin Hürlimann. I used to pore over this book, marvelling at Wells with its branching chapter-house staircase, the massive incised columns of the nave at Durham and the cloisters of Westminster and Gloucester. So York, for all its soaring splendour, seemed to me pretty basic as cathedrals go. And in a sense I was right. Not being a monastic foundation it has no cloisters, the chantries have gone, and what you see is what you get. So what this extraordinary mason's loft does for me on this bright May morning is reinvest the Minster with magic, and confounds that precociously disen-chanted boy who came here fifty-five years ago and was not impressed.

Nor is the magic quite over. The loft is still a bit of a junk room; the window sill, for instance, piled with old plaster casts made when delicate bits of moulding needed to be replaced, a boss, a shard of a vault . . . and there is more history here than one realises. Leaning against the wall by the door are some odd bits of wood, and as we're going out Louise Hampson idly sorts through them. One she picks out, recognising it from some eighteenth-century drawings she's been studying that morn-ing. It's a fragment of Gothic tracery from behind the medieval shrine of St William. Though the saint's bones are in the crypt, the shrine itself was looted and demolished by Henry VIII's commissioners in 1538. But lacking any religious imagery the doors were suffered to remain and weren't taken down until the eighteenth century, and here is some of their medieval tracery, a relic of the ancient shrine just gathering dust in the mason's loft. Suddenly I envy Louise her job.

County Arcade, Leeds

When in my early twenties I first went to Italy to Venice and Florence, I didn't at first understand why it all seemed so familiar. I had the feeling I had seen these buildings before, as indeed I had. I knew them because I'd been brought up in Leeds where so many nineteenth-century banks and commercial premises were modelled on and reproduced the palaces, baptisteries and bell towers of Renaissance Italy.

When in the sixties Leeds, like all the northern cities, was sacked by property developers much of its nineteenth-century inheritance was lost and what remained was cleaned. You can always tell when there's been some act of architectural murder because the surviving witnesses to it are all washed in dubious expiation. Lady Macbeth was probably an architect.

Among the happier survivors, though, are the arcades. There are some half a dozen arcades in Leeds. Thornton's Arcade was always the most exciting to me as a child because it had (and still has) a clock with moving figures. County Arcade was the poshest, though it never looked quite as posh as it does today when it has been nicely restored.

There was always something festive about County Arcade, an air of holiday and theatrical exuberance, but it wasn't until I was asked to compile this programme that I found out why. County Arcade is one of the few, as it were, lay buildings by an architect whose reputation rests on his design of Victorian and Edwardian theatres, Frank Matcham. Fifty years ago there was scarcely a town of any size in the United Kingdom that didn't boast one of Matcham's theatres and though scores have since been lost enough remain to testify to the achievement of someone who was undoubtedly this country's greatest theatrical architect.

Though this is not a theatre, it was built as part of a scheme involving one, the Leeds Empire lower down Briggate, which Matcham had designed – and which I remember as a child if only because it used to advertise some of its stalls as 'Fauteuils', a word both mysterious and unpronounceable. The Empire is long gone but here is County Arcade, which still somehow smacks to me of the seaside. I think it's because it's built in a material (glazed brick and terracotta tile) which is also the stuff of the grander hotels and boarding houses that line the front at Morecambe and Cleveleys.

As a child I was in this arcade more often than most (and I don't apologise that its charm has as much to do with memory as with architectural merit). I can remember the shops that used to be here and in particular a toy shop. At the start of the war toys were in short supply, and my dad had invested in a fretsaw and took to making toy animals. His speciality was penguins, which he mounted on a little four-wheeled cart. On his afternoon off he hawked them around the toy shops of Leeds without much success until one day he called here at a toy shop run by a Mr Baildon. 'Old Baildon', as Dad always called him, offered to take his entire output, though at a very modest rate. So, week by week, we would come down here with two dozen or so penguins and the occasional giraffe. They seemed to my brother and me a very dull toy, but did we ever see a child trailing one we would follow behind hoping to overhear some expression of pleasure, Dad presumably experiencing much the same frisson as an author does when he catches someone reading one of his books.

Many years after I saw one of these penguins in a shop window now elevated to the status of an antique. But the shop was closed and when I came back it had gone. One of the memories of my childhood is of rows and rows of penguins ranged on top of the wringing machine, uniform and without personality until Dad painted in the eye and suddenly they acquired a face.

Here used to be the Mecca Ballroom, which imparted a degree of whoopee to the arcade. It was thought, by me at any rate, to be a place of great wickedness, and boys in my class at school would sometimes go dancing there and come back swearing they had seen a prostitute, the cast-iron proof a chain worn round the ankle. Opposite the Mecca was Redman's the grocers, a grander version of the Maypole or Gallons, branches of which you found all over Leeds.

The window would be filled with great boxes of raisins and prunes and candied peel and you could buy homemade oatcakes here, Thompson's barley kernels and Allinson's brown bread – health food even then, though with none of the ideology that nowadays goes with it. And here, at the Vicar Lane end, was Cashdisia, the gents' outfitters where we got our school blazers but didn't get those great class indicators, the Cash's name tapes that better-class boys had sewn into all their clothes.

There are some surprising survivals: little milliner's shops, shops selling babies' knitwear, which somehow seem to cling on in the teeth of the fiercest economic gale. There was a *corsetières* here in the forties and the same *corsetières* is here now. It's a curious profession and not one I associate with the present day. *Corsetières* seldom had premises as it was a profession taken up by single ladies of a certain age, who did fittings in the home. My Aunt Eveline was briefly a *corsetière*, herself an ample lady and, like many of them, a model for the product she was marketing.

County Arcade runs between Briggate and Vicar Lane. In my day it marked the border of respectability because on the far side of Vicar Lane is Kirkgate and that other splendid survival, the covered market, and beyond the market is the slaughterhouse, or 'the yard' as my father called it. This is where the city began to be slightly disreputable and so here had lodged the less orthodox retail establishments: herbalists, shops selling surgical appliances, rubber goods, remedies for haemorrhoids or hair, wanted or unwanted, and remedies for babies too, wanted and unwanted.

Happy though I am to see this arcade so splendidly restored, if I'm honest it's just a bit too smart for me now – too done up, and the painted leaves make it look like Christmas all year round – but that's a small price to pay to keep it from the bulldozer. Oh that the financial institutions which rule our lives and which have helped to restore this arcade had learned the lessons of conservation twenty years earlier, in which case England would be a pleasanter place to live. As it is, I'd like to come back here in a few years' time when this particular restoration won't seem quite so synthetic. Time will have weathered it a bit, distressed these slightly too twee shopfronts, faded the lettering, and maybe some of those seedier backstreet establishments will have begun to creep back – a second-hand bookshop perhaps, a herbalist, shops for what people really want rather than what they can be persuaded to want. But I imagine babies' knitwear will still be hanging on like grim death.

Nowadays we live to shop. It's the only thing that holds us together. There's no such thing as society, said the Blessed Margaret, just shoppers. And if we can't shop we get depressed and feel oppressed, the deliverance of Eastern Europe not so much the restoration of freedom as the restoration of freedom to shop.

Small specialised shops selling chocolates, pot-pourri and scented candles, card shops with messages for all sorts of occasion, grave and gay, and straight, kitchen shops selling jams in esoteric combinations, rhubarb and ginger, apricot and almond, out-of-the-way mustards, pedigree vinegars – lovely, lovely shopping.

A Room of My Own

———————

'You're from Yorkshire and he's from Yorkshire. You're from a state school and he's from a state school. You're reading history and he's reading history. You seem to me,' and Rector Barber gave what I took to be a smile, 'you seem to me to be very well suited.'

So my first disappointment with Oxford was finding I was going to have to share. But the disappointment turned to consternation when I found I had been put in with someone with whom I had intermittently shared a barrack room and a bedroom for much of my two years in the army. He was amiable enough, much more so than I was (and far more convivial), but he was no more anxious to share with me than I with him. It was this depressing prospect that had emboldened me to knock on the door of the Lodgings the first day I arrived and ask to be moved.

Though a kindly enough man, Rector Barber had an air of death-in-life about him that is caught well in the Annigoni portrait, now hanging in Exeter College hall; a classicist from the age of Housman, he made even that austere figure seem jolly and certainly I got no joy that day. I came away thinking, 'Well, I'm here for three years and that's put paid to the first year.'

It hadn't, of course, but I have to say that, though I ended up staying at Oxford not for three years but for eight, the place inspires little nostalgia. Still, it was at Oxford that I first had a room of my own.

When, in Evelyn Waugh's *Brideshead Revisited*, Charles Ryder decorates his college rooms at Oxford he puts up a reproduction of Van

Gogh's *Sunflowers*, a poster by E. McKnight Kauffer and a screen painted by Roger Fry, bought at the closing-down sale of the Omega Work-
shops. Later, when Ryder meets Sebastian Flyte and is exposed to a more
sophisticated and idiosyncratic taste, these slightly shaming objects are
put away.

They're not shaming today, of course, when both the screen and the
McKnight Kauffer would be thought eminently 'collectable'. Still, Waugh
catches well the uncertainty of a young man called upon to stamp his personality on a room but who is not sure what he likes or what he should like.

For many undergraduates, though, and certainly in the mid-fifties
when I went up to Oxford, the problem did not arise. In my own college,
Exeter, most undergraduate rooms were papered in beige and even
rooms with eighteenth-century panelling were painted an unprepossessing cream; the furniture was heavy and uncomfortable and carpets
thin and violently patterned, the better to stand the strains and stains of
undergraduate occupation.

Billeted in rooms that resembled a cheap boarding house in Hull, few
of my contemporaries felt impelled to brighten up their surroundings or
even mitigate their discomfort. It wasn't only indifference, though, that
left the walls bare, so much as a shortage of anything with which to adorn
them. The glimpse of light, colour and good design that was the Festival
of Britain had been snuffed out and drabness was back. Even posters were
in short supply and there were no shops selling cheap reproductions.
Long-playing records were just coming in, however, and their covers were
often colourful and well designed, sometimes with good photographs;
these at least were readily accessible and several rooms that I remember
had record sleeves artfully arranged around the walls.

I myself was far from indifferent to questions of decoration, and having
a room that I could do up and arrange as I wanted was what made me look
forward to Oxford. University to me had less to do with broadening the
mind than finding a place I could call my own. I had never had a room to
myself; at home I had shared with my brother, and during my two years'
National Service had been in various barrack rooms. Some of this time,

though, was spent in Cambridge, which, perhaps because it boasted a School of Architecture, wasn't the design desert most provincial cities were.

At Joshua Taylor's there were pots by Lucie Rie which foolishly (and with only my army pay) I did not buy; Robert Sayle's had Isokon chairs and I didn't buy those either. The same shop did stock some hand-blocked wallpaper and though it was expensive, too, thinking of the room I was going to have I invested in a length. Few freshman undergraduates arrive at college, I imagine, with a single roll of wallpaper under their arm, but I did.

It was all to no purpose. Finding I was going to have to share meant that my precious wallpaper would have to wait. In an ideal world, I suppose we might have come to some arrangement about doing the place up together. But interior decoration was not high on my room-mate's list of priorities and so, since it was plain we were never going to be Colefax and Fowler, the wallpaper went back into the drawer.

At the time I had even less idea than Charles Ryder what it was I liked, though I didn't bother as much as he did about the impression I created, as none of my friends cared one way or the other. Exeter happened to have been the college of William Morris, and at the bottom of my staircase was a room enshrined to his memory, papered in green willow-patterned paper with his portrait over the mantelpiece along with various drawings by Burne-Jones. Together they had designed and furnished the college chapel, modelled on the Sainte Chapelle in Paris. I didn't care for it or Morris either, nor did the thick-necked women of Pre-Raphaelite portraiture much appeal. I would have liked Kelmscott had I seen it, but there was no hope of that. Too far to cycle, it was lost in the depths of the car-free countryside.

While not quite a sleepy provincial town, Oxford in 1954 was both quieter and dustier than it is today. Few college or university buildings had been restored or cleaned: the old emperors' heads around the Sheldonian were still shapeless and decayed, the stucco everywhere peeling and scrofulous. It smelled older too, some of it the smell of ancient meals in hall and buttery, and it's this smell rather than more obvious fragrances (wall-flowers, old books, cold stone) that calls the place back.

It was not until my second year that I achieved the sole occupancy of a set of rooms, under the eaves of the front quad and looking out at the back over Exeter garden and walls of the Divinity School. I could also see the towers of All Souls and the spire of St Mary's. Still, it was less the view than the interior I was interested in. I put my wallpaper up on the chimney breast and at the windows I hung long grey curtains of some shiny material which were purely for decoration because, since I was on the top floor, nobody could see in anyway. To the left of the fireplace I hung a plain gilded nineteenth-century mirror, which was falling to pieces then and is falling to pieces now where it still hangs at the top of my kitchen stairs. Below it in the photograph is a small black-and-white portrait of myself in profile. Though I am no artist, I was immensely pleased with it and mortified when it was later lost, the linen on which it was painted recycled, I've always thought, by a young painter for one of his own less distinctive efforts. I had painted a coloured portrait at the same time and this has survived. However, since I was the only subject I seemed able to tackle, I thought it was best, or at any rate healthiest, to cease production.

Also in the photograph is a red lacquer tea caddy, spotted in a junk-shop window as I was coming into Lancaster on the bus when I was about fifteen. I got off, ran back and bought it for five shillings and this, too, I still have, some dusty leaves of fifty-year-old tea a relic of that time. Next to it is a grey-and-blue mocha mug, also extant, and a Staffordshire dog which got the elbow (or the Charles Ryder treatment) sometime in the sixties. I note, too, that even I had succumbed to the lure of record sleeves – one of them, I believe, with a photograph of Prague, at that time an unvisitable place.

As a boy I felt myself a bit of an oddity for being drawn to such objects as those I now displayed on my college mantelpiece, as it was an interest unshared with any of my school friends. However, I'd been encouraged while I was in the army by reading (partly as an antidote to army life) the

527

Denton Welch Journals. The standard taste of the time was for insipid Georgian, but Denton Welch was more passionate and idiosyncratic than that and had an unashamed fascination with what he could turn up in wartime junkshops about which he wrote vividly in his diaries.

Oxford was still full of such shops then, and though I never ventured into the better class of antique shop on the High Street, there were plenty of others. Down Little Clarendon Street was Kyril Bonfiglioli, a colourful character, now I think revealed as possibly a spy and certainly an accomplished detective story writer. He sold me for a few pounds a little oil sketch of an Oriental market that he thought might be by W. J. Mueller (of whom I had never heard). Years later I took it into the Fine Art Society in Bond Street, where a young man glanced briefly at it before saying kindly, 'Ye-es. Well, Mueller painted some bad pictures, but I am afraid this is not one of them.' I've had other such humiliations down Bond Street which, in many different ways, I've come to regard as a street of shame.

I bought the supposed Mueller because it was a dark little painting with something of a glow about it and this reminded me of the glass paintings I liked at the time. Impossibly expensive today, the historical subjects, *The Death of Nelson*, for instance, or *The Trial of Queen Caroline*, were not cheap then but religious subjects could be picked up for a few pounds. Some were more votive than others – sickly depictions of the Virgin, say, or mawkish representations of the saints – but in others the strength of the colours and the primitive crudities of the style offset the, to me, slightly distasteful fact that these were in effect Stations of the Cross.

I stayed on at Oxford after I took my degree and in due course got larger rooms for which I could even buy furniture. Over Magdalen Bridge and just up the London road on the left, I bought a Victorian marble-topped chiffonier (£6) which is still in my kitchen today. In 1958 it had to be taken up the High Street on a handcart. The rooms I then had were at the end of Exeter's Broad Street building, my bedroom looking over the emperors to the Sheldonian and the Clarendon Building.

Where taste was concerned I never went through the Damascus-road experience like that occasioned in Charles Ryder by Sebastian Flyte, undergraduates who already knew what they liked being quite rare. One such, though, was Brian Brindley, with whom I overlapped at Exeter and whose much-reported death occurred last year in typically spectacular fashion when he collapsed in the middle of his seventieth birthday dinner at the Athenaeum. Brian's taste was for Soane and the Gothick, and his rooms were crowded with religious images and (though I did not know the word then) *bondieuserie*.

He was an outrageous figure, kinder than he would have liked you to think, but witty, camp and a bit of a bully. He once called on me at the top of Staircase 5, the call a mark of significant social favour and like a visit from Lady Bracknell. What I had done to my rooms can't have been to his taste at all but among my sparse possessions he spotted two blue Bristol-glass dishes, liners from some long-vanished salt cellars. He begged one from me in order to use it as an incense burner, and so overawed was I by this arbiter of taste that (though it had not been cheap and they were, after all, a pair) I gave it to him. I still have its fellow, and somewhere among the exquisite clutter of his Brighton flat (for his taste had not altered a jot since he was an undergraduate) languishes, I imagine, its twin.

No other personality that I came across was as colourful as Brindley or with such pronounced tastes, though mention of Brighton recalls John Morley, who was Director of the Royal Pavilion and Museums there. He, too, was an undergraduate at Exeter, though slightly younger than me and every bit as precocious and dogmatic in his tastes as Brindley. They both drew witty and elaborate Gothick extravaganzas in the college Suggestions Book rather like ecclesiastical versions of the *Punch* cartoons of Emmett. These days I feel there would not be time for such silliness, and talents so notable would already be being turned to profit or self-promotion. Then it simply seemed fun. Half a morning could be spent elaborating some confection in the Suggestions Book that only a few undergraduates would see and smile at. It was a community as enclosed and unworldly as a medieval monastery.

After I took my degree I stayed on at Oxford to do research in medieval history, and also taught a little. I now had rooms in Merton Street, the back looking over to the Botanic Gardens. Some of my pupils were already collectors and possessed of a good deal more expertise than I ever had. David Bindman, later Professor of Art History at University College, London, was a pupil and would show me old master drawings he had picked up for a song, and another pupil, Bevis Hillier, later the biographer of John Betjeman and writer on the arts generally, would fetch along ceramics; I knew little of either and could neither confirm nor deny the confident attributions both boys put forward. But they taught me a more useful lesson than I ever taught them, namely that my own taste was for surfaces.

I was no collector. I cared more for the look of an object than for what it was. My aim was to make a room look interesting or cosy. I didn't see paintings as art objects so much as objects in a setting, and had the unashamedly English notion of pictures as furniture. I preferred them above tables, behind flowers, say, dimly lit by lamps or even half hidden by books. I would never want a room in which a painting was spotlit; it smacks too much of a museum, or a certain sort of gallery.

It is for these reasons that almost my favourite museum is the Fitzwilliam at Cambridge. It has too much on the walls and there is furniture besides, but it adds up to just the kind of inspired clutter that has always appealed to me. When I was stationed in Cambridge in the fifties I used to go there on Saturday afternoons out of term when the museum (and the town) was virtually empty.

The first room I would head for was on the right at the head of the stairs. There were some grand pictures but they were mostly English paintings then – a portrait of Hardy by Augustus John, some Constable sketches and Camden Town paintings and, presiding over them all, another Augustus John, a portrait of Sir William Nicholson. He's in a long thin black overcoat, hand outstretched resting on his stick, urbane, disdainful and looking not unlike the actor in the films of the time who played Professor Moriarty to Basil Rathbone's Sherlock Holmes. I didn't even know then that William Nicholson was himself a painter; what it was I admired was his detachment and his urbanity to the extent that the first chance I got I bought a thin second-hand black overcoat which made me look as spidery as he did.

If I like the Fitzwilliam for its clutter, I also like another Cambridge museum for its lack of it, though Kettle's Yard is not a museum at all but the home of Jim Ede, who gave it to the university in 1966. It caters to all my notions of art and interior decoration; the paintings (Ben Nicholson, Christopher Wood, Alfred Wallis), while individually delightful, are integral to the overall decorative scheme, even starting at the skirting board; nowhere else have I seen pictures hung so close to the ground. Jim Ede, too, thought that paintings were not always best seen undeflected: 'I remember how in Arezzo,' he writes, 'I went to see the Piero della Francescas, and saw nothing but an old faded curtain by an open window making shadows across the pictures.'

And so it is at Kettle's Yard, the paintings part of an assemblage and subject to the changing light. There's a mixture of old and modern furniture and though I don't always like the stones and *objets trouvés* on top of tables and chests (the decorative charms of pebbles and driftwood for me strictly limited) and though I would never paint a room white . . . here the whole house glows.

I would be happy to live in Kettle's Yard, feeling that if I did my life would be better, or at least different. It passes one of the tests of a congenial interior, that you feel you would like the food that is cooked there. At Kettle's Yard you can practically smell it.

Denton Welch

A good subtitle for a biography of Denton Welch might be *A Bike in the Hedge*, so much are his leisure and his journals taken up with picnicking in fields, looking round country churches or exploring the overgrown parks of once grand houses. The bike would not be locked, as this was Kent in the 1940s, a county (though it had seen the Battle of Britain) still sunk in rustic tranquillity and seclusion.

> *June 7 1943 Monday* I am sitting in the cool in Capel Church under the medi-aeval fresco. Against a dim salmon pink ground two figures seem to be hang-ing long coats out of the window of a castle turret. Other figures seem to be banqueting.

He had been banqueting too.

> I have been eating my lunch in the fields nearby (Ryvita, cheese, apricot jam, chocolate bar of squashed dried fruits, coffee) sitting on my coral air-cushion, given me by May, reading for the fourth or fifth time an outline of the Brontë sisters' lives.

Having just had his first book published he identified with Charlotte and the prospect of fame. Earlier, not untypically, he had been watching a loutish boy picking cherries and another mowing a field.

> This is what goes on in nineteen forty three, the year of the greatest war to stop all wars, if I have the quotation right. Now I shall leave this cool church and this mediaeval fresco and get on my bike again.
>   This may be read about in years to come and then people will know about what I did on this June day.

There was no forgetting what he had been doing on the same June day eight years before. Then his bike hadn't been in the hedge but crushed on a Surrey road when, as a young art student, he'd been knocked down by a car, the injuries condemning him to the life of an invalid and leading ultimately to his death in 1948 at the age of thirty-three.

Tough, single-minded to the point of selfishness and often difficult to live with, he raged against the turn of fate that had wrecked his life, and though it's tempting to say that without it he would not have been a writer, I'm not sure this is true. From early childhood, as James Methuen-Campbell's book makes plain, he seems to have had a particular slant on the world and though his accident may have concentrated his energies it did not create his sensibility. A child who at the age of seven could remark 'in a slow, earnest, thoughtful voice that "a flea would despise the amount of lemonade I've got, Mother"' was never going to be ordinary, and his experiences with his family in China made their contribution. After holidays spent rooting through the junk shops of Shanghai and on a solitary walk coming across a severed human head in the undergrowth, it's hardly surprising he failed to fit in at Repton.

When Denton Welch began to write such occurrences were not slow to find their way into his stories and novels, which were nothing if not autobiographical. What the accident did was add urgency to the process, and though he regularly complained of how little his circumstances allowed him to accomplish, by the time of his death he had accumulated a substantial body of work and acquired a distinctive voice.

To begin with I knew nothing of his fiction, first reading about him when his journals were published four years after his death. In those days I could afford few books, certainly in hardback, and so wrote my name in them as I seldom do nowadays. My copy of the journals is also dated, with 'December 1952' written in my still-childish hand. This was a few months after I had been conscripted. Utterly unlike any person I had come across, I felt he was a sympathetic voice and – a characteristic of books read when young – seemed to be speaking particularly to me. So I took the book with me into the army as, I suppose, a token of a different sort of life, a 'civilised life' I probably thought of it then, though it was nothing like the life I'd known.

The military life meant regular kit inspections, your army belongings, boots, best BD, mess tins, etc. all laid out on the squared-off bed. Nor was it just the army side of things that was on display, as your locker had to be open too, your whole life available for scrutiny should the inspecting officer so choose. I imagined the journals being flicked open by a disdainful swagger stick at some offending page and read out with sarcastic comments for the benefit of the other conscripts.

Still, his work wasn't entirely unsuited to the barrack room, particularly during the war years, a time when reading (and writing) became almost an act of faith. Servicemen reading on barrack-room beds were testifying to their conviction that there was a world elsewhere. The early paperbacks slipped handily into the outside BD trouser pocket, as did *Horizon* or *Penguin New Writing*, and reading James Methuen-Campbell's account of his life it almost seems as if even *Vogue* was a light in the darkness. So though Denton Welch took and prided himself on taking no notice of the war, wartime and the austerity that followed were the time of his life.

In this regard, though, it's a blessing that his accident banished him from the metropolis. How much less idiosyncratic would his life have been, certainly to read about, had he landed up in Soho or Fitzrovia, the doings of which, particularly in that period, are amply documented and over-described.

Kent, where he spent most of his invalid life might seem dull by comparison, but had much to recommend it. The setting of Samuel Palmer's valley of vision, now with its evidences of war, was one of those evocative landscapes that Piper and Ravilious were recording elsewhere. But the war didn't interest Denton Welch, not in its scenic aspects anyway, and it never obtrudes onto his own canvases; no Nissen huts here or surrealist barrage balloons, no bomb damage even, his paintings resolutely personal and obscure (and not always very good).

But his journals are a different matter. Minor writers often convey a more intense flavour of their times than those whose range is broader and concerns more profound. Here the war is met with at every turn, but transmuted into an idyllic pastoral of soldiers bathing, prisoners harvesting and planes crossing the moonlit sky to the sound of distant singing from the pub. As drunken servicemen ride their girlfriends home on the handlebars, Welch's diaries sometimes read like the script for a documentary by Humphrey Jennings or notes for a film by Michael Powell.

In a letter to Barbara Cooper, secretary to John Lehmann, in October 1943 he gives his hobbies as 'old glass, china, furniture, little pictures and picnicking alone' and, though Ryvita has never had much charm for me, lovingly detailed as one of the ingredients of his wartime picnics even that gritty dimpled cardboard acquires glamour. Dashing off on his bike to antique shops (the prices absurdly cheap), exploring churches and dilapidated follies – to me in 1952 he sounded to have an ideal life. And a smart one, too. To a boy brought up in the provinces this ailing ex-art student seemed to have moved effortlessly into a charmed circle, with letters from E. M. Forster, lunch with Edith Sitwell and tea at Sissinghurst with Harold and Vita. It was probably only her suicide that stopped Virginia Woolf from figuring here.

What I didn't appreciate then was the guts Welch must have had and needed to have. At eighteen I thought that to be 'sensitive' was a writer's first requirement – with discipline and persistence nowhere – whereas he never allowed himself to languish. His spinal injuries no more kept him off his bike than sickness and high temperatures did from the typewriter, and it was this no-nonsense approach both to his disability and to his work that made him impatient of those occasional fans who sought him out expecting a wilting aesthete.

For the same reason he would probably have been uneasy to find himself on so many sensitive bookshelves in the late forties and fifties, when books said more about their readers than they do now. His writings would be found alongside such textbooks of proscribed affections as Housman's poems, the novels of Forrest Reid and Mary Renault and (as a chronicle of unhappy love) *The Unquiet Grave*: coded texts that spoke more plainly than their owners sometimes wanted or even knew.

Certainly much of what Denton Welch wrote trembled on the brink of sex, which gives it much of its energy, though in the journals it is never plain whether anything 'went on'. In 1952 I assumed he was of necessity exercising discretion, but, as James Methuen-Campbell makes clear, often catheterised and racked by his physical inabilities, Denton Welch was very much an onlooker and non-participant. But at eighteen I was an onlooker and non-participant myself, so that probably rang bells too.

In the description of the closeness between himself and his companion Eric Oliver, what I found reassuring was his frankness about the intensity of their association, at least on Welch's side . . . and one-sided associations were the ones with which I was myself familiar. And he plainly wasn't shy. Sitting chatting to naked boys in hay fields seemed fairly unshy to me, though the mixture of his knowingness and their seeming naivety was typical of the times and would not last. By the sixties it's not only the Nissen huts that have gone, but an innocence too.

Or perhaps not quite. In the early sixties I was in America for two years, during which time my parents took to reading the books I had left at home. This made me slightly apprehensive, though all it meant was that my father became an early and unlikely fan of Nancy Mitford and it was my mother who first took to reading Denton Welch's journals. What she picked up on were his visits to junk and bric-à-brac shops, since this was an inclination she shared. When he was younger my father had been a bit of a carpenter and made toys, so when she gave it to him to read what caught his fancy was the cleaning and restoration of the doll's house. What I had been apprehensive about, the sexual undertones, seemed wholly to pass them by, leaving it, ironically, to Philip Roth's *Portnoy's Complaint* as the first book of mine to which my father took real exception.

Scarcely reaching middle age, it's hard to think that had he lived Denton Welch would now be in his eighties. To me he will always be that frail, curly-haired high-foreheaded young man who sits at the chequerboard table with the lustres and the candles in the frontispiece to the journals that I bought in 1952.

His subject matter had a richness and a colour that links him with very unlike writers, such as Dylan Thomas, Edith Sitwell and Christopher Fry, all of whom were standing out against the drabness of their times. The nearest he had come to active service was in the battle against beige, so it was fitting that in June 1945 he should have had a picture in the Victory number of *Vogue*, 'a rendering of a room in his cottage in Kent, where colour plays an important part'. He writes, 'Do not think that brilliant colour is difficult to live with. It is always stimulating and refreshing; and change to a neutral-toned, colourless room would be exhausting, lowering and depressing.'

There was never much danger of that in his life or in his art; he went out still full of colour, and more than fifty years later it is unfaded.

England Gone: Philip Larkin

Larkin was such a fastidious critic of his own work that anyone making a selection from his poems finds the job virtually done already. It's true that since the publication of the *Collected Poems* in 1988 there turns out to be much more verse to choose from but, reviewing the poems I've selected (using and being very grateful for that volume), I find that I've chosen only a handful of poems that were not originally included in Larkin's best-known volumes of verse, *The Less Deceived* (1955), *The Whitsun Weddings* (1964) and *High Windows* (1974).

It may be, of course, that since these are the collections I know best familiarity has influenced my choice, but I think not. It was only with *The Less Deceived* that Larkin achieved his characteristic voice, that wry, lugubrious, thoroughly unheroic tone which can turn so unexpectedly tender and lyrical and which made him, apart from Betjeman perhaps, the best loved of contemporary English poets. There are echoes of this tone in the earlier poems, prefiguring phrases that one would like to single out and preserve, but Larkin as we have come to know him really dates from *The Less Deceived*.

At least one theme of Larkin's poetry, though, emerged before the style evolved with which he could express it and this is why the selection begins with 'Traumerei' (1946), which spells out Larkin's fear of death, the selection virtually ending with 'Aubade', which (thirty years later) does much the same. Between those fearful brackets I have arranged the poems in order of publication, beginning with poems taken from *XX Poems*

(1951) then *The Less Deceived, The Whitsun Weddings* and *High Windows*, finally folding in, as the cooks say, a few of the poems written after 1974 and which were first printed in the *Collected Poems*.

If Larkin does not require much selection nor does he need much introduction, his verse so lucid and explicit that his virtues as a poet require only the briefest tour. This, I'm sure, would be Larkin's own wish. Back in 1980 *The South Bank Show* did a TV programme on Larkin which, surprisingly, had his blessing, though he would not himself appear. I was interviewed and persuaded to say why I liked his poetry. This was a mistake. 'There's an awful lot of Alan Bennett,' he wrote to Anthony Thwaite, the letter as published kindly omitting what I'm sure were further strictures.

Fifteen years dead Larkin is still a looming presence so I will try and be terse. He writes with clarity and a determined ordinariness that does not exclude (and often underpins) the lyrical. He is always accessible, his language compact, though occasionally arcane. Fond of compound adjectives – air-sharpened, rain-ceased, bone-riddled – he shares this with Hardy, with whom he invites comparison though his sentiments are less gawky, what they have most in common a deep, unshiftable despair.

My perspective on Larkin is not the usual one in that I know his poetry chiefly from having had to read it in recitals and to record it on cassette. I understand little of metre or scansion or the structure of verse, but to read Larkin aloud is to become aware of his skill as a craftsman. The writing supports the reader but with some give: the verse feels sprung as a dance floor is sprung, with rhymes and half-rhymes turning up unexpected and unforeseen just when one needs them, stepping-stones across the poem. The rhymes are generally unobtrusive, widely separated and it sometimes takes three or four readings before one uncovers them.

Larkin spent most of his working life at the University of Hull, where he was the librarian of the Brynmor Jones Library. Hull suited him and England suited him and he never wanted to leave either, though he wouldn't have minded going to China, he said, if he could come back the same day.

He was a poet of England, or of England at a certain time, because to list Larkin's poetic locations is to realise now, less than two decades after his death, how diminished is the England he wrote about. It's not just 'The shadows, the meadows, the lanes/ The guildhalls, the carved choirs' that have gone. They haven't particularly, just changed their character under a deluge of visitors. What scarcely lasted his time was a much dingier world – churches, cemeteries, station hotels, digs, local trains, bikes, the seaside, parks, libraries. Larkin's world is no longer ours. The unvisited church is now so unvisited it has mutated into a car-pet warehouse or a furniture cave; the cemetery has been landscaped and incorporated into a heritage trail and the precinct (Larkin's poetry large-ly pre-precinct) has swallowed the coach-party annexes and the banquet halls up yards. The fumes and certainly the furnace glare of Sheffield are no more, his awful pie would be quality controlled and if Whitsun remains it's only on the Church calendar and provokes no rush to the altar; the 'Spring Bank Holiday Weddings' would not be quite the same.

Only the moon, strong, unhindered, dashing through the clouds or thinned to an air-sharpened blade . . . only the moon persists in a world that, even in Hull, has changed, if not beyond recognition certainly beyond any poetic impulse Larkin had in his sad unwriting years to recog-nise it. This change is acknowledged, just, in his last notable poem, 'Aubade' (1977). Unpack the phrase 'all the uncaring/Intricate, rented world' and you have much of what has happened to England since his death – or his two deaths, the death of poetry and the death of the man. Typical, he might grumble, that someone in such dread of death should be made to go through it twice.

Larkin's gloom has to be faced and sometimes, I've come to think, faced down. It gets under the skin as Hardy's never does. Though this may be because he's our contemporary, it's also that where melancholy is concerned Larkin is such a missionary. It's not enough that he sees the world as he does; we must see it too and feel as depressed about it.

'You're trying to preserve something,' he writes. 'Not for yourself but for the people who haven't seen it or heard it or experienced it.' Or:

People say I'm very negative and I suppose I am, but the impulse for producing a poem is never negative: the most negative poem in the world is a very positive thing to have done. The fact that a poem makes a reader want to lie down and die rather than get up and sock somebody is irrelevant.

Of course, a poem sometimes does both and the person one wants to get up and sock is Larkin himself.

Thus it is that whereas when I first read him it was his sadness that appealed, these days the poems I like best are those from which his depression and disenchantment are most absent – 'Church Going', for instance, 'The Whitsun Weddings', 'An Arundel Tomb', 'Maiden Name' and 'The Explosion' – none of them poems that can be said (perish the thought) to be cheerful: they would also include 'MCMXIV', which is not cheerful at all. But they are all poems in which the reader is not required to endorse or go along with what in some of the poems, 'Aubade', for instance, I now think of as a bullying (and, to my mind, specifically male) despair.

My perspective on this is of someone who has had to stand on the stage and read the poems, when it becomes a predicament. Declaiming lines like 'Life is first boredom then fear' or 'Courage is no good/It means not scaring others', and sensing an audience nodding I feel I want to dissociate myself from the poem and even slip in a disclaimer ('Just because I'm reading this doesn't mean that I believe it'). There is, after all, more to courage than that.

It would not be the same if Larkin himself were doing the reading, not that he ever (or very seldom) did, saying he didn't care for poetry recitals because he didn't fancy going round the country pretending to be himself. Yet anybody who does recite his poems has to some extent to pretend to be Larkin because if they're not then they haven't earned the right to preach the misery being Larkin seemed to involve.

Maybe all I'm saying is that his poems shouldn't be read aloud, at any rate in public. No great loss, he would have thought. Better read alone, under a lamp, hearing the noise of the wind.

Though I said at the start that, beginning with 'Traumerei' and ending with 'Aubade', this selection is bracketed by Larkin's fear of death, I have allowed one poem to escape those parentheses simply in order to finish on a relatively cheerful note. This is 'The Trees' and I've often thought that it makes a pair, a pendant as they say in art history, with Hardy's 'Proud Songsters' – the trees, as it were, and the birds in the trees, both poems coming as close to optimism as either poet allows himself.

I have read 'The Trees' often in recitals but once, when I was reading with Judi Dench, she was assigned the poem, the last line of which is:

Begin afresh, afresh, afresh.

I had read the poem umpteen times without sensing the obvious point that each 'afresh' should be differently inflected, which was how Judi read it. It was as if a bud was opening. I have never managed to read it like that myself but I'm sure that's how it should be done. It's unlikely, but it might even have pleased the poet.

Staring out of the Window

Writing about writing is a second best. For a writer the process is only of interest when he or she finds that they cannot do it (as today, 13 November 2001). If I could write . . . a play, a short story, anything . . . I would, writing about writing (or not writing) is just vamping till ready.

A writer only feels he or she is a writer at the point of performance, the moment of writing. Do anything else, even related activities like research or background reading, and the claim seems fraudulent. A writer is only a writer when writing. The rest is marking time. And your published books and plays don't count; they only prove that you were a writer yesterday but not today, not now.

Some might think this is an over-literal view. An actor is still an actor when he is off the stage; a singer still a singer when he or she is not in full flow. But it is not the same. Put down the pen or abandon the keys and a writer is always on the brink of fraud.

I have always been a late starter, and was as slow off the mark with writing as I was in other departments. Even when I was writing on a regular basis it was a long time before I dared to think of myself as a proper writer as distinct, I suppose, from someone who just wrote sketches. I was not to know then that writing sketches was not a bad way to begin since that was how Chekhov had started, as indeed had Harold Pinter.

Since it was a revue, sketches were obviously the stuff of the first stage production I had to do with, *Beyond the Fringe* done first here in Edinburgh over forty years ago. I went on writing sketches, chiefly for television, and when in 1968 I put together the stage play *Forty Years On* that too was still a bit of a hybrid, a play certainly but which included sketches, to the extent that some critics thought I ought to make up my mind.

But I never have and the stamp of my origins has stayed with me, and I still write in three-minute bursts so that beneath the most elevated stretch of dialogue or description lie buried the breeze blocks of revue.

By the time I'd written *Forty Years On* I was already thirty-four and had ceased to find reassuring Virginia Woolf's remark that one should never publish anything before one is at least thirty. I had understandably been consoled by this all through my twenties, though as so often with the pronouncements of writers on their trade (Auden is a prime example) this was simply the writer saying, 'All do as I do.' Virginia had kept quiet until she was thirty and so should we all.

When I hit thirty with still not much done I then took comfort from Proust, who had been an even later starter than Virginia Woolf: whatever else can be said about Proust, he did not hit the ground running.

In the end writing just seemed to sneak up on me. I was a writer after *Forty Years On*, not by virtue of having had a play produced but because by then I had started to do it (or to try and do it) every day. I still hesitated to lay claim to it as a profession, though, and it was only in the early seventies that I crossed out Teacher in my passport and substituted Actor/Author. The order is significant as I obviously thought at the time that the acting was a better bet than the writing; the actor would go on and the author might peter out, whereas it has tended to be the other way round.

Nowadays, of course, passports no longer require that one states (or confesses) a profession and rites of passage like mine are not so easily charted.

If I was slow off the mark it was also because it took me time to realise that I had a world to write about that was my own and not one that had been revealed to me through books or education. My Leeds contemporary the poet Tony Harrison had a similar experience. His class and social background were approximately the same as mine and like him I felt at first that 'the life . . . I lived didn't seem to be the stuff that literature could be made of . . . We didn't have books in the house,' he writes, 'so that my love of language and books always seemed different from the life I actually lived at home. Once I'd found a way of writing about that life, it all came back to me in the richest detail.'[*]

That wasn't quite my experience as I'm more light-minded than Tony Harrison and had (and maybe have) less of a grip on my vocation. It took me much longer to see that I had a childhood that could be written about and I couldn't truthfully say, as he does, that at sixteen or eighteen I loved language or had any notion that language or literature might be part of my future. But Tony went to a posher school than I did and a more snobbish one, and he suffered for his accent at school, was punished for his tongue as I never was, so it's hardly surprising if he sorted out his priorities quicker than I did.

For a long time, years even, it seemed to me I had nothing to put into what I wrote; and nor had I. I did not yet appreciate that you do not put yourself into what you write; you find yourself there.

When I realised that I ceased to worry. Or to worry about that anyway.

With a writer the life you don't have is as ample a country as the life that you do and is sometimes easier of access. My first play was set in an English public school, which was not an institution of which I'd ever been a pupil. I knew about it, though, and could write about it from the books I had read . . . memoirs, biography, school stories and indeed comics. State-educated, I had quite early on tried to write about the kind of school I had attended, a northern grammar school, but found it impossible and have never really managed to write about it since, perhaps because few others have managed it either.[†]

There was certainly not much state-school literature to draw on and definitely no tradition. Art comes out of art and to break new ground unassisted is not easy. Certainly I found it hard to do, whereas to write

---

[*] *Bloodaxe Critical Anthologies: Tony Harrison*, ed. Neil Astley, 1991.
[†] This was in 2001, since when I've slightly unexpectedly written *The History Boys* (2004), which is set in a northern grammar school.

about the oddities and eccentrics to be found teaching in a run-down public school was to release the imagination, facilitate the jokes and draw on much that I had read. It was not a life I craved or an education I envied but I found public school far easier to depict (or caricature) than the lives of the sometimes desperate and deeply disillusioned men who had taught me in state school . . . and whom I would perhaps have been better employed trying to understand and re-create.

Reading and going to the pictures as a child I had readily absorbed the inverse moral standards that prevailed in these alternative worlds. I needed no telling that the real villain in the gangster movie was not one of the small-time hoodlums and bully boys but the genial, white-haired and seemingly respectable mayor. In the story-book world, poor was better than rich and plain than pretty. Nothing was as it seemed.

So thoroughly did I absorb these topsy-turvy values, I expected them to prevail in the real world also. How could the French nobles on the eve of Agincourt not see that their overweening confidence and superior strength must inevitably doom them to defeat? Had they never read a fairy story? Or David and Goliath?

I was old enough to register the rout of the BEF in France in 1940 but the defeat and evacuation at Dunkirk to me made the victory at El Alamein and the D-Day invasion seem a foregone conclusion. Though it helped, of course, that that was also how the story was told.

If part of writing consists in smuggling the efforts of the imagination past an internal policeman or customs officer, one function of that official is as a monitor of taste. The precepts of taste are determined by the past and its precedents: the laws of taste are case law; they are a guide to what has been done and so can be done again with safety. And for some writers the constraints are no handicap at all; fences only become barriers if you choose to leap them.

But taste is no help to a writer. Taste is timorous, conservative and fearful. It is a handicap. It stunts. Olivier was unhampered by taste and was often vulgar; Dickens similarly. Both could fail, and failure is a sort of vulgarity; but it's better than a timorous toeing of the line.

Taste abuts on self-preservation. I have too much taste, find it hard to let go. And it is the audience that polices taste. Only if you can forget your audience can you escape. It was in an effort to evade this internal policeman that when I began to write sketches at Oxford I would often get drunk first, though since it's never taken much to make me tipsy a quarter bottle of whatever was enough to see me through the evening. To begin with it was gin, then I sickened of that, tried whisky, finally graduating to vodka, really because it has almost no taste at all. I never had any hesitation in telling my friends (who drank much more than I did) what I was occasionally up to and was surprised by how shocked they were, solitary drinking thought by them to be the first step to perdition. It seemed perfectly natural to me, a way of loosening up the mind and eluding the censor that narrowed one's scope, a thin vinegary voice which said, 'You can't write that. Other people can but not you. Not unless you want to make a fool of yourself.'

Sometimes, particularly in summers in New York, I have tried to write in shorts or with no shirt on and found myself unable to do so, the reason being, I take it, that writing, even of the most impersonal sort, is for me a kind of divestment, a striptease even, so that if I start off undressed I have nowhere to go.

The best moments in reading are when you come across something – a thought, a feeling, a way of looking at things – which you had thought unique and particular to you. Now here it is, set down by someone else, a person you have never met, someone even who is long dead. And it is as if a hand has come out and taken yours.[*]

To achieve this in writing must be satisfying, too, though short of being told so by readers (not easy if you're Montaigne, say) the writer may never know he has hit the spot.

Emerson writes:

> In every work of genius we recognise our own rejected thoughts: they come back to us with a certain alienated majesty. Great works of art have no more

[*] Words later put into the mouth of Hector, the old-fashioned schoolmaster in *The History Boys*.

affecting lesson for us than this. They teach us to *abide by our spontaneous impressions* [Emerson's italics] with good-humoured inflexibility most when the whole cry of voices is on the other side. Else tomorrow a stranger will say with masterly good sense precisely what we have thought and felt all the time, and we shall be forced to take with shame our own opinion from another.[*]

The same note is struck by Seamus Heaney, who, when he is analysing the need the poet has to write, describes first how he appeases that need by learning to find his own unique and distinctive voice but

> . . . then begins a bothersome and exhilarating second need, to go beyond himself and take on the otherness of the world in works that remain his own yet offer rights of way to everybody else . . . What poets do is to encourage our inclination to credit the prompting of our intuitive being. They help us to say in the recesses of ourselves . . . 'Yes, I know something like that, too. Yes, that's right. Thank you for putting words on it and making it more or less official.[†]

Never exactly a pushover, these notes of common humanity are harder to strike nowadays on account of competition from an unexpected quarter. Locating in one's own life or imagination those thoughts, impulses or experiences that may be part of the common stock is not without risk and can be shaming. Though a sympathetic reader may nod and say, 'I've thought that,' the less sympathetic may be outraged and think the writer a brute for even daring to set it down.

Most aware of this nowadays because of their more immediate access to an audience and its responses are not novelists or writers of autobiography. Today the keenest searchers after a currency that they hope is common are the stand-up comedians. Their coin is laughter bred out of recognition, their stock in trade riffs that begin 'Have you noticed that . . .' – there following some observation (less hard won, the poor novelist may feel, than his or hers) and the more shocking and intimate the better, the nearer the bone they come the more likely they feel that they will tap into thoughts so shaming or unspeakable we had thought them peculiar to ourselves (and wanted to keep them that way).

[*] Emerson, *Self-Reliance*, 1841.
[†] Seamus Heaney, *The Government of the Tongue*, Faber, 1988.

No longer. There is nothing nowadays that comedians cannot say. Jaded though one may feel their observations may be, their aperçus contrived and seldom so spontaneous or joyously incidental or indeed thrown off as they would have us think, nevertheless the comedians are at the same game as the rest of us. Playwrights, novelists, autobiographers, poets or comedians, it makes no difference; Proust is on a continuum that stretches past Billy Connolly to Eddie Izzard, Bernard Manning and beyond. And should you doubt that look up Proust's description of Charlus's behaviour when he first sees the young violinist Morel on the railway station; transposed, it is a routine by Jerry Seinfeld.

If there is a beneficiary of all this intrepid soul-searching and delving into our most intimate secrets by the nation's comedians seeking after common ground then I hope it will be a boy such as I was at fourteen, awkward, self-conscious and ridden by fears that seemed shameful and incommunicable. At the same time prudish and prurient, he feels himself set apart from his fellows and convinced of his own wickedness and hypocrisy. I hope there aren't as many such boys or girls as once there were and that the efforts of the writers and the routines of the stand-ups will set them free. But there will always be some, there being no enlightenment that can prevail against the ineluctable capacity of the human spirit to imprison itself.

If writing is a form of striptease it's easier when the author invents a satisfactory long-running eidolon such as Philip Roth's Zuckerman, for instance, or John Updike's Rabbit. I could have wished many (not that there are many) of my life's stories onto such a figure while at the same time maintaining my reserve. But I have not written enough fiction for that and plays seldom allow of sufficient continuity to feature a recurrent character.

Much of my work I have stayed outside. I do not find myself in *Forty Years On*, for instance, though much of my reading is there. I am in some of my other plays but can't find myself in others – *The Madness of George III*, for instance, or *A Question of Attribution* – and on the whole I prefer those plays from which I am absent to those in which I too clearly hear the sound of my own voice.

This absence from one's own work is abolished by death, or will be in my case, I imagine, because of having kept a diary. In life a journal is a separate thing, a commentary running alongside one's life even when (as in my case) extracts are occasionally published.

Death, though, coalesces all one's writings and wipes out the difference. Virginia Woolf is remembered as much for her diaries as for what she would have thought of as her proper work, but all now is just the work of Virginia Woolf.

Though there are diaries and diaries. Virginia Woolf's diary was livelier than her novels, as Philip Larkin's diary was probably livelier than his poems, though in a different way. Her diary enhanced her reputation; his (he felt anyway) wouldn't have, so his dutiful executrix put it into the shredder. Feeling as he did about death, the surprise to me still is that he cared.

When I do crop up in my own work I'm not a prepossessing figure. If I do write about (or at least around) myself the eidolon, the lay figure I advance into the picture and shelter behind, is generally downtrodden and middle-aged and often involved in some sort of pedagogic activity – a lecturer at a polytechnic, for instance (*Me, I'm Afraid of Virginia Woolf*), a teacher at the local comprehensive (*Intensive Care*). Even when I (if I can use the word) have a proper job, like the harassed provincial insurance man in *Kafka's Dick*, the job gets elbowed out of the way because of academic pursuits. Since teaching undergraduates is the closest I have ever come to having a normal job I suppose this is why, suitably disguised, it regularly smuggles itself into my written work.

That said, though, also evident is a deep uneasiness about learning and in particular books. It wasn't something I had been especially aware of when writing but I found quite late in the day that I had been writing and rewriting the same scene for half my life. In this set-up someone stands looking at a bookcase, baffled and dismayed by what one is expected to assimilate and despairing of ever doing so. It occurs in *Getting On*; in *The Old Country*; in the film of *Prick Up Your Ears*; and in *Kafka's Dick*. And the thought is always the same: 'How will I ever catch up?'

Though the character doing the looking and the despairing is often myself, the scene crops up even when I am nowhere to be found. I do not see myself in any form in *An Englishman Abroad* but sure enough here it is again, this time with Coral Browne looking at the books belonging to Guy Burgess. One couldn't get much further from an English provincial schoolboy than the Australian grande dame Coral Browne, but when she's looking at the bookcase in Burgess's Moscow flat that's what she is: me, as a boy or an undergraduate, baffled by the world of words.

Of course one isn't always able to make a certain identification. Am I – though it's no dream of mine – also the provincial boy in *The Old Country*, picked up by an establishment figure to spend an idyllic evening in his underpants looking at back numbers of *Country Life*? I hope not, but who am I to say?

I note another recurrence, or a preoccupation, something at any rate that seems regularly to crop up. I seem to have a fondness for, an affinity with, the maimed and the stigmatised. It is not charitable, still less Christian, and they don't get much sympathy or understanding. Indeed it occurs first just as a joke, part of the opening speech of my first play, *Forty Years On*. The headmaster addresses the school (which is also England) at his farewell speech day.

> Some of the older ones among you will remember Bombardier Tiffin, our Corps Commandant and Gym Instructor, lately retired. The more observant ones among you will have noticed that one of Bombardier Tiffin's legs was not his own. The other one, God bless him, was lost in the Great War. Some people lost other things, less tangible perhaps than legs but no less worthwhile . . . they lost illusions, they lost hope, they lost faith. That is why . . . chewing, Charteris. That is why the twenties and thirties were such a muddled and grubby time for lack of all the hopes and ideals that perished on the fields of France. And don't put it in your handkerchief . . .

Bombardier Tiffin was just the first of a series of less comic and variously maimed or stigmatised characters who turn up in plays over the years. There was Cross, a boy with a club foot who goes with an Edwardian cycling club on its outing to Fountains Abbey in *A Day Out* (1972).

551

In *The Old Country* (1977) there is a brief encounter with a child murderer; in *Marks* (1982) a boy stigmatises himself by getting tattooed; in *The Insurance Man* (1986) a young man is disfigured by a creeping eczema that gradually covers his whole body, and there are dozens of maimed characters besides as this is a play about Kafka and his job as accident and compensation assessor for a Prague insurance company. I suppose, too, though I had not thought of it, that George III was maimed mentally and physically by the attack of porphyria which is the subject of *The Madness of George III* (1991).

The prevalence of the damaged and disabled says something about me. It's not, as I might like to pretend, a plea for sympathy and understanding for the handicapped; this doesn't really come into it. However irritating and unfair it may seem to the actually disabled, these characters turn up out of a sense of identification because I do not think it is fanciful to suppose writing itself a form of disablement; it's certainly a handicap when it comes to getting on with things, writing in some sense a substitute for doing.

Roaring, which you occasionally do in the ordinary world with laughter, in Leeds means also to cry, 'Don't start roaring' a warning to a child to fetch it back from the brink of tears. I roared a lot when I was a child – out of shame, rage or simply because I couldn't see any other way out. Now, I suppose, the writing has replaced the roaring but the reasons are much the same.

When the young Stephen Spender told T. S. Eliot he 'wanted to be a poet' Eliot rather tartly responded, 'I can understand your wanting to write poems but I don't quite know what you mean by being a poet.'[*] Being a writer is not quite the same as writing. The evidence of a lifetime's work, his or her books ranged on the shelf (or shelves), ought to reassure someone who writes that he or she is indeed a writer. But nothing, not the books in the shop window or the play on the stage or shoals of letters from delighted readers, furnishes such assurance but only the act

---

[*] Ian Hamilton, *Against Oblivion*, Viking, 2002.

of writing itself, the fingers flying over the keys or, in my case, pushing the pen across the paper.

Still, it is always easier to be it than to do it, easier for the public, too, who prefer what they have had from a writer to what they might be given. Being it is comfortable, so far as the public is concerned: this is the writer they have got used to. Doing it is less comfortable: the writer might be wanting to try something new.

The real mark of recognition for a writer or any artist, perhaps, comes when the public begins to want him or her to die, so that they can close the book on that particular talent, stop having to make the effort to follow the writer any further, put a cork in the bottle.

Between being and doing, though, the writer sometimes has no choice. Larkin was someone who, on his own admission, ceased to be able to do it and just had to be it for the last ten years of his life, in the process becoming far more famous not doing it than he had ever been doing it. To E. M. Forster, too, this happened.

But any writer would say that, though the sales and plaudits come not with doing it but having done it, the useful medal to have would be one bestowed, as it were, on the field of battle, hung round your neck in recognition of yet another fruitless morning spent at the typewriter or after a week or even months spent staring out of the window.

Ups and Downs

A Common Assault

—————

'*Che cos'è la sua data di nascita?*'

I turn my head sideways on the blood-soaked pillow. '9–5–34.'

Expressionless, the doctor in the Pronto Soccorso writes it down as a thought occurs to me, and I raise my head. '*Domani il mio giorno natale.*'

Hardly a joke, in the circumstances it merits a smile, but from this mirthless young man nothing is forthcoming. I lay my head down again. At least I seem to have stopped bleeding.

Birthdays were never made much of in our family. Mine, as I told the Italian doctor, is on May 9 and my brother's too, though he is three years older than I am. The coincidence is always good for a laugh, particularly when it dawns that we must both have been conceived during the old August Bank Holiday, sex confined to the holidays perhaps, or unconfined by them. But that I should have had my beginnings in the cheerless surroundings of a boarding-house bedroom has always seemed to me a melancholy circumstance. Morecambe it would have been, or Filey, linoleum on the floor, jug and basin on the wash-hand stand, and the room smelling faintly of the methylated spirits my mother always brought for the pad on which she heated her curling tongs; meths for me, a lifetime later, still the smell of the seaside.

The kind of establishment we stayed in turned out its boarders, rain or shine, at ten in the morning and there was no coming back between meals, so it would have been done at night, the act itself stealthily undertaken, mindful of the strange bed and my two-year-old brother sleeping beside it and conscious, too, of the thin walls and the adjacence of other boarders, not sleeping perhaps, whose glances would have to be negotiated over the next morning's sparse breakfast. Other people were always very much a consideration in my parents' lives; mine, too, I suppose, so much of my timorous and undashing life prefigured in that original circumspect conjunction.

We were both born at home, my brother's an awkward birth requiring forceps, with my mother's screams said to have been heard down the street. I still have the bed, the polish at the foot of it scraped and scratched by my mother's feet during the initial stages of that reluctant arrival. Had mine been a difficult birth, the persistence with which untoward events occur on and around my birthday would, though I am no believer in astrology, make a kind of sense. But I seem to have come into the world with no fuss at all, my mother recalling only the bedspread, embroidered with flowers and butterflies, and how the midwife, making the bed after an examination, would always exclaim: 'Butterflies to the bottom!'

Neither my brother nor I ever had a party, the fact that our birthdays coincided not doubling the festivities but serving to cancel them out. By the time I was of an age to care about this the war was on, and parties and presents, like oranges and bananas, something that had been discontinued 'for the duration'. In later years things were to improve slightly, but unless we made a point of getting our own presents we'd build up a backlog of gifts ungiven that stretched back years. We were not particularly poor so there was no sense of deprivation about it. Whatever deprivation my brother and I felt was ceremonial: it was not so much the actual presents we missed as the want of occasion. Other people made more of their lives than we did. Wanting birthdays, parties and presents was just another instance of the way our family never managed to be like other families. Even where birthdays were concerned we could not achieve ordinariness.

We sometimes tried, though. My parents' birthdays came within a week of each other so, like ours, tended to coalesce and we would buy them a joint present. Dad was shy and undemonstrative so that, whatever the gift, the actual giving of it was guaranteed to put him off: he could never simulate the show of surprise and gratitude such occasions required. His coolest reception was for a coffee percolator, a present which ignored the fact that they had never drunk fresh coffee in their lives and weren't going to start now. Dad rightly detected a hint of social aspiration in the gift, the message being that it might be nice if we were the kind of family that did drink fresh-brewed coffee. Dad would have none of it. 'Faffing article' was his way of describing it and in due course the jug part ended up in the cupboard under the sink where it came in handy when washing his hair.

Presents were fraught with peril, the subtext to 'Many Happy Returns' so often 'I think you're the kind of person who'd like this (or I wish you were)'. Even the longed-for bike I got when I was ten came with the same sort of message: not the dashing, speedy bike other boys had, or a racer with drop handlebars like my brother's; mine was big, heavy and safe and, since it was still wartime, probably made out of the reconstituted iron railings that had been recently stripped from suburban walls in order to aid the war effort. Clumsy, upright and dependable, it was the kind of bike one went to church on, and I duly did.

Cut to twenty years later, and I have just learned to drive and am about to buy my first car. The general view seems to be that I need something solid and dependable, opinion favouring a Morris 1000 ('Your sort of car'). But in the nick of time I remember my old bike and switch to a scootier primrose-yellow Mini. With my next car I went even further and got a Triumph Herald, and while it didn't quite have drop handlebars, it was at least a convertible.

It was only when I reached fifty and started looking back that I began to think there might be something inauspicious about my birthday, and tried to count the occasions around that time when I'd strayed close to the edge of life, even been at death's door or somewhere in the vicinity. There had been the time in Sardinia in 1966, when I suddenly collapsed after vomiting blood. The island was still quite primitive, but was just beginning to be promoted as a holiday resort, chiefly by the Aga Khan, who had built a grand hotel but hadn't yet got round to providing a hospital. In the meantime, the only medical centre was a semi-monastic establishment run by the Frate Bene Fratelli, an order of Franciscan friars.

Dying, like much else in Italy, is something of a spectator sport and the steps of the monastery were lined with sightseers awaiting the arrival of the more spectacularly sick. As I was borne in on a stretcher, black-shawled ladies gazed down at me, raised their eyes to heaven, and crossed themselves: I was obviously a goner. In more sophisticated medical surroundings I would, of course, have been in no danger at all, as all that had happened was that a duodenal ulcer had burst and, without knowing it, I had been losing blood. Dramatic as it is, this is seldom a life-threatening condition (though my father had nearly died of something similar) and in normal circumstances a prompt blood transfusion will restore the drooping patient.

But these were not normal circumstances. Diagnostic equipment was primitive and the chief weapon in the therapeutic armoury of these delightful monks seemed to be prayer. It was some time, therefore, before my complaint was diagnosed, and when the remedy was agreed to be a blood transfusion it was still a long time coming, the monks seeming reluctant to fill what was so plainly a leaking bucket. So, for a few days, my life steadily drained away while the monks told their beads and somebody else told the *Daily Mirror*. 'Fringe Boy in Deathbed Drama' was the first my family heard of it.

At the lowest point of my fortunes my two companions went into Olbia to find some supper. I was feeling ghastly, but it only came home to me how desperate my situation was when one of them kissed me. Since she had never kissed me before, she plainly did not expect me to be there when she returned. It was the kiss of death.

There was another portent besides. Finding me alone, two novice monks chose this moment to give me a bed bath. I was lying on the bed, stark naked and virtually drained of blood, when one of them lightly lifted my dick (which, in the circumstances, was the size of an acorn) and let it drop again. '. . . è,' he said, the simple monosyllable given a melancholy falling inflexion, eloquent of pity and resignation. That, at any rate, was one message. The other was more implicit and more sinister: namely, that he was unlikely to take such a liberty were the body he was washing not, in effect, dead already.

Fortunately, that night they began to transfuse me and I eventually received twelve pints of blood, given mostly by sailors from the nearby naval base. It was customary, at any rate in Sardinia, for blood donors to follow their blood to its destination, perhaps to see that it had gone to a good home. So over the next ten days I would wake to find a mute Italian sailor by my bed, smiling and twisting his hat in his hands and nodding reassuringly. I was even visited by would-be donors, those who had tried to give me blood but who were from the wrong group. In those days I don't suppose there was all that much to do in Sardinia, visiting the hospital quite a high point. Nowadays, they probably go water-skiing.

I wasn't struck down again in the same way until May 1980, when I inadvertently took an aspirin. I remember looking in the glass and thinking that my face seemed to be acquiring an interesting artistic pallor, when I suddenly passed out, the aspirin having made my stomach bleed. That, too, was around my birthday, but in the intervening years the connection between birth and death had been maintained when I spent my fortieth birthday at Russell Harty's father's funeral. Russell had been sent round by his mother to give a neighbour the not unexpected news that Fred had died. 'Oh dear,' said the neighbour, 'I am sorry. Mind you, I had a shocking night myself.'

On my fiftieth birthday I was filming in Ilkley. Nothing untoward occurred until the evening, when I was taken out to supper by Michael Palin and Maggie Smith. Came my salad of mixed leaves and there, nestling among the rocket, were several shards of broken glass.

'*Very* mixed,' said Miss Smith.

'No,' said the waiter. 'It's a mistake.'

I reached the 1990s without mishap, though Miss Shepherd, the lady who lived for fifteen years in a van in my drive, died at the end of April 1989, after which the undertaker rang up wondering if May 9 would be a suitable day for her funeral.

'Why not?' I said. I was only surprised that I hadn't thought of it myself.

In the spring of 1992 I had arranged to go with a friend to Italy for the weekend. All being well, May 9 would find me in Todi. Writing that Italian name, I see it has a (German) death in it, but that is fanciful. What was not fanciful was that going to Italy meant that I would not be able to go to someone's funeral which, unsurprisingly, fell on my birthday.*

The friend with whom I was going on holiday was Rupert Thomas. At that time, May 1992, I am not sure that I would have called him my partner, or indeed known what to call him, though partners is what we are now. Friend, I suppose I would have said then, though in 1992 such a friendship is still novel enough for me not to know what to call it (and to hope to get away without calling it anything at all). Rupert is thirty years or so younger than I am and might easily be mistaken for my son. This embarrasses me, though not him, who has more reason to be embarrassed.

At that time we did not actually live together, though what was to happen in Italy was one of the factors that brought this about.

Even now, ten years after the event, I am reluctant to acknowledge these arrangements both because that is the way I have always led my life, but also because I would prefer them not to be made explicit, just taken for granted. But though what was to happen still does not make entire sense to me, without avowing this friendship it makes no sense at all.

Our plane was due to arrive in Rome at 9.30 on Thursday evening. We were to collect a hire car and had arranged to spend the night at Ladispoli, a small seaside town twenty kilometres or so to the north, from where we could make an early start for Todi the following morning.

Ladispoli is a modern town from what little we can see of it in the dark, and we drive down straight suburban streets lined with shuttered two-storey villas, looking for our hotel. There is no one about, no lights in the

---

* Lest I should be thought to be manufacturing these coincidences, I have since been in hospital twice more on my birthday, in May 1998 with appendicitis and in May 2000 with something similar.

houses hidden behind high walls hung over with a few dusty fig trees. It's a place of Chekhovian dullness, the centre a long tree-lined street ending in a square that scarcely qualifies as a piazza, with one or two cafés still open and a few people sitting outside. Some boys ride round aimlessly on mountain bikes; there is a closed funfair and festoons of dead fairy lights in the trees.

Booking in at the hotel, we find there is no food to be had, and so walk back to the square, where we have coffee and a sandwich. Paying the bill, I ask the woman at the counter the whereabouts of the sea and she points me down the road. It's now about 11 o'clock. And as I write these prosaic details down – the cashier, the time, the people sitting outside – I realise it's in an effort to find meaning in what is about to happen, as if the time might explain it, or the dullness of the place, something that I may have missed which might help it to make sense.

The distance from the café to what turns out to be a little promenade is only a few hundred yards along a sandy half-made road, past another line of shuttered villas. Rounding the corner onto the front, I see half a dozen young men sitting on the sea wall opposite. They are talking and some almost shouting, though not more vociferously than Italians often do.

The instant we appear, and it is the instant, with no time to size us up or to say, as one might have conventionally scripted them to do, 'Hello! Who've we got here?' – no, quick as thought, two of them are coming across the road to meet us. And though they effectively block our way so that we stop, there is no break in their excited chatter, except that it now seems to include us, as if we have arrived, somehow opportunely, to illustrate a point in their argument, the Italian they are speaking not eloquent or expressive, or pleasant to listen to, as Italian is, but harsh, assertive, jabbering almost.

In retrospect I see, as I run and re-run the scene in my head, that these two had come and stood too close, but there is no obvious threat or rancour, only a kind of feverishness to them which, retrospectively again (the debate never stopping), I put down to drink or drugs, or glue possibly (though too old for glue, surely?), like two boys seen once by the lake in

Regent's Park, pulling at their bags, then shouting hoarsely as if assailed, though no one was going near.

Suddenly the talking stops. The one blocking my way is smallish, with fair, curly hair, but his face now is a blank. Has he asked a question? 'We're English,' I say in Italian. 'We don't understand,' the nationality almost an excuse in itself, and I take a step back, meaning to go round and go on. Turning, I feel a blow across the side of my neck (I run my hand over it as I write, trying to decide if it is the neck I mean, or the throat), but not painful, a punch that has missed perhaps. Even so, it is surprise I register as much as alarm. But Rupert has become anxious at the same moment because the other youth is holding a cigarette far too close to his face. Rupert shouts and at the same moment we start to run back the way we have come.

Even at this point I feel surprise rather than alarm, but the scene plays and replays itself in my head, ragged, inexplicable and without sequence, and so unlike a film, though one searches every frame for a clue as to why it happened and how it might have been avoided.

There is no attempt to rob us, which would have been quite easy to do. Except now I wonder whether that was what they were saying when I said I didn't understand. Still, 'Hand over your wallet' isn't hard to convey, and I would have understood that. Or were they a gang and this bit of random promenade some special territory? Had there been a football match? Were we being punished for the skills of Gary Lineker?

As we run, I feel a heavy blow on the top of my head, the blow struck with a short length of steel scaffolding which Rupert sees the fair-haired youth pick up from the ground. Fortunately, the scaffolding doesn't come instantly to hand, and he has to spend a vital second or so disengaging it, which, since I am already on the move, probably saves me from a more direct blow on my skull. Had it landed squarely, I must certainly have been stunned and fallen, and so probably received more, the usual procedure nowadays when someone falls to kick them in the head. As it is, I stagger with the blow but run on, and we are now so close to safety and the lights of the café that the two give up the chase.

Looked back on, the few seconds of the assault seem intensely private and solitary. I do not see the blow, feel no pain, just sheer bewilderment as to why this is being done to me. It is as if I am a little boy again, which is the last time I was in a fight, an element of recollection there, or re-acquaintance: ah yes, now I remember! But I am not stunned in the least and retain enough sense of drama, as Rupert helps me towards the café, to note my blood falling in the dust around my feet, and to look forward to the looks of horror on the faces of the café clientcle that must shortly greet the arrival in their midst of this bloodstained apparition as the pizza turns to ashes in their mouths.

Actually they seem rather less horrified than I'd expected, some of them just looking away in a very English fashion, so I have time to wonder if maybe this isn't such an outlandish occurrence after all, and whether this establishment regularly welcomes blood-drenched casualties, staggering in from the promenade.

The proprietor of the café sits me down, while the cashier tries to staunch the blood, patting my head with paper napkins. There is so much blood that it seems to me (wrongly) that the wound must therefore be quite deep though I still feel nothing, and am not even dizzy. I am conscious of the blood, though, and apologetic about it; it splashes onto the café table and the café floor, the mosaic now littered with gory serviettes. I am conscious of it because this is 1992 and these days blood is no longer just blood, but can have dangerous overtones, hazardous propensities. So, sitting there, steadily, voluminously bleeding, though I am a victim I can see I also constitute a threat.

I wait in the café for a while, looking, I see in the counter mirror, quite dreadful. My head is now a little tender but I'm not otherwise in pain.

A taxi arrives, the driver concerned and helpful and not at all fussed about the blood on his upholstery; he drives us to the Posto di Primo Intervento, the Pronto Soccorso, which is not a hospital but some sort of emergency clinic, staffed by a doctor and two nurses.

The nurse lies me down on the table and starts to cut away some of my hair, as the doctor enquires about the circumstances of the injury. He has no English, Rupert has no Italian, so, despite being prone on the table, and being shaved and swabbed by the nurse, I struggle to answer with what little Italian I have. The doctor meanwhile is filling in a form, and it is now that I say ruefully that tomorrow will be my birthday. There is no smile, no interest even, and he glumly makes preparations to stitch my head.

I am expecting some kind of anaesthetic but none is forthcoming. Perhaps one cannot anaesthetise the surface of the skull, or perhaps, I think, as he takes a grip of my head, the surface of the skull feels no pain. I am soon disabused of this and, as he puts in his first stitch and draws the flesh together, my feet drum helplessly on the table with the pain of it, so that the nurse lies across my legs as he prepares the second stitch.

I watch him, trying to think who he reminds me of, and as he puts in the second stitch, and my feet start to bang, I realise that he is the young sheikh in John Huston's *Beat the Devil*. He, too, is ruthless and unsmiling, and finding Humphrey Bogart, Peter Lorre and Robert Morley cast up on his shores, plans to have them all shot. Bogart, however, discovers the sheikh's soft spot, a secret passion for Rita Hayworth, and saves their lives by promising the humourless young man an introduction to 'the peerless Rita' (the script was by Truman Capote).

If this equally humourless young doctor cherishes such showbiz longings I am not to know, as throughout this grisly embroidery he utters no word.

'Nearly done' or 'just one stitch more!' would have helped, even in Italian. But nothing is said: there is just this cold-blooded, cold bloodied, morose medic, plying his impassive needle, remorselessly hemming my head.

Between the twelve stitches it eventually takes, I have time to wonder about his life.

I wonder if he has a young wife, a baby perhaps, and if he was already in bed when the telephone rang, though his impassive demeanour and neat collar and tie betray no sign of him having been summarily rooted out. It will be one of those cheerless Continental apartments where

Formica-topped tables stand on rugless tiled floors, the sofa is protected by sheets of plastic and, in the unfrequented sitting room, the green metal blinds are never raised.

Had his ambitions once aimed higher than a casualty clinic in a run-down seaside town? Is he already sinking into a routine of frustration and inanition, like a doctor out of Chekhov, a drink in the same dull bar every night, a walk with the pram on Sundays and a coarsening wife to whom he finds less and less to say? Was the nightly quota of split heads and unexciting contusions diminishing what he had once thought of as a noble or at least profitable vocation? Does he hanker after a larger arena in which to vent his unwinking disdain?

A serious boy, thought promising at school, does he regret not hanging about with his racier classmates, now dashing about on their Lambrettas, and playing pool in the café? As he threads his needle for what I pray will be the final stitch, it occurs to me that he has missed his time, this expressionless, never altogether young man. Fifty years ago in a similar room and under the same unshaded lights, he could have been found lifting the eyelid of some near-insensible partisan; the heart checked, he gives a professional nod and watches while the victim's head is thrust back into the bucket.

He puts in the last stitch, my legs thrash for the last time as he neatly knots his thread; the nurse gets off my legs and the torture appears to be over.

Enter at this point a plump, middle-aged carabiniere, who is unshocked by the assault to the point of indifference, but with a touch of satisfaction that one more ingenuous member of the public now realises what the real world is like and the shit-heap it is that the police are toiling to clean up.

'Who were these people? What did you do to them?'

'Nothing,' I say.

'Well, they can't have been Italians. Were they black?' And to make sure I do not mistake his meaning, he draws a face on a pad and scribbles over it.

'No.'

'Were they Moroccans?'

'I don't know.'

The nurse cleans me up while medicine and the law confer.

'I would not go to a country where I did not speak the language,' says the doctor, confirming that Wilfred Thesiger he isn't.

Now Rupert and the nurse help me up from the table and suddenly, seeing us side by side, a solution to the crime presents itself to the policeman, a solution (the police being the same the world over) which hardly makes it a crime at all.

'This one,' he says, indicating me, 'is much older than the other one.'

The opinion of the law is given medical endorsement when Doctor Death nods thoughtfully. They consult our passports and I am revealed as old enough to be Rupert's father; perhaps they had hitherto thought I was his father – but not any more.

Now there is no longer any mystery about this crime in either of their minds: strolling down to the seafront at eleven at night, this oddly matched couple have been up to no good; what this sorry-looking, middle-aged Englishman is not saying is that on that seedy promenade some advance had been made, a gesture even, and the honour of the Italian male impugned. The wound I have received is virtually self-inflicted, an entirely proper response to an insult to Italian manhood for which a blow on the skull is perfectly appropriate. We had been cruising; it was our own fault.

That there was no truth in this assumption I hesitate to say again, as laying stress on one's innocence seems to presuppose the opposite. This happened is the most that one can say; to get into why it happened, why it should not have happened, or how one did nothing to make it happen, implies that there is an alternative story that could be sketched out, the denial in itself conferring some authenticity on the alternative. I see now how women who have been attacked find themselves incriminated when they are asked to explain it, and how, in classic fashion, by simply recounting the circumstances of an assault, the victim becomes the culprit. In Kafka (about whom I had written) it is almost a commonplace, the lesson (and this is in Kafka too) now written on my own flesh.

Just by telling the story one loses the facts, shakes them out and makes them available for interpretation and rearrangement. Instinctively, in telling the story one guards against misinterpretation, but to lay stress on the innocence of one's conduct is to imply that there have been other occasions, similar situations, dark nights with boys on seafronts where one's behaviour might be more blameworthy. But this too was false in my case, so far from the truth it was almost comical.

I have never been able to cruise and have never had much inclination to do so, though seeing it as a definite shortcoming, one of several masculine accomplishments I have never been able to master – throwing a ball, for instance, catching the barman's eye, pissing in public. It was partly that, never feeling I would be much of a catch, I saw no point in trawling the streets for someone who might feel differently. And then, too, I was quite hard to please.

Homosexual friends, I had noticed, never seemed all that choosy when they caught someone giving them the eye. Quick as a fish they were off on the trail of their quarry, a ritual of flight and pursuit that involved glances over the shoulder, looking in shop windows and hesitation at street corners, until when eventually one or other of the parties decided to close the gap and actually speak, it came as no surprise and was almost a joke.

It was a knack I did not have as well as a disinclination, and was reinforced by a fastidiousness that was disabling too. Friends invariably dramatised and romanticised such encounters, some of which must surely have been commonplace and many, though spiced up by the unexpected, downright dull. But what never ceased to astonish me (and fill me with a kind of wonder) was the persistent readiness for such casual flings and the rapidity with which, regardless of previous plans or engagements, they would, the opportunity unexpectedly presenting itself, dart away after some unknown man in response to a glance which, as often as not, I had not even spotted.

Some of these considerations I dramatised in the screen adaptation of Joe Orton's biography *Prick Up Your Ears*.

(*Orton sees a youth coming.*)

ORTON: Look at the package on this. He's lovely.

HALLIWELL: (*frantically*) Where? Where?

ORTON: Here. (*The youth looks back.*) We're on.

HALLIWELL: How? What did he do? I didn't see anything.

ORTON: What do you want, a telegram? Come on. (*They follow.*) He's built like a brick shithouse.

HALLIWELL: He's probably a policeman.

ORTON: I know. Isn't it wonderful?

HALLIWELL: We don't want it to make us late for the Proms.

ORTON: Listen, sweetheart, which do you prefer, him or Sir Malcolm Sargent?

Halliwell's wail of complaint is truly mine: my first consideration would always be Sir Malcolm Sargent, or whoever, until, that is, the moment passed, when I would be left wretched at my own timidity. 'One walks about the streets with one's desires,' wrote T. S. Eliot, 'and one's refinement rises up like a wall whenever opportunity approaches.' Still, living life in Orton's bold, head-on sort of way, which I was never able to do, seemed to me to have a morality of a sort. That all other fancies and preoccupations – the ties and tugs of social life, for instance, the need to keep appointments and the overriding obligations of work – should, at the prospect of sex, be straight away rendered provisional and be instantly dispensed with might be thought, if not admirable, at least praiseworthy; between keeping a promise and turning a trick no contest: it was a question of priorities.

It was as though life with all its engagements and obligations, its goals, duties and diversions, was for these rovers but a path beside a fast-moving stream of sex into which they were ready to plunge, literally at the blink of an eye. Half a smile, a second look – that was all it seemed to take. This was certainly not how I saw it, though strictly as an onlooker, as apart from anything else I was never quick enough off the mark to be a participant.

Besides, while the readiness was all, there were other necessary components: it required a certain self-esteem, for a start, a notion of oneself as meriting some interest, sexual or otherwise, and this I lacked; I could not see I was worth a second glance, let alone be worth pursuing. I did not like myself, so why should anybody else? Then, too, such encounters involved risk, of which a risk of rejection was not the least, a risk of being beaten up was another and, in our newly straitened circumstances, the risks attendant on any sex.

Such ease of encounter wasn't to be attained or even struggled after. Like so much else in life it was bestowed, though not on me.

Pierre Loti said 'I am not my type', and so it was with me. The predicament, if it is a predicament, is not unusual and those who find themselves in it can console themselves that they are luckier in the long run than those who find their reflection a cause for congratulation. Take Peter Cook, who, as a young man, always gazed at himself with both pleasure and interest, but for whom growing old must have been particularly depressing. Losing one's looks means less to those who have no looks to lose. Or should, but this is not the whole truth of it, naturally, as there can be few mortals who are not vain of something: in my case it is of always having looked younger than my age, owing to the inherited characteristic of having kept my hair, and my hair having kept its colour. So, too, did my father; on his deathbed at the age of seventy-one, his hair still as full and brown as it had always been. That apart, though, I look at myself and reflect that the face is not worth stopping for, and so, until I was well into my thirties, few did.

This was partly self-fulfilling. Had I liked myself more (or thought about myself less) things might have been different, or different sooner. Though it's the sort of reach-me-down psychology bandied about on afternoon TV shows, to like oneself more does, I see now, make one easier to like. I just wish I had come by the knowledge earlier in life.

Still, the walks I used to take every night around the streets of Headingley and Meanwood were, I suppose, cruising of a sort, and I wonder now whether that was the construction my parents put on my suburban rovings. It was not sex but the beauty of the city that had me in thrall, which might

571

seem eccentric, except that the Victorian painter Atkinson Grimshaw had found the same in the streets of Leeds, so I was in good company.

When I came home and filled my notebooks with descriptions of the sunset, treating it as if it were an ideal landscape and the clouds an alternative world, there was, I'm sure, a part of me that knew that the world I was really looking for and never found was darker and more furtive and not ideal at all.

But I was a romantic boy, and though to cruise meant employing skills I never managed to acquire, I felt my failure to acquire them was a disappointment rather than a disability, more regrettable than not being able to roller-skate or dance, but not much more.

In such matters, though, I retained an innocence long after it could be seen as becoming, and a timidity inappropriate in someone of forty, so that on the rare occasions when I was unambiguously approached I generally failed to divine the true nature of the encounter until it was too late. Asked by a perky young man for the time on the tube platform, I pointed to the clock a few yards away and got on the train, only to see him still waiting on the platform, smiling – I would like to think wistfully. I got off at the next stop and caught the next train back but he had, of course, gone.

Another similar exchange was more comic. I was walking in Regent's Park when another stroller stopped and (with no sign of a cigarette) asked me for a light. I explained that I had no matches as I had not long stopped smoking, but caught, as I stammered out this excuse, a flicker of amused despair, presumably that someone could be so stupid. As I walked on, the true nature of the approach dawned on me and I stopped and called back: 'But thank you very much for asking.' There, too, I went back five minutes later but to no purpose.[*]

Having a public face complicated things. Did one get looks, it was hard to sift one sort of interest from another, the searching look, the second glance, ascribable to having been seen on the screen rather than foreseen on the pillow.

_____
[*] An incident I later incorporated in the short story 'The Laying on of Hands'.

These failed encounters, though, invariably depressed for days after-wards, not because of a sexual opportunity missed but because they brought home to me my instinctive avoidance of risk. Risk was what I didn't want (or did), so I avoided not merely the risk but those areas where risk was likely to be encountered. To be bold was always my second thought, and always too late. With me, it's not a case of having left undone the things I ought to have done; I've left undone those things I ought not to have done too.*

I saw these fumbled passes as indictments of my own timidity; I had only to bring one off, I used to think, and my life would change its course. But I never managed it. So for this Italian policeman to assume that I had been attacked because I was doing something which had been persistently

---

* I note some of the times I have written about risks not taken: 'Another day, another ball had ended,' John Gielgud used to intone every night at the end of the first act of *Forty Years On*, as he remembered the years before the First World War, 'and life had not yielded up its secret. "This time," I always thought as I tied my tie, "perhaps this time." But there would be other nights and time yet, I thought.' That was about risk and a later play, the farce *Habeas Corpus*, was more specific:

> On those last afternoons in the bed by the door
> On the Clement Attlee Ward,
> When you mourn the loss of energy
> Even Lucozade cannot replace,
> And Sister Tudor thinks you may go any time,
> Do you think that you think
> Of the things that you did
> Or the things that you didn't do?
> The promise broken, the meeting you missed,
> The word not spoken, the cheek not kissed.
> Lust was it, or love? Was it false or true?
> Who cares now?
> Dying you'll grieve for what you didn't do.

(And, as they say, *passim.*) The notion of risks taken and not crops up in less likely plays. It's there in *The Lady in the Van*, for instance, when my own character remembers Miss Shepherd as the bold one: 'All those years stood on my doorstep, she was all the time on the run. Self-sacrifice, incarceration, escape and violent death – a life, this is what I keep thinking, a life besides which mine is just dull.' And, most unlikely of all I suppose, I am the bedridden ninety-year-old Violet, who in *Waiting for the Telegram* looks back to her doomed sweetheart who, on the eve of his departure for the front in the First War, wants to make love to her. In a moment she will regret all her life, she turns him down.

beyond my capacities to do, and which had defied all aspiration, seemed particularly unfair. If it was an offence, not only had I not committed it, but it was beyond my capabilities to commit.

'But I'm shy,' I should have protested, and that would have said it all. Or since making such an assertion on one's own behalf itself demands a degree of boldness, so to say you are shy you need to be quite unshy, I should have left it to Rupert. Except that he was not unshy too, so that made two of us. I suppose we must have looked like two prep-school masters, an older one and his much younger colleague, and though not quite Naunton Wayne and Basil Radford, hardly a predatory pair.

Later, when we were back in England, I wondered too (this wondering and the quest for certainties the most persistent feature of the whole episode) if some of the now evident hostility of this policeman and this doctor had to do with my poor Italian. I had, throughout, described our attackers as *ragazzi* which I took to mean 'young men', or rather 'youths'. Did it mean that, I wondered, or did it mean boys who were much younger? Was I describing an assault such as occurs in *Suddenly Last Summer* when Sebastian is, Orpheus-like, torn to pieces by street urchins?

'Youths' was what I meant, with its connotations of aimlessness, indolence and being on the loose, the associations of the specific the opposite of those of the general: youth is freshness, vigour and vitality; a youth is indolent, dull and up to no good.

'What did he look like?'

'He looked like a youth.'

That was what I wanted to say, but had I said it? Did *ragazzo* mean that? I subsequently discovered that that was exactly what it did mean, and so I need not have concerned myself; need not have concerned myself in any case since whether the culprits were youths or boys plainly did not concern that carabiniere. I was the real culprit; to him they were just specimens of affronted Italian masculinity.

The rest of the story is soon told. The carabiniere took Rupert off on a half-hearted run round the town and seemed surprised that the youths were not still hanging about at the scene of the crime. He told us that if we wanted we could report to the police station the next day, but that there would not be much point.

In this sorry saga the real Samaritan was the taxi driver who had ferried us to the clinic in the first place, horn sounding, white handkerchief hung out of the window; maybe he just liked the excitement. But he waited while I was patched up, and was there to take us back to the hotel in the small hours. No matter that his car must have been covered in blood, he went off without being paid, and ironically, in view of the carabiniere's eagerness to put the blame on blacks or Moroccans, he was an Egyptian.

Next day, we drove back to Fiumicino. Our plane tickets were invalid for immediate return so we spent £600 on new ones. Back in England, the travel insurance company, a large and reputable firm, refused to refund this fare on the grounds that we had not contacted them first for permission to return. So, unrobbed by our assailants, we ended up having our pockets picked by some respectable gentlemen in the City.

The wound had been covered in thick layers of elastoplast so we came back through Heathrow with me sporting this tipsy pink pill-box on the side of my head. I noted how invisible even a minor disability makes one, people preferring to look away rather than suffer embarrassment or fellow-feeling.

I put my bloodstained clothes in the washer (with Pre-Wash and Water Plus), wondering if this was how murderers went about it. At the dry cleaners I had to explain the state of my sports coat. The Spanish assistant shrugged: 'Then it's the same there as it is here.' But for days afterwards I kept coming across spots of blood on clothes I had not even been wearing and on my body, too. Several baths later, in a crack behind my ear, I found crystals of dried blood.

When, in due course, I took my head along to the local health centre, they were full of admiration for the neatness of the stitching on my cerebral sampler. Having yet again recounted the circumstances of the attack, I felt that, without saying so and with the kindest of smiles, they too felt that the carabiniere's interpretation came closer to the truth. I was past caring.

What remained for months afterwards was a thick welt across the crown of my head, like one of those mysterious marks that in SF movies single out those members of the human race who have been doctored by creatures from another planet.

While I still believe that a second blow, had it landed, would have killed me, I acknowledge that what happened on that shabby Italian seafront was no more than happens half a dozen times on a Saturday night in Glasgow or Leeds – or even Morecambe, another shabby seaside place which nowadays, I'm told, accounts for a disproportionate share of the personal injuries and assaults treated at one of our local hospitals. Bored youths are, I suppose, universal.

Never attacked or struck in anger since I was a child, I see my life as wrapped in almost Edwardian complacency. Even in New York, where one is primed to expect violence, I used to walk home in the 1980s through the empty streets of Tribeca at one or two in the morning and never came to harm. Before this I would no more have thought to cross the street to avoid the stumbling drunks who blunder at night around Camden Town than I would think twice before crossing a field of cows. Whereas the other evening, as I was walking up Bond Street, someone shouted and I nearly jumped out of my skin. And yet there are Asians in our cities for whom the likelihood of such incidents must underscore their every day.

I have described elsewhere[*] how my mother, while suffering from depression, spent a few days in the admissions ward of the local hospital and how, having seen patients with every species of mental disturbance, I walked the streets of Lancaster and saw madness on every corner. Having seen it plain in that terrible ward, I now saw variations of it in the faces of every other passer-by. And so it was for a while after Ladispoli. 'You could have done it,' I would think of some innocent eighteen-year-old, 'Why not you?' – violence like madness, discernible in every other face. In time this passed but violent scenes on film or television still leave me impatient,

[*] See *Untold Stories*, pp. 11–13.

injected very often into scripts out of the same vacuity with which, in real life, it is often inflicted – or was inflicted on me.

Least likely to be surprised by this account are unabashed homosexuals, or homosexuals who are less abashed than I am, and not so much in two minds, and whose dress and demeanour leave no doubt as to their preferences. To be attacked, beaten up or otherwise abused, and to find the police response one of indifference, is the not infrequent experience of homosexuals, and blacks too. But, reluctant to be enrolled in the ranks of gay martyrdom, reluctant, if the truth be told, to be enrolled in any ranks whatsoever, I kept quiet about this adventure. It has been another untold story, though it is better that it should be told. The police protect the respectable, of which I have always been one. So, to find ourselves in this grubby seaside town briefly and mistakenly cast out from respectability a while, and put outside the protection of the law, was, I hope, a salutary experience, though not one I would recommend.

Arise, Sir . . .

It's seldom that a week passes nowadays without an invitation to speak either at a literary festival or to some local literary society. Publishers are keen that their authors undertake these engagements, particularly the festivals, as the talk is often followed by a signing session when authors meet their readers and significant amounts of stock can be shifted.

I do fewer of these engagements than most authors partly because I am of an age now when I like to sleep in my own bed and also because I've found that, the large literary festivals apart, many of the smaller societies exist less to promote the written word than to beef up the social life of the organisers. Far too often one ends up in a provincial town at half past eleven at night having a Chinese meal up a back street somewhere with people you don't know.

When I do perform – and it is a performance, as Larkin, who refused as he put it to go round pretending to be himself, pointed out – I generally read from some of the stuff I've written, with my diaries the most popular (plenty of jokes), and then I take questions from the audience before finishing up with five minutes more reading, almost always ending with a speech from my 1980 play *Enjoy* in which a character describes the contents of a mantelpiece in a working-class household, a passage I have read so often it has become almost like an old-fashioned parlour recitation. It's fair to point out that, though I'm reluctant to undertake these engagements, generally speaking I enjoy them but feel it doesn't do to do them too often. The more I talk the less I write, and if I didn't write no one would want to hear me talk anyway.

I am not especially articulate so the question-and-answer segment might seem likely to expose my shortcomings, except that I have found that over a period of time the same questions tend to recur. Someone will always ask, for instance, if in the monologues I (used to) write I have in mind a particular actor or actress. Do I keep to a daily routine when writing and would I describe it? Why do I seem to prefer writing for women than men? Do I make notes on conversations that I overhear and in what circumstances?

It perhaps says something about the kind of audiences I attract but I'm seldom questioned about anything that requires much self-revelation. I was once asked how much money I made (it was by a boy at Bradford Grammar School) but my personal circumstances are generally left unprobed: I have never been asked if I live alone, for instance, or if not whom do I live with and why. The tentative confidences of my published diaries don't touch off requests for further information and, embarrassingly confessional though some of my writing occasionally seems to me to be, my audience perhaps sense that even this degree of opening up does not come naturally to me and don't enquire further. Maybe they're just not interested; or don't want to be thought to be the sort of reader who might be.

One slightly ticklish question I do get asked, though, and that is whether I have ever been offered any sort of official decoration. Why have I never figured in the Honours List?

Flattering though the assumption is that my failure to figure is some kind of omission, to date I have never answered this question directly, saying that, had I had such an offer and seen fit to turn it down, to acknowledge this would hardly be fitting; to have accepted an honour without fuss would seem less self-regarding than to turn it down then boast about it.

I wish I could dispose of the question by saying that I am a republican and then there would not be much more to be said. But while not a fervent monarchist (or a fervent anything much), I have no particular objection to

579

the monarchy, whatever its drawbacks, or even the honours system that comes with it. It seems a better way of going on than any presidential arrangement politicians could be trusted to devise and so, for reasons that are historical, sentimental and also practical, I would leave the monarchy alone.

So I then generally edge the question round to a discussion of honours in general and the shortcomings of the system, making some of the points I make here, though as I've got older I tend to feel less cagey about the whole subject and so can be more frank.

Out and out republicans apart, it's pretty safe to assume that those who refuse an honour are diffident about it and that this diffidence extends to keeping their refusal quiet. This, though, is voluntary. There is no requirement to this effect in the official notification. One is asked to let the prime minister's office know if the offer is not acceptable, and if it is acceptable not to mention the award until the list is published, with some implication that jumping the gun in this regard might result in the offer being withdrawn.

Voluntary though this discretion is, it accords with conventional notions of good behaviour and is therefore quite powerful. To refuse an honour and brag about it would seem bad form, but what makes the system self-sustaining is that those who complain about it can be presumed never to have been made an offer and so can be accused of sour grapes; just as those who have been preferred and have refused and come out and say so can be accused of showing off. It's not a very adult way of going on and the morality is that of the school playground, but it suits the Establishment as it precludes the possibility of change.

What should be plainly stated, though, is that the happiest temperament to have is one that accepts whatever distinction is offered, and accepts it graciously and without fuss or a lot of soul-searching. This is the nearest one gets to genuine modesty. Isaiah Berlin, on whom honours were heaped by the bucketful, never demurred. True, he said these marks of distinction were undeserved and made light of them, but he took them. But who is to say he was more or less modest than someone who refused because they don't care to be brought into the official fold? Or, as Updike puts it, 'Who will measure the selfservingness of self-effacement?'

Towards the end of 2003 a newspaper got hold of a list of those who had refused honours and published their names both in the paper and on the Internet so, while it did not altogether clear the air, the slightly absurd secrecy that has always surrounded the process was to some extent dissipated and it became possible to talk about honours less obliquely than in the past. Jon Snow, having turned down a distinction, did a TV programme about the subject and there was talk of reform. Whether that will happen remains to be seen but there is no doubt that nowadays the system is more porous and much more discussed.

If the bestowal of honours was not selective, came like the bus pass, say, on the attainment of a certain age, there would be nothing to talk about. And even allowing that some were singled out and others not, were there one honour and one honour alone undivided into ranks and categories (MBE, OBE, CBE and whatever) then the subject would lose much of its fascination. The more selection there is, the more grading and differentiation, the more occasion there is for snobbery.

I've nothing much against snobbery. It's a fairly harmless failing, though one to which the English are more prone than most peoples, and undoubtedly the honours system panders to it and is permeated by it.

Some critics blame the Queen for this, or at any rate the monarchy, but the English have never needed much encouragement to get themselves into clubs and cliques and, twiddling on their own particular eminences, however slight, pretend to be special and different, so that monarchy or no monarchy we would find ways of doing so.

Whether the French are the same with the Légion d'Honneur I am not sure, though I doubt it, and that's as far as my knowledge of other honours runs. I have the impression, though, that Europe (or what Mr Rumsfeld calls Old Europe) is generally more sensible than we are so I'm sure in this, as in many other departments, we could learn a thing or two from our hoped-for partners.

It's hard to object to the honours system, though, when it gives so much twice-yearly pleasure and is the occasion for such rich hypocrisy among the beneficiaries.* Perhaps I am unfortunate in my friends or in the corrupt metropolitan circles in which I move, but it's seldom I come across someone who has accepted a knighthood and done so with genuine pride and pleasure, still less anyone agreeing that it was well deserved. Nobody ever says that this is just what they have always wanted, though it's true that Kingsley Amis justified or at least excused his knighthood by saying that he took it because he knew so many people that it would annoy, which seems as good a reason for accepting it as any.

No, most of the knights I know are a bit shamefaced about it, disclaiming the title even when they have accepted it. They proffer a variety of excuses, their need to do so suggesting they are uncomfortable with their elevation or uneasy about the system altogether. They are anxious to show that they don't take it seriously and now they are knights or dames or whatever, could we please forget all about it.

This is probably not a general view. In the arts and on the left (which is often the same thing) genuine pride is, I would have thought, quite rare and honours seldom accepted without this note of apology or self-justification. In other sectors of society pride perhaps abounds. I imagine, for instance that those newspaper editors and TV commentators Mrs Thatcher thought it prudent to honour rejoiced in their advancement, though these honours were hardly a gift; there needs no money to change hands for honours sometimes to be a transaction. Still, whatever the circumstances, the majority of those singled out must be honestly pleased and accept with alacrity – which is nice, if not of much interest. More entertaining, though, are those who are in two minds and, when they do accept, feel the need to offer excuses.

Their mothers, for instance. Isaiah Berlin used to claim he had only taken a knighthood in order to give pleasure to his mother. And the moth-

* I leave aside the objections to the actual nomenclature or that many decorations come in the name of an empire that has long since disappeared. It's true this is antique and outmoded but, in my view, the more to be welcomed on that score. So too are pageantry and ceremonial, and after all, what is the Order of the Garter but an antique, and nobody so far as I know has suggested updating the name of that.

er doesn't need to be still around, as presumably Berlin's mother wasn't for most of the many honours that subsequently came his way. It's the thought of the mother that's important. After a lifetime on the left Eric Hobsbawm excused his acceptance of the CH by saying that it would have given his mother much happiness. Fathers are less often adduced, probably because they're beadier altogether and, dead or alive, are less likely to be taken in.

But as with mothers so with wives. A husband will often pass off his own snobbery as the aspirations of his wife. This is the 'little woman' argument, the husband posing as being above such petty considerations as knighthoods or whatever but not wanting to deprive the silly little creature of her fun. Meeting at a reception at Buckingham Palace, the playwrights John Osborne, Harold Pinter and David Hare are all said to have blamed their attendance on the curiosity of their wives, the wives, with more sense, probably not feeling it necessary to blame anyone at all.

Still, men being more decorated than women, wives have some reason to feel aggrieved and may think, quite rightly, that years of long-suffering loyalty entitle them to a share in the credit for their husbands' elevation and that it is proper, therefore, that a knight's wife should be ennobled, too, and be called a lady. That men, even when no less loyal, are not so long-suffering as partners perhaps explains why a wife appointed a dame throws no corresponding cloak of ennoblement over her husband. Nor, it hardly needs to be said, does a knight's elevation affect a partner if that partner is not a wife or if that partner is not of the opposite sex. As a convention, honours are nothing if not conventional.

Another strategy for acceptance is to take the honour as being bestowed on the institution, if such there be, or the firm to which one belongs, the assumption being that the staff or the employees thereby share in the honour. 'Oh yeah?' would seem a fair response to that, though it's sometimes more plausible than others. I can imagine the average Maltese being boosted by the George Cross awarded to the whole island for its record of resistance during the Second World War. Whether a thrill of pride went through the ranks of the RUC when the Queen decorated the Constabulary as a whole, I'm less sure.

I was once filming in a derelict factory in Bradford, the offices of which had not been touched since the firm closed down the previous year.

There is a ledger open on a desk, records and files still on the shelves. In a locker is a cardigan and three polystyrene plates, remnants of a last takeaway, and taped to the door a yellowing cyclostyled letter dated 12 June 1977. It is from a Mr Goff, evidently an executive of the firm, living at The Langdales, Kings Grove, Bingley. Mr Goff has been awarded the OBE in the Jubilee Honours and in the letter he expresses the hope 'that the People, who are the Main Prop in any endeavour, many with great skill and ability, will take Justification and Pride in it and will,' he earnestly hopes, 'feel that they will be sharing in the Honour conferred on me'.

(Writing Home)

The CH is at the other end of the scale from the OBE, and at the other end of the social scale, too, probably and a result of entirely personal achievement. Still, it can pay dividends in its actual bestowal, and Anthony Powell's account of a morning at Buckingham Palace and his interview with the Queen at which he was invested with the CH almost justified the award itself.

In the theatre the most direct route to honours is via Shakespeare, actors with the subsidised companies more likely to figure in the list (or to figure in it earlier) than their colleagues on Shaftesbury Avenue or on television. Hollywood isn't always helpful, as to make a good deal of money such as film stardom normally entails can put off elevation. There is a compensatory aspect to the Honours List; repertory Shakespeare is not well paid, the CBE therefore something of a top-up.

It's tacitly expected, certainly in theatrical circles, that most recipients of knighthoods or damehoods should not set too much store by the social cachet of such distinctions, the use of the title not to be insisted on. My own experience of the theatre began when there were relatively few knighted actors but it required only a brief acquaintance before they licensed the elision of the title and you were told to, 'Drop the sir.'

I never knew him but this was not true, apparently, of Terence Rattigan, who liked his handle used, perhaps because for all the usual reasons (absence abroad, earning too much money in Hollywood and dallying with his own sex) he'd been quite a long time acquiring it. Anyone making too much of such marks of distinction these days, though, runs the risk of being thought arrogant or foolish, the elevation is too small to insist upon without incurring ridicule. Besides knights, dames and commanders of the British Empire are now commonplace. Indeed there are so many it might save time (and some heartache) if the honour was just handed out along with the final diploma at drama school.

Opera singers and musicians generally don't have to wait so long and tend to be upgraded quite early in their careers, presumably because going to the opera or to concerts is one of the chief recreations of the great and the good who decide such things. If it takes longer in the theatre it's partly because plays can involve thought, more so anyway than opera, and so are a less satisfactory evening out for the great and the good, who have been thinking all day (or like to think so).

Sportsmen and women are less likely to figure in the upper reaches of the honours list because sport is popular and popularity is thought to be its own reward, though in more and more sports, football in particular, popularity equals advertising and that is not its own reward at all.

Still there is snobbery here. To sing like a bird and to run like the wind are both gifts of equal merit, the value society sets on them something else entirely. But an honours system that was truly democratic and which mirrored the public's concerns and enthusiasms would be just as unacceptable as the system now prevailing.

The occasions on which honours can be publicly displayed are limited, though I suppose a knighthood or even a CBE printed before or after one's name in a chequebook may procure you a deferential glance from the counter clerk, but how often these days do you see a counter clerk? And it won't cut much ice at the cashpoint.

One of the few occasions when honours can be flaunted is at a funeral, on top of the coffin, but that's hardly going to warm the heart. Alec Guinness was immensely pleased to be awarded the CH but said that since he was now too fat to get into his tails the only time anyone was likely to see it was when it was on his coffin. Even this unique opportunity was nearly let slip as when it came to the funeral the decoration was not to be found and only retrieved in the nick of time from the bottom of the wardrobe.

If English society was regularly on parade, graded in order of rank so that as honours accrued someone could see themselves move up towards the head of the queue, the knights ahead of the CBEs, the CHs ahead of the knights and the OMs out in front of them all . . . if everybody period-ically had to number off as one used to do on the parade ground there would be more to be said for the honours system. But the consolation of honours is for the most part private, sported perhaps in the bedroom or in front of the dressing-table mirror. An officer in the Scots Guards who won the MC for gallantry during the Anzio campaign referred in the mess to 'my new brooch' and honours at least enable men so inclined to indulge in a taste for jewellery. Or so Sir Steven Runciman used to say, whose breast bristled with Balkan baubles.

One drawback with honours nowadays is that they are not always per-manent and the Queen, particularly, is an Indian giver. I have never read a patent of knighthood or the terms of appointment to the various orders but I should be surprised if they find it necessary to emphasise that appoint-ments to the order are only during good behaviour and can be summarily withdrawn. This, though, can happen for a variety of offences, ranging from treason (Anthony Blunt), peculation (I. Jack Lyons) to fraud over VAT (Lester Piggott).

There was something unseemly about the speed with which Her Majesty demoted her ex-Keeper of Pictures when she had known for years what his situation was and enjoyed his jokes nevertheless. It may be, though, that snatching back the riband of a champion jockey distressed Her Majesty more than the demotion of a mere art historian.

Currently there is some discussion as to whether Jeffrey Archer's per-jury should lose him his peerage. I don't see why not, though it might be helpful for the future if honorands were given a tariff of possible offences, a guide to how low they are permitted to sink before they are summarily undubbed.

Another distinction that is more liberally distributed nowadays (and not, I think, retractable) is the honorary degree. However well deserved these bestowals are, it has to be said that, showbiz having penetrated every corner of the nation's life, university governing bodies nowadays tend to compose their annual honours list with an eye to maximum coverage in the media. Largesse has to be orchestrated.

John Gielgud was the most self-centred of men but paradoxically quite modest. Awarded an honorary degree by the University of Cambridge, he thought nothing of it, taking the conferring of this coveted distinction as not unlike one of the innumerable other award ceremonies in which he regularly figured. Finding he had a slight cold the day before the ceremony, he had no hesitation in telephoning to say he wouldn't be coming.

'But you must,' wailed the official in question (whom Gielgud should have been playing). 'We need you. You're top of the bill.'

As the pleasure of wives is adduced as a reason for accepting a knighthood, with honorary degrees, if justification is necessary, it's likely to be the pride of parents, particularly when the university in question is on home ground. It would certainly have given pleasure to my parents that the first honorary degree I was offered, an Hon.D.Litt., should have come from the University of Leeds, where I was born and brought up. Neither of my parents had been entirely clear what a university was, but by that time it had ceased to matter as my father was dead and my mother scarcely knew who I was, and whatever was left of my family did nothing to swell the (quite sparse) attendance.

Though I had never attended the university I knew it well, had been to lectures there and worked in its Brotherton Library, so I was pleased to have been approached. And I was glad in the finish to have gone through the process once at least, though it left me in the end thinking that it was not one I would be anxious to repeat.

I was teamed with the novelist Barbara Taylor-Bradford, who is also Leeds-born and indeed had been in the same class as me at primary school in Armley, though neither of us could remember the other. The proceedings involved two more or less formal meals with the ceremony sandwiched between them. For this one had to parade in a ludicrous hat and lurid gown (mine, I think, pink) and stand on a public stage alongside the University Chancellor while the Registrar read out a record of one's achievements.

The Chancellor of Leeds at this time was the Duchess of Kent and she did her job conscientiously and well, favouring me with a kindly (though occasionally quizzical) smile throughout this exhaustive recitation which I frequently wanted to interrupt if only to excuse what I saw as some of its less glowing achievements – appearances on *Countdown*, for instance, or *Desert Island Discs*.

The embarrassment attendant on the declamation of this well-meaning indictment I was not ever anxious to repeat and, since eating with people I don't know has always been a powerful deterrent, that and the two formal meals honorary degrees always seem to involve has been sufficient to put me off for good. Such offers as have come my way since I have managed to sidestep, saying generally that it's honour enough to have been thought of, which, indeed, is true. Still, it seems a touch mean-spirited, but there's an element of self-preservation in refusal also. Honorary degrees do not come without strings. While there is no formal obligation, an honorand must expect to be invited to address all sorts of gatherings of staff or students in the donor university, invitations which are hard to refuse once you're on the strength. If you enjoy such occasions all well and good, but talks have to be written and addresses composed and I write little enough as it is. Best to steer clear.

Better still, though, to be light-hearted about it. As President of the Royal Society and goodness knows what else, Sir Peter Medawar was showered with honorary degrees and used to say that his ambition was to get one from a university beginning with every letter of the alphabet. This seems as sensible a reason for accepting an honorary degree as any other, though hardly one to which most honorands aspire.

My own university is Oxford. I have an honorary fellowship at my college, Exeter, which gave me great pleasure when I was elected in 1987. It came as a surprise, though, in 1998 when I was asked if I would accept an honorary D.Litt. from the university itself, the surprise stemming (I hope) partly from modesty but also because I assumed the university had written me off a few years previously, a story best told in an extract from my diary.

10 August 1990. An invitation from the Vice-Chancellor at Oxford to a fund-raising dinner at Merton. 'It will be an opportunity,' he writes, 'to tell you something about the university's current achievements.' Since one of the university's current achievements is the establishment of the Rupert Murdoch Chair in Communications, I feel disinclined to attend, and write back saying that if the university thinks it's appropriate to take Rupert Murdoch's money perhaps they ought to approach Saddam Hussein to found a chair in Peace Studies. [A pained letter eventually comes back saying the university has been most careful to ensure the money came from *The Times* and not from the less reputable sections of the Murdoch empire. A visit to the university Department of Economics would seem to be in order.]

I'd had no communications from Oxford since that time so I was doubly surprised when in November 1998 the university was in touch again. More diary:

17 November. I'm looking forward to a quiet morning's work when out of the blue [*sic*] a letter comes from Oxford offering an honorary degree. This distinction is what Larkin called 'the big one' and when he got his letter he uncharacteristically bounded up the stairs to tell Monica Jones the good news. I sit looking at mine and wondering about it for most of the morning, wishing I could just say 'Delighted' and have done with it. But ever since the establishment of the Rupert Murdoch Chair in Language and Communication I've felt disaffected with the University. I'm aware of the arguments about bad money being put to good uses but I still think that Murdoch's is not a name with which Oxford should have associated itself. So, eventually, I write back saying no and explaining why.

Of course I am aware that writing (and publishing) this may be sneered at as showing off, and that if one does turn something down it's proper to keep quiet about it. But this refusal isn't for my own private moral satisfaction: Murdoch is a bully and should be stood up to publicly and so, however puny the gesture, it needs to be in the open.

I wish I could say that this refusal leaves me with a warm feeling of having done the right thing, but not a bit of it. I end up, as so often when I have tried to get it right, feeling I've slightly made a fool of myself, so that I wonder whether after more momentous refusals martyrs ever went to their deaths not in the strong confidence of virtue but just feeling that they had somehow muffed it.

There was some adverse comment in the press, notably from Paul Johnson, but nothing was said to make me feel I should have acted differently. What surprised and to some extent saddened me was that while I had quite a few letters in support from members of the public I had none from anyone in the University itself.

I don't know the circumstances and have never bothered to find out but I imagine the Murdoch post can't have been set up without some dissent at the time. If so it must have died down or been forgotten by 1998, when I made my own protest. Or it may be that university finances are now so tight that anyone involved in academic fundraising feels that they have to take money where they can find it. My closest friend at Oxford, David Vaisey, who had had to raise funds for the Bodleian Library, took this view, which I can sympathise with without thinking it right.

As it is I never read about some new depth to Murdoch's turpitude or the lies and hypocrisy of his newspapers without feeling that they demean the university which took his money to fund an appointment that bears his name. What, I wonder, do they teach there?

Finally I come back to that question from the audience with which I started and which I used to have to deflect. Nowadays, since it's no longer a secret and can be looked up on the Internet, I can go into the circumstances in more detail and without seeming to be showing off.

I was offered a CBE in the Birthday Honours in 1988 'for services to literature'. I didn't have much hesitation in declining it because, whatever doubts I may have about the honours system in general, the government through which the award came was still headed by Mrs Thatcher and I didn't want anything from that particular handbag.

It's true, though, that I had some regrets about refusing it because I longed to do it with a joke but couldn't think of one. There was a gap between the letter arriving and my letter of refusal and it might have been thought that I was agonising over the decision. In fact I just couldn't come up with a witty way of putting it. Of course in the unlikely event of the prime minister actually seeing my letter she was even more unlikely to have seen the joke: that was part of the trouble.

The list on which I did not figure was published on Saturday, 6 June, which happened also to be the day of Russell Harty's funeral. Russell would never have dreamed of refusing anything and would have been only too delighted to be singled out by Mrs Thatcher, or even by General Pinochet. Dead, and therefore knowing all things, he would have been infuriated by my piece of cheek.

Having turned down the CBE, I thought that would be the end of honours for me so I was more surprised to be offered a knighthood in the New Year's Honours for 1996. Admittedly it was quite a thin year so there may have been some scraping of the barrel, but I felt more ungracious saying no this time if only because it seemed kind that someone in the prime minister's office still thought it worthwhile to persist.

Again, though, I was mortified not to be able to get a joke out of this *gran rifiuto*. The nearest I got to humour was to think, quite genuinely, that being a knight would be like wearing a suit every day of one's life. This didn't seem quite funny enough, though, so I just said No, thank you. Richard Eyre claims that apropos honours I quoted Virginia Woolf as saying she had been brought up not to accept gifts from strangers. I've no recollection of this or of knowing that Virginia Woolf said anything of the sort. (It's a bit pert for her, I would have thought.) Still, it would have done at a pinch.

Suit, though, has something to do with it as I felt it wouldn't suit me, or would suit the me I was still trying not to be, though at sixty-one (my age when it was offered) I ought, I felt, to have a firmer grip on my character than I did or do. With writers, much more than actors, there must always be the suspicion that a knighthood means that they have arrived but at the wrong place. Self-regard, though, is boundless and, lest it be thought that this refusal has much to do with modesty, when the list of those who had turned down honours was leaked in the newspapers I cared enough to note (I hope wryly) how obscurely placed I was on the list and that sometimes I wasn't even mentioned at all.

Retrospective though most honours are, arising as they do out of services rendered, it's still hard not to feel that to be given an honour certainly at a higher level is to be in some sense enlisted or even leashed. It's a restraint, even if only in point of good manners: someone who has just been honoured by Downing Street might feel less ready on that score openly to criticise Downing Street. It's nothing so vulgar as being bought off; simply that most people would think it not quite the thing to do. An honour is not just a trinket; it's also a contract.

In my case, though, it would be hypocritical to pretend that I do not sometimes wonder about all these refusals and what lies behind them, and also that I do not have occasional regrets. Writing can be a pretty cheerless business and going through a bad patch I sometimes think it would be a consolation to be a sir . . . not that it would help. But it's not much of a regret and it passes.

Why I have this recusatory temperament, though, is quite hard to sort out but it must in part have to do with my father. He was naturally modest and reluctant to push himself forward and would never have thought he had anything to push himself forward about. As a child I was something of a show-off, which pained him, so I can see this refusal of honours has to do with atoning for that and is, in part anyway, an attempt to please my dead parent. It's futile, of course; there is no pleasing the dead and he would probably think I was making too much of a fuss anyway and would do better taking them and have done.

Still, I was brought up not to be beholden to anybody; my parents never liked to be under an obligation or to owe someone a favour, particularly someone outside the family – an attitude not uncommon in their class and circumstances. And this has, I think, been passed on to me, whose class and circumstances are very different.

If not being beholden is part of it and something that I've inherited, my own history plays a part and in particular something that happened in 1954 during my last months of National Service.

I had spent my obligatory two years very happily at the Joint Services School for Linguists, stationed most of the time at Cambridge where we wore civilian clothes, did no drill or military training and, though we enjoyed the status of officer cadets, it wasn't like being in the army at all and we were virtually undergraduates. Sometime in the spring of 1954 we were sent for three days to WOSB, a unit in Hampshire where we went through a series of tests to assess our suitability for a commission. These tests were to do with qualities of leadership, man management and nerve under fire. I had no hopes of passing but much to my surprise (and, I think, largely due to my acting abilities) I did. The next stage, though, involved a longer performance, a fortnight at Mons barracks in Aldershot. Still, it was reckoned to be a pushover and almost impossible to fail. I failed.

Those of us who had fallen at this or the earlier hurdle were then busted to private and spent the last month or so of National Service at the Intelligence Corps depot at Maresfield, the foulest camp I have ever been in and made worse by the fact that plain to view were those ten or so colleagues who had passed both stages and now idled about the camp with their swagger sticks and peaked caps as fully-fledged second lieutenants.

At the time it seemed a joke, this abrupt turnaround a farewell lesson in the absurdities of military service. But in retrospect I can see that it marked, if it did not actually cause, a change in my way of looking at things.

Mons had been a failure and, though I was only twenty, my life up till then had been one of unbroken success. I had passed the eleven plus, always been among the top of the class, done well in all but sport and after school and higher school certificates had ended up with a scholarship to Oxford. This army test, ludicrous though it was, was my first taste of failure, no less bitter because I knew the object of my ambition was contemptible in every possible way: I think I only wanted to be an officer because the uniform was smarter.

When I joined the army aged eighteen I had been a committed Christian, right-wing, censorious and, so far as I could predict, destined to become an Anglican clergyman. In the army this conventional façade began to break down and in a conventional way; I began to smoke and to swear and occasionally to get drunk. So if this failure at Mons was a turning point, like most turning points it had been in the offing for some time. But a failure it was. I had not got my platoon dry-shod across the flooded stream; the guerrilla attack I led scoured the Hampshire countryside and did not even locate the foe. And it mattered. Even after two years of its insanities I still believed in authority, even the authority of the army. No longer.

When a month or so later I was demobbed and went up to Oxford, something had happened. I had learned authority was not to be trusted. I was an Other Rank and I had better get used to it. Not a second lieutenant and so never a member of the Oxford Union or an actor in OUDS; I did not write for *Isis* or speak at the Labour Club. I led a thoroughly domestic life in my own college and began to fancy myself an outsider (which I wasn't, though it saved me from making an effort). What I was not was a joiner. And so in due course not a CBE and not a knight. An Other Rank.

The greatest honour I have ever been given had nothing to do with the Honours List and thus evaded the strictures of my recusatory temperament and all my misgivings about authority. This was when in 1993 I was appointed a Trustee of the National Gallery. It was entirely unexpected and unlooked for; when I asked, 'Why me?' I was told that I represented the man in the street.

The position of Trustee carries with it one inestimable privilege, namely permission to go round the gallery out of opening hours. To be made free of the nation's pictures and to be allowed to roam the gallery at will seems to me a distinction of more substance and worth than any of those doled out in the Honours List, particularly since, though a Trustee serves for five or seven years, the privilege of out-of-hours entry is given for life. Even though I was for all sorts of reasons an indifferent Trustee, nothing I have ever been given has pleased me more.

The last word on honours, though, ought to be a joke. The painter Francis Bacon accepted nothing. He was asked in his seventies why he had not taken a knighthood or the OM and his reply, though camp, as so often with Bacon concealed a good deal of common sense.

'Oh, I couldn't. So *ageing*!'

An Average Rock Bun

'I remember when you were here last time,' says the nurse as she checks my blood pressure. 'It doesn't seem like five years.'

'It does to me,' I say, 'every minute of it.' I am lying on a trolley in a cubicle in the endoscopy unit of the London Clinic. With my gut scoured clean and awaiting scrutiny and naked except for a hospital gown, I am beginning to look forward to the Valium. The nurse goes out, pulling the curtains closed. Condemned cells have no door, I reflect, just a tastefully patterned curtain and a locker for your valuables.

Actually the curtains have changed since I was last here. Then they were a cheerful flowered print, Laura Ashley perhaps; now, it's a rather sombre design of African violets in blue and grey. Five years ago I glanced at the fabric as I was taken out, thinking that when I was wheeled back after the colonoscopy I would see this same pattern again but by then I would be in the clear and it would all be over and done with, though why it should have been the soft furnishings I fixed on I can't think; tasteful unto death perhaps.

It's a Friday afternoon and the unit is not busy. In the corridor, a few feet away, a doctor is telling some relieved woman that there is nothing amiss.

'No polyps?' she asks.

'Not to speak of. Nothing out of the ordinary. You can go home and prune the roses.'

Oh, the lives that doctors wish upon us! But if she has no roses, or garden at all, she is still overjoyed as he ushers her out and the corridor falls quiet. Soon it will be my turn.

I have never got used to the sight of blood. On the paper, in the pan, the toothbrush or the handkerchief, however innocent the explanation, it never fails to startle and to mar the day. At different times I have shat blood, coughed blood, spat blood, and of course bled blood; it has happened all my life, but seldom with serious consequences or from significant cause.

Still, the sight of it has generally been shock enough for me to seek medical advice as one is told to do, though, suffering occasionally from piles, to do so on every occasion was hardly practical or fair on the doctor. But I have had regular sigmoidoscopies as a precaution, the doctor looking up my bum with a telescope ('A touch of cold steel now'). Sometimes I felt that more people had seen the inside of my bum than had seen some productions at the National Theatre.

My first London GP, a saintly man who never made me feel a fool, as doctors sometimes have, was often required to reassure me in this area. I was once lying on the couch while he carried out a manual examination of my back passage.

'No,' he said patiently, 'I find nothing that concerns me here. Though of course' (and his finger was still up my bottom) 'it's always nice to see you.'

So, even though I was bleeding fairly regularly, it was without any particular feeling of alarm that I arranged to see the usual specialist and have one of my periodic sigmoidoscopies. This revealed the piles which would account for the bleeding, but that apart, the examination was reassuring; the specialist could see nothing alarming, though he did ask when I'd last had a colonoscopy.* He didn't press the point and whether or not to have one seemed up to me. One reason why one goes to a doctor is to try and make another person responsible for one's life. I wanted him to tell me

---

* No one has ever satisfactorily explained to me how, short of frequent colonoscopy, a physician sorts out benign bleeding from piles from a more sinister cause. And if it puzzles me, who has been through the process, I imagine it must puzzle other patients in the same predicament.

what to do but he didn't, and not being at all anxious and feeling reassured by the sigmoidoscopy, I don't know what it was that made me, nevertheless, decide on a more extensive investigation. Luck, I think now, or providence, or maybe there was still a doubt and I was hankering after perfect peace of mind. But in that curtained cubicle in June 1997 I was probably thinking that, as on previous occasions, it was all a fuss over nothing and I was being a bit of a fool.

On this point, at least, I was soon proved wrong. Dr W., the head of the unit, breezily explains the procedure, how I will be given some IV Valium with more if I need it, and that if I choose I can watch the proceedings on a screen while he gives a commentary.

The tube with the camera attached begins its track up my bowel. 'Very few people come out of here without a smile on their face,' murmurs Dr W. as he cruises past some unassuming piles. 'Nothing to worry about there.' The camera pushes on with its proctoscopic odyssey.

Suddenly the tone of his commentary falters as he rounds a bend and is brought up short before something huge and craggy. Once it may have been benign; now it's not benign at all. Even before Dr W. explains this, I notice how the two nurses, who are also watching the screen, instantly become more solicitous, one kneeling down and stroking my arm, whispering reassurance before I have entirely realised that reassurance is required.

The culprit is a polyp that has gone undetected, turned malignant and is now firmly attached to the wall of the bowel. It's a situation, I know, in which I am expected to be an adult, and Dr W. invites me to look at the screen and confront the agent of my misery. But openness has its limits and my eyes are firmly shut as he gives me another burst of Valium and edges the camera past the evil monster, even looping the cable round it and giving it a tug to show how rooted it is. And he must be a gardening man because, almost to himself, he says something that chills the heart.

My own gardening skills are limited and the pleasure I get from the garden in Yorkshire has always been mitigated by my almost Manichaean attitude to plants, which I divide into good and evil, with the evil obviously weeds, thistles, dandelions, bindweed and a particularly stubborn resident of our garden, ground elder. I see ground elder as a nineteenth-century evangelist saw sin, something to be rooted out wherever it breaks the surface. The trouble, though, with ground elder is that it doesn't always break the surface, spreading through the soil and strangling the roots of neighbouring plants, and weedkiller and meticulous sifting of the soil notwithstanding, never to be wholly eradicated.

So when, having tugged the polyp to no purpose, he mutters, 'Ground elder', I know that I am doomed. When I'm dressed he comes to see me off.

'I imagine you're the sort of person who can cope,' he says. I imagine that, too, though it remains to be seen.

'It's about the size of the average rock bun. It will wait a week but not a month.'

Still half cut from the Valium, I write a cheque for the £800 bill, noting at the desk that the receptionist finds it hard to look at me and that I, in my turn, feel shame that I have somehow failed.

When I came home that afternoon, for all the shock and the reeling anxiety and the collapse of any imaginable future, there was, nevertheless, a feeling, too, that this was what I had been waiting for all my life. Waiting for in my mother's life and my father's and always in my own.

This makes me sound more morbid than I am. It was just that of all the ways any of us might go, cancer has always seemed the likeliest because most often met with. And it was more likely than I then knew.

I had known that there was some family history of bowel cancer as my father's brother had died of it, and I knew, too, that it was something my father feared. It was only later, after I'd been operated on, in fact, that I found that he had reason to fear it because his father had died of bowel cancer too. However, my father seldom talked of it and an aunt, one of whose regular topics of conversation was that 'cancer was in the family', he thought morbid and self-dramatising. His reticence was understandable, though in the light of what happened to me thirty years later, misplaced. And even in the sixties, when my uncle died, the familial nature of bowel cancer was not a great deal emphasised and the notion that some forms of cancer might run in families tended to be thought of as hypochondria.

However, this rock bun I was sequestering was not hypochondria and, distraught though I was, I noted that there was some small satisfaction in being able to ring my GP over what was not, as was so often the case, a triviality or an ailment I was imagining. This was real. 'Steady,' I wrote in my diary. It's what Dad used to say to us children when we were coming down the steps of a tram or waiting to cross the road. 'Steady!'

My GP recommended that I see John Northover, Senior Surgeon at St Mark's Hospital and head of the colorectal unit of the Imperial Cancer Research Fund. Though he was an NHS surgeon and in private practice, living in Camden I was obviously outside his catchment area for the NHS, for which, in any case, there was a waiting list. Even his private list was oversubscribed, and it was only because a vacancy occurred at the last minute that I was able to be operated on within a week, and in the specialist colorectal unit of St Mark's, Northwick Park.

There is no doubt in my mind that it was the skill of John Northover and the expedition of the operation that saved my life or, since I am still in remission, saved it so far, and certainly for five years. At the time, this seemed an unlikely prognosis. Although the cancer was found to be quite compact, and had not yet breached the wall of the bowel, unseen on the scan beforehand a small patch of cancer had begun on the liver, and traces were found in one of the nearby lymph glands.

The outlook did not seem cheerful and Mr Northover gave me, with chemotherapy, a fifty-fifty chance of recovery, odds which I think I knew at the time were probably overstated for my benefit. Still, the operation was uneventful and before and afterwards I remained uncharacteristically cheerful. As indeed did every doctor I came into contact with.

'He's very positive,' I wrote in my diary. 'Sometimes one wonders why anyone ever dies of this disease, everybody's always so hopeful.' Still, cheerful or not, I did not at that time, July 1997, expect to last more than a couple of years.

But we managed jokes.

'All I ask,' said Rupert, my partner, 'is that you don't follow [the Murdoch-hating] Dennis Potter's example and christen the cancer Rupert.'

Jokes or no jokes, in some ways the diagnosis of a life-threatening disease is easier for the patient to bear than his or her loved ones, who have to stand by and watch it happen. The positive thinking which the conventional wisdom requires of a cancer patient was easier for me (who had at least something to do, even if it was only to undergo surgery). Had I been cast as help or support I would have found it hard to disguise my anxiety. Rupert, on the other hand, seemed never other than cheerful and gave no hint of what he must have been going through, an impeccable performance in a role that is largely unsung, but which must be played out every day in thousands of households, suddenly stricken with mortal illness.

Various entries from my diary:

18 July 1997. I suppose that I assume this disease abides by the programme doctors impose on it: I have now had the operation and will to some extent recover; then I will have chemotherapy for six months and will in due course recover from that. I imagine that it will be then, and only then, that I will have to start worrying whether anything else is happening, the disease meanwhile having bided its time . . . or with luck, been eliminated. But why should it bide its time? What is it waiting for? And yet people survive.

There were unlooked-for bonuses:

24 July 1997. One of the blessings of my situation is that I no longer feel obliged to recycle and am absolved from trips down to the paper bin, laden with the week's supply of newsprint; I don't feel the need any more to post my few bottles, brown, green or clear, through the bristled mouths of the bottle bank. Excused duties, I suppose it would be called.

25 July 1997. However hard I try (and I probably don't try very hard) I keep being caught off guard . . . by a photograph, for instance, taken a year ago ('If I'd been investigated then,' I think, 'I wouldn't be in this hole now') . . . something in the house ('When I bought that I wasn't poorly' . . . not that I *feel* poorly now). So, I suppose from henceforth it must always be BC and AC, before cancer and after. Mine was, indeed, the blood of a new testament.

30 July 1997. To look at me in the glass one might think nothing much had happened. I am slightly thinner, particularly in the face, but all there is to show besides is a thin red line two inches above my navel, going down to the borders of my pubic hair with a neat little bypass – or *chicane* – round the navel itself.

'The scar will fade with time,' the nurse tells me, an assurance that tactfully forgets that time is probably what I don't have.

I am still surprised, though, at my own good spirits, not that I deserve much credit on that score. People talk of courage as if there were a choice, whereas one shows courage very often because there doesn't seem to be much alternative.

Larkin's 'Courage is no good/ It means not scaring others' is slightly beside the point.

But I don't want my life, or what there remains of it, to be all about cancer, any more than I've ever wanted it to be about being gay.

In the few weeks that elapsed between the operation in early July and the beginning of chemotherapy in August, I made some enquiries about alternative therapy. These weren't systematic or unduly conscientious; I had made up my mind to undertake the precautionary chemotherapy and, while I had no intention of signing up for the full range of holistic and dietary therapies that were on offer, I did feel, after talking to my GP, that homeopathy might help. The oncologist, while dubious about the alternative therapies, had no objection to homeopathy and, on the recommendation of the wife of a friend, who had had breast cancer, I made an appointment at a reputable complementary health clinic in Harley Street, simply in order to explain the situation and arrange some homeopathy.

The clinic was plainly busy, the only appointment available at seven in the morning. The doctor who interviewed me told me that he had himself been a conventional therapist, and so was well placed to assess such claims as were made for conventional cancer treatment and, in particular, chemotherapy. I explained, though, that I'd decided on a course of chemotherapy, and simply wanted it to run in conjunction with some homeopathy, expecting him, in the circumstances, to soft-pedal any understandable misgivings he himself might have about such treatment. Not a bit of it. He proceeded to pour scorn on chemotherapy, the benefits of which he said were unproven, and when I didn't budge, rather sulkily conducted some finger-tip tests, which I took to be to do with the homeopathy, but done in such a perfunctory fashion I'm not sure he thought much of the point of this either. People kept coming in with whom he chatted, and throughout treated the whole business so casually and with such a disregard for my predicament, and presumed agony of mind, that it reminded me of the arrogant and unconcerned conventional doctors one used to come across thirty years ago.

21 August 1997. Try and read some of the literature the alternative doctor gave me, but since one of its objectives is to discredit chemotherapy, which I'm currently undergoing, I put it aside.

Of course, there's a lot of money at stake in both approaches, one can see that, and the two sides behave like commercial rivals, each trying to discredit the other, with the truth somewhere in the middle. Only the patient is in the middle too. It's like the claims of two brands of soap powder, only you're the fucking shirt.

I agreed to have a blood test to check the level of the various minerals etc. in my blood. A few days later a letter came back with the results. Again, the alternative therapist did not mince words. The results of the blood test, the letter said, 'turned out to be a lot worse than I thought they would be. Don't be alarmed, however, we can certainly put this right' and an analysis of the various vitamins etc. followed. 'Without sorting this out, your chances are much less than fifty-fifty.' The remedy was six weekly visits to the Centre's clinic, an hour out of London, for a course of intravenous vitamins. 'I trust you can see the arguments,' the letter ended.

All I saw was a barefaced attempt at medical blackmail and a doctor trying to panic me into using his clinic's doubtless expensive facilities. I showed the letter to my GP, who was less shocked than I was, I suppose because I had unthinkingly assumed that the practitioners of complementary medicine were more scrupulous than their orthodox counterparts. But why should they be? Besides, as my GP pointed out, even if the assumptions behind the analysis were correct, the benefits of intravenous as distinct from oral administration of vitamins were far from established.

To be told, though, that unless you abandon a course of treatment you've already decided on you are likely to die, hardly encourages; to engender such alarm and despondency in a patient the last thing a therapist, alternative or otherwise, is supposed to do. I did not go back to the clinic.

After a month or so's interval in which to recover from the operation I began a course of chemotherapy, consisting of twelve sessions at two-week intervals over a period of six months. These involved a fortnightly visit to the London Clinic, where I would arrive at noon on Tuesday, have a blood test and then, with luck, be hooked up to the IV drip around three, and which would continue night and day until I left late on Thursday morning. The therapy was precautionary rather than intensive, and meant to mop up any rogue cells that had escaped the surgery and were still in circulation.

I imagined, as most patients I should think do, that I would lose my hair (something in my case that might be thought long overdue) but my oncologist, Maurice Slevin, thought that this was unlikely, and nor did it ever happen. Or it hasn't happened yet. The other common assumption which I shared was that I would feel very sick but, conscientiously taking the necessary pills, I never did.

Still, it wasn't enjoyable and, as time went on, the two days every fortnight came to seem unending. I was restless, un-sick, always bored, though the nearest I came to actual discomfort was the feeling of having a slight hangover. As I wrote in my diary, 'It's as if every fortnight I have to fly to Australia.'

I had never met an oncologist before and it was curious (and perhaps this is common too) how I regarded him as torturer rather than nurse, hunter more than healer, oncology, as I thought then, not a branch of medicine in which the doctor could expect to be liked. I was wholly wrong and came to look forward to Dr Slevin's visits, and never felt other than encouraged and heartened. I think I was a dull case, though I make no apology for that. With cancer, a challenge isn't what you want to be.

After my first bout of chemotherapy (I never felt matey enough with it to shorten it to chemo), I came home and wrote:

> I note no ill-effects other than a persistent drowsiness. I keep feeling I ought to be more depressed or anxious than I am, but sitting outside in the shade and watching a blackbird, I'm not discontented . . . though I suppose it's best to avoid that slightly frantic cheeriness that some suf- ferers from cancer have, and which I've always found a bit wearing and hard to fall in with.

Just after the first session, I got home and promptly cut my finger. At which point Maggie Smith rang:

'Oh, I'll ring back, darling. You need every drop of blood you can lay your hands on.'

I am aware, though, that in all this I am leaving something unsaid.

Until it came to it, I had always thought that in the event of serious ill- ness I would always opt for the NHS. I have never been opposed to pri- vate medicine in itself, or seen any objection to the mixed arrangement whereby NHS hospitals have private wings for paying patients, provided, that is, that the treatment on offer in both public and private sectors is of the same standard.

In the treatment of cancer I think it is, and I was told that all the treat- ment I had, the operation itself and the chemotherapy that followed, was in every respect the same as I would have received on the NHS. The cir- cumstances of the private treatment may have been more comfortable (though not always), but – and this is its main selling point – the crucial difference is that private treatment can be arranged more quickly, and that in my case was vital. If there was a queue, I jumped it. There is no gain-saying that. Someone else may have died as a result. I didn't because I could pay, and this showed me up to myself.

Since, though, it also saved my life, I find it hard to regret, but it is not something of which I can be proud, the only extenuating factor that I paid for all my cancer treatment out of my own pocket. I have no medical insurance, believing, paradoxically perhaps, that it is the private insurance companies who have done most to damage the NHS.

But there were bleak moments, particularly when I was having chemotherapy in the London Clinic – if, say, they were late hooking me up to the treatment (which might mean paying for an extra day), when I felt I was the only patient in that institution who was actually paying his own way.

30 July 1997. A scan at the Princess Grace. They fetch me out of the crowded waiting room, and I undress in a cubicle. Then, clad in a hospital gown, I carry my clothes along a corridor, where builders are working, looking for a vacant locker. There is no more privacy or comfort here than you get or expect in the NHS; just (just!) speed of access to the service. I begin to feel still more shame that I've chosen this road rather than thrown in my lot with the rest of the nation.

But there were droll moments, too.

29 August 1997. Another medical bill this morning and, glancing at it, I think it's one I've already paid – X-ray, laparoscopy – it all seems familiar until I see that, unlike my bills (so far anyway) it ends with a fee for euthanasia.

It's the bill for Captain Beaky, A.'s cockatiel, who last week went into intensive care at the vet's in Keighley. £98 including VAT.

Tedious though the chemotherapy was and long though I did to be away home at the earliest opportunity, I never wanted to be disconnected from the drip until the last drop of life-giving poison had gone into the vein, to be followed by the saline that flushed through the dregs. 'This might be the drop', I used to think, 'that kills the cell that starts the secondary,' and I'd probably have licked out the sachet if I'd been allowed to. It was hardly positive thinking, or even picturing the enemy as one is recommended to do, and nearer superstition than either. I suppose the closest I got to positive thinking was to regard the folinic acid as strengthening medicine. But it got me through and I seldom came away other than cheerful and happy to be home.

Had the chemotherapy made me feel sick I might have thought differently, but the worst I ever felt was mildly hung-over. As time went on, though, it became harder each fortnight to find a viable vein, and I learned to bless and appreciate those nurses (the nurses invariably better than the doctors) who could slip a needle into the arm without pain or fuss. In the course of my treatment, most of the veins in my arms were used up (though they've since rejuvenated themselves). It's the addict's predicament, and I began to have to have the cannula fixed into the back of my hand, which was both painful and restrictive. Still, I was lucky. The nurses told stories of patients so shot up that the only useable vein was in the penis.

After each session of chemotherapy I would come home and make a stuffed marrow. It's not the most exciting of dishes, but what with precooking the rice and preparing the various ingredients, it became both a ritual and a celebration of life, a plain, wholesome and almost consciously life-affirming meal that we could polish off between us to mark the end of another treatment. And I noted in my diary, 'It still seems to me strange how unblighted so much of the time manages to be.'

While in no pain, though, and little discomfort, as time went on I found the chemotherapy sessions deadening and increasingly wearisome. This was less to do with the treatment than the circumstances in which it was administered.

The London Clinic is not a lively institution, nor a particularly convivial one. Time was measured out in the steady drip of the folinic acid and the slow deflation of the sacs of fluid sagging on the stand. One woke in the night as a nurse came out of the darkness to shake the sac and shine a torch on the tube to check the drip of the liquid across the optic and through the cannula into the arm. Sometimes it is a known face, or the nurse I had seen before I went to sleep, but more often it is a stranger whose name I do not know. There is not much acquaintance here. And if the nights were long, the days seemed scarcely less so. Though I could pass the time by a trip down the corridor, trailing my drip-stand, I seldom did, as there was never anything to see.

14 September 1997. In an armchair an old man in a dressing gown watches the coming and going of the lift, his son in a burnous gazing moodily out of the window at a blank wall. Glimpsed occasionally through open doors are motionless figures laid on their beds like premature effigies, locked in a private world of illness and solitude where, though the television is always murmuring, nothing diverts.

But for the bed-wide doors it might be a superior hotel in Coventry, say, or one of those featureless establishments on the edge of an airport. Nothing disturbs this privileged sepulchritude. Life is elsewhere.

With two and half days in hospital every fortnight for six months, in all I spent nearly a month there and not once did I get into conversation with another patient.

I am not a gregarious man but it was in every sense too high a price to pay for privacy. There was no fellowship in suffering (not that I was suffering, particularly) but how should there be? In free hospitals the sick tend to make common cause, if only with a cheap cheerfulness. It's salutary to see patients in worse nick than you are, if only because pity drives down self-pity. But in private hospitals (and it's their selling point) you seldom see the other patients at all. And why should you? Rubbing shoulders is what you are paying to avoid. 'If this is the lap of luxury,' I wrote, 'I don't care for it much.'

Glimpses of my fellow patients were rare enough for me to write them down:

2 October 1997. 10.15 a.m. and 356 units left to be pumped through. With luck I may be out by three. I seldom see any of the other patients, but this morning, while the nurse is here, the door is open, and I see a man wheeled past, my age, I suppose, but difficult to tell because he's egg-bald and on his way to or from whatever treatment has made him so. Then, this afternoon, as I'm leaving, I see another man older than me sitting out in the corridor with his wife. He's also bald, but his head is mottled with bluish-grey marks as though tattooed. The sight of these two fellow patients depresses me and makes me think beyond the immediate relief and pleasure of being outside again, to what may be the ultimate outcome and when.

I hail a taxi on the corner of Devonshire Place where a young man in pyjamas and dressing gown has been wheeled out onto the pavement to take the sun, his legs still in their white hospital stockings. The unselfconsciousness of him touches; it's something I wouldn't do, I think, unless I was fairly far gone, which perhaps he is. No one seems to be with him. He's just sitting on the corner of Devonshire Place in the afternoon sun.

When Alec Guinness came to see me he was surprised and even disappointed that I had not lost my hair, understandably perhaps, in someone who had been bald since he was a young man. He was not wholly convinced that my hair remained my own until he had contrived to tug it to make sure. This was not entirely a joke.

12 December 1997. Let out yesterday at two, this episode (no. 10) the most wearisome so far, and I imagine episodes 11 and 12 will be more of the same. I'm running out of veins now and the nurse who fixes the cannula tries the right arm, then the left, and has given up on both until, by chance, I bend my right arm and she is overjoyed to discover a plump, hitherto unpunctured, vein in my forearm. Part of the dreariness of the process is the taste in the mouth, or the absence of same. Then, too, there is the over-employed air of the London Clinic, no windows ever open, each breath (which, such is the expense, could probably be individually costed) a breath of the well-to-do sickness that pervades the place, where even the crockery (beige with white flowers) turns the stomach.

Towards the end of the programme my boredom got to such a pitch I even began to devise improvements to the machinery.

Tethered to the infusion pump one often has to go to the lav or move about the room, and for this it can be unplugged, working in the meantime on the battery. However, the lead invariably gets caught up with the intravenous tube in the arm and a lot of time is wasted unentangling it. A simple improvement would be to make the flex automatically retractable, as is the case nowadays with vacuum cleaners; and this would eliminate the tangled flex problem straight away. I even think of writing to the manufacturers to suggest this, except that I see from the label they are a Belgian firm, and the pumps themselves are manufactured in Japan.

Medical fees apart, the price one paid for board and lodging at the London Clinic was not much different than that for staying at the Connaught. Unsurprisingly, though, the food did not compare and meals were dull, tasteless and old-fashioned. Paying for them out of my own pocket perhaps made me more critical than the average patient, who was likely to be putting it down to insurance, and unlikely to be here for the food anyway, and eventually I wrote to one of the board of trustees, complaining in somewhat exaggerated terms:

One is paying what one would have to pay at the Connaught and getting food which would disgrace a boarding house in Fleetwood. No effort is made to tempt the appetite, and the London Clinic's notion of a salad is what one would be given in Leeds in 1947, namely a piece of lettuce, a slice of tomato and another of cucumber. It deserves a place in a museum of gastronomy.

With chemotherapy, one is always being asked if one is nauseous, which, thankfully, I have not been. The only time I have come near to nausea is when removing the dish-cover of my supper tray.

The nurses assured me that their food was even worse, but the irony of crusading for better conditions for some of the richest patients in the world was not lost on me, and eventually I took to having most of my food brought in, a practice I'd thought confined to the inmates of Turkish prisons.

When, later on, I spent time in UCH and the Middlesex, both NHS hospitals, I was reassured to find the food, though of course free, was of approximately the same standard as in the private sector. There were fewer frills but it tasted (or didn't) much the same as most institutional food tends to do. But there, at least, I wasn't paying through the nose for it.

The final session of my chemotherapy ought to have been at Christmas 1997, making one wonder if this would have involved any festive accompaniments (the holly and the IV) but it was put off until the beginning of January, and this marked the end of my treatment. Now all I had to do was wait and come in every three months to be examined, thus becoming in the course of the next four years a denizen of that quartier clinique that lies east of Marylebone and north of Oxford Street. Sometimes it was Harley Street, but on two occasions, both quite dramatic, I was taken into UCH and the Middlesex. More often than not, though, my visits were on my bike, as it's only fifteen minutes from home, and most of them were without event. There were, though, as there had been already, various low points.

In the course of chemotherapy a considerable volume of liquid is passed intravenously through the body, only part of it folinic acid, the rest saline. The passage of this out of my system seemed, in my case, quite slow (I tried to imagine it staying and doing some good) but this retardation had to be catered for. Never feeling particularly incommoded by the treatment, I would often go home to Yorkshire the following day, but on one occasion en route I was taken short and pissed my pants. It was the first time I had done this since I was a small child, and though the relief was so blessed it was almost celestial, I found the episode unexpectedly depressing. It was on King Lane in Leeds, and I have never passed the spot since without remembering it, one of the grid references in that private topography of memory, embarrassment and romance that is laid over the map of Leeds.

Incontinence featured at another low point, the first of a series of scans that punctuated my treatment. At the time I was filming the second series of *Talking Heads* at Twickenham, and had to come away from the filming of one of the monologues when it was not going well. The sense of still-ness, which to my mind is essential to the effectiveness of this form, had begun to give way to a busyness which betrayed an anxiety about the bleakness of the set-up. I wasn't directing the piece myself, but had already insisted on retakes, without managing to make it any less *mouve-menté* and I had the feeling when I came away that the director and the studio were glad to see the back of me.

There were retakes at the hospital, too. I had to drink a good deal of water, or radio-sensitive squash, so that my bladder and bowel would show up properly on the screen. The retakes here were themselves a cause for anxiety (what had they spotted that they needed to see again?), and as I lay on the table, being passed in and out of the scanner, I became more and more desperate to piss. In the event, I managed not to, and in that sense there's no point to the story, but the wretchedness I felt, which must be part of the ordinary commerce of such a place, remains vivid. As it was, I was sure that the film they had taken (and retaken) did not bode well. In this, happily, I was wrong. The film I had left at Twickenham was probably better than I had imagined, too, though there was no retaking that.

Another low point concerned the rogue trader and banker of Baring's Bank, Nick Leeson, not a character with whom I had much sympathy, or thought to have any connection. Shortly after he was gaoled in Singapore he developed cancer of the colon, the onset of the disease causing much comment in the press and, I would have thought, an undercurrent of sat-isfaction. Certainly, there was much speculation in the papers about colonic cancer in general, and on Leeson's chances of survival in particu-lar, journalists gleefully quoting the odds.

I tried to sidestep most of this, knowing it would depress, but one item caught my eye: an interview with Professor Gordon McVie, then the Director General of the Cancer Research Campaign. It had been well advertised in the press that, after establishing itself in the bowel, the cancer's next port of call was often the liver.

'And what', enquired one fearless newshound, 'are Leeson's chances if the cancer has reached the liver?'

'Zero,' said Professor McVie or (which may have been a very different thing) that was what he was reported as saying.

Now I knew from my original operation that the cancer had reached my liver, if only just. So, unlike the pronouncements of my surgeon, which at least gave me a fighting chance, this pronouncement offered no hope at all. It's to be hoped Professor McVie was indeed inaccurately reported, because even if what he said were true, it scarcely helped to say so, and there must have been thousands of patients like myself for whom it seemed to sound a death knell. Leeson is not an appealing figure and altogether too cocky for my taste, but cancer made us kin. He was not the only one. Around this time Ian Dury succumbed too, and I even felt some kinship with the far more unlikely figure of King Hussein of Jordan, whose last months with cancer were served up and lengthily dwelled on by the press.

My own liver was obviously a source of concern to the doctors, and in the first three years following the operation was repeatedly sounded and scanned, so far, anyway, revealing nothing, as they say, sinister.

'And,' the scanner would say, 'I've had a good look round, besides.'

Regardless of age, looks or gender, radiologists never know how close they come to being kissed.

Cancer licenses hypochondria. Watchful for the disease's recurrence, one feels there is no ache that can be safely neglected or symptom ignored. In early detection lies the best hope of cure: and having, as I saw it, neglected this precept in the past, I was anxious not to make the same mistake again. So, a sore knee or an hitherto unnoticed mole would send me to the doctor's, never knowing in what guise any new assault might occur. I was lucky in having an understanding GP, and the regular check-ups that an operation for cancer requires, particularly in the early post-operational stages, helped to keep me on an even keel, and in some respects ensure that my general health was better than it had been before.

It was discovered, for instance, that I was on the edge of diabetes which I would not otherwise have known, so that precautions could be taken accordingly; high blood pressure similarly. It's true that I had reached the age when such perils and prudences are the common thing but I owed it to cancer to remind me.

The regular check-ups which are part of the treatment of cancer helped allay any incidental anxieties. Did you get cancer in the elbow, I wondered, as mine was quite painful. Was the thumb a site? One of the blessings of the seriousness of the disease was that nobody seemed to mind one asking these fool questions. Every three months I had a blood test and saw either the surgeon or the oncologist, a routine I kept up throughout the five years and, though in the later stages this was probably more frequently than I needed to, suited me, and I was paying.

Still, I never made these appointments without foreboding and there were often anxious moments when the blood tests were not clear, and I was sent for an ultrasound or a scan. I learned to measure out my existence in these three-monthly spans. Life became a series of small paroles, and I never came away without a sense of reprieve, wheeling my bike back through Regent's Park often a time of idyllic happiness. For all these check-ups, though, when in due course illness did strike, it was sudden and unexpected.

In April 1998, nine months after my first operation, I was taken into hospital with a high temperature and pain in my right side. It was in the area of the appendix but, in the light of the cancer, the doctors at University College Hospital were at first reluctant to settle for that diagnosis, presumably thinking that the most likely explanation was a recurrence.

That seemed the likeliest explanation to me, too, but the truth was I felt so ill I hardly cared, every jolt of the ambulance taking me to hospital, agony. Eventually, I was transferred to the Middlesex, where appendicitis was finally diagnosed; the appendix itself not to be found having, presumably, disintegrated, and in its place an abscess which was lengthily and tediously drained. It meant that, as on several previous occasions in my life,[*] I was in hospital on my birthday.

Two years later I had a similar episode, which again was thought to be the cancer recurring but turned out to be the residue of the previous infection. Both episodes included sudden *rigors* during which I shivered so violently that I felt I'd been attached to an electronic machine; my teeth chattered and in the stiflingly hot room I was bitterly cold. It's not an unusual symptom, though alarming to experience and spectacular to watch and, as often in such circumstances, there was part of me, moaning and shaking as I was, that registered how seriously ill I must seem. Stripped of my bedclothes to fetch my temperature down, it seemed to me like the onset of death, but was, in fact, not grave at all. This, too, was around my birthday.

I hesitate to dignify such self-scrutiny as a writer's instinct as it seems to me often closer to self-dramatisation. But there is no doubt that knowing that one day (provided there is a one day) you may write about what is happening to you (or just write it down) is a solace not on offer to patients unblessed by a similar instinct. For a writer, nothing is ever quite as bad as it is for other people because, however dreadful, it may be of use. Living is something I've managed largely to avoid so, naked and shivering on the bed though I might be, for all that I could reflect that something at least was happening.

The most painful experience had, as I say, nothing to do with the cancer, the operation for which had left me only a little sore and with a scar so lengthy it was something of a trademark.

'Ah ha!' said a consultant at UCH, as he kneaded my belly a year or so later, 'I see you were operated on at St Mark's.'

This was shortly before a tube had to be introduced to drain the abscess on the appendix. I had assumed that this would be done under Valium, a drug I find so delightful I'm happy to submit to any investigative

---

[*] See 'A Common Assault', p. 557.

procedures that have to accompany it. Laid out on a trolley in the base-ment of the Middlesex, I kept expecting the needle on the back of the hand and the near-oblivion and telescoping of time that generally come with it.

It was only when I saw the professor in charge running his hand spec-ulatively over my abdomen, deciding where to insert the tube, that I realised this was to be done cold. It was kindly, if a sudden blow to the belly can be called kind, and it had to be weighty enough to force the tube through the stomach wall. But it did not end with that, as thereafter he followed the progress of the tube on a screen, while he guided it round my guts to try to reach the root of the infection. It was like being host to an angry hornet that was crawling around one's insides, stinging as it went. The martyrdom of St Erasmus, whose intestines were wound round a wheel, must have begun in much the same way.

I was probably crying out because a nurse who was passing stopped and held my hand. Perhaps no more than a gesture of fellow-feeling, it seemed to me at the time like the kindest thing anyone had ever done for me: he was an angel and I loved him. Then the tube must have got to the root of the abscess and the accumulated pus began to flow out in gratifying quan-tities, as the professor rejoiced. I did not care. All I cared about was that the pain had stopped. The nurse wiped my face and went on his way.

The two sessions I had in UCH and the Middlesex gave me a chance to compare them with the treatment I'd had in private hospitals. Some com-parisons could be direct. I have had scans, for instance, in all three, and while there is little to choose between the performance of the scan itself, even in the attendant circumstances the NHS came out of it quite well. There was no greater degree of privacy in the private or the public sector; the waiting area was just as crowded at the Princess Grace as at the Mid-dlesex; the *class* of people was different and sometimes their nationality, but in both one had no choice but to traipse around in a hospital gown in full view of one's fellows, so if what you think you're paying for is seclu-sion, certainly in the treatment room, it's money wasted.

On the ward, I'm not sure that money spent on privacy is not wasted, too. However rotten I was feeling, I never felt so low on a public ward as when in expensive isolation. It's partly that on a public ward one comes to know the nurses and their routines; one sees the changeover from the night to the day shift, the daily formality of the ward round and the comings and goings of consultants of varying age and exaltedness. Something is always going on and with the same cast. Because what is above all comforting and professionally reassuring is that the same faces recur day after day. It seems to me incontestable that outside the specialist units of the private hospitals, where there is a permanent staff, the general ward nursing in the NHS is better than in the private sector, and it is better principally because there is more continuity.

Even though the NHS nowadays draws on more and more agency nurses, you are still much more likely on the NHS to be nursed by a regular team, or by nurses who have seen you before and are familiar with your case. Nurses in private hospitals seem to change from day to day. They may familiarise themselves with your case, but it's from your notes, not from personal observation.

It's my impression, too, that whatever the rates of pay in the respective sectors, one is more likely to meet with a degree of selflessness in the NHS than in the private hospitals. At UCH and the Middlesex I still had a sense that for most of the nurses this was a vocation; in private hospitals one is never sure it's not just a job.

And yes, the loos may not be so clean, and you don't have your own private facilities, but it's not worth £500 a day or whatever the premium BUPA extracts in lieu. And (no small recommendation in my book) with the NHS there are more jokes.

Jokes or no jokes, though, cancer was hard to forget, and though it often seemed more like a predicament than the siege it is always represented, what brought it home was any circumstance that required projection into the future. Having recently acquired a bus pass, shortly after being diagnosed I had to renew it. Looking at the expiry date a couple of years hence, I realised I might not be alive by then, and that was a shock.

Not long after the operation I remade my will, though without making any of those far-reaching, tax-saving provisions I could have made had I felt able to project a future running to at least seven years. This, as it turned out, was foolish, but I was so convinced of my impending death, I could not see the point. My solicitors and accountant were handicapped by my presumption of an early departure and a little embarrassed by it, though it's a situation that solicitors, in particular, must often find themselves in. Would-be testators often lived for years with such a diagnosis, they assured me; better to take the longer view. I would have none of it, made my dispositions as if they were shortly to be executed, got on my bike and cycled briskly home.

I wish I could record that the prospect of death threw open the creative floodgates, but it was not so, and short of the autobiographical scribblings which became the TV series *Telling Tales*, and which I thought a bit of an indulgence, I found it no easier to write.

When the expected apotheosis didn't happen, I kept reminding myself that time was short and I should behave accordingly, even enjoy myself, though how I wasn't sure. I had no wish to travel or to see exotic parts of the world; the round-the-world odysseys that Aids sufferers tended to take were not for me. A neighbour in Yorkshire, diagnosed with the same condition and around the same time, had spent Christmas in Bali. I'd no desire to do that or anything much outside my usual routine.

Nor did the prospect of impending death seemingly improve the character. Always grudging in my appreciation, benevolence did not come to me in a rush and I was as wanting in magnanimity as ever I was: a good review for a fellow playwright could still make me grieve, football fever depress, the *Telegraph* incense, when all this, as I had understood it, was supposed to fall away. So there was none of the expected serenity, or the disengagement from the world: just more of the same.

Before I was ill, I had more or less completed a second series of the *Talking Heads* monologues, and even before the operation these were hurriedly put into production. But so far as future projects were concerned, plots came no easier nor did my pace of writing quicken, as I felt it was only fair it should. But cancer has never had much to do with fairness, or death either, so instead I began, I suppose, to tidy up.

I have kept a spasmodic diary since the early seventies, extracts from which I regularly publish in the Christmas number of the *London Review of Books*. The bulk of the diaries, though, remained untranscribed, many of them written in my not easily decipherable longhand. So another consequence of the diagnosis was that I put in hand the transcription of a quarter of a century or so of these journals in the hope that I would at least be able to correct as much of the typescript as I could while I was still around.

I've never envisaged publishing the diaries in their entirety, either in my lifetime or posthumously. They will require stringent editing, not because of the scandalous material they contain, but because so much of the stuff is tedious, complaining and workaday. A substantial endeavour when it was begun, Kathy Burke and Susan Powell, who have done the job, are now nearing its completion, confirming me in my assessment that much of it is banal, but worth doing for all that.

Unexpected, though, at the start was a sense of luck. This didn't come out of any moral effort or a determination to count my blessings; I've never been very good at that. It came, I suppose, partly from not actually feeling ill, and so being able to enjoy the time I thought I had left, particularly with Rupert. Visits to Yorkshire, always a treat, now became much more so, and evening visits to the empty National Gallery, which had always been a privilege, were now doubly blessed.

As time went on, this unlooked-for sense of good fortune has tended to fade, though it has never entirely gone away, and helps to mitigate what is an habitually depressive temperament. Though I'm far from jolly, I suppose I feel, as I suspect many people do, that they have both had less than their due, but more than they deserve, and always, in my case, a lot of luck.

These would nowadays, I suppose, be called 'positive feelings', the sort one is supposed to try and generate in 'the battle against cancer'. In my case, they didn't come out of any striving, and always with misgivings that they are an elaborate form of self-deception, a front put up by the self to shield one against approaching pain and extinction. But I don't think so.

Not long after I'd been diagnosed and operated on, I compared notes with a friend who was in the same boat and, like me, was in no current discomfort. She said how surprised most people would be to find that cancer isn't a constant companion, and that for long periods of time one forgot one had it – or had had it – the uncertainty about the tense encapsulating the uncertainty about the disease.

Still, as I wrote in my diary in that unforgettable July: 'This is a real bummer (and in every sense of the word).'

There were to be other blessings, though. I have never lived with anyone in my life, and I was so set in my ways (some would say spoiled) that even having someone briefly staying in the house I found irritating and disruptive of my routine. When I was diagnosed in 1997, Rupert Thomas and I had been together for five years but he had never moved in. Now there was no choice. I could not manage alone, or at least not until I was over the immediate effects of the operation.

That time came and went and, my convalescence ended, we found that living together by necessity we had evolved a way of going on and so more or less settled down. Of all the mercies – I would not say side-effects – arising from this affliction, this unlooked-for conjunction has been far and away the most blessed.

The condition seldom had to be named. Excusing myself from some speaking engagement, I would explain that I'd just had a serious operation. If this didn't do the trick, I added that I wasn't sure how well I was going to be, and how soon. Only then, when the person concerned persisted, did I open up with the sixteen-pounder, and say, 'Listen, I've had cancer.'

It always seemed unfair and almost cruel, so instant was the withdrawal and total the embarrassment.

I never at any point looked satisfactorily ill, and some weeks after I'd been in hospital I ran into a neighbour who enquired how I was.

'I've just had an operation.'

'Really? Well, you look very fit on it. I should have another.'

I didn't enlighten her and, indeed, outside my own immediate circle, told few people that I had (or had had) cancer. This was for an assortment of reasons, chief among them the desire to keep it out of the newspapers. I had no desire to become a celebrity cancer sufferer, or to occasion supposedly caring articles headed 'Playwright Fights Cancer'. There had been very little fighting so far anyway, though of course the mere question of facts wouldn't deter such as the *Daily Mail*, the favourite trick of which is to pick up an item of news, illness, say, or the break-up of a marriage, and present it as if the person concerned had gone to the paper and wept on its ever-caring shoulder.

The *Mail* did, indeed, get wind of it, and a couple of times sent a reporter round who, having enquired of neighbours, then rang my bell. My face, like my father's, is always red, sufficiently so to deceive and disconcert this nervous youth ('I hear you've been ill?'). Despite having the door shut in his face, he must have reported sadly that I was still in rude health and so never came round again. The *Daily Mirror* tried the same tack, a young woman this time, ringing up to say, 'I hear you're fighting the battle against cancer. Would you like to tell us about it?' The startled yelp of journalists when they realise the phone is being put down on them never fails to please.

The truth was I did not want to die in the pages of a newspaper as, say, John Diamond had died, or Ruth Picardie, or, however good the cause, Roy Castle. I read some of the literature their deaths occasioned and I did not want to write it. I had no more wish to give newspapers copy in death than I had in life.

Others struggling with cancer at the same time as I was included the actors Michael Bryant, Nigel Hawthorne, John Thaw and, more lately, Harold Pinter and Alan Bates. Michael and Nigel I knew, and had worked with, but disinclined as I was to belong to any kind of cancer club (as I think they were too) I did not contact them or check on their progress, just hoping they were faring as well as I seemed to be. Both their deaths came as a shock and brought home to me my own luck, as did, latterly, the death of Alan Bates.

Another reason why I was anxious to keep my illness to myself was that, like many writers, I imagine, I get letters from readers, the number varying on how much I'm putting out, but a significant element in the day's work for all that. I have no secretary and answer most letters in longhand, so even though readers' letters often call for no more than a postcard, they add to the burden.

There was no doubt in my mind that if the news of my illness got out this correspondence would swell and its content would change. The letters I usually get are what might be called letters of fellow-feeling, readers writing to say that my stuff has rung bells, or that my experiences have chimed in with theirs. Learning that I had cancer, readers would, I'm sure with the kindest of motives, write with similar experiences of their own and with advice as to how to cope and – a particular dread – their fool-proof remedies.

To be bombarded with suggestions for alternative treatments, dietary regimes or mental exercises seemed to me a predicament best avoided. A cancer patient feels particularly vulnerable to suggestion, never sure that he or she might not be neglecting the one bit of advice that might lead to a cure. However well I felt I was doing, I did not trust my own strength of mind to resist the well-meant and passionately held blandishments of my readers.

For the same reason I tended not to read articles about cancer in the newspapers, and only someone who has suffered from the disease will know how many that is. I do not use, and would not know how to use, the Internet, so that is another source of information I was not tempted to explore. Five years down the road I still find the contemplation of cancer quite hard, and even hate having to write the word.

12 August 1997. Depressed by an item in the paper about yet another cancer breakthrough at Bristol re caffeine, concentrated doses of which are reckoned to have a better effect on bowel cancer cells in particular, which, so the news item says, are more resistant to chemotherapy. Time was when my interest in this would have been at most theoretical; now it's a question of life or the other.

I realise that there will be other sufferers who will regard this selfblinkering as cowardice, and who may have found comfort and purpose in immersing themselves in the whole culture of cancer – mastering the facts regarding its forms and their treatment and, of course, its myths, in a course of action which the Internet has made feasible and available to all.

But to go down that road seemed to me to succumb to cancer in a different way. I did not see cancer as a way of dramatising my life, the lurid light of approaching death endowing even the most trivial event with a long shadow. Cancer, like any other illness, is a bore.

I cannot remember when I was last in a fight, from early boyhood my natural instinct always to walk (or slink) away. Even the metaphorical fight that cancer obligatorily involved, at any rate if the newspapers were to be believed, seemed inappropriate, the metaphor in my case not of struggle and engagement, but evasion and absence.

There was nothing adversarial in it for me. Once I'd had the operation and the chemotherapy that followed, I just hoped to edge by and to go unnoticed. In my case the metaphor was nearer that of crime, or of enemy occupation. I wanted to be ordinary, dull, my papers (and my results) not worth a second glance. I was a quarry, I knew that, but I still tried to evade the round-up, if only by not registering or identifying myself as a sufferer. Life became warier, more circumspect, but I hoped to slide by and to pass as cured (which is to be cured, perhaps).

I did not say so, or put it into words at all – I was too superstitious for that, one concomitant of cancer that I became much more superstitious. And, in retrospect, I seem to have done so little it didn't amount to much more than keeping my fingers crossed.

But I ducked the fight, which is a strategy like any other, and which some might see as not so much combating the disease as colluding with it.

The dietary precautions I took were of the simplest, avoiding red meat, eating a good deal of broccoli (which I don't care for), taking a vitamin supplement and also drinking green tea, the beneficial properties of which seem to me well-authenticated.

These apart, I tended to steer clear of cancer, seldom reading about it in the papers, their coverage of the subject almost carcinogenic in itself, forever hunting after drama or pathos, and garbling what few certainties there are and, it seemed to me, altogether relishing a subject which (like the deaths of children) is always a good column filler.

This fastidiousness might, of course, be one of the reasons I got cancer in the first place. There is a notion, canvassed by no less an authority than the poet Auden, that cancer is almost a product of reticence, or at least of being buttoned up, a disease less likely, therefore, to affect the busy, the brash or the outspoken.

It's the kind of reach-me-down psychology you find nowadays on daytime TV, where, if reserve is indeed carcinogenic, the audience must be largely immune. Seemingly handpicked for their coarseness and social inadequacy, these vociferous assemblies take readily to the notion that restraint is uncalled for, and indeed perilous to psychic health. In this age of glandular freedom, the adrenalin must flow untrammelled as even manners carry a risk, to all the other drawbacks of shyness now added that of malignant disease.

Early in 2000 I had to go up to St Catherine's College at Oxford to take part in a discussion and question-and-answer session with Nicholas Hytner, who was at that time Cameron Mackintosh Professor of Theatre Studies. The Senior Tutor of St Catherine's was Michael Gearin-Tosh, who, five years or so before, had been diagnosed with multiple myeloma and given six months to live.

With some courage, it seemed to me (and with a certain relish for the dramatic), Gearin-Tosh had rejected the few conventional treatments that were on offer at this late stage of the disease, particularly the gruelling chemotherapy that offered the only hope. Instead, after reading all the literature to do with his condition (which in itself takes a good deal of nerve) and with the help of medical colleagues and the goodwill of his college, he embarked on a course of treatment virtually of his own devising.[*]

This was a regime of some rigour and expense which Gearin-Tosh has himself described, the efficacy of which, certainly to begin with, must

---

[*] *Living Proof*, Michael Gearin-Tosh, Scribner, 2001.

have seemed an almost lunatic act of faith, and with all the hallmarks of a crank. There was a daily regime of two caffeine enemas; every morsel of food had to be organic and, even so, all fruit and vegetables needed to be washed with Malvern water. This obsessive hygiene calls up thoughts of Howard Hughes. When I met him in February 2000 at sherry in the college common room, always on the edge of the conversation hovered a young man with a jug of carrot juice, a beaker of which Gearin-Tosh sucked through a straw, the straw, like Coward's cigarette-holder, a punctuation for his wit.

Tall and not undemonstrative, and with a swooping voice, and hands clasped high on his chest, Gearin-Tosh was an exotic figure, Lytton Strachey without the beard, but what was astonishing about him was that against all the odds he was alive at all. He is not cured but he has survived ten years since the original diagnosis and, carrot juice always at his elbow, still survives, very much in the pink and always in exuberant spirits.

Had we not to some extent both been in the same boat, I might have regarded this extravagant figure, and the ambient carrot juice, as almost a joke, and someone to be remembered and maybe written about. As it was, I tried to glean what tips I could, both of us, I suspect, recognising straight away that I was never going to be able to run to the whole package, 'Don't eat salt' the only one of his injunctions I now remember, as he explained the part salt played in the mechanism of cancerous cells.

After Nicholas Hytner's lecture I didn't stay for dinner in hall, though I would have been interested to see more instances of Gearin-Tosh's diet, and how it compared with the more Lucullan regime of the other dons. Perhaps the spectacle of Gearin-Tosh's extraordinary survival and his unending struggle ought to have cheered me, but I came away from Oxford that night naggingly depressed. I did not know if, all things considered, such a rigorous regime would work for me (though nor did Gearin-Tosh until he'd tried it). Besides, all things hadn't been considered. I hadn't gone into the nature of my condition as Gearin-Tosh had; I hadn't weighed up the pros and cons. I knew that I didn't want the treatment to become my life and who was to say that all the painstaking effort notwithstanding this exotic treatment might not be a gamble that would work for him but not for me? What I did know was that I was too disorganised, too all over the place, even to give it a try. Had I been Gearin-Tosh, to do all the preliminary reading and investigation that his diet required would have taken me all the six months that were supposedly left to him. How could I employ somebody to ply me with carrot juice or swill every bit of produce I ate with Malvern Water? And who, I thought irreverently, swilled the Malvern water?

No, his was an epic struggle and, as Lindsay Anderson told me many times, I was not suited to epic. I could say that this was being a fatalist and that I was just hoping to muddle through. More truthfully, I was lazy and my laziness persisted even into the grave. It was indolence unto death.

In this, though, I suspect I resemble the general run of humanity more than I like to think. With cancer, submission to the disease and deference to the doctors is the usual form, perhaps because the patient is in the presence of a mystery. Or two mysteries . . . the condition itself and the death it so often entails. Nothing that the patient can do about it, one would like to think. Wait and see the order of the day.

Back in the endoscopy unit, there have, thankfully, been no surprises.

'I'm coming out now,' says the doctor. 'All well.' I open my eyes and venture to watch on the screen the last leg of the camera's journey down my gut, which looks like a tunnel out of Disney. We pause for a reverent moment to gaze at the titanium clip which marks the spot where, five years ago, Mr Northover snipped out the offending section of my bowel, and neatly joined the ends together, the clip looking not unlike a coffee bean.

Wheeled back to my cubicle, I lie for half an hour or so, recovering from (and actually still enjoying) the effects of the Valium; then I get up, pay my bill at the desk and come home. It's another of those small reprieves which have marked out the last five years, more momentous than the others, perhaps, in that it *is* five years, but the habit (and the precaution) of treating whatever happens as provisional is hard to lose. So, though I'm cheerful, I don't rejoice or dare to think I'm cured – though in statistical terms, five years without a recurrence would qualify. Actually I daren't think that lest I activate the laws of irony and the opposite happens.

Having been given the all-clear I pay my routine visit to my surgeon, who now feels able to tell me that he had put the odds against my survival much higher than he had ever dared reveal. Having told me they were fifty-fifty the truth, apparently, was nearer one in five.

So far from feeling encouraged or even triumphant at this news I had a difficult few days, wondering now whether I was truly as well as I felt and why it was that I'd been singled out for survival.

In time these misgivings subsided, leaving me with a feeling to which I can honestly attest, though it's both surprising and slightly ridiculous, and that is pride. It's surprising because pride is normally something I'd shy away from and it's ridiculous because that I have survived – or survived so far – is entirely without merit on my own part. The credit lies with John Northover and Maurice Slevin, who treated me, and with my GP Roy Macgregor who had helped me at every stage of the journey; and of course my partner Rupert Thomas. If my own frame of mind has contributed to my recovery, that never cost me much conscious effort and was as much thanks to them as to any determination on my part.

And yet, more than in anything that I have written or otherwise achieved in my life, against all sense and logic, I feel pride in having come through, or come this far. Unlike so many others, much worse afflicted, I did not even have to fight. Yet I am thereby enrolled as a member, I hope a long-term member, of the exclusive aristocracy of those who have survived cancer.

Thankfully, it's a growing aristocracy, and one day, I'm sure, such survival will seem commonplace and hardly worth mentioning. Meanwhile, I am one of many who are here when they did not expect to be here. Take heart.

Acknowledgements

My thanks are due to Mary-Kay Wilmers and her band of youthful and pitiless scrutineers who edit the *London Review of Books*, where many of these pieces first appeared. Also to Kathy Burke, Sue Powell and Janet Macklam who have deciphered and transcribed my hand-written diaries.

I am also grateful to the staff of Lancaster Public Library and Leeds Reference Library, an institution which nurtured me as a boy and happily remains largely unchanged. Rupert Thomas at *The World of Interiors*, Mary Kalemkerian of BBC7, Lyn Haill of the Royal National Theatre, Ruth Rosenthal and Colin Smith of the BBC have all at various times nudged me into writing some of the pieces included here, several of which, particularly those to do with Oxford and National Service, are illustrated with photographs by Adrian Bedson, who almost alone of my friends at that time bothered to record the passing scene.

I am glad Faber and Profile Books have been able to collaborate over the publication of the book as during the last fifteen years I have worked happily with both. Dinah Wood and Charles Boyle have taken the text on the first stage of its journey and seen it through the press and Kate Griffin will manage it thereafter. I am indebted to them all for their tact, energy and understanding.

I have also had expert help much nearer home as my partner, Rupert Thomas, is an editor himself. He has shared many of the not always pleasant experiences the book recounts and sometimes they were not much fun; but without him nothing would have been any fun at all.

TEXT: 'Untold Stories' was first published, in part, in the *London Review of Books*. 'Seeing Stars', 'Spoiled for Choice', 'Lindsay Anderson', 'A Common Assault' and extracts from the Diaries were also first published in the *London Review of Books*. Other articles first appeared in *The World of Interiors* ('A Room of My Own', published in the supplement, *Interior Worlds*, December 1999; and 'Making York Minster', September 2001); and the *Independent* ('Going to the Pictures', 1993). 'The National Theatre' was written for the National Theatre programme in 2001. The prefaces to *The History Boys* and *The Lady in the Van* were written for the Faber editions. 'Denton Welch' appeared as the Introduction to *Denton Welch: Writer and Artist* by James Methuen-Campbell (Tartarus Press, 2002). 'The Last of the Sun' was first recorded in 2002 and together with this introduction was first broadcast on BBC7 in 2004. 'Hymn' was written for the Medici String Quartet's 30th anniversary and was recorded for the BBC Radio Collection. 'Portrait or Bust' was first transmitted on BBC2 in 1994, and was published in booklet form for the Leeds City Art Gallery. 'County Arcade' was written for the BBC2 series, *Building Sights*, in 1991.

Extract from Sonnet XXVI, 'The World's a Stage', *Sonnets and Verse* by Hilaire Belloc (copyright © The Estate of Hilaire Belloc 1923, 1938) is reproduced by permission of PFD (www.pfd.co.uk) on behalf of the Estate of Hilaire Belloc. 'The Odd Couple' by F. Pratt Green from *New Poems 1965* (Hutchinson), originally published in *The Listener*, 27 April, 1964. 'The Things that Matter' by E. Nesbit from *The Rainbow and the Rose* (Longman). 'Aubade' and 'The Trees' from *Collected Poems* by Philip Larkin (Faber and Faber Ltd); 'Church Going' from *The Less Deceived* (Marvell Press) and also in *Collected Poems*. 'The Send-Off' by Wilfred Owen from *Collected Poems* (Chatto and Windus Ltd) by kind permission from the Owen Literary Estate. 'We are on a kind of stair' by Ian Hamilton, first published in the *London Review of Books*, reprinted by kind permission of the Estate of Ian Hamilton.

PLATE SECTION: all photographs are from Alan Bennett's private collection, except: 19, © BBC Photo Library; 21, © Cecil Beaton, by courtesy of Cecil Beaton Studio Archive, Sotheby's; 32, © Donald Cooper; 34, 37, 38, © Adrian Bedson; 35, © Derry Moore; 36, © Ivan Kyncl; 43, 44, © Bill Batten.

PICTURES IN TEXT: p. 453, *The Wilton Diptych*, late 14th century (egg tempera on oak), by unknown artist © The National Gallery, London; p. 459, *Adriana van Heusden and Her Daughter at the New Fishmarket in Amsterdam*, c.1662 (oil on canvas), by Emmanuel de Witte © The National Gallery, London; p. 460, *The Family of Darius before Alexander*, 1565–70 (oil on canvas), by Paolo Veronese ©

The National Gallery, London; p. 463, *Mr and Mrs Andrews*, c.1750 (oil on canvas), by Thomas Gainsborough © The National Gallery, London; p. 470, *The Taking of Christ*, c.1598 (oil on canvas), by Caravaggio, courtesy of the National Gallery of Ireland and the Jesuit Community who acknowledge the generosity of the late Dr Marie-Lea Wilson; pp. 472–3, *The Baptism of Christ*, 1450s (egg tempera on poplar), and *The Nativity*, 1470–75 (oil on wood), by Piero della Francesca © The National Gallery, London; p. 474, *The Vendramin Family*, mid-1450s (oil on canvas), by Titian © The National Gallery, London; p. 479, *The Adoration of the Kings*, 1510–15 (oil on wood), by Jan Gossaert, also called Mabuse © The National Gallery, London; p. 484, *Hambletonian, Rubbing Down* by George Stubbs, c.1800, Mount Stewart House (The National Trust) © NTPL; p. 487, *Lorenzo and Isabella* by John Everett Millais, 1849, National Museums Liverpool (Walker Art Gallery); p. 489, *Southwold, 1937* © Estate of Stanley Spencer 2005, All Rights Reserved, DACS; p. 499, *The Shadow of Death*, 1870–73 (oil on canvas), by William Holman Hunt © Leeds Museum and Art Galleries (City Art Gallery) UK, www.bridgeman.co.uk; p. 500, *Christ Returning from the Temple with His Parents* by Rembrandt van Rijn, Rosenwald Collection, Image © 2005 Board of Trustees, National Gallery of Art, Washington, 1654, etching and drypoint (White/Boon 60.only); p. 501, *Park Row, Leeds, by Moonlight*, 1882 (oil on canvas), by Atkinson Grimshaw © Leeds Museum and Art Galleries (City Art Gallery) UK, www.bridgeman.co.uk; p. 502, *The Hope of Venus*, c.1818–20 (marble), by Antonio Canova © Leeds Museum and Art Galleries (City Art Gallery) UK, www.bridgeman.co.uk; p. 504, *A Ploughed Field*, c.1807 (pencil and w/c on paper), by John Sell Cotman © Leeds Museum and Art Galleries (City Art Gallery) UK, www.bridgeman.co.uk; p. 505, *Barges on the Thames*, 1906 (oil on canvas), by André Derain (1880–1954) © Leeds Museums and Galleries (City Art Gallery) UK/Bridgeman Art Library/© ADAGP, Paris and DACS, London 2006; p. 506, *Interior with Nude*, c.1907 (oil on canvas), by Spencer Frederick Gore © Leeds Museum and Art Galleries (City Art Gallery) UK, www.bridgeman.co.uk; p. 509, *Bust of Jacob Kramer*, 1921 (bronze), by Jacob Epstein © The Estate of Jacob Epstein/Tate, London 2005.

Index

Beckett Park, Leeds 137, 145
Beckham, David 271
Bede, Venerable 202
Beecham, Sir Thomas 203
Beeching, Dr Richard 489
Beeston, Leeds 176
Beevor, Antony 251
Bell, Julian 353
Bell, Vanessa 508, 511
Belle de Jour (film) 278
Bellini, Giovanni: *Agony in the Garden* 457
Belloc, Hilaire 300
Bellow, Saul 268
Belmarsh Prison 349, 364
Belsen concentration camp, Germany 171
Bennett, Alan (ex-chorister, King's College, Cambridge) 258
Bennett, Flo (née Rostron; AB's aunt) 21
Bennett, Geoff (AB's cousin) 22
Bennett, George (AB's uncle) 19, 21, 22, 54, 55, 69, 85, 278
Bennett, Gordon (AB's brother) 5, 19, 21, 29, 30, 43, 66, 68, 76, 89–92, 97, 108, 111, 117, 119, 120, 525, 558
Bennett, Grandad (AB's paternal grandfather) 19–20
Bennett, Jill (no relation) 424, 445, 449
Bennett, Lilian (née Peel; AB's mother) 3–16, 18, 20–9, 31–8, 40–41, 43–8, 51, 58–9, 61, 67, 76, 81–2, 88, 90, 96, 99, 100, 103–123, 125, 135, 144, 147, 149, 260, 293
Bennett, 'the Gimmer' (Walter's stepmother) 19, 20, 51
Bennett, Walter (AB's father) 3–16, 19, 20–21, 25, 26–32, 34–5, 36–9, 39, 41, 42, 43, 44, 45, 46–51, 54, 61, 65, 66, 67, 76–7, 88, 97, 99, 104–5, 109, 120, 121, 124–5, 136, 142–9, 152, 162, 174, 199, 293, 314, 410, 412–14, 521, 536, 558–9, 599
Benny, Jack 418
Benson, Albert 228
Bentley, Phyllis 58, 299

Berenson, Bernard 211, 454–8, 465, 495
Bergman, Ingrid 168
Berkeley, Michael 294, 406
Berlin, Isaiah 219–22, 236, 237, 369, 580, 582–3
Berlin Philharmonic Orchestra 327
Bermejo, Bartolomé: St George and the Dragon 478–9
Betjeman, Sir John 530, 538
Beyond the Fringe (Bennett, Cook, Miller and Moore) 74, 77, 152, 153, 167, 169, 213, 227, 245, 308, 310, 318, 363, 443, 454, 543
Bielby, East Riding 4
Big Brother (television series) 284
Billy Liar (film) 448
Bin Laden, Osama 300, 326
Bindman, Professor David 530
Bingham, Tom 325
Birth of Shylock and the Death of Zero Mostel, The (Wesker) 218
Blackburn 288
Blackburn, Nurse 93, 95
Blackheath, London 185
Blackpool 74, 81, 166, 421, 439
Blair, Tony 209, 316, 325, 326, 331, 333, 345, 352; see also mostly under Bush
Blake, William 244
Blé en Herbe, Le (film) 183
Blitz, the 417
Bloody Sunday shootings 265
Bloom, Allan 268
Blunkett, David 251, 313, 364
Blunt, Anthony 465, 586
Boccaccio 486, 487
Bodleian Library, Oxford 206, 326, 590
Boer War 17
Bogart, Humphrey 566
Bohème, La (Puccini) 262
Boleyn, Ann 318
Bolton Abbey 74, 181, 205
Bond, Edward 283
Bond Street, London 488, 528
Bonfiglioli, Kyril 528
Booker Prize, 304

City Square, Leeds 66, 162
Clark, Alan 238, 254
Clark, Kenneth 231, 457
Clarke, Kenneth 228, 229, 238
Classic FM 181, 182, 188–9, 215, 252, 278
Clause 28, Local Government Bill 155
Clausen, George 503
Cleveleys 490, 521
Clifford, Max: John Bayley no slouch in comparison with 304
Clifford's Tower, York 337
Clifton cinema, Bramley, Leeds 159
Closing of the American Mind, The (Bloom) 268
Clothes They Stood Up In, The (Bennett) 317
Clyde, Jeremy 207
CNN 209
Cobb, Richard 239–40, 278
Cockburn High School 402
Cockersands Abbey 351
Cocktail Sticks (Bennett) 144
Coffee House, Northumberland Avenue, London 263
Coghill, Nevill 358
Cohen, Ghita 386
Collected Poems (Causley) 332
Collected Poems (Larkin) 538, 539
Collins, Joan 168
Colman, Ronald 148, 163–4
Colt, Maximilian 244
Comedy Theatre, London 196
Commercial Street, Leeds 163
Commonplace Book (Lyttelton) 321
Condom, France 234
Connaught Hotel, London 610
Connaught restaurant, London 273
Connolly, Billy 549
Connolly, Cyril 394
Constable, John 463, 530
Contractor, The (Storey) 446
Cook, Peter 246, 306, 308, 311, 312, 439, 571
Cookham 490

Cookridge, Leeds 29, 146, 297
Cooney, Ray 283
Cooper, Barbara 535
Cooper, Diana 207, 208
Cooper, Tommy 420
Corbis Corporation 183
Corden, James 342
Cordilleros farm, Swaledale 224
Corn is Green, The (film) 355
Cornford, John 353
Cornish, Kimberley 254
Correr museum, Venice 183, 184
Cortot, Alfred 372–3
Corvo, Frederick Rolfe, Baron 358
Cosmo restaurant, Finchley Road, London 445
Costello, John 255
Cotan, Juan Sanchez 464
Cotman, John Sell 483–4, 503–4
Cottesloe Theatre, London 274, 347, 383
Countdown (television game show) 427, 588
County Arcade, Leeds 520–23
Coventry 265
Coverham Abbey 225, 414
Coward, Noël 227–8, 245, 425, 439, 442
Coxon, Edna 'Gin': good value girlfriend of Henry Moore 231
Craven, Yorkshire 179
Crawford, Joan 165, 166, 302
Crazy Gang 439
Cream Cracker Under the Settee, A (Bennett) 438
Criminal, The (film) 169
Crimp, Martin 340
Crittall, Ariel 223–4
Cromwell, Oliver 213
Cromwell, Thomas 213, 320, 338
Cross, Beverley 193
Crowley, Bob 343, 347
Crown, Leeds 68
Crown Hotel, Harrogate 98
Cruise, Tom 208